PEOPLE
OF THE
EARTH

Carolina Algonquian Indians around a fire, painted by John White in the late sixteenth century. Thomas Hariot wrote of the Indians, "They are verye sober in their eating and trinkinge, and consequently verye longe lived because they doe not oppress nature. . . . I would to God we would followe their exemple."

Seventh Edition

PEOPLE OF THE EARTH

An Introduction to World Prehistory

Brian M. Fagan

University of California, Santa Barbara

HarperCollins*Publishers*

TO *All the dozens of archaeologists and students who have read and used this book in its various editions and sent me their comments and criticisms. This is the only way I can thank them all and expose them for what they are—honest and unmerciful critics. I am deeply grateful.*

And as usual, to our cats, who disapprove of authors in general and my writing efforts in particular. Their contribution was to tread on the manuscript—with muddy paws, of course.

Sponsoring Editor: Alan McClare
Project Editor: Karen Trost
Editorial Assistant: John H. Matthews
Text Design: Robin Hoffmann
Cover Design: Lucy Krikorian
Cover Photo: © 1991, David Ryan
Photo Researcher: Mira Schachne
Production Manager/Assistant: Willie Lane/Sunaina Sehwani
Compositor: ComCom Division of Haddon Craftsmen, Inc.
Printer and Binder: R. R. Donnelley & Sons Company
Cover Printer: The Lehigh Press, Inc.

For permission to use copyrighted material, grateful acknowledgment is made to the copyright holders on pp. C1 – C7, which are hereby made part of this copyright page.

PEOPLE OF THE EARTH, Seventh Edition

Library of Congress Cataloging-in-Publication Data
Fagan, Brian M.
    People of the Earth : an introduction to world prehistory / Brian
M. Fagan.—7th ed.
        p.   cm.
    Includes bibliographical references and index.
    ISBN 0-673-52167-2
    1. Man, Prehistoric. 2. Civilization, Ancient. I. Title.

GN740.F3 1992
930—dc20
                                                    91-16049
                                                     CIP

91 92 93 94   9 8 7 6 5 4 3 2 1

BRIEF CONTENTS

DETAILED CONTENTS

Part III   The Spread of Homo Sapiens   167
(45,000 to Modern Times)

Part IV   Farmers   287
(c. 12,000 Years Ago to Modern Times)

Part V   *Old World Civilizations   415*
(5000 Years Ago to Modern Times)

Part VI   *State-Organized Societies in the Americas*   *559*
    (3550 Years Ago to A.D. 1530)

TO THE INSTRUCTOR

People of the Earth has been part of my archaeological life for nearly 20 years, years that have seen momentous changes in our understanding of world prehistory. This edition of the book, the seventh, bears little resemblance to the first, written at a time when archaeology was still a much less sophisticated discipline than it is today. Successive editions have reflected this increasing complexity and the multidisciplinary nature of research into the prehistoric past. To my surprise, the book is used as a text in courses as varied as archaeology, physical anthropology and archaeology, world history, and of course, world prehistory. *People* is used in Australia, in New Zealand, at European universities, and even in Africa. I am flattered to have had correspondence from Chinese colleagues, who have consulted and critiqued its pages. They are only a few of the many correspondents from near and far who take the trouble to write and tell me about their varied researches. As a result, I have learned about archaeological fieldwork that I otherwise never would have discovered. This book now reflects not only my own firsthand archaeological experience but also the insights, advice, and research of hundreds of instructors, research archaeologists, and thousands of students. It is flattering, too, to meet occasional colleagues who remember reading *People* as a first undergraduate text—and to hear that it got them interested in archaeology. All of this makes the monotonous and seemingly never-ending task of revision a unique opportunity to look at the world of archaeology on the broadest possible canvas.

Like its predecessors, the seventh edition aims to communicate the work of scientific archaeologists to the widest possible audience. There are still some people who believe that modern archaeology is all an elaborate folderol and hoax. Archaeologists are under attack from religious fundamentalists who believe that the scriptures offer the only true account of human history, as well as from those who believe with the same religious fervor that their theories about the settlement of the Americas or the origins of civilization are the only possible truth. This book is based on scientific research, not religious belief or wild speculation. Its purpose is to provide the student with a straightforward account of human prehistory from the earliest times to the advent of literate civilization. As such, *People* provides an answer to the critics of our discipline, for its pages show that we know much more about human prehistory than our critics suspect, or want to believe. What this book does *not* attempt is a frontal attack on either creationists or diffusionists. Not only is this a fruitless pastime, for you cannot shake people's sincerely held beliefs, but also I believe that instructors should tailor their courses to suit their audiences. All *People* can do is provide some theoretical background and basic data as a framework for teaching. It is up to you to defend archaeology against its critics, however ignorant they may be. To my mind, one of the best defenses is a well-taught undergraduate course based on good data. And this is what *People* attempts to provide.

This seventh edition of *People* differs considerably from earlier editions, and I have changed over half the book this time around. For the first time, I have included boxes in the text, which serve to describe key sites in more detail, introduce historical figures, quote some important archaeological writing, or describe a topic that is covered briefly in the main text. The illustration program has been completely revised, and the chronological tables simplified and revamped. An entirely new chapter on complex hunter-gatherer societies and the early Holocene has been added, and I have followed reviewers' advice and put the background material on the Ice Age in boxes that accompany relevant chapters. At a more detailed level, I have rewritten, updated, expanded, and culled to reflect important advances in our knowledge of human prehistory since the last edition. This is a period of rapid advances in world prehistory, sparked in part by a new emphasis on regional studies, which are yielding important information on early state formation in the Near East, the Andean region, and many other parts of the world. Perhaps the most important advances of the past 5 years have been the exciting new discoveries of human seafaring at least 30,000 years ago in the southwestern Pacific, which are described in Chapter 8. I have also incorporated new information on Maya civilization from recent advances in decipherment and on the spectacular Moche burials from Sipan, Peru. And I am very grateful to Mr. Christopher Edens of Harvard University for his meticulous comments and wise insights into early Mesopotamian archaeology.

Some of the latest research in areas such as Egypt, Mexico, Peru, or Sumer is so detailed that it has little impact on a basic text such as this, except perhaps in the addition of a reference, a few sentences, or a brief paragraph. The publication of many highly important pieces of research, foreshadowed by preliminary reports cited in earlier editions, has been noted.

There is no question that the basic formula for *People* has worked well. Almost all users have supported the broad geographic coverage of the book, so this remains a feature of the seventh edition. All too often, we teach students about the Americas, Europe, and the Near East and forget that insights from less well-known areas can often illuminate problems nearer to home. One has only to look at the research on early Australian aboriginal adaptive patterns or living archaeology in the Kalahari Desert in southern Africa to get the point. If I have sometimes skimped on detailed coverage of well-known areas, I am unrepentant. The omissions are more than outweighed by the interests of balanced coverage. Talking to many instructors over the years, I have found that they use the text as a basis for making their own comparative analyses of, say, Mesopotamian and Mesoamerican civilization or of the emergence of food production in China and Peru. This is the purpose for which it is designed—to give both student and instructor a narrative basis for a comprehensive course on the prehistory of humankind.

Anyone writing a book on world prehistory is poised on the horns of a sharp-pointed academic dilemma. Should the book be heavy on theory, perhaps encased in a specific theoretical framework? Or is it better to compile a basic culture history of the world with relatively little emphasis on theory? Most reviewers and colleagues seem to feel we have achieved a realistic balance. *People* is written without an overriding theoretical framework and with plenty of descriptive passages in the knowledge that different instructors use the book in different ways, each bringing his or her theoretical bias to the material. If there is a pervasive theoretical theme for the book, it is the gradual progress of humankind as a member of the world ecological community. If there are three overriding developments in world prehistory in recent decades, they are a massive expansion of field research to all parts of the world, the widespread adoption of scientific and quantitative methods, and a much greater concern with theoretical models. *People* navigates among these developments with sedulous care and tries to avoid excesses of scientific and theoretical bias. Presently, archaeologists seem intoxicated with science, sometimes to the extent that they forget they are studying human beings, with all their complex motivations and thought processes. Perhaps the greatest message of world prehistory is not that we humans are different but that our behavior is so strikingly similar. You have only to compare the archaeological record from Egypt and Peru to see what I mean. And this is a theme that I feel should pervade our world prehistory courses, a theme far more important than the latest nuances of archaeological theory or excavation technique.

Everyone working with students who are new to archaeology must balance strict scientific accuracy and terminological precision against the dangers of misinformation and overstatement. I have tried to avoid a catalogue and have deliberately erred on the side of overstatement. After all, the objective in a first course is to introduce students to a fascinating and complex subject. Overstatement is more likely to stick in their minds and can always be qualified at a more advanced level. The complexities of academic debate will be left to more specialized syntheses and to advanced courses.

As always, the new edition has benefited greatly from the detailed criticisms and frank advice of dozens of colleagues. I owe a particular debt to Professor Katharina Schreiber of the University of California, Santa Barbara, who critiqued the Peruvian chapters for me.

I wish to thank the following professors: Gary Feinman, University of Wisconsin, Madison; Leslie Freeman, University of Chicago; Donald L. Hardesty, University of Nevada, Reno; Charles McNutt, Memphis State University; Donald Proulx, University of Massachusetts, Amherst; Irwin Rovner, North Carolina State University; and Richard Yerkes, Ohio State University.

Last, a warm word of thanks to Alan McClare and the editorial staff at Harper-Collins, and especially to Karen Trost. Without them, this seventh edition would never have been completed. They have made the task of revision a (comparative) pleasure.

Brian M. Fagan

TO THE READER

People of the Earth is an attempt at a straightforward narrative of human history from the origins of humankind to the beginnings of literate civilization. To make the book accessible to those who have not previously studied archaeology, I keep technical terms to a minimum and define them where they do occur.

Anyone who takes on a task having the magnitude of a world prehistory must make several difficult decisions. One such decision was to gloss over many heated archaeological controversies and sometimes to give only one side of an academic argument. But the Bibliography of World Prehistory at the back of the book is designed to lead you into the more technical literature and the morass of agreement and disagreement that characterizes world prehistory. The essential point is that much of what we know about prehistoric times is still based on very inadequate data. The important thing about archaeology, as with any other science, is that it deals not with absolute truth but with successive approximations of the truth.

The structure of *People of the Earth* is comparatively straightforward. Part I deals with general principles of archaeology, theoretical views of the past, and the climatic background. The remainder of the book is devoted to the story of human prehistory. All measurements are given in both English and metric units. Chronological tables are provided at the beginning of most chapters, putting cultural names, sites, dates, and other subdivisions of prehistory into a framework. Key dates and terms appear in the margins to give you a sense of chronological direction throughout the text. I would draw your special attention to the following note, which is fundamental to your understanding of the chronology of world prehistory.

Chronological Note

All dates cited in the text earlier than about 1000 B.C. (before Christ) are expressed in years before present (B.P.), *present* being defined as A.D. 1950, the conventional year taken to reflect modern times. We switch to B.C./A.D. dating after about 1000 B.C. as this appears to be conventional usage, and people are more familiar with such a chronology when talking about, say, the Assyrians or the Maya.

Brian M. Fagan

PART I

PREHISTORY

We are concerned here with methodical digging for systematic information, not with the upturning of earth in a hunt for the bones of saints and giants or the armory of heroes, or just plainly for treasure.

Sir Mortimer
Wheeler

PART I CONTAINS THE ESSENTIAL BACKGROUND ABOUT THE STUDY OF ARCHAEOLOGY NEEDED FOR ANY EXAMINATION OF HUMAN PREHISTORY. WE MAKE NO ATTEMPT TO GIVE A COMPREHENSIVE SUMMARY OF ALL THE METHODS AND THEORETICAL APPROACHES USED BY ARCHAEOLOGISTS. RATHER, PART I TOUCHES SOME OF THE HIGH POINTS AND BASIC PRINCIPLES BEHIND ARCHAEOLOGISTS' EXCAVATIONS AND LABORATORY RESEARCH. OUR NARRATIVE IS, IN THE FINAL ANALYSIS, BASED ON THE SYSTEMATIC APPLICATION OF THESE PRINCIPLES.

CHAPTER 1   ARCHAEOLOGY

Preview

- The systematic study of world prehistory started in the late nineteenth century as anthropologists began to study human diversity. At the same time biologists and social scientists were exploring the implications of biological and social evolution.

- Archaeology is the study of past human societies and is an integral part of anthropology. Archaeologists have three objectives: the study of culture history, the reconstruction of past lifeways, and the explanation of cultural process.

- Culture is a theoretical concept formulated by anthropologists to define the adaptive systems unique to humanity, for culture is the means by which we humans adapt to the challenges of the world's diverse environments.

- A culture is a complex system, a set of interacting variables that serves to maintain the population in equilibrium with its environment. No cultural system is ever static. It is always changing in ways that can be studied in the archaeological record.

- The archaeological record is the data amassed from archaeological survey and excavation. Preservation factors play an important part in the amount of information that can be obtained from the archaeological record.

3

- Every archaeological find, be it an artifact, a site, or food remains, has a context in space and time. The study of patterns of artifacts in space depends on the Law of Association, the notion that an object is contemporary with the other objects found in the same archaeological level.

- Relative chronology is based on the Law of Superposition, which holds that the lowest occupation level on a site is older than those that have accumulated on top of it. Chronometric dating provides an estimate of the age of materials in calendar years and is developed by a number of methods, including potassium argon dating, radiocarbon dating, obsidian hydration, dendrochronology, and cross-dating by using objects of known age.

- Archaeological survey and excavation are carried out by using carefully formulated research designs. Excavation methods vary with the type of site being investigated and the kind of information sought.

- Archaeologists have developed sophisticated classification methods to describe artifacts and other finds; the classifications provide the basis for theorizing about archaeological cultures.

- Recent interpretations of early prehistory have come to rely heavily on several new approaches: experimental archaeology, replication of ancient technology and lifeways under controlled conditions; ethnoarchaeology, the study of living hunter-gatherer and agricultural societies; and a new body of middle range theory designed to bridge the gap between the dynamic present and the static archaeological record. All these approaches enable us to derive general theories about the relationship between human behavior and archaeological debris.

INTRODUCTION

The two men paused in front of the doorway bearing the seals of the long-dead pharaoh. They had waited six long years, from 1917 to 1922, for this moment. Silently, Howard Carter pried a hole through the ancient plaster. Hot air rushed out of the small cavity and massaged his face. Carter shone a flashlight through the hole and peered into the tomb. Gold objects swam in front of his eyes, and he was struck dumb with amazement.

Lord Carnarvon moved impatiently behind him as Carter remained silent.

"What do you see?" he asked, hoarse with excitement.

"Wonderful things," whispered Carter as he stepped back from the doorway.

The door was soon broken down. In a daze of wonderment, the discoverers wandered through the antechamber of Tutankhamun's tomb. They fingered golden funerary beds, admired beautifully inlaid chests, and examined the pharaoh's chariots stacked against the wall. Gold was everywhere—on wooden statues, inlaid on thrones and boxes, in jewelry, even on children's stools. Soon Tutankhamun was known as the golden pharaoh, and archaeology as the domain of buried treasure and royal sepulchers.

Gold, silver, lost civilizations, unsolved mysteries, grinning skeletons . . . all are part of the romantic world of archaeology in most people's minds. Archaeologists seem like romantic adventurers, digging into pyramids and finding long-forgotten inscriptions in remote places. Like Indiana Jones of movie fame, we seem to be students of sunken continents and great migrations, experts on epic journeys and powerful civilizations. A century ago, many archaeologists were indeed adventurers. Today, however, archaeology has become a complex and demanding scientific pastime that studies over 2.5 million years of human existence. On the face of it, modern scientific archaeology may seem dull and highly technical, but the fascination of great adventure has been replaced by all the excitement of the detective story. Fictional detectives take a handful of clues and solve apparently insoluble murders. Archaeologists take a multitude of small and apparently trivial archaeological finds and use them to answer basic questions about human behavior.

Even as late as the 1870s, you could go out digging in the Near East and find a long-lost civilization. German businessman-turned-archaeologist Heinrich Schliemann was convinced that Homer's Troy had actually existed. Armed with a copy of the *Iliad*, he went to Turkey and cut great trenches into the ancient mounds at Hissarlik. Schliemann found the remains of nine cities stratified one above the other and announced that the seventh was Homer's Troy (Ceram, 1953; Fagan, 1985). His discoveries caused an international sensation. So did Frenchman Emil de Sarzec when he unearthed Sumer in desolate southern Mesopotamia, a civilization that soon turned out to be one of the earliest in the world and the society where the Flood legend in Genesis probably originated (Fagan, 1979).

The twentieth century has seen archaeology turn from a casual treasure hunt into a science. There have been dramatic discoveries by the dozens—Tutankhamun's tomb in 1922; the royal cemetery at Ur of the Chaldees in Iraq in 1928; the spectacular early human fossils discovered by the Leakey family in East Africa during the last quarter century; and in the 1980s, magnificent royal burials in China, Guatemala, and Peru. Although these finds have stirred the popular imagination, archaeologists have been engaged in a less conspicuous but just as fascinating adventure of discovery—through 2.5 million years of prehistoric times.

In the 1840s, most scientists assumed that humankind was only a few thousand years old, perhaps no more than the 6000 years allowed for by the biblical account of the Creation in Genesis (Grayson, 1983). By the late nineteenth century, archaeologists believed that the first human beings had lived on earth some tens of thousands of years ago, perhaps as many as 100,000 years before the present. Modern scientific archaeology, with its elaborate dating methods and close ties to the natural sciences, has drawn back the curtains on a much longer prehistoric stage. Thanks to radiocarbon and potassium argon dating techniques, we know that our ancestors emerged in East Africa at least 2.5 million years ago. For more than a million years, our early ancestors lived on wild vegetable foods and by scavenging meat from predator kills. Then, about 1 million years ago, hunters and gatherers spread from the savanna regions of Africa into more temperate latitudes. These larger-brained people were

In 1872, an earnest banknote engraver turned clay tablet expert named George Smith was sorting through the fragments of King Ashur-bani-pal's royal library in London's British Museum. Suddenly, he came across a tablet that contained a reference to a large ship grounded on a mountain. Immediately, he realized he had found an account of a flood that bore a remarkable resemblance to the biblical story of the Flood in Genesis. A prophet named Hasisadra is warned of the gods' intention to destroy all of sinful humankind. He builds a large ship caulked with bitumen, into which he loads his family, "the beast of the field, the animal of the field. . . ." The flood destroys "all life from the face of the earth." The ship goes aground on a mountain. Hasisadra sends out a dove, which returns. Eventually a raven is dispatched and does not return. So Hasisadra releases the animals, becomes a god, and lives happily for ever after.

Smith's discovery caused a public sensation at a time when people believed in the literal historical truth of the Scriptures. Seventeen lines of the story were missing, so the London *Daily Telegraph* paid for him to go to Nineveh to find the missing fragments. Incredible though it may seem, Smith found them within five days. The tablets can be seen in the British Museum to this day, duly labeled "DT"—"Daily Telegraph."

apparently capable of articulate speech and gave way some 400,000 years ago to the immediate ancestors of modern human beings, *Homo sapiens*.

For most of the past 2.5 million years, the rate of human biological (and cultural) evolution was glacially slow at best, but about 150,000 years ago, the evolutionary pace quickened with the emergence of early *Homo sapiens*. *Homo sapiens sapiens* settled in all parts of the world, in the extremes of arctic and tropical climates. Modern people crossed into the New World from Siberia, settled in the deserts of Australia, and developed the first artistic traditions. Far from being only big-game hunters, many of them specialized in gathering wild vegetable foods, fishing, or collecting shellfish. And more than 10,000 years ago, some of them began to cultivate the soil and domesticate sheep, goats, and other animals—a true revolution in the cultural basis of human existence.

The new economies took off like wildfire. It took only 8000 years for most of the world to turn to food production. Agriculture and stock raising were well established throughout the Near East by 9500 years ago and had spread to Europe a millennium later. The Chinese were cultivating by 8000 years ago, the New Guinea highlanders by about the same time, perhaps much earlier. Only in such places as game-rich Africa and isolated Australasia, and in areas like the Canadian arctic, which were unsuitable for agriculture, did hunter-gatherer economies survive into recent times. The inhabitants of much of sub-Saharan Africa started growing crops and herding only about 2000 years ago. The native Americans took to food production by 7000 years ago, domesticating wild cereal grasses and squash as well as root crops like the sweet potato. Food production was probably the most significant watershed in human prehistory, for it enabled the development of much more complex societies and, ultimately, our own industrial civilization.

Many of us live in cities with populations in the millions. Yet only 10,000 years ago, most humans lived in tiny camps or small sedentary villages. The inexorable cultural forces of the agricultural revolution soon led to the emergence of literate, urban civilizations, first in Mesopotamia and Egypt, then in the Indus Valley, the Aegean, and the Far East. The civilizations of the Americas—the Olmec and Maya of Mesoamerica, the coastal and highland civilizations of Peru—subsisted on maize, squash, potato, and bean cultivation. And in the Old World, small-scale city-states

Right. An epigrapher studies the cuneiform script on a clay tablet from the archives at Tell Mardik, Syria.

Below. Excavations on the earliest European settlement at St. Mary's Maryland. This type of horizontal excavation exposes features like buildings, wells, and storage pits.

Bottom left. An exemplary excavation of an eighteenth-century kitchen at Colonial Williamsburg, Virginia. Large tree roots had damaged the north foundation. Behind it lies the H-shaped foundation for the chimney.

Bottom right. Recording details of an archaeological excavation. The overhead lights are for photography. All archaeological excavation depends on precise recording of the context of features and artifacts found in the trenches of the dig.

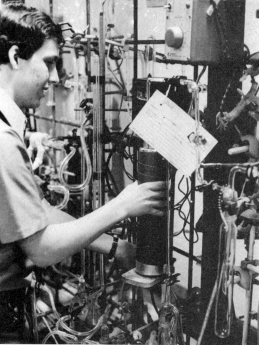

Above. A student archaeologist doing laboratory work; she is sorting through midden debris for small bones and artifacts.

Upper right. A technician working in a radiocarbon laboratory; he is dating archaeological samples from 500 to 50,000 years old.

Below. Excavation in progress on an early Kodiak Eskimo settlement at Karluk, Alaska.

Lower right. Field crew at work measuring a pre-historic Easter Island statue for the Rock Art Archive of the Institute of Archaeology, Los Angeles, California.

and valley civilizations were followed by the imperial civilizations of Persia, Greece, and Rome, which linked many diverse cultures into much larger hegemonies. Whereas the preindustrial civilizations relied on abundant cheap labor for their prosperity, the industrial civilization of today evolved from a preindustrial base, propelled to ever greater technological complexity by the use of fossil fuels, the advances of science, and the industrial revolution.

The fascinating chronicle of world prehistory has been written from the testimony of millions of chipped stones, animal bone fragments, and potsherds; from Sumerian clay tablets, pollen grains from Scandinavian bogs, and ancient Peruvian textiles. Archaeology is, as more than one author has reminded us, the science of rubbish (Fagan, 1991b). The data may seem trivial, but the results are not. World prehistory is of vital concern to everyone, for it records the collective cultural heritage of all humankind.

Scientific archaeology developed out of early intellectual curiosity and treasure hunting. It is a process of careful research design, site survey, excavation, laboratory analysis, and interpretation. In fact, it is no coincidence that the first large-scale scientific excavations in Europe were conducted by a retired British general and German archaeologists who came from a strongly military cultural tradition. It was they who imposed the first discipline on archaeological excavation, a discipline that continues to this day. To most people, archaeology *is* excavation—trenches, careful troweling and shoveling, and the clearance of burials with paintbrushes and dental picks. However, as the accompanying picture essay shows, modern archaeology is far more, involving everything from walking the countryside to sophisticated remote-sensing techniques and many months of quiet laboratory analysis. Archaeology is a complicated form of teamwork, involving not only experts but also volunteers from every walk of life. Many college students go on an excavation as part of their learning. If you are lucky, you will find an unusual artifact or help the archaeologists interpret a complicated sequence of long-collapsed buildings. You can spend your spare hours sorting shellfish and bone fragments from Indian shell middens, become an expert on a particular prehistoric pottery, or operate a computer program that holds the data from months of fieldwork. Your work may seem trivial, sometimes even dull, but the results are another tiny part of the great jigsaw of world prehistory. None of our attempts to explain the rise of civilization or the origins of humanity would mean anything unless they were based on scientifically recovered archaeological data.

People of the Earth takes you on a 2.5-million-year journey through prehistory, from the very earliest times to the emergence of the first urban civilizations. However, we begin by explaining some of the basic principles, methods, and theories of archaeology so that you will be better equipped both to understand prehistory and to participate in archaeology yourself as a volunteer if you so desire. Good luck with your adventures in the past!

WHY STUDY WORLD PREHISTORY?

Before starting our journey, we deal with another fundamental point. Why study world prehistory at all? Some people believe that any form of archaeology is a harmless luxury, a low priority in a world beset by inflation, famine, and geopolitics. Why look to the past, they ask, when all our energies should be devoted to preparing for an uncertain future? How can one look at the future, though, without an understanding of the past and, above all, of our own behavior? Whether we like it or not, we live with the legacy of the recent and remote past. Our civilization derives many of its most cherished institutions from classical Greece, whereas city life was developed between the Euphrates and Tigris rivers in Iraq more than 5000 years ago. Famine, slavery, warfare, and poverty are nothing new; they were familiar phenomena to the ancient Egyptians, the Chinese, and the Sumerians. In reality, we live with the consequences of decisions and actions that were enacted centuries or even millennia ago. The study of prehistory gives us a balanced perspective on our behavior and on our responses to pressing problems that are not new, even though they threaten us on a larger scale.

Western civilization has a written chronicle that extends back to Sumerian times, more than 5000 years ago. However, many of the world's societies have very limited written historical records and are known to us only through scattered folk memories or archaeological excavations. The Aztec people of Mexico first came into contact with the Spanish in 1519. Within a few years their civilization was in ruins, their written chronicles burned by zealous missionaries. As a result, our knowledge of Aztec history is a patchwork of incomplete data from dozens of sources, yet a knowledge of this history is vital not only for fostering a sense of identity among the surviving Aztec people and for nation building in Mexico but also for understanding the ways in which ancient Mesoamericans solved the problems of living (Schele and Friedel, 1990). It is no coincidence that many African nations have active archaeological programs, designed to reconstruct a national history from a morass of obscure tribal histories and excavations at archaeological sites. Likewise, some American Indian groups have become involved in archaeological research, in a search for their remote cultural roots (Kirk, 1975). In prehistoric times, most societies focused on living in equilibrium with their environment, existing in a world that was assumed to have been the same in the past and that would remain unchanged in the future. Today industrial civilization, with its concern with cultural roots and cultural identity, dominates the world, so there are compelling reasons for every society to have at least some sense of its cultural origins. In many cases, archaeology provides the only way of gaining this insight.

We live in a biologically and culturally diverse world, a world that is shrinking rapidly in this age of the jetliner, the satellite, and instant communications. Even half a century ago the world was a large place. Today the world, in all its bewildering diversity, comes right into our living rooms. We can contact Peru within seconds and watch wars on the other side of the globe as they are being fought. Confronting this diversity is often an uncomfortable experience, especially since we tend to perceive the differences between various societies as much greater than they really are. By looking back over the long millennia of prehistory, we obtain a quite different perspective of a world in which people have worked out solutions to extremely challenging problems with brilliant success, problems such as food shortages, rapidly growing populations, and catastrophic environmental changes. Very often the solutions of various societies, although they are separated by thousands of miles, have been remarkably similar: the advent of writing, the development of cities, or the formation of a state-organized society. What is striking is not the diversity of humankind but the remarkably similar ways in which we respond to external challenges. Societies may wax and wane, civilizations rise and fall, but something new always arises in their place. To look back at prehistory is to acquire a faith in humanity's ability to innovate and respond to changing circumstances. We are surrounded by doomsday prophets, by people who forecast the imminent demise of civilization, of humanity itself. Any serious student of prehistory can have no doubt that humankind will rise to the challenges of the twentieth century. We shall survive.

A final compelling reason to study world prehistory is simply for its fascination. Archaeology is a serious profession practiced by thousands of people in the United States and all over the world. They spend their lives gazing back at an extraordinary landscape of biological and cultural evolution, at our very origins among the nonhuman primates, at the first migrants to the New World perhaps 15,000 years ago, and at remarkable civilizations as widely separated as the Indus Valley and Peru. We are surrounded by awesome ruins that have survived the centuries to enlighten our age: Monk's Mound at Cahokia, Illinois, planned and constructed by Mississippian people nearly 1000 years ago; the magnificent pueblos of the Southwest; and the brooding stone circles of Stonehenge in southern Britain, to say nothing of the Pyramids of Giza, erected more than 4500 years ago, and the vast plazas and temples of the ancient city of Teotihuacán, Mexico. Most of us contrive to visit at least one major archaeological site during our lifetimes, to marvel at the achievements of our predecessors on this planet. An understanding of world prehistory enables us not only to better appreciate these monuments but also to recognize them for what they are, an integral part of the cultural heritage of all humanity.

People use scientific data from all over the world to outline the prehistory of humankind. This narrative is based on one basic assumption: The theory of biological evolution and natural selection provides a viable framework for the study of human prehistory.

ANTHROPOLOGY

Anthropology

Anthropology encompasses the whole range of human cultures, both Western and non-Western (Pelto, 1966; Penniman, 1965). As the study of humanity, anthropology is a holistic discipline that uses comparative methods to examine variations in every aspect of human society. Anthropologists are interested in comparisons between different cultures and in biological and cultural evolution. The comparative and evolutionary aspects of anthropology make it unique among the social sciences.

Archaeology

Archaeology is the study of the lives and cultures of ancient peoples. Archaeologists study and interpret the material evidence of past human activity. Archaeology has three main objectives, all of which involve interpreting the data of the archaeological record by using sophisticated analytic techniques, the natural processes that created the data, and controlled experiments and analogies from present-day societies. These objectives are the study of culture history, a reconstruction of past lifeways, and an explanation of cultural process. There are many types of archaeologists, each having distinctive objectives, methods, techniques, and theoretical approaches. *Classical archaeologists* study Greek and Roman civilization; *historical archaeologists* study relatively recent sites such as colonial American towns or medieval cities. *Anthropological archaeologists* (prehistorians) are concerned with sites of all ages, but they tend to concentrate their research efforts primarily on prehistoric settlements. *Paleoanthropologists* study the earliest human cultures of all.

Physical anthropology

   Physical anthropologists study the emergence and subsequent evolution of humankind and why human populations vary from one another (Weiss and Mann, 1988). Early human evolution is documented by fossil human and prehuman remains found in archaeological sites and geological levels. Physical anthropologists are deeply involved in modern human biology, trying to find out why different human populations have adapted physically to widely differing natural environments. *Primatologists* are physical anthropologists who are experts on ape and monkey behavior. Their work provides information relevant to the study of early human behavior.

History

   History is the study of our past through written records; such records extend back only 5000 years, and then only in Mesopotamia and Egypt. *Prehistory*, the millennia before documentary history, goes back at least 2.5 million years.

HUMAN CULTURE

Culture

   Culture is a term we will use again and again in these pages. Anthropologists study human cultures, and all of us live within a culture. Most cultural descriptions can be qualified by one or more labels, such as *middle class, American, mountain-dwelling,* or *Masai.* This qualification often becomes associated in our minds with certain behavior patterns or features that are typical of the culture so labeled. One such attribute for "middle-class Americans," for example, might be the hamburger.

   Culture is a concept developed by anthropologists to describe the distinctive adaptive system used by human beings (Jochim, 1981). Culture can be called a people's (or a society's) traditional systems of belief and behavior, as understood (or adapted) by individuals and the members of social groups, and manifest in individual or collective behavior. It is also part of our way of adapting to our environment.

   Until the emergence of humanity, all animals adapted to their environments through biological evolution. If an animal was well adapted to its environment, it prospered. If it was not, it evolved into a new species, moved away, or became extinct. The forces of biological evolution gave the polar bear a thick coat and layers of fat to protect it from the arctic cold, but Eskimos, the human occupants of the Arctic, do not have layers of fur. They wear warm clothing and make snow houses to shield themselves from the environment. Their tools and dwellings are part of their culture—their adaptive system that coincides with the polar bear's fur.

   Ordinarily, when animals die their experience dies with them. However, humans, once biological evolution had led to the development of speech, were able to communicate their feelings and experiences from one generation to the next. They could share ideas, which in turn became behavior patterns that were repeated again and again. We see abundant traces of this development throughout prehistory when the same types of tools and sites are found, almost unchanged, over millennia. A good example of this phenomenon is the stone hand ax, a multipurpose tool that remained in use for more than 1 million years (Figure 4.9).

Human beings use the symbolic system of language to transmit ideas and their culture. Culture is learned by intentional teaching as well as trial and error and simple imitation. Since people share ideas by teaching, the same artifacts and behavior continue from one generation to the next. Culture is an ongoing phenomenon that changes gradually over time.

Unlike biological adaptation, culture is nongenetic and provides a much quicker way to share ideas that enable people to cope with their environment. It is the adaptive nature of culture that allows archaeologists to assume that artifacts found in archaeological sites are patterned adaptations to the environment.

Cultural system   A culture is a complex system, a set of interacting variables—tools, burial customs, ways of getting food, religious beliefs, social organization, and so on—that function to maintain a community in a state of equilibrium with its environment. When one element in the system changes, say hunting practices as a result of a prolonged drought, then reacting adjustments will occur in many other elements, so that the system stays in a state as closely approximating the original system as possible. It follows that no cultural system is ever static. It is always changing in big and small ways, some of which can be studied in archaeological sites.

Archaeologists tend to think of culture as possessing two broad components:

- The individual's own version of his or her culture, the diversified individual behavior that makes up the myriad strains of a culture.

- Shared culture, the elements of a culture that are shared by everyone. These can include cultural activities like hunting or farming, as well as the body of rules and prescriptions that go to make up the whole of the culture. Shared culture is the system of behavior in which every individual *participates.* Not only do you share it with other members of society but you participate in the cultural system as well. Both sharing and participation, however, could not take place without language as a vehicle of communication.

Culture, then, can be viewed as either a blend of shared traits or a system that permits a society to interact with its environment. To accomplish more than merely working out chronological sequences, however, the archaeologist has to view culture as a complex set of interacting components. Unless the processes that actually operate the system are carefully defined, these components would remain static, which is why archaeologists are deeply concerned with what is called *cultural process,* the processes by which human societies changed in the past.

Cultural changes take place through time, most being gradual and cumulative. Inventions and design improvements result in dozens of minor alterations in the ways people live. Generally, cultural evolution was gradual in prehistoric times, although there are cases of sudden change, such as the Roman conquest of Gaul. Dramatic cultural modification can result from the diffusion from neighboring areas of a new idea or invention, such as the plow (Chapter 2). Culture change is proceeding at a dizzying pace in our own society, to the extent that we have problems adjusting to its constancy.

The cumulative effects of long-term culture change are easily seen. A comparison of the simple flaked stone tools of the earliest humans and the sophisticated contents of the Egyptian pharaoh Tutankhamun's tomb will help one to understand the power of cumulative change over thousands of years.

Modern archaeology swirls with controversy about the goals of research. Earlier archaeologists often were content just to collect and classify their finds into long sequences of human cultures. They described changing cultures but made no effort to explain *why* change took place and *what* changes meant. Today's archaeologist is concerned with explanation as well as description of ancient cultures, with processes of cultural change through time. The term *process* is used in archaeology to refer to mechanisms by which cultures change. These processes of culture change are studied by looking at variables in cultural systems that could lead to cultural change (Chapter 2). Then there is the archaeological record itself. Just trying to understand how it came into being is a far less obvious process than might be apparent (Binford, 1983).

THE ARCHAEOLOGICAL RECORD

Archaeologists study human cultures of the past and have to be content, for the most part, with the surviving, more durable evidence of prehistoric culture (Deetz, 1967; Fagan, 1991a). Any excavator is like a detective piecing together events from fragmentary clues.

What we can find out about the past is severely limited by soil conditions. Stone and baked clay are among the most lasting substances, surviving under almost all conditions. Wood, bone, leather, and metals are much less durable and seldom remain for the archaeologist to find. In the Arctic, however, whole sites have been found frozen, preserving highly perishable wooden tools or, in Siberia, complete carcasses of extinct mammoths (J. D. G. Clark, 1965). Water-logged bogs in Denmark have preserved long-dead victims of human sacrifice, and wooden tools survive well in such sites too. Everyone has heard of the remarkable tomb of the Egyptian pharaoh Tutankhamun, whose astonishing treasure survived almost intact in the dry climate of the Nile Valley for more than 3000 years (Romer, 1981). Still, in most archaeological sites only a few durable materials survive, and reconstructing the past from these finds is often difficult.

Archaeological record

The *archaeological record* is the data amassed from survey and excavation: We might think of it as the archival raw materials of world prehistory.

The inevitable result of having only durable remains to study is that many prehistoric cultures are interpreted solely on the basis of such imperishable tools as stone axes or clay potsherds. The only way archaeologists can combat this emphasis is by meticulous study of sites where preservation conditions are outstanding; through careful examination of the arrangement of artifacts in the soil, archaeologists may discover a clue about the activities or social status of the artifacts' owners.

Until recently, most archaeologists simply accepted the limitations of the archaeological record. They made little effort to understand the ways in which the record was formed. Consider for a moment a newly abandoned hunter-gatherer campsite in the Illinois valley of the Midwest. The inhabitants leave collapsing houses, newly extinguished hearths, broken-up bones, acorn husks, and all manner of domestic debris as well as worn-out artifacts behind them. The years pass. Rain and wind destroy the houses, and they become a scatter of foundation stones and postholes. The acorn husks and bones decay and vanish. Soon the site is covered with dense woodland and grass, soils accumulate, and there are no surface traces of the site left. Once buried, the surviving structures, hearths, and artifacts undergo still further change as a result of processes resulting from the distinctive soil chemistry on the site. Hundreds, if not thousands, of years later some archaeologists come along and dig up the site. All that they will unearth are the surviving remnants of generations of decay processes. These processes vary from site to site and are little understood (Chapter 2).

Since our understanding of these processes is very much in its infancy, most archaeologists still rely heavily on sites where preservation conditions are exceptional and on the assistance of scholars from other disciplines. Botanists and zoologists can identify seeds and bone fragments from ancient living sites to reconstruct prehistoric diets. Geologists study lake beds, gravels, and caves, the geological contexts of the many tools from early millennia. Paleontologists and paleobotanists specialize in the evolution of mammals and plants, studying bones from extinct animals and pollens from long-vanished plants. They help reconstruct ancient climates, which have fluctuated greatly through our long history. Chemists and physicists employ radioactive methods of dating for volcanic rocks and organic substances such as bone and charcoal. These techniques have produced a rough chronological framework for more than 2.5 million years of human life. Modern archaeology is truly a multidisciplinary team effort, depending on scientists from many fields of inquiry. In one afternoon, an excavator may call on a glass expert, an authority on seashells, an earthworm specialist, and a soil scientist. Each has a piece to fit into the archaeological puzzle.

THE FINITE ARCHAEOLOGICAL RECORD
AND CULTURAL RESOURCE
MANAGEMENT

The records of written history are preserved in manuscripts, in books, and on clay tablets or papyrus—archives of the past that can be photocopied, transcribed, and traced. The archives of world prehistory are the sites, artifacts, and other material remains of human behavior that make up the archaeological record. This record is finite, an intricate association of individual archaeological phenomena and geological or occupation layers, the context in time and space in which they occur. Every time someone picks up an artifact or excavates a site or constructs a highway through an ancient Indian village, the archives of the prehistoric past are destroyed, or at best modified. The archaeological record is quite different from a forest. Trees can regerminate; forests can be reseeded. But once disturbed the archaeological record is gone forever. Prehistory is nonrenewable.

Many of the fine artifacts displayed in museums can be admired as magnificent examples of prehistoric technological skill. But most have been wrenched from their sites without regard for their archaeological context, the information they could yield about prehistoric times. The archives of the past consist of far more than fine artifacts in public museums. They consist of archaeological sites and the information, as well as the artifacts, within them. Once disturbed, these cannot be replaced.

Prehistory is under siege—from unscrupulous art dealers and amateur "pot hunters"; from industrial activity, road construction, and urban sprawl; from deep plowing and strip mining. Every month, hundreds more sites vanish under the bulldozer or plow, scattered into historical oblivion. Some experts believe that there will be virtually no undisturbed archaeological sites in Europe, parts of Mesoamerica, and North America by the end of this century (McGimsey, 1973).

Many archaeologists are now engaged full-time in a frantic scramble to save sites from destruction. These activities—environmental impact studies and field projects, salvage excavations and complex regional surveys—are called *cultural resource management,* the process of managing archaeological sites and other cultural resources as nonrenewable parts of the landscape. Cultural resource management involves complicated legal and management decisions, some of which can conflict directly with the purely academic task of studying prehistoric times (D. D. Fowler, 1987; Knudsen, 1986), but the mass of information being acquired from such activity shows promise of transforming our knowledge of North American prehistory.

Cultural resource management

Although organizations like the Society for American Archaeology are frantically trying to stem the tide of destruction, the future of the past depends not only on archaeologists but also on the public at large. Many people still think of archaeology as a glorified treasure hunt, of archaeological sites as potential treasure troves. But for a significant part of the archaeological record to survive in the twenty-first century there must be concerted effort not only by professionals but also by every member of the public. You can do your bit by reporting all archaeological finds to responsible authorities, never collecting prehistoric artifacts or digging into sites, and respecting native American burial grounds.

The future of world prehistory depends on all of us.

ARTIFACTS, SITES, AND CONTEXT

World prehistory is recorded in thousands of archaeological sites and artifacts, each of which has a precise place in space and time, that is, in its context. Some knowledge of the ways in which archaeologists study the dimensions of space and time is essential to an understanding of prehistory (Dunnell, 1971).

Context

Archaeological context is the culturally significant location of a find spot of any object in an archaeological site (Fagan, 1991b). *Cultural context* is a subcategory that represents the position of an object; was it found in a pit, in a room, on a surface? Metric data are used to define the position of the object uniquely. The time component of the context is the date of the object in years or its position in the layers of an archaeological site relative to other artifacts and layers. The time and space context of an archaeological find provides the basis for building up long sequences of archaeological sites in time and space.

Artifact

An *artifact* is "anything which exhibits any physical attributes that can be assumed to be the results of human activity" (Dunnell, 1971). The term *artifact* covers

BOX 1.2

A Case of
Archae-
ological
Looting

Slack Farm lies near Uniontown, Kentucky, close to the Ohio River, the site of a large, undisturbed archaeological site occupied by native Americans sometime between A.D. 1450 and 1650, a time when Europeans were making their first contacts with communities in the general area. For years, the owners of Slack Farm preserved the site, but the property changed hands. In the fall of 1987, the new owners received $10,000 from ten pot hunters from Kentucky, Indiana, and Illinois for the right to "excavate" Slack Farm. They rented a tractor and began bulldozing their way through the village midden to reach graves. They pushed heaps of bones aside and dug through dwellings, and the potsherds, hearths, and stones associated with them. Along the way, they left detritus of their own—empty pop-top beer and soda cans, scattered on the ground alongside prehistoric pottery fragments.

Slack Farm looked like a battlefield—a morass of crude shovel holes and gaping trenches. Broken human bones littered the surface and fractured artifacts crunched underfoot.

Two months passed before local residents complained about the digging. Kentucky State Police arrested the diggers under a state law that prohibits desecration of a venerated object. Eventually, the charges were dropped. A team of archaeologists is now trying to record what is left of the site, but a vital chapter in Ohio Valley prehistory is gone forever.

It is not making headlines, but looting on the scale of Slack Farm is commonplace throughout the United States, from the Bering Strait to the Virgin Islands. If the present pace of scandalous destruction continues, there will be precious little archaeology left for our grandchildren to study.

every form of archaeological find—from stone axes to clay pots, butchered animal bones, and manifestations of human behavior found in archaeological sites.

Site

Archaeological sites are places where traces of ancient human activity are to be found. The Great Pyramid of Giza is an archaeological site; so is a tiny scatter of hunter-gatherer artifacts found on the surface of the Utah desert. Sites are limited in number and variety only by preservation conditions, by modern destruction, and by the activities of the people who lived on them. Some, like the early bone caches at Olduvai Gorge, Tanzania, were used for only short periods of time (M. D. Leakey, 1971). Others, such as the great Mesopotamian city mounds or *tells,* like Ur of the Chaldees, were occupied for thousands of years (Lloyd, 1963; Woolley, 1934). Archaeological sites are often classified according to the activities that took place on them—living sites, kill sites, burial sites, religious sites, art sites, and so on. Many archaeological sites contain evidence of different activities: those of individual households; of entire communities; or perhaps even of a single craftsperson like a potter, whose artifacts lie in a pattern as they were abandoned.

Features

Features are humanly manufactured structures found in archaeological sites, and they can take many forms. These include hut foundations, temples, humble storage pits, graves, fences, and fortifications.

SPACE

The archaeological context of space can run from a simple spatial relationship between two artifacts to the distance between several households, or even to the relationships between an entire regional network of communities (Flannery, 1976). Context in space is closely tied to cultural behavior. Archaeologists infer behavior from artifacts and their associations, from the patterning (spatial arrangement) of tools around, say, an abandoned bison carcass. A single projectile point dug up out of context at this particular site would allow us nothing more than the reasonable inference that it was part of a weapon. However, the patterning of many such weapon points in association with the butchered remains of the bison can tell us much about how the animal was killed and cut up. The relationships between the carcass and the tools in the ground are our primary source of information on human behavior there.

Association

The *Law of Association* is based on the principle that an object is contemporary with the other objects found in the precise archaeological level in which it is found (Figure 1.1): The study of space is the study of associations between artifacts within their archaeological cultures. It also involves the study of the distribution of human settlements against a background of the ancient environment in which they flourished.

TIME

World prehistory extends through at least 2.5 million years of gradually accelerating cultural change. The measurement of this enormous time scale has been a preoccupation of archaeologists for years.

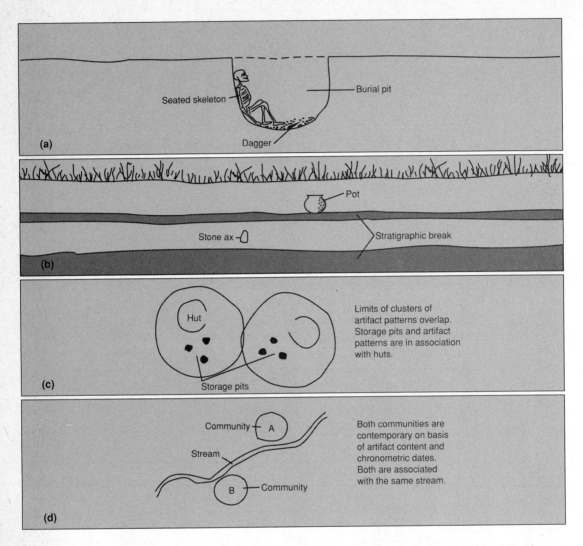

FIGURE 1.1   The Law of Association. (a) A skeleton associated with a single dagger and level II; (b) a pot and a stone ax, separated by a stratigraphic break, not in association; (c) two contemporary household clusters associated with one another; (d) an association of two communities that are contemporary.

Relative Chronology

At the end of the eighteenth century, people began to realize that the earth's rocks were stratified, or laid down in layers, one after another. The notion of geological stratification was soon applied to archaeological sites and is now a cornerstone of *relative chronology,* the correlation of prehistoric sites or cultures with one another by their relative age.

Superposition   Stratification is based on the *Law of Superposition,* which says that the lowest occupation level on a site is older than those accumulated on top of it. The principle can be readily understood if you place a book on a flat surface, then place a second book on top of the first. Obviously, the first book was put on the table earlier than the second that lies upon it. Unless you took a stopwatch and timed the exact interval in minutes and seconds between the time you placed the first and second books on the surface, you have no idea how much *time* separated the two events. All you know is that the second book was placed on the first at a *relatively later* moment. Figure 1.2 illustrates the principle of superposition in archaeological practice.

Superpositions are established by careful excavation and observation of archaeological layers. These layers are excavated with great care, and the artifacts associated with them are carefully studied relative to the stratigraphy of the site. We have stated that artifact styles change slowly though time. Every artifact style, however elaborate or simple, has a period of maximum popularity. This can be a few short months in

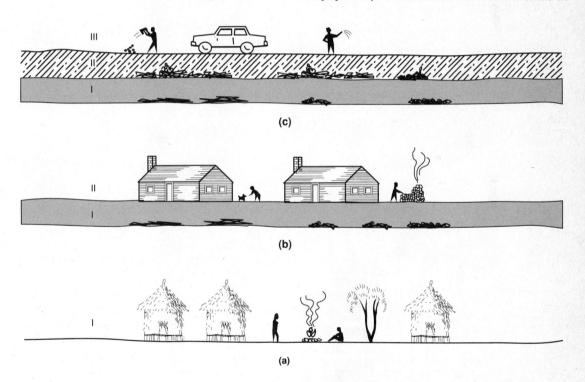

FIGURE 1.2   Superposition and stratigraphy. (a) A farming village built on virgin subsoil. After a time, the village is abandoned and the huts fall into disrepair. Their ruins are covered by accumulating soil and vegetation. (b) After an interval, a second village is built on the same site, with different architectural styles. This in turn is abandoned; the houses collapse into piles of rubble and are covered by accumulating soil. (c) Twentieth-century people park their cars on top of both village sites and drop litter and coins, which when uncovered reveal to the archaeologist that the top layer is modern.

An archaeologist digging this site would find that the modern layer is underlain by two prehistoric occupation levels; that square houses were in use in the upper of the two, which is the later (Law of Superposition); and that round huts are stratigraphically earlier than square ones here. Therefore, Village 1 is earlier than Village 2, but when either was occupied or how many years separate Village 1 from Village 2 cannot be known without further data.

the case of a dress fashion or tens of thousands of years for a stone tool type. By careful study of artifacts such as pottery found in the successive layers of several archaeological sites in a single region, it is possible to develop a relative chronology of changing artifact styles that is based on the assumption that the period of maximum popularity of a particular pottery type, or series, is the one in which it is most frequently found (see Figure 1.3). By using these plots of artifact frequencies, we can develop a relative chronology that later can be used to place isolated sites into the sequence on the basis of their artifact content. This type of ordered or *seriated* relative chronology is not expressed in years unless it can be checked by some dating method that provides dates in years (Deetz, 1967; Marquardt, 1978).

Seriation

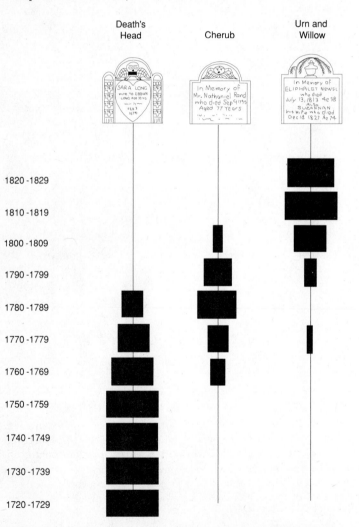

FIGURE 1.3   Seriation. The changing styles of New England gravestones from Stoneham, Massachusetts, between 1720 and 1829, seriated in three different styles. Notice how each style rises to a peak of maximum popularity and then declines as another comes into fashion.

Cross-dating

These ordered sequences of sites and layers can be expanded very effectively by a technique known as *cross-dating*. This requires a well-studied sequence of different artifacts whose development through time has been established by excavation, seriation of the artifacts, and stratigraphic observations. In the Tehuacán Valley in Mexico, Richard MacNeish (1970) was able to assign a relative date to isolated settlements by careful analysis of their pottery. (For a Peruvian example, see Menzel et al., 1964.) He counted the different vessel forms and decorative motifs at each site, then simply placed them in chronological order by matching the percentages of forms and motifs at undated sites with those in a dated sequence nearby. For example, a site with 60 percent red painted bowls is dated to 150 B.C., so it is a reasonable supposition that an undated comparable settlement with the same proportion of similar vessels (and of course, comparable percentages of other features) is of approximately the same date. Cross-dating like this has been used over wide areas of Mexico to compare sites in different valleys and environments.

Another type of cross-dating has proved useful in European sites. The early civilizations of the Near East traded extensively with the Minoan and Mycenaean civilizations of Greece and Crete as well as with Barbarian Europe (Childe, 1958; C. Renfrew, 1972). They exchanged luxuries such as semiprecious stones and ornaments with the illiterate Europeans for copper, salt, and other raw materials. Some of these luxuries can be dated very precisely in their home countries, so much so that their discovery on an archaeological site in central Europe enables one to say that the level in which the dated foreign object was found dates to the time of the import or later. Since the date of the artifact is known at its source, the settlement in which it is found can be relatively dated to a period contemporary with, or younger than, the exotic object of known age. For instance, a Roman coin minted the year Julius Caesar invaded Britain and found in an undated French village would date that settlement to a time no earlier than 55 B.C.

Chronometric (Absolute) Chronology

Chronometric dates are dates in calendar years. Prehistoric chronologies cover long periods of time, millennia or centuries as opposed to days or minutes. Some idea of the scale of prehistoric time can be gained by piling up 100 quarters. If the whole pile represents the entire time that humans and their culture have been on earth, the length of time covered by historical records would equal considerably less than the thickness of one quarter.

How do we date the past in years? Numerous chronometric dating techniques have been tried, but only a few have survived the test of continual use (Table 1.1) (Michels, 1973; Taylor and Meighan, 1978).

Historical Records (Present Day to 5000 Years Ago)

Historical records can be used to date the past only as far back as the beginnings of writing and written records. The Sumerian King Lists of Mesopotamia are some of the first attempts to record past events (Kramer, 1963). Many areas of the world, such as New Guinea or tropical Africa, entered the realms of recorded history only in the

Table 1.1   Dating methods in prehistory

Date B.P.	Method	Major Events
Modern times (after A.D. 1)	Historical documents; dendrochronology; imported objects most useful	European settlement of New World; Roman Empire
4500 B.P.		Origins of cities
	Radiocarbon dating (organic materials)	Origins of agriculture
		First Americans
70,000 B.P.	Obsidian hydration	Homo sapiens neanderthalensis
		Homo sapiens sapiens
500,000 B.P.		Homo erectus
	Potassium argon dating (volcanic materials)	Homo Australopithecus
5,000,000 B.P.	Uranium series dating	

These conventions have been used in the tables throughout this book:

——— A continuous line means the chronology is firmly established.

———▶ A line terminating in an arrow means the time span continues beyond the arrow.

———| A line terminating with a horizontal bar means the limit of chronology is firmly established.

- - - - - A broken line means the chronology is doubtful.

?Escale A question mark beside the name of a site means its date is not firmly established.

last century, and continual historical documentation began in the Americas with Christopher Columbus (Fagan, 1991c).

Dendrochronology

TIME SPAN: Present day to sites dating to 332 B.C. in the American Southwest, to earlier than 3000 B.C. in Europe.

PRINCIPLES: Many years ago Dr. A. E. Douglass of the University of Arizona used the annual growth rings of trees in the southwestern United States to develop a nonarchaeological chronology for this area that extends back 8200 years (Bannister and Robinson, 1975). Douglass studied the sequoia and other slow-growing trees to develop a long master series of annual rings that he used to date fragments of wooden beams found in Indian pueblos. By analyzing cycles of rings from dry and wet series of years, he was able to set up an archaeological chronology for the Southwest that extends back to 322 B.C. Dendrochronology has been used in other areas of the world as well—in Alaska and the American Southeast and with great success in Greece, Ireland, and Germany. European experts have linked rings from living oak trees to prehistoric trunks found in bogs and archaeological sites. A tree-ring sequence in northern Ireland goes back 7272 years, another from Germany 6000 years.

APPLICATIONS: The chronology of southwestern archaeology described in Chapter 14 is developed from dendrochronology. Tree-ring chronologies are used to calibrate radiocarbon dates from Europe as far back as 7200 years ago.

Tree rings have been used to date Roman sites in Germany and even the oak boards that formed the backings for paintings by old Dutch masters (Baillie, 1982).

Radiocarbon Dating (C14)

TIME SPAN: Approximately 40,000 years ago to A.D. 1500.

PRINCIPLES: The radiocarbon (C14) dating method, developed by physicists J. R. Arnold and W. F. Libby in 1949, puts to use the knowledge that living organisms build up their own organic matter by photosynthesis and by using atmospheric carbon dioxide. The percentage of radiocarbon in the organism is equal to that in the atmosphere. When the organism dies, the carbon 14 (C14) atoms disintegrate at a known rate. It is possible then to calculate the age of an organic object by measuring the amount of C14 left in the sample. The initial quantity in a sample is low, so the limit of detectability is soon reached, although efforts are being made to extend the limit beyond 70,000 years (Grootes, 1978).

Radiocarbon dating is most effective for sites dating between 50,000 and about 500 years before the present (B.P.). Dates can be taken from many types of organic material, including charcoal, shell, wood, or hair. When a date is received from a C14 dating laboratory, it bears a statistical plus or minus factor; for example, 3621 ± 180 years (180 years represents 1 standard deviation), meaning that chances are two out of three that the true radiocarbon age is between the span of 3441 and 3801. If we double the deviation, chances are 19 out of 20 that the span (3261 to 3981) is correct. Most dates in the book are derived from C14 dated samples and should be recognized for what they are—statistical approximations (Fagan, 1991c; Sharer and Ashmore, 1987).

The conventional radiocarbon method depends on measurements of a beta-ray decay rate to date the sample. Accelerator mass spectrometry allows radiocarbon dating to be carried out by direct counting of carbon 14 atoms, rather than by counting radioactive disintegrations (Gowlett, 1987). This method has the advantage of allowing very tiny samples to be dated, especially for the time period between 10,000 and 30,000 years ago. Accelerator dating distinguishes between carbon 14 and carbon 12 and other ions through its mass and energy characteristics. The samples required are so small that it is possible, for example, to date an individual tree ring or a small wood fragment preserved in the socket of a bronze ax. Accelerator dating is playing an important role in dating the first settlement of the Americas and late Ice Age sites in Europe.

CALIBRATION: Radiocarbon dating was at first hailed as the solution to archaeologists' dating problems. Later research has shown this enthusiasm to be a little too optimistic (C. Renfrew, 1973). Unfortunately, the rate at which C14 is produced in the atmosphere has fluctuated considerably because of changes in the strength of the earth's magnetic field and alterations in solar activity. By working with tree-ring chronologies from the long-lived California bristlecone pine and European oaks, a number of C14 laboratories have agreed on correction tables for C14 dates between approximately 7200 years ago and A.D. 1950. The discrepancies between radiocarbon and calibrated dates differ widely, but a typical adjustment is that for 10 B.C. $+$ 30, which has a calibrated interval of 145 B.C. to A.D. 210. We summarize the agreed correction tables at the end of this book (Pearson, 1987; Stuiver and Kra, 1986).

APPLICATIONS: Radiocarbon dating has been used to establish most of the chronologies described in this book for sites dating to between about 40,000 years ago and A.D. 1500. It has been used to date early agriculture in both the New and Old Worlds, the beginnings of metallurgy, and the first settlement of the Americas. Without the C14 method, world prehistory would be almost entirely undated.

Obsidian Hydration

TIME SPAN: Recent times to about 800,000 years ago.

PRINCIPLES: Obsidian is a natural glass substance often formed by volcanic activity. It has long been prized by humankind for its sharp edges and excellent qualities for toolmaking. A new dating method takes advantage of the fact that a freshly made surface of obsidian will absorb water from its surroundings, which forms a measurable hydration layer that increases with the passage of time. Thus, the depth of hydration on the fractured surface of a stone tool represents the time since the artifact was manufactured or used. Hydration is observed with the aid of microscopically thin sections of obsidian from artifacts that are ground down to about 0.003 inches. The thickness of the layer is measured through the microscope in units of microns. Although there are still some problems with such unknown variables as temperature changes and their effects on hydration, the method holds great promise for the future.

APPLICATIONS: Obsidian hydration is a useful way of ordering large numbers of artifacts in relative series, simply by using their micron readings as they increase with age. It can also be used for dating sites, provided one has some other form of chronology, like tree rings, to check the results. Some of the world's earliest sites have yielded obsidian, and this method has been tried experimentally with settlements as early as 780,000 years ago.

Uranium Thorium Dating

TIME SPAN: Earlier than 300,000 years ago, sometimes up to a million years ago.

PRINCIPLES: As uranium decays by alpha and beta emission to lead, it forms many elements. By studying different isotopic pairs in the uranium decay series, a scientist can measure the amount of time that has passed since they were disrupted. Most uranium-disequilibrium dating systems are used to date deep-sea cores, but they have occasionally been used to date terrestrial carbonates deposited in caves. Uranium thorium methods are very useful, for calcium carbonate excludes thorium from its structure during crystallization but includes significant parts of uranium. As time passes the amount of ^{230}Th increases because of the decay of both ^{234}U and ^{238}U in the sample. Uranium thorium samples have dated finds of early human fossils in southern European caves dating to between 100,000 and 300,000 years ago.

Potassium Argon Dating

TIME SPAN: From the origins of humankind down to approximately 250,000 years ago.

PRINCIPLES: Potassium (K) is an abundant element in the earth's crust and is present in nearly every mineral. Potassium in its natural form contains only a small proportion of radioactive ^{40}K atoms. For every one hundred ^{40}K atoms that decay, 11 percent become argon 40, an inert gas that can easily escape from its material by diffusion when lava and other igneous rocks are formed. As volcanic rock forms by crystallization, the argon 40 concentration drops to almost nothing, but the process of ^{40}K decay continues, and 11 percent of every 100 ^{40}K atoms will become argon 40. Thus it is possible, using a spectrometer, to measure the concentration of argon 40 that has accumulated since the volcanic rock formed.

APPLICATIONS: We are fortunate that many of the world's earliest archaeological sites occur in volcanically active areas. Human tools are found in direct association with cooled lava fragments or ash from contemporary eruptions. Potassium argon has been used to date Olduvai Gorge and other famous early sites (Chapter 3) (Dalrymple and Lamphere, 1970).

Experimental Methods

A number of newly developed dating methods promise to amplify both potassium argon and radiocarbon techniques.

Fission track dating uses the principle that minerals and natural glasses contain uranium atoms that decay by spontaneous fission (Fagan, 1991c; Fleischer, 1975). The decay rate can be measured in volcanic rocks and has been used to date some samples from Olduvai Gorge. Fission track dating may have applications for sites between a million and 100,000 years old.

Thermoluminescence dating involves measuring the radioactive properties of baked clay vessels. Sudden and violent heating of the vessel allows the scientist to study stored energy and radioactive impurities in the clay. Thermoluminescence may one day provide a means of dating clay vessels as old as 10,000 years. It is also being used to date Ice Age sediments and cave deposits in Europe, Australia, and the Near East. Thermoluminescence dates for early human settlement in Australia may exceed 50,000 years (Roberts et al., 1990).

Historical records, dendrochronology, radiocarbon, and potassium argon dating are the staple dating methods for world prehistory.

However effective and accurate a chronometric method, it is useless unless the dated sample—be it a fragment of a wooden beam, a handful of charcoal, or a lump of cooled lava—is interpreted correctly. For instance, a lump of lava associated with an early stone tool does not date the tool; it dates the moment at which the lava cooled. It is up to the archaeologist to establish that the tool is contemporary with the lava. Beams may be used years after their parent tree was cut down. All these factors have to be taken into account when interpreting chronometric dates. The most securely dated sites are those with a chronology derived from several methods, say a combination of tree rings, thermoluminescence, and carbon 14.

ARCHAEOLOGICAL SURVEY AND EXCAVATION

How do archaeologists find sites? Many large sites, such as the pyramids of Giza in Egypt or Teotihuacán in Mexico, have been known for centuries. Evidence for less conspicuous sites may be accidentally exposed by water or wind erosion, earthquakes, and other natural phenomena. Burrowing animals may bring bones or stone tools to the surface on ancient settlements. Farmers plow up thousands of finds. Road makers and land developers move massive quantities of earth.

Survey

Most archaeological sites are discovered as a result of careful field survey and thorough examination of the countryside for both conspicuous and inconspicuous traces of the past (Crawford, 1953; Schiffer and House, 1977). A survey can cover a single city lot or an entire river basin, a reconnaissance that could extend over several years. The theoretical ideal is to locate all sites in the survey area, but this is impossible because many sites leave few traces above ground and the best that one can hope for is a sample of what is in the area. The most intensive surveys are made on foot, with field-workers spaced out at regular intervals so that as little as possible is missed. Surface finds from newly discovered sites can provide clues about the identity of the occupants, although even scientifically collected surface finds are no substitute for excavation. Surface sampling is of great use not only in site location but also as a way of making decisions about modifying research designs for sites that are already being excavated (Redman, 1987).

Originally, archaeologists looked for individual sites, which they then excavated on a large scale. Today, the environmental context of a site is often as important as the settlement itself, so much so that regional surveys of prehistoric sites and their settlement patterns are as important as excavation. *Settlement patterns* are distributions of prehistoric occupation on the landscape. Establishing such patterns requires a large investment of time and money. It took William Sanders and his colleagues a decade to survey the evolving settlement pattern in the basin of Mexico over the

Settlement patterns

millennia that preceded the emergence of Aztec civilization in the fifteenth century A.D. (Sanders, Parsons, and Santley, 1979). They relied heavily on remote-sensing methods, among them aerial photography. This approach has long been used to plot more conspicuous sites; it works well with prehistoric agricultural systems, Roman road networks, and other large-scale archaeological phenomena.

The days of uncontrolled archaeological excavations are long gone. Yet the destruction of archaeological sites proceeds at a breathtaking pace. Since the archaeological record is being destroyed faster than it can be conserved, archaeologists are more and more avoiding destructive excavation where at all possible and turning to side-scan radar, satellite imagery, and other sophisticated remote-sensing devices to study the past without digging (Colwell, 1983; Ebert, 1984). Remote sensing enables us to look at ancient landscapes and peoples' imprints upon them, and through computerized data bases to begin to predict densities of archaeological sites in different landscapes. As the number of undisturbed archaeological sites dwindles, we can expect all forms of remote sensing to assume much greater importance than conventional excavation. All kinds of new approaches to site survey are being developed, among them sophisticated computer simulations that help predict where sites will be located. Other computer programs are used to create "site profiles" that aid in the recognition of actual sites in the field.

Excavation

Archaeological excavation has developed from a form of treasure hunting into an exact and precise discipline. The fundamental premise of excavation is that all digging is destructive, even that done by the experts. The archaeologist's primary responsibility, therefore, is to record a site for posterity as it is dug because there are no second chances.

Research design

Every excavation is undertaken to answer specific questions, according to a formal *research design* that is worked out beforehand. The research design can ask questions about the chronology of the site, the layout of the settlement it contains, or changing artifact styles within the levels to be excavated (Binford, 1964; Mueller, 1975). By meticulous digging and careful sampling of the archaeological deposits, the excavator implements the research design and digs up and records the data that are used to test the hypotheses developed as part of that research design. Most archaeologists distinguish between two basic excavation methods (Figure 1.4) (P. Barker, 1983; Joukowsky, 1981; Wheeler, 1954):

Area excavation

1. *Area or horizontal excavation,* in which the objective is to uncover large areas of ground in search of houses or entire settlement layouts. This type of digging is on a relatively large scale and is designed to uncover household and other activities that are normally discoverable only by digging over an extensive area.

Vertical excavation

2. *Vertical excavation or trenching,* designed to uncover stratigraphic information or a sequence of occupation layers on a small scale. This type of excavation often is practiced when chronology or artifact samples are a primary concern.

FIGURE 1.4   Area (horizontal) and vertical excavations. Although archaeologists excavate in many ways and sometimes use sampling techniques, there is a basic distinction between area and vertical methods.

An area excavation of a stone circle at Strichen, Scotland, is designed to expose large segments of ground on a site so that buildings, all other structures, and even the layout of the entire settlement can be traced over a much larger area than would be uncovered in a vertical excavation. Area excavation is widely used when the budget is not a problem and the archaeologist is looking for settlement patterns.

A vertical excavation of Maiden Castle, Dorset, England, shows how a narrow trench is cut through successive layers of an earth rampart. Notice that only a small portion of the layers in the trench walls has been exposed. The objective of this excavation was to obtain information on the sequence of layers on the outer edge of the earthwork and in the ditch that originally lay on its exterior side. Only a narrow trench was needed to record layers, the finds from them, and the dating evidence.

The numerous archaeological sites described in this book fall into several broad categories, each of which presents special excavation problems. The most common are *living sites,* the places where people have lived and carried out a multitude of activities.

Living sites

Much of our knowledge of the earliest hunters and gatherers is found by excavating abandoned living sites. These people favored lakeside camps or convenient rock overhangs for protection from predators and the weather, availability of abundant water, and ready access to herds of game and vegetable foods. Olduvai Gorge in Tanzania is renowned for its prehistoric sites, small lakeside locations used by early humans for a few days or weeks before they moved on in their constant search for game, vegetable foods, and fish (see Figure 3.10) (Hill, 1984; M. D. Leakey, 1971).

Fortunately for archaeologists, these people abandoned food bones and tools where they were dropped. Crude windbreaks were left and might have been burned down by the next brush fire or blown away by the wind. In Olduvai, the gently rising waters of a prehistoric lake slowly covered the bone caches and preserved them for posterity, with the tools lying where they were dropped. Other people lived by the banks of large rivers. Their tools are found in profusion in river gravels that were subsequently jumbled and re-sorted by floodwater, leaving a confused mass of artifacts, not undisturbed living floors, for the archaeologist to uncover (Oakley, 1964).

Caves already occupied more than half a million years ago were reoccupied again and again as people returned to preferred spots. Many natural caves and rock shelters contain deep occupation deposits that can be removed by meticulous excavation with a dental pick, trowel, and brush. The sequence of occupation layers can be uncovered almost undisturbed from the day of abandonment (Deacon, 1979; Movius, 1977).

In contrast, farmers usually live in larger settlements than hunters, for they are tied to their herds and gardens and move less often. Higher population densities and more lasting settlements left more conspicuous archaeological sites from later millennia of human history. In the Near East and many parts of the New World, farming sites were occupied time after time over several thousand years, forming deep mounds of refuse, house foundations, and other occupation debris. These *tells* require large excavations and extensive earthmoving if anything is to be understood about how towns and settlements were laid out.

Tells

Kill sites

Kill sites are places where hunter-gatherers killed large mammals, then camped around the carcass for several days as they butchered their prey. The most famous kill sites are in the American Great Plains, at which entire bison herds have been found trapped in narrow defiles where they were driven to their death (see Figure 7.5) (Wheat, 1972). The stone projectile heads, scraping tools, and butchering artifacts used by the hunters have been found around the carcasses. *Ceremonial sites* may or may not be part of a living site (Weaver, 1981). Mesopotamian temples formed the focus of a city, and the pyramids, temples, and plazas of the Maya city of Tikal were an integral part of a city that presided over a scattered settlement pattern of towns and villages in the countryside (Figure 22.9). Some structures, like the Great Serpent Mound in Ohio (Fagan, 1991b) or Stonehenge in England (Figure 20.6) (Chippindale, 1983), were sites that served the religious needs of a wider community around them.

Ceremonial sites

Burial sites

Burial sites can yield important data from periods later than 70,000 years ago, the time when the first deliberate burials were made (J. E. Anderson, 1969; Brothwell, 1985). Skeletons and their accompanying grave goods give us a rather one-sided view of the past—funerary rites (Figure 17.5). Among the most famous prehistoric burials are those of the royal kings deposited at Ur of the Chaldees in Mesopotamia during the second millennium B.C. (Chapter 16) (Woolley, 1934), as well as the Shang graves in China, where charioteers and many retainers accompanied the royal dead (Figure 19.5) (Chang, 1980). The celebrated mounds of Pazyryk in Siberia show us other spectacular burial customs (Chapter 21) (Rudenko, 1970). Important people were buried with their chariots and steeds, the latter wearing elaborate harness trappings preserved by ice that formed when water entered the tombs and froze.

STUDYING THE FINDS

Archaeological finds take many forms. They may include fragmentary bones from game or domesticated animals (Binford, 1981). Vegetable foods such as edible nuts or cultivated seeds sometimes are found in archaeological sites where preservation conditions are good (Ford, 1985; Pearsell, 1989). Pottery, stone implements, iron artifacts, and occasionally bone and wooden tools all build up a picture of early technical achievements.

Archaeologists have developed elaborate classification systems that set down certain criteria for their finds. They also apply sophisticated analytic techniques for both classifying and comparing human artifacts (Watson, LeBlanc, and Redman, 1984). They use collections of stone tools, pottery, or other artifacts like swords and brooches for studying human culture and its development. Whatever the classificatory techniques used, however, the objective of analyzing bones, pottery, and other material remains is the study of prehistoric culture and of cultural change in the past. We classify the remains into arbitrary groups either by their shape or design or by their use, the latter a difficult task (Figure 1.5). We fit them together to form a picture of a human culture.

From time to time we shall refer to archaeological groupings like the Acheulian culture or the Magdalenian culture, which consist of the material remains of human culture preserved at a specific space and time at several sites; these finds are the concrete expressions of the common social traditions that bind a culture. When we speak of the Magdalenian culture, we mean the *archaeological culture representing a prehistoric social system, defined in a context of time and space, which has come down to us in the form of tools or other durable objects.* The description *Magdalenian* is quite arbitrary, derived from the cave site at La Madeleine, France, where the tools of the culture were first discovered. Such labels as Magdalenian are devised by archaeologists for their convenience.

Archaeological culture

The geographic extent or content of any archaeological culture is also defined somewhat arbitrarily but as precisely as possible, so that an archaeological word has an exact implication for other scholars. Much of the archaeological data summarized in this book consist of carefully compiled chronological sequences of archaeological cultures often extending over thousands of prehistoric years. The workings of archaeological research compare one collection of artifacts with assemblages from different layers in the same sites or other sites near or far away from the original find. Our record of human activity consists of innumerable classified and catalogued archaeological finds whose relationships determined much of the story of human culture that follows in these pages.

How did our forebears live? What animals did they hunt? What plant foods did they collect, or did they plant cereal or root crops or herd cattle or llamas? We study ancient subsistence by examining the fragmentary animal bones that survive in archaeological sites, as well as the seeds, pollen grains, and other traces of plant foods. These studies often throw important light on the hunting and herding practices of ancient peoples. For example, at 'Ain Ghazal in Jordan, Stone Age farmers of 9000 years ago herded and penned goats. We know this because the goat bones from the

FIGURE 1.5   Inference from an artifact. This Chumash Indian parching tray from southern California shows how inferences can be made from an archaeological find. Clearly, the range of inferences that can be made from artifacts alone is limited, especially when the find has no context in a site.

Context   The archaeological context of the tray is defined by its position in a site and what it is associated with, level, square, etc.; its relationship to other features, such as houses, is also recorded. Unless this information is known, the tray is an isolated specimen devoid of a cultural context or even a date. Context cannot be inferred from an artifact alone.

Construction and materials   The tray was made of reed, its red-brown color determined by the reed, known from modern observations to be the best material available. The steplike decoration on the tray was dictated by sewing and weaving techniques of basketry. The diamond patterns were probably added as a personal touch by the craftsperson who made it. The shape and decoration of the tray are repeated in many others that have been found and are evidently part of a well-established Chumash basketry tradition. More information about an artifact's construction and materials can be learned than about any other category of inference.

Function   The flat, round shape of the tray is determined by its function, for such trays were used to roast seeds by tossing them with embers in the tray. The function of a tray normally cannot be inferred from its shape, but identical modern versions have been found that are used for parching. We employ the technique of analogy, inferring that the archaeological find had the same function as the modern tray.

Behavior   The parching tray reveals something about the cooking techniques of the Chumash, but again only by analogy.

settlement show the characteristic marks of tethering (Chapter 10). Tiny seeds are collected by using sophisticated flotation methods that collect small organic fragments by passing the soil through water. This method was used at Koster, Illinois, where Archaic peoples of 4000 years ago not only foraged intensively for wild plant foods but also grew some native plants to supplement the annual yields from wild harvests (Chapter 8).

Reconstructing prehistoric diets is extremely difficult, for it is hard to establish the exact proportions of, say, game and plant foods in the diet or the degree to which a group relied on domesticated rather than wild plant foods. One technique involves identifying types of plant foods from the isotopic analysis of prehistoric bone and hair. By using the ratio between two stable carbon isotopes—carbon 12 and carbon 13 in animal tissue—one can establish the diet of the organism. For example, a population that shifts its diet from wild vegetable foods to domesticated maize experiences a shift in dietary isotopic values. This technique has been used with success to study the changeover from plant foraging to maize agriculture in the Tehuacán Valley, Mexico (Chapter 14). Another approach uses plant phytolith analysis. Opal phytoliths are created from hydrated silica dissolved in groundwater that is absorbed by a plant's root and carried through its vascular system (Piperno, 1988). Silica production is continuous throughout the growth of a plant, and samples are taken in much the same way as pollen samples. For example, in Venezuela's Orinoco River Valley, Anna Roosevelt (1980) found that the percentages of grass phytoliths increased dramatically at the very moment when maize was introduced to the area. Both these new approaches offer opportunities to study not only the introduction but also the spread of agriculture in many parts of the world (Part IV).

Anthropological archaeology is much more than inference and induction from the archaeological record, for our ultimate aim is to explain the past, not simply to describe it. As we shall see in Chapter 2, until recently most archaeologists concentrated on descriptions of sites and artifacts, and on discovering how particular cultures changed and evolved through prehistoric times.

Modern archaeology is changing. New theories seek to explain the past and explore the processes by which human cultures have changed. The archaeologists of the 1990s try and explain culture change and variation in the archaeological record by examining the behavioral content of the material remains of the past. The concern is with long-term changes in the ways people have adapted to their environments. British archaeologist Clive Gamble (1986b) calls the archaeological record of world prehistory a record of observations of "items of lost energy." These include artifacts, features, food remains, sites, and environmental data. It follows that students of world prehistory have a major concern with how this archaeological record was formed and with different ways of interpreting the static data of past human behavior—stone artifacts, broken bones, and so on—in terms of what was once dynamic human behavior in prehistoric times. To acquire this information, archaeologists use several innovative approaches, including ethnographic analogy, controlled experimentation, and middle range theory, a body of theory designed to bridge the gap between past and present.

SITE FORMATION PROCESSES, ANALOGY, AND EXPERIMENT

Site formation processes

There is nothing obvious in the archaeological record. We cannot just pick up stones, bones, or potsherds and ask them what they can tell us about human behavior. The past in the form of artifacts does not come down to us unchanged, for complex processes have acted on these objects, be they tools, dwellings, burials, food remains, or other manufactured or humanly modified items. Archaeologists must untangle the many events and processes that contribute to the great variability in the archaeological record. The factors that create the archaeological record are known as *site formation processes,* the agencies, natural or cultural, that have transformed the archaeological record. They can be the result of human actions (e.g., rebuilding houses) or natural phenomena such as floods or earthquakes. Archaeologist Michael Schiffer (1983) refers to a time machine that he calls "archaeological process . . . the principles and procedures that we as scientists apply to material traces in the historical and archaeological records. If we desire to obtain views of the past that are closer to reality . . . then we must build into our time machine a thorough understanding of formation processes."

The archaeological record must be decoded with a precise methodology if we are to understand artifacts and other human remains in terms of human behavior. Archaeological data are the results of behavior, not the behavior itself. This behavior can be observed only in a living cultural system. So in a sense, modern approaches to world prehistory can be called a form of behavioral code cracking.

Middle range theory

Archaeology, like history, is based on the principle of *uniformitarianism,* the assumption that the present provides observational data that enable us to unlock the information in written and unwritten records of the past. The term *middle range theory,* taken from sociology, is the current "buzzword" for a body of theory that is being formed as archaeologists try to bridge the gap between what actually happened in the past and the archaeological record of today. Middle range theory is based on the assumption that the archaeological record is a contemporary, static phenomenon, formed not by human behavior but by all manner of natural and humanly caused factors that buried artifacts, destroyed sites, rebuilt other settlements on them, covered them with windblown sand, and so on. These site formation processes are the critical link between long-extinct, dynamic human behavior in the past and the static material properties common in both the past and the present—the artifacts that we examine, pots that were used in the past, and similar types of vessels still used today (Binford, 1978, 1981; Raab and Goodyear, 1984).

Ethnographic analogy

Ethnographic analogy, comparing prehistoric societies with living peoples, has been a backbone of prehistoric archaeology for more than a century. Early analogies were simplistic, sweeping comparisons that assumed, for example, that the Inuit of the Arctic were living examples of Stone Age hunter-gatherers who had flourished in southwest France near the end of the Ice Age (Sollas, 1910). As we have seen, such arguments were closely tied to ideas of universal human progress.

Another form of analogy became popular in North America, where prehistory

Direct historical
approach

was, and still is, regarded as a form of anthropology in the past. This was the so-called *direct historical approach,* in which the archaeologist starts with a historical baseline, then excavates stratified sites that link the known, historical present with much earlier prehistoric cultures. A. V. Kidder (1927) used this approach with great success at Pecos pueblo in the Southwest in the 1920s, developing an outline chronology of pueblo occupation that extended back more than 2000 years. Given the long continuity of Indian culture in this area, the approach was fundamentally sound. Unfortunately, however, this direct and comprehensive way of comparing ancient and modern society is simply too elementary (for a discussion of analogy, see Wylie, 1985).

The modern attitude toward analogy is far more rigorous. During the past quarter century, archaeologists have refocused analogy in much more specific terms. They approach it in the context of a carefully defined problem, such as the function of an artifact, ways in which garbage was discarded, and so on. Here again, though, there are serious problems because the earlier the site, the more likely it is that site formation processes and other variables have affected the patterning of artifacts, food remains, and other phenomena in the ground.

Artifact analogies

Many archaeologists have turned to highly specific *artifact analogies* and have made exact replicas of prehistoric tools and weapons that they then tested under controlled conditions. Nicholas Toth (1985) has replicated hominid artifact assemblages from East Turkana and Olduvai Gorge in East Africa, artifacts more than 1.75 million years old. His experiments have demonstrated that our earliest toolmaking ancestors were adept stoneworkers, who were primarily interested in sharp flakes for cutting, sawing, and butchery (Chapter 3). Toth has even been able to show that some of the earliest toolmakers were left-handed by studying the flake scars on discarded cores and flakes. Jeffrey Flenniken (1988), an archaeologist of the American Northwest, learned how to make Paleo-Indian projectile points, which he tested against live animals. Combining studies of edge wear on ancient artifacts and modern replicas with careful "retrofitting" of flakes to discarded cores has proved a fruitful approach to the study of prehistoric stone technology.

Experimental archaeology has taken many other forms, too, and can be regarded as a form of analogy using controlled experimentation as a means of comparison. British archaeologist John Coles (1973) fabricated exact copies of European Bronze Age shields and swords, which were tested one against the other, showing that such weaponry was highly effective. Another fashionable form of experimental archaeology has been to build prehistoric settlements, then find volunteers to live in them for months, acting out the ancient lifeway as closely as possible. Such experiments are informative, and when conducted under carefully controlled and specific circumstances, they are of great value. Artifact by artifact, even dwelling by dwelling, it is sometimes possible to make illuminating analogies about the ancient use of specific artifacts.

Modern archaeology still grapples with the problem of deciding the role of an artifact in prehistoric society. Since this "functionalist" approach considers an artifact as an integral part of the larger society in which it occurs, it should be possible to establish its role in the society. An analogy is set up between the modern society that most closely resembles the archaeological culture—and those least removed from it in time—in subsistence, technology, and environment. It is now realized that artifact analogies have somewhat limited value. In recent years, archaeologists have turned increasingly to microscopic studies of edge wear on stone tools and to painstaking attempts to refit tools to the flakes and cores from which they came. In each case, they are looking behind the artifact for insights into the human behavior of long ago. These approaches, and other controlled experiments, are more precise forms of analogy that lead logically into broader attempts to use modern hunter-gatherers or farming societies as a way of interpreting the past. This form of ethnographic analogy is called ethnoarchaeology, or "living archaeology."

ETHNOARCHAEOLOGY

Ethnoarchaeology *Ethnoarchaeology* is a form of ethnography with a strongly materialist bias (R. A. Gould, 1978). It is not just a mass of observed data on human behavior, the sort of simple, isolated analogy that Sollas made. It is the study of dynamic processes in the modern world. For example, the South African anatomist Raymond Dart claimed that the australopithecines, who lived in southern Africa more than a million years ago, made bone tools by twisting, fracturing, and hammering animal bone fragments. This, he claimed, was the first human culture, evolved long before people used stone artifacts. Biologist C. K. Brain tested Dart's hypothesis against a set of controlled observations on modern hyena dens. He was able to show that the bone accumulations in australopithecine caves had been created by predators, not hominids (Brain, 1981; Dart, 1957).

The most famous ethnoarchaeological studies have been carried out among hunter-gatherers: the San of the Kalahari Desert in southern Africa and the Nunamiut Eskimo caribou hunters of Alaska. The San research began when anthropologist Richard Lee (1979) undertook a long-term study of !Kung hunter-gatherers. He collected a mass of data on hunting and gathering, including residence patterns, that was of potentially vital use to archaeologists working on prehistoric hunter-gatherer bands. Then an archaeologist accompanied the research team and made detailed studies of butchery techniques as well as plans of abandoned settlements of known, historical age. John Yellen's research (1977) yielded a treasure trove of data on house and camp arrangements, hearth locations, population densities, and bone refuse. For example, he points out that a San camp develops through conscious acts, such as the construction of windbreaks and hearths, as well as through such incidental deeds as the discarding of refuse and manufacturing debris. Yellen recognized communal areas, open spaces where dancing and distribution of food took place. Then there were family hearths for food processing and cooking. These and other activity areas leave different tracks in the archaeological record.

Lewis Binford's Nunamiut research (1978) concentrated on the food procurement systems of a group of caribou hunters. In a carefully designed piece of research, he wanted to find out as much as he could about their hunting and food-processing systems by studying the animal bones that resulted from the chase. He studied not only seasonal hunting but also the storage systems that carried the group from one year to the next—fresh meat is available only two months a year. By close study of the Nunamiuts' annual round, as well as their butchery and storage strategies, Binford was able to develop indices that measured the way the Eskimo used different caribou body parts and utilized their primary food resource. The Nunamiut research provided a mass of empirical data on human exploitation of animals and also showed just how local many cultural adaptations are. Thus, argues Binford (1983), many of the artifact differences recognized in the archaeological record are, in fact, reflections of highly localized adaptations to the environment.

The archaeological record contains evidence for the study of long-term processes. The problem for archaeologists is to gain access to this information. It is hardly surprising that prehistorians have used living societies as analogies for interpreting ancient ones. After all, they are the living cultural systems that are most relevant for understanding the patterning in prehistoric cultural materials. Nevertheless, anyone who uses ethnographic analogy is steering a course into dangerous waters. As Clive Gamble (1986b) eloquently says, "With increasing frequency it is possible to spot, in current archaeological studies, glimpses of the Nunamiut, !Kung, and other groups faintly camouflaged in palaeolithic costume." Martin Wobst (1978) warns of what he calls the "tyranny of the ethnographic record," which provides well-focused glimpses of living human cultural systems. There is a strong temptation to freeze these glimpses and use them as wide-ranging prototypes that are perceived as "fitting" observed patterns of prehistoric materials (for an admirable and sophisticated discussion, see Gamble, 1986b).

Using the living world as a means of interpreting prehistoric times will never be easy. The fact remains, however, that we can only understand the past through the present since there are no direct ways of observing prehistoric human behavior (Spaulding, 1968). Ethnographic analogy does not consist of making isolated observations and fitting them to prehistoric examples. Rather, ethnoarchaeology provides a way to explore the relationship between behavior (dynamics) and its material remains (statics). Living societies, especially varied hunter-gatherer adaptations, allow us to examine this critical relationship, to think about ways of investigating causes of variation in the archaeological record. Understanding the causes of variation in modern hunter-gatherer adaptations gives us a potentially powerful foundation for predicting and investigating adaptations just as varied in the remote past. And understanding such ancient adaptations is a critical element in developing explanations of cultural change in prehistory, a preoccupation of theorists for more than a century.

GUIDE TO FURTHER READING

Binford, Lewis R. 1983. *In Pursuit of the Past*. New York: Thames and Hudson.
  A personal account of developing ideas in archaeology that is a marvelous introduction to archaeological reasoning. You may not agree with everything Binford says, but he makes you think.

Ceram, C. W. 1953. *Gods, Graves and Scholars*. New York: Knopf.
  This probably is the best-known book on archaeology ever written. A classic account of early archaeologists and the discovery of the early civilizations written for a popular audience.

Fagan, Brian M. 1991a. *Archaeology: A Brief Introduction*, 4th ed. New York: Harper-Collins.

    A widely ranging brief introduction, with major coverage of subsistence and settlement patterns.

————. 1991b. *In the Beginning*, 7th ed. New York: HarperCollins.

    A comprehensive survey of method and theory in archaeology that covers everything from stratigraphy to cultural resource management.

Renfrew, Colin, and Bahn, Paul. 1991. *The Practice of Archaeology: A Handbook of Ideas and Methods.* New York: Thames and Hudson.

    A superbly illustrated and perceptive textbook on archaeological methods.

Sharer, Robert, and Ashmore, Wendy. 1987. *Archaeology: Discovering the Past.* Palo Alto, CA: Mayfield.

    Another detailed introduction to anthropological archaeology that is especially strong on American examples. Excellent bibliography.

CHAPTER 2 APPROACHES TO WORLD PREHISTORY

Preview

- Although biological evolution resulted in the emergence of humankind, cultural evolution assumed the dominant role in our prehistory. It became humankind's unique means of adapting to the natural environment.

- Early archaeologists confronted with the problem of classifying and dating the past were at a loss until Christian Jurgensen Thomsen developed the three-age subdivision for prehistory. This scheme was verified by excavation and widely adopted during the nineteenth century.

- The social scientist Herbert Spencer developed the notion of cultural and social evolution. Along with Edward Tylor and Lewis Morgan, Spencer believed in unilinear cultural evolution, under which all humankind progressed from a state of simple savagery to civilization.

- Later scholars showed that these schemes were too simplistic when tested against data from archaeological excavations. We describe the primary cultural processes—invention, diffusion, and migration—and give examples of their application.

- Franz Boas and V. Gordon Childe fostered detailed studies of sites, peoples, and artifacts that placed scientific archaeology on a new footing. Boas collected minute details of dozens of societies. Childe believed in cultural evolution in which technology played a major role.

- Anthropologists Julian Steward and Leslie White played an important role in showing cultural evolution to be a major cornerstone of world prehistory. Steward demonstrated that all human cultures interact with their natural environments and stressed the importance of constantly changing adaptations. White conceived of cultures as complex systems whose various parts interact with each other and with the natural environment.

- From these researches developed two concepts—cultural ecology and diverse cultural evolution—both based on the notion that each human culture evolved independently and as a result of changing adaptations to its ever-changing environment.

- Multilinear evolutionary approaches have led to the development of four arbitrary stages of sociopolitical evolution in prehistory. Smaller societies were organized in bands, tribes, and chiefdoms, while state-organized societies were centralized on a regional scale and included social ranks.

- Our narrative of world prehistory is based on gradual, multilinear cultural evolution and on an evolutionary perspective that envisages increasingly effective human adaptations to the natural environment through prehistory. These have resulted in the dangerous overexploitation of resources commonplace today.

- Hunting and foraging theory plays an important role in interpreting world prehistory. We describe the forager-collector and optimal foraging strategy models.

- Notions of interconnectedness, of emerging world systems, are assuming increasing significance in world prehistory.

"Descended from apes! My dear, let us hope that this is not so, but if it is, that it does not become known." The worthy Victorian minister's wife who uttered these words more than a century ago would be horrified by the literature of world prehistory today. She would discover that important implications of Charles Darwin's theory of evolution and natural selection have become cornerstones of anthropology and archaeology (Campbell, 1985; Foley, 1984b). Darwin's theories offer an explanation for the biological evolution of humankind. They provide the framework of the evolutionary story of world prehistory, of a pattern of gradual change that can be traced in the archaeological and paleontological record of more than 2 million years.

The antiquity of humankind, sequences of fossils and stone tools, different species of hominids and early humans—these are the familiar landmarks of this story, many of them easily described. But what do these changes mean? How can we explain and analyze this provocative chronicle in meaningful terms? Why did human beings originate in tropical Africa? Why did they spread into other continents and adapt to much colder environments during the later Ice Age? Why, eventually, did human beings start cultivating the soil and living in cities? These are the questions of world prehistory, the questions that scholars have been trying to answer for more than a century, using a variety of theoretical approaches described in this chapter.

One general statement is obvious. We modern people do differ from our predecessors; we have adapted successfully to the world's many environments as a result of our superior intelligence, gradually acquired during biological evolution. The evolutionary process of *adaptive radiation,* whereby animal species branch off from a common ancestral form, has led to an order of primates and a family of *Hominidae,* of which modern people (*Homo sapiens,* the wise human being) are only one member and the sole survivors. (For the basics of human biological evolution, see Lewin, 1988a; Weiss and Mann, 1988.)

Humankind is unique in its use of culture as a means of adapting to the natural environment, and our culture has evolved to great levels of complexity since the appearance of the first human beings more than 2 million years ago. The study of world prehistory is the study not only of biological evolution but also primarily of cultural evolution and the ways in which people have adapted to their natural environment. The cultural diversity of humankind is truly amazing and extremely difficult to explain. Ever since scholars first began to study world prehistory, they have tried to explain this diversity and to account for its origins and for the reasons some societies achieved a much greater cultural complexity than others. Why, for instance, did the Australian Aborigines never take up agriculture but did develop a highly complex social life? Why did their contemporaries, the ancient Egyptians, enjoy a literate civilization that lasted for thousands of years? The explanations for cultural diversity must come from anthropological archaeology, the primary source of data on early human history.

Much of the prehistory recounted in these pages is fundamental culture history, based on hundreds of sites and cultural sequences and millions of individual artifacts. These culture histories from all areas of the world have been constructed by using the basic principles mentioned in Chapter 1. Culture history alone, however, does not explain culture change, nor does it provide information on the ways in which people have adapted to or exploited the natural environment. It is only in recent years that archaeologists have attacked the complex problems of reconstructing past lifeways and studying cultural process, with the aid of digital computers, sophisticated statistical methods, and enormous new bodies of excavated data from all over the world. A whole new battery of analytic approaches has been brought to bear on the archaeological record, approaches that rely heavily on detailed theoretical models, some derived from evolutionary theory (Binford, 1983; Fagan, 1991a).

Today's theoretical models and methodology cannot be considered in isolation from earlier attempts at interpreting world prehistory (Trigger, 1989). Our approaches to the past are cumulative in the sense that they are based on the contributions of many earlier scholars, who worked with inadequate data and much less sophisticated models than those of today. We must, therefore, first examine the intellectual debt we owe our predecessors.

Adaptive radiation

PROGRESS AND CULTURAL DEVELOPMENT

If there is one persistent theme that runs through all theories about world prehistory it is the explicit, or implicit, assumption that human cultures have progressed through the millennia, from very primitive beginnings to the lofty pinnacle of industrial civilization. How can one account for this progress and for the obvious fact that by no means all human beings live in highly complex, urban societies?

Archaeology in the modern sense really began in the eighteenth century, when curious landowners dug into European burial mounds and ancient settlements with such frenzy that they acquired an enormous mass of miscellaneous artifacts. This horrendous jumble made no sense at all until Christian Jurgensen Thomsen, curator of Denmark's National Museum in Copenhagen, rearranged the prehistoric galleries of the museum in 1817. Boldly he laid out the exhibits to represent three great ages of prehistoric time: a Stone Age, when metals were too expensive, a Bronze Age, and an Iron Age. Thomsen worked strictly with tools, each of his three ages in fact representing a stage of technological development in prehistoric times. His three-age system soon was adopted widely throughout Europe, and its broad labels are still used as convenient terms (Daniel, 1981; Grayson, 1983).

Three ages

Thomsen concerned himself with how the level of technology affected the evolution of cultures. The essential validity of his theory of cultural development was proved not long after he proposed it by excavations all over Europe. These early-nineteenth-century digs raised a whole new set of questions about the three ages. The three-age system implied that all humankind had passed through comparable broad stages of technological development, but what about economic development? In 1838 another Dane, zoologist Sven Nilsson, invented an economic model for the past, arguing that humankind had developed through a series of stages—from a state of savagery to one of herder-agriculturalist and on to a final phase, civilization. He based his economic model on both archaeological and anthropological observations. Nilsson's model was not in conflict with Thomsen's theory; it merely addressed a different aspect of the fact of evolution. What Nilsson did was to concentrate not on technology but on how in different societies lifeways always seemed to change in the same direction.

Economic model

Archaeology and "The European Century"

The later development of archaeology as an intellectual discipline was part of a much wider movement that also saw the foundation of geology and evolutionary studies (Mayr, 1982). Archaeology, and prehistoric archaeology in particular, gained respectability during a period of widespread and fundamental social change during the nineteenth century. Clive Gamble (1986b) points out that archaeology developed during what some historians call "The European Century [1815–1914]," a time that saw the culmination of three long-term historical processes stemming from the industrial revolution: the development of a world economy, the creation of the administrative and political apparatus of the modern state, and the rise of science. Science, and

(text continues on page 46)

BOX 2.1

Early
Pioneers of
Archae-
ology

The early days of archaeology were a period of high adventure and spectacular discoveries in Egypt, Mesopotamia, and Mesoamerica. Some of the archaeologists who dug in these areas were colorful characters and brilliant writers (Fagan, 1985).

Austen Henry Layard set out to ride overland to India in 1839. When he arrived in what is now Iraq, he was so fascinated by the ancient city mounds there that he stayed. In 1845, he dug into ancient Nimrud and two years later into Kuyunjik (Nineveh). He discovered palaces adorned with bas-reliefs of hitherto unknown Assyrian kings. "The portly forms of kings and viziers were so lifelike . . . that they might almost be imagined to be stepping from the walls," he wrote. He tunneled his way along the walls of each room looking for spectacular finds, sometimes supervising as many as 600 men. It was he who found King Assur-bani-pal's royal library at Nineveh and the famous bas-reliefs of a royal lion hunt and of King Sennacherib's siege of Lachish, mentioned in the Old Testament (2 Kings 18:13). Layard was a brilliant writer. His descriptions of Assyrian life are immortal. He wrote of the lion-decorated gateway of Sennacherib's palace: "Between them Sennacherib and his hosts had gone forth in all their might and glory to the conquest of distant lands, and had returned rich in spoil and captives. . . . Through them, too, the Assyrian monarch had entered his

Austen Henry Layard supervises the removal of a human-headed lion from the gates of a palace at Nineveh, Iraq.

Stela S at Copan, drawn by Frederick Catherwood, the English artist who accompanied John Lloyd Stephens in search of the Maya. His drawings have a photographlike quality that is quite extraordinary.

capital in shame, after his last and fatal defeat." He even found the ruts made by Assyrian chariot wheels in the roadway. Layard gave up archaeology in 1853 while still a young man.

John Lloyd Stephens was a New York lawyer and political operative, who took to foreign travel after a nervous breakdown drove him from the law in 1834. While traveling in the Near East, he discovered a talent for writing. Back in New York, he joined forces with English artist Frederick Catherwood for an expedition to investigate rumors of ancient palaces and temples in the rain forests of Mexico and Guatemala in 1839. They made their way to the tiny Honduran village of Copán, where "around them lay the dark outlines of ruins shrouded by the brooding forest. The only sound that disturbed the quiet of this buried city was the noise of monkeys moving among the tops of the trees." While Catherwood drew the intricate hieroglyphs on the Maya stelae, Stephens tried to buy the site for $50, so he could transport it piece by piece to New York. The deal fell through when he found that he could not float the antiquities downstream. Stephens and Catherwood visited Palenque, Uxmal, Chichén Itzá, and other sites in their two expeditions, vividly described in two famous books. Stephens was the first to recognize the Maya as the builders of these great sites: "These cities . . . are not the works of people who have passed away . . . but of the same great race which still . . . clings around their ruins." Stephens also gave up archaeology and perished while surveying a possible route for the Panama Canal through Nicaragua.

archaeology as part of it, developed because of a radical shift in the way people conceived of nature, investigated it, and used it.

These three historical processes had a profound effect on the development of archaeology. The nineteenth century was a time of rising wealth, of unprecedented exploitation of natural resources and intensification of agriculture to feed mushrooming European populations. The industrial revolution spawned public works, railroad and canal building, and massive disturbance of the modern land surface. Vast quantities of prehistoric artifacts came to light under the picks and shovels of the manual workers who transformed the landscape. Inevitably, these many finds began to arouse far more than idle curiosity—they began to acquire a real significance in the order of things.

Prehistory in the form of the three-age system and the stone artifacts found in ancient river gravels were not essential to the Victorian perception of human progress. But archaeology tended to reinforce the ideologies of progress and nationalism that were so much a part of nineteenth-century European popular thinking. The Victorians lived in rapidly changing times, when progress was a natural condition. It was comforting to them to find that change had also taken place in remote prehistory. Progress was inevitable, an integral part of civilization. The Danes used prehistoric archaeology to provide a link between themselves and the cultural heritage of the nation (Kristiansen, 1981). Nationalism, national identity, and progress were the very essence of nineteenth-century ideology. Age and antiquity became a way in which social value was to be given to contemporary change, by showing they had profound roots in older traditions.

Cultural Evolution

Prehistory, then, was seen as a scientific study of progress in prehistoric times (Trigger, 1981, 1989). In the decades following the acceptance of the antiquity of humankind in 1859, biological evolutionary theory was distorted into a simplistic, ordered way of charting human progress. Gabriel de Mortillet, an expert on French Stone Age caves, classified different prehistoric cultures into rigid geological layers that he implied were to be found all over the world. "It is no longer possible to doubt the great law of the progress of man," he wrote in 1867 (Daniel, 1981). Inevitably, this corruption of biological theory led to ethnocentric value judgments that linked levels of cultural development to ideas about racial inferiority and lesser intelligence in technologically unsophisticated, non-Western societies like the Tasmanians and Australian Aborigines. According to many nineteenth-century archaeologists, progress in prehistory was achieved by advances in human intellect that could be detected by changes in fossil skulls and, above all, by changing designs of stone tools (Gamble, 1986b).

Ideas of inevitable progress were also popular among pioneer social scientists of the day, scholars like Herbert Spencer (1820–1903). Spencer (1855) hailed Victorian civilization as the pinnacle of human achievement, a state to which all humankind aspired. He and his contemporaries wondered whether human culture had evolved, just as our bodies had. They developed the notion of *unilinear cultural evolution*—the idea that human societies evolved from simple hunter-gatherers to complex civilizations, but along a single evolutionary line. Theoretically, then, every society could achieve the highest reach of civilization. This form of cultural evolution provided not

Spencer's cultural evolution

only a rationale for ideas of racial superiority but also grounds for thinking of early prehistory as a mirror of the contemporary world, as remote eras when long-vanished peoples enjoying much the same level of culture as, say, the Tasmanians or Inuit lived on earth. The more complex these prehistoric societies, the more advanced they were—the dead equivalents of specific, still existing, non-Western societies. These ideas reached their extreme in the work of William Sollas, an early twentieth-century geologist turned prehistorian, who called the San of Africa and the Inuit of the Arctic "living fossils," examples of late Ice Age peoples (Sollas, 1910).

Tylor, Morgan, and Marx

This ethnocentric view of the past had its roots not only in ideas of progress but also in the writings about human diversity of two early anthropologists. Sir Edward Tylor (1832–1917) was a gentleman of leisure who became interested in anthropology during a visit to Mexico in the 1850s (Hatch, 1973). He was the first to attempt a chronicle of the full extent of human diversity. He argued that human beings had behaved in a commonsense and rational way since the earliest times. This rational behavior led to cultural evolution over time, while processes of selection, akin to those of natural selection in biological evolution, had made human institutions more efficient and complex. Tylor (1871) proposed three broad stages of human development akin to those of Sven Nilsson—savagery, barbarism, and civilization. His evolutionist view was far too simplistic, but he based his work on two research methods that are still widely used today:

- He used living, non-Western peoples at the same general level of cultural development to throw light on imperfectly known prehistoric societies—*ethnographic analogy.*

- He developed techniques for sampling the culture of dozens of different peoples—the *comparative method.*

The American anthropologist Lewis Morgan (1818–1881) was another ardent social evolutionist; he thought that social evolution occurred as a result of human societies adapting to the stresses of their various environments (M. Harris, 1968). Morgan identified no fewer than seven stages of social evolution in his classic work, *Ancient Society* (1877), beginning with "Lower Status of Savagery," a stage of simple food gathering, and culminating in "Civilization," when a society developed writing.

Morgan's ideas on cultural evolution had a profound influence on Karl Marx (1818–1883). Marx used Morgan's seven stages but argued that each stage was brought on by economic factors. Changes in material production, and also in the control of the means of production, were *the* forces that determined social, political, and legal aspects of society. This is historical materialism, which regarded economic developments as the prime movers of social evolution. Marx's ideas persist in some archaeological theories to this day.

Neither Morgan's nor Tylor's linear evolutionary schemes have stood up against the sheer complexity of human cultural diversity as we know it today. Their work and that of other nineteenth-century pioneers made one lasting contribution to world prehistory—the assumption that human cultures did, in general, proceed from the simple to the complex. The issue that has preoccupied archaeologists since is, of course, how and why they did so.

PRIMARY CULTURAL PROCESSES: INVENTION, DIFFUSION, AND MIGRATION

Spencer, Tylor, and Morgan may have believed in human progress, in unilinear schemes of cultural evolution, but their contemporaries were already pondering one of the fundamental questions of archaeology: By what processes did cultural change take place? How, for example, did humankind first acquire bronze weapons? Did one people invent metal tools and then spread their innovation to other parts of the world? Or did metallurgy develop in many widely separated areas? Did culture change result from the invention of the same idea in many different places, through gradual, parallel evolutions? Or did it stem from the diffusion of ideas or from actual migrations of people carrying new cultures with them?

Two Scandinavian scholars, J. J. A. Worsaae and Oscar Montelius, were among the first to study these processes, now called *primary cultural processes*—invention, diffusion, and migration (Worsaae, 1849). They used minute differences in bronze pins, swords, and other artifacts to trace artifact changes from southeast Europe into Scandinavia. Modern culture history studies stemmed in part from their work. Both the comparative method and increased use of ethnographic analogy played an important part in the refinement of the study of the primary cultural processes.

Invention
Invention involves creating a new idea and transforming it—in archaeological contexts—into an artifact or other tangible innovation that has survived. An invention implies either modifying an old idea or series of ideas or creating a completely new concept. It can be made by accident or by intentional research. Inventions are adopted by others if they are useful; if sufficiently important, they spread rapidly. The transistor, for example, is in almost universal use because it is an effective advance in electronic technology.

There is a tendency to think of inventions as dramatic discoveries, the products of a moment of inspiration. In practice, though, most inventions in prehistory were the result of prolonged experimentation, a logical extension of the use and refinement of an existing technology or a response to changes in the surrounding environment.

People once searched for the site where the first solitary genius planted grain and invented agriculture. Today's archaeologists are still investigating the origins of food production, but they are finding dozens of major and minor changes in peoples' lifeways that cumulatively resulted in a shift from hunting and gathering to agriculture and animal domestication. The toolkits and subsistence activities that archaeologists have found show evidence of changes over a long period. In the Tehuacán Valley of Mexico, for example, people experimented for thousands of years with maize cultivation, and their toolkits reflect an increasing dependence on cereal agriculture (MacNeish, 1970), but the old hunter-gatherer tools and practices still appear in the archaeological record long after maize cultivation had become commonplace.

Culture change is cumulative—that is, people learn the behavior patterns of their society. Inevitably some minor differences in learned behavior will appear from generation to generation; minor in themselves, they do accumulate over time, especially among isolated populations. This snowballing effect of slow-moving cultural evolution can be detected in dozens of prehistoric societies, among them the Archaic peoples of midwestern river valleys in North America, who developed more and more efficient ways of exploiting animal, aquatic, and plant resources. Eventually they developed more complex, sedentary societies with elaborate burial rites and religious beliefs (Fagan, 1991b).

Diffusion

Diffusion is the label for those processes by which new ideas or cultural traits spread from one person to another or from one group to another, often over long distances. These ideas are socially transmitted from individual to individual and ultimately from group to group, but the physical movement of many people is not involved. Instances of diffusion are legion in prehistory, cases in which ideas or technologies have spread widely from their place of origin. A classic modern example is tobacco smoking, a favorite pleasure of the North American Indians that was adopted by Elizabethan colonists in the sixteenth century. Within a few generations, tens of thousands of Europeans were smoking pipes and enjoying the narcotic effect of American tobacco. Tobacco smoking soon reached every corner of the Old World, carried there not by thousands of people migrating from America to Europe but by small numbers of seamen and traveling merchants, by word of mouth, and through the human habit of adopting new, fashionable ideas. Smoking became socially acceptable and remains so to this day in many societies (although not necessarily in ours). There are numerous examples of the diffusion of religious beliefs in prehistory, transmitted through trading contacts and simply by the spread of ideas.

Migration

Migration involves the movement of a people and is based on a deliberate decision to enter new areas and leave the old. English settlers moved to North America, taking their own culture with them; the Spanish occupied Mexico. Such population movements result not only in the diffusion of ideas but also in mass shifts of people and in social and cultural changes over a wide front. Migration implies a complete, or at least an almost complete, transformation in culture. Perhaps the classic instance of migration in prehistory is that of the Polynesians; they settled the remote islands of the Pacific in consequence of deliberate explorations of the open ocean by their skilled navigators (Bellwood, 1987; Jennings, 1979). These superb seamen learned the lore of the heavens and made long-distance voyages of discovery, whereby they found such remote islands as Hawaii and Easter Island. In most cases, they returned safely to their homelands with detailed sailing directions that could be followed by later colonists. No one knows why the Polynesians set out on voyages to the unknown. Perhaps population pressure and political considerations played their part. Undoubtedly, many long voyages of exploration were undertaken simply because the navigators were curious to learn what lay over the horizon.

Boas on data

The early students of diffusion and migration often carried their ideas to ridiculous extremes, claiming, for example, that all civilization originated among the ancient Egyptians and then spread over the globe in a series of great voyaging adventures. Soon the experts reacted violently against these simplistic notions with much more sophisticated research projects. One such expert was Franz Boas (1858–1942), an anthropologist of German birth who immigrated to the United States and became a professor at Columbia University. Boas attacked those who sought general comparisons between non-Western societies; he helped to establish anthropology as a form of science, applying more precise methods of collection and classification of minute details of human cultures, especially those of North America. He and his students sought explanations of the past based on meticulous studies of individual artifacts and customs. Boas instilled respect for the notion that data should not be subordinated to elaborate theoretical schemes. The myriad data provided by Boas and others gave great emphasis to the use of the comparative method and ethnographic analogy in archaeology (Hatch, 1973).

THE COMPARATIVE METHOD

Artifact comparisons were used by pioneer anthropologists like Morgan and Tylor, as well as by early European prehistorians like Worsaae and Montelius in the nineteenth century (Daniel, 1981). But the real proponent of the method was Boas, who devoted a long career to studying and comparing hundreds of American Indian societies. His preoccupation with the minute details of artifacts (as well as other, less tangible aspects of human society) strongly influenced archaeologists of the 1930s and 1940s. Even today, archaeologists spend a great deal of time in comparative studies of artifacts, settlement patterns, and art styles in different archaeological cultures. The comparative method in archaeology is closely tied to the classification and analysis of artifacts such as pottery and stone tools. Much of what we know of the prehistory of Bronze Age Europe is based on the study of swords, brooches, and pins, for example. Archaeologists of the American Southwest rely heavily on changing styles and distributions of painted pottery to construct the culture history of the region. Until the advent of radiocarbon dating in the 1950s, European archaeologists made great use of comparative studies of pottery and metal artifacts to refine their crossdatings of cultures far from the Mediterranean civilizations in which such artifacts had their origin.

V. Gordon Childe

Perhaps one of the best-known experts on the comparative method was an Australian-born archaeologist named Vere Gordon Childe (1892–1957) (Childe, 1958; Trigger, 1980; Tringham, 1983). Childe was a brilliant linguist who made his life's work the study of the diffusion of civilization throughout prehistoric Europe. He became familiar with even the most trivial sites and artifact assemblages and with obscure central European journals that few English-speaking archaeologists read. He used his encyclopedic knowledge to develop a thesis that Europe was a province of the Near East, an area that had received agriculture, metallurgy, and other major inventions by diffusion from the East. He traced these traits from one end of Europe to the other by comparing cultural sequences and artifact distributions from area to area. Childe combined cultural evolution and diffusionist ideas into unexpected notions of human prehistory. He believed, for instance, that farming was introduced into Europe from the Near East and that local cultures developed their own distinctive economies and social institutions in later millennia.

Childe on cultures

Childe's aim was to distill from archaeological remains "a pre-literate substitute for conventional history with cultures instead of statesmen as actors and migrations instead of battles" (Childe, 1942). He drew together approaches to the past from various schools, including the Marxists (he was a self-professed Marxist). He was convinced that humanity had made rational, intelligent progress from its earliest development. Childe was a brilliant and articulate popular writer whose syntheses of prehistoric times were—and still are—widely read by archaeologists as well as the general public.

Such was Childe's influence on world prehistory that it is only recently that his methods can be seen in historical perspective (Tringham, 1983). He was a consummate synthesizer, someone whose ideas were embraced totally or condemned out of hand. Childe was an idealist, a dreamer, whose theoretical models of the past were far ahead of his time and of the ability of archaeologists of the day to test them. His historical models, with their strong grounding in anthropology, have been of benefit to American archaeologists, and the scientific rigor of contemporary North American archaeology has brought greater credibility to some of the social, economic, and environmental models that have superseded Childe's visions of prehistory.

American archaeologists adopted the comparative method as a result of Boas's work and developed their own elaborate classification systems for New World prehistory that correlated local cultural sequences over thousands of miles (Willey and Sabloff, 1980). Between 1930 and 1960, they constructed hundreds upon hundreds of local sequences of culture history based on pottery styles and other artifacts.

To berate Childe and his contemporaries of the 1930s to 1950s for ignoring the environment as a factor in human history is to miss the point. They worked at a time when the science of ecology was hardly born, when much less was known about prehistory anywhere. Their view of the past was based on long-held ideas about the condition of early human beings, well expressed by Lewis Morgan in 1877: "Mankind commenced their career at the bottom of the scale and worked their way up from savagery to civilization through the slow accumulation of experimental knowledge." This statement was a good basis for understanding the nature of human evolution, the belief that progress was slow and inevitable, culminating in civilization. In a way, it was as if evolution had its own internal driving motor. The limitations of human mental capacity acted as a brake on evolutionary progress. Evolution's motor was believed to be such that archaeologists had no incentive to investigate the forces of selection that acted on human culture and biology (Gamble, 1986b). Archaeology, then, was a way of reconstructing a timetable of technological innovations—toolmaking, fire, housing, burials, art, and metallurgy. This timetable was outlined regionally—in southwest France, Europe, the Near East, and North America—within a broad and flexible framework of slow progress. The Victorians were concerned with what happened when, not with the forces that caused prehistoric peoples to settle in different areas. It is to Childe's credit that he began to grapple with a far more fundamental and often ignored problem: Why did people change and colonize new regions?

CULTURE AS ADAPTATION

Culture history, the kind of archaeology that characterized world prehistory before the 1960s, and is still a vital part of it today, was basically the study of regional cultural sequences, using refined dating methods and stratigraphic observations. Comparisons between different regions and sites were based on artifact analyses and assemblage composition. Many parts of this book are still based on culture history sequences from all parts of the world, for there are many areas where data are still thin and research has hardly begun. But as the archaeologists of the 1950s began to realize, culture history is narrowly focused on minute details of artifacts and artifact styles. The archaeological record was thought of in tidy, economical terms, as something orderly and simple.

Childe, Boas, and their contemporaries were concerned for the most part with precisely this type of culture history, the material remains of human behavior. They paid relatively little attention to prehistoric lifeways. Although Danish archaeologists were identifying animal bones from coastal shell middens as early as the 1840s, and Californian scholars examined seasonality by using bird remains in San Francisco shell middens during the 1920s (Fagan, 1991c), it was not until the 1950s that some archaeologists turned from culture history toward ecology and the study of prehistoric lifeways.

The British prehistorian Grahame Clark applied pollen analysis to a 10,000-year-old hunter-gatherer site in northeast Britain in the late 1940s with spectacular results. By using both pollens and fragmentary red deer antlers from the site, he showed that Star Carr was occupied during the spring and summer months (J. D. G. Clark, 1954). The preservation conditions at the swamp site were so good that he was able to recover other evidence of prehistoric lifeways, too, including a canoe paddle, rolls of birch bark, and the remains of a brush platform built out toward the water's edge. At about the same time, University of Chicago archaeologist Robert Braidwood led a multidisciplinary research team to the Near East on a broad-based study of the origins of agriculture. He excavated the 8000-year-old farming village of Jarmo in the Zagros foothills of Iraq, while zoologists studied domestic animal bones and geologists studied the evidence for recent climatic change in the area (Braidwood and Braidwood, 1983). These studies were the forerunners of the much more sophisticated multidisciplinary researches done today.

Currently, there are many avenues of research that provide information on hunting and gathering practices and on agriculture, pastoralism, and even long-distance trade. Here are some major lines of evidence:

1. *Artifacts* such as axes, plow shares, and digging sticks, to say nothing of stone spear points, provide evidence for subsistence activities. The discovery of a plow share, for example, implies a more complex set of tools for cultivation, which penetrate deeper into the ground and can be used on a much wider range of soils, as happened in prehistoric Europe after 4200 years ago. But the evidence for hunting, gathering, and food production that comes from tools is necessarily limited. Very often, the food remains themselves provide more precise insights.

2. *Settlement data,* in the form of house foundations, temple ruins, and the surviving traces of complete camps, villages, towns, or cities, tell us much about the changing ways in which people have exploited their ever-changing environment (Wilk and Ashmore, 1987). Archaeologists working in the Valley of Mexico have shown how the prehistoric population distributions changed in response to the growth of the Aztec Empire and later as a result of the Spanish Conquest (Sanders, Parsons, and Santley, 1979).

3. *Rock paintings* and other art objects can sometimes provide information on ancient subsistence. Witness Figure 6.2, which shows a San hunter from southern Africa with his toolkit. Sometimes such evidence can also be used to interpret the function of incomplete artifacts found in archaeological deposits nearby (J. D. Clark, 1959).

4. *Indirect evidence* of subsistence activities comes in several ways, not only from geological studies but also from surprisingly esoteric sources. For example, we can learn much of the subsistence ecology of the early hominids at Olduvai Gorge by examining the cut marks on the broken animal bones associated with their tools (Bunn and Kroll, 1986; Potts, 1984a). These marks show that the hominids concentrated on meat and marrow-rich bones. It seems possible that our earliest ancestors competed with predators for much of their game meat, scavenging it from carnivore kills in hasty forays. If so, they were opportunistic foragers rather than true hunters, such as were found among later humans.

    Fossil pollens from prehistoric swamps, and organic remains from wet sites like Ozette in Washington State and Monte Verde in Chile tell us much about ancient natural vegetation and also about more perishable artifacts made of wood, netting, or fiber (Fagan, 1991c). Pollens can reveal abrupt changes in tree cover resulting from forest clearance by early farming communities. Prehistoric farmers in Denmark and northern Germany, for example, burnt off and cleared forests for their fields 6000 years ago. As the forests were destroyed, characteristic cultivation weeds that infest newly planted wheat fields appeared in the pollen diagrams for the first time. Both pollen analysis (palynology) and zooarchaeology (the study of ancient animal bones) enable one to look at the constantly changing relationship between a human cultural system and its environment, as well as at the ways in which people made their living. And as time went on, both archaeologists and anthropologists began to look more closely at this very subject, called cultural ecology, which we discuss on the following pages. They found, for example, that there was a quantum jump in the number of archaeological sites in the Valley of Mexico once the Aztecs developed a distinctive form of swamp agriculture that doubled maize productivity over thousands of acres of hitherto unexploited land. By the time of the Spanish Conquest, the Indians were occupying every acre of potentially cultivable land in the area. This was in sharp contrast to earlier times, when far more selective, usually nonirrigation, agriculture was practiced (Fagan, 1984a).

5. *Food remains,* such as animal bones or seeds, offer direct evidence for types of food eaten and, by sophisticated analyses, can provide insights into overall dietary patterns as well. The remains of domestic animals or game can be identified by such parts as teeth, jaws, horns, and sometimes the articular ends of limb bones. One can not only establish the proportion of the diet that each type of animal supplied but also, in some cases, obtain invaluable data on butchery practices, the ages at which animals were killed (determinable by study of the teeth), and even the seasons at which the site was occupied. When Joe Ben Wheat excavated the 8000-year-old Olsen-Chubbock bison kill in Colorado, he found

the bones of 16 calves only a few days old. He concluded from known data about bison breeding seasons that the kill took place in late May or early June (Wheat, 1972; see also Speth, 1983).

Seeds are much harder to come by than animal bones and are often recovered through a flotation method: The soil is passed through water so that the fine seeds float on the surface (Ford, 1985; Hole, Flannery, and Neely, 1969). Dry caves in the United States and Mexico have yielded tens of thousands of once-edible seeds. Those from caves in the Tehuacán Valley in Mexico have shown how the inhabitants scheduled their gathering of wild plants with great care. The seeds yield an excellent chronicle of their early experiments with maize and other crops (Ford, 1985; MacNeish, 1978; J. Renfrew, 1973).

Food remains can come in many other forms, too. Fish and bird bones are highly informative and often provide evidence of specialist hunter-gatherer activities. Human feces can be subjected to detailed analysis and provide a fascinating insight into the diet of a site's inhabitants (Bryant, 1974). The ultimate objective of studying food remains is to understand the minutest details of a prehistoric society's adaptation to its environment.

CULTURE AS ADAPTATION—CULTURAL ECOLOGY

Since the 1950s, new views of human culture and its relationship to the natural environment have transformed ways in which archaeologists study world prehistory. Today, the notion that humans adapt to their natural environments seems obvious. But ecological interpretations of prehistoric times are a surprisingly new concept, partly because it is only recently that researchers have developed methods for studying ancient environments. At first they used isolated techniques, studying animal bones or employing pollen analysis. Then in the 1950s and 1960s, a new body of ecological theory emerged, which owed much to the basic concepts of systems theory in the natural and physical sciences. The assumptions and statements of intent in this research led to new notions of culture—culture as adaptation.

Steward on environment

The American anthropologist Julian Steward was one of those who developed the idea that human cultures were adaptations to the subsistence and ecological requirements of a locality. Steward saw this adaptation as constantly changing. "No culture," he wrote, "has ever achieved an adaptation to its environment which has remained unchanged over any length of time" (1970). This viewpoint contrasted sharply with that of many archaeologists of the time, who felt that human cultures were built by the accumulation of cultural traits through diffusion and not as responses to ecological factors.

White on equilibrium

Another famous anthropologist, Leslie White (1949), argued that human culture is made up of many structurally different parts that interact; they react to one another within an overall cultural system. He pointed out that cultures could change in response to changes in the environment but that one part of a cultural system could not change without triggering change in other segments—a prelude to the adoption of systems theory in archaeology. There is a relationship between a human cultural system and its natural environment, and the system is constantly adjusting to environmental changes. Steward and White assumed that successful adaptive patterns continue in use and act as an important stabilizing influence over a long period of time. From their work has developed a new recognition of the importance of cultural evolution in prehistory, not the cultural evolution of Tylor and Morgan, which implied that some human races are superior to others, but evolution based on many and increasingly complex adaptations to the natural environment. The study of the total way in which human populations adapt to and transform their environments is called *cultural ecology.*

Cultural ecology   Archaeologists who study cultural ecology are primarily interested in human cultures as systems interacting with other systems: other human cultures, the biotic community (other living things around them), and the physical environment. They are concerned not only with cultural evolution but also with reconstructing ancient environments and ways in which past cultures made their living (Fagan, 1991a; Sharer and Ashmore, 1987).

ENVIRONMENTAL ARCHAEOLOGY

The ultimate goal of environmental archaeology is to understand the relationships between human cultures and their environments, which involves, among other things, defining the characteristics and processes of the biophysical environment. This environment is the matrix for studying the human ecosystem, the interaction between human cultures and their natural surroundings. Archaeological sites, or distributions of them, are part of the human ecosystem (Butzer, 1982).

Biosphere   Human societies are a segment of the *biosphere,* which encompasses all the earth's living organisms interacting with the physical environment. The biosphere model is organized both vertically and horizontally. Vertically, genes and cells are found at the base; organisms, populations, and communities occur above them. Horizontally, the community, all the biological populations in a given area, functions together with the nonliving environment, in a biome.

Biomes   *Biomes* are the largest terrestrial communities, major biotic landscapes on earth
Habitats   in which distinctive plant and animal groups live in harmony together. *Habitats* are the areas within a biome where different populations and communities flourish, each
Sites   with hundreds of individual *sites,* specific locales with their own immediate settings. There are often transition zones between different habitats, and frequently there are areas of considerable importance to human communities exploiting specific re-
Ecotones   sources, such as certain game or vegetable foods. These are known as *ecotones.*
Ecology   *Ecology* is a study of functional relationships rather than genetic or phylogenetic
Niche   ones. This purview is reflected in the concept of the ecological *niche,* the tertiary space occupied by an organism, its functional role in the community, and how it is constrained by other species and external factors.

Every ecosystem is maintained by the regulation of trophic levels (vertical food chains) and by patterns of energy flow (Figure 2.1). The complexities of even modern ecosystems make them difficult to study empirically; prehistoric ones are impossible to reconstruct completely. Yet the broad conceptual framework of the ecosystem serves as a very useful research tool for archaeologists.

Human ecosystems differ from biological ecosystems in many ways (Figure 2.2). Information, technology, and social organization all play much greater roles. Human

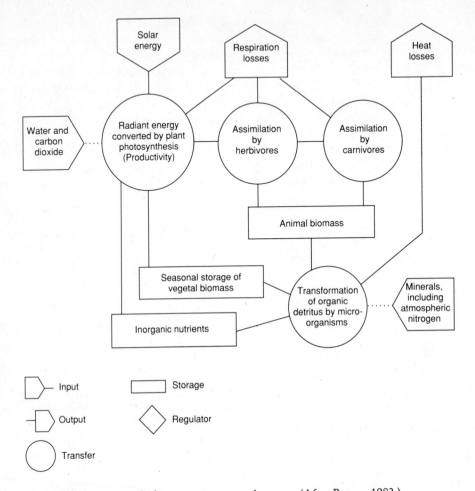

FIGURE 2.1   A simplified energy cycle for an environmental system. (After Butzer, 1982.)

beings, both as individuals and as groups, have unique capacities for matching resources with specific objectives. They not only think objectively about such matching but also transform the natural environment to meet their objectives. Value systems and goal orientation are important to human ecosystems, as are group attitudes and decision-making institutions, especially in more complex societies. Any attempts to reconstruct prehistoric environments must take into account not only environmental resources and constraints but also the ways in which humans utilized resources and intervened in the environment and changed it.

GEOARCHAEOLOGY

Geoarchaeology   *Geoarchaeology*, archaeological research using the methods and concepts of the earth sciences, is a cornerstone of environmental reconstruction (Butzer, 1982). Until

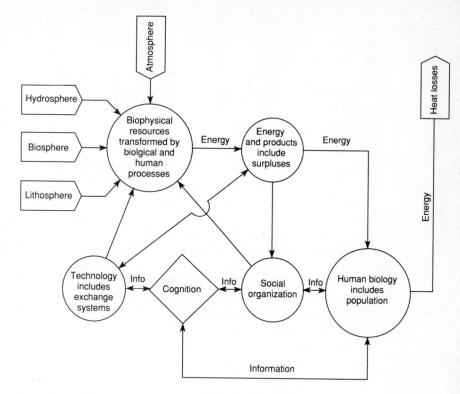

FIGURE 2.2   A much simplified energy cycle for a human ecosystem. This one does not include provisions for storage of food and other resources. (After Butzer, 1982.)

recently, geoarchaeology was little more than a battery of scientific techniques used for such things as radiocarbon dating and pollen analysis. But as archaeologists have concentrated more and more on environmental matters and on changing human settlement distributions over long periods of time, they have come to appreciate the great importance of an integrated approach to environmental reconstruction. The new geoarchaeology fills this role (Butzer, 1982).

Ideally, and whatever their expertise, geoarchaeologists should be members of a multidisciplinary research team. They should work alongside the excavators in the field, collecting pollen and soil and dating samples, recording stratigraphic profiles, relating the site to its landscape by topographic survey, and so on. Working closely with survey archaeologists, geoarchaeologists locate sites on the natural landscape with the aid of air photographs, satellite images, and other remote-sensing devices. They examine geological exposures and study the stratigraphic and sedimentary history of the entire region in a wider context vis-à-vis the sites found within it. In the laboratory, they analyze maps and soil samples. Studying the sediments, they work out the microstratigraphy of the site, down to the centimeter, relative to that of the surrounding area. They also analyze site deposits for such properties as pH, organic content, and so on, to establish the effects of human activity on the sedimentary sequence. The ultimate objective is to establish the ecological and spatial frameworks for the prehistoric data that emerge from archaeological excavations and surveys.

This approach has been tried with success in many places, including the Nile Valley, where Karl Butzer (1981) has argued that the ancient Egyptians constantly modified their state and economic structure to overcome external and internal crises, while maintaining the same basic adaptation to a floodplain environment for millennia.

Geoarchaeology is definitely not geology since it deals not only with sediments but with human activity as well. People are geomorphic agents, just as the wind is. Accidentally or deliberately, they carry inorganic and organic materials to their homes. They remove rubbish, make tools, build houses, abandon tools. All these mineral and organic materials are subjected to all manner of mechanical and biochemical processes during and after the time the site is occupied. The controlling geomorphic system at a site, whatever its size, is made up of both natural elements and a vital cultural component. So the geoarchaeologist is involved with archaeological investigations from the very beginning and is concerned not only with the formation of sites, and with the changes they underwent during occupation, but also with what happened to them after abandonment.

Site formation processes

Thus, geoarchaeologists are deeply involved in the study of what are called *site formation processes* (Schiffer, 1987). These are the processes by which an abandoned prehistoric site is transformed into the archaeological record, the pattern of artifacts, food remains, and so on that archaeologists investigate today. Site formation processes are still imperfectly understood because archaeologists have only just begun to look at this type of environmental archaeology in which a site decayed after abandonment. Wind, earthworms, cattle trampling, even human feet can shift the position of artifacts, erode and deposit soil, and cause artifacts and food remains to disappear or change shape. Geoarchaeologists use sedimentation studies, soil samples, and chemical analyses to study site formation processes.

Environmental archaeology involves, then, not only the study of ancient environments but also an examination of the highly localized environmental context in which the archaeological record of a site or area is created.

We return to geoarchaeology in Chapters 3 and 4, when we consider the environmental background to world prehistory.

PARTICIPATING IN CULTURE

Culture as adaptation—this phrase is behind most contemporary interpretations of world prehistory. Leslie White (1949) called culture "man's extrasomatic means of adaptation." Culture is the result of human beings' unique ability to create and infuse events and objects with meaning that can be appreciated, decoded, and understood (Gamble, 1986b). To espouse this definition of culture as adaptation means that culture is *participated in* as well as *shared by* human beings (for extended discussion, see Binford, 1965). However, this participation and sharing differ greatly from place to place and from time to time, resulting in variations in prehistoric material culture—the data for studying prehistory. This viewpoint contrasts somewhat with that of culture historians, who tend to argue that all variability can be accounted for by a view of culture that explains patterning in the archaeological record as the result of shared ideas and cultural norms. (Note that this is a gross simplification of a complex issue.)

The debate between culture historians and those who believe that we do not know all the causes of variability in the archaeological record has gone on for more than a decade. As Clive Gamble (1986b) points out, it is really a debate about how the archaeological record is formed. Are artifact assemblages generated by a shared set of experiences and deposited as a result of that phenomenon? Or does a cultural system leave behind a highly complex record of an adaptive strategy that defies easy interpretation?

Multidimensional model

The new school of thought uses a much more complex, *multidimensional model* to investigate the significance of patterning and variation in archaeological finds (Binford, 1983; Gamble, 1986b). This model is based on two fundamental assumptions:

• Since resources are not uniformly distributed within an environment, humans must expend energy in collecting and gathering them. They have to employ some form of adaptive strategy to minimize risk and make use of seasonal phenomena, such as availability of vegetable foods and game migrations. These seasonal strategies rely on the potential of available technology, food storage capacity, and so on. Among hunter-gatherers, for example, these strategies utilize the mobility of individual groups and their flexible social organization to divide them into bands of different sizes, membership, duration, and purpose (Jochim, 1976).

• Under this approach, human activities and their cultural residues are distributed over the landscape through time and space. This scattering results from variations in the distribution and organization of energy. In other words, the archaeological record of world prehistory varies *over the landscape* as a result of past behavior related to adaptive strategies (Foley, 1981; Gamble, 1986b). Thus, no one site can be taken to represent an entire adaptation; the focus for studying world prehistory must be regional.

The fundamental point is that human behavior, both today and in the prehistoric past, is an adaptation not to a single site but to environmental regions. Thus, to understand individual sites and artifact patternings, the archaeologist has to study regions. Robert Foley (1981) calls this *off-site archaeology,* the notion that the archaeological record, certainly of hunter-gatherers, should be perceived not as a system of structured sites but as a continuous pattern of artifact distribution and density over the landscape. As individuals and groups hunt and forage their way across this landscape, they leave behind material remains of their presence, a record that reflects their continual behavior within the region.

The off-site approach uses an ecological concept—a home range—as a way of establishing a link between the principles of ecological organization and the variable artifact densities that reflect mobile adaptations by people using the landscape (Foley, 1981). This approach allows the archaeologist to investigate variable artifact densities over a landscape "as signatures of long term adaptive strategies that have withstood many environmental changes and taken place within wider contexts of social and political change" (Gamble, 1986b, where a lengthy discussion appears).

MULTILINEAR CULTURAL EVOLUTION
AND WORLD PREHISTORY

The approaches to world prehistory embodied in analogy, experiment, and middle range theory are concerned with understanding long-term processes through millennia of prehistoric times. They seek to interpret cultural variation and adaptation on a regional basis, especially among highly mobile hunter-gatherer populations. As we have seen, the relationship between ecological and social systems is a critical part of this approach.

These same social systems have evolved through the long millennia of prehistory, not in the simple linear way espoused by Victorian scholars but in increasingly complex ways. Each human society pursues its own evolutionary course, determined by the long-term success of its adaptation, via technology and social institutions, to its natural environment (Sahlins and Service, 1960). This concept of *multilinear evolution* (multiple-lined evolution) now is widely accepted as a general framework by students of world prehistory.

Growth cycles

Some societies achieve a broad measure of equilibrium with their environment, in which adaptive changes consist of little more than some refinements in technology and the fine tuning of organizational structures. Other societies become involved in cycles of growth that are triggered by environmental change or from within society. If these changes involve either greater food supplies or population growth, there can be accelerated growth resulting from the need to feed more people or the deployment of an enlarged food surplus. Continued growth can place additional strains on the society, triggering technological changes, adjustments to social organization, or alterations in the belief system that provides the society's integrative force.

Every society has its growth limits imposed by the environment and available technology, and some environments have more potential for growth than others. Certain types of sociopolitical organization, such as centralized control of specialized labor, are more efficient than others. The emergence of food production and the beginnings of urban civilization in Mesoamerica are both cases of societies entering on a major growth cycle after centuries of relatively slow cultural evolution. Adaptive changes have triggered technological innovation that has led to increased food supplies and higher population densities. Our own society is embarking on such a cycle today—with open-ended and dangerous consequences.

This sophisticated concept of multilinear evolution has led a number of anthropologists to talk of stages of social development in prehistory (Service, 1962). Many archaeologists think in terms of two broad groups: prestate societies and state-organized societies.

	Prestate			
	Band	**Tribe**	**Chiefdom**	**State-Organized Societies**
Total Numbers	Less than 100	Up to few thousand	5,000 - 20,000+	Generally 20,000+
Social Organization	Egalitarian Informal leadership	Segmentary society Pan-tribal associations Raids by small groups	Kinship-based ranking under hereditary leader High-ranking warriors	Class-based hierarchy under king or emperor Armies
Economic Organization	Mobile hunter-gathers	Settled farmers Pastoralist herders	Central accumulation and redistribution Some craft specialization	Centralized bureaucracy Tribute-based Taxation Laws
Settlement Pattern	Temporary camps	Permanent villages	Fortified centers Ritual centers	Urban: cities, towns Frontier defenses Roads
Religious Organization	Shamans	Religious elders Calendrical rituals	Hereditary chief with religious duties	Priestly class Pantheistic or monotheistic religion
Architecture	Temporary shelters  *Paleolithic skin tents, Ukraine*	Permanent huts Burial mounds Shrines 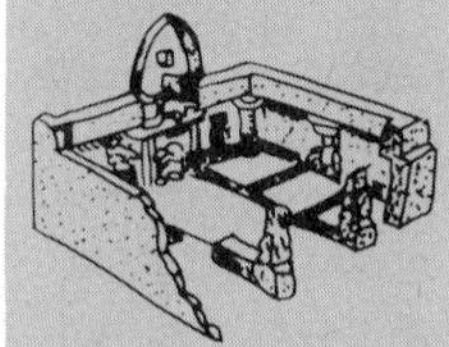 *Neolithic shrine, Çatal Hüyük, Turkey*	Large-scale monuments  *Stonehenge, England - final form*	Palaces, temples, and other public buildings  *Pyramids at Giza*  *Castillo Chichén itzá, Mexico*
Archaeological Examples	All Paleolithic societies, including Paleo-indians	All early farmers (Neolithic/ Archaic)	Many early metalworking and Formative societies Mississippian, USA Smaller African kingdoms	All ancient civilizations e.g. in Mesoamerica, Peru Near East, India and China; Greece and Rome
Modern Examples	Eskimos Kalahari San Australian Aborigines	Pueblos, Southwest USA New Guinea Highlanders Nuer and Dinka in East Africa	Northwest Coast Índians, USA 18th-century Polynesian chiefdoms in Tonga, Tahiti, Hawaii	All modern states

FIGURE 2.3   General categories of prehistoric human societies. (Modified from Renfrew and Bahn, 1991.)

Prestate societies

Prestate societies are societies on a small scale, based on the community, band, or village. They vary greatly in their degrees of political integration and are sometimes divided into three loosely defined categories (Figure 2.3):

1. *Bands* are associations of families that may not exceed 25 to 60 people. These bands are knit together by close social ties; they were the dominant form of social organization for most hunter-gatherers from the earliest times up to the origins of food production.

2. *Tribes* are clusters of bands that are linked by clans. A clan is a group of people linked by common ancestral ties, which serve as connections between widely scattered communities. Clans are important because they are a form of social linkage that gives people a sense of common identity with a wider world than their own immediate family and relatives. They are much more of a kin than a political unit and, as such, are not used as one of the major stages of social evolution in themselves.

3. *Chiefdoms* are societies headed by individuals with unusual ritual, political, or entrepreneurial skills and are often hard to distinguish from tribes. The society is still kin-based but more hierarchical, with power concentrated in the hands of kin leaders responsible for the redistribution of resources. Chiefdoms tend to have higher population densities and to display the first signs of social ranking. They vary greatly in their elaboration. For example, Tahitian chiefs presided over powerful, constantly quarreling chiefdoms, frequently waging wars against their neighbors. The elaborate Mississippian chiefdoms of the Midwest and South flourished during the early second millennium A.D., maintaining elaborate trade networks and ritual contacts over long distances.

State-organized
societies

State-organized societies operate on a large scale with centralized political and social organization, class stratification, and intensive agriculture. They have complex political structures and many permanent government institutions, and they are based on notions of social inequality. Such societies were ruled by a tiny elite, who held monopolies over strategic resources and used force to enforce authority. State-organized societies of the past were first ruled by priest-bureaucrats, then gradually came under the rule of secular kings, who sometimes became despotic monarchs, often with alleged divine powers. This type of social organization was typical of the early literate civilizations and was the forerunner of the classical civilizations of Greece and Rome.

There has been some criticism of this model (Dunnell, 1980; Plog and Upham, 1983). Most of the criticism is directed not at the stages themselves but at uncritical use of them. All too often, archaeologists have tended to use the stages as a way of fleshing out an incomplete record of the past (Creamer and Haas, 1985). To assume, for example, that a prehistoric society that displays some of the features of a tribal society actually had all of them is very naive, an interpretation far out of touch with reality. What is the point of studying ancient societies if they are carbon copies of modern ones in their social organization? Today's researches concentrate on using the archaeological record to expand and revise our understanding of different stages of human social organization. Archaeology is a unique and highly effective way of studying human cultural change in the past, and as such it adds a time dimension to studies of cultural evolution and helps explain how cultural change takes place.

CULTURAL PROCESS, SYSTEMS, AND EVOLUTION

In recent decades not only has a mass of new information become available to archaeologists but also new and much more complex methods of studying cultural process have been developed. At the heart of the new methodology is an insistence that archaeological investigations be based on formal scientific methods. This type of inquiry begins with formal research designs and testable hypotheses, which are then compared against data collected in the field.

Systems theory

Multilinear cultural evolution is the vital force that combines systems theory and cultural ecology into a closely knit, highly flexible way of studying and explaining cultural process (Sanders and Webster, 1978). When systems theory first came into fashion in archaeology during the 1960s, it was regarded as the solution to all theoretical problems. Kent Flannery (1968a) studied early agriculture in Mexico's southern highlands. He discovered that between 10,000 and 4000 years ago the highland peoples relied on five basic food sources—deer, rabbits, maguey, tree legumes, and prickly pears—for their sustenance. By careful prediction of the seasons of each food, they could schedule their hunting and gathering at periods of abundance and before animals gained access to the ripe plants. Flannery assumed that the southern highlands and their inhabitants were part of a large, open environmental system consisting of many subsystems—economic, botanical, social, and so on—that interacted with one another. Then something occurred to jolt the food procurement system toward the deliberate growing of wild grasses. Flannery's excavations at dry sites dating to between 7000 and 4000 years ago showed wild maize cobs slowly increasing in size and other signs of genetic change. He suggested that the people began to experiment with the deliberate planting of maize and other grasses, intentionally expanding the areas where they would grow. After a long period of time, these intentional deviations in the food procurement system caused the importance of wild grass collecting to increase at the expense of other collecting activities until it became the dominant one (Figure 2.4). Eventually, the Indians created a self-perpetuating food procurement system, with its own vital scheduling demands of planting and harvesting, that competed with earlier systems and won out because it was more durable. By 4000 years ago, the highly nutritious bean and corn diet of the highland peoples was well established.

FIGURE 2.4   Excavations at Guilá Naquitz, Valley of Oaxaca, Mexico.

Flannery's Mexican research dramatizes the importance of looking at cultural change in the context of the interrelationships among many variables. There is no one prime agent of cultural evolution but rather a series of important variables, all with complex interrelationships. When we seek to explain the major and minor events of prehistory, we consider the ways in which change took place, the processes and mechanisms of change (cultural evolution, experimentation), and the socioeconomic stresses (population pressure, game scarcity, and so on) that trigger these mechanisms (Flannery, 1972).

The problem is that testing such multicausal models is a difficult task, involving rigorous methodologies for identification of the variables in the archaeological record and comparative studies of these variables in regions where a particular development (say, the emergence of civilization) occurred and where it did not, as well as in societies that flourished immediately before its development (Redman, 1978).

CURRENT DIRECTIONS

Evolutionary theory has yet to be explored systematically in archaeology. Flannery's methods are still fundamentally based on the anthropologists' notions of cultural evolution, a view that tends to emphasize variability in human culture as a whole at the expense of individual human actions and decisions. Just how important was the individual in prehistory, as opposed to biological, cultural, and environmental forces? Much current archaeological research is trying to move us closer to understanding the frameworks within which cultural process took place. Some of the exciting new directions of this research are included in the following sections.

Structural Archaeology and the Individual

Some archaeologists believe that there is much more to human culture than functions and activities. Behind all activities of any society, ancient or modern, are the logic and coherence that have to be understood in their own terms (Hodder, 1982). This "structure" of prehistoric society is defined as "the codes and rules according to which observed sets of interrelations are produced," the set of rules, as it were, that can be likened to those in chess or Pictionary. They are followed as people go about the business of surviving, adapting, and making a living. Structural archaeology is an attempt to see objects as they were perceived by their original owners; the symbolism of burial rites; and ultimately the reasons why societies remain static, change, collapse, and so on. Structural archaeology is in its infancy since few areas provide the enormous quantities of archaeological data that are needed to trace and observe the subtle changes in artifact patterning over time.

Evolution and World Prehistory

Without question, the greatest theoretical advances in world prehistory currently involve neoevolutionary theory. They have special relevance for the study of early prehistory. The principle of natural selection has long been the central dogma of evolutionary thought, accepted as a basic mechanism for evolution but little analyzed (Mayr, 1982). All this has changed in recent years. A whole new body of evolutionary theory has equipped biologists with methods of investigating the processes as well as the patterns of evolution (Foley, 1984b). This wealth of new theory is finally having an impact on world prehistory (Dunnell, 1980), for natural selection may prove to be a means of explaining patterns of variation in human morphology and behavior. There are several approaches.

Sociobiology

Sociobiology attempts to account for patterns of behavior among living populations in terms of increasing fitness (Chagnon and Irons, 1979; E. O. Wilson, 1980). Sociobiologists believe that cultural expression is a flimsy blanket for genetic imperatives. In other words, human behavior is partly explained by a form of genetic determinism—our actions are much more genetically directed than we might think. In contrast, most anthropologists believe that the greater part of human behavior is produced by our unique culture.

Behavioral ecology

In another of the growing links between anthropology and biology, *behavioral ecologists* are using a comparative approach to biological evolution to place human characteristics within a general framework of animal variability. This and other emerging evolutionary approaches are concerned with the analysis of human adaptation from a biological perspective. All assume that patterns of adaptation in prehistoric times were the products of natural selection and can be interpreted in these terms. These new approaches assume that human biological evolution and human prehistory cannot be isolated from one another. Human biological and cultural evolution must be placed in two contexts: the evolution of the animal community as a whole and that of local ecology. Human adaptation in prehistory is the result of ecological and evolutionary adaptations between humans and other species that make up the biological community (Foley, 1984b).

Community ecology

It is both useful and more convincing to assume that natural selection conferred some reproductive advantage on some of the bearers of early human culture. Their thoughts and actions evolved in directions that were adaptive for an evolving humanity (Mithen, 1989). As a result, very diverse human societies with very different institutions and beliefs tend to think and act in the same general ways. Archaeologists of an evolutionary persuasion believe that one can understand the ways in which people behave by comprehending the constraints placed on the human mind by a long evolutionary heritage. It should be remembered, however, that the environment in which humankind evolved is very different from that in which we have lived for many thousands of years and still live today.

It follows from this argument that the common behavioral characteristics that are the product of biological evolution serve to link modern humans with prehistoric, anatomically modern people, and ultimately with earlier hominids as well. On these grounds alone, the validity of evolutionary approaches to archaeology is probably established beyond a reasonable doubt.

The modern evolutionary approach to archaeology considers adaptation as a continual response to ever-changing environments. Thus, flexible behavior and creative thought on the part of individuals are the driving forces behind decisions to change social and physical environments. Until now, most evolutionary studies in archaeology have been more concerned with prehistoric subsistence and interaction with the natural environment. In the future, research will be directed more toward identifying the extent to which individual choices and the patterns in the archaeological record that resulted from them can be explained in adaptive terms. It will involve developing new methodologies that integrate evolutionary ecology and human psychology, as well as ways of relating short-term individual behavior to the inevitably generalized data from the archaeological record.

HUNTER-GATHERER STUDIES AND WORLD PREHISTORY

For most of their existence on earth, humans have lived by hunting and foraging for wild plant foods. The evolutionary approaches to prehistory just outlined have a particular relevance to the study of both prehistoric and living hunter-gatherers, and a new group of theories of great relevance to world prehistory is emerging from recent research (Bettinger, 1987).

When they have engaged in theoretical discussion, hunter-gatherer scholars have tended to do so in comparative and evolutionary terms. Until the 1960s, they depicted hunter-gatherers as primitive societies living on the edge of starvation, people with underdeveloped cultural and social institutions. These were simple social Darwinian kinds of models that considered hunter-gatherers the least developed form of human culture.

The classic studies of anthropologist Richard Lee (1979) and others (Lee and Iwen, 1976) among the !Kung San hunter-gatherers of southern Africa's Kalahari Desert led to radically new perceptions (Figure 2.5). Lee showed that hunters did not struggle constantly against food shortages and other perils; indeed, they had more leisure time than farmers. No longer was it possible to call them backward or less developed. Lee and his contemporaries turned to cultural ecology, stressing the importance of understanding local environments. Now hunter-gatherer behavior was considered rational and adaptive, the result of group behavior that strove always to keep the group in equilibrium with its environment.

Lewis Binford (1978) combined cultural ecology and archaeological and ethnographic data in his well-known study of Alaska's Nunamiut Eskimo caribou hunters. From this material he developed the so-called "forager-collector" model of hunter-gatherer societies. He wrote of "foraging systems," where people living in warm climates without seasons when food was scarce did not store food but "mapped onto" resources, moving their camps constantly to allow easy access to food. In contrast, "collector systems" developed where there were sharp seasonal contrasts in the availability of food supplies. Collectors then developed carefully planned and organized hunting and foraging strategies designed to acquire a large food surplus, which was stored for use during lean months. Collector systems involved a more structured relationship between human populations and their food resources, that is, more efficient technologies and a well-developed storage system. Collectors tended to live in more diverse environments, which they exploited from a variety of settlements that were used again and again. The forager-collector model is a useful conception, pro-

FIGURE 2.5   San women foraging for mugongo nuts.

vided one realizes that there was a continuum between the two systems. Only very rarely were hunter-gatherer societies exclusively foragers or collectors.

Hand in hand with such models goes the notion of an *optimal foraging strategy.* This set of theories about how people make rational decisions about limited resources came to anthropology from economics and biology. From the archaeological perspective, optimal foraging strategy often assumes that under certain well-defined circumstances, human decisions are made to maximize the net rate of energy gain. These decisions can revolve around food choice and diet competition or site location and use of resources. The most common applications of optimal foraging strategy in archaeology revolve around diet models (Bettinger, 1987; E. A. Smith, 1983; Thomas, 1989).

The basic diet model argues that hunter-gatherers confront a range of animal and plant foods in their daily rounds. These resources vary greatly in the amount of energy they produce and in the effort required to acquire and process it from the food resource once it has been selected. Every hunter-gatherer society must select a combination of resource items that maximizes net energy captured and minimizes the amount of energy expended in the chase or while foraging. Behind this model lie three assumptions. First, the amount of time and energy needed to extract energy from a resource and the amount it yields are fixed commodities. Second, when decisions are made about dietary alternatives, normally those with a higher rate of energy return will be selected. Third, a food resource is either on the optimal set of choices or it is not.

The only variable in this model, with its assumptions of fixed extraction costs, is the abundance of food resources in the environment. If all resources were infinitely abundant, one's food choices would depend on two variables—the time needed to acquire resources and their energy benefits. Thus, ideally, people would choose only the item that yielded the highest possible energy intake under optimal circumstances, or a combination of items with the highest rates of potential return.

This selection is fine in a world where everything is infinitely abundant. In practice, resources vary greatly in distribution and abundance, even in areas such as, say, the Peruvian coast, where fish and sea mammals are very plentiful year-round. A new twist now enters the universe of optimal foraging strategy, that of contingency. Hunters may be looking for deer in the Little Tennessee Valley, but on the way, they come across a teeming rabbit warren. In a few minutes they acquire six rabbits and forget about a deer. Opportunistic response has led to a new course of action, to decisions based on anticipated energy expenditure and immediate food needs. Such "contingency models" are important, for they bring out an important point about human behavior in prehistory. As food resources decline in abundance, the time required to search for them increases, and the breadth of the hunter-gatherer diet widens to compensate for this reality. Conversely, as resources become more abundant, selectivity increases.

Optimal foraging strategy seems like an attractive model for interpreting hunting and gathering in prehistory, but serious criticisms can be made. First, is it best to measure the efficiency of hunter-gatherer societies in strictly energy terms? What about nutrition and other important variables? Second, should one treat hunting and gathering as an endless series of individual responses to momentary opportunities, or did such activities operate within an overall plan or strategy? Finally, what kind of genetic mechanisms or learned behavior could cause people to hunt or gather in optimal fashions (Bettinger, 1987)?

All these attempts to explain the long, ever more complex prehistory of humankind are based on an incomplete archaeological record that has accumulated from more than a century of scientific research in all parts of the world. Many of these explanations revolve around the major developments in prehistory—the origins and early evolution of humankind, the peopling of the globe, the beginnings of food production, and the rise of state-organized societies. As we shall see in the chapters that follow, they form the explanatory framework for our infinitely long and remote prehistoric past.

GUIDE TO FURTHER READING

Binford, Lewis R. 1983. *In Pursuit of the Past.* New York: Thames and Hudson.
> *A basic account of processual archaeology, with lengthy discussions of ethnoarchaeology and middle range theory.*

Butzer, Karl. 1982. *Archaeology as Human Ecology.* Cambridge, Eng.: Cambridge University Press.
> *A basic account of cultural ecology and environmental archaeology from a geological perspective.*

Fagan, Brian M. 1991. *In the Beginning,* 7th ed. New York: HarperCollins.
> *The early chapters of this textbook cover major theoretical developments.*

Gamble, Clive. 1986. *The Palaeolithic Settlement of Europe.* Cambridge, Eng.: Cambridge University Press.
> *Probably the most important synthesis of new approaches to prehistoric archaeology in a generation. Definitely a book for advanced readers.*

Harris, Marvin. 1968. *The Rise of Anthropological Theory.* New York: Crowell.
> *A magnificent, if occasionally polemical, survey of theory in anthropology that covers many personalities mentioned in this chapter.*

Meltzer, David, Fowler, Don D., and Sabloff, Jeremy A., eds. 1986. *American Archaeology Past and Future.* Washington, DC: Smithsonian Institution Press.
> *A series of essays that analyze the history and future of American archaeology. Essential reading for any serious student of world prehistory.*

Watson, Patty Jo, LeBlanc, Steven, and Redman, Charles L. 1984. *Archaeological Explanation: The Scientific Method in Archaeology.* New York: Columbia University Press.
> *A description of the basic principles of processual archaeology, widely used by serious students.*

Wolf, Eric. 1984. *Europe and the People without History.* Berkeley: University of California Press.
> *Essential reading on world systems perspectives.*

PART II

THE FIRST HUMANS

(c. 4 MILLION TO 40,000 YEARS AGO)

The art of fabricating arms, of preparing aliments, of procuring the utensils requisite for this preparation, of preserving these aliments as provision against the seasons in which it was impossible to procure a fresh supply of them—these arts, confined to the most simple wants, were the first fruits of a continued union, and the first features that distinguished human society from the society observable in many species of beasts.

Marquis de Condorcet

WE DESCRIBE THE ORIGINS OF HUMANKIND AND THE EARLY EVOLUTION OF HUMAN CULTURE FROM THE FIRST TOOLMAKERS TO THE EMERGENCE OF MODERN HUMANITY.

Chronological Table A

Million Years B.P.	SITES		Culture
	Asian	European	
	(see Chapter 4 ↑)		
1.5			
2.0	Koobi Fora	Olduvai Gorge	OLDOWAN
	East Turkana		
3.0	Hadar		
		Laetoli	
4.0		Middle Awash	
5.0			
5.5			

Note on Chronological Tables

A chronological table appears at the beginning of most subsequent chapters; it covers the sites and cultures mentioned in the narrative. These sites and cultures, and their dates, are also listed in the chapter headings or in the margins opposite the place where they are mentioned. *Only sites and cultures in the headings or margins are listed.*

In addition to being keyed to the text, the chronological tables are labeled A, B, C, and so on and are cross-referenced at the beginning of each chapter. They form an interlocking sequence; the beginning and end of each chart are keyed to earlier and later chapters. The following key is used throughout the tables:

──────────── A continuous line means that the chronology is firmly established.

───────────▶ A line terminating in an arrow means that the time span continues beyond the arrow.

───────────┤ A line terminating with a horizontal bar means that the limit of chronology is firmly established.

- - - - - - - - A broken line means that the chronology is doubtful.

Hadar A name in italics is an archaeological site, normally named after the locality at which it occurs.

?Hadar A question mark beside a site name means that its date is not firmly established.

ACHEULIAN A name in capital letters is an archaeological culture or complex, usually named after a type site, which in turn is labeled after a geographic location.

B.P. These initials mean years before present (see page 24).

CHAPTER 3   HUMAN ORIGINS
THE EMERGENCE
OF "HANDY PERSON"

(4.0 MILLION TO 1.6 MILLION YEARS AGO)

Preview

- The Great Ice Age, or Pleistocene period, was the climatic backdrop for the biological and cultural evolution of humankind. About 2.5 million years ago, glaciation intensified on earth, with at least nine periods of intense cold during the past 700,000 years.

- An evolutionary radiation of hominoids began in the Late Miocene, between 8 and 5 million years ago. It produced four lineages, at least one of which, human beings, is known to have been considerably modified.

- The apelike animals that formed the hominoid segment were probably tree living, with long arms and legs and broad chests. They eventually became bipedal, walking on two limbs.

- Molecular biology suggests that chimpanzees and humans shared a common ancestor some 6 to 7 million years ago.

- Early hominids faced three major adaptive problems: They were large mammals; they were terrestrial primates; and they lived in an open, tropical savanna environment. They solved these problems by widening territorial ranges, scheduling food gathering, broadening their diet, and achieving great mobility and behavioral flexibility. Life on the savanna was adaptive for bipedal posture and a highly mobile lifeway.

- It is possible that a small, bipedal hominid identified as A. *afarensis,* living about 4 million years ago, was ancestral to later hominids. There were at

73

least three, perhaps four, different hominid forms in East Africa by 2 million years ago, among them *Australopithecus africanus,* the more robust *Australopithecus robustus,* and a hominid with a larger brain but apelike limbs—*Homo habilis.* There is general agreement that *Homo habilis* is the probable ancestor of later human species—*H. erectus* and *H. sapiens.*

- The first toolmaking hominids were both hunters and scavengers, who relied heavily on wild vegetable foods. They returned habitually to places where they cached stone implements and processed parts of animal carcasses.

- Oldowan technology, the technology of *Homo habilis,* was based on the opportunistic production of sharp flakes and perhaps choppers. It was in use from perhaps as early as 2.5 million years ago to about 1.5 million years ago. This type of flaking required the stoneworkers to be able to think in three dimensions, but it did not result in the kind of relatively standardized artifacts found in later prehistory. Increasing use of bifacial flaking techniques is thought to have developed over the million years or so that Oldowan technology was in use.

- Although capable of vocal communication, *Homo habilis* was probably incapable of articulate speech, a characteristic of human beings that developed later in prehistory.

Chronological
Table A

The great Victorian zoologist Thomas Huxley called it the "question of questions," the nature of the exact relationship between humans and their closest living relatives such as the chimpanzee and the gorilla. Ever since his day, scientists have been locked in controversy over human origins, as they try to trace the complex evolutionary history of humanity back to its very beginnings.

THE GREAT ICE AGE

The story of humanity begins deep in geological time, during the later part of the Cenozoic era—the age of mammals. For most of geological time, the world's climate was warmer and more homogeneous than it is today. As long ago as the Miocene epoch (Table 3.1), land began to rise up in many places and mountains began to form, continuing through the Pliocene into recent times (Butzer, 1974). During the Oligocene epoch, some 35 million years ago, the first signs of glacial cooling appeared with the formation of a belt of pack ice around Antarctica. This development was followed by a major drop in world temperatures between 14 and 11 million years ago. As temperatures lowered, glaciers formed on high ground in high latitudes. About 3.2 million years ago, large ice sheets formed on the northern continents, locking up enough water to lower world sea levels by about 130 feet (40 m). Then, about 2.5 million years ago, glaciation intensified still more, and the earth entered its present period of constantly fluctuating climate. These changes culminated during the Quaternary period, or Pleistocene epoch, the most recent interval of earth history, which began about 1.6 million years ago (Goudie, 1983; Haq et al., 1977). This period is sometimes called the *Age of Humanity,* for it was during that time that human beings first populated most of the globe. The major climatic and environmental changes that

35 million years

2.5 million years

Pleistocene
1.6 million years

Table 3.1   Geological epochs from more than 60 million years ago. The curve demonstrates lasting temperature changes on earth since the late Miocene. Notice that the general trend is toward cooler temperatures with fluctuations (Pleistocene temperatures are shown in Table 3.2).

Millions of Years B.P.	Geological Epochs	Global Temperatures		
		← Lower	Today	Higher →
2	Pleistocene			
3	Pliocene			
10				
	Miocene			
20				
30	Oligocene			
	Eocene			
40				
50				
60	Paleocene			
70	Cretaceous			
75				

took place during the Pleistocene were the climatic backdrop for some of the most important stages in human evolution.

The Pleistocene period had constant fluctuations between warm and intensely cold global climates. For long stretches of time, the northern parts of both Europe and North America were mantled with great ice sheets, the last retreating only some 15,000 years ago. There were at least nine of these glacials during the last 700,000 years, which is why the Pleistocene is sometimes called the Great Ice Age. Interglacials, with climates as warm as or warmer than that of today, were rare, and the

BOX 3.1

Studying the Ice Age

Geologists have used a variety of methods to reconstruct the complex history of the Great Ice Age. The branches of science involved are botany, zoology, geomorphology (the study of land forms), nuclear physics, and oceanography (Nilsson, 1983).

Deep-sea cores yield columns of sediment that give a continuous record of Pleistocene events that can be fixed at key points by absolute dates. They also reveal information on changes in the earth's magnetic field (Chapter 4). The core sediments include the skeletons of tiny marine organisms that once lived close to the ocean's surface. By measuring the ratio between two oxygen isotopes in the calcium carbonate of the skeletons, scientists can calculate evaporation rates. They use the foraminifera and other marine microfossils to estimate the sea's surface temperature changes through time.

Glacial deposits in North America, the Alps, and Scandinavia have yielded information on the advances and retreats of major ice sheets. Such

studies are combined with other land observations.

Loess deposits are deep layers of windblown dust laid down under dry, arctic steppe conditions during glacial periods. Loess covers much of northern China, central Europe, and parts of North America. These layers can be correlated with major glacial episodes.

Pollen analysis (palynology) uses fossil pollen grains from lake deposits, peat bogs, and other layers to study vegetational change during the Ice Age. One lake core in northern Greece records vegetational change over more than 600,000 years. Pollen analysis is most effective for vegetational change over the past 130,000 years.

Animal bones are a useful but crude indicator of climatic change. For example, fossilized elephant teeth provide evidence of dramatic change in elephant populations during the Pleistocene. Small mammals such as rodents tend to be more sensitive to climatic change than larger animals.

---

constant changes repeatedly displaced plants and animals from their original habitats (Kurten, 1968; Kurten and Anderson, 1980; Martin and Klein, 1984). During colder cycles, plants and animals usually fared better at lower altitudes and in warmer latitudes. Populations of animals spread slowly toward more hospitable areas, mixing with populations that already lived there and creating new communities with new combinations of organisms. This repeated mixing surely affected the direction of evolution in many ways. No one knows how many mammal species emerged during the Pleistocene, although paleontologist Björn Kurten once estimated that no fewer than 113 of the mammal species now living in Europe and adjacent Asia appeared during the past 3 million years.

Deep-sea cores lifted from the depths of the world's oceans have produced a complex picture of Pleistocene climate. These cores have shown that climatic fluctuations between warm and cold were relatively minor until about 800,000 years ago.

Since then, periods of intense cold have reoccurred about every 90,000 years, with minor oscillations about 20,000 and 40,000 years apart. Many scientists believe that these changes are triggered by long-term astronomical changes, especially in the earth's orbit around the sun (Covey, 1984), which affect the seasonal and north-south variations of solar radiation received by the earth.

The earliest chapter of human evolution unfolded during a period of relatively minor climatic change, indeed before the Pleistocene truly began. Between 4 and 2 million years ago, the world climate was somewhat warmer and more stable than it was in later times, and the African savanna, the probable homeland of humankind, contained many species of mammals large and small, including a great variety of the order of primates, of which we humans are part.*

THEORIES ON THE ORIGINS OF THE HUMAN LINE

Primates

All of us are members of the order primates, which includes most tree-living placental mammals. There are two suborders: anthropoids (apes, humans, and monkeys) and prosimians (lemurs, tarsiers, and other "premonkeys") (Huxley, 1863). The research of more than a century has shown that the many similarities in behavior and physical

Hominids

characteristics between the hominids (primates of the family *Hominidae*, which includes modern humans, earlier human subspecies, and their direct ancestors) and the pongids (our closest living primate relatives) can be explained by identical characteristics that each group inherited millions of years ago from a common ancestor. (For an overview of human development covered in Part II, see Table 3.3.)

Thomas Huxley spelled out his own opinion about the divergences between humans and apes in his classic *Man's Place in Nature* (1863): "The structural differences which separate man from the gorilla and chimpanzee are not so great as those which separate the gorilla from the lower apes." Huxley realized, though, that humans are separated from the higher apes by a gap between parallel lines, not a gap between locations along a single line. The gap measures divergent evolution from a common ancestor.

The question is, When did humankind separate from the nonhuman primates? Experts disagree vigorously about the answer (Klein, 1989).

Aegyptopithecus to Sivapithecus

Some 35 to 30 million years ago, large bands of small, fruit-eating primates known to paleontologists as *Aegyptopithecus* trooped through the lush, wet forests of the Nile Valley. These creatures were no larger than a fox and weighed no more than 9 to 10 pounds (4 to 4.5 kg). Elwyn Simons (1984) has found their jaws and skulls near

---

*Specific details on later Pleistocene climatic change are to be found in Chapters 4, 5, and 6. Table 3.2 gives a general outline of the Great Ice Age for reference purposes.

Table 3.2 Geological events, climatic changes, and chronology during the Pleistocene (highly simplified), with approximate dates.

Temperature (Lower ← → Higher)	Dates (B.P.)	Periods	Epochs	Subdivisions	European Glacials/ Interglacials	North American Glacials/Interglacials	Human Evolution	Prehistory	Three-Age System
									Iron Age
								Cities, agriculture	Bronze Age
		Holocene	Holocene	Holocene	Holocene	Holocene	Homo sapiens sapiens	Settlement of New World	Neolithic
	10,000								Mesolithic
			Brunhes	Upper Pleistocene	Weichsel (Würm)	Wisconsin			Upper Paleolithic
	118,000	Quaternary			Eemian	Sangamon	Homo sapiens		
	128,000				Saale (Riss)	Illinoian		Hunter-gatherers	Lower and Middle Paleolithic
				Middle Pleistocene	Holstein	Yarmouth			
					Elster (Mindel)	Kansan	Homo erectus		
	730,000		Matuyama	Lower Pleistocene					
Uncertain climatic detail before 130,000 years ago		Tertiary	Pliocene — Olduvai Event				Early hominids and Australopithecus		
	1,600,000								

Note for the advanced reader and the instructor: Throughout this book I have used the glacial terminology applied to northern Europe in discussing the successive glaciations and interglacial periods in the Old World. This system follows Karl Butzer's definitive synthesis, *Environment and Archaeology*, 3rd ed. (Chicago: Aldine, 1974). Many still use the Alpine names preferred in earlier literature, but I have chosen to reduce confusion and recognize that not everyone will agree. For the newcomers, here are the equivalent names: *Alpine terms:* Würm Riss Mindel *Northern European terms:* Weichsel Saale Elster

Table 3.3   Human development: 10 million to 10,000 years ago.

Date (B.P.)	Technology	Economy	Brain Changes	Body Changes
10,000	Bows and arrows	Food production		
20,000				
31,000	Art in Europe			
37,000	Mounted tools		Fully developed brain and speech	Modern humanity
200,000				First *Homo sapiens* forms
250,000	Fire in use		Premodern speech	
500,000			Rapid brain expansion	
2,000,000	Stone toolmaking	Hunting and gathering	Reorganization of brain and slow expansion	Bipedalism is perfected—change in forelimbs / Bipedalism begins (?)
10,000,000				

Note: The developments on this table began at the period indicated by the placement. They are assumed to continue until being either replaced or refined.

the Fayum Depression west of the Nile. The bones bear some resemblance to those of later primates in East Africa dating to the Miocene epoch, which lasted from 23.5 to 5.2 million years ago. It was in Africa that apes and humans diverged from the monkeys, but no one knows when this divergence took place. Was *Aegyptopithecus* the basic primate stock from which the great apes and humans radiated, or did the separation occur during the Miocene?

Seventeen million years ago the world looked very different from what it is today. Continental drift linked Africa and Arabia with Europe and Asia. Hitherto they had been separated by sea. New mountain ranges like the Alps formed, and the climate became cooler as atmospheric and oceanic circulation patterns changed. As a result, previously separated animal species came into contact via the new land bridges, which led them into new habitats.

Several species of apes, some of which are now extinct, were already flourishing in Africa at the beginning of the Miocene, including a tree-dwelling, baboon-sized, hominoidlike primate named *Proconsul africanus* (Rose, 1984; Ward and Kimbel, 1983) *(Hominoidea;* superfamily that includes apes and humans). *Proconsul* fossils may date to as early as 22 million to around 18 million years ago (Pilbeam, 1985, 1986). *Proconsul* was an unspecialized primate. Its successors in Africa are unknown, but other Miocene hominoids occur in Europe and Asia, including *Ouranopithecus* from Greece and a better known, quite different form from Turkey, India, and Pakistan known as *Sivapithecus,* ranging in age from about 12 to 7 million years ago. *Sivapithecus* resembles the modern orangutan in facial anatomy (see Figure 3.1) but otherwise is quite different. Its teeth and other features vary greatly from those of later hominoids, such as *Australopithecus* (see later). *Sivapithecus* is thought to have been an active climber and spent most of its time in the trees.

Let it be said at once that there is so little fossil evidence that any hypotheses are little more than intelligent guesswork. The basic anatomical pattern of the large hominoids appears in the Middle Miocene, 18 to 12 million years ago. One lineage of that first evolutionary radiation survives in modified form as the modern orang (Pilbeam, 1986). A second radiation begins in the Late Miocene, between 8 and 5 million years ago. This radiation eventually produces four lineages, at least one of which, human beings, is known to have been considerably modified. It is interesting to note that a similar evolutionary pattern occurs among other herbivores, such as elephants. Early Miocene archaic elephant forms are replaced by a more modern radiation at the Early/Middle Miocene boundary. Late Miocene extinctions wipe out much of this radiation, but it also gives rise to a second Late Miocene radiation that produces most Pleistocene elephant lineages. In both cases, the patterns are monitor-

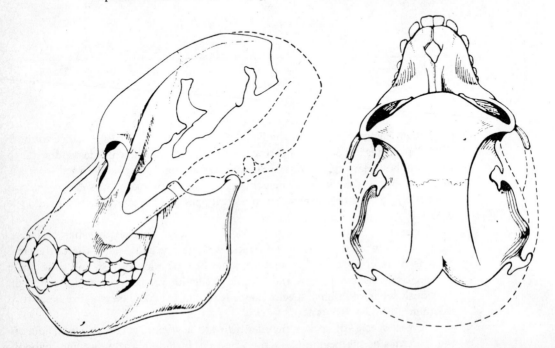

FIGURE 3.1   Side and top views of a reconstructed skull of *Proconsul africanus* (two-thirds actual size).

ing changing climates and habitats—from warmer, less seasonal, more forested regimens to colder, more seasonal, and less forested conditions. Such changes occurred throughout the past 25 million years, but there were major, pulselike shifts between 17 and 14 million years ago and again between 8 and 5 million years ago. These reflected changes in the configuration of continents, mountain systems, and antarctic ice (Figure 3.2) (Barry et al., 1985). Everyone agrees that the critical evolutionary radiation that produced the hominid line occurred in Africa.

Unfortunately, a vast chronological gap lies between *Ouranopithecus*, *Sivapithecus*, and the earliest hominidae, the australopithecines, which date to approximately 4 million years ago. Donald Johanson and Maitland Edey (1981) refer to this gap rather picturesquely as a "black hole" in our knowledge of early human evolution. The critical period was between 10 and 5 million years ago, when the segment of the African hominoid lineage radiated to produce gorillas, chimpanzees, and hominids. In the absence of key fossils, we can only speculate about the nature of the apelike animals that formed the hominoid segment during these millennia.

David Pilbeam (1986) has used existing fossils and evolutionary theory as well

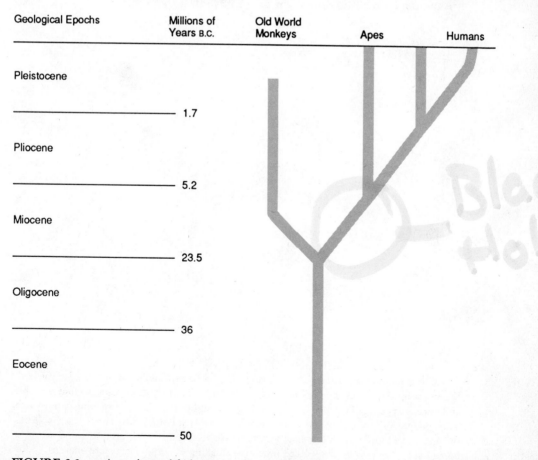

FIGURE 3.2   A much-simplified version of how Old World monkeys, apes, and humans evolved. For later human evolution, see Figure 3.11.

as molecular biology to guess—he can do no more—that these animals were mostly tree living, like *Sivapithecus*, with long arms and legs and a broad chest. They would have used all four limbs in the trees, occasionally scrambling on the ground and even standing on their rear limbs at times. There was a marked difference in size between males and females, females perhaps weighing around 44 pounds (30 kg), males about double. At least one of the Late Miocene hominoid lineages led to the gorilla, a much larger, more terrestrial form.

Pilbeam goes on to speculate that a later hominoid lineage divided into western and eastern parts at least 5 million years ago. The western segment, the "proto-chimpanzee," remained dependent on fruit and other tree foods, scattered resources that required a flexible social organization. To the ancestors of modern chimpanzees, who enjoyed a specialized adaptation to the forest, tree-living behaviors remained essential. Knuckle walking (see Figure 3.3), which provides an excellent power thrust for jumping into a tree or a short sprint (think of a football lineman), was adaptive in the forest because long arms and hands as well as grasping feet were still vital for climbing. In contrast, today's humans are the descendants of the generalized common hominoid ancestor who underwent an adaptive shift to a different ecological zone,

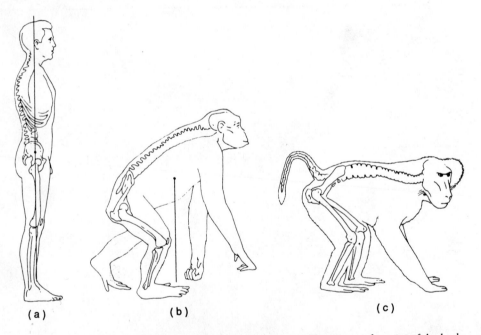

(a)   (b)   (c)

FIGURE 3.3   Bipedalism and quadrupedalism. (a) Human bipedal posture. The center of gravity of the body lies just behind the midpoint of the hip joint and in front of the knee joint, so that both hip and knee are extended when standing, conserving energy. (b) A knuckle-walking chimpanzee. The body's center of gravity lies in the middle of the area bounded by legs and arms. When the ape walks bipedally, its center of gravity moves from side to side and up and down. The human center of gravity is displaced much less, making walking much more efficient. (After Zihlman.) (c) A baboon. Baboons are quadrupedal and adapted to living on the ground.

the savanna. Early hominids became bipedal, walking on two feet, over a long period of time, perhaps as a result of spending more and more time feeding on food resources on the ground. Bipedalism is a posture that is configured for endurance rather than power or speed. Walking is highly effective for wide-ranging foraging or running a marathon. It might have social advantages, too, allowing males to monitor females more efficiently when they were dispersed over larger areas (Pilbeam, 1985, 1986).

Molecular Biology and Human Evolution

Some years ago, two biochemists, Vincent Sarich and Alan Wilson, developed a means of dating primate evolution. They assume that the albumin protein substances found in primate blood have evolved at a constant rate (Sarich, 1971, 1983). Thus the difference between the albumins of any pair of primates can be used to calculate the time that has elapsed since they separated.

Sarich and Wilson have shown that the albumins of apes and humans are more similar than those of monkeys and humans. Thus, they argue, apes and humans have a more recent common ancestry. They estimate that apes and Old World monkeys diverged approximately 23 million years ago, the gibbon and humankind only 8 million or so years ago, and that the chimpanzee, gorilla, and human last shared a common ancestor 6 to 7 million years ago. The apparent separation of apes and humans is so recent that statistically reliable numbers of differences have not yet accumulated.

Newer ways of comparing proteins and DNA are now refining the original "time clock" of evolutionary change and strongly imply some regular pattern of change along independent lineages. The new studies confirm that African apes and humans are similar, orangs roughly twice as distant, and gibbons a bit more dissimilar than orangs. Intense controversy surrounds the relationships among humans, chimpanzees, and gorillas (Pilbeam, 1986), but many biologists agree that chimpanzees are humans' closest relatives. The precise relationships between any genetic differences and the geological time scale are still uncertain and are the subject of much discussion (see Gingerich, 1985).

We are unlikely to achieve a greater understanding of very early human evolution unless we discover hominoid fossils dating to between 10 and 5 million years ago. Even when we do, the fossil record will probably be inconclusive simply because the hominoid populations of Africa were probably very heterogeneous. A major focus of research will also be the environments to which such (still hypothetical) hominoids adapted. These 5 million years were periods of major environmental change. As recently as 5.5 million years ago, the Mediterranean basin dried up when it became separated from the Atlantic. This development must have had major effects on the climate and ecology of Africa as well as the evolution of many species. That such evolution took place seems certain. During this critical period the African savanna, with its residual forests and extensive grassland plains, was densely populated by many mammal species as well as specialized tree dwellers and other primates. Both the chimpanzee and the gorilla evolved in the forests, surviving from earlier times. On savanna plains other primates were flourishing in small bands, probably walking upright, and conceivably making tools. No fossil remains of these creatures have been found, so we do not know when primates first achieved the bipedal posture that is the outstanding human physical feature. Only future fossil discoveries will resolve the question. We can, however, provide models of some of the ecological problems our earliest ancestors encountered.

THE ECOLOGICAL PROBLEMS FACED BY
EARLY HOMINIDS

Selection

The evolutionary process is based on selection, which can be viewed in several ways (Foley, 1984b). For example, one can consider the emergence of the first humans in terms of adaptive, evolutionary change. Organisms are mostly in balance with their environment. Mutations are the original source of variation in a population. They occur constantly and consistently, providing a reservoir of new variation. It is this variation, always present in a population, that occasionally provides significant advantage to some individuals, especially in cases of ecological transitions. Thus, a minority of the members of a population may increase their numbers through time because they have a selective advantage that may represent an improvement. As far as the behavioral evolution of the hominids is concerned, this process gives a model of terrestrial primates living in the increasingly dry environments of tropical Africa. Among one hominid group, mutations led to adaptive shifts—bipedalism, toolmaking, meat eating, and so on. These shifts put the group at an advantage over other terrestrial primates.

Problem solving

Another approach sees evolutionary changes arising as solutions to problems faced by the organism in its environment. New adaptations are selected if they solve problems effectively. The selective agent is the organism's environmental problems. Under this scenario, the characteristics of a hunter-gatherer adaptation would persist among hominids if they were solutions to problems faced in the environment. One viewpoint sees a species' problems as the other species it eats, those with which it competes, and those that eat it. In other words, an evolutionary advance made by one species in an ecosystem can be seen as a deterioration of the environment for another. Thus, environmental problems are not inanimate forces but dynamic, evolving processes. An organism has to evolve as rapidly as possible just to maintain its current ecological adaptation. L. van Valen, the biologist who developed this approach, calls it the "Red Queen" model: "Now *here*," the queen remarks in Lewis Carroll's *Alice Through the Looking-Glass,* "you see, it takes all the running *you* can do, to keep in the same place."

Red Queen
model

The Red Queen model is one appropriate theoretical framework for studying the behavioral evolution of the earliest hominids (Foley, 1984c). These populations underwent adaptive changes through natural selection to solve environmental problems caused by the broader ecological community. To analyze these changes requires identification of the ecological problems faced by the early hominids and understanding of the relationship between these problems and the evolution of the tropical savanna community as a whole.

Adaptive Problems

Early hominids faced three major adaptive problems. They were large mammals; they were terrestrial primates; and they lived in an open, tropical savanna environment.

Large mammals

Human beings are large relative to the majority of warm-blooded animals. Hominids have become larger through their evolutionary history, a change that has led to additional food requirements because of higher metabolic rates. This means that every individual has to range efficiently over a larger area to obtain food. Population densities must fall because the carrying capacity of any territory is finite. There will be an increase in dietary breadth, for metabolic requirements will decrease relative to body size. It is interesting to observe that hunter-gatherers use a wider range of foods, many of lower quality, than do nonhuman primates. Larger mammals are more

Range and mobility

mobile than their smaller relatives. They cover more ground, which enables them to subsist off resources that are unevenly distributed not only in space but also at different seasons. Mobility allows larger-bodied animals to incorporate unpredictable, often seasonal resources in their diets. Larger mammals can also tolerate extremes of heat and cold, a capacity that may have contributed to the expansion of humans out of tropical latitudes later in prehistory. Bipedal humans have sweat glands and are heavily dependent on water supplies. These glands are a direct adjunct to bipedalism, for they enhance endurance for long-distance foraging. Efficient heat transfer aided early hominids because both large and small animals are at a disadvantage if attacked at high noon.

These and several other factors—such as increased longevity and brain enlargement—created adaptive problems for emerging humans. These problems resulted in a variety of solutions: wider territorial ranges, the need to schedule food gathering, broadening of diet, a high degree of mobility, and much greater behavioral flexibility. This flexibility included enhanced intelligence and learning capacity, parental care, and new levels of social interaction.

Being a Terrestrial Primate

An upright posture and bipedal gait are the most characteristic hominid physical features. Upright posture is vital because it frees the hands for other actions, like toolmaking. Knuckle walking, used, for instance, by chimpanzees, is a specialized way of walking in which the backs of the fingers are placed on the ground and act as main weight-bearing surfaces. Human arms are too short for us to be comfortable with this posture, used by football linemen and runners at the starting block. However, this posture is highly adaptive in forest environments, where apes jump into trees and need the power of a fast, short sprint. In contrast, bipedalism favors endurance and the covering of long distances, important considerations on the open savanna. Bipedalism was a critical antecedent of both hunting and gathering and toolmaking (Tuttle, 1972).

Open environments

The fall in temperatures during the Late Miocene resulted in increasingly open environments in tropical latitudes. With this reduction in forested environments there probably came a trend toward terrestrially adapted species. The main constraint on arboreal primates is body size. Thus, to be part of the general trend toward larger body size among mammals, such primates would have to be at least partially terrestrial in their habits. Some 40 or more extinct and living primates, including the hominids, have adapted to a terrestrial existence. This secondary adaptation among tree-living forms may have occurred some time after 10 million years ago—expressed in the simplest terms, primates "came down from the trees" (Foley, 1984a). Coming down from the trees created three immediate problems:

Coming down from the trees

- Locomotion difficulties arise for animals with limbs adapted to moving through forests, which are less efficient for moving on the ground. All terrestrial primates underwent some modification of their way of getting about—in the case of hominids a shift to bipedalism. We know that this selection was a powerful one. It was in existence at least 4 million years ago.

- Shelter becomes an acute problem in open country, where predators abound. Arboreal primates have special sleeping areas and are safe in the trees. Those adapted to living in open country return to trees at night or use cliff faces or caves, even if they have to disperse. Large hominids that are safer from predators make ground nests, where they sleep and also seek shade on hot days—"home bases." Exactly what forms these home bases take is a matter of constant scientific debate.

- Competition for food is another pressing problem for primates who require high-quality plant food, abundant in the forests. Such foods are dispersed widely in open country. There are two possible solutions—either specialize in a small spectrum of plant foods and become an effective competitor or maintain a broad dietary niche and expand the range of foods consumed. It is striking that such a broad-based niche is characteristic of later hunter-gatherers in tropical environments. And as part of human evolution, hominids expanded their food range to include meat.

Living in a Savanna Environment

Water supplies

Terrestrial primate populations can live in drier grasslands and woodlands, environments that present another set of challenging problems. Water supplies are certain to be restricted in distribution and by season, a critical environmental reality for hominids that need regular access to liquids. The distribution of water and hominid populations are closely connected. Further, plant foods in a savanna are of lower quality, and hominids had to compete for them with other animals. Most species were seasonal and of low productivity, so a great deal of time would have been expended in searching for and processing the foods. A whole range of species would have been needed to ensure year-round food supplies.

Plant foods

Most plant species that do occur in the savanna are grasses, which are largely unsuitable for primates—but not for a diverse population of herbivores. This secondary biomass of animals could have been a valuable walking food source if the hominids found a way of tapping it. But there were competitors—a great diversity of predators, who would also have eaten an occasional hominid if the opportunity arose.

The long-term solutions to living in the savanna centered around an adaptation that involved exploiting a broad but patchy subsistence base. The lifeway was highly mobile, the range dependent on restricted water supplies. Meat became part of the diet as a way of coping with long periods of plant scarcity. Among mammal species, these characteristics are associated with a trend toward larger brain size (Eisenberg, 1981).

The Adaptive Behavior of Later Hunter-Gatherers

Characteristic behavior

Hunting and gathering have been the primary subsistence base of all human societies for more than 99 percent of human prehistory, in some areas, like the Arctic and parts of Africa and South America, until modern times (Foley, 1984c; Lee and DeVore, 1976). Hunters and gatherers are human beings who survive by exploiting resources as they occur in the wild. It follows that they exert little control over their natural environment or its resources. This universal way of life shares certain general characteristics, which appear to relate directly to the problems faced by the earliest hominids (Binford, 1979, 1980):

- Hunter-gatherers live at relatively low population densities.

- Their home ranges are larger than those of equivalent-sized mammals and primates.

- They live in small social units, often called bands, based on kin ties that regulate reproductive activity.

- They usually enjoy a mobile lifeway, focused on central places that are used for many activities.

- They tend to be omnivorous; the proportion of meat, plant foods, or other resources they consume varies greatly from environment to environment.

- They employ some division of labor. The men hunt; the women collect plant foods and tend infants (for female roles see Fedigan, 1986).

- In general, hunter-gatherer adaptations are highly flexible, and this flexibility has a direct relationship to the available resource base, territory, and band size.

This is a very general description that subsumes a great variety of hunter-gatherer adaptations, even within apparently uniform environments. But it describes, in general terms, human subsistence throughout most of prehistory. If the ecological model is on track in assuming that this lifeway evolved in response to selective pressures in the open savanna more than 2 million years ago, we must examine the archaeological and fossil evidence to see at what point hunting and gathering appeared. Were the hominids of 2 million years ago true hunters and gatherers? Or were they far more apelike in behavior than their successors?

THE FOSSIL EVIDENCE FOR HUMAN EVOLUTION

Between 9 and 4 million years ago, the last common ancestral hominoid stock split into two main lineages, which evolved into apes and humans. The details of this split are still a complete mystery, largely because fossil beds dating to this critical period are very rare in Africa (Figure 3.4). The fossil record proliferates after about 5 million

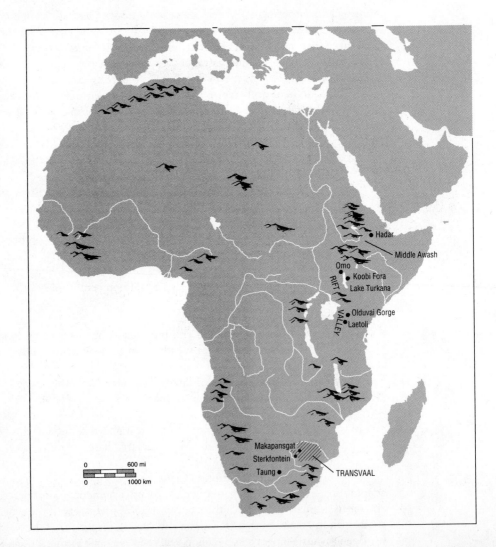

FIGURE 3.4   Archaeological sites in Africa mentioned in this chapter.

years ago but is still fragmentary. The later record of human evolution has become a veritable battlefield between paleoanthropological titans (Lewin, 1987). The controversies are aired within the pages of scientific journals, in popular magazines, even on television talk shows. We can only navigate cautiously between the various schools of thought.

Australopithecus **and** Homo

In 1925, an anatomist named Raymond Dart identified a fossil primate in South Africa that displayed both human and apelike features. He named his find *Australopithecus africanus* (Latin for southern ape of Africa) (Figure 3.5). *A. africanus*

FIGURE 3.5   *Australopithecus africanus* from Sterkfontein, South Africa. *A. africanus* was probably 42 to 50 in. (107 to 127 cm) tall; the females, weighing 40 to 60 lbs (18 to 27 kg), were somewhat lighter than the males. The posture was fully upright, with the spinal curvature that places the trunk over the pelvis for balanced walking. (Apes do not have this curvature, nor are their legs proportionately as long as those of *Australopithecus.*) The foot was small, with a well-developed big toe. *Australopithecus* looked remarkably human but with a snout that was less prominent than the ape's. The canines were small, and the incisors were vertical in the jaw, whereas the ape's slope outward. A flat nose was combined with a well-developed forehead, and the brow ridges were much less prominent than those of modern tree-living relatives. The brain had a minimum size of about 450 cc, much smaller than that of a modern human male (1450 cc) and slightly larger than that of the chimpanzee (400 cc).

A. africanus

A. robustus

was a gracile, small creature, in contrast to a second, more robust form that turned up among the dozens of australopithecine fragments found in later years. This has been named *Australopithecus robustus*, a squat, massively built primate with a crested skull (Figure 3.6). None of the South African australopithecines could be dated by potassium argon methods, but they are estimated to be between 3 million and 800,000 years old (Dart, 1925; Pfeiffer, 1985; Rak, 1983).

For years, paleoanthropologists thought that *A. africanus* was the direct ancestor of humankind, that human evolution had proceeded in a relatively linear way through time. Then hominid fossils began turning up in East Africa, finds that showed human evolution to be much more complicated. The many fossil finds are confusing, so we describe them in chronological order (see Table 3.2).

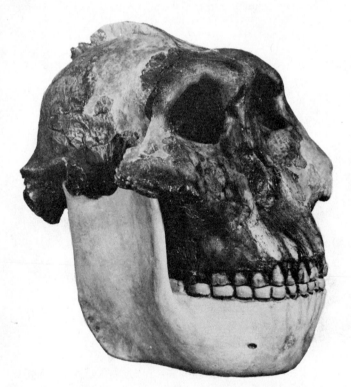

FIGURE 3.6   A robust australopithecine from Olduvai Gorge, Tanzania. The robust australopithecine was both larger and heavier than the *africanus* forms, with a more barrel-like trunk. The biggest contrasts were in the facial appearance and the teeth. *Australopithecus robustus* had a low forehead and a prominent bony ridge on the crest of the skull, which supported massive chewing muscles. Its brain was slightly larger than that of *A. africanus*, and *A. robustus* had relatively well-developed cheek teeth as well as larger molars. There was considerable variation among the robust australopithecines (see text).

Awash and Hadar

Middle Awash
**4.1 to 3.9
million years
ago**

The earliest australopithecines from East Africa are very fragmentary. The Middle Awash area of Ethiopia has yielded some skull fragments and a solitary thigh bone piece, found in deposits of potassium argon dated to between 4.1 and 3.9 million years ago. The skull fragments come from an australopithecine with almost no forehead and brow ridges intermediate between those of apes and humans.

Hadar
**3.0 to 3.75
million years
ago**

By far the most complete australopithecine finds earlier than 3 million years ago come from Hadar in northern Ethiopia (Johanson and Edey, 1981; Johanson and White, 1979; Kalb et al., 1984). When Maurice Taieb and Donald Johanson discovered a remarkably complete skeleton of a small primate at Hadar on the Awash River, they named it Lucy. Lucy was only 3.5 to 4.0 feet (1.0–1.2 m) tall and 19 to 21 years old. Nearby, they found the remains of at least 13 males, females, and children. Potassium argon dates for Hadar range between 3.00 and 3.75 million years ago. The Hadar hominid fossils are all from a single species of hominid, despite great variations in size. Some individuals stood 5 feet (1.5 m) tall and probably weighed approximately 150 pounds (68 kg), a far cry from the small, slender Lucy. These small creatures, however, were powerful, heavily muscled individuals, thought to be as strong as chimpanzees. All were fully bipedal, with arms slightly longer for their size than the arms of humans. They had humanlike hands, except that their fingers were slightly more curved. The Hadar hominids had brains approximating the size of chimpanzee brains, ape-shaped heads, and forward-thrusting jaws. There is no evidence that they made tools.

The Hadar finds are of great importance, for they demonstrate that the fundamental human adaptation of bipedalism *predates* the first evidence of toolmaking and the expansion of the brain beyond the level found in our nearest living relatives, the African apes. Bipedalism also implies that later hominids were preadapted to utilize their hands for toolmaking.

Donald Johanson and Tim White (1979) believe that Lucy and the other Hadar hominids are a species of primitive australopithecine, the common ancestor of all later hominids, including Dart's *Australopithecus africanus*. They named this species *Australopithecus afarensis*, a designation that has caused intense controversy (Figure 3.7). Are the Hadar hominids a primitive form of the later *A. africanus*, or do they represent more than one hominid species? There are just too few specimens to tell. Whatever the classification of the Hadar finds, they demonstrate that bipedalism was a hominid characteristic by 3.75 million years ago.

Bipedalism at Laetoli

Laetoli
**3.6 million
years ago**

Dramatic confirmation of hominid bipedalism by 3.75 million years ago comes from fossil-bearing beds at Laetoli in northern Tanzania, excavated by Mary Leakey and potassium argon dated to 3.75 to 3.59 million years ago. They have yielded not only the bones of extinct animals but also the incomplete jaws and teeth of at least 13 hominids (M. D. Leakey and Harris, 1990). The Laetoli hominids share many characteristics with those from Hadar, to the extent that Johanson believes they are the same

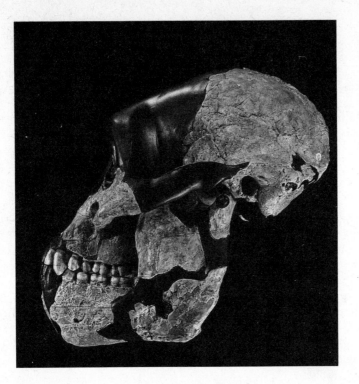

FIGURE 3.7   The reconstructed male cranium of *Australopithecus afarensis*.

species. The most remarkable finds came from the buried bed of a seasonal river, where thin layers of fine volcanic ash once formed a pathway for animals traveling to water holes. The hardened surface of the ash, dated to more than 3.59 million years ago, bore the footprints of elephants, rhinoceroses, giraffes, a saber-toothed tiger, and many species of antelope. Leakey also identified a trail of prints of a fairly large bipedal primate, which she estimated stood nearly 4 feet (102 m) tall (Figure 3.8). "The tracks," she wrote, "indicate a rolling and probably slow-moving gait, with the hips swiveling at each step, as opposed to the free-striding gait of modern man." Unfortunately, no traces of bones of this primate have come from the excavations so far.

The footprints now fully excavated are those of an adult male and an adult female carrying a child. This slender clue may be the first direct evidence for a human nuclear family, for pair bonding between male and female. The male prints are a step or two in front of the female, as if he was in a defensive role. This discovery strongly implies that these hominids were not only pair bonding but also sharing foods (see p. 116).

Turkana and Olduvai

The modern era of paleoanthropology dawned in 1959, when Mary and Louis Leakey found the skull of a robust australopithecine at Olduvai Gorge, a find potassium

FIGURE 3.8   Pliocene hominid footprints from Laetoli, Tanzania.

argon dated to 1.75 million years ago and named *Zinjanthropus boisei* (Figure 3.6) (L. S. B. Leakey, 1951; M. D. Leakey, 1971). The gorge is a spectacular rift in the great Serengeti Plain of northern Tanzania, a place where earth movements have exposed hundreds of yards of lake beds belonging to a long-dried-up Pleistocene lake (Table 3.4). Later, a more gracile hominid came from a level slightly lower than that of the original robust skull, a fossil Louis Leakey named *Homo habilis,* on the grounds that it was something quite different from the robust australopithecine nearby. The same levels yielded not only broken animal bones but also crude stone choppers and flakes that were more primitive than any previously discovered in the world (see pp. 111–113).

By the mid-1960s, there were hints that some form of more advanced hominid had lived in East Africa at the same time as *Australopithecus.* The evolutionary picture was further complicated by discoveries of fossil-bearing beds on either shore of remote Lake Turkana in northern Kenya. Richard Leakey and an international team

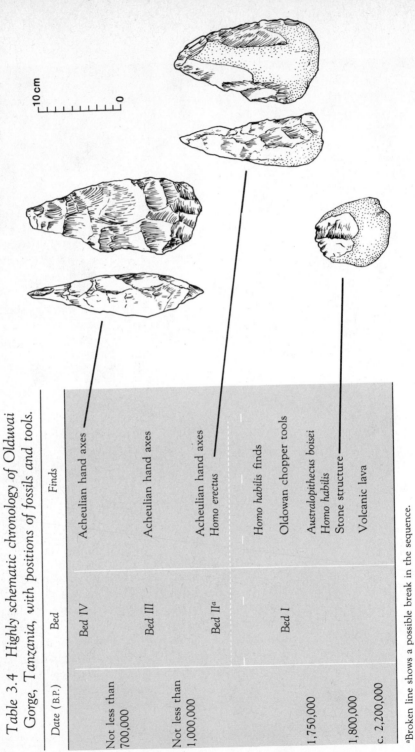

Table 3.4 Highly schematic chronology of Olduvai
Gorge, Tanzania, with positions of fossils and tools.

Date (B.P.)	Bed	Finds
Not less than 700,000	Bed IV	Acheulian hand axes
Not less than 1,000,000	Bed III	Acheulian hand axes
	Bed II[a]	Acheulian hand axes Homo erectus
	Bed I	Homo habilis finds
		Oldowan chopper tools
1,750,000		Australopithecus boisei Homo habilis Stone structure
1,800,000		
c. 2,200,000		Volcanic lava

10 cm

0

[a]Broken line shows a possible break in the sequence.

of experts located hundreds of square miles of Pliocene and Lower Pleistocene fossil-bearing sediments. The hominids include both australopithecines and individuals with unmistakably larger brains, including the famous Skull 1470 (Figure 3.9), which dates to about 1.8 million years ago (Leakey and Lewin, 1977; Lewin, 1987).

Homo habilis

Koobi Fora
**2.5 million
years ago**

Olduvai Gorge
**1.75 million
years ago**

Even specialists are confused by the proliferation of hominids in East Africa by 2 million years ago, not only gracile and robust australopithecines but also other hominids with much larger brains. These hominids come from Koobi Fora and from Olduvai in Kenya and have cranial capacities between 650 and 800 cc. These larger-brained individuals are generally assumed to represent the appearance of the genus *Homo*. Louis Leakey was the first to identify one of these hominids at Olduvai, so his label *Homo habilis* has stood the test of time.

If you had encountered *H. habilis* 2 million years ago, you would have seen little to distinguish the new hominid from *Australopithecus*. Both were of similar height and weight, about 4 feet, 3 inches (1.3 m) tall and about 88 pounds (40 kg). Both were bipedal, but *H. habilis* would have looked less apelike around the face and skull. The

FIGURE 3.9   A tentative reconstruction of Skull 1470 from East Turkana. Provisionally identified as *Homo*, this cranium is remarkable for its large brain capacity and rounded back.

head was higher and rounder, the face less protruding. Some of the most significant anatomical differences involve the teeth. The molars were narrower; the premolars smaller; and the incisors larger and more spadelike, as if they were used for slicing. However, microscopic wear studies of the teeth have shown that both *Australopithecus* and *H. habilis* were predominantly fruit eaters, so there does not seem to have been a major shift in diet between the two forms.

The first *Homo habilis* fragments, which came from Bed I at Olduvai Gorge in the early 1960s (Figure 3.10), consisted of some skull and postcranial fragments of a larger-brained hominid. Then Richard Leakey found the famous Skull 1470, a large-brained, round-headed cranium that confirmed the existence of *H. habilis* in no uncertain terms. Thigh and limb bones from Koobi Fora and from Olduvai confirm that *H. habilis* walked upright. The hand bones are somewhat more curved and robust than those of modern humans. This was a powerful grasping hand, more like that of chimpanzees and gorillas than humans, a hand ideal for climbing trees. An opposable thumb allowed both powerful gripping and precise manipulation of fine objects. With the later capacity, *H. habilis* could have made complex tools.

The discovery of 1.8-million-year-old *Homo habilis* skull and limb bones at Olduvai Gorge has shown that this was a tiny hominid, standing about 3 feet (1 m) tall, about the same size as Lucy from Hadar. There was probably considerable difference in size between males and females (the new Olduvai specimen, labeled OH 62, is thought to be female) (Johanson et al., 1987). This find throws important new light on hominid evolution between 4.0 and 1.5 million years ago; it shows that the small size of *Australopithecus afarensis* persisted for much longer than had been suspected.

Three major anatomical changes took place during the 2.5 million years between *Australopithecus afarensis* and the emergence of much larger and more advanced *Homo erectus* some 1.6 million years ago (see Chapter 4). Brain size increased from about

FIGURE 3.10   Olduvai Gorge, Tanzania.

450 cc in *A. afarensis* to 1000 cc in *H. erectus.* There were further modifications to hips and limbs for bipedal locomotion and a reduction in sexual dimorphism (size difference due to sex). The latest Olduvai *Homo habilis* shows that the primitive body form and sexual dimorphism characteristic of earlier hominids vanished only with the emergence of the much more advanced *H. erectus.* These observations have important implications for deciding just how "human" *H. habilis* was.

The specimen OH 62 suggests that *Homo habilis* was distinctly less human than had been thought. Skeletal anatomy from many finds gives a mosaic picture of both primitive and more advanced features, of a hominid that both walked bipedally and retained the generalized hominoid ability to climb trees. A telling clue comes from OH 62's upper arm bones, which, like Lucy's, are within 95 percent of the length of the thigh bone. The chimpanzee has upper arm and leg bones of almost equal length, whereas modern human upper arms are only 70 percent of the length of the leg bones. Almost certainly *H. habilis* spent a great deal of time climbing trees, an adaptation that would make them much less human in their behavior, and presumably social structure, than had been assumed even a few years ago.

From Hominids to Homo

There is general consensus among the experts that *Homo habilis* is the probable ancestor of the later human species *Homo erectus* and *Homo sapiens.* The sharp disagreement begins when one examines the evolutionary relationships between *Australopithecus afarensis* and later hominids and between *H. habilis* and the australopithecines. As British physical anthropologist Chris Stringer (1984) puts it, "The field is littered with abandoned ancestors and the theories that went with them."

Earlier models argued that evolution had proceeded through unidirectional, gradual change, as if evolutionary mechanisms were simple. One such model designated *Australopithecus africanus* as the direct ancestor for subsequent members of the genus *Homo,* with *Homo habilis* an evolutionary stage intermediate between *Australopithecus* and *Homo erectus.* This simplistic scheme has been rendered obsolete by a spate of discoveries in Ethiopia and East Turkana. Perhaps the most important recent discovery has been that of the so-called "Black Skull" in 2.5-million-year-old deposits on the western shore of Lake Turkana. This robust male australopithecine displays primitive facial features that are more in common with *Australopithecus afarensis* than the later *Australopithecus boisei* find from Olduvai Gorge (Walker et al, 1986). Some scientists now believe there are grounds for creating no fewer than three robust australopithecine species—*A. boisei* from Olduvai; *A. robustus* from southern Africa; and a new one, *A. aethiopicus,* to accommodate the Black Skull. This and other lesser finds have caused major revisions to the human evolutionary tree.

Figure 3.11 and Table 3.5 summarize the fossil evidence and two major hypotheses for early human evolution. Hypothesis A argues that *Australopithecus afarensis* (Lucy) was the common stem from which came the eastern African "robust" australopithecine lineage and another lineage that led ultimately to the southern African "robust" form (*A. robustus*) and to *Homo* via a common ancestor in *A. africanus,* the gracile australopithecines. The *Homo* line led ultimately to *H. habilis* and *H. erectus.*

Hypothesis B argues that the robust australopithecines from eastern and southern Africa are a single evolutionary branch. *Australopithecus afarensis* is thought to

(text continues on page 100)

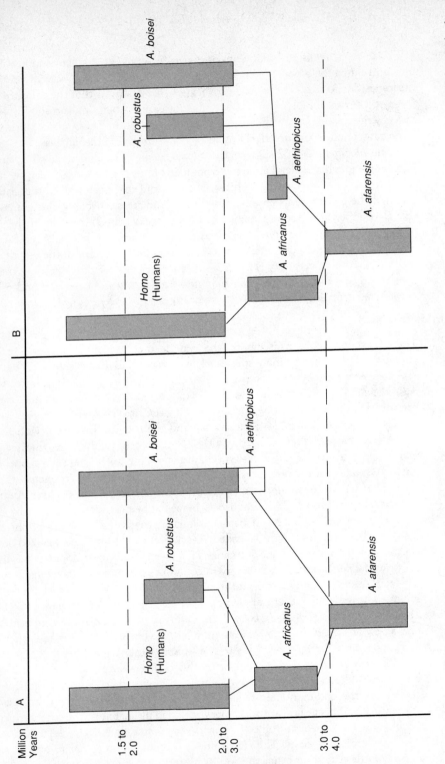

FIGURE 3.11 Two widely discussed, somewhat linear theories of early human evolution referred to in the text. Compare these with the "cladogram" in Figure 3.12, which reflects much current evolutionary thinking.

Table 3.5 Four tentative groups of East and South African hominids, much simplified for this book.

Variables	Hadar/Laetoli Group	Gracile Group	Robust Group	Homo Group
Brain size	Comparable to a chimpanzee	450–550 cc	500–550 cc	650–775 cc
Teeth	Small back teeth; large front teeth	Large front and back teeth	Very large back teeth; relatively small front teeth	Variable; generally smaller than robust and gracile forms
Limbs	Bipedal; arms slightly longer than *Homo sapiens*'s		Some elements of limb bones differ from those of modern humans	Bipedal, but lower limbs still partially adopted to arboreal life
Species and sites	*Australopithecus afarensis* East Africa: Hadar and Laetoli	*Australopithecus africanus* South Africa: Taung, Sterkfontein, Makapansgat East Africa: Omo?, East Turkana	*Australopithecus robustus* South Africa: Swarkrans, Kromdraai *Australopithecus boisei* East Africa: Olduvai, East Turkana, Omo *Australopithecus aethiopicus* East Turkana	*Homo* East Africa: Olduvai and East Turkana South Africa: Sterkfontein
Dates	East Africa: c. 4 million to c. 3 million B.P.	East Africa: c. 3 million to c. 1.5 million B.P. South Africa: no reliable dates	East Africa: c. 2.6 million to c. 1 million B.P. South Africa: no reliable dates	East Africa: c. 2 million to c. 1.5 million B.P.

be the last common ancestor of the robust australopithecine line and the lineage leading to humans. Under this theory, *A. africanus*, or a form like it, was the fore-bear of *Homo*. The robust taxa are grouped into a separate genus, *Paranthropus* (Delson, 1986). This scheme raises the possibility that the later australopithecines and *Homo* radiated rapidly and separately from a common ancestor. If such a rapid radiation took place, it was a unique event. Did hominids achieve some dramatic breakthrough in physiology or behavior? Was there a dramatic climatic change? We do not know.

A CLADISTIC THEORY OF HUMAN EVOLUTION

In reality, the fossil hominid record compares poorly with that of many other mammalian groups, to the point that any theorizing about the relationships between the hominids of 4.0 to 1.5 million years ago is invalidated by the limitations of the field evidence.

However, there have been great changes in the interpretation of human evolution in the past decade, resulting from both many new discoveries and new theoretical advances (Mayr, 1982). The most important development is a realization that hominid evolution involved a far greater level of species diversity than was previously thought (Foley, 1987). As Stephen J. Gould puts it (1977), human evolution is like a bush rather than the ladder that has been used as an analogy for so long.

Human evolution can be seen as one or more adaptive radiations rather than a simple, one-way evolution of successive species. This view stems from *cladistics*, an analytic system for reconstructing evolutionary relationships first proposed in the 1950s. Classical evolutionary analysis is based on morphological similarities between organisms. So is cladistics, but with a difference—cladistic analysis concentrates not only on features that identify common ancestry but also on those that are derived independently and are unique to specific lineages. Inevitably, cladistics tends to emphasize diversity over homogeneity.

The current view of human evolution begins with a widely accepted assumption that the sequence of hominid evolution began with the australopithecines, followed by the emergence of *Homo habilis* through *H. erectus* to *H. sapiens*. But cladistics emphasizes considerable diversity at each stage, so much so that one cannot think of human evolution as simply a trend toward anatomically modern forms (Figure 3.12). As we have seen, the australopithecines were remarkably diverse, with the primitive *afarensis* form, the lightly built and later *A. africanus*, and the much more massive *A. robustus*. Between 5 and 1 million years ago, there was considerable adaptive radiation of australopithecines. The earliest members of the genus *Homo* were probably part of that radiation, *Australopithecus*-like forms with larger brains relative to body size. These forms are all classified as *H. habilis*, but it seems certain that there was considerable variability and that several subspecies will be identified in the future. *Homo erectus* appeared about 1.6 million years ago and may also have been part of this adaptive radiation.

Homo erectus has long been considered the single human form to have lived on earth during much of the Lower and Middle Pleistocene (Foley, 1987). However,

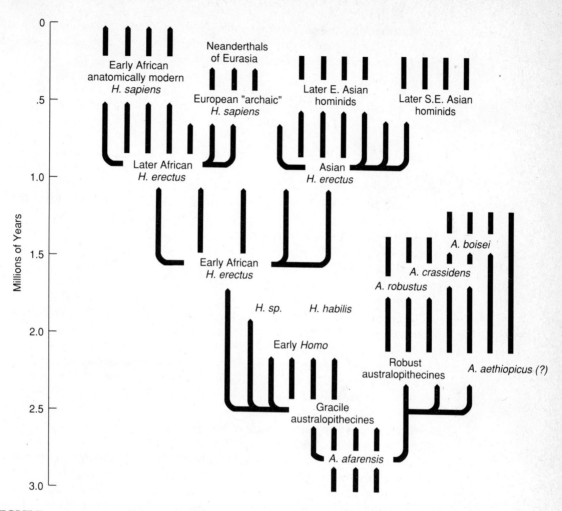

FIGURE 3.12   A diagram that sees the process of human evolution as a series of adaptive radiations. The basis for each radiation was a mixture of adaptations to local conditions and geographic isolation, isolation being especially important in later prehistory. The result was the evolution of diverse behavioral and ecological strategies and different species and subspecies. This model bears a much greater resemblance to models for other mammalian families, for it is a mistake to think of human evolution as different from that of other animals. (After Foley, 1987.)

cladistic theorists argue that this all-embracing classification is based on primitive features that link the various fossils from Africa, Asia, and Europe. Derived features, such as some of the massive features found on Asian *H. erectus* skulls, may in fact be evidence for several geographically defined forms, only one of which evolved into *H. sapiens.* This view sees *H. erectus* as an adaptive radiation of hominids in the Lower and Middle Pleistocene, with only a small part of this evolution resulting in the emergence of *H. sapiens.* Under this theory, the archaic forms of *H. sapiens* in Europe and Asia were merely local continuations of primeval local populations. It was only in Africa that *H. erectus* gave rise to modern *H. sapiens* (Braüer, 1984). In other words, the pattern of human evolution based on the adaptive radiation seen with the australopithecines persisted into much later times.

ARCHAEOLOGICAL EVIDENCE FOR EARLY HUMAN BEHAVIOR

Studying early human behavior is complicated by both poor preservation conditions and the vast time chasm that separates us from our remotest ancestors. In general terms, there are three lines of evidence that offer opportunities for testing hypotheses about early human behavior. One is scatters of artifacts and food remains that form the archaeological record for hominid activities, perhaps at predator kills, home bases, or meat caches. A second is manufactured artifacts; because of preservation conditions these are mainly objects made in stone. The transport of raw materials used to make these tools is also an important consideration. Finally, surviving food remains, almost entirely fragmentary animal bones, can reveal valuable information about our remote forebears.

Evidence for "Central Places"?

Later hunter-gatherers made habitual use of "central places," places where they returned to sleep, fabricate tools, cook food, and engage in a wide variety of social activities. Did the earliest humans have similar central places?

The only archaeological evidence comes from East Turkana and Olduvai Gorge, where a number of concentrations of bones and stone tools dating to around 2 million years ago and later have been excavated and studied with meticulous care. It is important to note that no such concentrations have been found with the earlier Laetoli or Hadar hominids.

Living floors

For years, Louis Leakey and other pioneer paleoanthropologists believed that these scatters were "living floors," places where our ancestors slept, made tools, and butchered game. These were central places, they argued, on the assumption that the hominids who created the artifact concentrations were hunters and gatherers behaving like primitive versions of living bands. Recent thinking on the subject regards such assumptions as dangerous. First, the archaeological record is very ancient, so much so that the only way one can hope to interpret it is with a thorough knowledge of the geological and other processes that have affected the bone and tool scatter since it was abandoned by its makers. Second, we now know much more about living hunters and nonhuman primates, enough to undermine confidence that direct analogies from such populations have any validity when dealing with 2-million-year-old hominid behavior. Third, a whole new generation of research involving controlled experimentation, edge wear studies, and other sophisticated approaches has thrown doubt on the notion that *Homo habilis* was a hunter at all (see Chapter 1).

If the Koobi Fora and Olduvai scatters are not central places, what behavior do they represent? Some of the earliest manufactured tools in the world, some in association with animal bones, come from the Koobi Fora area of East Turkana (Isaac, 1981a; Isaac and Harris, 1978). Several localities have been excavated, among them a dry streambed where a group of hominids found the carcass of a hippopotamus about 1.8 million years ago. They gathered around and removed bones and meat from the dead animal with small stone flakes. The deposits in which the stones and flaked debris are found are so fine-grained that they contain natural pebbles no larger than a pea. Thus, every lump of rock at the site was carried in by the hominids to make

Bone and stone accumulations

tools at the carcass. Some of the cores came from nearly 9 miles (14 km) away, presumably so the people could strike off sharp flakes to butcher the carcass. This site provides clear evidence of toolmaking, raw material transport, and butchering. We simply do not know whether the hominids killed the hippopotamus. The site may represent a place where they paused briefly to scavenge meat from a predator kill or an animal that had died of natural causes. It was certainly not a central place.

Site FxJj50, also at Koobi Fora, is in an ancient watercourse, a place where the hominids could find shade from the blazing sun, located close to water and abundant supplies of stone for toolmaking (Figure 3.13) (Bunn et al., 1980). The site consists of a cluster of stone artifacts: choppers, crude scrapers, battered cobbles, and sharp-edged flakes. Approximately 2100 bones representing at least 20 vertebrates, mainly antelope, are associated with the tools, some of them bearing carnivore chewing marks. There are clear signs that the bones were smashed and cut by hominids, for reconstructed fragments show signs of hammer blows and fine linear grooves that can have resulted only from cutting bone with stoneworking edges. The excavators noted the lack of articular ends of bones, a characteristic of bone accumulations resulting from carnivore kills. Perhaps the hominids simply chased away lions and other predators, then moved in on a fresh kill; we cannot be sure. There is a strong

FIGURE 3.13   Excavation at site FxJj50, Koobi Fora, Kenya.

possibility that successful hunting played a relatively limited role in hominid life at this early time.

Another site consists of a scatter of stone tools and broken animal bones, these from several antelope and larger mammals. The scatter lay on the surface of a dry streambed where water could still be easily obtained by digging in the sand. The banks of the watercourse were probably shaded by dense stands of trees that provided both shelter and plant foods. Perhaps the people who left the tools and bones climbed into these trees at night. The site was so sheltered that even minuscule stone chips were still in place, unaffected by the strong winds that sweep over the area; the leaves, too, left impressions in the deposits. The nearest source of toolmaking stone is 2 miles (3.2 km) from the site, so the inhabitants must have carried in their tools and, in all probability, portions of the several animals whose bones accumulated at the site. This type of behavior—the carrying in of food to a fixed location—is fundamentally different from that of the nonhuman primates.

Much of our present knowledge about the lifeways of the earliest hominids comes from Olduvai Gorge, where Mary Leakey plotted and recorded sites in Bed I at the base of the gorge (M. D. Leakey, 1971). The *Zinjanthropus* floor at Olduvai was found to be 1239 feet square (115 m²), consisting of more than 4000 artifacts and bones. Many artifacts and bones were concentrated in an area some 15 feet (4.5 m) across. A pile of shattered bones and rocks lay a short distance away, the bones perhaps piled in heaps as the marrow was extracted. A barer, arc-shaped area between these bone heaps and the pile of more complete fragments remains unexplained. Leakey wonders whether it was the site of a crude windbreak of branches since the area lies in the path of today's prevailing winds.

Recent researches have approached the Olduvai locations from several angles (Bunn and Kroll, 1986; Potts, 1984a). Careful examination of the bones revealed that many of them had lain on the surface for considerable periods of time, perhaps as long as four to six, even ten, years, to judge from weathering patterns on modern East African bones. The bones of many different animals are found in the assemblages, and the remains of carcasses are from a very ecologically diverse set of animals. Limb bones predominate on the "floors," as if these isolated bones were repeatedly carried to the site. Furthermore, the stone tools found on the Olduvai surfaces were all imported from raw material sources some distance away.

What is one to make of this pattern of meat- and marrow-rich bones concentrated in a small area with stone tools? The percentage of carnivore bones is somewhat higher than the natural environment would suggest, about 3 percent in the Olduvai assemblages, as opposed to 1 percent for the local environment today (in one case the figure was as high as 21 percent). Was there then intense ecological competition for game between hominids and other carnivores? It seems possible that the presence of carnivores restricted the activities of hominids at Olduvai. They may have grabbed meat-rich bones from carnivore kills, then taken them to a place where they had a collection of stone tools. There they could have hastily cut off meat and extracted marrow before abandoning the fresh bones to the carnivores hovering nearby. The Olduvai sites may not have been safe from carnivores, and without fire or domesticated dogs, *Homo habilis* probably had to rely on opportunistic foraging. As we have already noted, many of the Olduvai bones bear both carnivore teeth marks and stone tool cuts, perhaps a reflection of competition for game. It is also worth noting that one hominid bone found at Olduvai had been gnawed by carnivores.

Whatever their actual purpose, we can be sure that the Olduvai bone and artifact accumulations were places that were used only on a very transitory basis. Were they locations to which hominids returned to sleep, feed their dependents, and carry out other activities, or were they merely used occasionally for breaking up and eating meat? We know that the hominids transported toolmaking stone and portions of animal carcasses from one place to another. We cannot be sure that they actually lived at the places where these objects were abandoned, in the way that later hunter-gatherers did. Several experts believe that the accumulations were useful caches of stone artifacts to which bones and other food resources were taken for processing (Potts, 1984b). Perhaps these caches lay near water supplies or predictable food resources. Perhaps, too, they were maintained throughout a group's range, so the hominids did not have to carry meat or stone very far. However, a consistent pattern of caches spread throughout a territory requires a level of forethought, planning, and memory that may have been beyond the intellectual capacities of the Olduvai hominids.

All archaeology currently tells us is that the early Olduvai sites were places to which stone and food resources were carried. These may have been the predecessors to hunter-gatherer central places, which were to come into use in later prehistory, conceivably with the regular use of fire for heat and protection.

Hunting and Scavenging

Taphonomy, microwear studies, and other highly sophisticated approaches to the archaeological record of 2 million years ago have shown again and again the sheer folly of basing theories about early hominid behavior on crude analogies with contemporary hunting societies. Just for a start, the hominids belonged to a quite different species. Furthermore, their behaviors are not displayed by any living ape, nor indeed by all early hominids, some of whom never accumulated bones. At this stage, just about all we can do is pose fundamental questions about early lifeways:

- Did *Homo habilis* hunt game, merely scavenge meat, or do both? There seems to be some agreement that such humans were scavengers at least part of the time (Bunn and Kroll, 1986).

- What kind of scavenging was the rule? Was it casual scavenging when the opportunity arose? Or did the hominids deliberately chase away predators from their kills while they seized pieces of the carcass?

- Did early hominids just take small game, animals that were less powerful than themselves, only scavenging meat from larger species? Or did they hunt larger animals as well?

- How much of the diet was meat? Do the bones at the Olduvai scatters represent many meals or one major meat-eating event?

- How important was foraging for plant foods? Did the hominids make a practice of sharing food, with both hunters and foragers returning to a central place to distribute their spoils among other members of their group?

For some time, paleoanthropologists have assumed that the meat and foraging diet was associated with central places where food was shared, with momentous consequences for the evolution of human behavior (Isaac, 1984). Proponents of this school argue that meat is easily carried back to base and is a rich source of necessary amino acids. However, such explanations must be supplemented by information on the ecological conditions under which early hominid meat eating occurred (for a detailed discussion, see Potts, 1984b).

As we have seen, diverse carnivore and ungulate communities developed in eastern and southern Africa by 4 million years ago, with a wide diversity of hominids as part of the mammalian community. Some scientists believe that new ways of adapting to a heterogeneous environment like that of the East African savanna developed opportunistically. Under some ecological conditions, they argue, an opportunistic shift in the use of a food source such as meat could have led to a breakthrough in human behavior that had long-term significance.

In contrast, the Red Queen model (see The Ecological Problems Faced by Early Hominids) argues somewhat differently—that species within communities are highly interdependent and competitive. With a wide diversity of predators in the savanna, hominids consuming meat would have to have competed successfully with carnivores to obtain it. This competitive ability was selected because meat eating became vital to survival and reproductive success, and the dangers of competing with carnivores were more than outweighed by the advantages of more available food supplies and increased reproductive success because of better nutrition and easily transportable meat for social feeding.

At present, it is difficult to choose between these very general ecological models.

The Olduvai sites contain bones of smaller animals for the most part, species that were less powerful than hominids. Rather than scavenging, hunters may have run down their quarry and thrown it to the ground before killing it. This is more of an apelike form of behavior, although apes have been observed scavenging meat from predator kills (Hasegawa et al., 1983).

Some microscopic evidence from very early archaeological sites at Olduvai Gorge suggests that scavenging may have been much more important. Pat Shipman (1984) and others have examined dozens of broken animal bones from Olduvai, peering at minute but distinctive cut marks resulting from such activities as butchery, disarticulation of carcasses, and skin removal. They made high-fidelity replicas of bone marks and then examined them under a scanning electron microscope, comparing the results with those obtained from a 2300-year-old agricultural settlement in Kenya, where the inhabitants were actively engaged in disarticulation, butchery, and other activities. They found that 90 percent of the 2300-year-old bones showed cut marks resulting from the disjointing of carcasses, but only 45 percent of those from Olduvai showed the same marks. This was also true with butchery marks, those made when removing meat from bones. In contrast, about 75 percent of both the Olduvai and the 2300-year-old bones show the characteristic marks left by skin and tendon removal, which are especially visible on the lower limb bones since they had little meat on them.

Both disarticulation and butchery were surprisingly uncommon at Olduvai, so it seems doubtful the hominids were butchering and disjointing large animals and carrying them back to base. They seem to have obtained meat without cutting up too many carcasses. It is possible that they scavenged it from predator kills. A tantalizing clue came from 13 Olduvai bones on which both carnivore and humanly made markings were present. In 8 instances, the human marks *overlay* carnivore tooth marks, as if the humans had scavenged the bones from carcasses that had already been killed by lions or other predators (see Potts, 1984a).

The diversity of animals, including nonmigratory species, represented in the Olduvai bone accumulations is striking. Richard Potts (1984b) believes that this represents the variety of animals found in a resident rather than a migratory ungulate population, where only a few species are represented. He argues that the hominids depended at least partially on resident animals in a situation in which the generalization about large carnivores being hunters *and* scavengers might apply. Thus, the Olduvai hominids were hunting resident mammals as well as competing with other carnivores in scavenging activity.

By studying body part frequencies in Olduvai accumulations, Potts (1984b) has shown that carnivore bone assemblages contain a high proportion of forelimbs, the body part usually removed first from a carcass by a scavenger. In accumulations where hominid activity had taken place, higher forelimbs are also common but hindlimbs are relatively abundant as well, as if the hominids were obtaining meat both early and later in the sequence of carcass disarticulation.

A variety of ecological and zoological approaches argue for the Olduvai hominids not being just scavengers; their bone collection activities were generally similar to those of some modern mammal carnivores. They probably hunted and scavenged. Judging from the mix of fore- and hindlimbs, some of the scavenging was opportunistic.

Plant Foraging and the Early Hominids

Beyond some microscopic wear traces from plant tissues on early stone artifacts, there is as yet no archaeological evidence for plant foods being consumed by early hominids. Yet a scanning electron microscope focused on tooth microwear has shown that some Lower Pleistocene hominids had diets very similar to those of modern nonhuman primates (Walker, 1981). The recent discovery of *Homo habilis* limb bones revealed an unexpected inconsistency, for their anatomy was far more arboreal than that previously assumed for a terrestrial, bipedal primate of 2 million years ago. Such adept tree climbers are certain to have relied on fruit and other plant foods, perhaps enjoying a diet closer to that of modern apes than to that of hunter-gatherers. Clearly, plant foods were a major element in a broadly based early hominid diet, even if the archaeological evidence tends to stress meat eating over foraging.

TOOLMAKING

Other animals like chimpanzees make tools (Figure 3.14), but human beings manufacture tools regularly and habitually as well as in a much more complex fashion. In other words, we have gone much further in the toolmaking direction than other primates

FIGURE 3.14   Chimpanzee using a stick as a tool to fish for insects. Chimpanzees also use objects for play and display and carry them in their hands. Sometimes, they improve their sticks slightly with their teeth. They use leaves for cleaning the body and sipping water. Chimpanzees have inherited behavior patterns far closer to our own than to those of any monkey (Goodall, 1986).

(Gowlett, 1984). One reason is that our brains allow us to plan our actions much more in advance. Prehistoric tools in all their simplicity and sometimes extraordinary complexity provide a record of ancient decision-making processes. By analyzing the ways in which prehistoric stone artifacts—the most enduring of all technologies—were made, we can gain insights into the mind processes of the people who created them.

All studies of stone artifacts are based on the assumption that a sequence of removing flakes ultimately produced a finished artifact, whether simple or complex, to be used for a specific purpose (Figure 3.15). Many details of the world's earliest stone technology are debated, but there is no doubt that it was the work of individuals with an impressive knowledge of the properties of stone. They knew how to select the right rock, could visualize in three dimensions how to put it to use and flake it, had mastered the routine steps needed to create a tool, and were capable of passing this knowledge on to others.

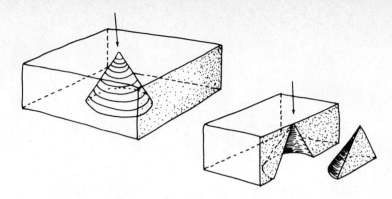

(a)

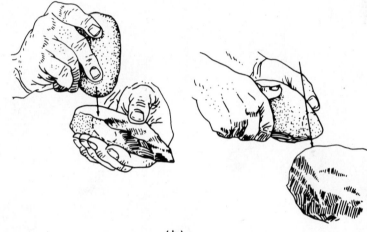

(b)

FIGURE 3.15   Early stone technology. The principles of fracturing stone were fully understood by early stoneworkers, who used them to make simple but very
effective artifacts. Certain types of flinty rock fracture in a distinctive way,
as illustrated in (a). Early stoneworkers used a heavy hammerstone to
remove edge flakes or struck lumps of rock against anvils to produce the
same effect, as shown in (b). Oldowan tools were frequently made by
removing a few flakes from lava lumps to form jagged working edges. Such
flakes have been shown by modern experiments to be remarkably effective
for dismembering and butchering game. Perhaps it is small wonder that this
simple stone technology was so long-lasting. (a) When a blow is struck on
flinty rock, a cone of percussion is formed by shock waves rippling through
the stone *(left)*. A flake is formed *(right)* when the block (or core) is hit at
the edge, and the stone fractures along the edge of the ripple. (b) Using
a hammerstone *(left)* and anvil *(right)*.

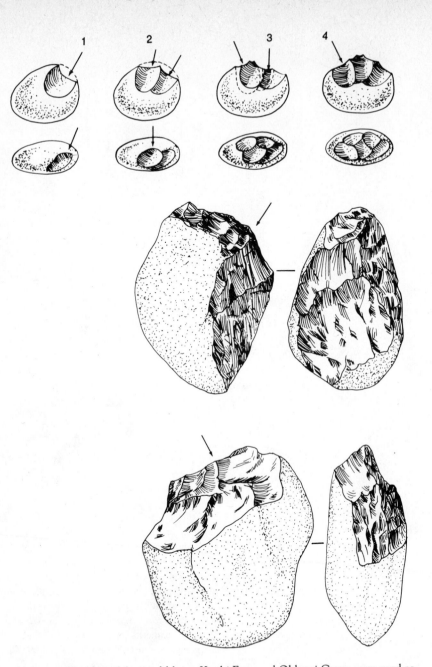

FIGURE 3.16 Oldowan technology. Many cobbles at Koobi Fora and Olduvai Gorge were used as cores to produce sharp-edged flakes. The technology was simple in the extreme. First, sharp blows were struck near the natural edge of a pebble to remove flakes. The pebble was then turned over and more blows struck on the ridges formed by the scars of the earlier flakes. A core with a jagged edge, perhaps sometimes used as a chopper, resulted. Many cores were "mined" for as many flakes as possible before being discarded. The figure shows two Oldowan cores from Olduvai Gorge. Arrows show flake edges. Front and side views (three-fifths actual size).

The Oldowan Industry

Everyone has always assumed that the earliest stone technology would be very simple (Toth and Schick, 1986). When the Leakeys found crudely chipped stones in the long-buried lake beds at Olduvai Gorge, they were indeed nothing much to look at (Figure 3.15). (The Leakeys called their early tool assemblages Oldowan, after the gorge where they were first identified.) Most were broken pebbles and flakes, with flakes in the majority. Some Oldowan tools were so crude that only an expert can tell them from a naturally fractured rock, and the experts often disagree. All the Oldowan choppers and flakes strike one as extremely practical implements; many are so individual in design that they seem haphazard artifacts, not standardized in the way later Stone Age tools were. Classifying them is very difficult, for they do not fall into distinct types. The tools cannot be described as primitive since many display a sophisticated understanding of stone's potential uses in toolmaking. We now know that the Olduvai hominids were adept stone toolmakers, using angular flakes and lumps of lava to make weapons, scrapers, and cutting tools. The tools themselves probably were used to cut meat and perhaps wood. In all probability, the hominids made extensive use of simple and untrimmed flakes for many purposes.

Oldowan industries have been found on several sites in East Africa dating to between about 2.5 and 1.5 million years ago. There appears to be relatively little variability between different toolkits, and the artifacts show certain common technological features:

- Use of pebbles as raw material

- Cores with edges flaked from both sides (Figure 3.16)

- Some of the cores possibly fashioned into deliberate core tools (were these choppers?)

- Both heavy- and light-duty tool forms, some modified into crude scrapers

There is a tendency to describe the Oldowan as a very simple technology. It is true that there are few formal Oldowan tool types, but the artifacts show a skilled appreciation of basic stone-flaking techniques and flaking sequences that were envisaged in the mind's eye.

For years, archaeologists have thought of the Oldowan as a static technological stage without any perceptible change. As more sites come to light and analytic techniques are refined, though, the Oldowan appears in a different light—as a simple, highly effective technology that grew more complex over time, with the appearance of crude bifacial working, in which cores were flaked on both sides (Figure 3.17) (Gowlett, 1986).

Mary Leakey (1971) studied the Oldowan choppers and flakes from the early hominid levels at Olduvai and divided the artifacts into different morphological forms. Her classification remained unchallenged until Nicholas Toth and a new generation of scholars approached early stone technology from a more holistic per-

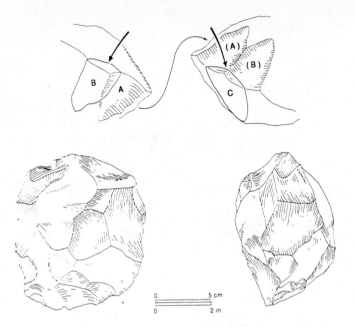

FIGURE 3.17   Making Oldowan bifaces. *Top,* a simplified picture of the process required for bifacial flaking. *Bottom,* a large Oldowan diskoidlike artifact from Chesowanja, East Africa, in plan and side views. The stoneworker used this bifacial technique but did not fashion the biface along a long axis, as later humans did (see Chapter 4). (After Gowlett, 1984.)

spective (Toth, 1985). The objective of their studies is to learn as much as possible about early hominid behavior from the stone artifacts left behind. Such research is based firmly in experimental archaeology and middle range theory. It is founded on every aspect of technology, from raw material acquisition through artifact manufacture and use to discarding and incorporation of the tools into the geological record. As part of his work, Toth became an expert stone toolmaker and carried out edge wear and taphonomic studies on sites in East Turkana.

Toth emerged from his work with a very different view of the Oldowan. He points out that conventional approaches to the stone artifacts are based on the idea that the makers had premeditated artifact forms in mind. His experiments replicated thousands of Oldowan cores and flakes and led him to argue that much of the variety in Oldowan artifacts was, in fact, the result of flake production. Many of the choppers from Olduvai and Koobi Fora are actually "waste," cores discarded when as many flakes as possible had been removed from them. Toth also observes that the size of available raw material can profoundly affect the size and variety of choppers and flakes at an Oldowan site (Toth and Schick, 1986).

Toth's experiments with replicated tools revealed that sharp-edged flakes are far more effective for butchering animal carcasses, especially for slitting skin. Flakes, then, were of much greater importance than hitherto suspected—but this does not mean that all choppers were just waste. Some may have served as wood-chopping and adzing tools or for breaking open bones for their marrow. Microwear studies of the few Oldowan flakes made of fine-grained materials have hinted at three possible uses: butchery and meat cutting, sawing and scraping wood, and cutting soft plant matter.

What are the implications of Toth's studies for our knowledge of early hominid cognitive skills? Toth believes our earliest ancestors had a good sense of the mechanics of stone tool manufacture and of the geometry of core manipulation. They were able to find the correct acute angle needed to remove flakes by percussion. Not even modern beginners have this ability; it takes several hours of intensive practice to acquire the skill. Although chimpanzees use sticks and crack nuts with unflaked stones, they rarely carry their "artifacts" more than a few yards. In contrast, the Koobi Fora and Olduvai hominids carried flakes and cores over considerable distances, up to 8 miles (13 km). This behavior represents a simple form of *curation*, retaining tools for future use rather than just utilizing convenient stones, as chimpanzees do. Toth hypothesizes that the hominids tested materials in streambeds and other locations; transported the best pieces to activity areas; and sometimes dropped them there, carrying the rest off with them. He also points out that they must have relied heavily on other raw materials, like wood and bone, and that stone artifacts do not necessarily give an accurate picture of early hominid cognitive abilities.

The archaeologists' traditional view of the Oldowan considers it a "protohuman culture," with its simple stone artifacts a first step on the long evolutionary trail to modern humanity. Perhaps this view has been colored by analogies with modern hunter-gatherers and by overoptimistic interpretations claiming that early hominids aimed and threw stone missiles, shared food, and so on. Another viewpoint argues that the Oldowan hominids were at an apelike grade of behavior, on the grounds that all the conceptual abilities and perceptions needed to manufacture Oldowan tools also appear in ape-manufactured tools like termite-fishing tools and sleeping platforms (Wynn and McGrew, 1989). Furthermore, not only Oldowan hominids but also chimpanzees scavenge and hunt for game, chasing down small animals, carrying meat over considerable distances, and using "extractive technology" to break open animal bones and nuts. Chimpanzees, like early hominids, use the same places again and again, pounding nuts at the same locations and carrying food to their favorite eating sites. Even if the specifics vary in some instances and the natural environments are different, the behavioral pattern of Oldowan hominids is generally similar to that of apes. There are, however, two behavioral differences between apes and early hominids. First, hominids were at an advantage in that they were bipedal, a posture that is far more efficient for carrying objects than walking on four limbs. Second, the Oldowan humans were adapted to savanna living, where they had to organize and cover far larger territories in open country than their primate relatives in the forest. In the long term, this may have resulted in new concepts of space and spatial organization, concepts that were definitely reflected in more complex stone tool forms after a million years ago.

It would be naive to claim that the behavior of early hominids was entirely apelike, for this means ignoring the importance of the evolution of enlarged primate brains. We can be certain that there were significant differences between nonhuman primates and hominids 2 million years ago, but these changes may not be reflected in stone artifacts. Without question, our ancestors became more and more dependent on technology. The opportunistic nature of primeval stone technology is in sharp contrast to the better designed, much more standardized stone artifacts of later humans.

THE DEVELOPMENT OF LANGUAGE

Cooperation, the ability to get together to solve problems of both subsistence and potential conflict, is a vital quality in human beings. We are unique in having a spoken, symbolic language that enables us to communicate our most intimate feelings to one another. One fundamental question about early prehistory surrounds this development: At what point did hominids acquire the ability to speak?

Washoe the chimp

Our closest living relatives, the chimpanzees, communicate with gestures and many voice sounds in the wild, whereas other apes use sounds only to convey territorial information. However, chimpanzees seem to have a natural talent for learning symbolic language under controlled conditions. A famous chimpanzee named Washoe was trained to communicate with humans, using no fewer than 175 sign language gestures similar to those of American Sign Language (Gardner and Gardner, 1969). After more than a year, Washoe could associate particular signs with specific activities, such as eating and drinking. Another chimpanzee, named Sarah, was taught to read and write with plastic symbols and acquired a vocabulary of 130 words, to the extent that she obeyed sequences of written instructions given with the symbols (Premack and Premack, 1972). The research continues, but there is no evidence that chimpanzees can combine visual symbols to create new meanings or use syntax. Sequences of signs produced by trained chimpanzees may have a superficial resemblance to the first multiword sentences produced by children, but beyond the stage of learning isolated symbols, an ape's language learning is severely restricted (Terrace, Sanders, and Bever, 1979).

Endocasts

Clearly, articulate speech was an important threshold in human evolution because it opened up whole new vistas of cooperative behavior and unlimited potential for the enrichment of life. When did hominids abandon grunts for speech? There are only two potential lines of research. One uses *endocasts,* natural casts of the interior of the brain case. Dean Falk (1984) has studied the convolutions of early hominid endocasts and found that those of the early australopithecines are apelike. The brain cell of Skull 1470 (Figure 3.10) is about 300 cc larger, and the frontal lobe of its endocast is more humanlike, especially in the Broca's area, where speech control is located.

Endocast research is much more generalized than detailed anatomical studies of the position of the voice box, the larynx, using both comparative anatomy and actual fossils to study differences between apes and humans. Jeffrey Laitman (1984) poses the two fundamental questions:

- What was the anatomy of our ancestors' vocal cords?

- How does it compare to that of modern humans?

The second line of research has been done by Laitman and others who studied the *position* of the larynx in a wide variety of mammals, including humans. They found that all mammals except adult humans have a larynx high in the neck, a position that enables the larynx to lock into the air space at the back of the nasal cavity. Although this position allows animals like monkeys and cats to breathe and swallow at the same time, it limits the sounds they can produce. The pharynx—the air cavity part of the food pathway—can produce sounds, but animals use their mouths to modify sounds since they are anatomically incapable of producing the range of sounds needed for articulate speech.

Until they are about 18 months to 2 years old, human children's larynxes are also situated high in the neck. Then the larynx begins to descend, ending up between the fourth and seventh neck vertebrae. How and why are still a mystery, but the change completely alters the way the infant breathes, speaks, and swallows. Adult humans cannot separate breathing and swallowing, so they can suffocate when food lodges in an airway. However, an enlarged pharyngeal chamber above the vocal cords enables them to modify the sounds they emit in an infinite variety of ways, which is the key to human speech.

Fortunately, the shape of the base of the skull is highly informative. Most mammals have flat-based skulls and high larynxes, but humans have an arched skull base associated with their low larynx. Using sophisticated statistical analyses, Laitman (1984) and his colleagues ran tests on as many complete fossil skulls as possible. They found that the australopithecines of 4.0 to 1.0 million years ago had flat skull bases and high larynxes, whereas those of *Homo erectus,* dating to about 1.5 million years and later, show somewhat more curvature, suggesting that the larynx was beginning to descend to its modern position. It was only about 300,000 years ago that the skull base finally assumed a modern curvature, which would allow for fully articulate speech to evolve.

So it seems that language was a relatively late development, albeit one of vital importance. The real value of language, apart from the stimulation it gives brain development, is that with it we can convey feelings and nuances far beyond the power of grunts or gestures to communicate. We may assume that the first humans had more to communicate with than nonhuman primates, but it appears that modern articulate speech was a more recent stimulus to biological and cultural evolution.

THE EARLY ADAPTIVE PATTERN

The few early sites that have been excavated show that the first phase of human evolution involved shifts in the basic patterns of subsistence and locomotion as well as new ingredients—food sharing and toolmaking. These led to enhanced communication, information exchange, and economic and social insight, as well as cunning and restraint. Human anatomy was augmented with tools. Culture became an inseparable part of humanity.

Opportunism

Archaeologist Glynn Isaac (1984) believes that opportunism is a hallmark of humankind—a restless process, like mutation and natural selection. The normal pressures of ecological competition were able to transform the versatile behavior of ancestral primates into the new and distinctive early hominid pattern. The change required feedback between cultural subsystems, such as hunting and sharing food. Weapons and tools made it possible to scavenge and butcher larger and larger animals. Vegetable foods were a staple in the diet, protection against food shortages. Foraging provided stability, and it may also have led to division of labor between men and women. The savanna was an ideal and vacant ecological niche for hominids who lived on scavenging, hunting, and foraging combined.

By a million years ago, the hominid lines had been pruned to the extent that one lineage, *Homo*, remained. Judging from the abundance of finds from East Turkana, the hominids of 2 million years ago appear to have been about as common as baboons are in the savanna today (Lewin, 1988a). The microwear patterns on the tooth surfaces of *Australopithecus* and *Homo habilis* show that both creatures flourished on a diet very similar to that of chimpanzees. But this pattern can be produced by all kinds of combinations of vegetable and meat foods, to the extent that the two species may have been ecologically separated by their different dietary preferences. Otherwise it would not have been possible for them to share the same area for very long. But this is purely intelligent speculation. The archaeological deposits in which both fossils and artifacts are found are simply too coarse-grained to allow detection of even fairly major climatic and ecological changes.

The only clue to this separation may lie in the appearance of *Homo habilis* at about the same time as the first stone tools. These artifacts must have been connected with new ways of getting and processing foods, even with entirely new forms of diet. *H. habilis* had a much larger brain, a development that was probably associated with an increase in economic and social complexity, and perhaps food sharing as well.

What sort of social organization did *Homo habilis* enjoy? However much we look at contemporary nonhuman primates, we cannot be sure. Most primates are intensely social and live in groups in which the mother-infant relationship forms a central bond. The period of infants' dependency on mothers found in, say, chimpanzees was probably lengthened considerably with *H. habilis.* The larger brain size would mean that infants were born with much smaller heads than adults, at an earlier stage of mental maturity. This biological reality would have had a major impact on social organization and daily habits.

Chimpanzees have flexible, matriarchal social groups. They occupy a relatively small territory, one with sufficient vegetable resources to support a considerable population density; this pattern contrasts sharply with the average hunter-gatherer band, typically a closely knit group of about 25 people of several families. The kind of systematic hunting such people engage in requires much larger territories and permits much lower densities per square mile. The few sites that have been excavated suggest that *Homo habilis* tended to live in bands that were somewhat more akin to those of modern hunter-gatherers. However, it would be a mistake to assume that they lived in actual hunter-gatherer bands. In all probability their social organization resembled more closely that of chimpanzees and baboons, which are very different from those of humans.

Chimpanzees and baboons live in a world created in their brains by the integration of sight, sound, smell, and touch. The more complex the inputs and their neural processing, the more complex the inner world built by the brain. It may well be that this increase in complexity is what underlies the cumulative growth in brain size that is such a distinctive feature of mammalian evolution, from amphibians to reptiles, then through mammals to humans. The world of *Homo habilis* was much less predictable and more demanding than that of even *Australopithecus.* What was it that was more complex? Why do we have to be so intelligent? Not for hunting animals or gathering food but for our interactions with other people. The increased complexity of our social interactions is likely to have been a powerful force in the evolution of the human brain. For *H. habilis,* the adoption of a wider-based diet with a food-sharing social group would have placed much more acute demands on the ability to cope with the complex and unpredictable. And the brilliant technological, artistic, and expressive skills of humankind may well be a consequence of the fact that our early ancestors had to be more and more socially adept.

GUIDE TO FURTHER READING

Foley, Robert, ed., 1984 *Hominid Evolution and Community Ecology: Prehistoric Human Adaptation in Biological Perspective.* London: Academic Press.
> *A provocative set of essays on the ecological background to the evolution of human-kind. Crammed with thoughtful commentary and imaginative theorizing on the emergence of humanity. Essential for the serious student.*

Isaac, G. Ll. 1984. "The Archaeology of Human Origins." *Advances in World Archae-ology* 3:1–87.
> *An authoritative account of the archaeological evidence from East Africa.*

Johanson, Donald C., and Edey, Maitland A. 1981. *Lucy: The Beginnings of Human-kind.* New York: Simon & Schuster.
> *A well-written, racy account of the Hadar hominids that ranges widely over the major controversies of paleoanthropology. Superb descriptions of the research process and dating methods.*

Klein, Richard. 1989. *The Human Career.* Chicago: University of Chicago Press.
> *A summary of human biological and cultural evolution for more advanced students.*

Lewin, Roger. 1987. *Bones of Contention.* New York: Simon & Schuster.
> *An entertaining account of the major personalities and controversies surrounding paleoanthropology. Admirable for the general reader.*

———. 1988. *Human Evolution,* 2d ed. Oxford, Eng.: Blackwell Scientific Publica-tions.
> *A lucid, multidisciplinary account of human origins; full of stimulating ideas.*

Toth, N., and Schick, K. D. 1986. "The First Million Years: The Archaeology of Protohuman Culture." *Advances in Archaeological Method and Theory* 9:1–96.
> *A synthesis of recent research into the archaeological record of early prehistory.*

Weiss, Mark L., and Mann, Alan E. 1990. *Human Biology and Behavior,* 5th ed. New York. HarperCollins.
> *A standard undergraduate text that presents the biological background to human evolution. Excellent graphics.*

Holocene Present *(handwritten)*
Upper Pleistocene *(handwritten)*
Middle Pleistocene *(handwritten)*
Lower Pleist. *(handwritten)*

Years B.P.	Africa	Europe and the Near East	Asia
10,000 *(handwritten)*			
20,000		(see Chapter 5 ↑) Upper Paleolithic	Tabon
	Late Stone Age	Saint-Césaire Hahnofersand Combe Grenale	Long Rongrien Niah
40,000		La Ferrassie Le Moustier (and other sites) Mt. Carmel Teshik-Tash Regourdou Qafzeh Monte Circeo Shanidar	
100,000	Border Klasies Cave River		
128,000 *(handwritten)*			Maba
200,000	Kapthurin	Steinheim Swanscombe Torralba/Ambrona Arago (?)	Dali Narmada
300,000		Terra Amata	

400,000		Petralona
		       Torralba/Ambrona
		           (?)
			Zhoukoudien

500,000			Lang Trang Lan-t'ien Q'en-Xia-wo
	Kilombe	Isernia La Ubeidiya Pineta	Ban Mae Tha
750,000			
73,000 *(handwritten)*			Java
1.0 Million	Olduvai Gorge		
1.5 Million	East Turkana Chesowanja Swartkrans		
1.6 Mya *(handwritten)*		(see Chapter 3 ↓)	

CHAPTER 4

HOMO ERECTUS AND HOMO SAPIENS

(1.5 MILLION TO 40,000 YEARS AGO)

Preview

- *Homo erectus* and *Homo sapiens* evolved during the Lower and Middle Pleistocene. The Lower Pleistocene began about 1.6 million years ago and lasted until 730,000 years ago, when the world's magnetic polarity changed at the Matuyama/Brunhes boundary.

- The Middle Pleistocene lasted from 730,000 to 128,000 years ago and was marked by constant cycles of cold and warm climate, with the world's climate in transition from one extreme to the other most of the time.

- *Homo erectus* first evolved in tropical Africa about 1.6 million years ago and was apparently the first hominid to adapt to climates as diverse as tropical forest, temperate, and near arctic. Anatomically, *H. erectus* was fully adapted to bipedal posture, had much more humanlike limbs than *Homo habilis,* and had a brain capacity that ranged between 775 and 1300 cc.

- *Homo erectus* may have been the first hominid to tame fire, to use it for protection, warmth, and cooling.

- About 1 million years ago, *Homo erectus* moved from Africa into Asia and Europe. This spread coincided with a radiation of tropical carnivores and ungulates into temperate latitudes. The earliest known European human settlement is at Isernia La Pineta, Italy, dating to this time. The Zhoukoudien Caves of China were visited by *H. erectus* bands from about 600,000 to some 230,000 years ago.

- The successful colonists of northern latitudes were those who could exploit game animals distributed unevenly over a landscape with a climate of sharp seasonal contrasts. The key to this new adaptation was mobility, an opportunistic adaptation based on knowledge of resource distribution.

- *Homo erectus's* stone technology was oriented toward the making of stone axes, a wide range of flake tools, and choppers. Acheulian hand axes were shaped symmetrically around a long axis, multipurpose tools like the flake artifacts favored at many locations. Human technology between 1.5 million and 150,000 years ago shows considerable diversity, probably associated with different local adaptations and the availability of toolmaking stone.

- *Homo erectus* hunted and foraged for food, perhaps developing effective social mechanisms to foster collaboration and enhanced communication in pursuit of large game. Torralba/Ambrona, Spain, and Terra Amata, France, provide examples of European settlements occupied by such early hunter-gatherers.

- Anatomically modern humans *(Homo sapiens sapiens)* are thought to have evolved in tropical Africa some time before 100,000 years ago and to have spread into the Mediterranean Basin and the Near East about 45,000 years ago.

- The Neanderthals first appeared in Europe, the Near East, and Asia well before 100,000 years ago and flourished until replaced by modern humans about 35,000 years ago. Their more robust postcranial skeleton and skeletal anatomy set them apart from *Homo sapiens sapiens.*

- Middle Paleolithic technology used techniques developed by Acheulian stoneworkers but yielded a wider variety of finished artifacts, some of them composite tools. Prepared and disk core technologies came into use and were important after 150,000 years ago. However, the Neanderthals used techniques that varied considerably from one location to the next for many reasons, among them availability of raw materials, climate, different activities, and subsistence needs.

- The Neanderthals were the first human beings to bury their dead, suggesting at least rudimentary spiritual beliefs.

Chronological Table B

Human evolution should not be thought of in terms of neat ladders of progression from one form to the next, improved form. With only a handful of fossils to work with, and those fragmentary at best, there has been a tendency even for experts to think in linear terms. However, since human evolution has probably followed the pattern of that of other animal groups, we are likely to find more rather than fewer species in our ancestry. Instead of a ladder, one should think of a bush, with different branches representing new species that all became extinct, except for the one surviving form—*Homo sapiens.* We are a rarity in nature in that we are all from one species (Lewin, 1988a).

In Chapter 3, we noted how opportunism and adaptability were hallmarks of the first hominids, in terms of both diet and ecological exploitation. The australopithecines were not as adaptable as some of their hominid contemporaries. They lived at a time when baboons and other competitive primates were evolving rapidly, and they probably became extinct as a result of competitive exclusion. Their successors and those of *Homo* were humans capable of a far more complex and varied lifeway. These were hominids who used fire, made systematically manufactured rather than opportunistic tools, developed seasonal central places, and were the first to settle outside Africa.

PLEISTOCENE BACKGROUND

The evolutionary developments described in this chapter begin at the start of the Pleistocene and unfolded during a prolonged period of ever-changing Ice Age climate. These changes were the background both to an accelerating pace of human biological and cultural evolution and to the first peopling of the Old World outside Africa by human beings.

Lower Pleistocene (1.6 million to c. 730,000 Years Ago)

1.6 million B.P.

As we mentioned in Chapter 3, the Pleistocene began about 1.6 million years ago, after an intensification of glaciation after 2.5 million years ago (Table 3.2). This arbitrary boundary coincides with a major geomagnetic reversal in the earth's magnetic field, which can be recognized on a worldwide basis (Haq et al., 1977). By this time, great mountain chains had formed in the Alps, Himalayas, and elsewhere. Landmasses had been uplifted; connection between these latitudes and southern areas was reduced, lessening their heat exchange and causing greater temperature differences between them. Three million years ago, northern latitudes were still warmer than today, but they were much cooler by the beginning of the Pleistocene.

The Lower Pleistocene is distinguished by surviving Pliocene animal forms and by the appearance of horses, cattle, elephants, and camels. Deep-sea cores tell us that climatic fluctuations between warmer and colder regimens were still relatively minor during this, the first million years of the Ice Age (Kurten, 1968). This was a critically important time, when *Homo erectus* evolved in Africa and moved out of the tropics into Asia and Europe.

Middle Pleistocene (c. 730,000 to 128,000 Years Ago)

730,000 B.P.

An abrupt reversal of the earth's magnetic field, back from reversed to normal, occurred about 730,000 years ago, an event that has been identified all over the world in both deep-sea cores and terrestrial deposits. This Matuyama/Brunhes boundary, named after the geologists who first identified it, marks the arbitrary division between the Lower and Middle Pleistocene (Butzer and Isaac, 1975). The seesaw pattern of sea-core changes tells of constant climatic change from this point on. Consistently,

BOX 4.1

Deep-Sea Core V28–238

The deep-sea core that serves as the standard reference for events during the past 700,000 years comes from the Solomon Plateau in the Pacific Ocean (Shackleton and Opdyke, 1973). This core is a long way from the great ice sheets of Europe and North America, but as do many other cores, it records events of local climatic significance like glacial advances on a global scale. In this core, the Matuyama/Brunhes boundary occurs at a depth of 39.3 feet (1200 cm). Above it, a sawtoothlike curve identifies eight complete glacial and interglacial cycles, a far more complete record of the Middle and Upper Pleistocene than comes from land sediments (Gamble, 1986b; Goudie, 1983).

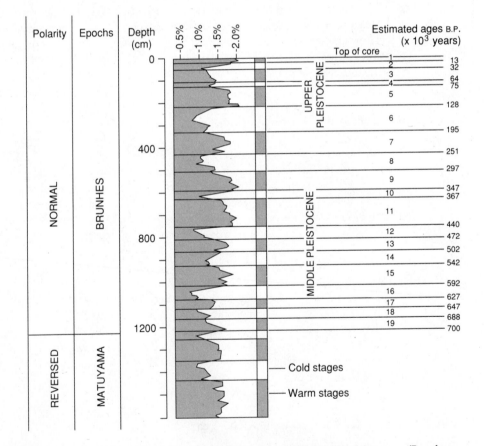

Stratigraphic record of the Pleistocene from deep sea core V28–238. The Matuyama/Brunhes boundary occurs at about 730,000 years ago. The sawtoothlike profile chronicles the relative size of the world's oceans and ice caps. (After Shackleton and Opdyke, 1973.)

the cores tell us, ice sheets formed gradually, but deglaciation took place with great rapidity, during phases that geologists call *terminations.* These correspond with major sea level rises that flooded low-lying coastal areas. Street (1980) estimates that glaciers covered a full third of the earth's surface during glacial maxima. Great ice sheets mantled Scandinavia and the Alps, as well as much of northern North America (Figure 4.1). The glaciers were about as extensive as they are today during interglacials (warmer periods). Thus, during interglacials, sea levels were within 18 to 20 feet (5 to 10 m) of present shorelines. Much less is known about changes in tropical regions, although it is thought that the southern fringes of the Sahara Desert expanded dramatically during cold periods: High percentages of windblown desert sand have been found in contemporary sea cores taken in West African waters.

Elster
525,000 B.P.

The outlines of Middle Pleistocene climatic change are still imperfectly known, but we know that there was a major glacial episode, known to European geologists as the Elster glaciation, about 525,000 years ago. At its height, there was ice as far south as Seattle, St. Louis, and New York in North America, and sea levels were about 650 feet (197 m) below modern levels. In contrast, there were periods of more temperate conditions between about 515,000 and 315,000 years ago, with colder incidents breaking up the warmer climate. It was during this interglacial that human settlement of temperate latitudes really took hold, as small bands of hunter-gatherers exploited the rich animal and plant resources of European and Asian river valleys and woodlands (see below).

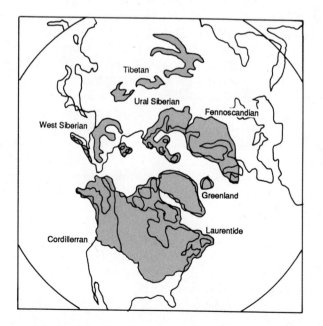

FIGURE 4.1   Pleistocene glaciers in the northern hemisphere at their maximum extent. Shorelines caused by low sea levels are not known.

Saale
180,000 to 128,000 years ago

The Middle Pleistocene ended with another intense glaciation, the Saale (known as the Illinoian in North America), that lasted from about 180,000 to 128,000 years ago. As we shall see, this colder cycle coincides in general terms with the period when anatomically modern humans were evolving in tropical Africa.

Both *Homo erectus* and *Homo sapiens* evolved during a period of constant climatic transition between warmer and colder regimens in northern latitudes. Experts believe that the world's climate has been in transition from one extreme to the other for over 75 percent of the past 730,000 years, with a predominance of colder climate over the entire period. These constant climatic changes played an important role in the spread of archaic humans throughout temperate and tropical latitudes (Gamble, 1986b).

The climatic events of the Upper Pleistocene are described at the beginning of Chapter 5.

HOMO ERECTUS

Homo erectus
1.5 million to ?200,000 B.P.

Lake Turkana
1.6 to 1.5 million B.P.

The earliest unquestioned specimen of *Homo erectus* comes from East Turkana in Kenya, a skull dated to between 1.6 and 1.5 million years ago (Figure 4.2) (Leakey and Lewin, 1977). This fossil, with its massive brow ridges, enlarged brain size, and high forehead, is morphologically very close to examples of *H. erectus* dating to a million years ago and earlier.

Richard Leakey and anatomist Alan Walker have recently discovered the virtually complete skeleton of a 12-year-old *Homo erectus* boy on the western shores of the same lake, dating to about the same time period. The footprints of hippopotamuses and other animals nearby suggest that the decomposing corpse was trampled to pieces. From the neck down, the boy's bones are remarkably modern looking. The skull and jawbone are more primitive, with brow ridges and a brain capacity perhaps as high as 700 to 800 cc, about half the modern size. The skeleton shows that the boy stood about 5 foot, 6 inches (1.8 m) tall, taller than many modern 12-year-olds. This new Turkana find tends to confirm many scientists' view that different parts of the body evolved at different rates, the body achieving fully modern form long before the head.

Java
900,000 to 600,000 B.P.

These finds are earlier than the classic finds of *Homo erectus*, which were made as early as 1891. A Dutch doctor named Eugene Dubois found the skullcap, but no tools, of an apelike human in the gravels of the Solo River near Trinil in central Java (Pfeiffer, 1985). When, a year later at the same site, he found an upper limb bone that displayed many human features, he named his discovery *Pithecanthropus erectus* ("apeman who walks upright"). A vicious outcry greeted his announcement; Dubois was accused of heresy and his findings dismissed with contempt. Then in 1928, a Canadian anatomist named Davidson Black announced the discovery of human teeth at Zhoukoudien Cave near Beijing (Weidenreich, 1946). A year later, the Chinese archaeologist W. C. P'ei recovered a complete skullcap from the same cave; it closely resembled Dubois's Java finds. The human remains were associated with stone tools, crude bone artifacts, and the bones of hundreds of animals. A Dutch physical anthropologist, G. H. R. von Koenigswald, discovered more fossils in Java, examined

Zhoukoudien
400,000 to 230,000 B.P.

FIGURE 4.2 Skull KNM-ER3733, East Turkana, Kenya.

the Chinese and Japanese remains, and described a new human form: *Homo erectus* (Figure 4.3) (Symon and Cybulski, 1981).

Homo erectus is known to have lived over a wide area of the Old World. Louis Leakey found a skullcap of *H. erectus* in the upper levels of Bed II at Olduvai Gorge (Lewin, 1988a). This specimen came from levels dating to approximately a million years ago. In contrast, the Chinese finds are now estimated to date to between 500,000 and 350,000 years ago, and new *H. erectus* finds from the Trinil area of Java have been potassium argon dated to between 900,000 and 600,000 years ago (Weiss and Mann, 1988). *Homo erectus* fossils have come to light in Morocco and Algeria and in Hungary and West Germany. None of the European finds can be dated, but they probably belong to approximately 500,000 years ago. Further, although fossil remains of *H. erectus* are rarely encountered, their distinctive toolkit of stone axes and other artifacts is relatively commonplace and tells us much about their distribution and adaptations.

During *Homo erectus*'s long history, humanity adapted to a far wider range of environments, ranging from tropical savannas in East Africa to forested Javanese valleys, temperate climates in North Africa and Europe, and the harsh winters of

Olduvai Gorge
1 million B.P.

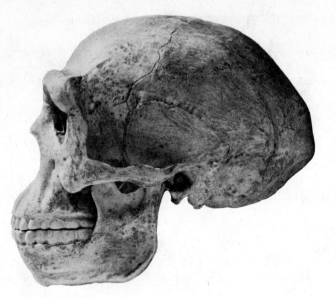

FIGURE 4.3   A plaster cast of *Homo erectus* from Zhoukoudien, China. The skull bones of *H. erectus* show that these hominids had a brain capacity between 775 and 1300 cc, showing much variation. It is probable that their vision was excellent and that they were capable of extensive thought. The *H. erectus* skull is more rounded than that of earlier hominids; it also has conspicuous brow ridges and a sloping forehead. With a massive jaw, much thicker skull bones, and teeth with cusp patterns somewhat similar to those of *Australopithecus africanus* and modern humans, *H. erectus* had limbs and hips fully adapted to an upright posture. It stood over 5 feet, 6 inches (1.8 m) and had hands fully capable of precision gripping and many kinds of toolmaking.

China and northern Europe. *Homo erectus* was certainly capable of a far more complex and varied lifeway than previous hominids, and with such a wide distribution, it is hardly surprising that some variations in populations appear. For example, some had more robust skulls than others, although it is said that the Zhoukoudien skulls display a gradual increase in brain capacity from about 900 cc in 600,000-year-old specimens to about 1100 cc in 200,000-year-old individuals. In any case, *H. erectus* was far more "human" than *H. habilis*, a habitual biped, who had probably lost the thick hair covering that is characteristic of nonhuman primates. Unfortunately, we are unlikely to know when we lost our dense facial hair because soft parts are never preserved. But it seems possible that this occurred when the dramatic enlargement of hominid brains recycled the developmental "clock"—perhaps with *H. habilis* (Lewin, 1988a). In any case, *H. erectus* certainly had abundant sweat glands and, presumably, in common with most tropical primates and humans, relatively dark skin.

FIRE

Fire caused by natural conflagrations was certainly part of the savanna environment in which our earlier ancestors lived. Great grass and brush fires swept across open and wooded country during the dry months, especially, perhaps, when markedly drier conditions were widespread in East Africa about 1.7 million years ago (Clark and Harris, 1985). This was a time when the faunal communities of East Africa adapted to drier, more open grassland conditions. It was also about the time that *Homo erectus* first emerged. From this point on, there are signs that human behavior changed. The first archaeological sites appear at higher East African elevations, and less densely vegetated areas are more intensively occupied. Butchery sites containing the remains of large animals are more common. Stone technology becomes more complex, evidenced by the appearance of more elaborate hand ax-like artifacts and flake tools.

Swartkrans
Chesowanya
1.6 million B.P.

The earliest traces of what may be humanly tamed fire come from Swartkrans in South Africa, dating to about 1.6 million years ago, and from Chesowanya in the Kenya Rift Valley. Both are assumed to be the work of *Homo erectus.* Chesowanya yielded evidence of hearthlike arrangements of stone artifacts, fragmentary bones, and baked clay that had been hardened in antiquity. Unfortunately, it has not proved possible to demonstrate that the inhabitants controlled the fire that hardened the clay. It is not until between 1 million and 700,000 years ago that fire is well documented in the archaeological record—significantly, in temperate China.

It is not unreasonable to assume that the early hominids had learned to live with natural fires and were not afraid of them (Clark and Harris, 1985). Fire offers protection against predators and an easy way of hunting game, even insects and rodents, fleeing from a line of flames. The toxins from many common vegetable foods can be roasted or parched in hot ashes, allowing people to use a wider range of plants in their diet (Stahl, 1984). The prevalence of such toxins may be the reason chimpanzees eat so many insects—still an important protein source for many African peoples and perhaps for early hominids, too. Perhaps *Homo erectus* had the habit of conserving fire, taking advantage of long-smoldering tree stumps ignited by lightning strikes and other natural causes to kindle flames to light dry brush or simply scare off predators.

Hominid body size had increased dramatically with the appearance of *Homo erectus.* An ecological consequence of enlarged body size is extension of the home range, a fact well documented from animal behavior studies (Foley, 1984b). Larger quantities of food are needed because of higher metabolic rates. This may have been the time when hominids not only relied on smoldering tree stumps but also began to carry simple firebrands as protection against large predators. The new weapon would also allow them to move into more open country, where trees were much rarer, and to increase their home ranges into unfamiliar habitats.

Clark and Harris (1985) think it not unlikely that the conservation and taming of fire—as much as food sharing, meat eating, and new forms of sexual behavior—helped to forge close-knit family groups among hominid bands. The distribution of archaeological and hominid sites approximately 1.5 million years ago may reflect greatly increased home ranges and, perhaps, the time when humans domesticated fire. It may be no coincidence that the earliest human settlement of Europe and Asia, of more temperate latitudes, occurred after *Homo erectus* appeared in East Africa and, perhaps, mastered fire.

THE RADIATION OF *HOMO ERECTUS*

African hominids had to adapt to cyclical alterations among savanna, forest, and desert after 1 million years ago (Roberts, 1984). They could do so by migrating with the changing vegetational zones, as many other mammals did, or they could adapt to new environments, changing their dietary emphasis from meat to plant foods. Finally, they could move outside tropical latitudes altogether, into habitats that human beings had never occupied before.

Paleoanthropologists now believe that *Homo erectus* adapted to changed circumstances in all these ways, with hominids radiating out of Africa by way of the Sahara, when the desert was capable of supporting human life. Neil Roberts (1984) has likened the Sahara to a pump, sucking in population during wetter savanna phases and forcing hunter-gatherers out toward the Mediterranean during drier cycles. In radiating out of Africa, *H. erectus* behaved just like other mammals in its ecological community (Fagan, 1990).

Hominids were carnivores and plant eaters, and thus linked ecologically with other predators. There was widespread interchange of mammals between Africa and more temperate latitudes during the Pliocene and Lower Pleistocene. A major change in the mammalian populations of Europe took place about 700,000 years ago. Hippopotamuses, forest elephants, and other herbivores and carnivores like the lion, leopard, and spotted hyena seem to have migrated northward from Africa at this time. Migrations by the lion, leopard, and hyena—the animals with which hominids shared many ecological characteristics—were in the same direction as that taken by *Homo erectus*. Many paleontologists have noticed that the first European lions, leopards, and spotted hyenas reached enormous sizes, as if they had enjoyed a successful adaptation in areas that were subject to far greater seasonal temperature fluctuations than the tropics. That the first successful human settlement of Europe and temperate Asia coincided with a radiation of a tropical mammal community from Africa seems plausible.

Earliest Human Settlement in the Near East and Europe

Ubeidiya
700,000 B.P.

The earliest recorded human settlement in the Near East comes from the Ubeidiya site, near the confluence of the Jordan and Yarmuk rivers in Israel. Some human and animal bones are associated with simple choppers and some crude hand axes at this lakeside site. Unfortunately, Ubeidiya's dating is somewhat controversial, but an estimate of about 700,000 years ago, close to the Matuyama/Brunhes boundary, seems likely (Bar-Yosef, 1975).

Isernia La Pineta
c. 730,000 B.P.

The earliest securely dated human artifacts yet found in Europe come from lake beds at Isernia La Pineta, southeast of Rome, Italy, stratified under volcanic deposits that have been potassium argon dated to some 730,000 years ago. The artifacts include flakes, scrapers, and choppers associated with bison, elephants, and other animals (Gamble, 1986b; Segre and Asconzi, 1984). None of the claims for even earlier European settlement have yet withstood close scrutiny, but by at least 350,000 years ago, human groups were living throughout western and central Europe and perhaps even farther east.

Homo erectus in Asia

In the present state of research, there is general agreement that Africa was probably the cradle of humankind. Despite several claims to the contrary, no australopithecine or *Homo habilis* fossils have come from tropical Southeast Asia. Nor is there evidence of tropical radiation of hominids during the Lower Pleistocene. *Homo erectus* is the earliest human being documented either in Southeast Asia or in the Far East (G. G. Pope, 1984).

Southeast Asia

Ban Mae Tha c. 700,000 B.P.
The earliest traces of human settlement consist of three artifacts found in gravel deposits at Ban Mae Tha in northern Thailand. These split and flaked cobbles are dated through paleomagnetic and potassium argon studies to about 700,000 years ago (Pope et al., 1986). Given what we know about the earliest prehistory of Southeast Asia, it seems almost certain that these tools were made by *Homo erectus.* Dubois's *H. erectus* finds and other more recent discoveries from Indonesia are thought to date to no earlier than about 700,000 years ago (G. G. Pope, 1984), a point that appears to coincide with the appearance of similar hominids in Europe and perhaps in China as well. Five *H. erectus* specimens dating to about 500,000 years ago have recently come from Lang Trang Caves in Vietnam, the earliest securely dated human fossils in Southeast Asia.

Lang Trang c. 500,000 B.P.

Homo erectus may have reached east Asia in the very late Lower Pleistocene, perhaps via the so-called Sunda shelf, low-lying ground that joined many of the Southeast Asian islands during cooler cycles. This shelf appears to have acted as a faunal filter, preventing many tropical ungulate species from reaching the east. Southeast Asia was a tropical forest environment, with extensive patches of dense forest even during the driest periods of the Pleistocene. Geoffrey Pope (1984) believes that bamboo and other wood resources from these forests were of vital importance for the highly portable toolkit used by *H. erectus* in this environment. He also points out that fire, perhaps tamed by these people, is an important component in forest technology. Thus, the crude stone choppers and flakes that may have formed the simple stone technology of Asia for tens of thousands of years were only a limited part of forest material culture. Such implements are all that remain of a Stone Age lifeway that was based not on the pursuit of large savanna animals but on smaller game and forest resources, many concentrated around natural springs, sinkholes, and caves.

(a)

FIGURE 4.4   (a) Zhoukoudien Cave, China; (b) (facing page) a crude chopping tool from Zhoukoudien, front and side views (one-half actual size).

China

Lan-t'ien
Q'en-Xia-wo
600,000 B.P.

There are two or three artifact assemblages from China that are claimed to date to the Lower Pleistocene, but the dates of all of them are uncertain (Chang, 1986). The earliest widely accepted traces of human activity date to after 700,000 years ago, during the Middle Pleistocene. The Lan-t'ien and Q'en-Xia-wo sites in central China have yielded specimens of *Homo erectus* that probably date to the early Middle Pleistocene, before 600,000 years ago.

The most famous and largest Middle Pleistocene site in China is the

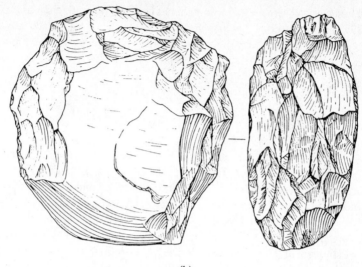

(b)

Zhoukoudien
**460,000 to
230,000** B.P.

Zhoukoudien Caves, 28.5 miles (46 km) west of Beijing. Zhoukoudien consists of many caverns and fissures, the most famous of which is Locality I, where both stone implements and human fossils have been found. These caverns were visited by *Homo erectus* over an immensely long period of time, from about 600,000 to 230,000 years ago (Chang, 1986; Institute of Vertebrate Paleontology, 1981; Rukang and Shenglong, 1983). At least 40 *H. erectus* individuals have been found at Zhoukoudien, most of whom died before they were 14 years old. Many of them appear to have perished from injuries; according to some physical anthropologists, some skulls were smashed open at the base to extract the brain, perhaps evidence for the earliest cannibalism in the world (Hooton, 1948).

The Zhoukoudien people visited the caves when the climate was perhaps a trifle warmer and moister than today. They hunted deer and other animals; more than 60 species are represented in the deposits. Lewis Binford, who examined some of the bones very briefly, claims that they were brought into the cave by scavenging predators, but the sample he studied was extremely small, and his conclusions are disputed (Binford and Ho, 1986; Binford and Stone, 1986). Charcoal, burned bone fragments, and ash accumulations that formed hearths show that *Homo erectus* used fire (Binford and Stone, 1986, claim that the people were not using fire).

About 100,000 stone implements come from Zhoukoudien, most of them made on flakes of rough-vein quartz. The people made choppers and scrapers, awls, crude points, and many multipurpose artifacts (Figure 4.4). The toolkit evolved through the 100,000 years of occupation, with the earliest artifacts tending to be larger and made with simple percussion techniques. As time went on, the toolmakers produced smaller implements, many of them made of finer raw materials.

Taken together, the Asian fossils are remarkably homogeneous. They have broad-based skulls; low, receding foreheads; and prognathous faces. The upper skull bones are thick and show every sign that these humans had strong chewing muscles.

These people were up to 5 feet, 6 inches (1.67 m) tall and had a brain capacity between 775 and 1300 cc. One has the impression of a biologically conservative human population that changed little over enormously long periods of time. The latest *Homo erectus* finds come from Java and Narmada in India and date to about 230,000 years ago.

Choppers and Chopping Tools

In 1948, the Harvard archaeologist Hallam Movius divided the archaic world of early prehistory into two vast cultural provinces. The grasslands and woodlands of Africa and Europe were the home of Acheulian hand ax makers, who also flourished in the Indian continent and far into Eurasia. A second province lay in the East, he wrote, an enormous region of woodland and forest and great environmental diversity. Here stone technology was far cruder and more conservative. Crude stone choppers and the simplest of flakes remained in use for more than three-quarters of a million years, in the hands not only of *Homo erectus* but of modern humans as well. Movius felt that Asia was an area of cultural retardation. It could never have played a "vital and dynamic role in early human evolution, although very primitive forms of Early Man apparently persisted there long after types at a comparable stage of physical evolution had become extinct elsewhere" (Movius, 1944). For generations, prehistorians thought of this "chopper-chopping tool complex" as culturally backward, as a culture that had developed in isolation.

More recent interpretations take a different tack. They assume that far from being backward, the early Asians took full advantage of the forest resources available to them. Instead of stone, they turned to wood, fiber, and bamboo, all of them organic materials that survive poorly in archaeological sites. In other words, our view of early Asia is biased simply because we lack evidence of the whole range of their forest cultures. Tropical forests are rich in animal and plant foods, but they are widely dispersed. Thus, human groups subsisting off forest foods must move constantly, carrying their artifacts with them. Under these circumstances, it is logical for people to use for their toolkits bamboo, wood, and other fibrous materials—the most convenient materials at hand. There was no need for the specialized, often complicated implements used in open country in the West, either for spear points or for the butchering tools used on bison or large antelope. Geoffrey Pope (1989) points out that the distribution of "chopper-chopping tool" sites coincides very closely with the natural distribution of bamboo, one of the most versatile materials known to humankind. Bamboo was efficient, durable, and portable. It could be used to manufacture containers, sharp knives, spears, weapon tips, ropes, and dwellings. To this day, it is widely used in Asia as scaffolding for building skyscrapers (Figure 4.5). It is an ideal material for people subsisting not off large game but off smaller forest animals such as monkeys, rats, squirrels, lizards, and snakes as well as plant foods. Simple stone flakes and jagged-edged choppers would be ideal for working bamboo and may, indeed, have been used for this purpose over many millennia.

We still know little of the world of *Homo erectus,* beyond a certainty that humans

FIGURE 4.5   Bamboo scaffolding in use to build a modern highrise.

had radiated far from their tropical homeland in Africa. By 700,000 years ago, *H. erectus* had settled in temperate Europe and the Near East, was probably living in India, and was certainly present in Southeast Asia and China. Human beings had now adapted to a far wider range of environments than ever before, where fire and efficient shelter were essential to survive dramatic contrasts in summer and winter climates. As far as is known, however, *H. erectus* did not settle in extreme arctic latitudes, in what is now the USSR and Siberia. Nor did they develop the watercraft needed to cross from island Southeast Asia to Australia, a landmass that remained isolated by the ocean throughout the Ice Age.

The Settlement of Temperate Latitudes

We must think of the first human settlement of temperate latitudes as part of a broader set of ecological processes, one of them the simultaneous radiation of modern grazing animals and new vegetational communities into Europe and other northern latitudes of the Old World. Humans were part of this vast animal community. Their long-term success resulted from their ability to adapt to the cyclical changes in the Ice Age environment, from temperate to much colder, then to full glacial conditions and an abrupt deglaciation as the climate warmed up again rapidly. Karl Butzer (1982) believes that these early human populations flourished in regions where dense, abundant, and predictable resources were to be found, isolated from other regions where similar conditions existed. The climatic changes of the Ice Age sometimes brought these isolated populations together, then separated them again, ensuring gene flow and genetic drift and continued biological and cultural evolution over the millennia.

The British prehistorian Clive Gamble (1986b) argues that the first settlement of temperate latitudes was not simply a case of an opportunistic species seizing a set of favorable environmental circumstances. He believes that by 730,000 years ago hominids had mastered the necessary hunting and foraging strategies to survive in much more diverse environments than tropical savanna. Most regions of the temperate world had the energy and resources for hominid settlement even when *Homo habilis* flourished. *H. habilis* had not evolved the long-term solutions, such as tailored clothing, for coping with cyclical climatic change and all the resource changes that resulted from it.

Gamble points out that most evidence for Middle Pleistocene settlement, between about 730,000 and 130,000 years ago, falls in periods when the climate was colder than today but not fully glacial, as it has been for most of the past 700,000 years, times when grazing animals formed the principal food resource in cooler latitudes. Plant and marine foods were much more costly to exploit and often sparse. The successful colonists of northern latitudes were those hominids who could exploit game animals distributed unevenly, at times very densely, over the landscape.

That is not to say, of course, that the hominids lived by hunting alone. They had to cope with long, sparse winter months, when their prey dispersed so widely that it was beyond human capacity to hunt them effectively. Gamble (1986b) hypothesizes that the people searched for frozen animal carcasses, a winter strategy that was adaptive for highly mobile predators like humans. They had one advantage over other predators—their technology of sticks and wooden probes that could be used to unearth food buried in ice fissures or snowdrifts. This would have been a lower-risk strategy if a large group worked together, searching for the predictable refrigerated carcasses of large animals that died during the winter months.

During the spring and summer the people would concentrate on hunting migratory game, eating their kills quickly and stripping them of meat before other predators moved in. Both winter and summer lifeways of this type required compact territories, where the people remained highly mobile year-round. We can thus expect to find Middle Pleistocene sites clustered in regions with large areas of uninhabited country between them. Gamble (1986b) points out that many known sites are near lakes and streams, perhaps the places where the bands most commonly hunted and also where wood might have been found for tools and for the fires used to thaw frozen meat. The key to this entire adaptation was mobility; the bands could respond quickly to changes in resource distribution by moving into new areas. Gamble believes this was a primarily opportunistic adaptation based on knowledge of resource distribution rather than the result of deliberate planning.

THE TECHNOLOGY OF *HOMO ERECTUS*

Oldowan technology was simple and opportunistic and developed slowly over more than a million years ago. There is good reason to believe that the same primeval toolmaking survived long after *Homo habilis* had vanished as an integral part of later toolmaking traditions. We can be fairly certain, too, that Oldowan stoneworking methods formed part of the legacy of the first hominids to later prehistory.

Neither *Homo habilis* nor *Homo erectus* relied exclusively on stone, for we can say with confidence that our remote ancestors also made use of wood, one of the most versatile raw materials known to humanity. Unfortunately, timber rarely survives in the archaeological record. The earliest known wooden artifacts consist of a wooden spear tip (or possible snow probe) from Clacton in eastern England, dating to about 200,000 years ago (Figure 4.6), and a 150,000-year-old wooden spear from Lehringen in Germany. Most insights into the technology of *H. erectus* come from stone tools and the by-products associated with them.

Both Oldowan technology and the artifacts fashioned by *Homo erectus* remained in use in various forms for immensely long periods of time. Oldowan stoneworking lasted for as much as a million years, its more diverse successor for nearly half as long again. There is a tendency to think of both technologies as monolithic, unchanging chronicles of human prehistory, fixed stages in human cultural evolution, partly because of the time scales involved and also because stone tools appear to have changed so little over hundreds of thousands of years. In fact, the technology of *H. erectus,* like that of *H. habilis,* displays considerable variability and development.

Hand Axes and Other Tools

In Africa, Europe, and some parts of Asia, *Homo erectus* is associated with a distinctive toolkit that includes not only a variety of flake tools and sometimes choppers but also bifacially flaked hand axes. These hand ax industries are grouped under the technological label *Acheulian,* after the town of St. Acheul in northern France, where many such artifacts have been found. Hand axes come in many sizes and shapes; they are sometimes artifacts of great refinement and beauty (Figure 4.7), so much so that people ignore all the other tools *H. erectus* made. In fact, human technology between 1.5 million and 150,000 years ago shows considerable diversity, probably associated with local adaptations and the availability of suitable raw materials.

The hand ax is one of the most common exhibits in the world's museums. It has been found over a vast area of the Old World in all shapes and sizes, from crude

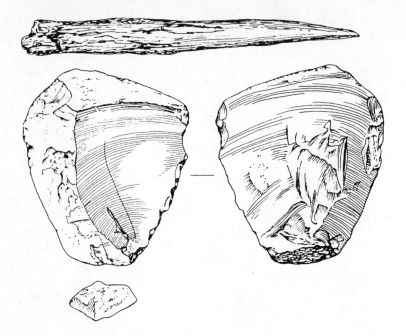

FIGURE 4.6   European wood and stone tools. *Top,* a wooden spear tip (perhaps a snow probe) from Clacton, England, dating to about 200,000 years ago (approximately one-eighth full size). *Bottom,* views of a flake from the same location. The upper surface is shown at left, the flake (lower) surface on the right. The striking platform is at the base (one-third actual size).

tear-shaped forms to ovals, tongue-shaped axes, and occasional finely pointed specimens that were evidently made with considerable care. Unlike the crude scrapers and choppers of the Oldowan, the Acheulian hand ax was an artifact with converging edges, which met at a point. The maker had to envisage the shape of the artifact, which was to be produced from a mere lump of stone, then fashion it not with opportunistic blows but with carefully directed hammer blows. Acheulian hand axes come in every size, from elegant oval types a few inches long to heavy axes more than a foot (0.3 m) long and weighing 5 pounds (2.3 k) or more. They must have been a versatile, thoroughly practical artifact to have continued in use for so long.

What exactly were hand axes used for? Almost certainly they were held in the hand rather than being hafted on the end of a wooden shaft. They were simply too cumbersome, and in any case, hafted tools probably did not come into use until much later. Conventional wisdom has it that they were multipurpose artifacts, used for grubbing up roots, working wood, scraping skins, and especially skinning and butchering large and small game. There is no question that they were highly effective butchery tools. Many archaeologists have tried not only cutting up antelope carcasses but also slicing through hippopotamus and elephant hide—with great success. In some ways, the hand ax was ideal for this purpose because it could be sharpened again and again, and when it became a useless lump of stone, it could be recycled into flake tools. But you can achieve effective butchery with simple flakes as well, and a number of researchers have wondered whether the hand ax, which took longer to make, was not used for other purposes.

In contrast to the earlier Oldowan, the Lower Paleolithic technology of *Homo erectus* varied greatly throughout its duration, reaching considerable heights of delicate artistry (Figure 4.8). In addition to hand axes, the new technology resulted in scrapers and other artifacts for woodworking, skinning, and other purposes. But hand axes remain the most characteristic artifact of many *H. erectus* populations.

Acheulian culture
1 million to 60,000 B.P.

Hand axes have been found over an enormous area of the Old World (Figure 4.9). Fine specimens are scattered in the gravels of the Somme and Thames rivers in northern Europe, in North African quarries and ancient Saharan lake beds, and in sub-Saharan Africa from the Nile Valley to the Cape of Good Hope. Acheulian tools are common in some parts of India, as well as in Arabia and the Near East as far as the southern shores of the Caspian Sea and perhaps even farther north. They are rare east of the Rhine and in the Far East, where chopping tools were commonly used until comparatively recent times (Butzer and Isaac, 1975; J. D. Clark, 1970; Howell and Clark, 1963). No one has been able to explain why hand axes have this distribution. Were such multipurpose tools used only in big-game hunting camps? Was their use restricted by the availability of flint and other suitable raw materials? Did environmental conditions affect the hunters' choice of toolkits? Or were they used as projectiles in areas where big game abounded? We do not know.

Hand Axes and the Evolution of the Human Mind

While we recognize that *Homo erectus* made a wide variety of artifacts, the fact remains that the Acheulian hand ax is the most characteristic and one of the most widely distributed tools made between 1.5 million and 150,000 years ago. It also provides us with an opportunity to consider the relationship between an artifact and the evolution of the mind.

John Gowlett (1984, 1986), who has thought profoundly about this relationship, believes that manufacture of the hand ax and the remainder of *Homo erectus's* toolkit was the result of a series of ideas, some derived from previous stoneworking experience and perhaps also from observation of the environment or from woodworking. We do not know where hand axes first evolved. It is reasonable to assume that the technology began in Africa, where *H. erectus* developed and where the earliest sites with such artifacts are found. Gowlett believes that a discoidlike artifact, a cobble flaked bifacially on all sides, was the general prototype for the hand ax. Discoids occur in Olduvai Beds I and II and at other early sites, like Peninj in Kenya and perhaps in East Turkana. Elongate these discoids and make them on large flakes, and you are approaching the shape of the hand ax, an artifact based on a design that stressed symmetry around the long axis.

Kilombe
700,000 B.P.

Hand axes were the logical end result of long-used stone technology, made to a degree of standardization unimaginable in earlier times. Gowlett (1978) has studied the hand axes from Kilombe, Kenya, a site that dates to over 700,000 years ago. He found a very high statistical correlation among length, breadth, and thickness, stan-

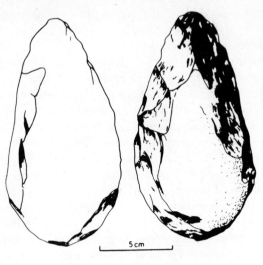

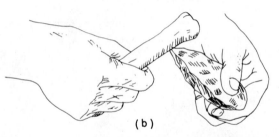

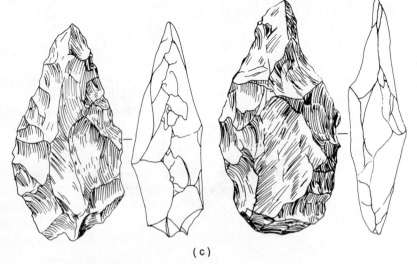

FIGURE 4.7 Acheulian technology. Hand axes were multipurpose artifacts that were shaped symmetrically around a long axis. (a) As the hand ax from Kilombe, Kenya, of 700,000 years ago shows, the stoneworker would sometimes use a minimum of blows

dardization within a length of 3.14 to 9.40 inches (8–24 cm), which implies a well-defined mental image of the ideal end product shared by more than one person (Figure 4.10). "The artifacts which we see, and can measure, were present in the mind," he writes. *Homo erectus* had a geometrically accurate sense of proportion, which was imposed accurately on stone. Gowlett (1984) believes that this technology formed part of the fundamental preconditions for the much later development of art and mathematics.

Acheulian technology was far from static. Another East African site, Kapthurin, near Kenya's Lake Baringo, contains hundreds of late Acheulian hand axes dating to about 230,000 years ago. The stoneworkers there used elaborately prepared cores, fashioned with perhaps 40 or more strokes, as the blanks for a single large flake, a dramatic contrast to the three or four flakes removed in earlier millennia (Figure 4.10). The large flake that resulted was then bifacially flaked into an elegant, versatile hand ax in a wide variety of useful shapes.

Gowlett and others believe that the problem-solving abilities needed to fashion Acheulian artifacts of all types were much more complex than has sometimes been assumed. One suspects that *Homo erectus* was capable of implementing elaborate hunting and foraging strategies and engaging in social interactions that were a quantum jump beyond those of much more apelike *H. habilis.*

Kapthurin
230,000 B.P.

Hominid Species and Stone Tools

The cladistic theory of human evolution highlights a basic phenomenon of early prehistory: The human artifacts of the Pleistocene are patterned in space and time in a general way that mirrors the pattern for early hominids. The earliest Oldowan stone artifacts appear at the same time as the genus *Homo,* and bifacially worked hand axes become commonplace as *Homo erectus* emerges in Africa. Later, the world divides into two broad technological provinces, a western province with hand axes and an Asian without. The end of the Middle Pleistocene brought local changes throughout the Old World, technological changes like the prepared core techniques of stone tool manufacture that are found in Europe and Africa.

(text continues on page 142)

---

to achieve the desired shape. Simple hammerstones were used to make many early hand axes and blanks for far more finished products. (b) Sometimes a hammer made of animal bone served to strike off the shallow flakes that adorn the margins of these tools.

Later hand axes assume many forms, among them the finely pointed shape in part (c), which shows front and side views of two early hand axes from Bed II, Olduvai Gorge, Tanzania (three-quarters actual size). Cleavers are thought to have been butchering tools, artifacts with a single, unfinished edge that has proved effective in modern experiments for skinning and dismembering game. As time went on, the stoneworkers used carefully prepared cores to fashion large flakes that served as blanks for axes and other artifacts. They also produced flakes that were used as opportunistic artifacts, for woodworking, and for many other purposes (see Figure 4.4).

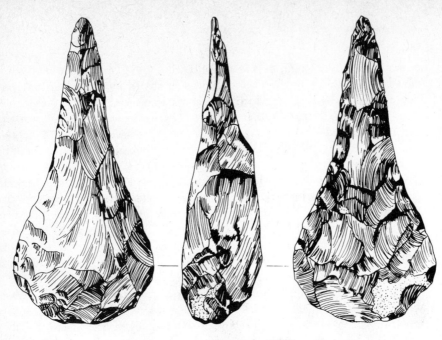

(a)

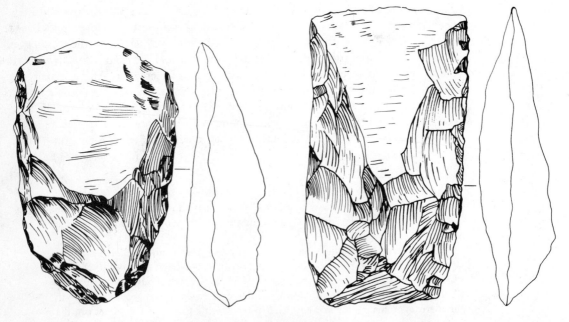

(b)

FIGURE 4.8   Hand ax technology. (a) Acheulian hand ax from Swanscombe, England (one-third actual size). (b) Two Acheulian cleavers, from Baia Farta, Angola *(left)*, and Kalambo Falls, Zambia *(right)* (both one-half actual size).

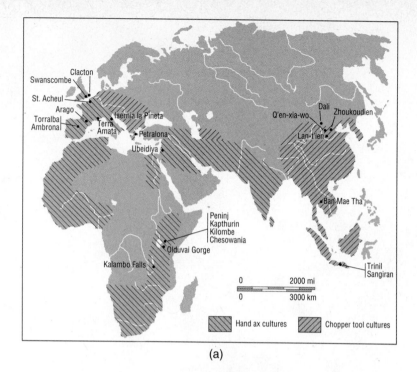

(a)

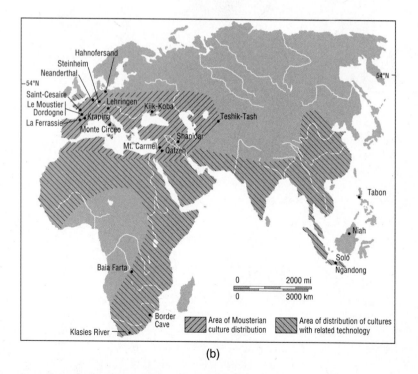

(b)

FIGURE 4.9   (a) Distribution of Lower Paleolithic hand axes and other stone tools, also showing location of sites mentioned in the first half of this chapter. (b) Distribution of Middle Paleolithic cultures, with locations of sites mentioned in text.

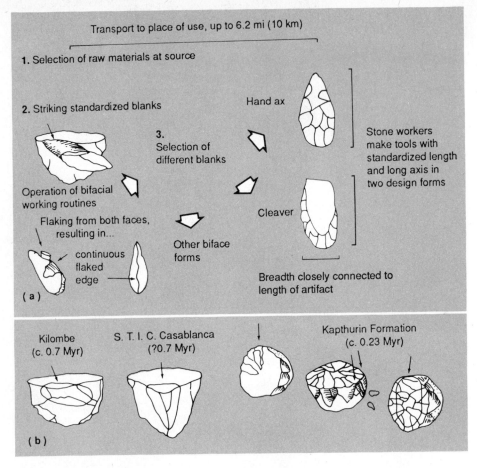

Transport to place of use, up to 6.2 mi (10 km)

1. Selection of raw materials at source

2. Striking standardized blanks

Operation of bifacial
working routines

Flaking from both faces,
resulting in...

continuous
flaked
edge

(a)

3.
Selection of
different blanks

Other biface
forms

Hand ax

Cleaver

Stone workers
make tools with
standardized length
and long axis in
two design forms

Breadth closely connected to
length of artifact

Kilombe
(c. 0.7 Myr)

S. T. I. C. Casablanca
(?0.7 Myr)

Kapthurin Formation
(c. 0.23 Myr)

(b)

FIGURE 4.10   Making Acheulian bifaces. (a) The complex process used about a million years ago. (b) Early and late methods. The simple flaking process of 700,000 years ago *(left)* used in East and North Africa, compares with the expertise of the stoneworkers at Kapthurin, Kenya, 230,000 years ago *(right)*. They prepared elaborately shaped cores to create flakes about 6 inches (16 cm) long as hand ax blanks. (After Foley, 1984b.)

Everywhere except tropical Africa, the technological continuity is striking, with hand axes being used by Mousterians in Europe and chopping tools lasting until late in prehistory in Asia. In Africa, the hand ax tradition gave way to the so-called Middle Stone Age over 200,000 years ago. This characteristic technology, with its scrapers and crude projectile points, was made for the most part on simple flakes. But in some places, like Klasies River Cave in South Africa, people were making parallel-sided blades, which they fashioned into simple tools as early as 70,000 years ago. Everywhere else in the Old World, in Europe and Asia, blade technology appeared suddenly and abruptly between 40,000 and 25,000 years ago. The new technology was far more varied and specialized than anything ever used before (Figures 4.11–4.13).

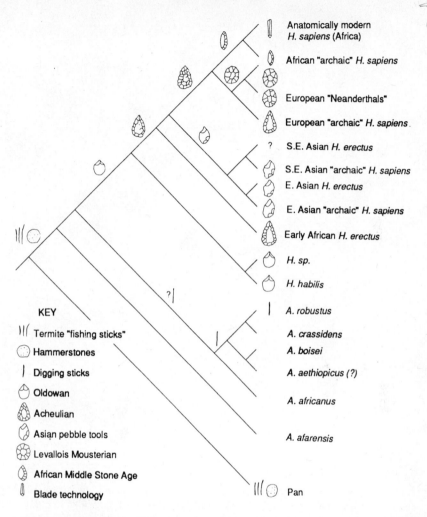

FIGURE 4.11   A cladogram of human evolution that emphasizes the divergence of human taxa and associates stone tool technology with each taxon. British anthropologist Robert Foley (1987) uses this diagram to infer the origin of each at the branching points of the different lines.

Evidence for Behavior: Torralba and Terra Amata

What do we know of the behavior of these archaic tribes? Without question, *Homo erectus* hunted and foraged for food, probably in far more effective ways than *H. habilis*. Time and time again, hand axes and other butchering artifacts have been found in association with the bones of large game animals, which they were used to butcher. No one doubts that *H. erectus* butchered such animals. But did the hunters actually kill such formidable herbivores as the elephant and rhinoceros? To do so would require social mechanisms to foster cooperation and communication abilities far beyond those of *H. habilis*.

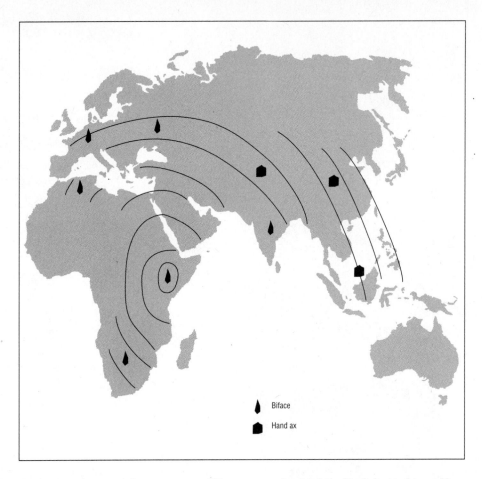

FIGURE 4.12   Foley's (1987) view of the expansion of *Homo erectus* from Africa. He believes that as *Homo erectus* colonized Asia and Europe, they diverged biologically. In cultural terms, the tradition of making hand axes persisted in Europe, whereas it was lost in Asia.

Torralba
**400,000 or
200,000 B.P.**

Evidence for butchery and perhaps big-game hunting comes from two remarkable Acheulian sites, at Torralba and Ambrona, northeast of Madrid in Spain (Gamble, 1986b; F. C. Howell, 1966). The Acheulians probably lived in this deep, swampy valley either 200,000 or 400,000 years ago (the date is disputed). Torralba yielded most of the left side of a large elephant that had been cut into small pieces, and Ambrona contained the remains of 30 to 35 dismembered elephants. Concentrations of broken food bones were found all over the site, and the skulls of the elephants had been broken open to get at the brains. In one place, the elephant bones had been laid in a line, perhaps to form stepping-stones in the swamp where the elephants had been dispatched (Figure 4.14). Both kill sites were littered with crude hand axes, cleavers, scrapers, and cutting tools.

The elephant bones at both sites were buried in clays that were once treacherous

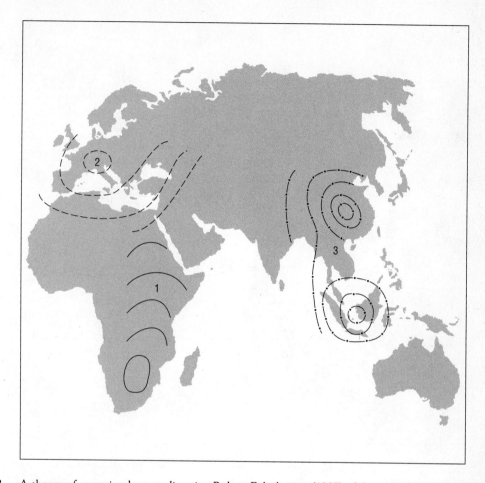

FIGURE 4.13   A theory of emerging human diversity. Robert Foley's view (1987) of the end of the archaic world about 130,000 years ago, when the descendants of African *Homo erectus* had diverged to form local centers for later human evolution. Foley identifies three populations: (1) sub-Saharan Africa, the ancestors of modern humans; (2) Europe, the Mediterranean Basin, and central Asia, the Neanderthals, Mousterian, and related cultures; and (3) east Asia, archaic hominids with chopper or chopping tool cultures. This is probably a gross simplification of a very complex situation.

marsh. The original scenario for the sites had hunters watching the valley floors where the elephants roamed. At a strategic moment several bands would gather quietly, set brushfires, and drive the unsuspecting beasts into the swamps, where they could be killed and butchered at leisure. Karl Butzer (1982) argues that Torralba and Ambrona were on important game trails between summer and winter grazing areas. The hunters thus preyed on migrating elephants each spring and fall (Figure 4.15), dispersing into smaller groups during the other seasons. Other archaeologists believe that the hunters were actually scavenging meat from animals that perished when enmired (Gamble, 1986b; Shipman and Rose, 1983).

FIGURE 4.14   From Torralba, Spain, a remarkable linear arrangement of elephant tusks and leg bones that were probably laid out by those who butchered the animals.

Terra Amata
300,000 B.P.

Terra Amata, excavated by Henry de Lumley, was occupied some 300,000 years ago (de Lumley, 1969). De Lumley excavated what he thought was a series of oval huts that consisted of shallow hollows 26 to 50 feet (8 to 15 m) long and 13 to 20 feet (4 to 6 m) wide, with an entrance at one end (Figure 4.16). When he cleared the hollows, he uncovered a series of posts approximately 3 inches (7 cm) in diameter that had once formed the walls. The bases of the posts were reinforced with lines of stones. The roofs were supported by center posts, and some huts had a hearth in the center. The excavators recovered the bones of wild oxen, stags, and elephants, as well as those of small rodents. There were even imprints of skins once laid on the floors. De Lumley records that the inhabitants never cleaned out their huts. They lived among butchered bones, discarded stone tools, and even their own feces. The feces yielded numerous fragments of nuts and seeds that had flourished in the late spring and early summer. De Lumley concluded that Terra Amata was a seasonal camp, occupied by a band of hunter-gatherers who returned to the same locale year after year in search of vegetable foods and shellfish, another common find at the site.

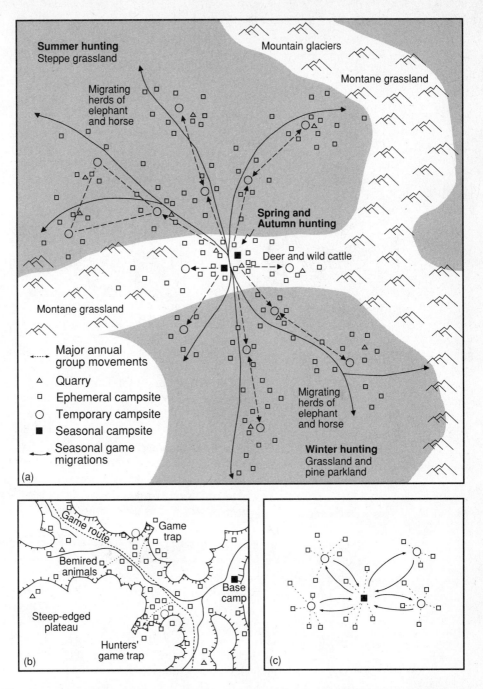

FIGURE 4.15 Reconstructed model for seasonal movement by Acheulian hunters at Torralba-Ambrona, Spain. (a) Interception of migrating animals in spring and fall. (b) Use of topography to secure game. (c) Schematic model of how the populations moved. The reconstructions were made by using information recovered from excavations (Butzer, 1982).

FIGURE 4.16   Henry de Lumley's controversial reconstruction of a hut at Terra Amata, France.

Paola Villa (1983) threw serious doubt on this original interpretation when she tried refitting flakes from the site to one another in order to reconstruct stoneworking activity there. Over 40 percent of the refitted flakes came from different levels, implying that many specimens had been displaced vertically some 8 inches (21 cm). She believes that undetected natural phenomena such as soil creep, ice action, animal burrowing, and even earthworm tunneling transformed Terra Amata after its abandonment—to the point that de Lumley's houses of reeds and brush may not actually have existed. Terra Amata and many other sites of this age may have been disturbed so extensively since they were occupied that our interpretations of them will always be somewhat suspect.

Improvements in language and modes of communication are thought to have been a distinctive feature of *Homo erectus*'s style of life. With enhanced language skills and more advanced technology, it became possible for people to achieve better cooperation in gathering activities, in storage of food supplies, and in the chase. Unlike the nonhuman primates, who strongly emphasize individual economic success, Middle Pleistocene hunter-gatherers depended on cooperative activity by every individual in the band. The economic unit was the group; the secret of individual success was group success. Perhaps individual ownership of property was unimportant since neither individuals nor groups as a whole had tangible possessions of significance. People got along well as individuals, as families, and as entire groups.

THE ORIGIN OF *HOMO SAPIENS*

For hundreds of thousands of years, archaic humans, subsumed under the general taxonomic label of *Homo erectus*, flourished in the tropical and temperate regions of the Old World. Except for an overall increase in brain size, *H. erectus* remained remarkably stable in evolutionary terms for more than a million years, until less than 500,000 years ago. Eventually, *H. erectus* evolved into early *H. sapiens,* but we do not even know when the gradual transition began or how it took place. Some researchers believe it began as early as 400,000 years ago, others much later, some time around or after 200,000 years ago.

Homo sapiens sapiens means the "wise person," and the controversies surrounding the origins of modern humanity, of ourselves, rank among the most vigorous in world prehistory (Fagan, 1990). We are the clever people, the sage humans, animals capable of subtlety, of manipulation, of self-understanding. What is it that separates us from earlier humans, scientists wonder? First and foremost must be our ability to speak fluently and articulately. We communicate, we tell stories, we pass on knowledge and ideas all through the medium of language. Consciousness, cognition, self-awareness, foresight, and the ability to express oneself and one's emotions—these are direct consequences of fluent speech. They can be linked with another attribute of the fully fledged human psyche: the capacity for symbolic and spiritual thought, concerned not only with subsistence and technology but also with defining the boundaries of existence and the relationship among the individual, the group, and the universe. Fluent speech, the full flowering of human creativity expressed in art and religion, expert toolmaking—these are some of the hallmarks of anatomically modern humans. With these abilities humankind eventually colonized not just temperate and tropical environments but the entire globe. With the appearance of *H. sapiens sapiens* we begin the study of people biologically identical to ourselves, people with the same intellectual abilities and potential as ourselves. It is hardly surprising that controversy surrounds the appearance of our remote ancestors.

Continuity or Replacement?

Over generations of debate, two major, and diametrically opposed, hypotheses have developed to explain the origins of modern humans (Mellars, 1989):

- The so-called candelabra model hypothesizes that *Homo erectus* populations throughout the Old World evolved independently, first to archaic *H. sapiens,* then to fully modern humans. This continuity model, sometimes also called the Neanderthal phase hypothesis, argues for multiple origins of *H. sapiens* and no migrations. Thus, modern geographic populations have been separated from one another for a long time, perhaps as long as a million years (Wolpoff et al., 1984).

- The Noah's ark model takes the diametrically opposite view. According to it, *Homo sapiens* evolved in one place, then spread to all other parts of the Old World. This replacement model implies that modern geographic populations have shallow roots and were derived from a single source of relatively recent times.

These two models represent extremes, which pit advocates of anatomical continuity against those who favor rapid replacement of primeval populations. Until fairly recently, most anthropologists strongly favored the candelabra model. They did so because finds from western Europe and the Near East dominated academic discussion, largely because the largest numbers of fossils came from these areas. Furthermore, many deep, well-excavated caves and rock shelters appeared to document technological change from simple, relatively unsophisticated toolkits to the much more elaborate artifacts characteristic of *Homo sapiens*.

A torrent of new discoveries has turned our conception of Europe from one of the cradles of modern humans into somewhat of a backwater. The candelabra hypothesis was based in part on two famous 200,000- to 300,000-year-old European fossil skulls, from Swanscombe in England and Steinheim in Germany, thought to represent "Presapiens" humans with larger brains than *Homo erectus* and other modern features (Figure 4.17) (Ovey, 1964; Roe, 1981). Today, more sophisticated cranial analysis has shown that both skulls display many archaic features, which are shared by newer European finds, among them the Petralona skull from Greece (400,000 to 300,000 years ago) and the Arago skull and jaws from the French Pyrenees (about 200,000 years ago). These finds appear to represent not Presapiens populations but a very heterogeneous group of archaic humans whose descendants were the Neanderthals of the last interglacial and Weichsel glaciation.

Apart from the fossil evidence, basic principles of evolutionary biology make it appear unlikely that populations of *Homo sapiens* were living in central and western Europe for 200,000 years so isolated from one another that two different lineages could form.

Another important group of finds lent support to the candelabra model. These were the highly variable fossil populations found in the Mt. Carmel Caves in what is now Israel just before World War II (Garrod and Bate, 1937)—Neanderthals displaying startling anatomical variation compared with their European contemporaries.

Was the Near East a cradle of *Homo sapiens?* Many new discoveries from Southwest Asia and from sites like Qafzeh in Israel have confirmed that Near Eastern populations were very heterogeneous between 100,000 and 40,000 years ago. However, there is a considerable morphological gap between more archaic and only slightly older fossils and those displaying more modern features, such as reduced brow ridges, more rounded crania, and larger limbs. Eric Trinkaus (1982, 1984) and other experts believe that the differences between these individuals make local evolution of *H. sapiens* from Neanderthals unlikely.

Such an evolution would require an adequate amount of time for anatomical change to take place. This time frame does not appear to exist in Europe, for recent finds of Neanderthal-like individuals from Hahnofersand near Hamburg, Germany, and Saint-Césaire in the Charente (France) date to as late as 36,000 to 31,000 years ago. Anatomically modern humans were living in western Europe by this time. Very likely there was a period of coexistence and probably hybridization between the Neanderthals and the modern populations at about this time, when the latter had already replaced Neanderthals in the Near East (Fagan, 1990).

Everything points not to anatomical continuity in Europe and the Near East but

---

Petralona
400,000 to 300,000 B.P.

Arago
200,000 B.P.

Mt. Carmel
50,000 B.P. and earlier

Qafzeh
92,000 B.P. and later

Hahnofersand
Saint-Césaire
36,000 to 31,000 B.P.

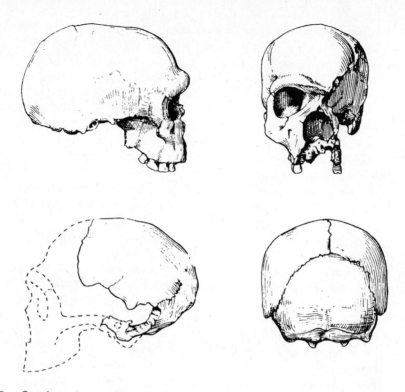

FIGURE 4.17   Steinheim *(top)* and Swanscombe *(bottom)* skulls (one-fourth actual size). The Swanscombe skull is shown with a tentative reconstruction of the missing parts.

Considerable controversy surrounds the classification of these and other European human fossils dating from about 300,000 to 120,000 years ago. Are they *Homo erectus* or archaic *Homo sapiens*? Chris Stringer and other paleoanthropologists have suggested that specimens like these and other well-known finds, such as the Petralona skull from Greece and the Arago specimens from France, be placed in "grades" of *H. sapiens*. Under this scheme, Steinheim and Swanscombe would be in *H. sapiens* Grade 1, modern *H. sapiens* being in Grade 3 or 4, depending on the scheme. This system is coming into widespread use as a convenient way of classifying Middle Pleistocene human fossils. It does not necessarily imply any evolutionary relationship between different grades (for full discussion, see Stringer et al., 1979).

to replacement of primeval populations by *Homo sapiens.* Furthermore, Near Eastern excavations make it certain that *H. sapiens* populations were living there as early as 92,000 years ago, earlier than they were in Europe. This may indeed have been the area from which modern people—perhaps we can call them *proto-Cro-Magnons*—spread into the north and replaced the Neanderthals some time later. The Noah's ark model, then, seems to fit the available evidence better. But the central question remains unanswered. Where did the proto-Cro-Magnons come from? We know from distributions of Neanderthal finds that there were contacts and gene flow with North

Africa. Might tropical Africa have been the ancestral homeland of modern human beings?

Homo sapiens in Africa

Africa may have been the cradle of humankind, but for years it was regarded as a backwater in later prehistory, a place where modern humans arose very much later than they did in Europe. This long-held view coincided with what was known of late Stone Age archaeology in tropical Africa, where cultural innovations such as blade technology and art were thought to have appeared very late (J. D. Clark, 1970), arriving with *Homo sapiens* from the north. These ideas were formulated before radiocarbon chronologies and were based on a mere handful of fossil finds, among them the famous robust Broken Hill skull from Zambia, an archaic-looking cranium that seemed to epitomize a backward continent.

A new generation of research based on radiocarbon dates and sophisticated cave excavation has painted a radically different picture of African life after 200,000 years ago. We now know that Acheulian hand ax technology gave way to "Middle Stone Age" culture, with its more sophisticated flake tools and much more versatile toolkit, between 200,000 and 130,000 years ago in both eastern and southern Africa. The excavators of the Klasies River Mouth Caves in southeastern Africa were able to correlate Middle Stone Age occupation with deep-sea cores and date it to between 120,000 and 70,000 years ago. Numerous fragmentary human remains dating to between 125,000 and 95,000 years ago came from the Middle Stone Age levels, remains that displayed astoundingly modern features at a date far earlier than anything from the Near East or Europe (Singer and Wymer, 1982).

> **Klasies River**
> **120,000 to**
> **70,000 b.p.**

Nor are the Klasies River finds unique. Border Cave, also in southern Africa, has yielded anatomically modern human remains dating to between 115,000 and 90,000 years ago (Beaumont, 1980). There are also scattered finds from East Africa (for a review, see Brauer, 1984).

> **Border Cave**
> **115,000 to**
> **90,000 b.p.**

Günter Brauer (1984) believes he can identify at least three "grades" of *Homo sapiens* in sub-Saharan Africa. An "early archaic *Homo sapiens*" form was widely distributed from southern to northeast Africa some 200,000 years ago. These archaic populations had evolved from earlier *H. erectus* populations and had larger cranial vaults and many other anatomical features akin to those of anatomically modern humans. The Broken Hill skull from Zambia belongs in this group. Brauer's second group—"late archaic *Homo sapiens*"—includes fossils with mosaics of both archaic and modern features, with the latter tending to predominate. These specimens date to 100,000 years ago and earlier. His last group are anatomically modern individuals, with only a very few archaic features.

Brauer (1984) believes that very early anatomically modern *Homo sapiens* was widely distributed in eastern and southern Africa as far back as the early Upper Pleistocene, some 115,000 years ago, perhaps even earlier. He also believes that the developments that led to the emergence of *Homo sapiens* in eastern and southern Africa had run their course as early as between 100,000 and 70,000 years ago, far earlier than any equivalent developments in Europe or the Near East. At this time, the evolution of the classic and late Neanderthals had run its course in those areas.

In evolutionary terms, the transition from *Homo erectus* to archaic *Homo sapiens* seems to have occurred not quickly but relatively slowly and continuously. It is difficult to draw a line between the two species. In contrast, the "modernization" of the human skull into its present configuration took place considerably faster, some time at the very end of the Middle Pleistocene or the beginning of the Upper Pleistocene, by 100,000 years ago.

Molecular Biology and *Homo sapiens*

Molecular biology has played a significant role in dating earlier human evolution and is now yielding important clues to the origins of *Homo sapiens* (Cann et al., 1987). Researchers have zeroed in on mitochondrial DNA (mtDNA), a useful tool for calibrating mutation rates because it accumulates mutations much faster than nuclear DNA. Mitochondrial DNA is inherited only through the maternal line; it does not mix and become diluted with paternal DNA. Thus, it provides a potentially reliable link with ancestral populations. When genetic researchers analyzed the mtDNA of 147 women from Africa, Asia, Europe, Australia, and New Guinea, they found that the differences among them were very small. Therefore, they argued, the five populations were all of comparatively recent origin. There were some differences, sufficient to separate two groups within the sample—a set of African individuals and another comprising individuals from all groups. The biologists concluded that all modern humans derive from a 200,000-year-old African population, from which populations migrated to the rest of the Old World with little or no interbreeding with existing, more archaic human groups. Although the mtDNA research tends to confirm what we know from archaeological evidence, it should be stressed that the results are highly provisional and the methodology still in its infancy.

Cann and her fellow biochemists (1987) assumed that there was a constant rate of mitochondrial DNA mutation of about 2 to 4 percent every million years in several vertebrate species. They used this rate to calculate a date of about 200,000 years for the primeval population of *Homo sapiens*. They also estimated that the second split, which separated *Homo sapiens sapiens* in Africa from those who moved out, occurred between 180,000 and 90,000 years ago, perhaps around 140,000 years ago. The reliability of this chronology is hard to assess and will have to be checked against fossil finds. At present, the earliest archaeological evidence for anatomically modern humans in sub-Saharan Africa comes from Omo in Ethiopia and dates to between 130,000 and 100,000 years ago, whereas the Klasies River finds belong in the 100,000-year range. With so few fossils to work with, all we can be sure of is that there was considerable anatomical variation in Africans between 200,000 and 100,000 years ago. It is also entirely possible that anatomically modern humans evolved in many locations south of the Sahara in highly varied and very isolated African populations. (For a critique of the mitochondrial evidence and chronology, see Mellars, 1989.)

Ecology and *Homo sapiens*

For generations, anthropologists have tended to treat the origin of *Homo sapiens* as a unique event that took place outside the processes of evolutionary biology. The molecular research reminds us that this was not so. As Robert Foley (1984c) argues, one can understand this event only within a comparative ecological framework. Foley points out that modern humans were most likely to have originated within a single location. The savanna woodland of Africa around 100,000 years ago was an ideal environment for promoting the speciation of modern humans, he believes. Foley has studied monkey evolution in Africa and found that the widely dispersed populations had diverged; they did not continue on a single evolutionary course. Africa experienced considerable habitat fragmentation and re-formation during the alternating cold and warmth of the Pleistocene, fluctuations that enhanced the prospects of speciation among the continent's animals and plants. For example, Foley found that one monkey genus alone radiated into 16 species at about the same time that modern humans may have evolved on the continent. These environmental shifts cannot have been too rapid or too severe or the indigenous populations would have moved away or become extinct. The tropical environments of Africa consisted of a constant mosaic of changing environmental patterns, a mosaic that tended to foster local evolution. This phenomenon contrasted with higher latitudes, where environmental changes were more marked and animal distributions changed significantly and rapidly over short periods of time.

Foley's monkey studies have convinced him that modern humans evolved in such a mosaic of tropical environments, developing distinctive characteristics that separated them from their archaic predecessors. Within tropical Africa's patchy environments were areas where food supplies were both predictable and of high quality. In response to such regions, some humans may have developed wide-ranging behavior, lived in larger social groups with considerable kin-based substructure, and been highly selective in their diet. As part of these responses, some groups may have developed exceptional hunting skills, a technology so effective that they could prey on animals from a distance with projectiles. With more efficient technology, more advance planning, and better organization of both hunting and foraging, our ancestors could have reduced the unpredictability of the environment in dramatic ways.

This ecological approach to modern human origins is still untested against archaeological evidence. Even at this stage in research there are unexplained anomalies between biology and archaeology. Once modern human beings had evolved, they manufactured a sophisticated tool technology, based on antler, bone, wood, and stone blade manufacture. This technology was far more advanced than anything made by their predecessors. In Africa, at sites like the Klasies River, the first modern humans were still making archaic toolkits and their hunting skills were less developed than those of later millennia. Conversely, in Europe, there are instances of the new technologies being associated with Neanderthal fossils. The link between technology and anatomy is very loose, as if ideas and genes had moved at different rates. A number of lines of evidence strongly suggest that *Homo sapiens* originated in Africa and spread from there into other parts of the Old World.

The Spread of *Homo sapiens*

If tropical Africa was the cradle of modern humans, how and why did *Homo sapiens* spread into Europe and Asia (Brauer, 1984)? The critical period was between 100,000 and 45,000 years ago, the date by which *H. sapiens* is known to have been living in the Near East. The only major barrier to population movement between tropical Africa and the Mediterranean Basin is the Sahara, today some of the driest territory on earth. During the early Weichsel, the Sahara went through phases of relative aridity and greater rainfall. A cooler and wetter climate prevailed in the desert from before 100,000 until about 40,000 years ago and again between 32,000 and 24,000 years ago. For long periods, the country between East Africa and the Mediterranean was passable, supporting scattered game herds and open grassland. The Nile Valley was always habitable, even during periods of great aridity in the desert. Thus, anatomically modern *H. sapiens* may have hunted and foraged across the Sahara into the Nile Valley and the Near East in the early Weichsel. Then as the Near East became increasingly dry and less productive, the newcomers may have responded to population pressure and food shortages by moving across the wide land bridge that joined Turkey to southeastern Europe 45,000 years ago, spreading into the more productive steppe and tundra regions of Europe and western Asia (Fagan, 1990).

How did *Homo sapiens* appear in eastern Asia?

HOMO SAPIENS IN ASIA

For hundreds of thousands of years, from over 750,000 years ago until perhaps later than 200,000 years ago, *Homo erectus* populations flourished in East and Southeast Asia. These archaic humans adapted to a wide range of environments, but the adaptations were conservative ones, especially in the tropical forests and woodlands of Southeast Asia, where bamboo may have been an important toolmaking material.

Although physical anthropologists argue over the anatomical differences between different Asian *Homo erectus* populations, no one doubts that there were gradual changes in human anatomy through time. Unfortunately, there is such a dearth of fossils and accurate dates for them that the experts can do little more than speculate intelligently about human fossils often separated in time by as much as 250,000 years. In China, there are scattered finds of what are said to be archaic forms of *Homo sapiens,* as opposed to anatomically modern people, dating to about 200,000 years ago from such sites as Dali and Maba. By this time, Chinese biologists believe they can recognize distinctive "Chinese" anatomical features, and there is general agreement that brain sizes were increasing by that date. Despite theories that anatomically modern people flourished in China as early as 70,000 years ago, there is a yawning fossil gap until finds in the 35,000-year-old range, much later in prehistory.

In Southeast Asia, where there is a similar chronological gap, physical anthropologists Milford Wolpoff and Alan Thorne (1984) compared a *Homo erectus* fossil from Sangiran in Java, estimated to be some 700,000 years ago, with a large sample of *Homo sapiens sapiens* skeletons from Kow Swamp in southern Australia

(Chapter 8). On the basis of comparisons of selected anatomical features like the jutting forward of the face, they argued that there was strong evidence of anatomical continuity between *H. erectus* and more modern Asian populations. They and Chinese scholar Wu Zin Xhi (1984) believe that there was interbreeding of *H. sapiens sapiens* populations from centers of greater morphological variation like the Near East with archaic populations further east (Groves, 1989; Hapgood, 1989). The further one got from the "centers," they argue, the later the appearance of modern humans. One of the outer regions was mainland Southeast Asia, where *H. erectus* apparently survived far longer than in Africa and Europe.

Noah's ark critics of this candelabra form of hypothesis argue that Wolpoff and Thorne's research is based on a careful selection of a few anatomical features, some of which may be primitive retentions, and on fossils that are separated by hundreds of thousands of years of prehistoric time. It has to be admitted that if the Noah's ark hypothesis is correct, the date when anatomically modern humans spread into Asia and the processes by which they did it are a complete mystery.

The earliest well-documented *Homo sapiens sapiens* fossils date to long after modern people were living in the Near East. A poorly dated *H. sapiens sapiens* skull from the great cave at Niah in Borneo is believed to be about 40,000 years old, and an anatomically modern skull from Tabon Cave in the Philippines may date to about 23,000 years ago. Both of these specimens are said to display features that link them to gene flow from further north in Asia. The earliest anatomically modern fossils in China date to somewhere between 50,000 and 37,000 years ago (Fagan, 1990).

The earliest dated mainland site that might be attributed to *Homo sapiens sapiens* is the Long Rongrien cave on the west end of the Thai-Malay Peninsula in the thick rain forest. The lowest occupation levels date to at least 37,000 years ago and are marked by small scrapers, some worked pebbles, and three antler or bone tools. We can only hypothesize about the inhabitants of mainland Southeast Asia between 100,000 and 40,000 years ago. In the forests, as Long Rongrien shows, there was no need for sophisticated stone artifacts when easily split and sharpened bamboo and other woods would suffice for weapons and knives.

In short, we do not know when anatomically modern people settled in Asia, but an intelligent guess would be after 75,000 years ago, by which time *Homo sapiens sapiens* was well established in the Near East and Africa.

ARCHAIC *HOMO SAPIENS* IN EUROPE: THE NEANDERTHALS

We have hypothesized that anatomically modern humans moved into Europe during the last glaciation. It was there that they encountered the Neanderthals, indigenous inhabitants of Europe and Eurasia, who are still the subject of great controversy among physical anthropologists. Some people use the word *Neanderthal* to describe dim-witted, ugly people who are like apes, an insult aimed at those they consider dumb. This stereotype and that of the shambling cave people so beloved by cartoonists come from mistaken studies of Neanderthal skeletons in the early years of this century. In fact, the Neanderthals were strong, robustly built humans with some archaic features, like bun-shaped skulls and sometimes eyebrow ridges, when compared with modern people. There is every reason to believe they were expert hunters and beings capable of considerable intellectual reasoning.

There are, of course, striking anatomical differences between Neanderthals and modern humans, both in the robust postcranial skeleton and in the more bun-shaped skull, sometimes with heavy brow ridges and a forward projecting face (Figure 4.18). These features are the reason this extinct hominid form is classified as *Homo sapiens*

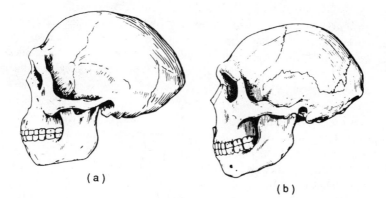

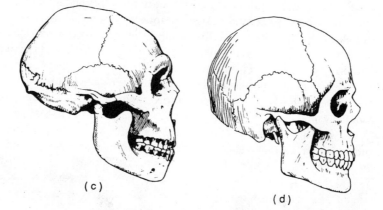

FIGURE 4.18 Comparisons of four fossil skulls and jaws. (a) The reconstructed *Homo erectus* skull has prominent brow ridges, a bun-shaped rear to the cranium, and a retreating chin. (b) A "classic" Neanderthal skull found at Monte Circeo, Italy, still has well-marked brow ridges and bun-shaped cranium but an increased brain capacity. The skull is lower and flatter than those of modern humans, and the jaw is chinless. (c) The Shanidar Neanderthal from Iraq is a less extreme example, with a higher forehead, somewhat reduced brow ridges, and a much more rounded skull. (d) Modern skull with well-rounded contours, no brow ridges, high forehead, and a well-marked chin.

neanderthalensis, a subspecies of *Homo sapiens,* and not as *Homo sapiens sapiens,* a fully modern human.

In the century since the first Neanderthal skull from the German village of that name was unearthed, substantial numbers of Neanderthal individuals, most in western Europe, as well as contemporary human fossils from the Near East, Africa, and Asia have been unearthed. They first appeared during the Eem interglacial, well before 100,000 years ago, but they were apparently few in number. Large Neanderthal sites occur in the Dordogne area of southwest France, where deep river valleys and vast limestone cliffs offered abundant shelter during the Weichsel glaciation (Bordes, 1968; Gamble, 1986b). The skeletons found in French caves look like anatomical anachronisms, with massive brow ridges and squat bodies. The Neanderthals walked upright and as nimbly as modern humans. They stood just over 5 feet tall (153 cm), and their forearms were relatively short compared with those of modern people. This "classic" variety of Neanderthal is confined to western Europe and is more noticeably different from *Homo sapiens* than its contemporary populations found elsewhere, especially around the shores of the Mediterranean and in Asia (Figure 4.7). We find much variability among nonclassic Neanderthals, who most often display less extreme features, particularly brow ridges and other cranial features, than the classic variety of western France. It is well demonstrated at the Mt. Carmel sites of et-Tabūn and es-Skhūl in Israel as well as at Krapina in central Europe (Stringer, 1988; Trinkaus and Howells, 1979).

Morphological differences

The morphological differences apparent between many Neanderthals and modern *Homo sapiens* are startling. How do these heavily built, beetle-browed people fit into the picture of human evolution? The great French physical anthropologist Marcellin Boule believed, in the 1930s, that the classic Neanderthals were clumsy, shambling people, so specialized that they became extinct while other populations provided the evolutionary basis for modern humans (Boule and Vallois, 1957). Erik Trinkaus and William Howells (1979) reviewed Neanderthal populations from all over Europe and the Near East and point out that their anatomical pattern took approximately 50 millennia from 150,000 years ago to evolve, then stabilized for another 50 before changing rapidly to essentially modern human anatomy within a brief period of 5,000 years approximately 40,000 years ago. They indicate that Boule was mistaken, partly because his definitive studies were made on an elderly individual suffering from arthritis and partly because much more skeletal material is now available. The Neanderthals had the same posture, manual abilities, and range and characteristics of movement as modern people. They differed in having massive limb bones, often somewhat bowed in the thigh and forearm, features that reflect the Neanderthals' greater muscular power. For their height, the Neanderthals were bulky and heavily muscled, and their brain capacity was slightly larger than that of modern humans. Their antecedents are in the *Homo erectus* group, from which they inherited their heavy build, an adaptation so successful that it lasted for more than 100,000 years.

EARLY *HOMO SAPIENS* ADAPTS

Although many details of the biological evolution of early *Homo sapiens* remain unresolved, we know a great deal about the many and diverse adaptations of these

Mousterian
culture
?100,000 to
40,000 B.P.
(Chapter 5)

people. Their distinctive hunter-gatherer culture, which continued in the basic homi-nid tradition, is known from hundreds of sites in Africa, Asia, and Europe. The Neanderthals' *Mousterian* technology (named after the Le Moustier rock shelter in southwest France) was far more complex and sophisticated than its Acheulian prede-cessor, with many regional variations (Trinkaus, 1983a). Many of the Neanderthals' artifacts were made for specific purposes. Like their *erectus* predecessors, the early *Homo sapiens* bands occupied large territories, which they probably exploited on a seasonal round, returning to the same locations year after year when game migrated or vegetables came into season. The Neanderthals were skilled hunters who were not afraid to pursue large game animals like the mammoth as well as reindeer and wild horses. They also caught birds and fish. It appears that many western European bands lived in caves and rock shelters during much of the year as a protection against arctic cold. During the summer months they may have fanned out over the tundra plains, living in temporary tented encampments (for details, see Gamble, 1986b).

Clive Gamble (1986b) argues that the Neanderthal adaptation in Europe was significantly different from that of earlier human populations. He points to significant changes in human settlement patterns, that is, to a greater use of rock shelters and caves as well as repeated use of open sites as temporary stopping places for people away from the larger main group. This may have been a time when technology was more organized, when planning assumed greater importance—to reduce the risk of starvation. People were now developing hunting and foraging strategies based on four main herd species—bison, horse, red deer, and reindeer. Gamble theorizes that storage assumed much greater importance for surviving winter shortages, maximizing the meat culled from seasonally migrating animals. There may have been higher population densities, greater population stability, and more adaptive stability, with less risk of local populations dying out in times of stress.

For the new adaptive strategies, environmental knowledge was the key to effec-tive planning. Factors such as herd size, migration seasons, and predictability of animal movements assumed vital importance. This pattern of adaptation resulted in considerable interregional differences within the Neanderthal world. The southwest-ern areas of Europe, with their deep river valleys and large rock shelters, were occupied constantly, whereas more open areas to the north and east were more extensively exploited during periods of warmer climate and largely abandoned during glacial times. It is interesting to note that no Neanderthal sites have yet come to light north of 56°N (see Figure 4.9b).

STONE TOOL TECHNOLOGY

Middle
Paleolithic
technology

The stone technology used by the Neanderthals and other early *Homo sapiens* forms has often been subsumed under the label Middle Paleolithic, on the grounds that the techniques used were distinct from those of *Homo erectus*. In fact, the basic differences are much less radical than has often been assumed. There is a basic continuum in stoneworking skills that begins in the Lower Paleolithic and continues through the Middle into the Upper Paleolithic and even later in prehistory. Even the technologi-cal changes associated with the spread of *Homo sapiens sapiens* after 40,000 years ago have a strong basis in much earlier, simpler technologies (Chapter 5).

Levallois and Disk Core Reduction Strategies

At Kapthurin and other East African sites, Acheulian stoneworkers demonstrated a remarkable skill at preshaping cores to produce large flakes for making axes and other artifacts. With such prepared core techniques, which were to assume great importance after 100,000 years ago, the core is shaped to predetermine the flake or blade that is to be removed. The *Levallois technique,* named after the Paris suburb where it was first found, produces broad, flat flakes, large blades, and triangular points (Figure 4.19). The *disk core technique* is designed to produce as many flakes of varying size as possible and results in residual cores with an approximate round shape. The size of the raw material lumps available to the stoneworker probably had a major effect on the flakes produced, for both techniques as well as simpler flaking were widely used in Europe, Africa, and Asia.

Tool Forms and Variability

Mousterian and other Middle Paleolithic tools were made for the most part on flakes, the most characteristic artifacts being points and scrapers (Figure 4.19). Some of these were *composite tools,* artifacts made of more than one component—for example, a point, a shaft, and the binding that secured the head to the shaft, making a spear. The edges of both points and scrapers were sharpened by fine trimming, the removal of small, steplike chips from the edge of the implement (Figure 4.20). These artifacts, almost universally distributed in Middle Paleolithic sites, were used in the chase, in woodworking, and in preparing skins. However, recent microwear researches have revealed that many untrimmed flakes were used for cutting, scraping, and other tasks; they were convenient working edges when needed at a moment's notice (Gamble, 1986b).

The complexity of Mousterian technology is striking. The French sites have yielded a great diversity of Mousterian artifacts and toolkits. Some levels include hand axes; others, notched flakes, perhaps used for stripping meat for drying or pressing fibrous plants. Subdivisions of Mousterian technology have been identified by the prevalence of specific tool types. The French archaeologist François Bordes (1968) excavated the Combe Grenal cave in the Perigord and studied a stratified series of intermittent Mousterian occupations between 90,000 and 40,000 years ago. Bordes identified no fewer than 60 different Mousterian tool types, made with a variety of toolmaking techniques, including the Levallois method, and with carefully prepared disk cores. He also identified four distinct toolkits in the Combe Grenal levels: one associated with small hand axes, another with thousands of heavy-duty side scrapers, a third with a high proportion of saw-edged flakes, and some that contained an even balance of different tool types.

Such wide variation in Mousterian toolkits is found not only at Combe Grenal but also at other Neanderthal sites throughout Europe and the Near East and in North Africa where other archaic *Homo sapiens* made similar tools. Bordes (1968) believed that the Combe Grenal toolkits reflected four different Neander-

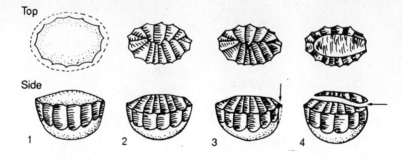

Top

Side

1 2 3 4

(a)

1   2

(b)

FIGURE 4.19 Prepared core techniques. Prepared cores were carefully flaked to enable the toolmaker to strike off large flakes of predetermined size.

    The Levallois technique meant that the stoneworker would shape a lump of flint into an inverted bun-shaped core (often compared to an inverted tortoise shell). The flat upper surface would be struck at one end, the resulting flake forming the only product from the core. Another form was the disk core, a prepared core from which several flakes of predetermined size and shape were removed. The core gradually became smaller, until it resembled a flat disk. Disk cores were often used to produce points and scrapers. (a) Making a Levallois core: (1) The edges of a suitable stone are trimmed; (2) the top surface is trimmed; (3) a striking platform is made, the point where the flake will originate, by trimming to form a straight edge on the side; and (4) a flake is struck from the core and removed. (b) (1) A Levallois core from the Thames Valley, England, with the top of the core (bottom), shown from above and the end view (top). (2) A typical Levallois flake: upper surface (center), lower (flake) surface (right), and cross section (left). Both artifacts are one-third actual size.

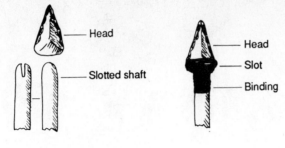

Head

Slotted shaft

Head

Slot

Binding

(a)

Western European point

French Mousterian
side-scraper

Mount Carmel point

Zimbabwe Middle Stone Age
point (Stillbay type)

cutting edge —

French denticulated
flake

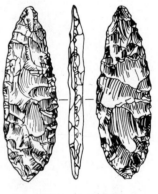

German point

(b)

FIGURE 4.20   Middle Paleolithic tools and technology. This technology was based on simple stone techniques that were used for tens of thousands of years before the emergence of early *Homo sapiens*. By 100,000 years ago, artifacts of many types were of *composite* form—made from several different parts. A wooden spear might have a stone tip, a flint scraper, a bone handle. Unfortunately, we know almost nothing about the bone and wood tools used. (a) Stone-tipped Mousterian spear (a hypothetical example). The spear was made by attaching a pointed stone head to a wooden handle to form the projectile. The head probably fitted into a slot in the wooden shaft and was fixed to it with resin or beeswax; a binding was added to the end of the shaft. (b) Mousterian artifacts.

thal groups who all visited the same location but who lived in almost complete isolation and rarely had any contact with one another. Others hypothesize that the variations in toolkits were the result of slow cultural change, with different tools, like the side scraper, in fashion at different times (Mellars, 1973). In contrast, Lewis and Sally Binford argue that Bordes's traditions reflect various distinct activities carried out within the same cultural system at different times of the year (Binford, 1983; Binford and Binford, 1966). Harold Dibble (1987) has studied Mousterian scraper technology, on the assumption that the various shapes of these artifacts represent a "reduction continuum," that is, a continuous process of flaking the edge of flake blanks. Thus, collections with more large side scrapers represent *less* intensive utilization of scrapers than those with greater variability in scraper forms. He argues that neither style nor function was the overriding factor in stone tool variability. Rather, the Neanderthals were using a fundamentally very simple stone technology, with both flaking techniques and reduction processes varying considerably in response to all kinds of external factors—availability of raw materials, size, climate, differing activities, and subsistence needs among them.

The Neanderthals and their contemporaries were developing tools for different activities far more quickly than ever before, perhaps at a time of growing human populations and slightly enhanced social complexity. Fundamentally Middle Paleolithic technology was simple, highly variable, and a logical development of technologies refined over many millennia.

THE ORIGINS OF BURIAL AND RELIGIOUS BELIEF

The Neanderthals were hunter-gatherers and the world's population was still small, but life was gradually becoming more complex. We find the first signs of religious ideology, of a preoccupation with the life hereafter. Many Neanderthals were buried by their companions. Neanderthal burials have been recovered from the deposits of rock shelters and caves as well as from open campsites. Single burials are the most common, normally accompanied by flint implements, food offerings, or even cooked game meat (evidenced by charred bones). One band of Siberian mountain goat hunters lived at Teshik-Tash in the western foothills of the Himalayas. They buried one of their children in a shallow pit, surrounding the body with six pairs of wild goat horns (Klein, 1969).

Burials at Teshik-Tash

Shanidar

Another remarkable single burial came from the Shanidar Cave in the Zagros Mountains of Iraq (Trinkaus, 1983b). There a 30-year-old man was crushed by a rockfall from the roof of the cave. He was buried in a shallow pit. Other single graves from France and central Europe were covered with red ocher powder (Gamble, 1986).

La Ferrassie

One rock shelter, La Ferrassie near Les Eyzies in France, yielded the remains of two adult Neanderthals and four children buried close together in a campsite (Peyrony, 1934). Group sepulchers occur at other sites, too, more signs that the Neanderthals, like most living hunter-gatherers, believed in life after death. They may also have had beliefs that coincided with deliberate burial, but details will always remain hypothetical.

Some glimmers of insight into Neanderthal beliefs may come from their remarkable bear cults. The Neanderthals were skillful hunters who were not afraid to go after cave bears, which were about the size of Alaskan brown bears and weighed perhaps up to three-quarters of a ton. Like some modern northern hunters, the Neanderthals had a bear cult, known to us from bear skulls that were deliberately buried with ceremony. The most remarkable find was at Regourdou in southern France, where a rectangular pit lined with stones held the skulls of at least 20 cave bears (F. C. Howell, 1974). The burial pit was covered with a huge stone slab. Nearby lay the entire skeleton of one of the bears. It seems likely that the cave bear became an integral part of these hunters' mythology, an object of reverence and an animal with a special place in the world.

Evidence of an even more remarkable ritual appeared in the depths of the Guattari Cave at Monte Circeo, 60 miles (96.5 km) south of Rome. A Neanderthal skull was found in an isolated inner chamber surrounded by a circle of stones (Blanc, 1961). The base of the skull lay upward, mutilated in such a way that the brain could be reached. The right side of the skull was smashed in by violent blows. Near the circle of stones lay three piles of bones, from red deer, cattle, and pigs (Figure 4.21). Although ingenious explanations for this curious ritual have been proposed, we shall never know why this sacrificial victim was killed and beheaded outside the cave, his head then laid out as the centerpiece of an important ritual. Like the bear cult, cannibalism and other hunting rituals appear to have been part of human life and subsistence. We find in Neanderthals and their culture the first roots of our own complicated beliefs, societies, and religious sense.

Rituals at Regourdou

Monte Circeo

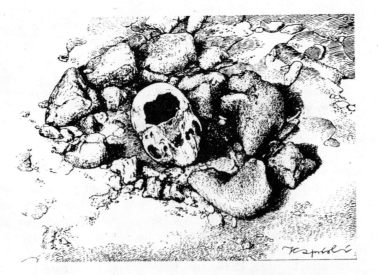

FIGURE 4.21   In the Guattari Cave of Monte Circeo, a human skull was found lying base upward in the center of a ring of stones. The condition of the skull, as well as other artifacts in the cave, gives evidence of a sacrificial murder.

GUIDE TO FURTHER READING

Bordes, François. 1968. *The Old Stone Age.* New York: McGraw Hill.
A simple manual on the Paleolithic period that is out of date except for its simple descriptions of basic Stone Age technologies and European tool types. Ideal for beginners.

Fagan, Brian M. 1990. *The Journey from Eden.* New York: Thames and Hudson.
A synthesis of the controversies surrounding the origins of modern humans for laypeople. Written in nontechnical language. Recommended for beginning students.

Gamble, Clive. 1986. *The Paleolithic Settlement of Europe.* Cambridge, Eng.: Cambridge University Press.
A full discussion of the fundamental issues surrounding the Middle Paleolithic adaptation in Europe. For advanced readers.

Mellars, Paul, and Stringer, Christopher, eds. 1989. *The Human Revolution*, vol. 1. Edinburgh: Edinburgh University Press.
A comprehensive series of essays on the origins of modern humans that summarizes not only biological and genetic evidence but archaeological as well. This is a comprehensively referenced, technical work.

Pfeiffer, John E. 1985. *The Emergence of Man*, 4th ed. New York: Harper and Row.
An articulate and complete account of early human evolution that focuses on behavior and culture as well as fossils.

PART III

THE SPREAD OF *HOMO SAPIENS*

(45,000 TO MODERN TIMES)

THIS PART RECOUNTS THE RAPID SPREAD OF *HOMO SAPIENS SAPIENS* THROUGHOUT THE OLD WORLD AND INTO THE AMERICAS AND EXAMINES SOME OF THE MANY HUNTER-GATHERER ADAPTATIONS THAT DEVELOPED AFTER THE ICE AGE.

"I want you to remind yourself," he said, "that you have now spent 1 field season of excavation, 15 years of analyses, and thousands of dollars of taxpayers' money to find out no more than this: what a family of five did during the autumn, on six different occasions, scattered over a 2,000-year period. I earnestly hope that the thought will keep you humble."

"Would you believe 'deeply depressed'?"

Kent Flannery,
Guilá Naquitz

167

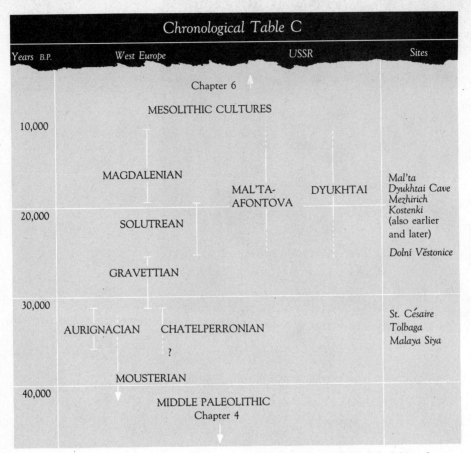

Chronological Table C

Years B.P.	West Europe		USSR	Sites
		Chapter 6 ↑		
		MESOLITHIC CULTURES		
10,000				
	MAGDALENIAN			Mal'ta
		MAL'TA-AFONTOVA	DYUKHTAI	Dyukhtai Cave
				Mezhirich
20,000	SOLUTREAN			Kostenki (also earlier and later)
	GRAVETTIAN			Dolní Věstonice
30,000				St. Césaire
	AURIGNACIAN	CHATELPERRONIAN		Tolbaga
		?		Malaya Siya
	MOUSTERIAN			
40,000		MIDDLE PALEOLITHIC		
		Chapter 4		

Note: There is probably considerable overlap between western European Upper Paleolithic cultures.

CHAPTER 5   EUROPEANS AND NORTHERN ASIANS

(c. 40,000 TO 8000 YEARS AGO)

Preview

- *Homo sapiens sapiens* spread rapidly through the Old World after 45,000 years ago, a marked biological and cultural break reflected by the sudden appearance of anatomically modern humans and of more refined and efficient tool technologies.

- Over the millennia after 40,000 B.P. there was an increasing trend toward greater specialization and flexibility in the hunter-gatherer lifeway.

- *Homo sapiens sapiens* populations may have replaced *Homo sapiens neanderthalensis* in most places rather than evolving from them.

- The technological changes of the Upper Paleolithic were foreshadowed tens of thousands of years earlier in tropical Africa and in the Near East. Complex adaptive forces, including the need for more economical methods of using fine-grained rock, led to the refinement of age-old technologies.

- Upper Paleolithic technology was based on both blades and flakes, producing a wide range of scraping and graving tools as well as backed knives. In time, antler and bone technologies assumed great importance in colder latitudes, perhaps as substitutes for, and to supplement, wooden artifacts.

- The transition between Middle and Upper Paleolithic in Europe was a rapid one, occurring after 40,000 years ago. The new cultures were characterized by frequent readaptations to changing climatic conditions, as people exploited a rich mammalian biomass. The sheer diversity of the Ice Age environment gave hunter-gatherer bands great flexibility and resulted in a considerable diversity and complexity among Upper Paleolithic cultures, especially the Magdalenian with its intricate artistic traditions. The Magdalenian flourished after about 18,000 years ago until the end of the Ice Age about 5000 years later.

• Upper Paleolithic settlement in Europe coincided with long-term trends toward a restructuring of social relations after 32,000 years ago, together with a great proliferation of tool forms. There may have been more structured relationships between different bands. These people may have subsisted off migratory game animals as well as other foods, and many may have lived in southwest France in smaller territories.

• The Upper Paleolithic cultures of southwestern France lived in relatively close juxtaposition. At certain times of the year, they may have come together for communal hunts and a variety of social functions.

• Upper Paleolithic art flourished for more than 20,000 years and involved a complex symbolism revolving around the relationships among animals, humans, and the natural environment. This art tradition died out after 13,000 years ago, when postglacial forest, river, and coastal adaptations replaced the big-game hunting traditions of the late Ice Age.

• In Russia and Siberia, big-game hunting traditions flourished during the last climax of the Weichsel glaciation. Siberia saw two distinctive Upper Paleolithic traditions—Mal'ta-Afontova and Dyukhtai—in existence about 18,000 years ago.

• The Dyukhtai tradition may have connections with Upper Paleolithic cultures to the south, in northern China, and has direct links to Paleoarctic cultural traditions in Alaska.

Chronological
Table C

In the final analysis, the long millennia of prehistory have seen humankind become ever more efficient at extracting energy from its environment. The first hominids branched out into unfamiliar environments that took them away from an almost total dependence on forest fruits. *Homo habilis* was a scavenger as well as a collector, perhaps even an occasional hunter, a lifeway that further deepened the scope of our predecessors' lives. *Homo erectus* radiated into temperate latitudes, into the Near East, Europe, and Asia. These more advanced hominids were hunters as well as scavengers, who relied on enhanced cooperation for success in the chase. Once they became serious hunters, people could tap rich supplies of energy-rich meat, as well as vegetable foods. Hunters were, at first, yet another carnivore in a world well populated by successful carnivores. The transition to the new lifeway must have been slow, at times painful, and may have occurred in several stages. There can be little doubt that increased efficiency as a carnivore played an important role in the emergence of both archaic *Homo sapiens* and anatomically modern *Homo sapiens sapiens.* In Chapter 4, we explored current thinking about the emergence of *H. sapiens sapiens* in tropical Africa and hypothesized that anatomically modern humans spread from the tropics into North Africa and the Near East about 45,000 years ago. From there, *H. sapiens* may have entered Europe at a time of low sea level, crossing the land bridge that connected the Balkans with Turkey across the Bosphorus (for a full discussion, see Fagan, 1990; Stringer et al., 1984). This chapter chronicles the cultural changes that resulted from this replacement of European Neanderthals by anatomically modern humans and looks at the vigorous hunter-gatherer cultures that flourished in the northern parts of the Old World between 40,000 years ago and postglacial times (Figure 5.1 shows sites in Chapters 5, 6, and 8).

Radiation of
Homo sapiens
45,000 B.P. and
later

THE UPPER PLEISTOCENE (c. 128,000 TO 10,000 YEARS AGO)

The Upper Pleistocene coincided with the last interglacial and glacial cycle of the Ice Age, which began about 128,000 years ago. The detailed picture we have of this cycle gives us important clues to the general nature of the Ice Age climate—gradual glaciation and rapid deglaciation in cycles of cold, dry weather prevailing over northern latitudes for some 60 percent of the past 730,000 years. Full interglacial conditions, when the climate was warmer than today, brought forest and woodland to Europe (Figure 5.2). The Upper Pleistocene is now divided into five stages, summarized in Box 5.1 (Gamble, 1986b), beginning with the Eemian interglacial, which lasted only some 10,000 years. About 118,000 years ago, global temperatures started to cool gradually with the onset of the Weichsel (or Wurm) glaciation. By 115,000 years ago, North American and European ice sheets were expanding again, and sea levels had already fallen some 230 feet (70 m). Glacial conditions were intense about 75,000 years ago, when the Neanderthals were flourishing in Europe and the Americas were still uninhabited, and again after 29,000 years ago, during the heyday of the Cro-Magnons, reaching their height about 18,000 years ago, when sea levels fell to about 425 feet (130 m) below modern levels. This drop led to the exposure of huge continental shelves in Southeast Asia and elsewhere, and the Bering Strait was dry land (Hopkins et al., 1982).

At the height of the last glaciation, world temperatures fell by as much as 60°F (15.5°C) near the ice sheets, between 37° and 48°F (20.6° and 26.7°C) in the tropics. The world's vegetation was very different at the height of the Weichsel glaciation (Figure 5.3). Treeless tundra vegetation extended south of the ice sheets, giving way to a wide belt of continental, cold steppe that extended from the Low Countries into China and from Siberia to the Mediterranean. The steppe was much narrower in North America, soon giving way to coniferous forest farther south. Huge zones of desert occupied more than half the earth's surface between latitudes 30°N and S, but some of today's desert areas—like the American Southwest, the northern Sahara,

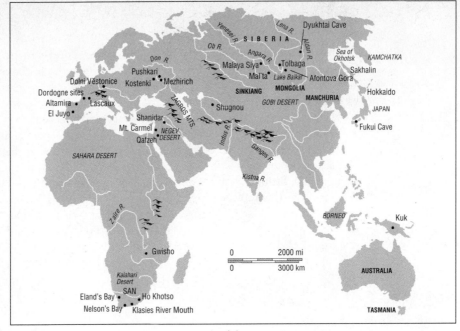

(a)

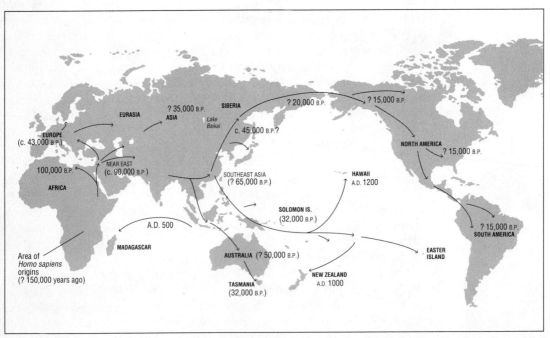

(b)

FIGURE 5.1   (a) Map showing archaeological sites mentioned in Chapters 5, 6, and 8. (b) The spread of *Homo sapiens sapiens* in the late Ice Age and later.

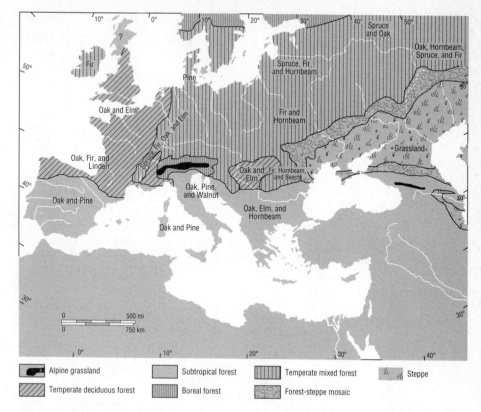

FIGURE 5.2   Generalized distribution of vegetation in Europe during the height of the Holstein interglacial. The succeeding Eemian interglacial was not quite as warm and was of shorter duration, but the same general vegetational patterns prevailed. (After Butzer, 1971.)

and the southern African deserts—were more hospitable, supporting scrub, grassland, and shallow lakes. The rain forests of tropical Africa and Asia gave way to open woodland and grassland; coral reefs and mangrove swamps contracted drastically as a result of cooler temperatures. However, despite the harsh world climate, humankind managed to survive and flourish in this very different world.

NEANDERTHALS AND *HOMO SAPIENS SAPIENS*

If anatomically modern *Homo sapiens* spread from Africa into the Near East and Europe, the question immediately arises, What happened to the Neanderthals? Their sudden disappearance and replacement by modern humans has sparked some of the most vigorous controversies in archaeology and some scintillating, if speculative, popular novels. How did the Neanderthals become extinct? Were they attacked and killed by anatomically more advanced newcomers? Or did they interbreed with

BOX 5.1

Stages of the Upper Pleistocene

Scientists conventionally divide the Upper Pleistocene into five broad stages:

Stage 1: Eemian Interglacial (128,000 to 118,000 years ago)

Global temperatures were between 1° and 3°C warmer than today. During this short-lived interglacial, archaic *Homo sapiens* lived in Europe and Asia, and anatomically modern humans in sub-Saharan Africa.

Stage 2: Early Last Glacial (Early Weichsel) (118,000 to 32,000 years ago)

This was a stage with two phases, the earlier before 75,000 years ago, when there was still temperate woodland in Europe but gradual cooling, and a later one with full glacial conditions after that date. There were occasional brief, warmer episodes, the last around 32,000 years ago. This was the period when Neanderthals lived in Europe and Eurasia and when *Homo sapiens sapiens* was in the Near East. Modern humans moved into Europe after 45,000 years ago.

Stage 3: Full Glacial (Main Wurm) (32,000 to 14,000 years ago)

Glacial conditions reached their maximum around 18,000 to 20,000 years ago, when the Scandinavian and North American ice sheets reached their maximum extents. At this point bitterly cold climate effectively blocked off huge areas of the world for human settlement. Barren polar deserts covered the dry northern latitudes of Siberia and Alaska, on both shores of the Bering Strait. Lower sea levels and cooler ocean temperatures resulted in less rainfall and atmospheric moisture.

Stages 4 and 5: Late Glacial (Late Weichsel) and Postglacial (Holocene) (14,000 years ago to the present)

Rapid deglaciation and rising sea levels usher in the post-Ice Age world, with climates acquiring basically modern characteristics by 7000 years ago (Chapter 6).

Note: Recent calibrations of radiocarbon dates achieved with the aid of uranium thorium tests on Caribbean coral suggest that current dates for Stages 3 and 4 may be up to 3500 years too recent. The new calibrations would place the Stage 3 maximum at about 21,500 as opposed to 18,000 years ago.

anatomically modern humans and adopt new cultural adaptations? It is hardly surprising that the fossil record gives no clues, for it is far too incomplete. Although some of the more pronounced facial features of the classic Neanderthals, like their brow ridges, did begin to recede in some later populations, this is far from a conclusive sign that the one population gave way to the other. The first *H. sapiens* populations, like the famous Cro-Magnon people of southwest France, although robustly built, show no anatomical signs that can be called transitional from the Neanderthals (Figure 5.4). Their robustness still lies within the range of variation of modern populations,

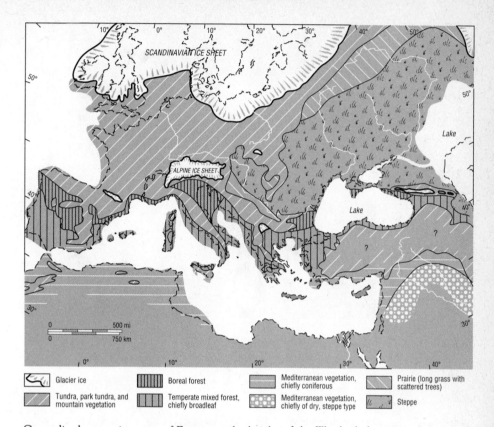

FIGURE 5.3   Generalized vegetation map of Europe at the height of the Weichsel glaciation, showing ice sheets. (After Butzer, 1971.)

albeit at the robust end. It seems most likely that the *H. sapiens sapiens* replaced *H. sapiens neanderthalensis* rather than evolving from them (Ronen, 1982).

Current thinking has it that *Homo sapiens sapiens* evolved from early *H. sapiens* in tropical Africa, and ultimately from *H. erectus,* by phyletic (evolution of different biological lines) change and by hybridization from earlier populations that displayed considerable variation (see Chapter 4). If this evolution took place in sub-Saharan Africa, did modern people evolve from the Neanderthals elsewhere? The most logical place to look is the Near East. There, *H. sapiens sapiens* was living at the Qafzeh Cave in Israel at least 92,000 years ago, almost as early a date as modern humans are known to have flourished in southern Africa (Stringer and Andrews, 1988). These fossils also imply that Neanderthals and anatomically modern people were living in the Near East at the same time and coexisted there without biological or cultural interaction for thousands of years, perhaps from before 90,000 until at least 45,000 years ago. Stone tools from Qafzeh, from caves on Mt. Carmel, and from the Negev Desert chart a slow evolution of human technology between 100,000 and 40,000 years ago. Does this mean that Neanderthals evolved into anatomically modern people in the Near East, as the candelabra hypothesis implies (Chapter 4)? Alternatively, did Neander-

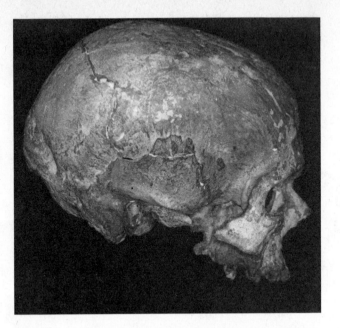

FIGURE 5.4   *Homo sapiens sapiens* from Cro-Magnon rock shelter, Les Eyzies, France, dating to between 40,000 and 35,000 years ago. (Courtesy of Milford Wolpoff.)

thal groups move south from Europe to escape extreme cold, perhaps as late as 50,000 years ago, settling in a region where anatomically modern humans from Africa were already living? At present, we do not know. What is significant, however, is that after 45,000 years ago new technologies based on fine stone blades and associated with *H. sapiens sapiens* become dominant in Near Eastern toolkits. Perhaps it was not until these new technologies developed that fully modern people had the competitive edge that enabled them to move northward into the new, challenging environments of late Ice Age Europe.

THE UPPER PALEOLITHIC TRANSITION

The biological transition from Neanderthals to *Homo sapiens sapiens* is still the subject of much debate; however, the replacement theory is most strongly favored. Can we, then, document the transition in technological and cultural terms (Hoffecker and Wolf, 1988)?

The final chapter of human biological evolution was accompanied by considerable technological changes, but these changes were far less dramatic than has sometimes been claimed. For generations, experts on the Stone Age assumed that the appearance of *Homo sapiens sapiens* was associated with the invention of radically new, much more advanced technologies that involved, among other things, the use of

punches to produce fine, parallel-sided blades and a proliferation of specialized tools, not only in stone but in antler and bone as well. Although there is no doubt that such innovations did appear in the Upper Paleolithic, careful examination of earlier technological traditions shows that they were foreshadowed tens of thousands of years earlier.

Africa and the Near East

Rock shelters and caves in eastern and southern Africa have yielded large tools made on blades fabricated by skilled percussion from carefully prepared cores. The same peoples of 100,000 years ago were using composite tools and a wider range of artifacts than many of their predecessors. In the Near East, great caves and rock shelters like et-Tabūn and Mugharet el-Wad at Mt. Carmel, Israel, and Shanidar, Iraq, document thousands of years of Neanderthal toolmaking. These sites were visited again and again by hunter-gatherer bands from more than 70,000 years ago right into modern times.

The Mousterian levels in these caves contain tens of thousands of carefully retouched flakes and side scrapers, as well as the bones of large deer and wild cattle (Marks, 1983). As Arthur Jelinik (1981) has pointed out, this technology was a very simple and conservative one that displayed considerable variability within fairly restricted limits. This variability included some horizons in which large bladelike blanks were made with sophisticated percussion flaking. The Mousterian levels are covered by further occupation levels containing different toolkits that gradually replaced earlier artifact forms and technologies. In these, the long, parallel-sided blades that were the first stage in making stone tools were removed from cylindrical flint cores with a punch and a hammerstone (Figure 5.5). Some blades were up to 6 inches (15.2 cm) long. The tools made from them varied greatly; many were designed for specific tasks and, in later millennia, mounted in handles. The great British prehistorian Dorothy Garrod (1951) believed that the occupation levels of the Mt. Carmel Caves and neighboring sites documented a technological transition from Middle to Upper Paleolithic toolmaking. Subsequent research has proved that Near Eastern technology was changing much earlier and that Upper Paleolithic toolkits and stoneworking may have resulted from new adaptive strategies because of climate change and other factors.

Anthony Marks (1983) believes that Upper Paleolithic technology resulted from far more than dramatic inventions and the rapid adoption of new ideas. He studied hunter-gatherer camps in Israel's Negev Desert and found an interesting change in ancient settlement patterns. The climate was wetter and the hunting population tended to concentrate in more circumscribed areas 45,000 years ago. As the climate dried up, the people were forced to become more mobile. Instead of camping close to convenient sources of toolmaking stone, they were forced to move around constantly, a reality that necessitated new ways of using precious fine-grained rock. Instead of using wasteful Levallois techniques (Figure 4.17), they experimented with more economical flaking methods, which evolved into the long, parallel-sided blades favored by Upper Paleolithic stoneworkers. So Upper Paleolithic blade technology

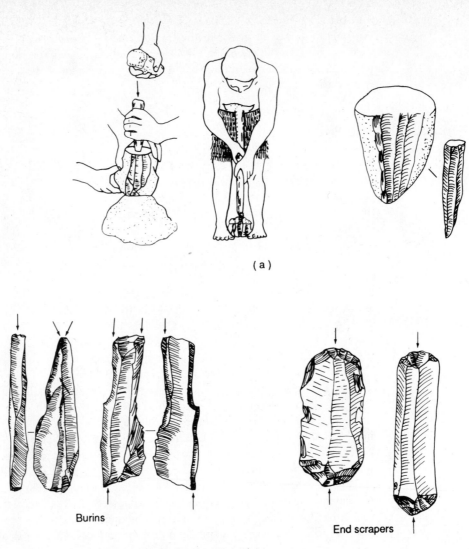

(a)

Burins

End scrapers

(b)

FIGURE 5.5 Upper Paleolithic technology. The classic stoneworking technology used for Upper Paleolithic tools was based not only on percussion and the use of bone hammers but also on punch-struck blades. Various methods were used to strike off the blades, using a hand-held or chest-impelled punch to produce parallel-sided blades (a). The punch allows intense pressure to be applied to a single point on the top of the core and channels the direction of the shock waves. Parallel-sided blades were made into a variety of tools, among them burins and scrapers, which were typical of all stages of the Upper Paleolithic. Burins (b) were used for grooving wood, bone, and particularly antlers, which were made into spears and harpoon points. The chisel ends of burins were formed by taking an oblique or longitudinal flake off the end of a blade. Burins also were used to engrave figures. End scrapers were used on wood and bone as well as skins. Arrows indicate the chisel ends of burins and the scraping edges of end scrapers. A strong trend toward the production of smaller blades developed in Europe and Asia after

was the logical result of millennia of gradual adjustment to more mobile lifeways, in which careful curation of toolmaking stone was essential.

MODERN HUMANS IN EUROPE

Why did it take *Homo sapiens sapiens* so long to move into Europe and Eurasia from the Near East? Environmental conditions may have militated against earlier settlement. From 100,000 to about 45,000 years ago, Europe was locked into extremely cold, full glacial conditions, with very long, severe winters. It may be no coincidence that *H. sapiens sapiens* first appears in continental Europe during a brief spell of more temperate climate after 50,000 years ago. Even then, climatic conditions and seasonal contrasts may have been severe enough to require new artifacts and more sophisticated hunting skills to exploit northern environments to the full.

Blade technology, with its highly portable cores and efficient small blanks, was highly adaptive for late Ice Age hunter-gatherers exploiting large periglacial hunting territories (periglacial: close to and around ice sheets). It has been likened to the Swiss Army knife, with its strong hinge and many blades. The knife is a foundation for many tool forms, as was the blade core (Fagan, 1990). The stoneworker knocked off numerous blade blanks, which could be fashioned into a great variety of scrapers, awls, and knives, to say nothing of fine-edged graving tools, or burins, as archaeologists call them (Table 5.1). This versatile stone technology produced the fine, sharp working edges necessary for grooving bone and antler, raw materials available in abundance in the periglacial north. The development of blade technology may well have enabled modern humans to move north from the Near East.

A scatter of radiocarbon dates and stone tools chronicles the spread of modern humans into late Ice Age Europe. Characteristic blade technology appears in Bulgaria as early as 43,000 years ago; in Hungary by 40,000 years ago; and in western Europe

(text continues on page 182)

20,000 years ago. Heat treatment enabled stoneworkers to use pressure and other new retouch methods to remove fine, flat flakes from artifact surfaces (Price et al., 1982).

Upper Paleolithic technology was based on efficient use of toolmaking stone, an important point in environments where such materials may have been hard to find. It also relied heavily on composite tools, of which stone elements were only a part. Many small blades and bladelets were mounted in handles or sockets, as barbs or knives. A diverse bone and antler projectile point technology came into use after 35,000 years ago, greatly enhancing hunting effectiveness. After 20,000 years ago, Upper Paleolithic people began to use another deadly, and highly effective, device, the spear-thrower. This leverlike artifact with a weight on the outer end extended the throwing arc and the range and accuracy of the weapon, an important consideration with large animals. After about 15,000 years ago, the Magdalenian people decorated many of their spear-throwers with finely crafted animals, often headless.

Many Upper Paleolithic stone tools were employed in woodworking, for the people made use of many perishable materials that do not survive in the archaeological record. A small imprint of three-braided plant fibers from the famous Lascaux Cave in southwest France shows that cordage may have been important for making nets and snares, both for use on land and for catching fish.

Table 5.1 *Much simplified outline of the Upper Paleolithic cultural traditions of western Europe from 40,000 to 8000 years ago.*

The most commonly accepted scheme has two parallel cultural traditions flourishing from about 34,000 until 30,000 years ago, the Chatelperronian, characterized by backed knife blades, and the Aurignacian, favoring scrapers and sharpened blades (opposite, bottom). The Gravettian, with its fine-backed blades, became dominant after 30,000 years ago. Thereafter, there were considerable regional variations.

The Solutrean, a culture that relied on sophisticated "cooking" of large pieces of flint so that it became porcelainlike in texture, flourished in France and Spain. The stoneworker could exert pressure on the flake edges to produce magnificent leaf-shaped spear points (opposite, right). Pressure flaking never took hold in central Europe, where many variations of Gravettian culture are found. In the west, the Magdalenian tradition, which relied heavily on antler and bone (opposite, top), emerged about 18,000 years ago.

It should be noted that all Upper Paleolithic cultures in this area relied heavily on blade technology and on scrapers, burins, and other simple blade artifacts.

With the retreat of the ice sheets after 12,000 years ago, Stone Age peoples adapted their cultures to more forested environments, where exploitation of woodlands and coasts was important to survival. These Mesolithic cultures, with their distinctive microlithic technology, lasted until farming spread into Europe about 8000 years ago, reaching the northwest about 7500 years ago.

Years B.P.	Climate	Cultures		Characteristics
8000	Temperate	Mesolithic Late Glacial		Forest and coastal adaptations. Microlithic technology. No cave art.
10,000	Warming up after 14,000		Magdalenian	Apogee of cave and antler art. Skillful bone and antler work. Most elaborate development in Spain and France.
15,000				Magnificent pressure-flaked bone heads. Bas-relief sculpture (France and Spain).
20,000	Very cold		Solutrean	"Venus" figurines, some cave art. Backed points and blades. Many regional variants in central Europe, where Gravettian survived until the end of the Ice Age.
25,000	Cold	Gravettian		
30,000	Somewhat temperate	Chatelperronian	Aurignacian	Some art, bone points. Aurignacian—notched, sharpened blades. Chatelperronian—backed knife blade points.
35,000	Cold	Mousterian		Middle Paleolithic technology

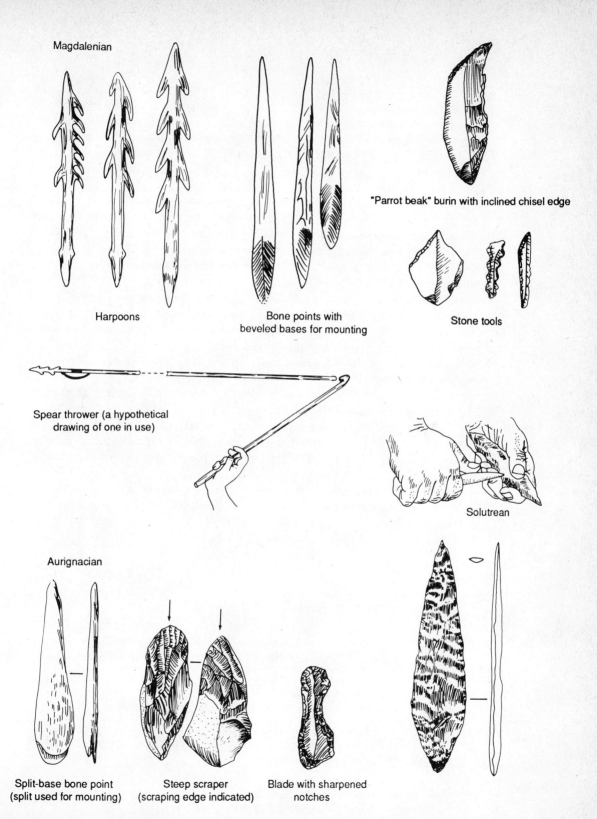

Magdalenian

Harpoons

Bone points with
beveled bases for mounting

"Parrot beak" burin with inclined chisel edge

Stone tools

Spear thrower (a hypothetical
drawing of one in use)

Solutrean

Aurignacian

Split-base bone point
(split used for mounting)

Steep scraper
(scraping edge indicated)

Blade with sharpened
notches

within a few millennia, perhaps as early as 40,000 years ago. There are clear signs that Neanderthals and newcomers lived alongside one another, for Mousterian occupation layers in some central European caves date to much later than 40,000, and there were Neanderthals making blade tools at Saint Césaire in France 36,000 years ago (Leveque and Vandermeersch, 1982). After 33,000 years ago, *Homo sapiens sapiens* was the only human form in Europe, and Upper Paleolithic blade technologies are universal.

Quite what form this population replacement took remains an enigma (Gamble, 1986b; Mellars, 1989; White, 1982). There may have been interbreeding between Neanderthals and anatomically modern Cro-Magnons. The resulting gene flow would have produced mosaiclike changes, which may be reflected in a degree of variability in early Cro-Magnon populations. Alternatively, the Neanderthals may have been pushed aside, forced to occupy hunting territories on the periphery, where they lived alongside the newcomers for some millennia. It was a long process of gene flow and small-scale population movement, and of cultural innovations also—new technologies and new strategies for the hunt. The flow of ideas may have been accelerated in situations in which hunters exploited large hunting territories and wandered far and wide in search of game and, perhaps, good toolmaking stone. Under such circumstances, technological innovation may have preceded gene flow and population movement, resulting in Neanderthals experimenting with more sophisticated artifacts, as apparently was the case at Saint Césaire.

The late Stone Age archaeology of Europe has been so well studied that we can discern a series of long-term trends that took hold in hunter-gatherer societies throughout the world after 35,000 years ago. The changes were by no means simultaneous, nor did they occur everywhere, but they were cumulative and led in the long term to major economic, social, and political changes everywhere, especially in areas such as southwestern France and parts of Australia, where food resources were abundant and seasonally predictable. Randall White (1982) lists the significant changes for late Ice Age Europe, many of which were mirrored elsewhere:

Upper Paleolithic trends

- A tendency toward high population densities after 35,000 years ago.

- More regular social gatherings.

- Much more stylistic variation in stone artifacts that were patterned in time and space. Perhaps these represent different territorial or social boundaries.

- Much greater emphasis on the working of bone and antler. Again, these tools display formal stylistic variation, perhaps with social significance.

- Some shift toward the hunting of herd animals that carry antlers for much of the year, especially in cold latitudes.

- Growing importance of personal ornamentation as a way of communicating corporate and personal identity.

- Acquisition of materials from distant sources, probably through structured exchange involving cooperation with other groups.

White believes there was a total restructuring of social relations during the critical transition period. It was then that corporate and individual identities became important and were enhanced by the skilled working of antler, bone, and stone, and by the use of ornaments. The Upper Paleolithic may have seen more structured relationships between the inhabitants of different geographic areas, expressed not only in trade but in better defined hunting territories and other social relationships. White believes that we should examine this transition on a very broad canvas. One of the most important questions is establishing whether *Homo sapiens sapiens* had to adapt to the close presence of other human groups as a matter of survival. In later prehistoric times, relationships with neighbors were to assume ever-increasing importance in adaptive strategies for long-term survival.

We cannot possibly describe the full diversity of hunter-gatherer peoples who flourished in all parts of the globe after 35,000 years ago, so our narrative concentrates on the following major developments:

- The hunter-gatherer cultures that flourished in southwest France and northern Spain between 35,000 and 8,000 years ago. These cultures are of particular importance because of their adaptation to the last cold snap of the Weichsel glaciation and their remarkable artistic traditions.

- The big-game hunting cultures that developed on the west Russian plains and Siberia.

- The early settlement of the arctic latitudes of northeast Asia, from which the first settlement of the New World may have developed.

- The first human settlement of the Americas and the cultural traditions that stemmed from it.

- The early history of surviving hunter-gatherers in tropical latitudes, especially the Australians and the San peoples of southern Africa.

EUROPEAN HUNTER-GATHERERS: 45,000
TO 8000 YEARS AGO

Central and western Europe was cold and dry during much of Upper Paleolithic times, with great ice sheets covering large expanses of northern latitudes. South of the ice sheets, thousands of square miles of steppe-grassland with occasional stands of trees covered much of the unglaciated land. There were many local variations, with extensive tree growth in deep river valleys and other sheltered areas. A rich mammalian community flourished in these diverse environments. It included bison, horses, reindeer, and mountain goats in more rugged areas; large herbivores like the mammoth, woolly rhinoceros, and wild ox were common on the open steppe. The human inhabitants could exploit not only a rich animal biomass but also a wide variety of plant foods, including blueberries, raspberries, acorns, and hazelnuts. The climate was changing constantly, so the people had to readapt by altering their diet, hunting and gathering strategies, and technology. Much of the great variability in Upper Paleolithic culture results from such readaptations.

The Upper Paleolithic of Europe began about 35,000 years ago and witnessed constant changes in human behavior over the next 25,000 years. These millennia have been subdivided into a series of cultural periods, each with its own technology and technological innovations (see Table 5.1; Figure 5.5) (Movius, 1973). At first French archaeologists, who developed this cultural sequence from excavations in caves and rock shelters, thought of each period as a rigid "epoch," like a geological layer. Today the cultural phases are seen as changes stimulated by a variety of complex and little understood factors (Laville et al., 1980). Some of them may have been responses to practical needs, others purely dictates of fashion or small technological innovations.

As time went on, major regional differences emerged throughout central and western Europe (Gamble, 1986a). These can be identified from stone and antler tool types by contrasting stone technologies. As Randall White (1986) remarks, it is almost as if barriers to communication were arising, as if there were regional dialects in Europe for the first time.

Settlement Strategies and Lifeways

The Upper Paleolithic peoples of southwest France have long been thought of as one of the prehistoric models for the cave people so beloved of twentieth-century cartoonists. Although it is true that much of our knowledge of their cultures comes from French caves and rock shelters, these were by no means the only settlements occupied after 40,000 years ago. Southwest France is remarkable for its high density of Upper Paleolithic sites within a restricted area, sites that were sometimes intensively occupied over long periods of time.

Diverse food resources

Between 35,000 and 12,000 years ago, the climate of this region was strongly oceanic, with cool summers and mild winters by Ice Age standards. Summer temperatures may have been in the 53.6° to 59°F range, with winter readings around 32°F (Mellars, 1985). The vegetation growing season was longer than on the open plains to the north and east, and snow cover was considerably less. Thus, food resources for large herbivores were more readily available, perhaps resulting in a much higher density of game animals as well as more plentiful edible foods. This was a region of diverse food resources (Jochim, 1983), reflected not only in tree pollens in sheltered archaeological sites but also in the range of animals recovered from them. The people were mainly subsisting off reindeer, but they also took wild ox, red deer, bison, ibex, chamois, woolly rhinoceros, and mammoth. The sheer diversity of the environment gave the human inhabitants economic security. In years when reindeer migrations were unpredictable, there were other sources of animal protein close at hand, to say nothing of plant foods.

Food resources

Many of these resources were relatively predictable. There were seasonal reindeer migrations, from the higher ground to the east in summer to the deep river valleys of the west in winter, where food resources could be found even in the coldest months. Paul Mellars (1985) believes that the hunters could intercept animals from a broad range of species, many of them migratory, from an ecological range extending perhaps some 62 miles (100 km) on either side of their central places. Michael Jochim (1983) argues that large-scale salmon fishing during seasonal runs was a major factor in the evolution of complex hunter-gatherer societies in this region. The concentration of settlement along riverbanks, at places where the salmon runs were most prevalent, was a logical response to predictable food resources. Unfortunately, Jochim's argument has a serious weakness, for very few salmon bones have been found in the region's Upper Paleolithic sites (Mellars, 1985). Although fish hooks and harpoons, as well as fine engravings of salmon and seals, are known from many later Upper Paleolithic sites, it appears likely that hunting of large mammals was the predominant subsistence activity between 35,000 and about 10,000 years ago. Fishing does seem to have assumed much greater importance at the very end of the Ice Age, perhaps as forests encroached on open grazing grounds and rising sea levels brought more fish to French rivers (Mellars, 1985; Pfeiffer, 1985).

Whatever the precise makeup of Upper Paleolithic diet in southwest France, there were direct adaptive responses to these highly favorable ecological conditions. Population densities were locally much higher than in other parts of Europe, with groups living in the same locations for much of the year, close to seasonal concentrations of food resources. They exploited these resources with high efficiency, Mellars believes, and some part of the population lived almost permanently in certain key locations. Smaller groups then exploited more distant resources in summer and according to need.

Settlement preferences

The people tended to choose many of their settlement sites with reference to plentiful water supplies and good views of the surrounding landscape, so they could observe game and perhaps their neighbors. More than 90 percent of all known sites are close to springs or riverbanks. The bands could live wherever they wanted, for they had the technology to survive hard winters in the open. Some of the largest cave and rock shelter sites lay close to river fords, places, perhaps, where migrating reindeer would cross each year. One such site is Laugerie Haute near Les Eyzies, where the skeletons of several reindeer lay between the great rock shelter and the river ford. When the people occupied a rock shelter or cave, it invariably faced south, so they could benefit from the sun's rays on cool days. They appear to have erected tents and hide curtains in the shelters for additional protection. Some overhangs lay near places where it was possible to stampede reindeer, horses, and other herd animals over precipitous cliffs. In the open, some groups laid out pavements of river cobbles as foundations for wood, skin, or sod structures. Sometimes they heated the pebbles first, perhaps so they could lay them over frozen ground to form a secure platform.

Social Life and Group Size

Many of the largest French Upper Paleolithic sites are close to places where seasonally abundant resources like reindeer could be exploited by large numbers of people.

Other settlements were much smaller, little more than temporary camps occupied by a few families. Perhaps it is significant that the larger sites—like Laugerie Haute and Laugerie Basse or La Madeleine, the type site of the Magdalenian—contain many more art objects. The bands may have come together into larger social units at locations where abundant resources were available for a few months or weeks to cooperate in the food quest. Such aggregations could not have lasted year-round, partly because the environment would not support so many people in one place for long. If modern hunter-gatherers are any guide, the bands probably had no mechanisms for resolving disputes, except that practiced by modern San—walking away. This is what anthropologist Richard Lee (1979) calls "voting with your feet."

Social structure

The days, weeks, even months of aggregation are the high point of the year in living hunter-gatherer societies, as they must have been in Upper Paleolithic times. This was the time of marriage and initiation ceremonies, of highly intense rituals, in which the fine art objects of the people may have played important roles. This was when shamans told tales and wove spells, when the forces of the ancestors and the spirit world were invoked to ensure the continuity of life and the success of the hunt. It was also a time when men and women exchanged artifacts, ornaments, and exotic raw materials from near and far. Seashells from the English Channel and the Mediterranean, Baltic amber, and other exotica—items that were sometimes imbued with special magical, social, or prestige value—were apparently exchanged from hand to hand. Many of these may have been given and received as gestures of social obligation between individuals and groups.

The Upper Paleolithic societies of southwest France lived in relatively close juxtaposition, in a diverse environment with rich, predictable food resources. For at least part of the year, these societies may have lived a relatively sedentary existence and come together in much larger aggregations. Under these circumstances, it is reasonable to expect that their social organization would become more complex than was normal among egalitarian band societies. The evolution of social complexity among prehistoric hunter-gatherer societies is a much-debated topic (for a set of essays, see Price and Brown, 1985), but in the case of the Magdalenian of southwest France, we can predict some social complexity with confidence.

Social complexity

Magdalenian culture was elaborate and sophisticated, to the point that we can predict that more sedentary living and larger group size might have resulted in social change, in more complex hunter-gatherer societies (Mellars, 1985) (for discussion, see Chapter 6). Certainly, the sometimes elaborate decorations of seashells, bracelets, even sewn clothing associated with the dead argue for complex spiritual beliefs, many involving abstract symbolic images of the Ice Age world that we will never be able to recover.

Upper Paleolithic Art

Nearly 200 caves bearing wall paintings and engravings are known from southwest Europe, mainly France and Spain. Some 10,000 sculpted and engraved art objects have come from Upper Paleolithic sites across Europe, far into Siberia, and in Africa. Upper Paleolithic people were brilliant artists in stone, antler, bone, clay, ivory, and wood. They used paint on rock walls, sculpted in bas-relief and the round, and made musical instruments (Bahn and Vertut, 1988). The artists created thousands of naturalistic images of animals, sometimes human and humanlike forms, and dozens of enigmatic signs. All this art conveys complex, long-forgotten ideas, a symbolic world of spirit animals and spirit humans, of forces benevolent and evil. Generations of archaeologists have grappled with the meaning of the art (Pfeiffer, 1982), so far with little success.

Cave art
32,000 B.P.

  The earliest artworks date to perhaps as early as 32,000 years ago. (There are some earlier scratched bones from Mousterian sites, but these hardly constitute art.) The earliest Cro-Magnon artists carved some animals in the round in ivory and made simple paintings or engravings of animals and human sexual organs. British archaeologist Mark Newcomer has made an exact copy of a 32,000-year-old bone flute and played it, evidence that musical sounds were made early in the Upper Paleolithic (R. White, 1986).

c. 25,000 B.P.

  Later artists executed incised engravings on walls and blew or brushed pigment against their hands to make imprints on cave walls. They also fashioned "Venus" figurines, sculptures and bas-reliefs of females, often with pendulous breasts, sometimes pregnant, and with exaggerated sexual characteristics (Figure 5.6). Many scholars believe these were female fertility figurines. They have been found from Russia in the east to the Dordogne of France in the west, most in deposits dating to about 25,000 years ago. We have no means of knowing whether, in fact, these were fertility figures, but they seem to have been associated with a relatively short-lived set of beliefs that was in use over a wide area of Europe.

  Bas-reliefs, friezes of animals like wild horses that adorn places where the people lived, came into fashion during the Solutrean. The Solutreans also painted animals on cave walls, but 80 percent of all known Upper Paleolithic art comes from the Magdalenian, beginning around 18,000 years ago. The earlier Magdalenian saw some remarkable cave painting, from places like Lascaux, painted some 17,000 years ago. Lascaux's walls were covered again and again with depictions of wild horses, bulls, reindeer, and many other animals. Many of the animals were painted with long, distorted necks and thick bodies, as if the artists were unaware of perspective (Figure 5.7). The paintings also include squiggles, spaghettilike patterns, and tentlike symbols (Windels, 1965). A Great Hall of the Bulls features four immense wild bulls, drawn in thick, black lines, with some of the body details filled in. Horses, deer, a small bear, and a strange unicornlike beast prance with the great bulls in a fantastic display of blacks, browns, reds, and yellows that truly brings the animals to life in a flickering light. It is hard to believe that the paintings are at least 17,000 years old.

Cave art
32,000 B.P.

  The earliest tradition reached its height with an explosion of antler and bone work after 18,000 years ago. The hunters decorated their harpoons, spear points, spear-throwers, and other artifacts with naturalistic engravings, fine carvings of wild animals, and elaborate schematic patterns. Even fine eye details and hair texture were shown by delicate graving strokes (Figure 5.8). But the Magdalenians are most famous for their beautiful rock art, paintings and engravings deep in the caves of northern Spain and southwest France. At Altamira, in northern Spain, you walk deep into the hillside to enter a low-ceilinged chamber, where the painters left fine renderings of bison in red and black (Figure 5.9) (Breuil, 1908). By painting and engraving the

Altamira

FIGURE 5.6   Paleolithic art. Venus figurines from Brassempouy, France *(left)*, and Dolní Věstonice, Czechoslovakia *(right)*.

animals around natural bulges in the rock, the artists conveyed a sense of relief and life. In cave after cave, the hunters left jumbled frenzies of large and small game and animals, hand impressions, dots, and signs, many of which must have had symbolic significance.

An enormous and highly speculative literature concerns the motives behind this remarkable art (Bahn and Vertut, 1988; Mellars, 1985; Pfeiffer, 1982). Originally, Henri Breuil and other experts (Breuil, 1952) argued that the caves were sacred places where the hunters gathered to perform rituals and sympathetic magic that would ensure the fertility of game and the success of the hunt. Even the signs on the cave walls were interpreted as snares and traps (Grasiosi, 1960). Today we know a great deal more about symbolic behavior and the art that goes with it and much more about how hunter-gatherer societies function. The latest cave art research has concentrated not only on the art itself but also on the contexts in which it appears. French prehistorian Andre Leroi-Gourhan argued in 1965 that the art was not random but part of a system of meanings, an expression of a world view that organized Upper Paleolithic life. By counting the associations of subjects and clusters of motifs, Leroi-

FIGURE 5.7   A giant stag painting from Lascaux, France.

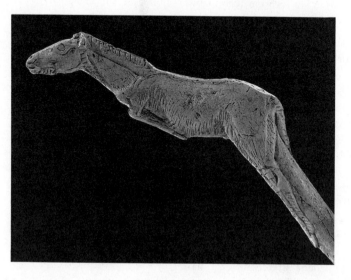

FIGURE 5.8   A superb example of the Magdalenian carver's art: a spear-thrower decorated with a horse.

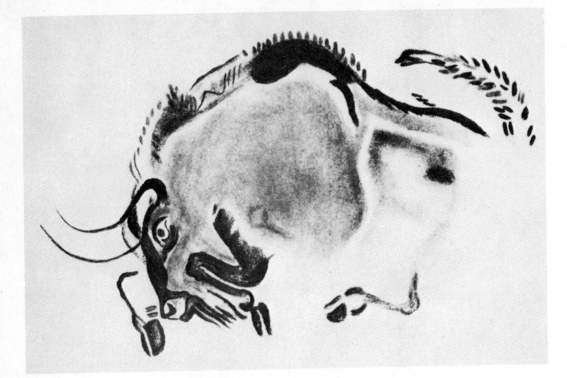

FIGURE 5.9   A bison in a polychrome cave painting from Altamira, Spain.

Gourhan found that certain themes, among them female figures, appeared in rock shelters and better lit locales, whereas others were in dark caverns. There are differences in the distribution of art, too. Bison, for instance, dominate northern Spanish cave walls, but they rarely occur on portable objects. Perhaps the social contexts of wall and portable art were different (Bahn and Vertut, 1988).

Alexander Marshack (1972, 1975) has carried out detailed microphotographic studies of Paleolithic art and shown that many of the visual forms are ecologically and seasonally related. Rather than concentrating on the naturalistic pictures of

Nonnaturalistic
pieces

animals, he has studied the hundreds of nonnaturalistic pieces, with their patterns of lines, notches, dots, and groupings of marks (Figure 5.10). On some pieces, the marks were made with different tools at different times. These pieces, which Marshack named "time-factorial" objects, were used, he believes, as sequential notations of events and phenomena, predecessors of calendars. Marshack has examined hundreds of specimens stretching back as far as the Lower Paleolithic. He found duplicated designs, systematic groups of dots and notches that were either counting tallies or the beginnings, he feels, of a writing system; but, he suggests, they differ from later, more formal writing systems that could be read by everyone: The Magdalenian and earlier notations were for the engraver alone to read, even if this person explained them to others on occasion. To formulate such a system required thought and

FIGURE 5.10   Engraved bone, 8.2 inches (21 cm) long, from La Marche, France, which was intensively studied by Marshack. The close-up shot shows tiny marks in two groups, each engraved by a different point, with a different type of stroke. (© Alexander Marshack, 1972.)

theoretical abstractions far more advanced than those hitherto attributed to hunter-gatherers of this age. Marshack's ideas are highly controversial and not widely accepted, but they come out of the type of ground-breaking research that produces exciting new interpretations and insights into Stone Age life.

Today, we know that many hunter-gatherer groups use ritual and art, creating and manipulating visual forms to structure and give meaning to their existence. Many ethnographic studies have shown how symmetry and other artistic principles may underlie the designs of many art traditions and characterize every aspect of daily life, from social relationships to village planning. The people may use relatively few symbols to communicate meanings. Very often it is the context of the symbols that reveals the meaning. For the Upper Paleolithic artists, there were clearly continuities between animal and human life and with their social world. Thus, their art was a symbolic depiction of these continuities. The artists did not choose just any wall or piece of antler or bone for their drawings nor just any animal or geometric form to depict. Their selections were deliberate, symbolic acts that provide clues to the significance of the world's earliest artistic tradition (Bahn and Vertut, 1988).

Some archaeologists believe that the underground art, with its accurate depictions of reindeer and other animals at different times of the year, may have been a kind of storehouse of knowledge about the environment, passed from generation to generation. One such 14,000-year-old sanctuary comes from El Juyo Cave in northern Spain. Inside a large, stone-walled dugout, there are four trenches, topped by four layers between 30 inches (75 cm) and 3 feet (1 m) high. The mounds were made up of layers of burnt vegetation, containing red ocher and animal bones, accompanied by more than 40 bone spear points, alternating with packed lots of fill, turned out from cuplike containers to form rosettelike patterns. A foot- (30 cm-) tall stone carved into a half-human, half-feline face stood erect atop one mound facing the cave entry. The excavators believe this was a sanctuary (Freeman and Echegaray, 1981; Pfeiffer, 1982; Bahn and Vertut, 1988).

About 13,000 years ago, the Magdalenians seem to have stopped painting and engraving deep caves. Most art after that appears at cave entrances and in rock shelters, always exposed to the light of day. The paintings and engravings were no longer naturalistic, and they vanished altogether about 11,000 years ago. By this time, much warmer climatic conditions had brought forest to the open plains, and the large Arctic animals depicted in the earlier art were largely extinct. The brilliant efflorescence of Magdalenian culture had been replaced by new adaptations—to forests, rivers, and coasts. By this time, cave and antler art had given way to a complex symbol system, much of it painted on flat pebbles (Courand, 1985).

RUSSIA AND SIBERIA

The vast, undulating plains of western Russia and central Europe as far east as the Ural Mountains were a much less hospitable environment for Stone Age hunter-gatherers than the deep, well-watered valleys to the west. There were no convenient caves or rock shelters. For warmth and shelter the inhabitants of this area had to create artificial dwellings with their own tools and locally available raw materials. It may be no coincidence that few archaeological sites are found on these frigid plains, with their nine-month winters and short summers, until Upper Paleolithic times. The Neanderthals and early Upper Paleolithic populations may have ventured onto the steppe during the warmer summer months. It took some significant technological innovations, providing better cultural adaptations to bitter cold, to allow people to live there year-round. One important invention may have been the perforated bone needle, which enabled people to fabricate tailored layers of clothing, for layered garments provide the best protection against subzero temperatures. Advances in bone and antler technology may also have played a decisive role in Arctic adaptation, for they allowed not only more efficient hunting but also the development of such important artifacts as the spear-thrower, a highly effective weapon against large, gregarious animals.

Only a few rivers dissect the west Russian plains, among them the Don and the Dnieper. It is no coincidence that ancient river terraces were the most common locations for Stone Age hunting settlements. These were often promontories overlooking the river, where the hunters could spy on the movements of the herds of Arctic elephant (mammoth), woolly rhinoceros, and wild horse that flourished in the valleys (Dolukhanov, 1982). At the height of the last glaciation, this area was a treeless periglacial landscape, a meadow steppe in warmer interstadials. It was a very inhospitable environment but one where hunter-gatherer societies flourished for thousands of years. Winter temperatures may have averaged −30° to −40°F, summer maxima rarely reaching 64°F.

Soviet archaeologists have found traces of human settlements in plains river valleys going back into Mousterian times, before 40,000 years ago. The earliest Upper Paleolithic sites, probably settlements of anatomically modern people, date to at least 35,000 years ago (Hoffecker, 1988). The most intensive Upper Paleolithic occupation dates to the period between 18,000 and 14,000 years ago, when scattered hunter-gatherer bands lived in what were often spectacular mammoth bone structures (Soffer, 1985). The Mezhirich site overlooks the Dnieper River southeast of Kiev; it

Mezhirich
15,000 B.P.

is a 15,000-year-old settlement of five houses, covering an area of some 110,000 square feet (10,219 m²) (Kornietz and Soffer, 1984; Soffer, 1987). Each house was about 13 to 22 feet (4 to 7 m) across and up to 850 square feet (78.9 m²) in area (Figure 5.11). Foundation walls of massive mammoth bones supported an intricate framework of smaller limb bones, vertebrae, and other parts, sometimes arranged in fine herring-bone patterns. The roof was supported by uprights that were stuck into holes broken through large mammoth bones, and the entire structure was almost certainly covered with elephant hide. Hearths and work areas lay inside the houses, which seem to have been occupied over long periods of time. More hearths and deep storage pits that kept meat refrigerated in the permafrost lay between the houses.

The Mezhirich dwellings are thought to have housed about 50 people, each dwelling taking 10 men about five or six days to complete, a considerable investment of effort. Since mammoth bone dwellings found at other locations are less elaborate, it may be that this settlement was of unusual importance. The inhabitants hunted not only mammoth but also other large mammals, as well as river fish and birds. Judging by the evidence from several sites, they pursued mammoth in autumn and winter, reindeer in spring and early summer, fur-bearing animals in winter, and waterfowl in summer (Dolukhanov, 1982). So many mammoth bones were used in house construction that the people may have scavenged them from carcasses on the plains in addition to using their own kills. Soviet archaeologists report that seashells from between 400 to 500 miles (643 and 804 km) away came from the Mezhirich houses, and amber, a stone thought by many prehistoric peoples to have magic qualities, was traded from 100 miles (160 km) away.

Mezhirich is far from unique. The famous Kostenki sites on the Don River have yielded large, irregular dwellings partially scooped out of the earth (R. G. Klein, 1969; McBurney, 1976). The floor plans are so irregular that it is difficult to be sure what the house plan was. In some cases, several circular structures up to 15 feet (4.6 m) in diameter were built together in a huge depression with a row of hearths down the middle. Bands of considerable size must have congregated in these tented areas (Figure 5.12).

Soviet central
Asia

To the east of the western plains stretches Soviet central Asia, a vast area of continental territory that covers not only northern Afghanistan but also the arid Turan depression and the central Asian highlands. The archaeology of this area is still little known, although research has made rapid strides in recent years (Davis,

FIGURE 5.11   Excavation of Dwelling 4 at Mezhirich, USSR.

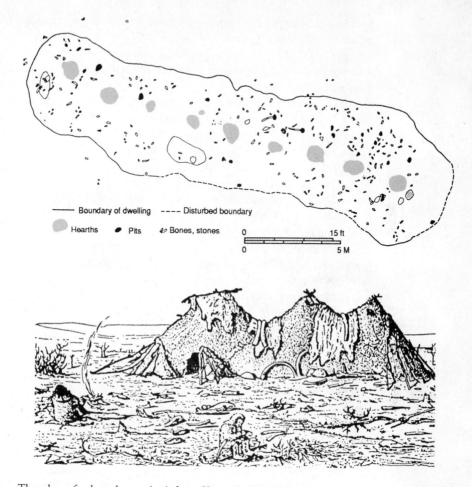

FIGURE 5.12 The plan of a long house *(top)* from Kostenki IV, USSR, and a reconstruction *(bottom)* based on the finds at Push Kari. The latter was nearly 40 feet long by 12 feet wide (12.0 by 3.7 m) and stood in a shallow depression.

1987; Ranov and Davis, 1979). There are numerous Mousterian sites dating to the early part of the Weichsel glaciation, as they do in the West, displaying different toolkit variations that probably reflect different seasonal activities. It is not yet known when the transition to the Upper Paleolithic took place, but one hunting camp at Malaya Siya on the White Iyus River west of Lake Baikal has been radiocarbon dated to about 34,500 years ago (Larichev et al., 1988). Here people hunted mammoth, horse, reindeer, and other steppe animals, which they also engraved on bone, some of the earliest art in the world. Undoubtedly, however, the human population of this harsh country was very small.

Malaya Siya
34,500 B.P.

The Upper Paleolithic of Soviet central Asia is known from a late Weichsel culture that was widespread in caves, rock shelters, and open sites but is still not well known. The Shugnou site southwest of the city of Samarkand lies at an altitude of 6700 feet (2000 m), one of the highest Upper Paleolithic sites in the world. Soviet archaeologists found five occupation layers in a site above a mountain river, yielding evidence of big-game hunting, of horses, wild oxen, wild sheep, and goats, dating to at least 20,000 to 15,000 years ago. Pollen grains suggest that weather conditions were somewhat cooler and wetter than today. The hunter-gatherer population of central Asia may have been sparse for thousands of years, perhaps because of unfavorable climate conditions, but this is pure conjecture. Population densities rose at the end of the Pleistocene, and human settlement expanded into higher elevations.

Mammoth skins, bones, sinews, and marrow were valuable to the Soviet central Asian peoples for many purposes. Bone was especially important for fuel; burned mammoth bones have come from Kostenki and other sites. House frames, digging tools, pins, needles, and many other small tools were made from the bones of the hunters' prey. Wood was naturally scarce in the treeless environment of the steppe. In this difficult environment, we would expect an economy based at least in part on lumbering beasts, whose carcasses could support many hungry mouths and fuel fires. The technology of the plains made much use of fire for warmth and for cooking. Indeed, fire was vital in the human armory as people moved outward to the arctic frontiers of the Paleolithic world.

Soviet central Asia was subjected to cultural influences from both the flake and blade traditions of the West and the chopper-chopping tool traditions of the Far East. Consequently, stone tools here frequently were based on stone cobbles and were simple, highly effective artifacts that rarely achieved the sophistication or artistry of Western traditions. The same amalgam of cultural traditions filtered into Siberia in Far Eastern Asia (Larichev et al., 1987).

Siberia

Remote from Atlantic and Pacific weather patterns, Siberia is dry country with harsh, dry winters and short, hot summers. Treeless plains predominate in the far north and extend to the shores of the Arctic Ocean. Rainfall was so sparse during the Weichsel glaciation that the great ice sheets of the West never formed here. Herds of gregarious mammoths grazed on the tundra and on the edges of the river valleys, where small bands of hunter-gatherers weathered the long winters. The archaeology of this enormous area and of northeast Asia is still little known, despite long-term excavation campaigns by Soviet archaeologists in recent years (Bryan, 1978; Muller-Beck, 1982). Nonetheless, Siberia and northeast Asia are of vital importance, for they were the staging areas from which the first settlement of the Americas took place, across the Bering Strait. A number of key issues confront anyone working in this area:

- What was the date of the first human settlement of the far northeast?

- Was there a pre-*sapiens* population in Siberia before 35,000 years ago?

- What technological and cultural traits are found in the Far East that can be identified in the New World?

Tolbaga
34,900 B.P.

Soviet archaeologists claim that sites contemporary with Malaya Siya lie east of Lake Baikal, including one at Tolbaga, said to date to as early as 34,900 years ago, but few details of the site have been published (Larichev et al., 1988). All these settlements contain well-developed blade technology but also artifacts made by using

Middle Paleolithic techniques. There is far less variation in tool forms than in later Stone Age cultures in the region.

By 25,000 years ago, two very different cultural traditions flourished in Siberia and into northeast Asia. The Mal'ta tradition is known from clusters of sites west of Lake Baikal and the Yenesei River Valley, many of them located in places sheltered from the prevailing northerly winds. The Mal'ta site itself, one of semisubterranean houses, covers more than 6458 square feet (600 m²) and may have been reoccupied many times. Mal'ta was probably a winter base camp of houses framed with large animal bones covered with a lattice of reindeer antler to support a skin or sod covering. The hunters pursued mammoth, woolly rhinoceros, and reindeer, as well as small animals. The Mal'ta people were expert bone workers who carved female and bird figurines (Figure 5.13).

The Afontova Gora-Oshurkovo tradition flourished over a much wider area, not only in the Yenesei River Valley, but also over an enormous area of northern Asia, perhaps all the way from the Altai to the Amur River. The oldest sites, Afontova

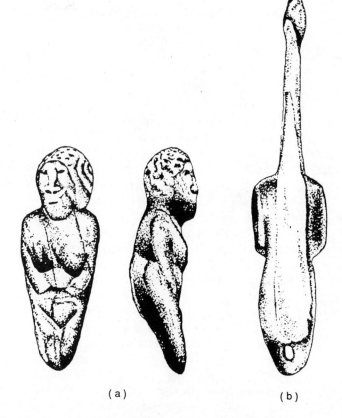

(a)   (b)

FIGURE 5.13   Figurines from Mal'ta, Siberia. (a) A bone figurine (actual size), two views. (b) An ivory bird (two-thirds actual size).

Afontova
Gora-Oshurkovo
tradition
21,000 B.P.

Gora itself on the Yenesei and Mogochino on the Ob' River, date to between 21,000 and 20,000 years ago. Again, the people hunted periglacial steppe mammals, making large tools fashioned on pebbles, blade artifacts, large pebble scrapers known locally as *skreblos,* and occasionally small blade artifacts fabricated on "microblades" (see pages 234–236).

There are many general similarities between the Mal'ta and Afontova Gora-Oshurkovo traditions, which tend to transcend the local differences between them. Together, they reflect a varied adaptation by *Homo sapiens sapiens* to an enormous area of central Asia and southern Siberia from well west of Lake Baikal to the Pacific Ocean far to the east. Late Ice Age populations in this harsh area were never large and were concentrated for the most part in river valleys and near lakes. In general terms, their lifeway may have resembled that of plains big-game hunters on the steppe-tundra to the west, but it would be a mistake to argue that these Siberian groups originated in western Eurasia. They may have moved north or northeastward onto the open steppe-tundra from more temperate environments, perhaps at about the same time as Cro-Magnons moved into Europe. Although Neanderthal settlements are known in the mountainous Altai region of Soviet Asia, there are no signs of Middle Paleolithic sites on the steppe-tundra itself. Anatomically modern humans may have been the first to venture north into periglacial regions.

DYUKHTAI AND THE FIRST SETTLEMENT
OF FAR NORTHEAST ASIA

The first human settlement of periglacial northeast Asia appears between 40,000 and 30,000 years ago and was well established just before the late glacial maximum of about 18,000 years ago. The Mal'ta and Afontova Gora-Oshurkovo traditions peter out as one moves north and east into the far frontiers of northeast Asia. As we shall see in Chapter 7, this harsh and unforgiving region of periglacial steppe-tundra and occasional large river valleys was the homeland of the first Stone Age people to cross into the Americas, probably across a low-lying land bridge that connected Siberia and Alaska during the last glaciation. If, as seems apparent, no pre-*sapiens* groups settled on the steppe-tundra, who were the first *Homo sapiens* groups to venture into these deserted lands?

Dyukhtai
tradition
**?18,000 to
12,000 B.P.**

Soviet archaeologist Yuri Mochanov has identified a far-flung late Ice Age culture that once flourished in the Middle Aldan Valley, far north and east of Lake Baikal. He excavated Dyukhtai Cave, close to the river floodplain. There he found mammoth and musk-ox remains associated with large stone choppers, bifacially flaked stone points, burins, blades, and some "microblades." The cave deposits were much disturbed by freezing, thawing, and other natural phenomena, but Mochanov was able to date the occupation levels to between 14,000 and 12,000 years ago. Soon he found more Dyukhtai-like sites on the banks of the Aldan, sites that contained not only points and choppers but also highly distinctive "microblades" and the characteristic wedge-shaped cores from which they were formed (Figure 5.14). Mochanov (1978) grouped these locations and many others scattered across far northeast Asia into the

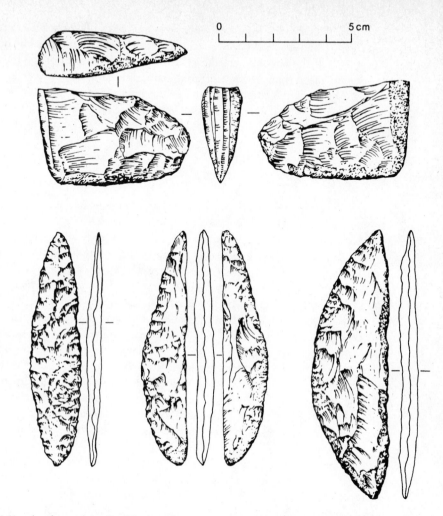

FIGURE 5.14   Artifacts of the Dyukhtai tradition. *Top,* four views of a wedge-shaped core, used to make tiny blades. *Bottom,* three bifacially flaked projectile heads. The wedge-shaped core is a characteristic artifact found on both sides of the Bering Strait in contexts of approximately 10,000 B.P. It is, of course, a by-product of the production of fine microblades.

Dyukhtai tradition and claimed that it flourished from as early as 35,000 years ago to the end of the Ice Age, some 12,000 years ago.

Since Mochanov's excavations, the chronology for the Dyukhtai tradition has been thrown in doubt. Many of his radiocarbon dates come from river terrace deposits that contain concentrations of animal bones and debris disturbed by seasonal freezing and thawing cycles in an environment of climatic extremes. In fact, the earliest well-dated Dyukhtai site is about 18,000 years old, with other locations dating to around 15,000 to 14,000 years ago.

The "microblades" and wedge-shaped cores of the Dyukhtai tradition are wide-spread throughout far northeastern Siberia after 14,000 years ago. The northernmost site at 71°N is the famous Berelekh cemetery near the mouth of the Indigirka River, famous for more than 140 refrigerated mammoth carcasses drowned during spring floods. The Dyukhtai site there contains the remains of two mammoths and dozens of arctic hares, as well as small "microblades" and some nondescript bone and ivory tools.

Bifaces, Microblades, and the First Americans

Clearly the Dyukhtai tradition owes little to the well-defined plains big-game hunting traditions of central and western Eurasia. It is marked by "microblades," also by bifaces and some stone spear points. Since this is the only known late Ice Age culture from extreme northeast Asia, it may be one of the cultural traditions from which the culture of the first Americans came. However, there are no signs of "microblades" in the earliest human cultures of the Americas, although these distinctive artifacts do appear later, in Alaska, by about 11,000 years ago.

The most important artifacts used by the first Americans were stone-tipped spears and stone knives, made from flakes of fine-grained stone struck off large cores, often themselves fashioned into bifaces so they could be carried around from one camp to the next. Such artifacts must also have been important on the steppe-tundra of northeast Asia long before "microblades" came into use. Unfortunately, we know so little of Dyukhtai that we can only guess that it may represent more than one cultural tradition, one using bifaces and stone-tipped spears, a technology that spread early into the Americas, and, perhaps, a later version that relied more heavily on "microblades."

The origins of "microblade" technology are somewhat better documented. We have put the word "microblade" in quotation marks up to this point, for this technology needs more precise definition. If there is one significant trend in human stoneworking technology during the late Ice Age, after 25,000 years ago, it is a progressive elaboration and diminution of stone tools. This trend is well documented in Africa, Europe, and southern Asia, and in the Far East as well. Chinese archaeologist Chen Chun (1989) believes that a primitive "microblade tradition" emerged in Asia quite soon after *Homo sapiens sapiens* appeared in the region. In time, microblade technologies were to dominate stone technology throughout northern China, Korea, Japan, and far to the northeast in Siberia and possibly extreme northwestern America as well.

Microblades are diminutive blades that were struck in the thousands off carefully prepared conical or wedge-shaped cores (Figure 5.14). By their very size, microblades were designed to be mounted in antler, bone, or wooden handles to serve as spear barbs, arrow points, or small knife or scraper blades. Microblade technology first appeared in northern China about 30,000 years ago and soon spread over an enormous area, even into tropical environments far to the south (Chung and Pei, 1986; Olsen, 1987). They were widely used in China by 20,000 years ago, in Japan by about the same time (A. Anderson, 1987; Reynolds and Barnes, 1984), and in Dyukhtai

Microblades

country by at least 18,000 years ago. With its microblades and wedge-shaped cores, then, the Dyukhtai tradition has links with well-established cultural traditions in northern China that were flourishing at least 30,000 years ago.

We can propose a scenario for what occurred. Perhaps microblade technology first developed in temperate Asia, in areas like the Gobi Desert and Mongolia, where people hunted over enormous areas. Here they needed a stone technology that was economical, easy to carry and manufacture, and yet capable of arming spears; and perhaps very late in the Ice Age, they needed bows and arrows with sharp, lethal points for taking game on the run in open country. In time, the same technology spread north and east into the harsh periglacial landscapes of Siberia, where small-scale and highly portable toolkits were highly adaptive, especially when used against such migratory periglacial animals as the reindeer. In time, small groups of microb-lade-using Dyukhtai people may have carried the same technology across the dry land of the Bering Strait into Alaska, perhaps after simpler biface and spear point toolkits had spread into the Americas (Fagan, 1990). This scenario receives some support from the dental researches of Christy Turner (1984). He has shown that the characteristic tooth features of native Americans include specialized attributes, such as shovel-shaped incisors, that are mirrored on northern Chinese skeletons dating to about 20,000 years ago. He calls this group of features "Sinodonty," features that are never found on European Stone Age teeth. Turner believes that the first Americans originated in northern China, reaching their new homeland through eastern Mongolia and northeast Siberia. With that momentous development, *Homo sapiens sapiens* eventually reached the Americas.

GUIDE TO FURTHER READING

Bahn, Paul, and Vertut, J. *Images of the Ice Age.* 1988. New York: Viking.
A superb general account of Paleolithic art, illustrated with magnificent photographs. Excellent on the motives behind the art.

Fagan, Brian M. 1990. *The Journey from Eden.* New York: Thames and Hudson.
A synthesis of the spread of Homo sapiens sapiens *for the general reader. Recommended for the beginning reader.*

Gamble, Clive. 1986. *The Palaeolithic Settlement of Europe.* Cambridge: Cambridge University Press.
Provocative essay on the European Stone Age. Essential for all serious students of the subject.

————, ed. 1990. *The World in 18,0000.* Cambridge: Cambridge University Press.
Specialist essays that review the Stone Age cultures of the Old World at the height of the last glaciation.

Pfeiffer, John. 1982. *The Creative Explosion.* New York: Harper and Row.
A wide-ranging popular treatment of early cave art for the general reader.

Soffer, Olga. 1985. *The Upper Palaeolithic of the Central Russian Plains.* New York: Academic Press.

> *An account of Mezhirich and other Upper Paleolithic sites. An exemplary essay on the Stone Age of the Ukraine.*

————, ed. 1987. *The Pleistocene Old World.* New York: Plenum Press.

> *A series of academic essays on late Ice Age cultures. Up-to-date and well-written specialist accounts.*

White, Randall. 1986. *Dark Caves, Bright Images.* New York: American Museum of Natural History.

> *Up-to-date, well-illustrated, and readable account of Cro-Magnons and their culture. Recommended for the general reader.*

CHAPTER 6 INTENSIFICATION AND COMPLEXITY

(BEFORE 12,000 YEARS AGO TO MODERN TIMES)

Preview

- The Holocene began after 12,000 years ago, about three millennia after the first glacial retreat at the end of the Weichsel glaciation. It was marked by major climatic changes, including major shifts in vegetational zones and rises in sea level.

- These environmental changes had profound effects on hunter-gatherer societies, who were often less mobile and more circumscribed in their responses to change. As a result, there was great localization of adaptations, more intensive exploitation of food resources, and, in many areas, a trend toward more sedentism and more complex hunter-gatherer societies.

- The trend toward localization is marked by a long-term diminution in tool-kits, and in more specialized artifacts for plant processing, fishing, and other activities. The bow and arrow came into widespread use.

- Mesolithic hunter-gatherers in Europe developed a broad range of responses to postglacial conditions. These responses included more intensive exploitation of food resources, and, in southern Scandinavia, the development of great social complexity.

- The stereotype of hunter-gatherers as mobile, band societies is now outmoded, for some, especially those in areas with abundant, seasonally predictable resources, achieved great social complexity.

- This complexity is marked by higher population densities, more intensive food exploitation, well-developed subsistence technology, exchange in exotic commodities and objects, and a degree of social ranking.

- The Levant provides a convincing scenario of emerging cultural and social complexity among the Natufian people, who were intensive foragers of cereals and nuts and expert gazelle hunters.

- Sedentism, emerging social ranking, and subsistence strategies aimed at reducing the risk of famine from environmental uncertainty in a sense preadapted hunter-gatherer societies in many areas for agriculture and animal domestication in later millennia.

Despite the harshness of late Ice Age climates, especially in northern latitudes, *Homo sapiens sapiens* adapted successfully to a remarkable range of global environments. The last 50,000 years of the Ice Age saw human settlement of the globe reach its premodern limits, with two major exceptions. The subarctic lands and eastern Arctic regions of North America were mantled by ice and were uninhabitable until long after the Ice Age (Chapter 7). The far offshore islands of the Pacific were not to be settled until much later, after the development of the twin-hulled offshore canoe and new navigational techniques that allowed seafarers to voyage far out of sight of land during the closing 5000 years of prehistoric times (Chapter 13) (see Figure 5.1).

All later developments in prehistory, including both a new focus on agriculture and animal domestication and on much more complex human societies, including the first civilizations, ultimately stem from this progressive settlement of the globe by *Homo sapiens sapiens* during the last glaciation (Fagan, 1990). The immediate consequences of the end of the Ice Age affected many hunter-gatherer societies scattered across the world when the great ice sheets finally retreated.

THE HOLOCENE (AFTER 12,000 YEARS AGO)

The world's climate remained extremely cold for about 4000 to 8000 years after the Stage 3 maximum of the Weichsel glaciation some 20,000 years ago. Global warming began in earnest after about 15,000 years ago. Then the great ice sheets began to retreat, at times very rapidly, ushering in postglacial Holocene times (Greek: *Holos* "recent"). Changes in ice distribution and sea levels were very irregular. Using core borings from coral beds off Barbados in the Caribbean, Richard Fairbanks (1988) has shown that sea levels at the glacial maximum were 396 feet (121 m) below modern levels. They rose by 66 feet (20 m) between about 17,000 and 12,500 years ago. Then there was an abrupt rise of 79 feet (24 m) in a mere 1000 years, a slight rise at about 11,000 years ago, and another 92-foot (28-m) rise after 10,500 years ago that culminated at 9500 years ago. These new levels led to major changes in world geography.

The Bering Strait was dry land as late as 15,000 years ago and ocean again by 10,000. By this time, sea levels were rising rapidly, especially in areas such as Scandinavia, where the earth's crust was depressed by the massive weight of retreating ice sheets. The North Sea was flooded, and Britain was separated from the continent by approximately 8000 years ago. Enormous areas of North America and northern Europe were exposed by retreating ice sheets and were available for human settlement for the first time in nearly 100,000 years.

We have hardly begun to understand the dramatic changes in temperature, rainfall, and vegetation that occurred during the early millennia of the Holocene, between about 15,000 and 7000 years ago. The most striking transformations took place in northern latitudes, in areas like western and central Europe, and in regions of North America contiguous to the great ice sheets. During the height of the Weichsel glaciation, for example, central Europe had been treeless periglacial tundra, and the Baltic Sea did not exist. Only 5000 years after the Scandinavian ice sheet began retreating, forests covered most of Europe and sparse human populations had settled on the shores of a newly exposed northern sea.

Throughout the world, game populations changed radically in the millennia after the Ice Age. By 12,000 years ago, the familiar mammoth and woolly rhinoceros hunted by the Cro-Magnons were extinct in central and western Europe, as were steppe bison and reindeer, all replaced by forest animals like the red and roe deer. In North America, mammoths, mastodons, camelids, and many other large animal species vanished abruptly about 11,000 years ago (Martin and Klein, 1984). Even in tropical Africa, the rich and diverse savanna faunas suffered losses at the end of the Ice Age. The extent to which humans were responsible for the rapid extinction of late Ice Age animals is a matter of great, and unresolved, controversy.

There were major and highly significant vegetational changes in warmer latitudes, too. For much of the Weichsel maximum, for example, the Sahara Desert had been as arid as it is today, but rainfall patterns changed at the end of the Ice Age, bringing large, shallow lakes and short grasslands to the desert. As late as 8000 years ago, hunter-gatherer populations flourished in the heart of the Sahara, in areas that are now arid wilderness. In the Near East, the late Ice Age climate of the Tauros and Zagros mountains was so cold and dry that no trees grew in the uplands. After about 11,000 years ago, new plant assemblages immigrated into the now warmer highlands, among them wild cereal grasses that were to become the ancestors of domesticated crops. These cereals had long been native to the region, having survived the late Ice Age in sheltered locales (H. Wright, 1977). With the onset of warmer conditions, their distribution expanded greatly, making them accessible to many more hunter-gatherer bands distributed over a vast area. In Mexico, the climate of 20,000 years ago was drier and colder than today. At the end of the Ice Age temperatures rose, bringing a rich forest of cacti and legume trees to the mountain valleys of Puebla and Oaxaca. This thorn-scrub-cactus forest included many wild ancestors of domesticated plants, including the maguey; squash; bean; and teosinte, the wild grass that was probably the ancestor of domesticated maize.

These and other Holocene climatic changes had profound effects in hunter-gatherer societies throughout the world, especially on the intensity of the food quest and complexity of their societies. Why had such changes not occurred earlier in prehistory? There had been climatic changes of similar, if not even greater, magnitude in early millennia, say during the early part of the last interglacial, some 128,000 years ago. The reason may be population density. Then, human populations were much smaller and a great deal of the world was uninhabited. It was possible for human populations living in large hunting territories to move around freely, to adapt to new circumstances by shifting their homeland, even over large distances. This ability enabled them to develop highly flexible survival strategies that took account of the constant fluctuations in food availability. If, for example, an African band experienced two dry years in a row, it could move away or fall back on less nutritious edible foods, perhaps species that required more energy to harvest.

By 15,000 years ago, circumstances were very different. The world's hunter-gatherer population was probably approaching about 10 million people (Hassan, 1981). The carrying capacity of the world's many environments still exceeded that of the human population, largely because humans were becoming more efficient in their exploitation of a broad spectrum of food resources. After 15,000, the population curve approached that of carrying capacity (Figure 6.1). This development might have set off behavioral changes resulting from restricted mobility and greater competition. Notable among them would have been a necessity to solve problems locally rather than just moving away from them. People would have tended to exploit a wider

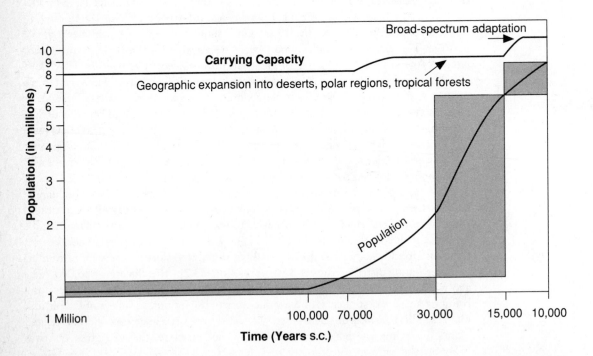

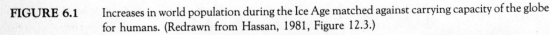

FIGURE 6.1   Increases in world population during the Ice Age matched against carrying capacity of the globe for humans. (Redrawn from Hassan, 1981, Figure 12.3.)

range of local resources, both to avert starvation and to protect themselves from food shortages caused by short-term droughts and other unpredictable changes.

In a sense, the world was full, or at least occupied sparsely by people who lived off its game, plant, and other food resources. *Homo sapiens sapiens* had settled in periglacial regions, in tropical rain forests, on offshore islands, and in the Americas. There were sparse hunter-gatherer populations throughout the world, many of them living in areas such as central Australia, for example, where carrying capacities of individual territories were very low indeed. Human populations had risen considerably, too, especially in areas with diverse and seasonally predictable food resources. Even in sparsely inhabited environments, hunting territories were more confined. There was less room to move around; there were often more mouths to feed; and new adaptive strategies were needed, strategies aimed at more efficient and productive exploitation of the environment. As a result of these new strategies, hunter-gatherer societies underwent profound changes, and in some areas acquired much greater complexity (Price and Brown, 1985).

COPING WITH ENVIRONMENTAL VARIATION

Increasingly during the late Ice Age and more frequently in Holocene times, prehistoric hunter-gatherer populations were confronted with new challenges, challenges created both by major climatic changes at the end of the Pleistocene and by local population growth. Everywhere, much more circumscribed hunter-gatherers were forced to improve their strategies for coping with local environmental variations, both in predictable seasonal resources and in unpredictable shifts in such phenomena as rainfall patterns or game migration routes. This shift can be seen clearly in the Americas. As we shall see in Chapter 7, the first Americans of 12,000 years ago were small in numbers, highly mobile, and sparsely distributed on the ground. They subsisted in part off Ice Age big game, which became extinct very rapidly after 11,000 years ago. The archaeological record now shows a much greater diversity of local adaptations over the millennia, as thousands of isolated hunter-gatherer groups became more and more restricted in their movements. The change is especially marked in areas of exceptional resource diversity like the Pacific Northwest coast, the southern California coast, and the fertile river valleys of the southern Midwest and southeastern United States. In all these areas, hunter-gatherer populations became more sedentary; developed often highly specialized technologies for hunting, foraging, or fishing; and in the process, developed some form of social ranking.

In strictly archaeological terms, the trend toward greater localization is reflected in several long-term, widespread technological changes that appear throughout the world in the late Ice Age in early Holocene times. In some areas, such as the North American Arctic, parts of Latin America, and southern Africa, the basic technologies developed at the end of the Ice Age were still in use into the nineteenth century A.D. For example, the San hunter-gatherers of the Kalahari Desert in southern Africa used wood and bone-tipped arrows and wooden digging sticks identical in design to those used by prehistoric hunter-gatherers in the same general area more than 3000 years earlier—and the artifacts from such sites were, in turn, used widely throughout the central and southern African savanna as early as 10,000 years ago. They also appear in prehistoric San rock art (Figure 6.2). The highly specialized and very effective salmon fishing technologies used by Northwest coast Indians to exploit seasonal salmon runs at European contact in the eighteenth century A.D. were in use at least 2000 years earlier, and probably long before (Figure 6.3).

The intensification of hunting and gathering was marked by two long-term technological trends that went hand in hand. The first was the gradual downsizing of stone artifacts and the perishable antler, bone, and wood toolkit that went with them. The second was the development of highly efficient, often very specialized sets of hunting weapons or food-processing implements designed for intensive exploitation of specific food resources such as reindeer, sea mammals, birds, or acorns.

The trend toward diminution in stone technology began during the late Ice Age and coincides in general terms with the last glacial maximum of about 20,000 years ago. Spear barbs and knife blades became smaller, more lightweight, as if the hunters were relying more heavily on spear-throwers for propulsion velocity. It was sometime during the late Ice Age, too, that the bow and arrow came into use, a weapon with many advantages, among them greater accuracy, enhanced portability, and the ability to fire off several missiles within a very short space of time. The bow was also far more versatile than the spear, for the hunters could carry many more lightweight, lethal

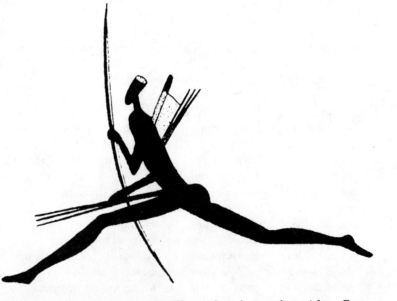

FIGURE 6.2   San hunter with weapons from Ho Khotso, Lesotho, southern Africa. From a late Stone Age painting colored purple-red. The figure is approximately 8 inches (21 cm) high.

FIGURE 6.3   Salmon fishing in the Pacific Northwest. Nineteenth-century painting by Paul Kane.

points with them in a small quiver, arrows that could be brought into use in a few moments. Under these circumstances, the chances of a kill were greatly enhanced (Figure 6.4).

We do not know exactly when the bow and arrow first came into use, but there is a good reason to believe that this versatile hunting weapon was in Europe by 15,000 years ago and perhaps in Africa and the Near East at about the same time. In contrast, it reached the Americas very much later, in some areas as late as 200 B.C. As early as 30,000 years ago, and even more intensively after 15,000 years ago, stone tool technologies were becoming more and more standardized and more and more oriented toward the production of parts of composite tools, especially small arrow and knife barbs, scrapers, and awls. In Europe and the Near East, this technology involved the production of thousands of small microliths, geometrically shaped barbs used on all manner of weapons (Figure 6.5). (The term *microlith* comes from the Greek *micros,* "small," and *lithos,* "stone.") These standardized artifacts were made by striking small bladelets off a conical core, then notching and snapping off the thicker end to form a small microlith. Microlith-tipped and barbed wooden arrows have been found intact in Danish swamps, environments where they were used to hunt forest game, rodents, and birds for many centuries.

The diminution of stone technology reflected a much greater emphasis on specialized but versatile toolkits that were modified to reflect local needs. The early Holocene saw a much greater localization of artifacts of all kinds, a development reflected in a proliferation of new archaeological "cultures"; these, in fact, reflected a world in which movement was more circumscribed, in which thousands of small bands and occasionally larger population groups adapted to constant local environ-

FIGURE 6.4   Eskimo demonstrating a sinew-backed bow and ivory-tipped arrow at Chicago's Columbian Exposition in 1893.

mental variation. This localization is well documented in areas like Europe, Australia, the Near East, and the North American Great Basin, as well as by Kent Flannery's important work on a microband who visited Guilá Naquitz cave, Mexico, between about 10,750 and 8670 years ago (Flannery et al., 1986) (see Figure 2.4). As Flannery has eloquently pointed out, the new local toolkits were part of a process whereby humans coped not only with long-term climatic change but also with the constant uncertainties of local climates. "Humans are well suited to the working out of resilient strategies for environmental variability," Flannery writes, "since they possess multi-generational memory and have unique methods for exchanging information and establishing cooperative relationships over long periods."

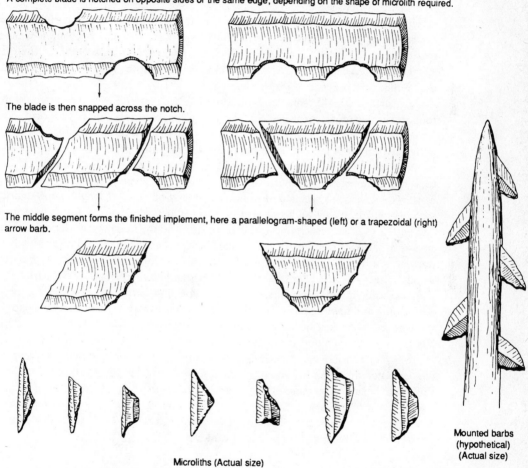

A complete blade is notched on opposite sides or the same edge, depending on the shape of microlith required.

The blade is then snapped across the notch.

The middle segment forms the finished implement, here a parallelogram-shaped (left) or a trapezoidal (right) arrow barb.

Microliths (Actual size)

Mounted barbs (hypothetical) (Actual size)

FIGURE 6.5   Microliths. Stages in manufacturing a microlith, a small arrow barb, or similar implement made by notching a blade and snapping off its base after the implement is formed.

The new subsistence strategies often involved highly intensive exploitation of locally abundant and predictable resources such as salmon or nuts. Such intensive exploitation was adaptive in environments where seasonal phenomena such as salmon runs, caribou migrations, or hickory harvests required not only the harvesting of enormous quantities of food in a short time but also their processing and storage for later use. Storage technology now assumed a new and pressing importance; thousands of fish were dried on racks in the sun or in front of fires, and the nut and wild cereal harvest was placed in basket- or clay-lined pits for later consumption. There was nothing new in the notion of storage; much earlier in prehistory, big-game hunters, for example, dried meat and pounded it up to make food on the march. What was new, however, was the notion of large-scale storage in more sedentary settlements, where mobility was no longer a viable strategy. By using storage and by careful seasonal "mapping" of game, plant, and aquatic resources, early Holocene hunter-gatherers compensated for periodic food shortages caused by short-term climatic change and seasonal fluctuations. At the same time, they broadened their diet to include foods that were at a lower trophic level, another way of ensuring fallback in the diet in the event of staple shortages.

As early as 20,000 years ago, and more markedly after 15,000 years ago, human toolkits display much greater specialization and elaboration. We have already mentioned the development of the needle as a catalyst for layered, tailored clothing in periglacial environments, and both the Magdalenians and the Ukraine big-game hunters used a wide variety of specialized, and sometimes elaborate, antler and bone tools in the chase and in domestic life (Chapter 5). Holocene hunter-gatherer societies worldwide developed specialized toolkits for many purposes. Many North American societies relied heavily on seeds and nuts. They developed many forms of grinders and pestles to process such harvests (Figure 6.6), and the rich organic deposits of such sites as the Hoko River and Ozette on the Olympic Peninsula in the Pacific Northwest document a highly effective halibut-fishing and whale-hunting technology based on wood, bone, slate, and fiber (Figure 6.7) (Croes and Hackenberger, 1987; Kirk, 1975). Canoes, bone-tipped fish spears, and wooden birding arrows were part of the specialized fishing and fowling toolkit of Holocene groups in northern Europe. Perhaps the ultimate in specialized hunting technology for sea mammals comes from the Bering Sea coasts of Alaska and the Thule culture of the Canadian Arctic (Chapter 7).

More circumscribed territories, less mobility, rising local population, and new strategies for dealing with seasonal and unpredictable environmental variations—these problems were common to postglacial hunter-gatherer societies throughout the world. A few of these societies, especially those living in areas with rich and diverse food resources that included fish or sea mammals, achieved a high degree of social complexity, with signs of some social ranking.

COPING WITH ENVIRONMENTAL UNCERTAINTY: MESOLITHIC HUNTER-GATHERERS IN EUROPE

European
Mesolithic
10,000 to 5500
B.P.

An excellent example of how late Ice Age hunter-gatherers adapted to global warming comes from northwestern Europe, where Mesolithic forest and coastal hunter-gatherers replaced tundra reindeer hunters after 13,000 years ago. [*Mesolithic* refers to the period of postglacial times in Europe that preceded the introduction of farming (J. G. D. Clark, 1975, 1979).] The European Mesolithic spans about 4500 years, from

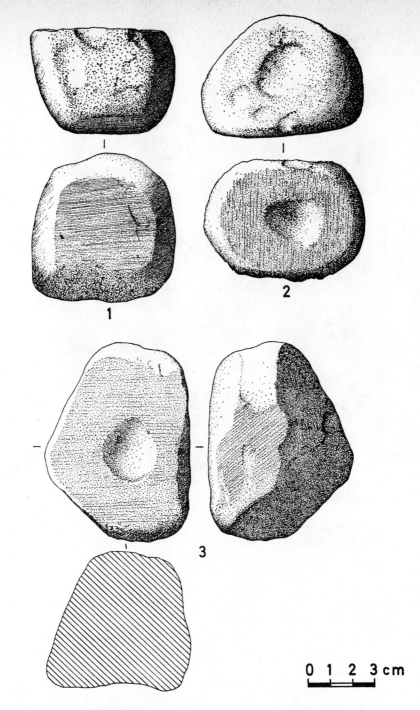

FIGURE 6.6   Pounders used for processing wild vegetable foods from the Gwisho late Stone Age hunting settlement Zambia, c. 3500 years old. The peck marks served to hold the grains.

FIGURE 6.7   Ancient wooden halibut hook and modern replica used for fishing from Hoko River Site, Olympia Peninsula, Washington.

about 10,000 years ago until the beginnings of farming in northwest Europe about 5500 years ago (Figure 6.8).

The environmental changes in Europe after 15,000 years ago were so dramatic that the Magdalenian and other late Ice Age cultures vanished relatively quickly. The traditional view held that Europe was now populated by impoverished Meso-lithic hunters and gatherers who had lost much of their capacity for economic and social relations (for discussion, see Rowley-Conwy, 1986). This notion of a cultural hiatus has crumbled in the face of recent sophisticated ecological researches. In-stead of impoverished environments, each change in postglacial forest composition probably brought greater ecological productivity. A range of forest ungulates such as red and roe deer replaced the migratory reindeer that were so important in Ice Age times. Plant foods such as nuts assumed much greater importance in Meso-

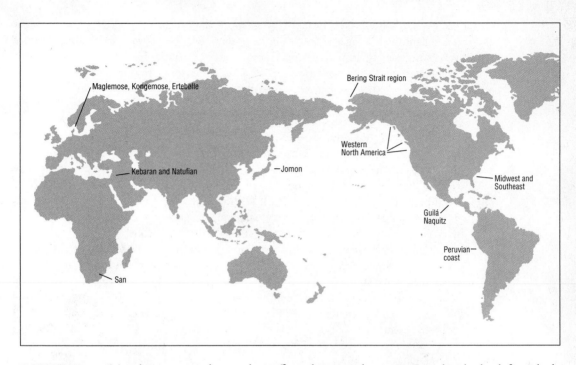

FIGURE 6.8   Map showing general areas where affluent hunter-gatherers mentioned in this book flourished.

lithic life. These food sources may have contributed to an increase in Mesolithic populations. Coasts, estuaries, and lakes were highly productive, especially with such seasonal resources as salmon, water birds, and sea mammals, many of them relying on seasonal plankton production in the oceans. Many of these aquatic foods could be taken and stored, especially by people who occupied relatively permanent encampments nearby. Thus, larger populations were possible in some areas among people who relied on seasonal resources and used such nonseasonal foods as shellfish to "plug" the gaps (Rowley-Conwy, 1986). Some of these more sedentary groups enjoyed a bounty of food sources and a complexity of life that has been called "affluent foraging."

Were all European Mesolithic groups affluent foragers? The interplay of different resources varied dramatically throughout Europe, with its seasonal climates and productive environments. This was not a hostile environment peopled by only minimally complex hunter-gatherer bands but one where a great variety of adaptations was possible. At least two general models have been proposed for Mesolithic Europe:

- Lower latitudes supported somewhat generalized environments, where highly mobile bands exploited evenly dispersed animal and plant resources, shifting camp regularly as local resources were exhausted (Binford, 1980).

- Higher-latitude environments were more uneven in productivity and resource reliability, having few species in large numbers. These were specialized environments, where human groups moved less often and frequently directed their moves toward the exploitation of a single seasonal resource such as caribou. Larger numbers of people sometimes congregated for seasonal hunts.

These are, of course, by no means the only models for Mesolithic life that could be put forward, but they serve to remind us that this was a period when European populations enjoyed a wide range of adaptations, from peoples with highly mobile lifeways to permanently settled, "affluent" peoples who dwelt in large villages or base camps, such as are found in northwest Europe and by the Iron Gates area of the Danube River (Rowley-Conwy, 1986). Without question, the Mesolithic was a period of broad variation in economic and social life, with some intensification of the food quest where uncertain environmental conditions dictated it.

Clive Gamble (1986a) points out that the adaptive trends seen in the European Mesolithic are not particularly innovative; indeed, most of them have their roots in a much earlier restructuring of the organization and use of resources with the arrival of modern humans in temperate latitudes some 35,000 years ago. The Upper Paleolithic saw much greater exploitation of regional resources and an enhanced ability to adapt to extremes of both glacial and fully interglacial climates. This restructuring gave Europeans the ability to solve the problems of exploiting not just a few resources but many different ones at once. This ability became vital at the end of the Ice Age, when food management strategies were able to cope with extremely varied combinations of food resources. These strategies included some elements that were of critical importance when people began to grow crops and tame animals: adaptations that were attuned to the scheduling of seasonal activities connected with growing and harvesting seasons and systems of information sharing. The Mesolithic hunters' schedule was comprehensive and flexible enough to cope with anything and could easily accommodate strategies that relied on deliberate cultivation of the soil or careful animal husbandry.

Efficient food management strategies involved more effective technology, too—more diverse toolkits for hunting forest animals and exploiting coastal resources such as sea mammals and shallow-water fish. The Mesolithic peoples who lived along the shores of the newly emerging Baltic Sea developed an astonishing range of fish spears, nets, harpoons, and traps, many of them preserved in waterlogged sites. Spears and arrows were tipped with tiny stone, bone, or antler barbs. Ground-edged tools were used for woodworking and processing forest plants. Large canoes, some of them dugouts hollowed from tree trunks, were in evidence. We know that Stone Age people were crossing open water as early as 12,000 years ago, for miners were visiting the island of Melos in the Mediterranean to collect obsidian that was traded far and wide (Torrance, 1986).

Many Mesolithic groups lived in larger, more permanent settlements, a number of them located on strategic bays or near lakes or rivers. Some locations were probably used year-round or certainly for many months, anchored by abundant aquatic resources nearby. There were smaller camps and specialist activity areas, too. Everything points to greater internal differentiation in society and to more intensive subsistence activities. Nuts and shellfish became far more important, and hunters took a far wider range of game than their Ice Age predecessors. It was not the dietary staples but merely the diversity of exploited food resources that changed.

Perhaps the most profound changes were those in population densities and social organization, both notoriously difficult phenomena to identify in the archaeological record. Grahame Clark (1979) has identified three major "social territories" at the end of the Upper Paleolithic, between the Netherlands, Poland, and southern Sweden. Three distinct cultures (Ahrensburgian, Swiderian, and Bromme) each covered territories of about 38,610 square miles (100,000 sq. km). As the postglacial wore on, these territories were rapidly reduced in size. By 8000 years ago, there were at least 15 territories in this same area, identified by different artifact styles or distributions of raw materials. Each of these zones was about 5791 to 7722 square miles (15,000 to 20,000 sq. km) in extent. This pattern may reflect major changes in the regional distribution, density, and social organization of Mesolithic populations. Douglas Price (1983) points out that as these changes were taking place, new artifact forms and presumably other innovations were spreading across wide areas of Europe. Among them was a characteristic trapeze-shaped microlith, widely used as an arrow barb by later Mesolithic peoples, that appeared all over the continent about 8000 years ago, perhaps somewhat earlier in southeast Europe (J. G. D. Clark, 1958). The Mesolithic ended with the rapid spread of agricultural economies into southeast Europe about 8000 years ago. From there they spread sporadically into central Europe by 6500 years ago and to the northwest after 5500 years ago.

The European Mesolithic testifies to a continuity in human culture from Ice Age times, but this continuity was based on continuous adjustment to changing postglacial environments. In time, the same Mesolithic societies readapted to the warmest millennia of postglacial times not only by shifting their hunting and foraging methods but also by taking up new subsistence practices, often within the context of their existing society (Price, 1983).

Mesolithic Complexity in Scandinavia

This continuity is well documented from waterlogged Mesolithic sites in Britain and Scandinavia, where three broad subdivisions of the northern Mesolithic are known (Price, 1985).

Maglemose
9500 to 7700
B.P.

The Maglemose Period (9500 to 7700 Years Ago)

The Maglemose was a time of seasonal exploitation of rivers and lakes, combined with terrestrial hunting and foraging. Inland late spring and early summer settlements are represented by the Ulkestrup site in Denmark, where the people lived in large huts with bark and wood floors on a peat island in a swamp by a lake. One hut lay close to poles where canoes were once moored. A large wooden paddle lay nearby. The Maglemose people fished with bone and antler barbed points; trapped birds; and hunted such animals as red deer, wild ox, and pig. In fall, the bands foraged for hazelnuts and other edible plant foods, killing elk and other game in winter, when apparently fishing was less important.

Kongemose
7700 to 6600
B.P.

The Kongemose Period (7700 to 6600 Years Ago)

Kongemose sites are mainly on Baltic Sea coasts, along bays and near lagoons, where the people exploited both marine and terrestrial resources. Many Kongemose sites are somewhat larger than Maglemose ones; among the better known is the now-submerged Segebro settlement in brackish water near the southwest Swedish coast. This settlement covered 164 by 82 feet (50 by 25 m) and was occupied year-round, but mainly in spring and summer. Carbon isotope analyses of human bones from Segebro show that fish and sea mammals constituted most of the diet, with no fewer than 66 species of animals found in the site. Not only freshwater and saltwater fish but also red deer, elk, boars, and seals were commonplace. Like the Maglemose people, Kongemose hunter-gatherers used small stone microlithic arrow barbs as well as artifacts and weapons of bone, antler, and wood.

Ertebølle
6600 to 5200
B.P.

The Ertebølle Period (6600 to 5200 Years Ago)

Ertebølle was the culmination of Mesolithic culture in southern Scandinavia (Price, 1983, 1987). By this time, the Scandinavians were occupying many coastal settlements year-round, subsisting off a very wide range of food resources indeed. These included forest game and waterfowl, shellfish, sea mammals, and both shallow- and deep-water fish. There were smaller, seasonal coastal sites, too, many for specific activities such as deep-water fishing, sealing, or hunting of migratory birds. The Aggersund site in Denmark was occupied for a short period in the autumn, when the inhabitants collected oysters and hunted some game, especially migratory swans (Price, 1985).

Inland, the Ertebølle people occupied both large and small summer and winter settlements. The Ringkloster site, also in Denmark, was occupied some 5500 years ago. The inhabitants concentrated on hunting wild boars but also collected nuts and trapped pine martens. Skinned carcasses are almost intact, for the hunters were after pelts.

Ertebølle technology was far more elaborate than that of its Mesolithic predecessors; a wide variety of antler, bone, and wood tools for specialized purposes such as fowling and sea mammal hunting were developed, including dugout canoes up to 32.8 feet (10 m) long.

With sedentary settlement comes evidence of greater social complexity. Some

Ertebølle communities buried their dead in cemeteries, with the bodies placed in various positions and also with dog interments. The Vedbaek Bogebakken cemetery in Denmark dates to about 6000 years ago and contains the graves of at least 22 people of different ages. Everyone was buried in an extended position, at least three people after injury or a violent death. Men and women were deposited with different grave goods, older people with red deer antlers. Other Ertebølle cemeteries from Denmark contain evidence of violent death; some people had projectile points in their ribs. There are also traces of cannibalism (Price, 1985). One 40-year-old man buried at Skateholm was deposited in a wooden coffin, his body sprinkled with red ocher and associated with an antler harpoon, ground stone axes, and other tools.

The trend toward more sedentary settlement, the cemeteries, and occasional social differentiation revealed by elaborate burials are all reflections of an "intensification" among these relatively "affluent" hunter-gatherers of 5000 years ago. Mesolithic societies intensified the food quest by exploiting many more marine species, making productive use of migratory waterfowl and their breeding grounds, and collecting shellfish in enormous numbers. This intensification is also reflected in a much more elaborate and diverse technology, more exchange of goods and materials between neighbors, greater variety in settlement types, and a slowly rising population throughout southern Scandinavia. These phenomena may, in part, be a reflection of rising sea levels throughout the Mesolithic, inundations that flooded many cherished territories. There are signs, too, of regional variations in artifact forms and styles, of cultural differences between people living in carefully delineated territories and competing for resources (Price, 1985).

Mesolithic cultures are much less well defined elsewhere in Europe, partly because the climatic changes were less extreme than in southern Scandinavia and because there were fewer opportunities for coastal adaptation. In many areas, settlement was confined to lakeside and riverside locations, widely separated from one another by dense forests. Many Mesolithic sites were located on ecotones (transitional zones between different environments) so that the inhabitants could return to a central base location, where for much of the year they lived close to predictable resources such as lake fish. However, they would exploit both forest game and other seasonal resources from satellite camps. In central Europe, for example, Michael Jochim (1976) believes that some groups lived during the winter in camps along the Danube, moving to summer encampments on the shores of neighboring lakes. In many areas like Spain, there appears to have been intensified exploitation of marine and forest resources. There was a trend nearly everywhere to greater variety in the diet, with more attention being paid to less obvious foods and to those, like shellfish, that require more complex processing methods than game and other such resources.

Thus, in parts of Europe, there was a long-term trend among hunter-gatherer societies toward more extensive exploitation of food resources, often within the context of a strategy that sought ways to minimize the impact of environmental uncertainty. In more favored areas such as southern Scandinavia, some such societies achieved a level of nascent social complexity that was to become commonplace among later farming peoples. When farming did come to Europe, this preadaptation was an important catalyst for rapid economic and social change (Chapter 11).

HUNTER-GATHERER COMPLEXITY

"Hunter-gatherers move around a lot and live in small groups." This statement has been a universal label for hunter-gatherer societies ancient and modern for a generation (Lee and DeVore, 1976). It paints a picture of hunter-gatherers in prefarming times who lived in small, temporary camps; were constantly on the move; and possessed a highly portable technology and flexible social system. These models were based in large part on anthropological researches among living societies like the !Kung San of the Kalahari Desert in southern Africa or the Inuit of the Canadian Arctic. Most of them are peoples living in areas of the world, like tropical rain forests, Arctic regions, or semideserts, where agriculture is an impossibility. Only a handful of hunter-gatherer societies, peoples like the Ainu of Japan or the Northwest coast Indians, enjoyed more complex adaptations at the time of European contact around the eighteenth century A.D. Generalizations about highly mobile, small-scale hunter-gatherer societies took little account of the great diversity among the many hunting and foraging societies that once existed on earth. This diversity, known almost entirely from archaeological researches, developed during the late Ice Age and Holocene. Above all, the archaeological record of the world of 15,000 to 6000 years ago reveals a global trend toward great complexity in hunter-gatherer societies in well-defined regions as widely separated as northern Europe, southern Africa, the Midwest, and coastal Peru.

Conditions for Greater Complexity

Complex hunter-gatherer societies did not appear everywhere, but they occurred in a remarkable variety of environments, from fertile river valleys to coastal deserts. Whatever the environment, however, certain general conditions were necessary. First, population movements had to be limited by either geography or the presence of neighbors. Thus, one could not move away from resource shortages; solutions had to be found on the spot. Second, resources had to be abundant and predictable in their seasonal appearance. Small, numerous organisms with high reproductive rates played an especially important role in intensifying hunting and gathering. Such organisms include fish, shellfish, nuts, and seeds (Hayden, 1981), species that are available in abundance and seldom exhausted. Third, population growth might reach a point at which food shortages occur and there is an imbalance between people and their food supply. Again, a solution was to intensify the food quest, an intensification that might result in a more complex society.

Attributes of Greater Complexity

What features distinguish a more complex hunter-gatherer society from its less elaborate neighbors? The following appear to be of fundamental importance:

- Higher than normal population, concentrated in relatively small and restricted territories, such as individual river valleys, where movement is circumscribed by either geography or neighbors.

- A more intensive, more diversified, and more specialized food quest. Selected species such as nuts and seeds become more important, and foods that were not exploited previously because they required more effort are taken into the diet. In some cases, people will deliberately plant wild plants to ensure an adequate harvest.

- A system of food storage and preservation.

- Permanent and nearly permanent settlements, often base camps of much greater size than in earlier times. Settlements are often linear, distributed along, say, river banks; contain different forms of structures; and are often associated with burial grounds, which may serve as territorial boundaries.

- Highly developed hunting, fishing, or plant-processing equipment.

- Division of labor not only by sex and age but also by activity, such as whale hunting or a craft specialty like canoe building.

- Some form of simple social ranking, probably based on lineages or other kin groupings, marked by differences in wealth, diet, and burial customs.

- Often quite intensive exchange in exotic objects and raw materials with neighboring groups.

- More elaborate ritual beliefs and ceremonial life.

Debates About Social Complexity

We do not know when the first more complex hunter-gatherer societies appeared, but it seems likely that at least some late Ice Age societies enjoyed some level of complexity. Possible candidates may include the Magdalenians of southwestern France and northern Spain as well as the plains hunters, with their mammoth-bone houses, who lived in the river valleys of the Ukraine 18,000 years ago (see Chapter 5). Complexity among hunter-gatherer societies became widespread after the Ice Age, especially in areas where freshwater or marine fish, shellfish, or sea mammals were available in abundance. Aquatic resources have the advantage of being both relatively plentiful and predictable, so much so that there are strong incentives for people to adopt sedentary lifeways along rivers and at lake and ocean shores. However, the full potential of marine and freshwater resources was only realized in a relatively few areas of the world, and then within the past 10,000 years.

The debates about social complexity among hunter-gatherers revolve around two opposing viewpoints. The first sees the oceans as a kind of "Garden of Eden" (Binford, 1983). Proponents of this theory point to the enormous abundance of shellfish in many areas of the world and to the great productivity of many estuaries and coastal waters easily exploited by shore-dwelling fisherfolk. This abundance allowed societies to become sedentary and to maintain population densities (Fladmark, 1978; Holmes, 1987; Moseley, 1975a).

In contrast, another group of archaeologists, many of them studying post-Ice Age hunter-gatherers in Europe, argue that aquatic resources were a strategy of last resort, a response to population pressure and shortages of terrestrial resources such as game and plant foods (Bailey, 1978; Gamble, 1986b). These authorities assume that marine and freshwater resources, no matter how productive, are more labor intensive to harvest and are less nutritionally valuable than food sources on land.

David Yesner (1987) has recently taken a somewhat different perspective. He argues that the shift to the exploitation of aquatic resources was the result of decisions made in periods of rapid environmental change, when population pressure was causing food shortages. The "optimal" strategy for people under these circumstances would be to turn to a resource that does involve more work and is, perhaps, as productive as big game.

All of these viewpoints assume, however, that maritime resources played a key role in the emergence of social complexity among Stone Age hunter-gatherers. The debate is unresolved, for we do not know exactly how decisive marine or riverine resources were in allowing dense populations and sedentary living, both essential prerequisites for social complexity. Nor do we know whether we can make comparisons between the elaborate and socially complex Northwest coast Indian cultures that flourished a few centuries ago and early Holocene hunter-gatherer groups living thousands of years earlier in prehistory.

HUNTER-GATHERER SOCIETIES IN THE
LEVANT

The Near East has provided a fascinating picture of emerging social and cultural complexity among hunter-gatherers at the end of the Ice Age. Between 14,000 and 10,000 years ago, the simple hunter-gatherer societies of the Levant, the coastal zone of Israel and Syria, gave way to more complex hunting and gathering societies and eventually to farmers (for a site map, see Figure 10.1). For years, scientists have discussed the origins of agriculture in the Near East, believing it to be a more radical transformation in human life than almost any other development in prehistory (see Chapter 9). In fact, recent researches have suggested that the earlier hunter-gatherer transition may have been much more profound.

The Levant was populated 14,000 years ago by small and highly mobile hunter-gatherer bands, subsumed under the general cultural name of Kebaran. Kebaran sites, marked by thousands of small, geometric microliths, occur not only in wooded country but also in the steppe and desert of the Negev and Sinai (Henry, 1989). The Kebarans are found in a wide variety of environments, which may account for the great variation in their toolkits (Figure 6.9). Everything points to the Kebarans having enjoyed a simple hunter-gatherer strategy, which placed a high premium on mobility (Bar-Yosef, 1987). In some areas, the people may have dispersed to the uplands in summer, moving into caves and rock shelters near lowland lakes in the winter. Apparently, plant foods were not overwhelmingly important, and the Kebaran toolkit lacks the specialized grinders and pounders found in later cultures, except at lower elevations, where some wild cereal grasses grew.

By about 11,000 years ago, warming temperatures throughout the Near East brought significant environmental and vegetational changes. During the late Ice Age, warmth-loving plants like wild emmer wheat and barley, oaks, almonds, and pistachio trees were restricted to refuge areas lying below modern sea level. These sandy-soiled areas would have given only poor yields of wild cereals. As early Holocene temperatures rose, these plant and tree species colonized higher country, where clayey soils produced much higher yields (Henry, 1989). New, denser cereal stands were now much more resistant to short-term climatic change and also harvestable over a longer period of time each year. After 11,000 years ago, many hunter-gatherer sites on higher ground contain ground stone tools—pestles and mortars, implements used to process seed harvests.

These abundant cereal and nut resources within the Mediterranean hill zone stimulated the development of more intensive foraging strategies, more sedentary settlement, and rapid territorial expansion until the most favored territories were filled. The emergence of these more plentiful plant resources coincided with the emergence of the Natufian culture from the earlier Kebaran, a culture that expanded

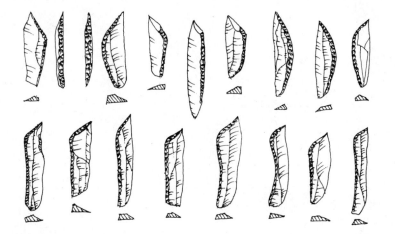

FIGURE 6.9   Geometric Kebaran microliths.

rapidly to the edges of the Mediterranean zone within about 1500 years, during a brief cycle of wetter climate that ended about 11,000 years ago.

The Natufians used a more complex hunting and foraging strategy than the Kebarans. They exploited wild emmer and barley intensively, as well as acorn, almond, and pistachio, all highly productive resources that were easily stored. The new subsistence strategies encouraged more sedentary lifeways and the development of much larger settlements, averaging about 7500 sq feet (700 sq. m) in area. These villages, which contained semisubterranean houses, storage pits, and pavements, were associated with nearby small, transitory camps, where food was collected and processed (Figure 6.10). The Natufian toolkit contains all manner of specialized plant-processing tools, including querns, grinding slabs, pestles, mortars, and bone sickles with flint blades (Figure 6.11). These bear a characteristic "sickle gloss" caused by the silica in cereal grass stalks.

Natufian hamlets are confined to the Mediterranean hill zone, where wild cereals and nut-bearing trees had their natural habitat. The larger sites are close to the boundaries between the coastal plains or grassland valleys and the hill zone.

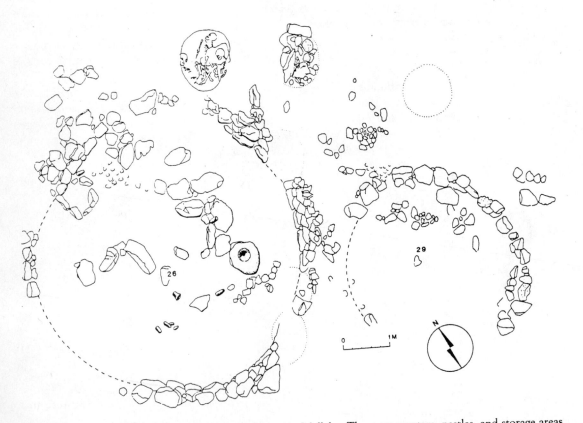

FIGURE 6.10   Natufian house foundations from Ain Mallaha. There are mortars, pestles, and storage areas in structure 26, and a group of burials outside the hut.

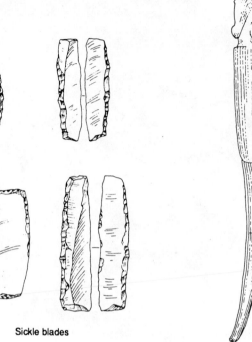

Sickle blades

Sickle handle

FIGURE 6.11   Natufian bone-handled sickle and flint blades.

Some were placed strategically to take advantage of good toolmaking stone. Such settlements enabled the Natufians to exploit spring cereal crops, fall nut harvests, and the game that flourished on the lowlands and on the rich nut mast on the forest floor in the hills above. Unlike their more mobile ancestors, the Natufians enjoyed many months of plentiful food by exploiting spring cereals and then following nut harvests up the slopes as they ripened at progressively higher elevations. Gazelle hunting assumed great importance at certain seasons of the year, with neighboring communities cooperating in game drives, ambushes, and other mass-hunting enterprises.

By the end of Natufian times, about 10,500 years ago, local populations were considerably higher than in earlier times. Natufian society offers intriguing glimpses at a new, more complex social order. The Natufians buried their dead in cemeteries, which have yielded a wealth of information on their society. There are clear signs of social ranking. One common and constantly recurring symbolic artifact, the dentalium seashell, is confined to a few burials, whereas elaborate grave furniture such as stone bowls with some individuals, including children, hints strongly at some form of inherited social status. Archaeologists Gary Wright and Johnson (1975) believe that this social ranking was the result of a need for the redistribution of food surpluses and to maintain order within much larger, sedentary communities. Also, the stone slab grave covers and mortar markers associated with the cemeteries may have served as ritual markers of territorial boundaries, perhaps of lands vested in revered ancestors.

After 11,000 years ago, the Natufians were faced with much drier climatic conditions at a time when their populations were expanding. The effect of increased aridity was to shrink the cereal habitats in the Mediterranean zone, causing the most productive stands to be found at higher altitudes. At the same time, the Natufians were forced to remain in sedentary settlements close to permanent water supplies, a fact of life that made the cost of harvesting cereals and nuts at remote locations much higher. How, then, could people living in a complex hunter-gatherer system solve the problem of declining staples? After nearly 2000 years' close involvement with cereal plants, they would have been well aware of what was needed to plant and grow cereal grasses deliberately. By deliberately planting cereals on a modest scale, the people tried to cope with uncertainty, to augment declining stands of wild wheat and barley with their own supplemental crops. As we shall see in Chapter 10, it was only a short time before full-time farming societies were flourishing over a wide area of the Near East. In a real sense, the development of a more complex hunter-gatherer society in this area preadapted the Natufians to plant crops.

The Natufian scenario from the Levant was mirrored under different circumstances in many parts of the world, where trajectories of cultural change followed many paths. In some areas, the new shape of the hunter-gatherer society preadapted people for the deliberate planting of cereal and root crops and for the domestication of animals. In other regions, such as southern California, that were marginal for subsistence farming, complex hunter-gatherer societies flourished until modern times. The chapters that follow describe the prehistory of hunter-gatherer societies from the arrival of *Homo sapiens sapiens* in all parts of the world.

GUIDE TO FURTHER READING

Clark, J. G. D. 1952. *Prehistoric Europe: The Economic Basis.* Cambridge, Eng.: Cambridge University Press.
> *The classic essay on prehistoric European economies. Still of immense value on Mesolithic life.*

————. 1975. *The Earlier Stone Age Settlement of Scandinavia.* Cambridge, Eng.: Cambridge University Press.
> *A fundamental synthesis on Mesolithic northwest Europe.*

Henry, Donald O. 1989. *From Foraging to Agriculture.* Philadelphia: University of Pennsylvania Press.
> *This essay on the Near East is excellent on the Natufian.*

Price, T. D. 1985. "The Mesolithic of Western Europe." *Journal of World Prehistory* 1 (3):225–305.
   A well-reasoned synthesis, which discusses complexity among hunter-gatherers.

Price, T. D., and Brown, James A., eds. 1985. *Prehistoric Hunter-Gatherers: The Emergence of Cultural Complexity.* Orlando, FL: Academic Press.
   Essays on emerging cultural complexity among hunter-gatherers in many parts of the world. A specialist volume.

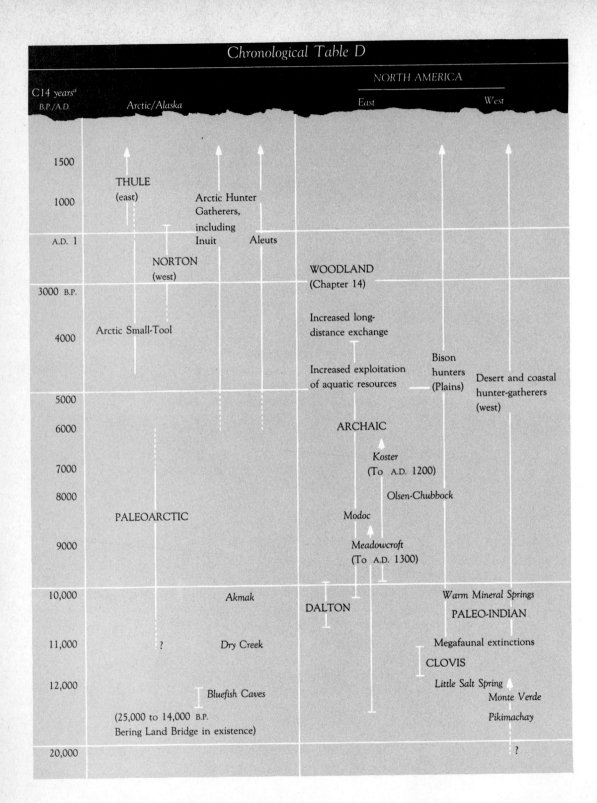

Chronological Table D

C14 years[a] B.P./A.D.	Arctic/Alaska	NORTH AMERICA	
		East	West
1500	THULE (east)		
1000		Arctic Hunter Gatherers, including	
A.D. 1		Inuit Aleuts	
	NORTON (west)	WOODLAND (Chapter 14)	
3000 B.P.			
4000	Arctic Small-Tool	Increased long-distance exchange	
		Increased exploitation of aquatic resources	Bison hunters (Plains) Desert and coastal hunter-gatherers (west)
5000			
6000		ARCHAIC	
7000		Koster (To A.D. 1200)	
8000		Olsen-Chubbock	
	PALEOARCTIC	Modoc	
9000		Meadowcroft (To A.D. 1300)	
10,000	Akmak	DALTON	Warm Mineral Springs PALEO-INDIAN
11,000	? Dry Creek		Megafaunal extinctions CLOVIS
12,000	Bluefish Caves		Little Salt Spring Monte Verde Pikimachay
	(25,000 to 14,000 B.P. Bering Land Bridge in existence)		?
20,000			

228

CHAPTER 7 THE FIRST AMERICANS

Preview

- The earliest human settlers of the Americas are now generally agreed to have come across the Bering Strait during the last glaciation. During the coldest millennia of that glaciation, a land bridge, part of a landmass named Beringia, connected Siberia and Alaska. It is known to have existed from about 25,000 to 14,000 years ago.

- The precise date of first settlement is much disputed. Some scholars believe that it was before 15,000 years ago; others, that it occurred at the very end of the last glaciation, when big-game hunters crossed into Alaska. However, the earliest dated human settlement of Arctic North America occurred around 12,000 years ago, at Bluefish Caves in the Yukon Territory.

- Further south in the Americas, there is possible evidence for human settlement by 14,000 years ago at Meadowcroft Rock Shelter in North America and slightly later at Monte Verde in northern Chile. Claims for earlier settlement in South America are highly controversial.

- The Clovis tradition of North America dates to between 11,500 and 11,000 years ago and was the first widespread big-game hunting culture as far south as Mexico. About 11,000 years ago, the Ice Age big game became extinct, and the human inhabitants of the Americas adapted by turning to more diverse hunting and foraging activities.

- Many varieties of hunting and gathering culture developed in the Americas after 10,000 years ago. The desert traditions of the Far West made efficient use of favored locations by lakes, rivers, and swamps, as well as coastal resources, while Archaic societies in the eastern woodlands developed highly effective ways of exploiting vegetable foods and aquatic resources. Many varieties of hunter-gatherer adaptation, often involving precise scheduling of gathering activities, developed in Central and South America during the same period. It was among some of these specialized foraging groups that early American agriculture began.

- The hunter-gatherer cultures of the Aleutian Islands and the Arctic developed from earlier Paleoarctic traditions based on fishing and sea mammal hunting. Aleut and Inuit cultures can be recognized in the archaeological record at least 3000, perhaps 4000, years ago.

Ever since the Americas were first colonized, people have speculated about where the pre-Columbian populations of the Western Hemisphere came from (Wauchope, 1962). Canaanites, Celts, Chinese, Egyptians, Phoenicians, and even the Ten Lost Tribes of Israel have been proposed as ancestors of the native Americans (Willey and Sabloff, 1980). By the early nineteenth century, field research and museum work had begun to replace the wild speculations of earlier scholars. People began to dig in Indian mounds. Spanish and American explorers rescued the temples of Mesoamerica from the rain forest.

In 1856 a wise and sober scholar named Samuel Haven summarized myths and legends about pre-Columbian Indian beginnings. He concluded that the New World was initially settled from across the Bering Strait, designating the earliest Americans as northeastern Asiatics who migrated into North America at an unknown date. (See Figure 7.1 for sites mentioned in this chapter.) Most archaeologists now agree with Haven that the first Americans set foot in the New World by way of the Bering Strait. The Bering route is accepted because at times the strait formed a land bridge between Asia and Alaska during the Wisconsin (equivalent to Weichsel) glaciation (Figure 7.2).

CONTROVERSIES OVER FIRST SETTLEMENT

Chronological Table D

For all the agreement about the Siberian route, intense controversies surround the beginnings of human settlement in the Americas (Adovasio and Carlisle, 1988; Fagan, 1987; Meltzer, 1989). These controversies revolve around three fundamental questions:

- How long ago did humans first settle in the Americas?

- What toolkit did they bring with them, and what was their lifeway?

- What was the ultimate ancestry of the first American Indians?

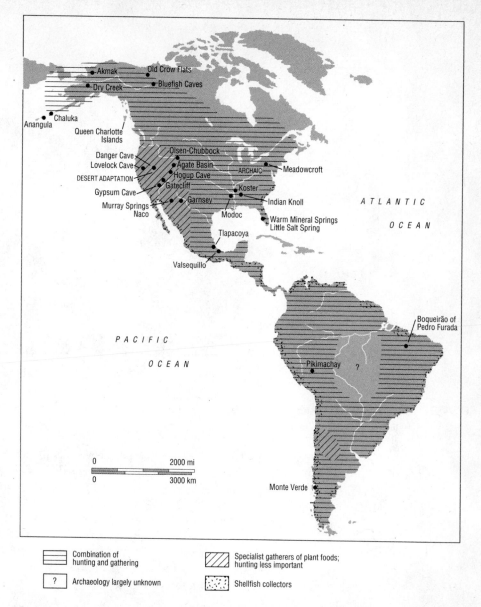

FIGURE 7.1   Prehistoric hunter-gatherers in the New World. Sites mentioned in the text are indicated. (For the Bering Land Bridge, see Figure 7.2.) The diagonally hatched areas show the distribution of specialized hunter-gatherers after 7000 years ago.

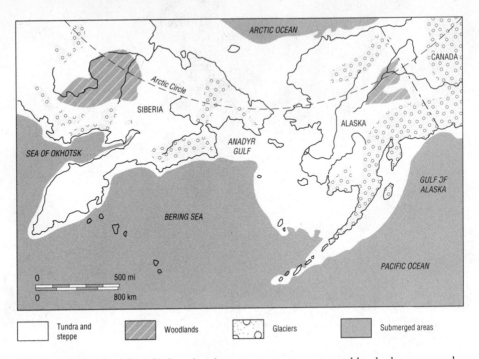

FIGURE 7.2   The Bering Land Bridge at the last glacial maximum, as reconstructed by the latest research.

Although a few scholars still believe that people were living in the Americas as early as 250,000 years ago, or before the emergence of modern *Homo sapiens* about 45,000 years ago, there are absolutely no valid archaeological grounds for such hypotheses. No generally accepted 200,000- or even 50,000-year-old sites have come from the Americas, nor have any human fossils other than those of anatomically modern individuals been discovered. Furthermore, the archaeological record in the Old World strongly suggests that no one occupied the northern latitudes of northeast Asia or the Siberian coasts of the Bering Sea this early (Fagan, 1987). On logical grounds, we are left with two competing hypotheses, each with passionate advocates:

- The *Pre-Clovis* hypothesis holds that the Americas were colonized by *Homo sapiens* some time during the Wisconsin glaciation, perhaps as early as 40,000 years ago or even earlier.

- The *Clovis* hypothesis argues that the first Americans crossed into the New World at the very end of the Wisconsin glaciation, perhaps as recently as about 15,000 years ago, and penetrated south of the Upper Pleistocene ice sheets as they retreated.

Intense controversy surrounds not only the specific archaeological evidence for the first settlement but also the criteria that can be used to establish it (for extended discussion, see Fagan, 1987). However, most archaeologists agree that securely radio-carbon dated, well-stratified cultural remains of undoubted human manufacture are the only acceptable evidence. So far, data whose quality is universally acceptable have eluded even persistent search, leaving one of the major mysteries of world prehistory still unsolved.

ICE SHEETS AND LAND BRIDGES

As we have seen in Chapter 6, human settlement in Siberia and far northeast Asia is documented as early as 18,000 years ago, perhaps somewhat earlier. These Dyukh-tai people remain somewhat of an enigma, for dating Siberian sites situated in subarctic landscapes requires sophisticated geological and geomorphological field-work. However, judging from western and central Europe, human settlement of extreme Arctic environments expanded about 18,000 years ago, a date that coincides well with the apparent first appearance of hunter-gatherer culture in the far north-east. If we accept the notion that *Homo sapiens* was living near the shores of the Bering Strait about 18,000 years ago, how did people cross into Alaska, only a short distance away?

At the time we are considering, world sea levels were as much as 330 feet (100 m) lower than today—so low that a land bridge stood where the Bering Strait now separates Asia and Alaska. (Sea levels drop when quantities of ocean water are frozen into continental ice sheets.) The strait formed part of a now almost submerged landmass known to geologists as Beringia. Only parts of west and east Beringia are dry land today—in Siberia and Alaska.

Bering Land Bridge

Since modern *Homo sapiens* emerged, the Bering Land Bridge has always con-nected Siberia to America, a land connection of varying width. The low-lying land bridge was a continuation of the Siberian steppe-tundra, a landscape that extended like a peninsula from Asia eastward to the vast Wisconsin ice sheets that covered North America (see Figure 7.2). We know from deep-sea cores that Beringia was a dry plain, with brief, warm summers; long, extremely cold winters; and continual winds. At first glance, the land bridge would seem like a most inhospitable place for human settlement, especially at the height of a glaciation. Its plains gave way to many marshy areas near rivers, which provided ample summer fodder for large grass-eating mammals like the mammoth, as well as for wild horses, musk-oxen, and other Arctic species. The Upper Pleistocene fauna of this general area included many species that are intolerant of deep snow, although they may have flourished in the dry environ-ment, moving from one grazing ground to another as the snow thawed during the summer. Judging from modern Arctic environments, the density of game may never have been high. This was no land teeming in milk and honey but a very savage climate indeed. Nevertheless, it may have been capable of supporting a human population of between 15 and 25 people per 386 square miles (1000 sq. km), a figure roughly equivalent to that for modern Eskimos living off the land and sea alone (for a fascinating set of essays on Beringia, see Hopkins et al., 1982).

Unfortunately, the Ice Age coasts are now deep below the Bering Sea, so we cannot say whether its coasts were rich in fish and sea mammals or whether the first settlers on the land bridge were fisherfolk rather than big-game hunters (Meltzer,

1989). However, the most likely period for humans to have used the land bridge was during or after the height of the Late Wisconsin glaciation, for it was then that Dyukhtai people were living in Siberia. Under these circumstances, we should look for traces of human settlement in Alaska, then eastern Beringia, sometime between 25,000 and 14,000 years ago.

Could the first Americans have made their way across the strait by boat? We know that people colonized the remote landmass of Australia before 30,000 years ago and that they could only have done so by crossing over some 55 miles (88 km) of open water even at the height of the glaciation, when sea levels were much lower than today. These were more benign tropical waters, where such hazards as floating ice, strong arctic winds, and the ever-present danger of hyperthermia were unknown. The risks in the far north were much greater. Even in summer, fogs and rough seas make the strait a chancy place, and to cross winter pack ice is to invite disaster.

Unfortunately, we have no means of knowing whether the coastal Dyukhtai people or their predecessors may have had skin boats, even kayaks, for their long-abandoned settlements lie under modern sea levels. We do know that the predominant dietary source for Arctic Stone Age hunters over an enormous area of Europe and Asia was big-game and land mammals of all sizes, with apparently much less concentration on seasonal vegetable foods, fish, and marine mammals (Kelly and Todd, 1988). To venture onto the Bering Land Bridge required no new skills, merely the big-game hunting skills that characterized generations of Ice Age hunters. That the first crossing into Alaska was by land rather than by boat seems likely, simply on deductive grounds. It may have been only later that Arctic peoples adapted to postglacial coasts and crossed freely from Asia to Alaska, maintaining social and cultural ties on both sides of the Bering Strait.

FIRST SETTLEMENT—ALASKA

If the Dyukhtai people were the first settlers, it would be logical to find similar artifacts in Alaska. Unfortunately, field research is very difficult because of the remote terrain and severe climate (Dumond, 1987a; Morlan, 1983). As Richard Morlan says, it is rather "like looking for a needle in a haystack (and a frozen one at that)."

The first Alaskans are still a very shadowy entity, known only from confusing scatters of stone artifacts and a few stratified locations. The earliest of these is the remote Bluefish Caves in the Yukon, about 40 miles (64.4 km) southwest of Old Crow. Some 15,000 years ago, the caves lay within sight of windswept glacial lakes. Jacques Cinq-Mars (1979) found a layer of tightly packed, undisturbed loess in the caves, with mammoth and other bones, microblades, a wedge-shaped core, and some trimming flakes. Cinq-Mars obtained bone collagen dates from several animal fragments and believes that this stratified site contains evidence of human occupation between 15,000 and 12,000 years ago, perhaps earlier. If this site is accepted as valid, it is one of the earliest in the Americas.

Bluefish may have been occupied while the land bridge was still dry land, but soon afterward the low-lying plain was submerged, although parts of the Alaskan coastline were up to 60 miles (96 km) offshore as late as 10,000 years ago. A handful

Bluefish Caves
?12,200 to
?24,800 B.P.

of sites documents human settlement in the millennia coinciding with and following submergence. Most of these contain microblades and small cores, bladelets that are far smaller than the normal Upper Paleolithic blade so well known from the Old World. So far, there are few signs of distinctive Upper Paleolithic blades in Alaska. A few sites, like Dry Creek in the northern foothills of the Alaska Range, offer tantalizing clues. The lower levels of this location have yielded cobbles, flakes, and thin bifacial knives but no microblades; they are radiocarbon dated to about 11,100 years ago (Powers and Hamilton, 1978). A later occupation, dated to about 10,700 years ago, does contain microblades and other small artifacts. Roger Powers believes the earlier Dry Creek level contains "Upper Paleolithic" tools similar to those from a Siberian site said by Soviet archaeologists to belong within the Dyukhtai tradition.

**Dry Creek
11,100 B.P.**

Elsewhere, isolated artifact scatters and dates lie between 12,000 and 11,000 years ago, but later sites almost invariably contain microblades and wedge-shaped cores belonging to an ill-defined "Paleoarctic" tradition dating to later than 11,000 years ago, by which time there was well-documented human settlement far to the south. This description in general terms probably masks considerable cultural diversity. The most famous locality is the 10,000-year-old site at Akmak, on the Onion Portage. Akmak lies in a river valley that has been a migration route for caribou since the earliest human settlement in the region (D. Anderson, 1970). This site consists of little more than a scatter of characteristic tools that once lay by a shelter long since eroded away.

**Akmak
10,000 B.P.**

Some archaeologists believe that there are some connections between the Dyukhtai artifacts of northeast Asia (Chapter 6) and those of the Paleoarctic tradition, but it would be unwise to pursue these analogies too far until many more sites have been dug on both sides of the Bering Strait. Some of the stoneworking techniques practiced by Paleoarctic groups are broadly similar to those used by Stone Age people in northern China as early as 20,000 years ago (Chung and Pei, 1986) and in Japan between approximately 14,000 and 10,000 years ago (Ikawa-Smith, 1978). Again, it would be easy to read a great deal into these parallels, but in fact their very existence has been barely established, from only a few widely separated sites.

The first settlement of Alaska most likely took place between 25,000 and about 14,000 years ago, perhaps toward the end of that period, when hunters followed mammoth and other game to higher ground. However, the earliest archaeological evidence for such settlement is at the most 15,000 years old, perhaps less.

The toolkits used by the first settlers may have been generally Upper Paleolithic. However, the earliest documented toolkits from either side of the Bering Strait are based on wedge-shaped cores and microblades, artifacts associated with the Dyukhtai tradition of Siberia and perhaps with caribou hunting.

As far as can be established, the predominant lifeway in extreme Arctic latitudes of Europe and Asia during the last glacial climax was based on big-game hunting (Gamble, 1986b). That this lifeway also predominated on the Bering Land Bridge and in Alaska during the same period seems unquestionable. Once the ice sheets retreated, however, many Ice Age big-game species became extinct, and big-game hunting bands had to adapt to a far more diverse tundra and birch forest environment. This environmental diversity is reflected in considerable toolkit variation within Alaska's Paleoarctic tradition.

A possible scenario for first settlement, then, has tiny groups of big-game hunters crossing into Alaska at a time when Ice Age mammals were still to be found, perhaps between 25,000 and 15,000 years ago. Some of these people, perhaps numbering only in the dozens, were the first to move southward into the temperate latitudes that lay beyond the great ice sheets covering much of Canada and the Rocky Mountains.

There remains one fundamental question: Why did humans settle in the New World at all? Was it an inner urge that caused the first Americans to endure the harsh climate of the Bering Land Bridge? Or was there some more prosaic reason?

Two great population dispersals occurred during prehistory, the first when *Homo erectus* emerged from the tropics about a million years ago. The second took place after the emergence of *Homo sapiens sapiens,* when the first human populations crossed from the Old World into the New and Australia was inhabited for the first time (Fagan, 1990). The exact dates of this later dispersal are still highly uncertain, but it seems to have occurred soon after modern people appeared. The explanation for these sudden dispersals seems to lie mostly in the fact that humans tended to behave as other animals did. Rather than responding to an inborn restlessness, the first Americans were probably behaving in the same way as other animal predators. They spent their days tracking the game herds that formed an important part of their subsistence, and when Siberian game herds moved onto the Bering Land Bridge during the coldest millennia of the last glaciation, their human predators followed. The higher ground to the east—Alaska—formed part of the same hunting grounds.

BIOLOGICAL EVIDENCE FOR THE FIRST AMERICANS

For more than a century, anthropologists have pointed to biological similarities between Siberians and North American Indians. Christy Turner (1984) of Arizona State University has studied the changing physical characteristics of native American teeth, especially their crowns and roots, and compared them with those of Old World populations. These dental features are more stable than most evolutionary traits, with a high genetic component that minimizes the effects of environmental differences, sexual dimorphism, and age variations. After examining more than 4000 individuals, ancient and modern, Turner has developed a series of hypotheses about the first settlement of the Americas based on dental morphology (Figure 7.3).

Sinodonty

Turner points out that prehistoric Americans display many fewer variations in their dental morphology than do eastern Asians. He calls these characteristics "Sinodonty," a pattern of dental features that includes incisor shoveling, single-rooted upper first premolars, triple-rooted lower first molars, and other attributes. Sinodonty occurs only in northern Asia and the Americas. Turner's earliest evidence for Sinodonty comes from northern China about 20,000 years ago, but he believes that it emerged much earlier, perhaps as early as 40,000 years ago. European Upper Paleolithic skeletons do not display Sinodonty. Turner believes that the Sinodont northern Chinese may have evolved from a primeval Southeast Asian *Homo sapiens* population, whom they resemble more closely than the northeast Asians and American Indians, who evolved from them.

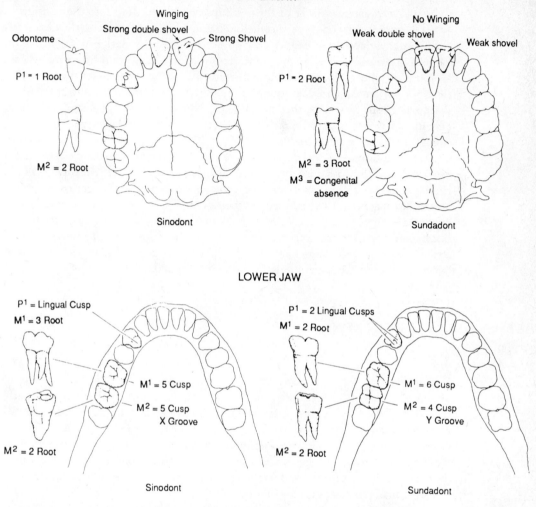

FIGURE 7.3   Dental morphology and the first Americans. Some of Christy Turner's theories about the peopling of America are based on differences between the teeth of so-called Sinodonts (northern Asians and all native Americans) and Sundadonts (eastern Asians). Sinodonts display, among other features, strong incisor shoveling (scooping out on one or both surfaces of the tooth), single-rooted upper first premolars, and triple-rooted lower first molars.

Using statistics to study evolutionary divergence, Turner has estimated the approximate dates at which Sinodont populations split off from ancestral Chinese groups. He hypothesizes that the first settlement of the Americas resulted from a population movement through east Siberia and across the now-submerged continental shelf around 14,000 years ago. Two subsequent population movements brought the present-day Athabaskan and Eskimo-Aleut populations into the Americas a few thousand years later. Neither of these groups penetrated deep into the continent.

If Turner is correct, there is some biological support for a late settlement date. His researches have been supported by studies of genetic marker distributions in modern American Indian populations. The research team found that more than 14,000 Central and South American Indians in their samples share the same Gm allotypes (variants in a protein found in the blood). Since interbreeding populations share sets of such variants, the genetic experts believe there was a single primeval migration of hunter-gatherers into the Americas, who evolved later by cultural differentiation (for discussion, see Fagan, 1987).

Dental morphology and genetic research hint strongly at a relatively late date for first settlement. So does the controversial linguistic work of Joseph Greenberg (1987). He has compiled a massive data base on the vocabulary and grammar of American Indian languages, which leads him to believe that there were three basic Indian linguistic groups: Amerind, Aleut-Eskimo, and Na-Dene (Athabaskan). Most American Indian languages are in the Amerind group, whose speakers Greenberg believes arrived before 11,000 years ago. It is only fair to point out, however, that some linguists consider Greenberg's classifications too broad.

THE CASE FOR LATE WISCONSIN SETTLEMENT

Exactly the same problem—lack of sites—arises when we look for archaeological evidence of Late Wisconsin settlement south of the great ice sheets. Until fairly recently, most archaeologists believed that first settlement took place about 13,000 years ago, after the retreat of the Laurentide ice sheet. Those who argue for earlier settlement point to the toolkits used by the human inhabitants of the Americas at that time, suggesting that their projectile points and hunting artifacts are quite unlike the Dyukhtai tools of Siberia. They developed, then, from an earlier technological tradition that still awaits discovery.

Everyone agrees that the connections between 13,000-year-old toolkits south of the ice sheets and the few of this age known from the far north and Asia are tenuous at best. Proponents of late settlement argue that this situation is hardly surprising given the long distances, the great isolation of the first Americans, and the diversity of environments. Those who support earlier colonization believe that we have yet to find the primeval American toolkit. Decades of ardent search have produced only a handful of sites that *may* date to earlier than 15,000 years ago (Adovasio and Carlisle, 1988; Fagan, 1987; Lynch, 1989).

The lack of evidence is depressing, to the point that many claims are based on emotionalism and specious argument from minimal data. There are numerous claims for early North American settlement based on poorly dated scatters of projectile heads and flaked tools from deep caves and open sites in many parts of the United States. Many of these have been disproved by later investigation, through improved dating methods or more sophisticated artifact analysis techniques (Fagan, 1987).

ICE-FREE CORRIDORS AND SEA COASTS

If tiny bands of hunter-gatherers penetrated the fastnesses of Beringia during the late Wisconsin glaciation, how, then, did they reach the heart of the Americas? Again, the first settlement is fraught with controversies about hypothetical routes and the boundaries of ice sheets.

North America was very different during the Wisconsin glaciation. We know from deep-sea core studies that the Wisconsin began some 117,000 years ago, with an inexorable cooling of world temperatures. Great ice sheets covered much of northern North America during the early Wisconsin, until about 60,000 years ago. Between 60,000 and about 25,000 years ago, there was a prolonged period of glacial retreat and sea levels rose. With the possible exception of a much reduced ice sheet around Hudson Bay, most of North America was freed of glacial barriers. For these 35,000 years, any (hypothetical) human settlers would have encountered environments not very different from modern tundra and boreal forest.

Late Wisconsin
25,000 B.P.

The Late Wisconsin, the earliest time period when human settlement seems possible, began about 25,000 years ago. The so-called Laurentide glaciers, centered on Labrador and the Keewatin areas of Canada, expanded south, west, and east, eventually fusing into a huge frozen wilderness. At its maximum about 18,000 years ago, the Laurentide ice sheet extended from the Atlantic seaboard across the Great Lakes region into southeast Alberta. The mountain ranges of southern Alaska and British Columbia were heavily glaciated at the time, forming the Cordilleran glacier complex in the west. The Cordilleran extended about 30 miles (48 km) south of Seattle as recently as 14,500 years ago, apparently reaching its maximum extent after the Laurentide.

Clearly, these great Late Wisconsin ice barriers would have inhibited travel between Beringia and the southern latitudes of the New World. Did they stop human settlement altogether? In the 1950s, Canadian geologists reported that the Cordilleran ice flowed down the eastern flanks of the Rockies but apparently did not join the Laurentide ice sheet. Despite a lack of reliable maps, the idea of an "ice-free corridor" soon took hold of archaeologists' imaginations. "Doubtless it was a formidable place," wrote Thomas Canby (1979) of the National Geographic Society, "an ice-walled valley of frigid winds, fierce snows, and clinging fogs . . . yet grazing animals would have entered, and behind them would have come a rivulet of human hunters." The picture is a compelling one—but was it reality?

The ice-free corridor has been mapped more thoroughly in recent years, to the point that we can be sure it was no superhighway for Stone Age hunters. In some places the ice sheets did merge. In others, especially in the far north and south, there was a corridor, but it twisted and turned through the roughest of terrain, country restricted by chill meltwater lakes, often with biologically sterile shores. At best the Late Wisconsin ice-free corridor was a barren and impoverished landscape. Even if it was passable, there is a good chance that there was no incentive to cross it between about 25,000 and 15,000 years ago, for much better food resources lay in Beringia. In any case, we lack evidence that human settlers had made Beringia their homeland earlier than 15,000 years ago (Carlisle and Adovasio, 1988).

If an interior route was used, chances are that it was traversed during a time of glacial retreat, sometime after 15,000 years ago, when the Laurentide glaciers shrank rapidly. If the ice-free corridor was a barrier to human settlement, could people have passed down ice-free coastal areas along the Alaskan and British Columbian coasts into temperate regions? Knud Fladmark (1978) believes that the Late Wisconsin northwest coasts were relatively warmer and more productive than other areas, to the extent that they might have sustained human life. Unfortunately, however, we do not know whether these areas were accessible from mainland Beringia or, indeed, whether there were Late Wisconsin populations on the land bridge at all. If such people did exist, their sites are buried deep beneath modern sea levels. The earliest documented settlement occurs on the Queen Charlotte Islands of British Columbia, between 12,000 and 10,000 years ago (Fladmark, 1978). Many archaeologists believe that much earlier coastal settlement is unlikely, on the (perhaps dangerous) assumption that everything we know about the earliest settlers suggests they were terrestrial hunters and gatherers, with a lifeway adapted in part to the pursuit of large Ice Age mammals.

Queen Charlotte Islands
12,000 to 10,000 B.P.

ARCHAEOLOGICAL EVIDENCE FOR LATE WISCONSIN SETTLEMENT

A number of sites throughout the Americas have been claimed as evidence for Late Wisconsin settlement, mainly caves and rock shelters (Dincauze, 1983; Fagan, 1987). The most important are worth individual review.

Meadowcroft Rock Shelter

Meadowcroft
12,000 B.P. (perhaps as early as 19,000 B.P.) to 700 B.P.

Meadowcroft Rock Shelter lies 30 miles (48.2 km) southwest of Pittsburgh, Pennsylvania, a sheltered location close to permanent water supplies. James Adovasio excavated and dated the 11 levels of the shelter with more than 70 radiocarbon dates. They show that it was occupied from nearly 700 years ago back to at least 12,000 and perhaps to 16,000 years ago (Adovasio et al., 1981, 1984, 1986, 1990).

Adovasio's meticulous excavations establish human occupation at 12,000 years ago beyond any doubt. Controversy swirls over the lowest levels of the rock shelter, which were claimed to date to as early as 19,600 years ago (Dincanze, 1989). The earliest date of human occupation at Meadowcroft has now been established as being between 2000 and 3000 years before 11,500 years ago, that is, perhaps as early as 14,500 years ago (Adovasio et al., 1990), a date that fits well with other estimates of first settlement. At the time of writing, there is no earlier evidence for human settlement in North America.

Mesoamerica and Latin America

The evidence for Late Wisconsin human occupation is also sparse south of the Rio Grande. Richard MacNeish believes there is evidence for a "chopper-chopping tool" stage of human occupation in Mesoamerica dating to more than 30,000 years ago

(MacNeish, 1986; MacNeish and Nelken-Terner, 1983). This probably mythical formulation consists mostly of undated surface finds and artifacts from river terraces.

Valsequillo
?21,850 B.P.

MacNeish's second stage, marked by "bone tools and a unifacial industry," is dated to between 30,000 and 15,000 years ago. One of his key sites is Valsequillo, near Pueblo in central Mexico, where 13 apparent unifacial stone tools lay with the bones of extinct animals at five locations. The finds came from stratified gravels, the upper levels of which contained bifacial tools. A date of 21,850 ± 850 years is claimed for a freshwater shell near one of the stone flakes (Irwin-Williams, 1978). Unfortunately, Valsequillo is questionable because the geology is suspect. The gravels containing the early artifacts may be 200,000 years old. Some scholars have questioned both the associations of animals and artifacts and the humanness of the earliest "tools."

Tlapacoya
24,000 to
22,000 B.P.

MacNeish places the famous Tlapacoya mammoth bones from near Mexico City in the same stage; they are claimed to have been found with simple flakes and other artifacts in contexts dating to between about 24,000 and 22,000 years ago. Unfortunately, there are again serious doubts about the validity of this association.

MacNeish is a fervent believer in early human settlement in Mesoamerica. It is only fair to point out that most scholars favor a later date, for the earliest indisputable finds date to about 11,000 years ago, roughly contemporary with early human occupation to the north (Figure 7.4).

Supporters of Late Wisconsin and even earlier settlement reserve their greatest enthusiasm for a series of finds from South America, scattered between Venezuela and northern Chile (Bryan, 1978, 1986). Alan Bryan has gone so far as to hypothesize that human settlers fanned out over South America long before 20,000 years ago.

Pikimachay Cave

Richard MacNeish excavated the deep Pikimachay Cave high in the Andes foothills of southern Peru (MacNeish et al., 1980, 1981). He identified three major occupation groups in the cave, a relatively recent one and a second occupation with large, crude

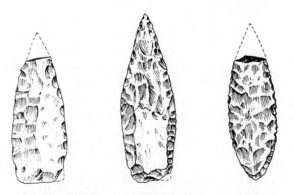

FIGURE 7.4   Points found with mammoths in Mexico. The length of the middle point is approximately 3 inches (8.1 cm).

Pikimachay
14,200 B.P.
(perhaps
earlier)

bifaces; some projectile points; and choppers as well as sloth, horse, camel, and puma bones radiocarbon dated to 14,200 ± 180 years. This single radiocarbon date identified one of the earliest postglacial occupations in the Americas.

The earliest Pikimachay level consists of jumbled earth and cemented soil containing deer and sloth bones as well as crude tools, radiocarbon dated to between 20,250 and 19,650 years ago. Quite apart from the large statistical errors for the dates, the crude artifacts are probably rock fragments from the cave walls, despite Mac-Neish's claims. The evidence for a 20,000-year-old occupation at Pikimachay is questionable.

Boqueirão of Pedro Furada

Boqueirão of
Pedro Furada
?30,000 B.P.

The Boqueirão of Pedro Furada rock shelter in northeast Brazil contains deep, sandy layers with pebbles and gravel beds (Guidon and Delibrias, 1986). Niede Guidon excavated 9.8 feet (3 m) into the cave and unearthed "traces of human occupation [that] succeed one another throughout the stratigraphic sequence." She believes the shelter was occupied again and again by a small human band, the earliest of whom left large circular hearths as well as stone pebble tools, mainly "pieces with blunt points obtained by . . . convergent flakings," along with a variety of other tools. Guidon claims occupation as early as some 47,000 years ago, with continuing occupation between 30,000 and 12,000 years ago. She believes she has found a piece of rock with two painted lines—the first American rock art—in a hearth dated to 17,000 ± 400 years ago.

The Pedro Furada deposits are claimed to contain the remains of camps alongside a stream, and the layers may well be part of a streambed themselves. Are the "hearths" actually of human origin? Were the proposed artifacts, which look unconvincing to the dispassionate eye, actually humanly manufactured? Have chemical analyses of the red pigment from the 17,000-year-old "painting" been completed? Until definitive answers to these questions are forthcoming, Guidon's claims lack scientific authority, and the site must remain doubtful.

Monte Verde

Monte Verde
13,000 to
12,500 B.P.

Located in a small river valley in southern Chile, Monte Verde is said to be a streamside settlement covered by a peat bog, so that not only stone and bone but also wooden artifacts survive. The site has been excavated very thoroughly and radiocarbon dated to between 13,000 and 12,500 years ago (Dillehey, 1984). Although some doubts have been expressed about the date and context of the finds, they are certainly remarkable. Thus far, only a portion of the site has been excavated, revealing two parallel rows of what are said to be rectangular houses, joined by connecting walls (Figure 7.5) (Dillehey, 1990). The skin-covered houses were 9 to 13 feet (3 to 4 m) square, with log and crude plank foundations and a wooden framework. Clay-lined hearths, wooden mortars, and large quantities of vegetable foods were found in the houses. A short distance away lay a wishbone-shaped structure associated with chewed bolo plant leaves (used today to make a form of medicinal

FIGURE 7.5   Excavations at Monte Verde, Chile.

tea), mastodon bones, and other work debris. This may have been a work area. The Monte Verde people exploited a very wide range of vegetable foods, including wild potatoes; they also hunted small game and perhaps mammals such as extinct camels and mastodons (it is possible that they scavenged such meat, however). Monte Verde was in a forest, with abundant vegetable foods year-round. The site was almost certainly a long-term campsite. What is fascinating is that 90 percent of the stone artifacts are crude river pebbles. It is clear that wood was the most important raw material. It was certainly used for spears and digging sticks and for hafting stone scrapers, three of which have survived in their wooden handles. Sites yielding simple flaked stone artifacts like those from Monte Verde have been found elsewhere in South America, as far south as Patagonia, but this is the first place that anyone has been able to make more complete discoveries.

The Monte Verde investigations are still in progress, although they hint that early American society may have been much more sophisticated than had been realized. Other locations like Pikimachay and Meadowcroft are located in more open country. The Monte Verde site shows just how scanty the archaeological record of the first Americans is and just how little we are likely to find out about them until more waterlogged sites come to light.

After more than a century of searching, the earliest archaeological sites in the Americas date to around 14,500 to 13,000 years ago, and even these occupations are poorly documented. As the years go on and the intensity of archaeological research throughout the New World picks up, the chances of finding indisputable evidence for Late Wisconsin or even earlier human settlement seem ever more remote. Add the realities of full glacial environments in the far north, the evidence from genetics and dental morphology, and the distribution of archaeological sites in northeast Asia as we know it, and a compelling case can be made for late settlement.

In all probability, the first Americans crossed into east Beringia (Alaska) from the Bering Land Bridge, perhaps at the very end of the last glaciation. Then, as the ice sheets retreated 14,000 years ago, a mere handful of people hunted their way southward into the heart of a virgin continent. In the millennia that followed, human predators underwent a population explosion in the new lands, adapting to a great diversity of local environments everywhere between the ice sheets and Tierra del Fuego.

THE PALEO-INDIANS

About 11,500 years ago, the highly distinctive Clovis culture appeared on the Great Plains of North America and much farther afield. These *Paleo-Indian* people are the first well-documented inhabitants of the New World, but many questions still remain about their ancestry and lifeway. What is certain, however, is that the Clovis culture was relatively short-lived. Judging from dated sites in the west, most sites were occupied during the five centuries after 11,500 years ago. We now move onto solid prehistoric ground, for the archaeological record suddenly mushrooms from nothing to a well-documented scatter of locations from coast to coast in North America, with well-established Paleo-Indian occupation in Mesoamerica and Latin America as well.

Clovis

Clovis
**11,500 to
11,000 B.P.**

Although Paleo-Indian occupation is known from both eastern and western North America, the Clovis culture is best known from the Great Plains. At the end of the Wisconsin glaciation, the areas in the rain shadow of the western mountains of North America were dominated throughout the year by the dry mid-Pacific air mass. Most rain fell, and still falls, in spring and early summer, supporting short grasses that keep much of their biomass beneath the soil. This structure helps retain moisture in the roots, providing mammoths, bison, and other ruminants with high-quality nutrients in the dry fall and into the winter. These grasslands expanded at the end of the Wisconsin and were colonized by herds of ruminants who were selective feeders. They were also the home of scattered bands of Clovis people. Within a few centuries, tiny hunter-gatherer bands had spread to both North American coasts and as far south as Guadalajara, Mexico, adapting to different environments they encountered.

The western plains of North America offer a highly diverse range of environments with a variety of protein-rich grasses and shrubs that once supported a browsing and grazing mammalian fauna, which in turn provided subsistence for a small number of hunter-gatherers (Frison, 1978). However, life was not easy for the bands, as they had to respond to different distributions of animals and plants each year, conditions that depended on rainfall, snowfall, runoff from the mountain peaks, and so on. The realities of the climate meant that the people had to collect dried meat and vegetable foods in the summer months and store them against the bitter winter. Each family group probably moved frequently, tending to visit the same campsites year after year, taking all their belongings with them. Archaeologically, they left very little behind, so the evidence for prehistoric occupation of the plains normally is limited to remains of large bison kills and scatters of broken flakes and projectile points.

The Clovis culture is known mainly from kill sites in the West. At Murray Springs, Arizona, for example, the people killed mammoth and bison, butchering them at separate locations, with a campsite nearby. Eleven bison died at Murray Springs, yielding enough meat to support up to 50 to 100 people, perhaps many fewer. Distinctive Clovis projectile points and other tools were found among the bones. At Naco, Arizona, no fewer than 8 points lay in one mammoth carcass. Perhaps between 4 and 8 hunters, a fifth of a band of about 20 to 40 people, killed the great beast. The hunters partially dismembered their quarry, sometimes making piles of the disarticulated bones. The Clovis people who camped in Blackwater Draw, New Mexico, a natural arroyo trap, could drive large animals into swampy ground. There they took mammoth, bison, horse, camel, and deer. Lehner, also in Arizona, is another well-known waterside site, where Clovis hunters may have killed 13 mammoth in one hunt.

Everyone agrees that the Clovis people hunted both big game and smaller animals, besides foraging for wild vegetable foods during spring, summer, and fall. Big-game hunting was probably the most important part of their subsistence. Large animals like the mammoth and bison could provide meat for weeks on end, as well as valuable byproducts for household possessions, tents, and even clothing. George Frison (1978) and others believe that Clovis hunters tended to concentrate on solitary mammoths, for their spear technology could not stop an elephant in its tracks, just wound it severely. They would stalk herds, concentrating on straying animals, sometimes perhaps driving them into swamps (for extended discussion, see Haynes, 1982). The hunters would wound an animal, then take their time to kill it with thrusting spears.

Clovis people, and other Paleo-Indian groups, used a portable toolkit that included bone, stone, and wood artifacts. Preservation conditions allow us to know most about their stone technology, often based on precious, fine-grained rock from widely separated outcrops. The hunters traveled great distances for their stone, trading it in core form for hundreds of miles. These cores were like a savings account, carried around so that flakes could be used to make finely pressure-flaked projectile points. The finished heads were mounted in wood or bone foreshafts set on the end of spear shafts (Figure 7.6). Once the spear penetrated an animal, the foreshaft would break off. The hunter could then rearm the spear with a new foreshaft in a few moments. Damaged points were resharpened and used again; some exceptionally large ones may even have been ceremonial artifacts.

Besides projectile points, the Clovis toolkit included butchering tools, scrapers, and dozens of untrimmed stone blades and flakes used as convenient knives. The people used bone, and presumably wood, for foreshafts, spears, and other artifacts. The origins of this technology are unknown but must lie in Upper Paleolithic big-game hunting traditions in the Old World. The fluted projectile point itself may have

FIGURE 7.6   Clovis points found with a mammoth skeleton at Naco, Arizona.

been an indigenous development in temperate North America (Haynes, 1982). Under this argument, big game and mammoths were to the Upper Paleolithic hunter what the reindeer is to the Laplander or the caribou to the inland Inuit. These authorities also believe that *general* similarities exist between Clovis stone and bone tools and those from classic mammoth-hunting sites in east Europe and the Ukraine. Thus, they speculate that the first settlement of North America was part of a primeval big-game hunting tradition that spread from northeast Asia into the New World. The descendants of these people wandered farther south, pursuing their favorite game, the mammoth. Eventually they reached the Canadian prairie, where they encountered new mammoth species and a greater bounty of other big game. Within a few centuries, Clovis people and their relatives were scattered all over the Americas.

This scenario for first settlement is almost as inadequately documented as those espousing earlier dates. However, the cumulative sum of the limited data tends to support rather than undermine it (Fagan, 1987).

BIG-GAME EXTINCTIONS

The Clovis people flourished for about 500 years, and then, about 11,000 years ago, they vanished abruptly, to be replaced by a multitude of hunting and gathering cultures. This sudden disappearance coincides with one of the great mysteries of modern science—the catastrophic extinction of Ice Age big-game animals in the Americas. Many large animals became extinct throughout the world at this time but nowhere as drastically as in the Americas. Three-quarters of the large mammalian genera there vanished abruptly at the end of the Pleistocene (Martin and Klein, 1984; Martin and Wright, 1967).

Speculations about this extinction have been long and lively. One theory that has long held on is that the large mammals were killed off by the Paleo-Indian bands' intensive hunting, as they preyed on large herds of animals that had formerly had relatively few predators to control their populations. This overkill hypothesis is weakened by the fact that many Pleistocene animals disappeared before the heyday of the Paleo-Indians. Besides, the Indians existed in very small numbers, and they had other subsistence activities as well. Surely the animals would have adapted to changed conditions and new dangers. Instead, the extinctions accelerated after the hunters had been around for a while; the modern bison, for example, never adapted to mounted hunters.

Change in climate gives a second hypothesis for the cause of extinction. Changing environments, spreading aridity, and shrinking habitats for big game may have reduced the mammalian population drastically. Strong objections face this hypothesis too. The very animals that became extinct had already survived enormous fluctuations in Pleistocene climate without harm. If they had once migrated into more hospitable habitats, they could have done so again. Furthermore, the animals that became extinct were not just the browsers; they were selected from all types of habitat. This too-simple hypothesis is supported by the notion that desiccation leads to mass starvation in game populations, an idea refuted by ecological research in Africa. What actually occurs is that the smaller species and those with lower growth rates adapt to the less favorable conditions, leaving the population changed but not defunct (R. C. D. Olivier, 1982).

A third hypothesis cites the great variation in mean temperatures at the end of the Pleistocene as a primary cause of extinction. In both the New and Old Worlds, the more pronounced seasonal contrasts in temperature climates would have been harder on the young of species that are born in small litters, after long gestation periods, and at fixed times of the year. These traits are characteristic of larger mammals, precisely those that became extinct. The less equable climate at the end of the Pleistocene, then, would have been a major cause of late Pleistocene extinctions in North America.

All three hypotheses contain some truth. Complex variables must have affected the steps that led to extinction, with intricate feedback among the effects of intensive big-game hunting, changing ecology, and the intolerance of some mammalian species to seasonal contrasts in weather. It may be that the hunters, being persistent predators, were the final variable, causing more drastic mammalian extinctions than might otherwise have occurred.

(Margin notes: Overkill *·* Climate change *·* Seasonal contrasts)*

LATER HUNTERS AND GATHERERS

As the world climate warmed up rapidly at the end of the last glaciation, New World environments changed drastically. The great ice sheets of the north shrank, mountain snow lines and sea levels rose, and forest vegetation established itself in hitherto glaciated regions. If one word can be used to describe these momentous changes, it is *diversity,* a great diversity of local environments—lush river floodplains, great deserts, grassy plains, miles upon miles of boreal and deciduous woodland. The late Paleo-Indians and their successors adapted to this great diversity with brilliant success and ingenuity. In general, the West and Southwest United States became drier, but the East Coast and much of the Midwest grew densely forested. The large Pleistocene mammals became extinct, but the bison remained a major source of food. In the Southeast, the more favorable climate brought drier conditions, which meant less standing water, markedly seasonal rainfalls, and specialization among humans for fishing or intensive gathering. Many areas had much economic diversity, as we see among the desert gatherer peoples of the Tehuacán Valley in Mexico. They flourished between 12,000 and 9000 years ago, at the same time hunter-gatherers in the Pacific Northwest were probably taking advantage of seasonal salmon runs in the fast-moving rivers.

North American climate and sea levels seem to have stabilized close to their modern configurations about 8000 years ago. Three thousand years later, human populations started to grow more rapidly. Almost everywhere in temperate North America the number of archaeological sites mushroomed within a millennium. The stage was set for rapid cultural, economic, and social change in many areas, which was still climaxing as European explorers and colonists arrived in the New World.

Eight thousand years ago, the human population of North America was still sparse, scattered in a myriad of isolated hunter-gatherer bands. Judging from sites in many areas, people spent most of the year living in small family groups, exploiting large hunting territories. They might have come together with their neighbors for a few weeks during the summer months at favored locations near rivers or nut groves. The bands would have held ceremonies, exchanged wives, and traded fine-grained rocks and other commodities. Then they would have gone their separate ways, following migrating game, trapping small animals, and foraging for wild vegetable foods.

At first there was plenty of vacant territory to go around, continues this hypothetical scenario. In time natural population growth and the low carrying capacity of the land combined to restrict mobility. Several long-term adaptive trends developed.

First, the extinction of the Ice Age megafauna meant that hunters focused on smaller mammals, especially the white-tailed deer. Inevitably, people turned to alternative food sources, including wild vegetable foods, birds, mollusks, and fish. Wild vegetable foods were a particularly favored dietary source, especially in areas like river valley bottoms and lakeshores, where they were seasonally abundant and diverse.

Second, there was a long-term trend toward less mobility, toward base camps that were occupied for many months of the year. These served as anchors for larger territories, which were exploited seasonally from outlying settlements. This settlement pattern was by no means universal, but it took hold in areas where there was an unusual diversity of food resources. Examples of base settlements are to be found in the desert West, in midwestern and southeastern river valleys, and in the Northeast.

Third, some areas witnessed a move toward sedentary settlement, occupation of the same settlement year-round or for most of the year. This type of settlement is different from a base camp used on a seasonal basis, even if the latter lasts for many months. It implies a permanent settlement within a highly restricted territory, a settlement lying within easy reach of sufficient game, vegetable, and aquatic resources to enable the occupants to stay through every season of the year. Sedentary settlement is hard to identify in the archaeological record, except through the presence of substantial dwellings or cemeteries. Such occupation was well established in some midwestern river valley bottoms by 4000 years ago and perhaps in favored coastal areas, such as southern California and the Pacific Northwest, somewhat later.

These trends coincided with accelerating population growth in more favored areas after 4000 years ago.

Such was the diversity of North American environments in Holocene times that only a few relatively limited areas witnessed sedentary settlement and large-scale population growth. Perhaps it is no coincidence that it was in some of these areas, notably midwestern and southeastern river valleys and the Southwest, that people turned to the cultivation of domesticated plants.

Surviving Big-Game Hunters

In only one region—the arid grasslands from the frontiers of Alaska to the Gulf of Mexico—did big-game hunting survive. This was the "Great Bison Belt," which lay in the rain shadow of the western mountains (Fagan, 1987). The short grass range of the plains was an ideal environment for the bison, one of the few Ice Age big-game species to adapt to Holocene conditions. The postglacial descendants of the Ice Age steppe bison have increased digestive efficiency to cope with the high-fiber, low-nutrient dead grass of winter. They can feed in deep snow and are less selective eaters than many of the Ice Age species that died out. By 10,500 years ago, bison were the dominant species in all archaeological sites through the bison belt.

10,500 B.P.

At first glance, the Great Plains appear homogeneous, even monotonous. Close examination reveals many subtle differences—stream courses and water holes where game congregated, places where longer grass and seasonal water favored larger bison herds. The late Paleo-Indians and their successors, who preyed on the herds right into historic times, could only survive by a careful, planned utilization of the plains' complex ecosystem (Frison, 1978).

10,000 B.P.

After 10,000 years ago, numerous variations of bison-hunting cultures appeared on the plains, all of them using portable toolkits that bear a strong resemblance to those of their Clovis ancestors. Stone-tipped projectile heads with carefully thinned and ground bases made spear-throwers and spears effective weapons for bison hunting. At least seven major forms are known, with names like Eden, Folsom, Plainview, and Scottsbluff—to mention only a few (Frison, 1978; Haynes, 1982; Irwin and Wormington, 1970). Whether all these forms actually represent distinct cultural entities is a matter of controversy. The entire Paleo-Indian toolkit was highly portable and capable of being used for a wide variety of purposes, everything from woodworking to bison butchery.

Many plains sites are kill locations, strategic places where mass game drives could be organized. Such drives were far from daily events, perhaps taking place every couple of years or so. To pursue bison on foot means days of patient stalking and an intimate knowledge of the animals' habits. Perhaps several bands would cooperate in a game drive. They would encircle a few beasts or, more often, stampede a herd into a swamp or a narrow defile. In some cases, they would drive the frightened animals over a cliff or into dune areas. The archaeological evidence for such activities comes from a series of sites, among them the Agate Basin site in eastern Wyoming, where, judging from the age of the animals, the hunters apparently maneuvered 10 to 20 animals into an arroyo bottom in late February or early March (Frison, 1978). The hunters then drove them upstream until they reached a natural trap in the gully, where the confused bison could be killed with stone-tipped spears.

Olsen-Chubbock 8000 B.P.   The Olsen-Chubbock site in Colorado is an example of a kill site, where approximately 200 bison of all ages were stampeded into a deep, narrow arroyo, probably during the summer or fall (Frison, 1978; Wheat, 1972). Because the skeletons of the prehistoric bison faced north, the excavators concluded that the wind was blowing from the south on the day of the hunt. The stampeding herd was driven into a gully and could not catch the scent of the people waiting for them at the arroyo. The hunters' artifacts were scattered around the carcasses of their quarry (Figure 7.7): scraping tools, stone knives, and flakes used for dismembering the bison.

Smaller communal hunts were probably much more commonplace. John Speth's (1983) excavations at Garnsey, New Mexico, chronicle such a kill. About 400 years ago, a group of hunters visited a small gully where they knew bison would congregate in late March or early April. Instead of killing every animal on sight, they tended to concentrate on the males because, Speth believes, male bison are in better condition in the spring, when their bone marrow has a higher fat content. Fattier meat is an important source of energy and essential fatty acids and is difficult to come by after the lean winter months. So if Garnsey hunters killed a cow, they consumed only the choice, fatter parts.

Bison hunting was practiced on the plains right up until the advent of the horse and the repeating rifle, but Paleo-Indian peoples flourished throughout North America. Clovis-like projectile points are known from many locations in the East. Herds of caribou may have provided sustenance in northern sites around the Great Lakes and in the Northeast at locations such as Robert, Nova Scotia, where caribou hunters flourished (Meltzer, 1988). Paleo-Indian hunting and gathering economies may have varied a great deal from region to region, some bands specializing in big game, others in fishing or gathering, depending on the resources available in each territory. This variation is reflected in Paleo-Indian archaeological sites that can vary from kill locations to shell middens. That hunting was important in places where large game was abundant seems unquestionable, but this activity diminished rapidly in importance as the big game became extinct.

The Desert West

Economic emphasis shifted in the arid West and Southwest. As big game became scarce, many hunting bands relied more heavily on wild vegetable foods that required much more energy to collect and process than game meat. In the Great Basin, smaller animals such as rabbits, squirrels, and deer became more common prey. At the same time, gathering of vegetable foods grew to dominate economic life, combined with some fishing and, in maritime areas, exploitation of shellfish. We are fortunate that arid climates in Utah, Nevada, and elsewhere have preserved many plant and vegetable foods eaten by these early hunter-gatherers. By 9000 years ago, a distinctive,

FIGURE 7.7   A layer of excavated bison bones from the Olsen-Chubbock site in Colorado, where a band of hunters stampeded a herd of bison into a narrow arroyo.

Desert tradition
**9000 B.P. to
modern times**

Danger Cave
Gypsum Cave
Lovelock Cave

Hogup Cave

desertlike form of Archaic culture had been developed over much of the western United States by small bands camping in caves, rock shelters, and temporary sites.

Excavations at later sites like Danger Cave in Utah and the Gypsum and Lovelock sites in Nevada reveal that the hunters were making nets, mats, and baskets, as well as rope (Figure 7.8) (D'Acevedo, 1986; Heizer and Berger, 1970; Jennings, 1957). Hogup Cave in Utah has yielded one of the world's most complete and longest archaeological culture sequences (Aikens, 1970). The site displays gradual adaptations at one settlement, changing it from a base camp to a short-stay camp that was associated with other base camps or with horticultural villages after people learned how to produce food. At all these sites the inhabitants used digging sticks to uproot edible tubers, and much of their toolkit consisted of grinding stones used in preparing vegetable foods. Most Great Basin peoples were obliged to be constantly on the move, searching for different vegetable foods as they came into season and camping near scanty water supplies. Only a few communities living near relatively permanent food sources or good fishing grounds could afford a more sedentary life.

The deposits at Gatecliff Rock Shelter near Austin, Nevada, are 40 feet (12.1 m) deep and span more than 8000 years of human occupation. The inhabitants lived by valleyside streams in the winter, then moved up to the shelter in the summer, gathering piñon nuts on the mountain slopes as well as hunting game, just as Shoshone Indians did in recent times (D. Thomas, 1973; Thomas and Bettinger, 1983).

Most western prehistoric societies continued to live by hunting and foraging right up to European contact. It was only in the most favored areas that people could stay in one place for months on end. One such location was Lovelock Cave in Nevada, where the base camp overlooked a lake rich in fish and waterfowl. The people hunted their prey with bows and arrows, using extremely lifelike reed duck decoys. Human feces show that over 90 percent of the Lovelock inhabitants' diet came from the lake area, including wetland grasses, such fish as chub, ducks, and mud hens (Heizer and Berger, 1970).

8000 B.P.

The southern California coast was another hospitable area, first exploited by small bands blending fishing with marine mammal hunting as early as 8000 years ago. The coastal population remained sparse except in favored areas, where much more elaborate societies evolved. For example, the historic Chumash people of the Santa Barbara Channel area congregated in large, more or less permanent villages ruled by local chiefs, who maintained trading contacts over extensive areas of the West (Moratto, 1985). Such sedentism was possible because of exceptional resource diversity. From November to March, the Chumash subsisted on dried meat and stored vegetable foods. They also collected shellfish and caught fish in the dense kelp beds close inshore. Come spring, they ranged far afield, collecting plants and tubers. Summer brought tuna and other warm-water fish to local waters. The people caught enormous quantities of fish from their canoes. Pine nuts and acorns were gathered in the fall and stored for the leaner months ahead. The Chumash hunted marine mammals and scavenged stranded whales whenever the opportunity arose. This maritime bounty resulted from upwelling that replenishes the surface layers of the Santa Barbara Channel with nutrients and zooplankton. At least 125 fish species flourished in local waters, part of an incredibly diverse range of food resources that enabled not only relatively sedentary settlement but also higher population densi-

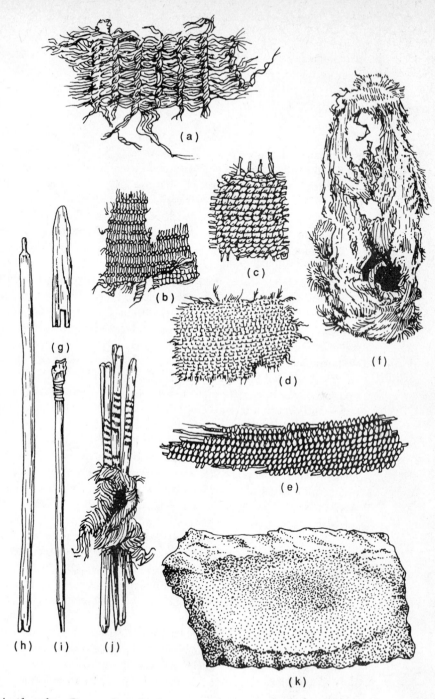

FIGURE 7.8   Artifacts from Danger Cave, Utah, preserved by the dry climate: (a and b) twined matting; (c) twined basketry; (d) coarse cloth; (e) coiled basketry; (f) hide moccasin; (g) wooden knife handle, 4.5 inches (7.4 cm) long; (h) dart shaft, 16 inches (41 cm) long; (i) arrow shaft with broken projectile point in place, 33 inches (84 cm) long; (j) bundle of gaming sticks, 11.5 inches (29 cm) long; (k) milling stone.

ties—as many as 15,000 people living near the shores of the channel and on the offshore islands at European contact.

Eastern North America

Whereas the Great Plains are dominated by grasslands, eastern North America, the region from the Mississippi Valley eastward, is covered by deciduous woodlands and the Southeast by evergreen forest. Superficially, this could be considered a homogeneous natural environment with no sharp geographic barriers to interaction between different human groups, but in fact the area includes an almost bewildering array of microenvironments (Caldwell, 1958; Stoltman and Barreis, 1983). As a result, it is almost impossible to generalize about cultural developments after first settlement some 11,000 years ago (for general and regional summaries, see Mason, 1981; Morse and Morse, 1983; Muller, 1986; B. Smith, 1986; Snow, 1980; Stoltman and Barreis, 1983).

Paleo-Indian bands settled widely over the eastern woodlands from as far north as Nova Scotia to southern Florida (Meltzer, 1988). The most dramatic, but atypical, finds come from natural sinkholes in Florida. During the early Holocene, when sea levels were much lower than today, many rivers left large sinkholes that were favored game areas and places where vegetable foods were also to be found. Carl Clausen, Wilburn Cockrell, and others (Fagan, 1987) have investigated several such locations. At Warm Mineral Springs in Sarasota County, a male burial dating to about 10,000 years ago lay on a ledge 42.6 feet (13 m) below the modern water level. Ground sloth bones and other extinct animal remains occurred in the same horizons as human remains higher up in the hole. Parts of the Warm Mineral Springs site may be older than 11,000 years. (For discussion, see Fagan, 1987.)

Little Salt Spring, not far away, yielded the collapsed shell of a giant tortoise killed about 12,000 years ago. The hunter thrust a wooden stake between shell and plastron, then turned the tortoise over and cooked the meat in the shell (Figure 7.9). A wooden boomeranglike artifact remarkably like those of modern Australian aborigines came from the same site.

The Florida Paleo-Indians and their contemporaries farther north combined hunting with foraging, turning to the pursuit of the white-tailed deer and other smaller mammals as the Ice Age megafauna vanished. By 10,000 years ago, a widespread shift to more generalized hunting and gathering was under way, as the peoples of the eastern woodlands exploited a broad variety of foods—forest resources, like gray squirrels and annual nut harvests, and pioneer seed-bearing grasses. It seems certain that small game, fish, mollusks, and vegetable foods assumed greater importance in the eastern diet after about 10,500 years ago. Inhabitants were part of the broad-spectrum hunting and gathering tradition known as the *Archaic*, which lasted until about 3000 years ago in many areas (for alternative terminology, see Stoltman, 1978).

During the many millennia of the Archaic, there was a long-term trend toward increased efficiency and success in exploiting forest and river valley resources, a shift called "Primary Forest Efficiency" by Joseph Caldwell (1958) in a landmark paper. The Archaic has been subdivided into early, middle, and late stages on the basis of stylistic changes in projectile points and the introduction of slate tools, copper

Margin notes:

Archaic tradition 10,500 to 3000 B.P. and modern times

Warm Mineral Springs 10,000 B.P.

Little Salt Spring 12,000 B.P.

10,000 B.P.

Archaic

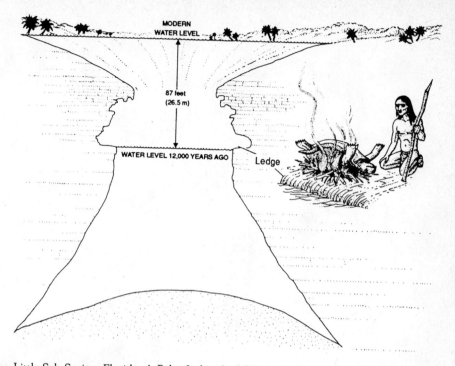

FIGURE 7.9   Little Salt Spring, Florida. A Paleo-Indian had fallen into the spring and swum to a dry ledge, where he found a turtle that he cooked for food. When the meat ran out, he starved to death.

artifacts, and other technological innovations (see Griffin, 1967, for details), but the basic patterns of Archaic life were established early on and are known to us from excavations and surveys in northeast Arkansas and the Little Tennessee River Valley (Chapman et al., 1982; Morse and Morse, 1983; B. Smith, 1986) (Figure 7.10).

Dalton
10,500 to 9500
B.P.

The Dalton tradition flourished over a wide area of the Southeast and Midwest from about 10,500 to 9500 years ago. Dan Morse and Phyllis Morse (1983) argue that in northeast Arkansas, Dalton band organization allowed a network of stable local family bands of 20 to 30 people who regularly used base camps centered on watershed territories. There they exploited easily accessible shallow-water fish, vegetable foods, seasonal nut harvests, and deer; the women married into neighboring bands in nearby river valleys, thereby maintaining trading links between each drainage, contacts that ensured ample supplies of fine-grained chert over large areas (see also Anderson and Hanson, 1988).

8000 B.P.

By about 8000 years ago, warmer and drier climates were developing in the East, culminating in the so-called Hypsithermal episode of 6500 to 6000 years ago (Delcourt and Delcourt, 1981). The major rivers of the Midwest and Southeast stabilized their courses, while prehistoric population densities were still low. The highest concentrations of population were in areas such as major river valley bottoms and lakeshores, which offered the greatest diversity of aquatic, game, and vegetable foods. In some favored areas, there was a slow trend toward

FIGURE 7.10   Artist's reconstruction of an Archaic camp on the Little Tennessee River, c. 8500 years ago. The houses are conjectural.

living within more circumscribed territories and toward more sedentary settlement, made possible by an abundant constellation of seasonal foods.

Koster
9500 b.p. to
a.d. 1200

The famous Koster site in the Illinois River Valley, with its 14 stratified occupation levels, provides an extraordinary chronicle of human exploitation of a midwestern river valley from about 9500 years ago until A.D. 1200 (Struever and Holton, 1979). The first visitors to camp at Koster were Paleo-Indians, but about 8500 years ago, an early Archaic camp there covered about 0.75 acre (0.3 ha). An extended family group of about 25 people returned to the same location again and again, perhaps to exploit rich fall nut harvests in the area. Between 7600 and 7000 years

7600 to 7000
b.p.

ago, there were substantial settlements of rectangular, pole, brush, and clay houses that were occupied for most if not all the year, covering about 1.75 acres (0.7 ha). During spring and summer the inhabitants took thousands of fish, gathering freshwater mussels and hickory nuts in fall and migratory birds in spring. Perhaps the people moved to the nearby uplands to hunt deer. As long as this middle Archaic population remained stable, they could find most of their food resources within 3 miles (4.8 km) of their settlement. It was not until much later, after 4500 years ago, that the Koster people began exploiting a wider range of food resources.

A similar trend toward exploiting a relatively narrow range of wild foods is documented at other midwestern sites, among them the Modoc Rock Shelter near the Mississippi River (Brown and Phillips, 1983; M. L. Fowler, 1958). Modoc was occupied between about 10,000 and 4000 years ago. As time went on, it became more and more of a base camp, where people lived for much of the year while they caught fish and exploited nut harvests. Both Koster and Modoc show that the middle Archaic adaptation was a conservative one, requiring at least a degree of careful scheduling to maximize the potential of nut harvests and to capitalize on the game that fed on the rich forest mast (undergrowth) each fall. In this sense, Caldwell's Primary Forest Efficiency was achieved very early in the Archaic.

By about 4500 years ago, there had been a dramatic increase in the use of riverine resources over much of the Southeast and Midwest, perhaps coinciding with the onset of the Hypsithermal, when the stabilized river bottoms provided an abundance of oxbow lakes and swamps, where fish abounded and native grasses, shellfish, and other foods were to be found. Some of the river valleys lay on seasonal waterfowl migration routes, too, providing a bounty of food in spring and fall. This enhancement of aquatic habitats increased potential food supplies over long sections of river floodplains. As Bruce Smith (1986) puts it, there was an "opportunistic response to the advantageous emergence of a localized, seasonally abundant, dependable, and easily collected resource." This response led to the gradual adoption of sedentary lifeways in many parts of the eastern woodlands. Perhaps it is better described as a shift toward centrally based wandering, which involved a seasonally mobile lifeway and regular returning to the same base location for much of each year, especially during the summers (see Figure 10.11).

Archaic populations in the East rose sharply after 6000 years ago, especially in favored areas. The Hypsithermal opened up vast areas of eastern Canada to caribou and human settlement. Rising sea levels and warming ocean temperatures allowed a steady northward expansion of fish and shellfish habitats. Flooded estuaries allowed more up-river fish runs in spring and fall. Nut-bearing forests spread farther north, into parts of the Great Lakes region, and river valley bottoms were exceptionally diverse and rich environments for Archaic hunter-gatherers (Yerkes, 1988).

In all probability, Archaic population growth was a response not only to environmental change but also to technological and subsistence advances, as well as new settlement patterns that took advantage of new riverine environments. The more sedentary living that accompanied the growth in many areas allowed people to store nuts and other winter foods on a much larger scale than if they were always on the move. This storage, in turn, created larger food surpluses, the ability to support higher population densities year-round, and opportunities for kin groups and individuals to play important roles in controlling labor and the redistribution of food and luxury goods. By the same token, people lived within more restricted territories, and there was far more local cultural variation.

There were also long-term changes in the ways people interacted with one another and their neighbors. The smaller territories inhabited by more people contained a diversity of food resources and raw materials, but there was always something

Modoc
10,000 to 4000
B.P.

4500 B.P.

lacking. Such items as obsidian for toolmaking had to be sought from elsewhere, by making a special journey or maintaining regular economic and social contacts with groups living nearer to the sources of what was needed. Over time, these trading connections assumed ever greater importance in the yearly round. They became a source not only of valued possessions and raw materials but also of social connections and prestige—a way of maintaining "diplomatic" relations with the outside world. These interactions also affected population densities, especially when demand for prestige items, such as copper objects or seashells, soared. More and more hands would be needed to increase the output of food and trade goods. The intensification of hunting and foraging to meet these demands would lead to population increases—and to the emergence of social ranks based on prestige and social and economic power within previously egalitarian societies.

Central Riverine
Archaic
6000 B.P.

Koster
**5900 to 4800
B.P.**

The late Archaic witnessed much greater regional variety in hunter-gatherer culture in the East (B. Smith, 1986; Snow, 1980). The so-called Central Riverine Archaic was the most elaborate and well developed of all eastern late Archaic traditions, for it was centered on midwestern and southeastern river valleys with a superabundance of aquatic, game, and vegetable foods. Between 5900 and 4800 years ago, a village covering 5 acres (2 ha) flourished at Koster, Illinois (Struever and Holton, 1979), housing perhaps 100 to 150 people in substantial homes. The inhabitants did not concentrate on faster-water fish like their predecessors. Instead they speared and netted thousands of shallow-water species such as bass and catfish. One Illinois fish biologist has estimated that the people could have taken between 300 and 600 pounds (136 and 272 kg) of fish flesh per acre from backwater lakes that covered hundreds of acres. The people still collected shellfish and exploited the fall hickory and acorn harvests, but they now collected many more seed plants including marsh elder, a swamp-side grass, grinding the seeds with pestles and mortars. In spring and fall, they would also shoot and trap thousands of migrating waterfowl. Everything from this late Archaic settlement points to greater efficiency at food procurement, accompanied by exploitation of a broader spectrum of potential foods.

Similar broad-spectrum exploitation is found at other midwestern sites, among them the celebrated Indian Knoll site in Kentucky (C. H. Webb, 1968), which has yielded more than 1000 burials. Judging from these graves, the people still lived in fairly egalitarian societies, even if a few individuals were buried with prized possessions, such as turtle-shell ornaments or copper ornaments from Lake Superior (for other late Archaic sites, see Jeffries, 1987; Winters, 1967).

By 6000 years ago, the diverse hunter-gatherer populations of the East were living under very different social conditions than their remote ancestors; in territories with restricted boundaries, they cherished tenuous social and economic links that connected individual to individual, kin to kin, through valleys and entire drainages, over hundreds, even thousands of miles of North America. The long-distance exchange of materials associated with these networks first appeared about 6000 years ago and escalated over the next 3000 years. Lake Superior native copper, hematite, Atlantic and Gulf Coast seashells, jasper from eastern Pennsylvania, chert and other fine-grained rocks—all these materials were exchanged between individuals and passed "down the line," just as obsidian was in the Neolithic Near East.

As studies of Lake Superior copper have shown, exotic artifacts and materials acquired greater prestige the farther they were traded (Figure 7.11). Within this

FIGURE 7.11   Archaic copper artifacts (approximately one-half actual size).

context of regular social gatherings and exchanges, a greater degree of social differentiation based on reciprocity may have developed in late Archaic society. This may have been nothing more than a ranking between younger and older members of society or perhaps the emergence of one kin group as the "ranking" one. Judging from burial customs, both kin-based and individual social ranking took place within a context of increasingly elaborate ritual life. Perhaps some of the richly adorned burials from late Archaic cemeteries are those of individuals who achieved social rank not by force or through virtue of birth but because of their personal qualities as traders and diplomats, as people who helped break down the social, economic, and political isolation that came with restricted mobility (Yerkes, 1988).

More intensive exploitation of food resources (even some cultivation of native plants), greater sedentism, regular social interaction and long-distance exchange, increased ceremonialism—these were the culminating elements in late Archaic life that were to persist into the last few centuries before Christ, when new, much more elaborate burial customs appeared in the eastern woodlands (Chapter 14). In some areas of the Northeast and eastern Canada, much of the Archaic hunter-gatherer tradition survived until modern times, until people came into contact with European explorers (Morison, 1971).

Specialized Hunter-Gatherers in Mesoamerica and Latin America

The hunter-gatherers of the central and southern portions of the New World enjoyed a wide variety of specialized adaptations after 9500 years ago. Sites of these specialized hunter-gatherer groups have been excavated from Mexico to Tierra del Fuego. One characteristic adaptation has been identified in the Andes, and another flourished on the uplands of eastern Brazil (Chauchat, 1988; Lynch, 1980; Rick, 1980, 1988). As in North America, intensified hunting and gathering concentrated the human population in favored localities such as lakeshores and seacoasts, where resources were unusually abundant.

Tehuacán
1000 B.P.

Sophisticated hunting and gathering strategies ensured food at all seasons. Kent Flannery (1968a) has shown, for instance, that the hunter-gatherers of the Tehuacán Valley in Mexico had a regular, almost scheduled, annual round of hunting an gathering activities that caused the population to gather in large camps during the plentiful season and scatter into small groups during the lean months. The people obtained a balanced diet by using different food procurement systems that varied in importance with the time of year.

Some of these specialized hunter-gatherers remained at the simple hunting and collecting level because of limitations in their environment and plentiful natural resources, making economic change unnecessary. However, in some areas of Mesoamerica and on the coast and highlands of Peru, hunter-gatherer bands began to experiment with the deliberate planting of vegetable foods, perhaps in attempts to expand the areas in which certain favored vegetable foods were found. These experiments became one of the vehicles of dynamic cultural change that resulted from the first development of agriculture in the New World (Chapter 14).

Fuegian Indians
**6000 B.P. to
modern times**

The southernmost extremities of Latin America were inhabited until recent times by scattered bands of hunters and fisherfolk. The Ona, Yaghan, and Alacaluf peoples are vividly described by early missionaries who settled among them. They lived in small bands, using only the crudest shelters of skins or grass and driftwood, with nothing but skin for body covering during the height of the antarctic winter. Shellfish, some game, fruits, berries, and fish provided a simple diet, and for tools they had none of the more sophisticated weapons made by more northern hunters. Tierra del Fuego, however, was occupied remarkably early, and it is thought that the Fuegian tradition began as early as 6000 B.P., if not earlier. Many roots of these most southerly prehistoric humans lie in early hunting cultures that elsewhere were replaced thousands of years before by more advanced farming cultures.

ALEUTS AND INUIT

We started the story of the first Americans with Alaska, and we now end with a brief return to Arctic latitudes to trace the origins of the Aleuts and Inuit, whose remarkable hunter-gatherer cultures survived long beyond European contact into recent times. The origins of both the Aleut and the Inuit go back many thousands of years into prehistory, and their ultimate ancestry may lie both in Asian roots and in local cultural evolution. The differences between them are more cultural than physical and reflect varied adaptations to Arctic maritime environments. It is logical for us to end this chapter with the Arctic, for the Inuit were the first native Americans to come into contact with Europeans, in Greenland and in the extreme continental Northeast (Dumond, 1987a,b).

As we have seen, the earliest cultural tradition that makes any archaeological

Paleoarctic
tradition
**11,000 to 6000
B.P.**

sense at the moment is the Paleoarctic tradition, which was flourishing by about 11,000 B.P. and had some connections with contemporary cultures in Siberia. The Paleoarctic people were tundra-dwelling hunter-gatherers, whose culture and language *may* be the ancestor of both Inuit and Aleut culture and language. It should be noted that both peoples are the most Asian of all indigenous Americans. By 9000 years ago, these two peoples had moved south as far as the Alaskan peninsula. Only a millennium later they had settled in the Aleutian Islands.

9000 B.P.

6000 B.P.

By 6000 B.P., there was more cultural diversity in the Arctic, as specialized adaptations developed on the coast and in the interior, and some American Indian groups moved northward into formerly glaciated regions in the interior. On the Pacific Coast and in the eastern Aleutians, the Aleutian tradition was among those that emerged.

Aleutian
tradition
**8700 B.P. to
modern times**

The Aleuts have been in their island homeland twice as long as the Inuit have been in Greenland (Laughlin, Marsh, and Harper, 1979). Their ancestors entered the archipelago at a time when the sea level was lower than it is today. Their ancestry is perhaps in the Norton tradition (see later; Dumond 1987a). The earliest occupation dates to approximately 8700 B.P. at Anangula, about a third of the way along the chain, at the terminus of the Bering Land Bridge. Anangula lies on a cliff 65.5 feet (20 m) above sea level and probably was occupied for at least 500 years by an estimated group of at least 100 (Aigner, 1970; Laughlin, 1980). The inhabitants lived by fishing, sea mammal hunting (Figure 7.12), and fowling, an ideal strategy for an isolated, stable marine environment. The nearby and later site of Chaluka carries the story of Aleutian occupation up to recent times. Radiocarbon dates suggest that the

FIGURE 7.12   Aleuts returning from a sea otter hunt, probably in the 1890s. They are wearing eye visors made of wood. Photograph by an unknown government surveyor.

eastern and western ends of the Aleutian archipelago were occupied approximately 3000 years ago, the people expanding outward from the Anangula area as the population density grew.

The origins of the Inuit (Eskimo) cultural tradition of modern times may lie in the Arctic Small-Tool tradition, a distinctive small-artifact technology that appeared in Alaska approximately 4300 years ago. The Arctic Small-Tool people may have had strong connections with Siberia and are thought to have been nomadic land mammal hunters who preyed on caribou and musk-ox. Some settled in Alaska; others wandered as far east as Greenland by 4000 B.P., becoming the first people to settle in the eastern Arctic. The eastern Small-Tool tradition eventually evolved into the long-lived Thule tradition, whose people were the first native Americans to come into contact with Europeans (Maxwell, 1985; Schledermann, 1990).

The Arctic Small-Tool tradition began to disappear in Alaska some 3500 years ago, to be replaced by cultures based on the intensive hunting of both sea mammals and land animals. This tradition, called the Norton tradition, in turn gave rise to the Thule tradition, which is thought to have originated among whale hunters in the Bering Strait. This tradition first emerged in the first millennium after Christ and developed into a highly distinctive sea mammal hunting culture with all the Inuit artifacts so well known from popular publications—among them, the kayak, the umiak (open skin boat), and toggled harpoons, as well as fine ivory work (Figure 7.13). Many of the Inuit, especially those who hunted whales, lived by then in larger settlements. In approximately A.D. 900 the Thule people started to expand to the south and then to the east. Thule whale hunters appeared in the Arctic islands of the east in approximately A.D. 1000, where their open-water hunting techniques could be used with great effect. By the time the Thule reached northwest Greenland, the Norsemen had been living in the southern parts of the island for some time (McGhee, 1984).

Inuit cultural traditions, like those of the Fuegians and other hunter-gatherer groups, continued to flourish after European contact, but within a few centuries, traditional lifeways were modified beyond recognition and exotic diseases decimated

Arctic Small-Tool tradition
4300 to 3500 B.P.

Norton tradition (west)
3500 B.P. to A.D. 500

Thule tradition
A.D. 500 to modern times

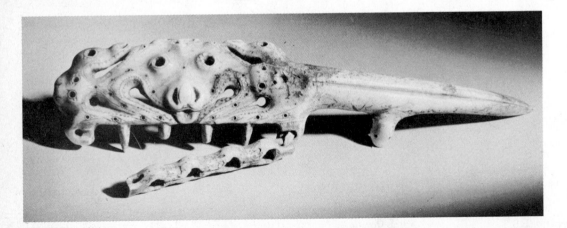

FIGURE 7.13   Ornamented ivory object, perhaps a comb, from the Seward Peninsula in Alaska (Northern tradition and style). Length: 10.2 inches (26 cm).

hunter-gatherer populations. Today, few of America's hunter-gatherers still practice their millennia-old lifeways; there are no longer the resources or the territory for them to do so.

GUIDE TO FURTHER READING

The following references will guide you through the morass of books and articles on this complex subject:

Carlisle, Richard, ed. 1988. *America Before Columbus: Ice Age Origins.* Pittsburgh: Department of Anthropology, University of Pittsburgh.
> *Conference papers that summarize the present state of knowledge about the first settlement. Technical content.*

Fagan, Brian M. 1987. *The Great Journey.* New York: Thames and Hudson.
> *A general, analytic discussion of the evidence for first settlement.*

———. 1991. *Ancient North America.* New York: Thames and Hudson.
> *A general summary of North American archaeology for beginning readers. Covers the entire spectrum from first settlement to historical archaeology.*

Hopkins, David M., et al., eds. 1982. *Paleoecology of Beringia.* New York: Academic Press.
> *A fascinating and highly technical set of essays about the Bering Land Bridge that discusses everything from animal life to sea level changes.*

Jennings, Jesse D. 1983. *Ancient Native Americans,* 2d ed. (2 vols.). New York: Freeman.
> *A comprehensive volume of essays on the archaeology of North, Middle, and South America, each written by an established authority. Up to date, highly technical, and crammed with useful information.*

———. 1988. *The Prehistory of North America.* Mountain View, Ca: Mayfield.
> *A textbook for undergraduates, which summarizes basic culture history and artifact forms.*

Keatinge, Richard W., ed. 1988. *Peruvian Prehistory.* Cambridge, Eng.: Cambridge University Press.
> *The first two chapters in this book summarize much of value on Latin American hunter-gatherers.*

Phillips, J., and Brown, J., eds. 1983. *Archaic Hunter-Gatherers in the Midwest.* Orlando, FL: Academic Press.
> *Essays on Archaic hunter-gatherers, some of which have broad application.*

Smith, Bruce D. 1986. "The Archaeology of the Southeastern United States: From Dalton to de Soto, 10,500–500 B.P." *Advances in World Archaeology* 5: 1–92.
> *A superb analytic synthesis of southeastern archaeology that has broad application elsewhere in the eastern woodlands. This is an excellent example of contemporary approaches to North American prehistory.*

Chronological Table E

C14 Years B.P./A.D.	Sub-Saharan Africa	Australia	New Guinea offshore islands
Modern Times	European contact ↑	European contact ↑	
A.D. 1	Gwisho	Continuous record of aboriginal settlement	Chapter 15
5000 B.P.	?SAN HUNTER-GATHERERS		
12,000	Eland's Bay	Kutikina · Purritjarra · Bone Cave · Devil's Lair Cave · Oenpelli Miriwun	
20,000	Nelson's Bay	Koonalda Malangangerr · Lake Mungo	Tabon Kosipe · Kilu · Kuk, New Guinea · New Ireland
30,000	MIDDLE STONE AGE CULTURES	Bluff Cave ORS 7 · Mammoth Cave	
40,000	Chapter 5 ↑	?First settlement 50,000	Bobongara (Huon)

264

CHAPTER 8 AFRICANS AND AUSTRALIANS

Preview

- Like hunter-gatherers in northern latitudes, the post-Pleistocene peoples of tropical regions adopted increasingly diverse economies after 10,000 years ago. They also made much use of the bow and arrow. Toolkits became smaller and more lightweight as a result.

- Judging from excavations in southern Africa, the postglacial populations of Africa may have turned their attention to smaller browsing animals, food gathering, and aquatic resources, continuously adapting to changing environmental conditions. The densest human populations were probably concentrated in areas of abundant water and diverse animal and plant resources. The result was probably a much greater diversity of hunter-gatherer societies throughout much of Africa, a diversity from which living societies like the San arose.

- The San of southern Africa flourished in savanna woodland country that was rich in game and vegetable foods. Their lively rock art depicts their hunting and gathering activities. These paintings and the waterlogged Gwisho sites in Central Zambia have shown that the San's portable toolkits changed little over the centuries. The San's highly flexible band organization of today doubtlessly ensured the continued viability of prehistoric hunter-gatherers as well. They also lived at small campsites, which were often reoccupied at certain seasons of the year for many generations.

- During much of the Weichsel glaciation, New Guinea and Australia formed a single landmass, called Sahul.

- It has been estimated that human settlement of Sahul goes back 70,000 to 50,000 years ago, although the earliest archaeological sites at present date to little more than 40,000 years ago.

- People using open-water craft had settled on some southwestern Pacific islands, including the Solomons, by 30,000 years ago.

- The first settlement of Australia dates to at least 40,000 years ago, perhaps earlier, but securely dated sites proliferate after 35,000 years ago, with late Ice Age hunters flourishing in Tasmania by 31,000 years ago.

- The archaeological record shows that the Australian lifeway changed little during its long history, but there were steady, slow changes in tool technology. The Tasmanians were isolated in their homeland as sea levels rose at the end of the Pleistocene and, as a result, did not acquire some of the later mainland tool types, such as the boomerang.

- Living archaeology and ethnographic analogy play an important part in our interpretation of the prehistory of tropical hunter-gatherers.

Chronological Table E

The end of the Weichsel glaciation had less profound climactic effects on tropical latitudes than on northern latitudes. However, it did result in minor shifts in rainfall patterns, which may have had a significant effect on the distribution of critically important game populations and cereal grasses. The archaeological record for the many hunter-gatherer populations of southern latitudes consists for the most part of thousands of stone implements from dozens of isolated sites (Allchin, 1966). Instead of attempting a detailed chronicle of isolated local cultures, we concentrate on two adaptations of particular interest—those of the San peoples of southern Africa and those of the Australian Aborigines. Both these peoples continue to display a wide range of relatively specialized adaptations that include not only hunting and gathering but fishing and exploitation of shellfish as well.

The modern hunter-gatherer populations of Africa and Asia are among the very few survivors of the longest-lived and perhaps most viable of all human lifeways. Only 15,000 years ago, probably everyone lived by hunting and gathering. Ethnographer George Peter Murdock (1968) has estimated that perhaps 15 percent of the world's population was still hunting and gathering at the time Columbus landed in the New World. We are fortunate that modern anthropological studies of the San and Australians have given us at least a few insights into the traditional lifeways of southern hunter-gatherers.

AFRICAN HUNTER-GATHERERS: PAST AND PRESENT

As we saw in Chapter 5, *Homo sapiens sapiens,* anatomically modern humans, probably evolved in Africa, perhaps as early as 100,000 years ago. The long millennia of the Weichsel glaciation saw the peoples of Africa developing ever more efficient ways of hunting and foraging. Some fascinating indications come from coastal caves in South Africa, among them Klasies River Mouth and Nelson's Bay (Binford, 1984; R. Klein, 1979). Richard Klein found that the people who inhabited these caves lived not only off vegetable foods but off game and marine resources as well. Klasies River was occupied between about 120,000 and 70,000 years ago, then abandoned until about 5000 years ago. The early inhabitants collected limpets and also pursued seals and penguins. They took few fish; they preferred game on the hoof, especially such docile animals as the eland and bastard hartebeest. They did kill some more formidable beasts like the buffalo, black wildebeest, and roan antelope but in much smaller numbers, and some of the meat was perhaps scavenged. Interestingly, the bones of these individual species came from either very old or young individuals, which is the sort of age pattern found with predator kills. Only the eland and bastard hartebeest were taken at all ages. Klein concluded that they may have been driven into traps or over cliffs.

The Nelson's Bay Cave was occupied by modern *Homo sapiens* populations after 15,000 years ago. Again, eland and bastard hartebeest were common and taken at all ages, perhaps by game drives. The Nelson's Bay folk took bush pigs and warthogs, much fiercer and more formidable prey. Not only that, they used nets and fish hooks to catch a wide range of ocean fish. They also lived off flying sea birds such as cormorants. One could argue, of course, that the Klasies River people simply preferred game on the hoof, but the relative abundance of wild pigs strongly suggests that the Nelson's Bay hunters were much more expert and capable of exploiting a far wider range of game. They may have used the bow and arrow. Although the eland lives in widely dispersed herds, other antelope do not and would have been much more vulnerable to efficient hunting. Klein (1979) notes that several large mammal species became extinct 12,000 to 10,000 years ago.

We know very little about the climate of sub-Saharan Africa at the height of the last glaciation, but John Parkington (1987) and others believe that the human populations living at the southern tip of the continent were sparse. Parkington notes that larger animals appear to have been more common before about 9000 years ago; small bands of hunter-gatherers may have roamed over large territories in search of large, gregarious animals. There is, however, almost no evidence to support this scenario, and much of the southern part of Africa may have been wet, cold, and windy during glacial times.

By about 9000 years ago, the world's southern oceans were warmer than today. It was not until 3000 years later, during the so-called postglacial climatic optimum, the northern seas achieved higher temperatures. This delay is due to different land and water distributions in the two hemispheres, with Antarctica being much colder than the Arctic Ocean. Warmer, drier conditions in southern Africa led to more succulent vegetation at the expense of grassland and heath, with major changes in human subsistence. These changes are hard to document. John Parkington (1987) has chronicled one changing scenario at Eland's Bay Cave in the far south. Thirteen thousand years ago, the inhabitants hunted large and medium-sized antelope. But between 11,000 and 9000 years ago, they turned their attention to smaller browsing animals, with estuarine and marine animals as well as limpets becoming ever more common. By 8000 years ago, the entire coastal plain was flooded, with only small

*Klasies River
Nelson's Bay*
**100,000 to
70,000 B.P.**

Eland's Bay
**13,000 to 8,000
B.P.**

browsing animals, mussels, and fish being taken. Then Eland's Bay Cave was abandoned suddenly, never to be reoccupied.

After 11,000 B.P. the quantity of food bones increases dramatically, as does the variety of ostrich eggshell beads, water containers, bone tools, decorated bone work, and other artifacts (Figure 8.1). Parkington believes that this intensification in domestic activity was due to environmental change, to the dramatic encroachments of the postglacial ocean. Eland's Bay Cave was first visited, then lived in for long periods of time as the coastal plain shrank. Finally, the people moved into the interior or elsewhere along the shore when this stretch of coastline was no longer productive. It would be a mistake to describe the major changes in artifact inventories or subsistence as evolving culture change. Rather, they may reflect continuous adaptation to rapidly altering climatic conditions, changes that were reflected by other adaptive shifts elsewhere on the coast, as at Nelson's Bay, and also in the warm interior.

The long-term trend over the past 15,000 years may have been toward smaller "food parcels" (Parkington, 1987). Many late Stone Age caves and rock shelters in southern Africa were used much more regularly in postglacial times, as if mountain and near-coastal locations were extremely favorable places to settle, places where smaller browsing animal herds would be concentrated. The warming trend in the earlier millennia of postglacial times may have led to increased aridity in many parts of the interior, with the densest human populations concentrated in areas of abundant water and diverse animal and plant resources. The result was probably a great diversity of hunter-gatherer societies throughout much of Africa.

Hilary Deacon (1979) has excavated several late Stone Age rock shelters and caves with exceptional care. He believes that there was a trend toward hunting smaller game and especially toward the exploitation of plant foods. Rabbits, tortoises, and both grasses and root plants became vital components in the hunter-gatherers' diet. Just when plant foods came to be of overwhelming importance is much debated, but they were especially significant after about 2000 years ago, when herding peoples were settled in extreme southern Africa (Chapter 12), perhaps when the newcomers squeezed hunter-gatherers into more limited territories, away from cattle-grazing grounds (for full discussion, see Parkington, 1987).

The same general trend toward increasingly specialized subsistence strategies may also have developed in other parts of sub-Saharan Africa, just as in other parts of the world. The peoples of the open savanna lived off the abundant game populations and supplemented their diet with seasonal gathering of the rich vegetable resources of the woodland. Other bands settled on the shores of lakes and on riverbanks and lived by fishing. This valuable and reliable source of protein encouraged more lasting settlement and increased specialization. The rain forest peoples of the Zaire River Basin in central Africa were unable to hunt as wide a range of game as their savanna counterparts, so they relied heavily on vegetable foods and wild roots.

The later Stone Age hunter-gatherers of the eastern and southern African savanna are comparatively well documented not only from archaeological sites but also from their own rock paintings and engravings. Rock paintings are notoriously hard to date, but it is possible that Stone Age artists were at work in southern Africa as early as 20,000 years ago. They were certainly painting the walls of caves they visited 8000 years ago. Modern ethnographic and historical records connect the San peoples who live today in the Kalahari Desert with this ancient artistic tradition.

0 1 2 3 cm

FIGURE 8.1   An ostrich eggshell bead necklace from Gwisho, Zambia, c. 3500 years old.

Their Stone Age lifeway survived into the twentieth century and appears to have changed relatively little for thousands of years.

The Gwisho hot springs in central Zambia provide evidence for a basically similar subsistence pattern at least 3500 years ago (Fagan and van Noten, 1971). Because the

Gwisho
3500 B.P.

lower levels of the sites among the springs were waterlogged, many organic artifacts and food remains have survived, giving an exceptionally complete picture of Stone Age life in the region. The economy and material culture of the Gwisho people show a striking resemblance to those of modern San peoples in the Kalahari, although, of course, there are environmental differences (Lee, 1979; Lee and DeVore, 1976; Yellen, 1977). The Gwisho people hunted many species of antelope and caught fish in shallow pools of the nearby Kafue River. The waterlogged levels contained more than 10,000 plant remains, from only eight species, all of which were apparently collected to the exclusion of many other edible species. Nearby lay some fine arrowheads and some of the wooden artifacts made by the inhabitants, including some simple digging sticks used for uprooting tubers. These tools are identical to those used by Kalahari San today. There were traces of a grass and stick shelter, of hearths, and of layers of grass that may have served as bedding. Thirty-five burials were deposited in the soil of the campsites. The deposits were littered with hundreds of stone arrow barbs and tiny scraping tools that lay alongside pestles and grinding stones used to process the vegetable foods that were an important part of the Gwisho diet. So little have gathering habits changed in the past 3000 years that a San from the Kalahari was able to identify seeds from the excavations and tell archaeologists what they were used for.

The Gwisho hot springs are informative, for they confirm ethnographic observations made about the present-day San. Like that of their modern successors, the toolkit of the Gwisho people was highly portable, and much of it was disposable. Except for bows and arrows, the Kalahari San improvise many of their tools from the bush as they need them, making snares from vegetable fibers and clubs from convenient branches. The women use digging sticks like the Gwisho artifacts for digging tubers and a softened antelope hide, or kaross, as a garment and carrying bag. Their only other artifacts are a pair of pounding stones for breaking up nuts. The Gwisho site contained both digging sticks and pounders. We know from cave paintings that the San used karosses for thousands of years, and we can assume they were used at Gwisho and elsewhere.

Like those of the San, the Gwisho home bases were little more than small clusters of brush shelters. The average present-day !Kung San camp holds approximately 10 to 30 people. The small population of !Kung territory leads to a continuous turnover of the composition of camp populations. This constant change is a reality reflected in the !Kung's highly flexible kinship system. Every member of a band has not only close family ties but also kin connections with a much wider number of people living all over !Kung territory. The !Kung kinship system is based on an elaborate network of commonly possessed personal names, which are transmitted from grandparent to grandchild. People with similar names share kin ties even if they live some distance from one another. This network is such that individuals can move to a new camp and find a family with which they have kin ties to accept them. The resulting flexibility of movement prevents total social chaos. Presumably, the prehistoric San had a similar social organization to aid survival.

The vivid San paintings and engravings depict the game hunted, the chase, and life in camp (Lewis-Williams, 1981; Vinnecombe, 1976). The San drew running hunters, people fishing from boats, and scenes of gathering honey and vegetable foods (Figure 8.2). The hunters can be seen stalking game in disguise, hotly pursuing

FIGURE 8.2   San hunters depicted in a rock painting in Natal, South Africa.

wounded quarry, and even raiding the cattle herds of their agricultural neighbors of later centuries. David Lewis-Williams (1981), who has studied ethnographic records of San bands, has shown convincingly that many of the paintings depict complex metaphors that represent symbolic values in the San world. Each superimposition of paintings and each relationship between human figures and animals had profound meaning to the artists and the people. For instance, many of the paintings depict eland with dancers cavorting around them (Figure 8.3). Lewis-Williams believes that the dancers were acquiring the potency released by the death of the eland. The dancers go into trances so powerful that they become eland themselves (Figure 8.4). This symbolism survived into the nineteenth century. When Victorian anthropologist George Stow (Lewis-Williams, 1981) showed some rock painting pictures to an elderly San couple, the woman began to sing and dance. The man begged her to desist because the old songs made him sad. Eventually he joined in, and Stow watched the couple reliving the symbolism of past days. Only now, more than a century later, are archaeologists trying to probe this forgotten world.

A.D. 1   Prehistoric hunter-gatherers enjoyed the savanna woodlands of eastern and southern Africa undisturbed until approximately 2000 years ago, when the first farming peoples (other African folk) settled by the banks of the Zambezi and Limpopo rivers (Phillipson, 1984). The San placed second in the resulting competition for land: The farmers wanted grazing grass and prime land for cultivating, so they drove off the bands of San hunter-gatherers, who had to retreat into less favored areas. Some took up the new economies and married into farming communities.
A.D. 1800   White settlement in South Africa increased the isolation of the San. As the pressure

FIGURE 8.3   A trance dance being executed by San shamans. Their elongated bodies convey the sense of being stretched out that is felt by people in altered states of consciousness. Dots along the spine of the central figure depict what the San describe as a "boiling" sensation as supernatural power rises up the spine and "explodes" in the head. The power is derived from certain animals, like the eland depicted to the right.

on their hunting grounds grew, the San moved into mountainous areas and desert regions. Even there they were harassed and hunted. Some of the white settlers made a sport of shooting them on Sunday afternoons. The doomed San of South Africa calmly continued to paint scenes of cattle raids and of European ships and wagons. They even depicted red-coated English soldiers on their expeditions into the mountains. By the end of the nineteenth century, there was no San painting in South Africa, and the art of stone toolmaking had all but died out. The last stoneworkers used glass bottle fragments to make their sharp arrowheads. They found this unusually pure "stone" vastly preferable to their usual quartz pebbles (Peringuey, 1911; Schapera, 1930).

A.D. 1890

SUNDA AND SAHUL: THE FIRST
SETTLEMENT OF ISLAND SOUTHEAST
ASIA

On the other side of the world, island Southeast Asia underwent far more profound change than tropical Africa after the Ice Age. Climatically, global warming brought generally drier conditions to the Australian interior and caused major changes in the distribution of tropical forests. Dramatic rises in post-Ice Age sea levels altered the geography of the off-lying parts of Southeast Asia beyond recognition. Therein lies one of the fascinating questions of world prehistory. The Australian Aborigines

FIGURE 8.4   A curing dance among the San from the Nyae Nyae area of Namibia. Dances like this may
have formed part of the ritual behind prehistoric rock paintings.

encountered by British navigator Captain James Cook and other early European
explorers in the eighteenth century A.D. were still living in the Stone Age (Figure 8.5).
For two centuries, anthropologists and historians have puzzled over the ancestry of
these remarkable people. Where did the Australians come from and how long ago
did people first settle on this remote continent (Allen, 1989; Lourandos, 1987; White
and O'Connell, 1982)?

　　At the height of the last glaciation some 20,000 years ago, sea levels were over
300 ft (100 m) below modern levels. Dry land joined Sumatra to Borneo, and the
Philippines and Malaya to the Southeast Asian mainland. Great rivers dissected the
now-sunken plains, known to geologists as Sunda (Figure 8.6). Further offshore,
nearly 19 miles (30 km) of open water separated Sunda from the island of Wallacea
(modern Sulawesi and Timor); 62 miles (100 km) further offshore lay a vast landmass,
Sahul, a combination of Australia, New Guinea, and a low-lying shelf between them
that is now the Arafura Sea. These are, of course, the coastlines of the glacial

Sunda
Wallacea
Sahul

FIGURE 8.5   An Australian aborigine with his lightweight hunting kit. This somewhat romanticized portrait was drawn by François Peron, a naturalist attached to the Baudin Expedition of 1802.

maximum, and sea levels were considerably higher for most of the last glaciation. For most of the period between about 100,000 and 15,000 years ago, people would have had to cross much wider stretches of ocean than those at the glacial maximum. Even at the height of the last glaciation, the colonization of Wallacea and Sahul would have required some form of watercraft and the technology to build them. This raises a

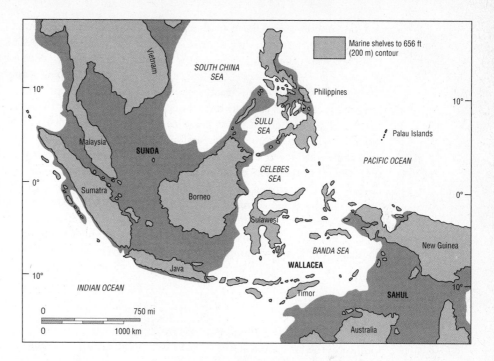

FIGURE 8.6   Ice Age, Southeast Asia. Low sea levels exposed dry land off Southeast Asia and between Australia and New Guinea during the last glaciation, creating Sahul and Sunda.

fundamental and deeply interesting question: How long ago did people go offshore and cross wide tracts of ocean, perhaps paddling out of sight of land?

   Despite intensive search, no traces of *Homo erectus* or archaic forms of *Homo sapiens* have come from the islands of Southeast Asia. Thus, it seems a reasonable assumption that anatomically modern people were the first to settle the off-lying landmasses. If *H. sapiens sapiens* had settled in Southeast Asia by about 75,000 years ago, as we hypothesized in Chapter 6, we can reasonably expect colonization to have occurred some time after that date. At the time, the plains of Sunda were relatively dry. Human settlement was probably concentrated in areas such as coasts, lakeshores, and rivers with more diverse and predictable food resources. As in the rain forests, easily split bamboo and other woods sufficed for many tasks. The coastlines that faced Wallacea and Sahul were lapped by relatively benign waters that probably offered a bounty of easily taken shallow-water fish and shellfish to supplement game and plant foods. Perhaps the people living along these shores fashioned simple rafts of bamboo and mangrove logs lashed together with forest vines (R. Jones, 1989). Such rafts would have served as stable platforms for fishing in sheltered, shallow water, for reaching offshore shell beds. Perhaps it was in such craft that some people crossed to Wallacea and Sahul well before the glacial maximum of 20,000 years ago.

Two routes led offshore to Sahul. One led from southern Sunda to Wallacea, then across to the Australian shore. The other was from southern China, across the Philippines and Borneo, and into New Guinea via Sulawesi (Figure 8.6). Whichever route was used, the process of colonization involved both island hopping and open-water travel, the earliest instance of seafaring by human beings. As is always the case with ocean crossings, scholars debate endlessly about whether the first settlement was accidental or deliberate. In the case of Southeast Asia, with its strong northerly monsoon winds of summer, colonization was probably the result of dozens of accidental driftings offshore over thousands of years. Computer simulations have shown that there are moderate chances of a raft drifting from Timor to Australia in about seven days in front of strong monsoon winds. Undoubtedly many of these strandings resulted in the group dying out, and computer simulations show that the chances of survival, even with men and women in the party, were very small. Eventually, however, a viable population (or populations) was established along the more than 1850-mile (3000-km) coastline of Sahul (Figure 8.7).

New Guinea

Bobongara
c. 40,000 B.P.

Much of Sahul was rolling, semiarid lowlands—what is now Australia, with New Guinea in the far north offering a quite different landscape of rugged mountains and highland valleys. The earliest evidence for human settlement in New Guinea comes from Bobongara on the Huon Peninsula, where archaeologist Les Groube found waisted ground axes and a single stone flake sealed under volcanic ash that dates to at least 40,000 years ago (Figure 8.8). Groube believes these waisted axes were used to ring trees and clear forests, perhaps to encourage the growth of plants on the forest

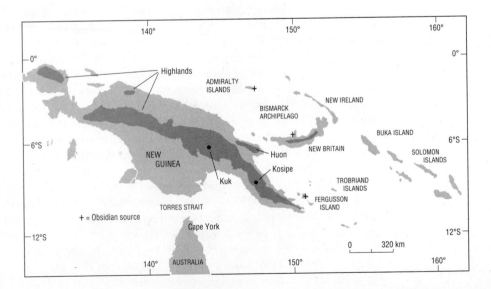

FIGURE 8.7   Map showing New Guinea and adjacent islands mentioned in Chapters 8 and 13.

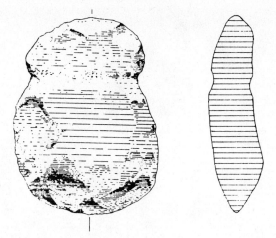

FIGURE 8.8   Waisted stone ax from the Huon Peninsula, New Guinea.

fringes—a form of deliberate manipulation of wild plants to enhance the growth of wild plant foods such as yams, sugarcane, and perhaps taro and fruit trees (Groube et al., 1986).

Kuk
c. 30,000 B.P.

The Kuk site in the New Guinea highlands contained fire-cracked and humanly transported rocks that have been dated to about 30,000 years ago (White and O'Connell, 1982). Both rock shelters and open sites such as the 24,000-year-old Kosipe site in the eastern highlands show that this occupation was widespread before the last glacial maximum.

The Solomon Islands

The Huon Peninsula faces the Bismarck Strait, with the island of New Britain only a 30-mile (51-km) or so passage offshore. From there, it is only a short voyage to New Ireland. These two islands are visible from one another but are separated by deep water and were never joined during the last glaciation. Open-water voyages were needed to colonize them, and excavations in four limestone caves on New Ireland

32,000 B.P.

have yielded traces of human occupation at least 32,000 years ago (Allen et al., 1989). These were expert fisherfolk, who took shellfish and fish and hunted bats, reptiles, and birds. By 20,000 years ago, their successors were regularly trading obsidian for toolmaking across 19 miles (30 km) of open water from west New Britain, from a source 217 miles (350 km) in a straight line from their home.

Kilu
28,000 B.P.

Even further offshore to the south, the Kilu Rock Shelter on Buka Island in the northern Solomons contains human occupation dating to between 28,000 and 20,000 years ago (Figure 8.9) (Wickler and Spriggs, 1988). Open-water crossings of at least 81 to 112 miles (130–180 km) would have been required to settle on Buka, depending on the route selected. Voyaging over this distance would certainly have

FIGURE 8.9   Excavations at Kilu Rock Shelter, northern Solomon Islands.

required some form of open-water craft, as well as foods that could be preserved for use during longer voyages. Substantial water containers would also have been essential. From Buka, it would have been an easy matter to colonize the rest of the Solomon chain, for the islands are separated by short distances (Allen et al., 1989).

Further offshore lay the limits of the late Ice Age world, for sea distances become much larger. More than 186 miles (300 km) lie between the Solomons and the environmentally impoverished Santa Cruz Islands, which were a much smaller target area even for expert navigators. The islands to the south and east lie within a region with no indigenous terrestrial mammals except bats and a progressively impoverished flora and fauna. Such remote oceanic environments were insufficient to support hunter-gatherers. It was not until much later that the development of larger offshore canoes, much more sophisticated navigational skills, and easily storable food crops enabled humans to colonize islands far offshore (Chapter 13).

Everything points to a relatively rapid spread of hunter-gatherer peoples with expert seagoing abilities through northern Sahul and contiguous islands at least as early as 40,000 years ago. This rapid colonization was aided by favorable climatic conditions, with generally good weather and predictable winds and currents that would carry people in small crafts from island to island without the necessity for elaborate technology. The Sunda-Sahul area was a superb "nursery" for seafaring expertise, and it is no coincidence that islanders in the western Pacific were venturing far offshore long before Westerners undertook ambitious voyages in the Mediterranean after 14,000 years ago (Irwin et al., 1990).

Australia

50,000 B.P.

The first settlement of Australia, like that of the Americas, is an issue thwart with controversy (Allen, 1989). The earliest absolutely indisputable evidence of human settlement dates to after 35,000 years ago, but there are finds of stone implements in river gravels and other sediments that are claimed to date back to 50,000 years ago, perhaps even earlier (Roberts et al., 1990) (Figure 8.10). It is, of course, possible that there was a long period of what archaeologist Jim Allen calls "invisible coloniza-

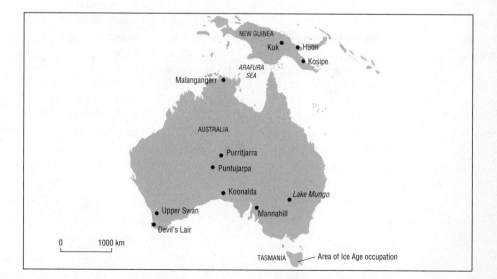

FIGURE 8.10   Archaeological sites in Australia and Tasmania.

30,000 B.P.

Devil's Lair
32,500 B.P.

Purritjarra
27,000 B.P.

Lake Mungo
26,000 B.P.

Koondalda
24,000 to
15,000 B.P.

tion" for thousands of years by peoples who are not represented in the archaeological record. Traces of human occupation immediately before and around 30,000 years ago have accumulated rapidly in recent years. Some hunter-gatherers visited the Devil's Lair Cave near Perth in the southwest part of west Australia as early as 32,500 years ago and used the site more regularly from 23,000 years ago to the end of the Ice Age (Dortch and Merrilees, 1973). The Purritjarra rock shelter in the arid center of Australia near the Northern Territory's Cleland Hills was occupied from at least 27,000 to about 6000 years ago.

Far to the east, in the Willandra Lakes region of western New South Wales, early sites cluster around long dried-up lakes. One group of sites includes shell middens located in dune systems dating to around 32,000 years ago, perhaps earlier. The 26,000-year-old Lake Mungo site comes from the same general area, a thin scatter of stone artifacts, hearths, fish bones, and other food remains (J. M. Bowdler, Jones, and Thorne, 1970). Humans were living in the arid zones of Australia, at places like Koondala Cave on South Australia's Nullabor Plain, by 24,000 years ago. People lived there until 15,000 years ago, visiting the site to quarry stone and making patterned lines or "flutings" on the cave walls during their stays (R. Wright, 1971). Arnhem Land in the north was certainly occupied well before 20,000 years ago, with radiocarbon dated occupations of about 22,900 years ago from Malangangerr Rock Shelter. Ocher pencils with traces of wear date to at least 19,000 and perhaps even to 30,000 years ago. It is possible that some of the earliest Arnhem Land paintings depict extinct animals, but the interpretation is much debated. Dates from coatings of "desert varnish" from engravings on rocky outcrops at Mannahill in South Australia are said to span a period from 31,000 to 16,000 years ago, but the dating method is still experimental (Dorn et al., 1988). There seems little reason to doubt, however, that prehistoric Australians were painting as early as artists in Europe and Africa (Figure 8.11) (Bahn and Vertut, 1988).

Hunter-gatherers were living around the coast and on the fringes of the central Australian desert by 20,000 years ago. By 10,000 years later, they were exploiting every major environmental zone. As for the first settlement itself, scientists are deeply divided. Some believe that initial colonization was a slow and gradual process along coasts and then into the interior by people who had had to adapt not only to a new maritime environment but also to unfamiliar animal and plant foods (White and O'Connell, 1982). Others argue for a rapid colonization, with small groups expanding rapidly over the continent as a result of their highly mobile lifeway (Allen, 1989). Anthropologist Joseph Birdsell (1977) hypothesized that a mere doubling of the Australian population every 20 years after the first settlement would have resulted in natural population growth to eighteenth-century levels within only 2000 years. Recent, remarkable discoveries of late Ice Age wallaby hunters in Tasmania tend to support his hypothesis.

Ice Age Wallaby Hunters in Tasmania

Tasmania is now an island, but it was connected to mainland Australia by a land bridge from 37,000 to 29,000 years ago, at about the time of the first securely dated settlement of Sahul. During much of the last glaciation, climatic conditions through-

FIGURE 8.11   Aboriginal bark painting from the Alligator River region, Northern
Territory. Representation of the inner organs of man and kangaroo
is characteristic of painting from this region.

out Tasmania were quite severe, with ice sheets on higher ground in the interior and
temperatures at the glacial maximum as much as 10.8°F (6°C) lower than today.
Archaeologist Richard Cosgrove has excavated the Bluff and ORS 7 rock shelters in
south-central Tasmania. The Bluff site was first occupied about 30,500 years ago,
whereas ORS 7 was in use 30,800 years ago. Both of these occupation levels contain
emu eggs, which can be collected only during late winter and early spring, a bitterly
cold time of year (Figure 8.12) (Allen, 1989; Cosgrove et al., 1990).

     Both sites were occupied before the glacial maximum, but people continued to live
in the rugged landscape of southwestern and central Tasmania through the coldest
millennia of the last glaciation. The Kutikina Cave was occupied between 20,000 and
14,000 years ago, when what is now dense forest land was open tundra and grassland.
The inhabitants hunted red wallabies, as did the people who lived in at least 20 other
occupied caves nearby. Slightly to the east, another rugged area, now rain forest, is
Bone Cave, occupied between 17,000 and 13,000 years ago. The groups in these areas
appear to have been part of a common social system that flourished over a large area for

Bluff ORS 7
31,000 B.P.

Kutikina
20,000 to
14,000 B.P.

Bone Cave
17,000 to
13,000 B.P.

FIGURE 8.12   Excavations at the Bluff Rock Shelter, Tasmania.

many thousands of years. Some groups used Darwin glass, a natural glass from a meteorite crater a minimum distance of 28 miles (45 km) from Kutikina and over 62 straight-line miles from the Bluff Cave area. Some of these people were painting hand stencils and other designs long before the end of the Ice Age.

These were the southernmost people living on earth during the last glaciation. With the severing of the land bridge, their successors remained isolated from the outside world for thousands of years until French explorer Marion du Fresne met some aboriginal Tasmanians face to face in A.D. 1772.

LATER AUSTRALIAN PREHISTORY

Between 25,000 and 10,000 years ago, the population of Australia may have reached approximately modern levels, an estimated 300,000 people. Cultural change was gradual right into modern times. The same traditions of stoneworking and bone technology found in early sites survived almost unchanged for thousands of years (Mulvaney, 1975; R. V. S. Wright, 1977). For instance, flakes showing wear patterns characteristic of adz blades made by modern aborigines date back as far as 20,000 years ago, and the same bone points used to fasten skin clothes in historic times have been found deep in the prehistoric levels of Devil's Lair. The Australian Aborigines were famous for their artistic traditions and elaborate ceremonial life. Abundant traces of ritual belief have been found in Australian sites. The Devil's Lair site yielded stone plaques, a deep pit, and human incisor teeth that had been knocked out with a sharp blow: Such evulsion of teeth was a long-lived Australian tradition.

Despite the essential conservatism of Australian stoneworking practices, some regional variations did appear over the millennia. Steep-edged scrapers, which were probably used as woodworking tools, were made over a wide area of Australia during much of the Upper Pleistocene. These and crude flake tools remained in use until recent times; they were joined after 6000 B.P. in some areas by stone points, set on shafts, and other microliths. There is good reason to believe that Aboriginal technology developed within Australia over a long period in response to local needs and without the benefit of cultural innovation from outside (Figure 8.13).

Some idea of the simple level of early Australian life can be obtained from the saga of the Tasmanians (Plomley, 1969). When the first European voyagers visited Tasmania in 1642, they found bands of hunter-gatherers living on the island. The Tasmanians lasted precisely 80 years after European settlement in 1802. They had no shafted tools (that is, tools made of stone heads or points with wooden shafts or handles) and relied instead on scrapers and choppers somewhat like those used by early hunter-gatherers on the mainland; they lacked the boomerangs, spearthrowers, shields, axes, adzes, and lightweight stone tools the Australians of the mainland had when they first entered written history. The result of Tasmania's isolation was that its populations, although forming part of the Australian cultural group, never received the later cultural innovations that spread through Australia after sea levels rose. Harry Lourandos and others have suggested that Tasmanian adaptations preserved a rather specialized lifeway that was typical of much of Australia during the late Weichsel into modern times (for discussion, see Lourandos, 1987).

Fortunately for archaeology, at least some investigations of Aboriginal culture have been made that have important bearing on the interpretation of the archaeological record. Richard Gould (1977) spent many months among the Ngatatjara people of the Western Desert, carrying out ethnographic investigations that had objectives somewhat similar to those of Richard Lee among the San in Africa: He was interested in their cultural ecology and in the ways ethnographic observations could be used to interpret the archaeological record. His aboriginal informants took him to Puntutjarpa Rock Shelter, a site that they still visited regularly. Gould excavated the occupation levels in the shelter and found that people had lived there for more than 6800 years. The later stone implements were almost indistinguishable from modern Ngatatjara tools, to the extent that Gould was able to compare the wear patterns on both ancient and modern artifacts and decide which 5000-year-old tools had been

Puntutjarpa

FIGURE 8.13   Australian Aborigines making stone tools.

mounted on shafts and which had not. He also compared modern living surfaces with equivalent features found in the rock shelter (Figure 8.14).

The study of living Aborigine bands shows just how conservative Australian lifeways have been. There were few major technological innovations during Australian prehistory. Indeed, it was possible for the prehistoric Australians to maintain a thoroughly viable lifeway with minimal technology and only the simplest of artifacts. The Tasmanians, for instance, used only two dozen or so tools to hunt and forage. The great elaboration of Australian and Tasmanian culture was in social and ritual life, neither of which can readily be recovered by archaeological investigation. That much of this activity was designed to maintain the delicate balance between the aborigines and the available resources in their environment was no coincidence (White and O'Connell, 1982). A belief in such balance lay at the very core of Australian life.

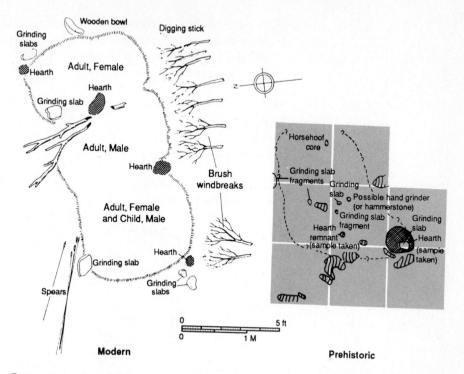

FIGURE 8.14   Comparison of a prehistoric campsite at Puntutjarpa Rock Shelter, Australia, with a modern aboriginal campsite in the same area. Note that the modern encampment can be subdivided into living areas by using informants' data and anthropological observation, whereas the archaeological site is devoid of such information, consisting merely of artifact patterns.

GUIDE TO FURTHER READING

Clark, J. Desmond. 1970. *The Prehistory of Africa.* London: Thames and Hudson.
   Still the best summary description of the Stone Age of sub-Saharan Africa, even if outdated in parts.

Fagan, Brian M. 1990. *The Journey from Eden.* New York: Thames and Hudson.
   A synthesis of the first settlement of Sunda and Sahul for the general reader. Also some descriptions of late prehistoric hunter-gatherer life.

Gould, Richard A. 1980. *Living Archaeology.* Cambridge, Eng.: Cambridge University Press.
   A definitive primer on ethnoarchaeology that covers most major field research conducted thus far. Excellent on basic principles.

Lee, Richard B. 1979. *The !Kung San.* Cambridge, Eng.: Cambridge University Press.
If there is one classic ethnographic study of hunter-gatherers, this account of the Kalahari San and their complex ecology is it. Strongly recommended to give the reader a clear understanding of hunter-gatherer lifeways.

Lewis-Williams, David. 1981. *Believing and Seeing: Symbolic Meanings in Southern San Rock Art.* New York: Academic Press.
A superb, well-argued study of the meaning of prehistoric rock art in southern Africa that should be read by anyone interested in this subject.

White, J. Peter, and O'Connell, James. 1982. *A Prehistory of Australia, New Guinea, and Sahul.* New York: Academic Press.
The definitive analytic synthesis of the prehistory of Australia. A superb, even masterly account but somewhat outdated by 1991.

PART IV

FARMERS

(c. 12,000 YEARS AGO
TO MODERN TIMES)

Agriculture is not to be looked on as a difficult or out-of-the-way invention, for the rudest savage, skilled as he is in the habits of the food-plants he gathers, must know well enough that if seeds or roots are put in a proper place in the ground they will grow.

Sir Edward
Tylor, 1883

THE BEGINNING OF FOOD PRODUCTION—OF AGRICULTURE AND ANIMAL DOMESTICATION—WAS ONE OF THE CATALYTIC EVENTS OF HUMAN PREHISTORY. PART IV NOT ONLY DESCRIBES THE SEQUENCE OF FARMING CULTURES IN ALL PARTS OF THE WORLD BUT ALSO ANALYZES SOME OF THE RECENT THEORIES ABOUT THE ORIGINS OF FARMING. WE WILL START WITH THE THEORETICAL BACKGROUND AND THEN STUDY FARMING IN GEOGRAPHIC AREAS. WITH THE BEGINNINGS OF FOOD PRODUCTION WE FIND THE FIRST SIGNS OF RAPIDLY ACCELERATING CULTURAL EVOLUTION, OF PROCESSES THAT ARE STILL OPERATING AT A RECORD PACE. HOWEVER, OUR UNDERSTANDING OF THE EARLY MILLENNIA OF FARMING IS INCOMPLETE. THE ARCHAEOLOGICAL EVIDENCE OUTLINED HERE IS EXTREMELY SKETCHY AND OFTEN STRETCHED TO THE LIMIT TO PRODUCE A COHERENT NARRATIVE. FUTURE RESEARCH IS CERTAIN TO MODIFY DRASTICALLY THE STORY SET FORTH IN THE FOLLOWING CHAPTERS.

CHAPTER 9 A PLENTEOUS HARVEST

THE ORIGINS

Preview

- Many early Holocene hunter-gatherers were preadapted toward the cultivation of plants and domestication of animals by changes in their lifeways after the Ice Age.

- Food production proved dramatically successful. Ten thousand years ago almost everyone in the world was hunting and gathering. By 2000 years ago hunter-gatherers were in a minority.

- The advent of food production brought more sedentary settlements, improved storage facilities, and new toolkits designed for agriculture and food storage. Population increases appear to have preceded, and followed, the beginnings of food production.

- The first theories for the origins of food production were formulated in terms of a single genius who invented agriculture. Others hypothesized that increased desiccation at the end of the Pleistocene concentrated plants, humans, and animals in a close symbiosis, which resulted in domestication. V. Gordon Childe refined this theory and postulated a Neolithic revolution.

- Modern theories have invoked social causes, population growth, and ecological factors as multivariate causes of food production. All argue that the development of food production was a gradual process, in which hunter-gatherers moved from scheduled gathering activities to experimentation with food crops.

- Kent Flannery's Guilá Naquitz research included a sophisticated computer simulation, which suggests that constant and unpredictable environmental change and irregular population shifts were major factors in the development of agriculture in Mesoamerica and perhaps in other areas.

- Studies of prehistoric diets tend to suggest a general decline in the quality and perhaps the length of human life with the advent of food production. People may have turned to agriculture only when no other alternatives were available.

- Domesticated herds assured a regular meat supply, isolating species from a larger gene pool for selective breeding under human care. As a result of domestication, animals and humans increased their mutual interdependence. The process of domestication took a considerable time, but in time, penned, gregarious animals became a food "reserve," protected, stored, and maintained against hard times.

- A long period of deliberate gathering and experimentation preceded the domestication of root and cereal crops throughout the world. With cereal grasses, this meant selecting for a tough rachis, the hinge that joined seed to stalk and allowed deliberate harvesting of the grain.

- Food production resulted in more sedentary human settlement, more substantial housing, elaborate storage technologies, and special implements for clearing, cultivating, and harvesting crops. All these new technological developments led to greater interdependence and to long-distance exchange of raw materials and finished artifacts.

It is sometimes hard for us to remember, buying our food from supermarkets, that for more than 99 percent of our existence as humans we were hunters and gatherers, tied to the seasons of plant foods, the movements of game, and the ebb and flow of aquatic resources. Food production, the deliberate cultivation of cereal grasses and edible root plants, is a phenomenon of the last 10,000 years of human existence. This relatively new human subsistence strategy is in large part responsible for the rapidly accelerating rates of population growth and cultural change in the past ten millennia. One of the major controversies in world prehistory surrounds the origins of food production: Why, when, and where did people first grow crops and domesticate wild animals?

THEORIES ABOUT THE ORIGINS OF FOOD PRODUCTION

As we saw in Chapter 6, changing environmental and demographic conditions at the end of the Ice Age, after 15,000 years ago, caused major long-term changes in hunter-gatherer societies. There was more localization, considerable technological innovation, and a trend toward sedentary settlement in areas with abundant and seasonally predictable food resources. And as we saw with the Natufian culture of the Levant (p. 224), many of these societies were, in many respects, preadapted for food production. Why, then, did they choose to grow their own crops?

Early Hypotheses

Late Victorian archaeologists were the first to speculate about agricultural origins. They envisaged a solitary genius who suddenly had the brilliant idea of planting seed (Roth, 1887). Today, no one looks for a single genius or for the earliest maize cob. Rather, modern theory concentrates on the complex processes that caused gradual changes in human subsistence patterns (G. Wright, 1971).

Childe's Neolithic Revolution

The best known and longest lived of the early theories was Vere Gordon Childe's "Neolithic Revolution." He proposed a major economic revolution in prehistory, which took place in the Near East during a period of severe drought, a climatic crisis that caused a symbiotic relationship between humans and animals in fertile oases. The new economies ensured a richer and more reliable food source for people on the edge of starvation after the Ice Age (Childe, 1936, 1952). Childe's simple theory was widely accepted, but it was based on inadequate archaeological and environmental data. It has long been surpassed by much more sophisticated formulations.

Braidwood's hilly flanks

Systematic fieldwork into the origins of food production began only in the late 1940s, when Robert J. Braidwood of the University of Chicago mounted an expedition to the Kurdish foothills of Iran to test Childe's theory. He soon rejected any notion of catastrophic climatic change, arguing that economic change came from "ever increasing cultural differentiation and specialization of human communities" (Braidwood and Braidwood, 1983). Thus, people were culturally receptive to innovation and experimentation with the cultivation of wild grasses. Braidwood believed that Stone Age hunters had domesticated animals and plants in "nuclear zones," areas such as the hilly flanks of the Zagros Mountains in Iraq and upland areas overlooking the Mesopotamian lowlands. He was convinced that the human capacity and enthusiasm for experimentation made it possible for people to domesticate animals. All modern theories of food production have their beginnings in Braidwood's work, which focused attention on the notion that people were culturally receptive to new subsistence practices.

Multivariate Theories

Now that we can look at world prehistory on a far wider canvas than the pioneers, we know that agriculture appeared in widely distributed parts of the world at approximately the same time in the Near East, China, south and Southeast Asia, and the Americas. This development has led some scholars to think in terms of worldwide population pressure that caused many hunter-gatherer societies to abandon gathering because their growing populations had reached the limit that their food resources

BOX 9.1

Foraging, Tending, Cultivation, and Plant Domestication

Paleoethnobotanist Richard Ford (1985) emphasizes that plant domestication was part of a long continuum of human interaction with natural vegetation. He divides this interaction into broad categories:

Foraging and unintentional tending. For thousands of years, prehistoric hunter-gatherers tended plants unintentionally, by using fire to encourage regeneration of edible grasses or by trampling seeds into damp ground in camp sites. Intensive exploitation of larger seeds at the expense of smaller ones, for example, can lead to long-term genetic changes that select against less desirable traits.

Cultivation. "Deliberate care afforded the propagation of a species." People disrupt the life cycle of a plant, usually to collect larger quantities of food or to harvest it with greater ease. Cultivation includes such casual tending activities as weeding, pruning wild fruit trees, or grubbing the soil with a digging stick to improve moisture

retention. Transplanting, digging up and replanting plants, and the sowing of seed help produce seasonal supplements to vegetable diets.

Plant domestication. Domestication is the final stage in the process, when cultural selection for useful traits results in new plants that depend on human beings for their existence. One increases their productivity by clearing special lands for them, ensuring a favorable environment, a process that Ford calls "Field Agriculture."

Some archaeologists refer to

Horticulturalists. Horticulturalists are cultivators who rely on simple methods such as slash and burn.

Agriculturalists. Agriculturalists are farmers who intensify food production with irrigation, plows, and other technological means to increase production.

These distinctions are not used explicitly here, as they seem self-evident.

Cohen's population pressure

could support (for full arguments, see Cohen, 1977). No one denies that food production led to higher population densities and indeed ignited a population explosion (see Figure 9.2) (Lewin, 1988a). But there is no evidence for very high population densities in the Near East or Mesoamerica during the millennia when agriculture was taking hold, certainly not for the sorts of density that cause chronic food shortages (Flannery, 1983; Stark, 1986).

Recent theorizing about the origins of food production revolves around complex, multivariate models that combine many factors (Binford, 1968; Flannery, 1965, 1968a). All these models take into account the emerging realization that many early Holocene hunter-gatherer societies were more complex and well preadapted to food production before anyone started planting wild cereal grasses or penning animals (for a survey, see Stark, 1986).

Barbara Bender (1985) argues for social factors. She theorizes that hunter-gatherer societies were becoming more complex, with far more elaborate, hierarchical social organizations. She points to the increasing abundance of trade objects and the appearance of richly decorated burials in preagricultural societies in the Near East, Europe, and elsewhere. Perhaps, she hypothesizes, an expansion of trade and of political alliances between neighboring groups created new social and economic pressures to produce more and more surplus goods, not only foodstuffs but other objects as well. This development, in turn, led to more sedentary lifeways. This social hypothesis tends to ignore the compelling factors of now well-documented environmental changes that were apparently one of the key elements in a move toward cultivation in areas like the Near East.

Another category of theories is based on relationships between populations and resources. This category is an extension of a famous argument by economist Ester Boserup, which points out that food production systems of any type are highly flexible. Thus, hunter-gatherers responded to favorable relationships between population densities and available resources by intensifying their hunting and gathering (Clark and Yi, 1983). Population growth in restricted areas with diverse resources can cause food shortages because there is less mobility and everyone has less territory to move around in, a situation that may have arisen in parts of the Near East (Chapter 10), northwestern Europe (Chapter 11), and the Americas (Chapter 14). These theories tend to concentrate on several interdependent factors: risk and population-resource imbalances. Apart from environmental change, all environments involve some form of risk for hunter-gatherer societies—drought cycles, long, cold winters, or unpredictable floods, to mention only a few possibilities discussed in earlier chapters. People respond to these risks by moving away, by developing new storage technologies for dried fish or plant foods, and by drying foods like powdered bison meat or salmon. A straightforward solution to rising populations, resulting food shortages, or risk factors may be to go one step further, to cultivate familiar plants and domesticate common prey so that people can draw on familiar "stored" resources in scarce months.

A third group of theorists focuses on ecological factors such as local variability in food resources and the interactive effects of human exploitation. Proponents of these ecological models talk of "opportunities" for the introduction of agriculture, of people turning to superior local resources when the moment arrived (see Minnis, 1985; Rindos, 1984). What happens is that some resources, say, wild wheat or barley or wild goats, are seen as attractive. People use them more and more, to the point that they are eventually domesticated. Kent Flannery (1968a) used this approach to examine the mechanisms by which Mesoamericans took up agriculture. The preagricultural peoples of the region adapted to a few animal genera and plants, whose range cut across several environments. These included deer, rabbits, cactus fruit, and wild grasses, including the wild ancestor of maize. They scheduled their annual round to be in the right place at the right time to harvest, say, cactus fruit. Over the centuries, genetic changes in the ancestor of corn made it more productive and progressively more important in the diet. As time went on, people spent more and more time cultivating it and rescheduled their annual round accordingly, thereby neglecting foods they once exploited in favor of cultivated crops.

The crux of ecological models is trying to identify the processes that caused people to make the shift to deliberate cultivation, again a very difficult task. For example, did cultivation enable people to widen their adaptive niches? Were these new cost-benefit realities that favored farming? What about such factors as the nutritive value and seasonal availability of foods? Did genetic changes in animals and plants play a role?

Most theories about the origins of food production are far from easy to test. It is difficult to link complex models with actual field data, largely because the models do not lend themselves to easy documentation. Such documentation will come from very meticulous excavations at single sites, which will be combined, eventually, into larger regional models. Such research has been conducted successfully at Abu Hureyra, Syria (Chapter 10), and at Guilá Naquitz, Mexico.

GUILÁ NAQUITZ

**Guilá Naquitz
10,750 to 8650
years ago**

As part of a long-term archaeological project in the Oaxaca Valley of Mexico, Kent Flannery and his research team excavated Guilá Naquitz Cave, a small shelter used about six times over a 2000-year period between 10,750 and 8670 years ago (Flannery et al., 1986). These sporadic occupations extend from the early Archaic, soon after the extinction of big game in the region, to a period when the occupants were using domesticated plants. The early Archaic occupants spent some of the year in large bands, splitting up to exploit larger areas of territory in much smaller groups, one of which used Guilá Naquitz upon occasion. The multidisciplinary research project revealed a wealth of information about the visitors to this shelter, identifying not only subsistence strategies but also the division of labor between women, who processed plant foods, and men, who did the hunting, through the distribution of artifacts and features in occupation levels. Most important of all, Flannery and his colleagues tried to answer two questions: What was the strategy that led to the choice of the wild plants eaten by the inhabitants, and how did this strategy change when they began planting?

Robert Reynolds (1986) developed a comprehensive and ingenious "adaptive computer simulation model" to approach these questions. He started with a hypothetical, and totally ignorant, band of five people who settle in the area. Over a long period of trial and error, they "learn" how to schedule 11 major food plants over the year, in an environment where the sequence of dry, wet, and "average" years is totally unpredictable. The collective memories of successive generations prove to be of vital importance, for past experience is the basis upon which they modify their strategies in future years that prove to be the same as already experienced ones. For example, a cycle of drought years may yield survival strategies that are remembered through the succeeding wet years, despite the passage of a generation or more, and are then used again. The strategies rank plants and vegetational zones in order of the size of the harvest, yielding collective decisions followed by the band. By the time the last preagricultural occupation occurs at Guilá Naquitz, the band is so efficient in all conditions that very few modifications improve the adaptation. Basically, there is a stable performance level.

The computer simulation produced a mix of plant species that matched that found in the occupation deposits very well. It also showed that the group used one set of strategies for wet years, when plant foods were available in abundance and a wide range of them was used, and another in dry years, when the people took fewer species and those with higher yields. Reynolds's simulation is based on the assumption that the first stages of agriculture were attempts to alter the densities of specific plants. The wet-year strategies were the ones that were the most flexible and most capable of incorporating experimentation without risk. At first, deliberate planting may have been a rarity, a strategy that was successful but only employed in wet years. It was a specialized strategy but one whose yields were seen eventually to have advantages, to the point that planting became more frequent, occurring not only in wet years but in dry ones as well, *once the experiment had been shown to work.* If the simulation is correct, the pace of experimentation was very slow, confined at first to wet years; at the same time, centuries-old foraging strategies continued. Reynolds's simulation suggests that bean cultivation near the cave itself allowed the people to collect more food and travel less, with ultimately a greater emphasis on foraging in the thorn forest near the site rather than further afield. At the same time, traveling time decreased and collecting time increased—acorns from the thorn forest become much more common, for example. Less time is spent on lower-yielding, more marginal wild plants, as greater emphasis is placed on beans, squash, and maize. As the group gained experience with planting, yields rose, and the people placed ever more emphasis on cultivation as opposed to foraging.

Reynolds's (1986) simulation corresponds well with the shifts in plant species found in the six occupation levels at Guilá Naquitz. When he added climatic change and population growth to the equation, he found that two sources of uncertainty, unpredictable climate fluctuations and population shifts, were the factors that led to the most rapid increase in the density of high-yielding domesticated plants near the site. Reynolds believes that a high level of annual climatic variation—with its frequent wet years, for experimentation, and dry years, which put pressure on people to be efficient—was a major factor in the shift to food production in Oaxaca. So were short-term as opposed to long-term fluctuations in population densities, which also led to an accelerating reliance on cultivation not only on hill slopes but also on river plains in Oaxaca, the environments in which the first larger villages are found.

This sophisticated, hypothetical model is remarkable in that it corresponds well with excavated data. Reynolds demonstrates that these Oaxaca people were well preadapted to food production. There was no "trigger" that started cultivation. The people simply added gourds, beans, and a simple form of maize to a much earlier foraging adaptation, at first as a wet year innovation, which came into use in average and dry years once it proved reliable. As Flannery (1986) says, "Human hunting and gathering is, after all, economic behavior." Foragers make decisions about distances to travel and the plants and territory to exploit. When they shift to agriculture, they are changing the pattern of their decision making, not in an irreversible way but probably as one of several alternatives open to them. This change "has to be understood in terms of their previous decision-making pattern, the options open to them, and that new situation." At the same time, too, this culturally based explanation emerges from circumstances arising from larger processes, among them a worldwide climatic change at the end of the Ice Age and long-term evolutionary processes. In time, for example, early farmers anywhere acquired a selective advantage by virtue of their ability to disperse seeds from "a group of plants whose genetic program they had altered, in defiance of natural selection."

Probabilistic ecosystem model

The Guilá Naquitz research, with its sophisticated computer simulations, is an example of what future research into agricultural origins holds. In the final analysis, Flannery (1986) seems to prefer what he calls a "probabilistic ecosystem model." This model allows people to respond to changes in the ecosystem in several ways. The Guilá Naquitz people reduced their search area for wild plants, which may have led to protein deficiencies. Their solution was to grow beans, a protein-rich crop that allowed them to reduce their search area still more. In other parts of the world, like southern California or the Pacific Northwest, they intensified fishing and sea mammal hunting, and agriculture was never adopted on any scale, even if the people were well aware of it. Agriculture was not the only option. It was one of many, and one that achieved remarkable success in the regions where it did develop.

Once successful, food production spread rapidly, partly because population growth after the fact prevented people from reverting to hunting and gathering. There remains an interesting question. Why did food production not take hold much earlier in prehistory? Surely there were many previous occasions during the Ice Age when conditions were favorable for people to start cultivating plants? Here population models for prehistory offer some clues. We know there was gradual population growth during the Stone Age. The constant, cyclical changes of the past 700,000 years must have led to conditions in some areas that presented human societies with the challenge of constant environmental change and population shifts. However, as we saw in Chapter 6, it was not until the end of the Ice Age that global populations rose sufficiently to circumscribe mobility, and the easiest strategy for people faced with food shortages is to move away. It must be significant that there was initially a slow and then a rapidly accelerating intensification of hunter-gatherer lifeways during and after the last glacial maximum, especially during Holocene times. This intensification preadapted many societies for food production for the first time (Stark, 1986).

DIFFERING DATES FOR EARLY FOOD PRODUCTION

As we shall see in Chapters 10 to 14, food production began at very different times in various parts of the world, being well established in the Near East by 9000 years ago, in Mesoamerica by 5000 years ago, but in tropical Africa by about 3000 years ago, and then only in some locations. What were the local variations that accounted for this time lag? David Harris (1978, 1980) argues that hunter-gatherers in subtropical zones such as the Near East and highland Mesoamerica were beginning to manipulate potential domesticates among wild grasses and root species at the end of the Ice Age. Dependence on such foods probably came earlier in these regions, where there were only a few forageable species. Such dependence was essential to long-term survival. In contrast, populations in more humid tropical regions, like the African and Amazonian rain forests, probably did little more than manipulate a few wild species to minimize risk in lean years; as a corollary, many African agricultural peoples turn to hunting and gathering in lean years to this day. The archaeological record shows that agriculture was established considerably earlier in the subtropical Near East, Middle and South America, Southeast Asia, and India than it was in humid, tropical zones, undoubtedly because that environment was rich in game and wild vegetable foods. Furthermore, domesticated crops and animals were more susceptible to irregular rainfall, locusts and other insect attacks, and endemic stock diseases. A strong and sustained incentive to obtain food must have been a prerequisite for a lasting shift from foraging to agriculture.

Harris points out that many variables must be understood before we can reconstruct the conditions under which agriculture was first regarded as a profitable activity. We are searching for a set of conditions in which population pressure, distribution of plants, the rate at which the environment is changing, and even techniques of harvesting wild grasses all play their part in making agriculture work. Then there are variations among the potentially domesticable plants and animals, some of which resist domestication because of their long life span or because parts of their lives take place outside human control. The seasonal distribution of wild vegetable foods or game could also have prevented experiments in domestication, when the seasons during which these wild foods were exploited coincided with the times of year when it was important that experimenting farmers stay near their growing crops. Under these circumstances, people would tend to pursue their traditional food-getting strategies rather than risk their lives for an uncertain outcome.

CONSEQUENCES OF FOOD PRODUCTION

The new food-producing economies proved dramatically successful. Ten thousand years ago virtually everybody in the world lived by hunting and gathering. By 2000 years ago most people were farmers or herders and only a minority were still hunter-gatherers. The spread of food production throughout the world took only about 8000 years. The problem for anthropologists is not only to account for why people took up agriculture but also to explain why so many populations adopted this new, and initially risky, economic transition in such a short time. Food production spread to all corners of the world except where an environment with extreme aridity or heat or cold rendered agriculture or herding impossible or where people chose to remain hunters and gatherers. In some places, food production was the economic base for urbanization and literate civilization; but most human societies did not go further than subsistence-level food production until the industrial power of nineteenth- and twentieth-century Europe led them into the machine age.

Food production resulted, ultimately, in much higher population densities in many locations, for the domestication of plants and animals can lead to an economic strategy that increases and stabilizes available food supplies, although more energy is used to produce them (Figure 9.1). Farmers use concentrated tracts of territory for agriculture and for grazing cattle and small stock if they practice mixed farming. Their territory is much smaller than that of hunter-gatherers (although pastoralists need huge areas of grazing land for seasonal pasture). Within a smaller area of farming land,

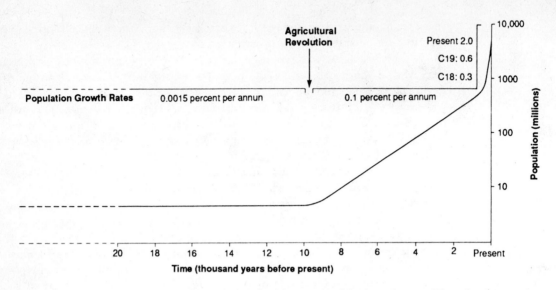

FIGURE 9.1   World population changes since the beginnings of food production. There has been an explosion in population densities in the past 10,000 years.

property lines are carefully delineated as individual ownership and problems of inheritance arise. Shortages of land can lead to disputes and to the founding of new village settlements on previously uncultivated soil (Childe, 1936; Struever, 1971).

More enduring settlements brought other changes. The portable and light-weight material possessions of many hunter-gatherers were replaced by heavier tool-kits and more lasting houses (Figure 9.2). Grindstones and ground-edged axes were even more essential to farming culture than they were to gathering societies. Hoes and other implements of tillage were vital for the planting and harvesting of crops. New social units came into being as more lasting home bases were developed; these social links reflected ownership and inheritance of land and led to much larger settlements that brought hitherto scattered populations into closer and more regular contact.

Food production led to changed attitudes toward the environment. Cereal crops were such that people could store their food for winter (Figure 9.2). The hunter-gatherers exploited game, fish, and vegetable foods, but the farmers did more; they *altered* the environment by the very nature of their exploitation. Expansion of agriculture meant felling trees and burning vegetation to clear the ground for plant-ing. The same fields were then abandoned after a few years to lie fallow, and more woodland was cleared. The original vegetation began to regenerate, but it might have been cleared again before reaching its original state. This shifting pattern of farming is called *slash-and-burn*, or *swidden*, *agriculture*. Voracious domesticated animals stripped pastures of their grass cover; then heavy rainfalls denuded the hills of valuable soil, and the pastures were never the same again. However elementary the agricultural technology, the farmer changed the environment, if only with fires lit to clear scrub from gardens and to fertilize the soil with wood ash. Hunter-gatherers had

Slash-and-burn (swidden) agriculture

FIGURE 9.2   A pole-and-mud hut typical of the Middle Zambezi Valley, Africa *(left)*. Such dwellings, often occupied 15 years or longer, are more lasting than the windbreak or tent of the hunter-gatherer. *Right* is a grain bin from an African village, used for cereal crops. Storing food is a critical activity of many hunters and farmers.

deliberately set fires to encourage the growth of new grass for their grazing prey. In a sense, shifting slash-and-burn agriculture is merely an extension of the age-old use of fire to encourage regeneration of vegetation.

Food production resulted in high population densities, but growth was controlled by disease, available food supplies, water supplies, and particularly famine. Early agricultural methods depended heavily on careful selection of the soil. The technology of the first farmers was hardly potent enough for extensive clearing of the dense woodland under which many good soils lay, so potentially cultivable land could only be that which was accessible. Gardens probably were scattered over a much wider territory than is necessary today. One authority estimates that even with advanced shifting agriculture, only 40 percent of moderately fertile soil in Africa is available for such cultivation (Allan, 1965). This figure must have been lower in the early days of agriculture, with their simpler stone tools and fewer crops.

In regions of seasonal rainfall, such as the Near East, sub-Saharan Africa, and parts of Asia, periods of prolonged drought are common. Famine was a real possibility as population densities rose. Many early agriculturalists must have worriedly watched the sky and had frequent crop failures in times of drought. Their small stores of grain from the previous season would not have carried them through another year, especially if they had been careless with their surplus. Farmers were forced to shift their economic strategy in such times. We know that the earliest farmers availed themselves of game and vegetable foods to supplement their agriculture, just as today some farmers are obliged to rely heavily on wild vegetable foods and hunting to survive in bad years (Scudder, 1962, 1971). Many hunter-gatherer bands collect intensively just a few species of edible plants in their large territories. Aware of many other edible vegetables, they fall back on these only in times of stress; the less favored foods can carry a comparatively small population through to the next rains. A larger agricultural population is not so flexible and quickly exhausts wild vegetables and game in the much smaller territory used for farming and grazing. If the drought lasts for years, famine, death, and reduced population can follow.

NUTRITION AND EARLY
FOOD PRODUCTION

Was food production a real improvement in human lifeways? For generations archaeologists have argued that human health improved dramatically as a result of agriculture, because people worked less and lived on more reliable food supplies (Butzer, 1982; Childe, 1952). In recent years, Ester Boserup (1965) and others have argued that in fact agriculture brought diminishing returns in relation to labor expended in the new systems that were adopted to feed many more people. Richard Lee's (1979) studies of the !Kung San of the Kalahari Desert tend to support her views. They show that these hunter-gatherers, and presumably others, had abundant leisure and worked less than farmers. Some nutritionists point out that foragers may have had better-balanced diets than many farmers, who relied heavily on root or cereal crops. Further, farmers, with their sedentary settlements and higher population densities, were much more vulnerable to famine than their hunter-gatherer predecessors. They would also have been more vulnerable to gastrointestinal infections and epidemics because of crowded village populations (Cohen and Armelagos, 1984).

While the theoretical controversies swirl, actual empirical data are still hard to come by. Some pioneer nutrition studies based on the skeletons of early farmers suggest some incidence of anemia and slow growth resulting from malnutrition. Signs of physical stress are even harder to come by. Ten regional studies of prehistoric populations have suggested a *decline* in mean age life expectancy in agricultural populations, which contradicts the commonly held perception. Taken as a whole, the paleopathological studies that have been published suggest a general decline in the quality, and perhaps the length, of human life with the advent of food production. It should be pointed out, however, that there are many unknowns involved, among them changes in fertility and population growth rates, which caused the world's population to rise even if general health standards and life expectancy fell. (For details, consult Cohen, 1988.)

What impact these studies will have on population pressure theories about the origins of agriculture is still uncertain. Certainly, any shift to food production caused by increasing population pressure could be reflected in a decline in the overall health and nutrition displayed by prehistoric skeletons. It is likely that the next generation of theories about early agriculture will be based on researches into the paleopathology of pioneer farming populations.

In the final analysis, people probably turned to food production only when other alternatives were no longer practicable. The classic example is the Aborigines of extreme northern Australia, who were well aware that their neighbors in New Guinea were engaged in intensive agriculture. They, too, knew how to plant the top of the wild yam so that it regerminated, but they never adopted food production simply because they had no need to become dependent on a lifeway that would reduce their leisure time and produce more food than they required.

HERDING: DOMESTICATION OF ANIMALS

Potentially tamable species like the wild ox, goat, sheep, and dog were widely distributed in the Old World during the Upper Pleistocene. New World farmers domesticated only such animals as the llama, the guinea pig, and the turkey, and then only under special conditions and within narrow geographic limits. It is possible that the domesticated dog crossed into the New World with the first Americans before 15,000 years ago or that it was domesticated elsewhere in the Americas, but the evidence is uncertain.

Having one's own herds of domesticated mammals ensured a regular meat supply. The advantages to having a major source of meat under one's control are obvious. Later, domesticated animals provided byproducts such as milk, cheese, and butter, as well as skins for clothes and tent coverings and materials for leather shields and armor. In later millennia, people learned how to breed animals for specialized tasks such as plowing, transportation, and traction (Clutton-Brock, 1981).

Domestication implies a genetic selection emphasizing special features of continuing use to the domesticator (Ucko and Dimbleby, 1969). Wild sheep have no wool, wild cows produce milk only for their offspring, and undomesticated chickens do not lay surplus eggs. Changes in wool bearing, lactation, or egg production could be achieved by isolating wild populations for selective breeding under human care. Isolating species from a larger gene pool produced domestic sheep with thick, woolly coats and domestic goats providing regular supplies of milk, which formed a staple in the diet of many human populations.

No one knows exactly how domestication of animals began. During the Upper Pleistocene, people already were beginning to concentrate heavily on some species of large mammals for their diet. The Magdalenians of southwest France directed much of their life toward pursuing reindeer. At the end of the Pleistocene, hunters in the Near East were concentrating on gazelles and other steppe animals. Wild sheep and goats were intensively hunted on the southern shores of the Caspian Sea. Gregarious animals are those most easily domesticated; they follow the lead of a dominant herd member or all move together.

Hunters often fed off the same herd for a long time, sometimes deliberately sparing young females and immature beasts to keep the source of food alive. Young animals captured alive in the chase might be taken back to the camp and grow dependent on those who caged them, thus becoming partially tamed. A hunter could grasp the possibility of gaining control of the movements of a few key members of a herd, who would be followed by the others. Once the experience of keeping pets or of restricting game movements had suggested a new way of life, people might experiment with different species (Flannery, 1969; Higgs and

Jarman, 1969). As part of domestication, animals and humans increased their mutual interdependence.

The archaeological evidence for early domestication is so fragile that nothing survives except the bones of the animals kept by the early farmers, and differences between wild and domestic animal bones are often so small initially that it is difficult to distinguish them unless very large collections are found. In the earliest centuries of domestication, corralled animals were nearly indistinguishable from wild species.

One way of differentiating between domestic and wild beasts is to age an animal find by its dentition—the number, kind, and arrangement of its teeth. Hunters normally kill animals of all ages but strongly prefer adolescent beasts, which have the best meat. However, herd owners slaughter younger sheep and goats, especially surplus males, for meat but keep females until they are no longer productive as breeding animals. In some early farming sites, such as Zawi Chemi in the Zagros Mountains in the Near East, the only way domestic sheep could be identified was by the early age at which they were slaughtered (Perkins, 1964).

The process of animal domestication undoubtedly was prolonged, developing in several areas of the Near East at approximately the same time. Although animal bones are scarce and often unsatisfactory as evidence of early domestication, most authorities now agree that the first species to be domesticated in the Near East was the sheep, about 10,500 years ago. Sheep are small animals living in herds, whose carcasses yield much meat for their size. They can readily be penned and isolated to develop a symbiotic relationship with people.

Cattle are much more formidable to domesticate, for their prototype was *Bos primigenius,* the wild ox much hunted by Stone Age people (Figure 9.3). Perhaps cattle were first domesticated from wild animals that were penned for food, ritual, and sacrifice. They may have been captured from wild herds grazing in the gardens.

It should be noted that some animals, such as sea mammals, resist domestication because much of their lives is spent out of range of human influence. As mentioned, most early successes with domestication took place with gregarious animals. Kent Flannery (1969) has pointed out that penned gregarious animals can, in a sense, be regarded as a "reserve" of food, protected, stored, and maintained against hard times—"grain or the hoof."

CULTIVATION: DOMESTICATION OF PLANTS

Many fewer wild vegetable foods were domesticated than foraged over the millennia (Pearsall, 1987; J. Renfrew, 1973). In the Old World, wheat, barley, and other cereals that grow wild over much of Asia and Europe became cultivated. In the New World, a different set of crops was tamed (Zohary and Hopf, 1988). These included Indian corn (*Zea mays*), the only important wild grass to be domesticated. Root crops such as manioc and sweet potatoes, chili peppers, tobacco, and several types of bean were all grown. Common to both Old and New Worlds are gourds, cotton, and two or three other, minor crops (Ford, 1985).

FIGURE 9.3   *Bos primigenius,* the aurochs or wild ox, as depicted by S. von Herbenstain in 1549. It became extinct in Europe in 1627, although recent breeding experiments have reconstructed this formidable beast.

Carl Sauer (1952) pointed out that seed crops such as maize were first grown in Mesoamerica, and root crops such as manioc and potatoes were grown more commonly in South America. This fundamental distinction also applies in the Old World, where tropical regions had many potential domesticates such as the yam and gourds. In Southeast Asia and tropical Africa, a long period of intensive gathering and experimenting with the deliberate planting of wild root crops probably preceded the beginnings of formal agriculture. Perhaps, however, the transition from gathering to cultivation of root crops was almost unconscious, for many tubers are easy to grow deliberately. The African yam, for example, can be germinated simply by cutting off its top and burying it in the ground. The hunter-gatherer bands who were familiar with this easy means of conserving their food supplies may simply have intensified their planting efforts to supplement shortages caused by changed circumstances. As with animals, however, certain heavily exploited species tended to resist domestication; among them were the long-lived trees like the oak and plants whose life spans were so long that they inhibited human selection. They also tended to cross-pollinate, a process that undoubtedly discouraged human efforts to trigger or control genetic variation.

In the Old World, the qualities of wild wheat, barley, and similar crops are quite different from those of their domestic equivalents (D. Harris and Hillman, 1989; Hillman and Davies, 1990). In the wild, these grains occur in dense stands. They can be harvested by tapping the stem with the hands and gathering the seeds in a basket as they fall off or by uprooting the plant. The tapping technique is effective because the wild grain is attached to the stem by a brittle joint, or *rachis.* When the grass is tapped, the weak rachis breaks and the seed falls into the basket.

The first cultivated wheat and barley crops were of the wild, brittle-rachised type,

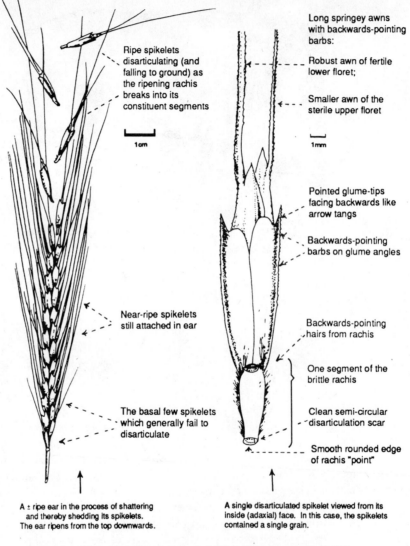

Ripe spikelets
disarticulating (and
falling to ground) as
the ripening rachis
breaks into its
constituent segments

1cm

Long springey awns
with backwards-pointing
barbs:

Robust awn of fertile
lower floret;

Smaller awn of the
sterile upper floret

1mm

Pointed glume-tips
facing backwards like
arrow tangs

Backwards-pointing
barbs on glume angles

Near-ripe spikelets
still attached in ear

Backwards-pointing
hairs from rachis

One segment of the
brittle rachis

The basal few spikelets
which generally fail to
disarticulate

Clean semi-circular
disarticulation scar

Smooth rounded edge
of rachis "point"

A ± ripe ear in the process of shattering
and thereby shedding its spikelets.
The ear ripens from the top downwards.

A single disarticulated spikelet viewed from its
inside (adaxial) face. In this case, the spikelets
contained a single grain.

Wild einkorn *(Triticum boeoticum)* showing its brittle-rachised ear and arrow-shaped
spikelets adapted for penetrating surface litter and cracks in the ground.

FIGURE 9.4   The features affecting seed dispersal and spikelet implantation in wild and domesticated einkorn wheat.

and the resulting crops would probably have been large enough to generate domestic-type mutants in the first 2 to 5 years (Figure 9.4). Selection for the semitough rachised forms was, of necessity, an unconscious process during the earliest stages of domestication. Computer simulations have shown that domestic, semitough rachised forms may have been rare at first, but they would have been fully domesticated within 20

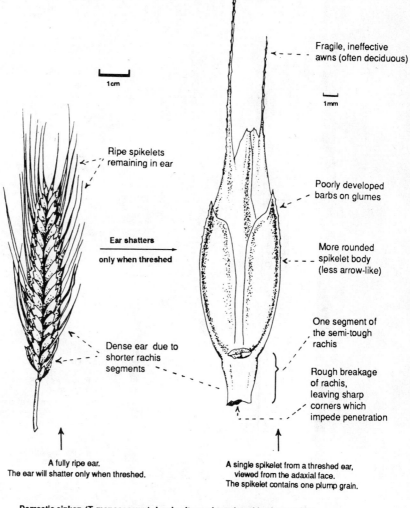

1cm

Ripe spikelets
remaining in ear

Ear shatters

only when threshed

Dense ear due to
shorter rachis
segments

A fully ripe ear.
The ear will shatter only when threshed.

Fragile, ineffective
awns (often deciduous)

1mm

Poorly developed
barbs on glumes

More rounded
spikelet body
(less arrow-like)

One segment of
the semi-tough
rachis

Rough breakage
of rachis,
leaving sharp
corners which
impede penetration

A single spikelet from a threshed ear,
viewed from the adaxial face.
The spikelet contains one plump grain.

Domestic einkon *(T. monococcum)* showing its semi-tough-rachised ear and its
plumper spikelets which have lost some key features neccesary for
self-implantation.

FIGURE 9.4 *(continued)*

to 30 generations—for these cereals, between 20 and 30 years. Even with less intense
selective pressures than those assumed in the experiment, domestication could have
been achieved within 1 or 2 centuries (Figure 9.5). (For a full discussion of this issue,
see Hillman and Davies, 1990).

Archaeobotanist Gordon Hillman believes that the farmers would have started
conscious selection as soon as the domesticates became sufficiently common to be
recognized, perhaps 1 to 5 percent of the crop. From then on, domestication would
have been completed in 3 or 4 years.

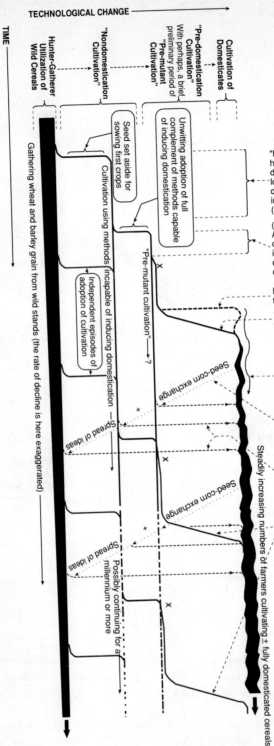

FIGURE 9.5 A summary of the principal events associated with the domestication of wheat and barley. For the sake of argument, this diagram assumes that domestication of each of the wheats and barleys occurred at several settlements independently.

Although the broad outlines of the process of domestication can be reconstructed through controlled experimentation and computer simulation, it is most
unlikely that anyone will ever find "transitional" grains in Near Eastern sites that will
document the actual process underway. The changeover from wild to domesticated
strains was so rapid that we are more likely to find wild seeds in one level and
domesticated ones in the next. This is precisely what has been found at Near Eastern
sites such as Abu Hureyra, where farming appears abruptly about 9700 years ago (see
Chapter 10).

TECHNOLOGY AND DOMESTICATION

The technological consequences of food production were, in their way, as important
as the new economies. A more settled way of life and some decline in hunting and
gathering slowly led to long-term residences, lasting agricultural styles, and more
substantial housing. As they had done for millennia, people built their permanent
homes with the raw materials most abundant in their environment. The early farmers
of the Near East worked and dried mud into small houses with flat roofs; these were
cool in summer and warm in winter. At night during the hot season people may have
slept on the flat roofs. Some less substantial houses had reed roofs. In the more
temperate zones of Europe, with wetter climates, timber was used to build thatched-
roof houses of various shapes and sizes. Early African farmers often built huts of grass,
sticks, and anthill clay. Nomadic pastoralists of the northern steppes had no concern
with a permanent and durable home, yet they, too, took advantage of the related
benefits of having a domestic food supply: They used the skins to make clothing as
well as tents to shelter them during the icy winters.

Agriculture is a seasonal activity, with long periods of the year in which the fields
are lying fallow or are supporting growing crops. Any farmer is confronted with the
problem of keeping food in ways the hunter-gatherer never has to ponder. Thus, a
new technology of storage came into being. Grain bins, jars, or clay-lined pits became
an essential part of the agricultural economy for stockpiling food for the lean months
and against periods of famine. The bins might have been made of wattle and daub,
clay, or timber (see Figure 9.2). Basket and clay-lined silos protected valuable grain
against rodents.

Hunter-gatherers use skins, wood containers, gut pouches, and sometimes baskets for carrying vegetable foods back from the bush. Farmers face far more formidable transport problems: They must carry their harvest back to the village, keep
ready-for-use supplies of foods in the house as opposed to storage bins, and store
water. Early farmers began to use gourds as water carriers and to make clay vessels
that were both waterproof and capable of carrying and cooking food (Figure 9.6).
They made pots by coiling rolls of clay or building up the walls of vessels from a lump
and firing them in simple hearths. Clay vessels were much more durable than skin
or leather receptacles. Some pots were used for several decades before being broken
and abandoned. Pottery did not appear simultaneously with agriculture. It came into
use at different times in many widely separated places. For example, the Jomon
hunter-gatherers of Japan were making simple clay pots at least 10,500 years ago. They
lived a more or less sedentary life by their shell middens, using clay vessels long before

FIGURE 9.6   Pottery manufacture. A common method of pot-making was to build up the walls from coils of clay *(top)*. The pot was then smoothed and decorated *(left)* and fired, in either an open hearth *(right)* or a kiln. These pictures illustrate Pueblo Indian pottery-manufacturing techniques from the Southwest United States and are, of course, not necessarily typical of all potters.

agriculture became part of their way of life (Aikens and Higuchi, 1981). In the Near East, however, pottery was first used by farmers approximately 8000 years ago (Mellaart, 1975).

For tens of thousands of years, people dug up wild edible roots with simple wooden sticks, sometimes made more effective with the aid of a stone weight. The first farmers continued to use the digging stick to plant crops a few inches below the surface, probably on readily cultivable soils. They also used wooden or stone-bladed hoes (and much later, iron) to break up the soft soil. These they fitted with short or long handles, depending on cultural preference. European and Near Eastern farmers made use of the ox-drawn plow in later millennia, at first with a wooden-tipped blade, then bronze, and later iron (Chapter 16). The plow was an important innovation, for it enabled people to turn the soil over to a much greater depth than ever before. Every farmer has to clear wild vegetation and weeds from the fields, and it is hardly surprising to find a new emphasis on the ax and the adz. The simple axes of pioneer farmers were replaced by more elaborate forms in metal by 4500 years ago in the Near East. Present-day experiments in Denmark and New Guinea have shown that the ground and polished edges of stone axes are remarkably effective in clearing woodland and felling trees (Figure 9.7) (Cranstone, 1972). In later millennia, the alloying of copper and bronze and, later, the development of iron cutting edges made forest clearance even easier.

New tools meant new technologies to produce tougher working edges. At first the farmers used ground and polished stone, placing a high premium on suitable rocks, which were traded from quarry sites over enormous distances. Perhaps the most famous ax quarries are in western Europe, where ax blanks were traded the length of the British Isles and Grand Pressigny flint from France was prized over thousands of square miles. In the Near East and Mexico, one valuable toolmaking material, not for axes but for knives and sickles, was obsidian, a volcanic rock prized for its easy working properties and its ornamental appearance. Early obsidian trade routes carried tools and ornaments hundreds of miles from their places of origin. By using spectrographic techniques, scientists have been able to trace obsidian over long distances to such places of origin as Lipari Island off Italy and Lake Van in Turkey (Renfrew and Dixon, 1976; Torrance, 1986).

All these developments in technology made people more and more dependent on exotic raw materials, many of which were unobtainable in their own territory. We see the beginnings of widespread long-distance trading networks, which were to burgeon even more rapidly with the emergence of the first urban civilizations.

We still know tantalizingly little about the ways humankind began to exercise control over food resources. We know that in the Near East there was a dramatic shift in human subsistence patterns 9000 years ago, in northern China about 7000 years ago, and in Mesoamerica some 5000 years ago. Some fascinating clues suggest that people were exercising some sort of control over their food supplies very much earlier. Perhaps Upper Paleolithic people who specialized in hunting reindeer or mountain goats made some attempts to manage the prey herds. Conceivably, too, hunter-gatherers living on the fringes of tropical rain forests could have engaged in deliberate opportunistic horticulture, planting yams and other food plants that could be regenerated for future use. The beginnings of the agricultural revolution may have taken hold many thousands of years before the explosion came. After all, we should never

FIGURE 9.7   Using a stone adz to fell a tree. A Tefalmin farmer at work in 1966, in New Guinea.

forget that humans have always been opportunistic, and the planting of food crops and the first taming of animals may have been the simple result.

GUIDE TO FURTHER READING

Childe, V. Gordon. 1936. *Man Makes Himself.* London: Watts.
    Classic Childe arguments for a Neolithic Revolution that summarize all the evidence in favor of a revolutionary change in prehistory when food production began.

Cohen, Mark. 1977. *The Food Crisis in Prehistory.* New Haven, CT: Yale University Press.
    An original and thought-provoking essay on the origins of agriculture that advocates population as a major factor.

————. 1989. *Health and the Rise of Civilization*. New Haven, CT: Yale University Press.
> An essay on paleopathology and the origins of more complex societies that contains much original thinking.

Flannery, Kent V. 1986. *Guilá Naquitz*. Orlando, FL: Academic Press.
> A case study of a site occupied during the transition from hunting and gathering to food production, with excellent theoretical discussion.

Pearsall, Deborah. 1987. *Paleoethnobotany: A Handbook of Procedures*. Orlando, FL: Academic Press.
> A basic discussion of paleoethnobotany, which reviews fundamental techniques.

Rindos, David. 1984. *The Origins of Agriculture: An Evolutionary Perspective*. New York: Academic Press.
> A provocative discussion of the origins of agriculture that evaluates competing theories.

CHAPTER 10 THE ORIGINS OF FOOD PRODUCTION IN THE NEAR EAST

Preview

- The Near East was cool and dry from about 20,000 to 15,000 years ago, with dry steppe over much of the interior. Human populations were sparse and highly mobile until conditions warmed up at the end of the Ice Age and forests spread. The development and spread of agriculture took place under unusually favorable environmental conditions.

- Stone Age hunter-gatherers expanded south into the Negev and Sinai as conditions warmed. Occasional larger settlements situated on ecotones appeared, some apparently occupied for much of the year. One such culture was the Natufian, which flourished as early as 12,000 years ago. There was a trend toward a more sedentary life, associated with intensification of hunting and gathering, and also a shift toward the deliberate planting and harvesting of cereal grasses.

- The Neolithic of the Levant began about 10,500 years ago and lasted until about 5750 years ago. Archaic Neolithic sites date to between 10,500 and 9600 years ago in this area. Most were small settlements, but Jericho was protected with a stone wall and watchtowers and covered a much larger area.

- The farmers of the Archaic Neolithic hunted gazelles, wild goats, and other species. They were efficient, selective hunters. Sheep and goats abruptly replaced gazelles at Abu Hureyra and other sites after 9000 years ago, as if herding was introduced to the Levant at this time.

- In the Zagros Mountains, herding was well established by 10,000 years ago, by which time farmers were living on the Mesopotamian lowlands to the south.

- Anatolia was a diverse, favorable environment for hunter-gatherers in the early Holocene. Agriculture and animal husbandry developed in this area at least 9500 years ago. Widespread trading in obsidian and other exotic materials connected Neolithic villages in Anatolia with others hundreds of miles away. Some settlements, like Çatal Hüyük, occupied 7500 years ago, achieved considerable complexity as a result of trading activity.

- Cultural development proceeded separately in each area of the Near East described in this chapter. In each, food production emerged independently, although there were trading links between regions. It was only later, after 7000 years ago, that broader cultural unity developed.

Much of the theorizing about early food production has stemmed from archaeological research in the Near East, where many early farming settlements are found (Figure 10.1) (G. Wright, 1971). Agriculture and settled life developed in three regions of the Near East: Anatolia, the Zagros Mountains and Mesopotamia, and the Levant. The Neolithic time when food production began is called the *Neolithic*, the "period in which a pattern of village settlement based on subsistence farming and stockbreeding became the basis of existence for communities throughout the Near East" (Moore, 1985). The Neolithic of the Near East began about 10,000 years ago nearly everywhere and lasted until the sixth millennium B.C. in Mesopotamia and until as late as 6000 years ago in the Levant (Henry, 1989).

THE HOLOCENE ENVIRONMENT

Deep-sea cores and pollen studies tell us that the Near Eastern climate was cool and dry from about 20,000 to 15,000 years ago, during the late Weichsel (Moore, 1985). Sea levels dropped more than 300 feet (100 m); much of the interior was covered by dry steppe, with forest restricted to the Levant and Turkish coasts. Between 15,000 and 10,000 years ago, climatic conditions warmed up considerably, reaching a maximum about 5000 years ago. Forests expanded rapidly at the end of the Ice Age, for the climate was still cooler than today and considerably wetter. Many areas of the Near East were richer in animal and plant species than they are now, making them highly favorable for human occupation. The development and spread of agriculture took place in unusually favorable environmental conditions (Bar-Yosef and Belfer-Cohen, 1989).

About 10,000 years ago, human occupation was confined in the main to the Levant and the Zagros Mountains and its western foothills. Within the inhabited areas, there were some locations that were more densely populated than others, among them the Jordan Valley, the Damascus Basin, the Middle Euphrates Valley in the east, and some valleys of the Zagros region. These may have been the loca-

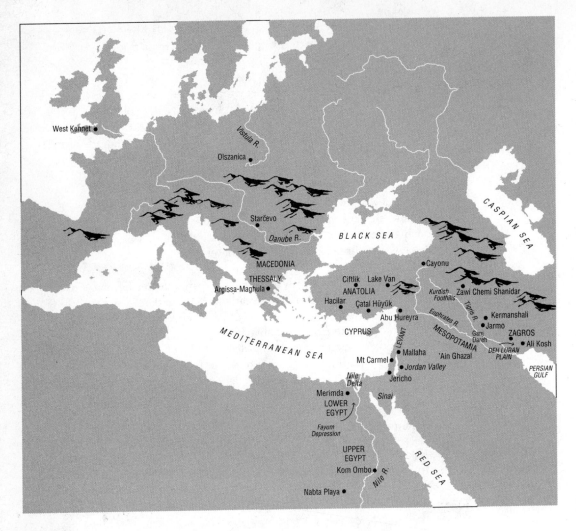

FIGURE 10.1   Early farming sites in the Near East, Europe, and the Nile Valley.

tions where the transition from hunting and gathering to food production, the growing of wheat and pulses and domestication of sheep and goats, took place (Moore, 1989).

HUNTER-GATHERERS IN THE LEVANT

In Chapter 6, we described the dramatic changes in hunter-gatherer life throughout the Levant during the early Holocene. We described the simple, highly mobile Kebaran culture, which flourished over a wide area of the coastal zone and inland at a time of more severe climate than today. Kebaran evolved into the much more sedentary and more complex Natufian culture. These people exploited the Mediterranean zone intensively, foraging on the slopes for cereal grasses and nuts, while exploiting gazelle and other game on the grassy lowlands. This same pattern of specialized hunting and gathering is documented elsewhere in the Near East about 11,000 years ago. The inhabitants of the Abu Hureyra site in Syria were hunting gazelle virtually to the exclusion of all other species. More than 80 percent of the mammal bones in this small settlement were from gazelle, while at the same time the people exploited only a few species of plants. To this extent, they were managing and tending their environment to a significant degree (Moore, 1989).

Natufian sites occur over much of the coastal strip from southern Turkey to the fringes of the Nile Valley and in parts of the interior (Bar-Yosef and Belfer-Cohen, 1989). The largest Natufian sites and cemeteries contain considerable evidence for social ranking and for a large volume of intercommunity exchange in such commodities as seashells, obsidian, and stone bowls. By 10,500 years ago, favorable environmental conditions in the Mediterranean zone were giving way to much drier and unpredictable conditions. It was at this point that many Natufian communities turned to at least some deliberate cultivation of wild cereal grasses. One can speculate that much the same conditions of unpredictable environmental change and shifting population densities were major factors in the changeover from foraging to agriculture some 10,000 years ago.

THE NEOLITHIC OF THE LEVANT

How, then, did the transition from hunting and gathering to food production take place in the Levant? The models for the transition described in Chapter 9 were developed on the basis of entire regions, for example, not only the Levant but Mesopotamia and the Zagros as well. They tend to invoke such factors as population increase, ecological changes, or social imperatives, and they are drawn in very general terms. As far as the Levant is concerned, Andrew Moore (1985, 1989) believes that these three factors were all important at different times. His long-term excavations at the Abu Hureyra site near the Euphrates have led him to believe that agriculture and stock herding developed in this region of the Levant remarkably quickly, perhaps in no more than a few hundred years around 10,500 years ago. The adoption of the new economy was accompanied by a major relocation of settlements, two related events brought about by population growth and environmental deterioration (Moore, 1985).

Under Moore's scenario, pre-Neolithic groups were, in many respects, preadapted to food production. They lived more sedentary lives than their predecessors, hunted a few game species intensively, perhaps even penning some, and probably deliberately planted some plants such as einkorn to supplement wild stands. Then, about 10,500 years ago, agriculture and stockbreeding assumed much greater importance, although hunting and foraging continued to be important until about 8000 years ago.

Abu Hureyra began life as a small village settlement of pit dwellings with simple

reed roofs supported by wooden uprights (Moore, 1979) (Figure 10.2). Using fine screens and flotation equipment, the excavators recovered thousands of wild vegetable foods, including wild einkorn, rye, and barley. Abu Hureyra lies outside the present-day range of these wild cereals. However, between 11,500 and 10,000 B.P., when the site was first occupied, the climate was somewhat warmer and damper than it is today. As a result, the village lay in a well-wooded steppe area where animals and wild cereals were abundant. At any rate, some hunter-gatherer groups such as the Hureyra people came together in more permanent settlements and harvested wild cereals as a deliberate subsistence strategy. The inhabitants also had access to a reliable meat source, Persian gazelles that arrived from the south each spring. The arrivals were apparently killed en masse each year and the meat stored. With such a favorable location, Abu Hureyra slowly increased in size to 300 to 400 people, until deteriorating climatic conditions, and perhaps deforestation due to heavy firewood consumption, caused them to leave. In its heyday, its people may have enjoyed a higher degree of social organization than that found in nomadic hunter-gatherer societies (Lewin, 1988b).

Abu Hureyra c. 11,500 to 10,000 B.P. c. 9700 to 7000 B.P.

Just about half a millennium separated the first, gazelle-hunting settlement at Abu Hureyra and the subsequent, much larger farming settlement. About 9700 years ago, a new village, which grew to cover nearly 30 acres, rose on the low mound. At first, the inhabitants still hunted gazelle intensively. Then, about 9000 years ago, within the space of a generation or two, they switched to herding domesticated sheep and goats and to growing einkorn, pulses, and other cereals. Visitors to the village would have found themselves wandering through a closely knit community of rectangular, one-story, mud-brick houses, joined by narrow lanes and courtyards. The multiroom dwellings had black burnished plaster floors, sometimes decorated with red designs. Each was probably occupied by a single family.

Archaic Neolithic 10,500 to 9600 B.P.

Abu Hureyra is not, of course, unique. Archaic Neolithic sites dating from about 10,500 to 9600 years ago are found in the Aleppo region of Syria as far south as the southern Sinai, but only as far east as the interior plateau, with just a few outliers in the Euphrates Valley. Most lie on low ground, near well-watered, easily cultivable land. Every settlement was considerably larger than earlier hunter-gatherer camps. The people lived for the most part in circular or oval one-room houses, often partially dug into the ground. These stone, mud, or mud-brick dwellings were between 13.0 and 19.6 feet (4 and 6 m) in diameter, densely clustered together in tightly knit communities.

Most Archaic Neolithic villages covered at most a couple of acres. In dramatic contrast, the settlement at Jericho extended over at least 9.8 acres (4 ha). A tem-

---

FIGURE 10.2   Abu Hureyra, Syria. *Top:* The mound of Abu Hureyra from the southwest. The site, which overlooks the Euphrates floodplain, consists of two superimposed settlements. The earliest dates to between c. 11,500 and 10,000 B.P. A later farming village was occupied c. 9500 and 7000 B.P. *Bottom:* The earlier settlement consisted of a series of interconnecting pits dug into the natural subsoil. These were roofed with poles, branches, and reeds to form huts. Part of a later rectilinear house can be seen near the top of the picture.

porary Natufian camp had flourished at the bubbling Jericho spring at least 10,500 years ago (Kenyon, 1981), but a more lasting farming settlement quickly followed. Soon these people, whose technology did not include clay vessels, were building massive walls around their settlement. A rock-cut ditch more than 9 feet (2.7 m) deep and 10 feet (3.2 m) wide was bordered by a finely built stone wall complete with towers (Figure 10.3). The beehive-shaped huts of Jericho were clustered within the defenses. The communal labor of wall-building required both political and economic resources on a scale unheard of a few thousand years earlier. Why

FIGURE 10.3   Excavated remains of the great tower in early Jericho.

walls were needed remains a mystery, but they must have been for defense, resulting from group competition for scarce resources. Some recent geomorphological researches hint that the walls may have been flood-control works, but the theory is controversial (Bar-Yosef, 1986).

The earliest Archaic Neolithic populations were descended from Stone Age peoples, for many of their simple artifacts and their circular houses strongly recall those of earlier times.

The population of the Levant increased considerably between 9600 and 8000 years ago. More than 140 sites are known, scattered throughout the Levant and far east onto the Syrian plateau. Many of them, like the later settlement at Abu Hureyra, are much larger than the earlier sedentary villages.

Types of houses similar to those at Abu Hureyra occur at Jericho and other contemporary settlements, where the dead were buried within the settlement, sometimes under house floors. At Jericho, 'Ain Ghazal in Jordan, and elsewhere, the people would sever the head and deposit it alone or with a cache of skulls. At both sites, they sometimes modeled the features of the deceased in painted plaster, perhaps in some form of ancestor cult (Figures 10.4 and 10.5). There are no signs of differences in individual status in society.

The farmers of 10,000 years ago hunted gazelles, wild cattle, pigs, goats, and other game species. None of the bones shows the characteristic morphological features of domesticated animals. Judging from the proportions of immature gazelles at some sites, the people were very efficient, selective hunters. This pattern of animal exploitation began millennia earlier, during the Upper Paleolithic. Sheep and goats very rapidly replaced gazelles as the principal meat supply at Abu Hureyra and elsewhere after about 9000 years ago. At the same time, there are signs that cattle and pigs were subject to increasing human control. By this time, the domestication of sheep and goats had proceeded to the point that their morphology is clearly that of domesticated animals (see Moore, 1985, for references). About 8500 years ago, it appears that the local gazelle herds were depleted: Sheep and goats now composed 60 percent of all meat consumed (Legge and Rowley-Conwy, 1987).

Emmer wheat, barley, lentils, and peas were grown in the Archaic Neolithic from as early as 10,000 years ago. Even quite early on, agricultural methods were relatively sophisticated, cereals being rotated with pulses to ensure high crop yields and sustained soil fertility. An effective system of allowing fields to lie fallow also enabled larger sites. Abu Hureyra and Jericho were occupied continuously over many centuries as a result. Many settlements became trading centers, for the numbers of imported materials and exotic objects rise dramatically after 9000 years ago. The farmers were using obsidian from Anatolia, turquoise from Sinai, and seashells from the Mediterranean and Red Sea. The volume of trade was such that many villagers used small clay spheres, cones, and disks to keep track of commodities traded. These tokens are thought to have been a simple recording system that later evolved into written script (Schmandt-Besserat, 1978).

By 8000 years ago there was considerable variation in farming culture throughout the Levant, caused by local cultural developments. But the farmers maintained fleeting contacts with communities many hundreds of miles away, even with peoples living in quite different culture areas in the Zagros and Anatolia.

FIGURE 10.4   Plastered Neolithic skull from Jericho, perhaps evidence for an early
ancestor cult.

THE ZAGROS AND MESOPOTAMIA

As in the Levant, the sequence of Neolithic cultures in the Zagros foothills and
Mesopotamia can be divided into an earlier stage, from about 10,000 to 8000 years
ago, and later Neolithic, lasting until about 7000 years ago. There were sporadic
contacts between these areas and the Levant, but cultural developments in this region
were parallel to and independent of those at Abu Hureyra, Jericho, and other western
locations.

Thanks to the pioneering work of Robert Braidwood (L. S. Braidwood, 1982),
who looked for agricultural origins on the hilly flanks of Mesopotamia, we know more
about the highlands, where agricultural conditions were less favorable, than we do
about early food production on the lowlands, the undulating northern Mesopota-

FIGURE 10.5   Plaster figurines from 'Ain Ghazal, Jordan.

mian steppe, where the Assyrian civilization flourished. To the south, the sandy Mesopotamian plain accumulated deep layers of silt throughout the Holocene. Early farming settlement there is probably buried under several feet of alluvium. Only small farming villages preserved under great city mounds like those of Ur and Eridu tell us anything about early farming settlements in these regions, and they date to not much earlier than about 7000 years ago.

During the late Ice Age, human groups probably lived on the warmer lowlands. In the very early Holocene, the mountains were cool and dry, so agriculture probably began on the lowlands first, a natural habitat for wild cereals and pulses. As the climate warmed up, people moved into the mountain valleys of Zagros, open steppe country with seasonal resources spaced vertically up hill slopes. This was ideal country for herding sheep and goats, to the extent that herding may have developed earlier here than in other parts of the Near East (Moore, 1985).

Zawi Chemi Shanidar 11,000 B.P.

Some 11,000 years ago, wild goats were a primary quarry for the hunters and gatherers exploiting the resources of the foothills. The people of a small encampment named Zawi Chemi Shanidar in the mountains of Kurdistan were hunting and gathering at this time, living in small, circular huts. Dexter Perkins (1964) studied the animal bones from the site and found that the inhabitants were killing large numbers of immature sheep, as if they had fenced in their grazing grounds for efficient, intensive hunting. Zawi Chemi may have been a summer encampment on the steppe. Pollen studies show an increase in cereal grasses during the occupation, perhaps evidence of cultivation (Moore, 1985).

Ganj Dareh 10,500 B.P.

High in a mountain valley near Kermanshah lies another early farming village named Ganj Dareh, first occupied about 10,500 years ago (P. E. L. Smith, 1978). The earliest settlement was probably a seasonal camp used by hunters and gatherers, but a later occupation, around 9000 years ago, consisted of a small village of rectangular mud-brick houses, some two stories high. The lower stories may have been used for storage because clay bins have been found there. Ganj Dareh represents the beginnings of permanent settlement in the Zagros, based on goat and cattle herding and possibly agriculture. Contemporary sites contain clear evidence for changes in goat bone morphology indicative of full domestication.

Jarmo 7000 B.P.

One of the best-known Zagros farming villages is Jarmo, a permanent hill village southeast of Zawi Chemi occupied more than 7000 years ago (Braidwood and Braidwood, 1983). Jarmo was little more than a cluster of 25 houses built of baked mud, forming an irregular huddle separated by small alleyways and courtyards. Storage bins and clay ovens were an integral part of the structures. The Jarmo deposits yielded abundant traces of agriculture: Seeds of barley, emmer wheat, and minor crops were found with the bones of sheep and goats. Hunting had declined in importance—only a few wild animal bones testify to such activity—but the toolkit still included Stone Age-type tools with sickle blades, grinding stones, and other implements of tillage. Jarmo contains exotic materials such as obsidian, seashells, and turquoise traded into the Zagros from afar. There are also numerous clay tokens, perhaps again evidence for a recording system connected with long-distance trade. Jarmo was a fully permanent, well-established village engaged in far more intensive agriculture than its predecessors. More than 80 percent of the villagers' food came from herds or crops.

Ali Kosh 10,000 to 8000 B.P.

Below, on the lowlands, farming began along the eastern edge of the flat Mesopotamian plain at least as early as in the Levant. The well-known Ali Kosh site on the plains of Khuzistan, north of where the Tigris and Euphrates join waters, chronicles human occupation from as early as 10,000 years ago. Ali Kosh began life as a small village of mud-brick rectangular houses with several rooms (Hole et al., 1969). As time went on, the houses became larger, separated from one another by lanes or courtyards. The people herded goats and sheep, which may have been driven to highland pastures in the mountains during the hot summer months. This transhumance pattern continues in the area to this day. Emmer, einkorn, barley, and lentils were cultivated from the earliest days of Ali Kosh. Hunting and gathering were important, as were fish and waterfowl from a nearby marsh. This well-excavated site documents more than 2000 years of farming and herding on the lowlands, a time span that saw the development of improved cereal strains and the first appearance of irrigation as a way of intensifying agricultural production.

Agriculture and herding were well established in the lowlands when Ali Kosh was founded some 10,000 years ago. As in the Levant, cereal cultivation and animal husbandry were probably developed by hunter-gatherer groups in the very early Holocene. (For details of the late Neolithic in the Levant and these areas, see Moore, 1985.)

ANATOLIA

Anatolia (Turkey) was a diverse, favorable highland and lowland environment for human settlement from early on in the Holocene. However, the earliest evidence for farming and animal herding there dates from about 9500 years ago. We can only assume that the new economies were developed in this region somewhat earlier and that sites to document the transition await discovery. Certainly, there is no reason food production could not have developed here as early as 10,000 years ago.

**Çayönü
9400 to
8000 B.P.**

Çayönü in southeast Turkey was occupied from about 9400 to 8000 years ago (L. S. Braidwood, 1982; R. J. Braidwood and Cambel, 1980). The first phase of occupation lasted about 650 years, when the inhabitants lived in separate rectangular houses of various designs. The people cultivated cereals and pulses, collected wild vegetable foods, and relied increasingly on domesticated sheep for meat after 8700 years ago. Çayönü represents a relatively developed form of farming life, remarkable only for the sudden adoption of sheep herding, a phenomenon also found at Abu Hureyra in Syria. Perhaps the inhabitants of both sites started herding sheep as a result of contact with shepherd peoples from the highlands to the east, who had been herding small stock for a long time (Moore, 1985; Ryder, 1982).

**Hacilar
8700 B.P.**

On the Anatolian plateau, James Mellaart (1975) excavated a remarkable early farming village at Hacilar, which was founded approximately 8700 years ago. Seven phases of occupation took place at Hacilar before its inhabitants moved. They lived in small rectangular houses with courtyards, hearths, ovens, and plastered walls.

No pottery was used at Hacilar, but basketry and leather containers probably were. Barley and emmer wheat were cultivated, and some wild grass seeds were also eaten. The bones of sheep or goats and cattle and deer are present, but there is no evidence for the domestication of any animal except the dog. Hacilar was a simple and unsophisticated settlement, probably typical of many communities in the Near East in the early millennia of farming.

Most Neolithic sites in central and east Anatolia were within easy reach of the rich obsidian sources near Lake Van and elsewhere. Villages close to the volcanic flows where the fine stone came from used it almost exclusively for artifacts, trading a great deal of obsidian to communities near and far in the form of prepared blade cores. Small quantities of Anatolian obsidian traveled hundreds of miles into the Levant and as far as the Persian Gulf (Renfrew and Dixon, 1976). Trace element analyses of artifacts from many sites show that the patterns of exchange were exceedingly complex, as different sources came into and went out of fashion (Moore, 1985).

The simplicity of many Anatolian farming villages contrasts dramatically with a more complex settlement engaged in widespread trading activity. The great mound of Çatal Hüyük covers 32 acres (13 ha); it was a town of numerous small houses built of sun-dried brick, which were designed to back onto one another, occasionally separated by small courtyards. Roofs were flat, and the outside walls of the houses provided a convenient defense wall (Figure 10.6). The town was rebuilt at least 12 times after approximately 8000 years ago, presumably when the houses began to crumble or the population swelled.

A most remarkable feature of Çatal Hüyük is its artistic tradition, preserved in paintings on carefully plastered walls and in sculptures, some of them parts of shrines (Figure 10.7). Most depict women or bulls. Some paintings show women giving birth to bulls. Much art was about fertility and the regeneration of life, and figurines of women in childbirth have been found.

Much of Çatal Hüyük's prosperity resulted from its monopoly on the obsidian trade from quarries in nearby mountains. Obsidian was only one of many materials traded by Near Eastern farmers after 10,000 years ago. Marine shells, jadeite, serpentine, turquoise, and many other exotic commodities moved from village to village through a myriad of barter transactions. Perhaps these regular exchanges were used not only to obtain exotic materials but also to cement social relationships. Andrew

Çatal Hüyük
8000 to 7000
B.P.

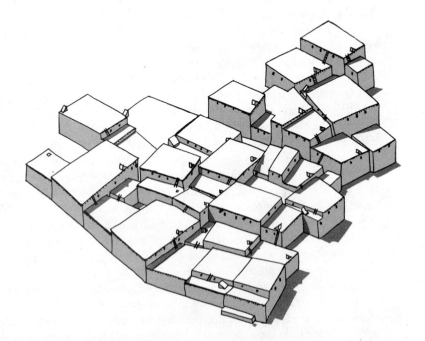

FIGURE 10.6   Schematic reconstruction of houses and shrines from Level VI at Çatal Hüyük, Anatolia, showing their flat-roof architecture and roof entrances.

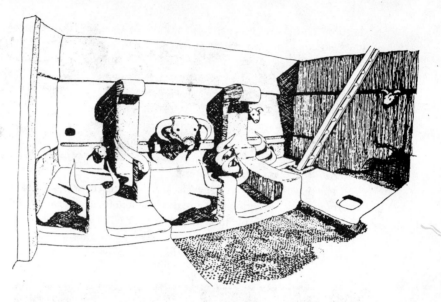

FIGURE 10.7   Reconstruction of the east and south walls of Shrine VI.14 at Çatal Hüyük, Anatolia, with sculptured ox heads, horns, benches, and relief models of bulls and rams. The shrine was entered by the ladder at right.

Moore (1985) believes that this widespread exchange of raw materials accelerated the diffusion of all manner of innovations far and wide, among them sheep herding, the introduction of pottery, and eventually copper and bronze metallurgy.

Just how important the obsidian trade was in the area has been shown by spectrographic analyses of fragments of the volcanic glass in hundreds of sites between Turkey and Mesopotamia. The trace elements in obsidian are so distinctive that it is possible to identify the natural source of the glass by this analysis and to reconstruct the distribution of obsidian from dozens of localities. Colin Renfrew and others were able to identify no fewer than 12 early farming villages that had obtained obsidian from the Ciftlik area of central Turkey (Renfrew, Dixon, and Cann, 1966). The study showed that 80 percent of the chipped stone in villages within 186 miles (300 km) of Ciftlik was obsidian. Outside this "supply zone," the percentages of obsidian dropped away sharply with distance, to 5 percent in a Syrian village, and one-tenth of a percent in the Jordan Valley. Renfrew and his colleagues argue that regularly spaced villages were passing approximately half the obsidian they received to their more distant neighbors. Much early farming trade probably was a form of "down-the-line" bartering that passed various commodities from one village to the next.

Until about 7000 years ago, cultural development proceeded independently in each of these three regions. In each, herding and agriculture emerged separately—not that they were isolated one from another, far from it. There were no regular trading contacts between each area, contacts that may have led to the spread of cereal crops, herding, pottery, and other innovations. In time, these well-established barter networks helped spread both economic and technological innovations throughout the ancient Near East and is why similar developments and intensifications of agricultural production occur at about the same time in several places. Cereal agriculture and herding occurred much earlier than the Near Eastern Neolithic, among late Ice Age hunter-gatherers. The Neolithic saw the culmination of these developments; at this time the new economies became the foundations of human diet throughout the Near East. Major changes in settlement patterns ensued. Sustained population growth took hold some time after farming became commonplace and agriculture sufficiently productive to feed many more people.

The development of the new food-producing economies took place in two stages. The first saw some agriculture and control of animals, but most of the diet came from game and wild vegetable foods. Then, about 8000 years ago, more productive cereal grains and the domestication of cattle, sheep, goats, and pigs created the fully agricultural and stock-raising economy that was to persist into historic times, albeit in elaborated forms.

This was a time of profound social change, when human societies developed new mechanisms for social control, settlement of disputes, and regulation of the cultivation and inheritance of land. Evidence for ranked socieites appears in the form of richly adorned burials at Çatal Hüyük and, perhaps, the plastered skulls from Jericho; both were large, important settlements that were the focus of long-distance exchange and important religious rituals. Some scholars even refer to these large centers as towns, or "protocities," locations where new forms of ranked society first developed in the Near East. For the most part the new societies were still egalitarian, their economies based on the productive abilities of the household and the nuclear family. Just as in many modern-day subsistence farming societies, the plastered skulls from 'Ain Ghazal, Jericho, and other Neolithic sites (Figures 10.5 and 10.6) and complex rituals and ancestor cults were already defining the relationship between living people and the spiritual world, the world of soil fertility, bountiful crops, and revered ancestors.

GUIDE TO FURTHER READING

Bar-Yosef, O. 1987. "Late Pleistocene Adaptations in the Levant." In Olga Soffer, ed., *The Pleistocene Old World: Regional Perspectives,* pp. 219–236. New York: Plenum.
    An authoritative synthesis of late Upper Paleolithic cultures in the Near East designed for the serious reader.

Hole, Frank, Flannery, Kent V., and Neely, J. A. 1969. *The Prehistory and Human Ecology of the Deh Luran Plain.* Ann Arbor: Museum of Anthropology, University of Michigan.
    An exemplary monograph on a lowland Mesopotamian excavation. Excellent discussion of subsistence changes after 10,000 years ago.

Kenyon, Kathleen. 1981. *Excavations at Jericho,* vol. 3. Jerusalem: British School of Archaeology.

    The *monograph on the early levels at Jericho. A fascinating specialist publication.*

Mellaart, James. 1975. *The Earlier Civilizations of the Near East.* London: Thames and Hudson.

    A summary of early farming societies in the Levant and Turkey. Excellent for advanced students.

Moore, Andrew T. 1985. "The Development of Neolithic Societies in the Near East." *Advances in World Archaeology* 4:1–70.

    A comprehensive and thoroughly up-to-date synthesis of the subject matter covered by this chapter. Strongly recommended for its clarity and taut thinking.

Chronological Table F

C14 Years B.P.	NEAR EAST		Egypt	Tropical Africa	Anatolia	Temperate Europe and The Balkans
	Lowlands	Foothills				
			Chapter 17 ↑	Chapter 17 ↑	Chapter 20 ↑	Chapter 21 ↑
4,000				?Agriculture in West Africa		
5,000		Chapter 16 ↑	UNIFICATION			Stonehenge
			Merimda	Saharan cattle herders		Megaliths Cardial ware
6,000			Fayum			Brzesc Kujawski / CHASSEAN BANDKERAMIK TRIPOLYE
7,000	Jericho	Jarmo / ?Early agriculture				Starčevo
8,000			Nabta Playa Bir Kiseiba		Çatal Hüyük	
9,000	A R C H A I C N E O L I T H I C	Ali Kosh / Mugharet el-Wad	QADAN		Hacilar / Çayönü	KARANOVO Argissa-Maghula / Mesolithic hunter-gatherers
10,000		Abu Hureyra / 'Ain Mallaha				
		Ganj Dareh				
11,000	NATUFIAN	Zawi Chemi Shanidar				
12,000	Chapter 6 ↑		↓			Chapter 6 ↑

328

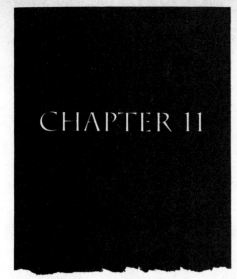

CHAPTER 11   EARLY EUROPEAN FARMERS

Preview

- Mesolithic hunter-gatherers flourished in Europe from about 10,000 years ago until the introduction of food production. Many of these societies were well preadapted to the new economies.

- Agriculture and animal husbandry in southeast Europe probably developed partially as a result of indigenous adaptive shifts to more intensive exploitation of cereals and wild sheep, and also because of the "drift" of domestic animals and cereals from the Near East. Cereal cultivation and animal domestication are known from Greece as early as 8000 years ago.

- The Bandkeramik complex documents the first settlement of southeast European farmers in the Middle Danube and on the light loess soils of central Europe just after 6000 years ago.

- Food production began over most of Europe during the subsequent millennium, largely by indigenous Mesolithic people adopting sheep, pottery, and cereals, which they considered of immediate advantage to them.

- The megalithic tombs of the Mediterranean Basin and west Europe document a trend toward greater cultural diversity after 6000 years ago. They are thought by some observers to be symbols of the continuity of human life.

MESOLITHIC PRELUDE

Chronological
Table F
**10,000 years
ago**

In Chapter 6, we described the Mesolithic hunter-gatherers of central and western Europe, the indigenous peoples of these densely forested regions concentrated by seashores, lakes, and rivers and in forest clearings (J. G. D. Clark, 1975). The Mesolithic lasted for about 4500 years, from about 10,000 years ago until the introduction of farming in northwest Europe about 5500 years ago. This temperate and boreal forest adaptation displayed considerable location variation. Except in areas of abundant aquatic resources and predictable food supplies, population densities were very low. In some areas, such as the Danube's Iron Gates region and the Baltic shores of Scandinavia, population densities were higher than normal, and there are some signs of social ranking and great complexity in some late Mesolithic groups (Price, 1987).

These trends toward greater complexity, more sedentary lifeways, and more intensive hunting, foraging, and fishing took hold in Mesolithic societies throughout Europe at a time when Near Eastern societies were already experimenting with the deliberate cultivation and domestication of crops and animals. After about 8000 years ago, farming was well established in parts of the Aegean and in southeastern Europe. During the 2500 years that followed, European Mesolithic societies apparently embraced these new subsistence practices quite readily (G. Barker, 1975), abandoning the hunter-gatherer lifeways that had sustained their immediate and more remote ancestors for hundreds of thousands of years. (For detailed discussion and regional surveys of the European Mesolithic, see Zvelebil, 1986; also Price, 1987.) The details of this transition are still little understood, but it can be argued that the Mesolithic population was preadapted to cultivation and animal domestication, especially in areas where short-term population shifts and local environmental change may have required conservative subsistence strategies.

8000 years ago

THE TRANSITION TO FARMING IN EUROPE

Did farming spread into Europe as a result of diffusion from the Near East, or did food production develop independently in the temperate zone? There are almost as many theories about this controversial subject as there are archaeologists; the theories pit diffusionists against those who argue that Europeans developed their own farming culture in southeast Europe more than 8000 years ago.

Radiocarbon Dates and Prehistoric Europe

The conventional wisdom that agriculture and metallurgy had spread into temperate Europe from the Near East was overturned by radiocarbon chronologies, which have radically altered our view of European prehistory. V. Gordon Childe and his diffusionist contemporaries worked before radiocarbon dates were available. All chronologies of epochs before approximately 5000 years ago, when civilization emerged in the

Near East, were based on artifact typologies and inspired guesswork. The first radiocarbon dates showed that agriculture and metallurgy had begun in Europe much later than in the Near East, and there seemed nothing wrong with the traditional hypotheses.

When people started to calibrate radiocarbon dates against tree-ring chronologies, they found that European time scales between 3500 and 7000 years ago had to be corrected several centuries backward (Fagan, 1991a; Klein et al., 1982; C. Renfrew, 1970; Suess, 1965). Egyptian historical (that is, from the written record) chronology from 5000 years ago now agrees more closely with calibrated C14 dates rather than being several centuries too recent, as it was before.

British archaeologist Colin Renfrew (1973) has now moved the dates for temperate Europe back far enough to rupture the traditional diffusionist links between the Near East and Europe (Figure 11.1): That is, it is now apparent that events in Europe were contemporary with those in the Near East and not a later result of the spread of Near Eastern culture. Using historical dates for the Mediterranean has thrown what Renfrew aptly calls a "fault line" across the Mediterranean and southern Europe. This line marks a chronological boundary, to the west of which radiocarbon (C14) dates after 5000 years ago have been pushed back by calibration, making them

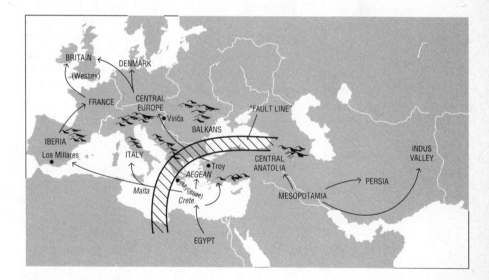

FIGURE 11.1 Chronology of Europe and calibration of C14 chronology. With the uncalibrated chronology, the traditional view of European prehistory had agriculture and other innovations spreading northwestward from the Near East and eastern Mediterranean into continental Europe. The calibrated chronology has hardly affected the dates after 5000 B.P. for the eastern Mediterranean and sites to the southeast of the fault line. The calibrated dates after 5000 B.P. for sites to the west and northwest of the fault line, however, have been pushed back several centuries, so that the old notion of innovation from the east is replaced by new theories postulating less eastern influence (Renfrew, 1973).

older than the accurate, historically attested dates for the eastern Mediterranean and the Balkans, which are east of the fault. Of course, this fault line is a methodological boundary, but it serves to show that prehistoric Europeans were much less affected by cultural developments in the Near East than Childe had suggested. They adopted metallurgy and other innovations independently just as many such inventions were being brought into use in the Near East.

Greece and the Balkans

One reason that everyone assumed for so long that agriculture spread into Europe from the Near East was that they thought of Europe as one geographic entity and Turkey and the rest of the Near East just across the Dardanelles as another (Dennell, 1983). This artificial barrier combined with the assumption that rising population densities caused surplus farmers to spill over into Europe, bringing goats, sheep, and Near Eastern cereal crops with them. There is no evidence of uncomfortably high population densities anywhere in Anatolia at this time (although our knowledge is incomplete). Furthermore, the earliest farming sites in southeast Europe are situated in very favorable places, which could only have been familiar to people who had lived in the region for many generations. However, it is undeniable that food production began in the Near East about 10,000 years ago and some 2000 years later in southeast Europe. How, then, are we to account for the chronological gradient?

The assumption that the natural distributions of wild cereals and of potential animal domesticates have remained unchanged since the early Holocene is at best questionable (Dennell, 1983). As many authors have pointed out, human activity alone may have drastically reduced present-day ranges to the point that all we record are residual distributions. Late glacial and early Holocene pollen diagrams from northern Greece demonstrate that barley and perhaps other cereals were present in **8000 years ago** southeast Europe long before farmers appeared, about 8000 years ago. Cereal grasses may have moved into temperate Europe ahead of woodlands in early Holocene times. Pulses may also have grown in Europe—the evidence is uncertain. As for potential animal domesticates, wild sheep are known to have flourished, albeit in scattered groups, in Upper Paleolithic Europe. At least one of these groups survived in southern France into postglacial times.

Robin Dennell (1983) argues that the development of food production in southeast Europe went through three phases: First, climatic conditions in the early Holocene favored more plant growth. Grasses like einkorn and barley became more abundant, growing in dense stands that could be harvested in sufficient quantities to support a family for a year (for a modern experiment, see Harlan, 1967). However, in reality, most groups probably relied on shorter-term supplies, as wild plant harvests were unpredictable. So they moved on and obtained much of their diet from hunting and other foraged foods.

A second stage began when trees colonized the areas previously occupied by grasses. This change would have scattered grass stands, decreasing the amount of grasses worth harvesting by human groups. The grasses were worth maintaining as a seasonally important food, so the people may have ring-barked tree trunks or burned the forest to clear space for wild grasses to grow. The harvested plots would gradually revert to woodland, where young shoots would attract deer, wild sheep, and other animals. Dennell (1983) believes that a simple interdependence between plant harvesting and animal exploitation developed in areas where woodlands were expanding at the expense of cereals. In such areas, human beings lived in small transitory settlements, many of them seasonal camps—just the kinds of sites found in the southern European Mesolithic (see Zvelebil, 1986).

A third phase saw the establishment of permanent agricultural settlements. Through either local bartering or natural means, large-grained tough-rachis cereals were introduced into southeast Europe. These were Near Eastern cereals like emmer and bread wheat that were more predictable and productive than wild cereals. They required much more work to cultivate and careful sowing in specially prepared and selected fields. The farmers had to weed and protect their growing crops. All this extra effort involved creating special fields and gardens for crops, a mosaic of cultivated land based on carefully chosen soils and a rotation system that allowed exhausted soils to rest. Both domestic emmer and bread wheat extract large quantities of nutrients from the soil, which could be replaced by underplanting nitrogen-fixing legumes and using animal manure. This new farming habitat involved the integration of cultivation and animal husbandry into a closely knit subsistence strategy based on individual households supplying their own food needs.

This model envisages food production in southeast Europe as a largely indigenous development, stimulated in part by the immigration of some domestic plants and animals from across the Dardanelles. It also accounts for the chronological gradient, a time lag that resulted from the gradual "drift" of new crops and domesticated animals from the Near East.

The earliest known evidence of food production in Europe comes from the Argissa-Maghula village mound in Greek Thessaly (Figure 11.2). The inhabitants cultivated emmer wheat and barley. Domestic cattle, sheep, and pig bones in the lower levels of the site date to before 8000 years ago. The Franchthi Cave in southern Greece was occupied in Mesolithic times and continued in use for many thousands of years. Farming appeared there about 8000 years ago. These people had trading contacts with the Aegean islands (Dennell, 1983; Jacobsen, 1981). Since domesticated crops appeared abruptly at Franchthi, it is reasonable to suppose that cereal agriculture had been developed somewhat earlier or elsewhere.

In the Balkans to the north, the earliest farmers settled on fertile agricultural soils on floodplains and elsewhere (Tringham, 1981; Whittle, 1985). Many of them lived in compact villages of one-room dwellings built of baked mud plastered on poles and wicker (Tringham et al., 1980). These Karanovo culture settlements were occupied over long periods. Farming villages were built on brown forest soils and alluvial river plains, and the economy was based on cultivated wheat and barley and domesticated sheep and goats. A number of culture traits, including *Spondylus* shells (a characteristic Mediterranean mussel much valued because it could be used for ornamentation), clay seals and figurines, and reaping knives, show continuing connections with the Mediterranean world. This is an area with great environmental variability and ranges in temperature. For example, there are fertile plains and spring areas where the soils are permanently moist. It was here that many farming communities settled in the

Argissa-Maghula
8000 B.P.
Franchthi
8000 B.P.

Karanovo culture

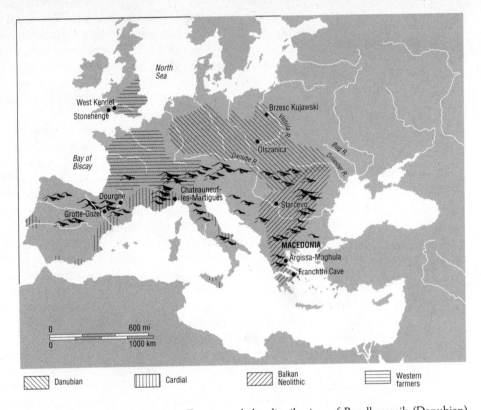

FIGURE 11.2 Archaeological sites in temperate Europe and the distribution of Bandkeramik (Danubian) pottery, Cardial ware, and western Neolithic.

same locations for centuries, just as Near Eastern and Anatolian farmers had done. The largest mounds are found where good arable soils are most widespread. It was in this area that metallurgy developed approximately 5000 years ago (see Chapter 20).

THE SPREAD OF FARMING INTO
TEMPERATE EUROPE

8000 years ago

The beginnings of farming in Europe have traditionally been explained as a process of colonization from the Near East (G. Barker, 1985). Under this theory, the newcomers spread across Europe from about 8000 years ago, ending with the introduction of farming to northwestern Europe about 5500 years ago. The new economies effectively terminated hunter-gatherer societies in Europe. In fact, the process was much more complicated, a combination of both local and intrusive developments.

The adaptive processes and population movements involved are still little understood. These temperate zones have year-round rainfall and marked contrasts between winter and summer seasons. Timber and thatch replaced the mud-brick architecture used so effectively for houses in Near Eastern villages (Melisauskas, 1978). Agricultural techniques had to reflect the heavier soils and perennial rainfall of European latitudes, but the first introduction of farming coincided with a warm, moist phase, when midsummer temperatures were at least 2°C higher than today (Butzer, 1974). The forest cover was mainly mixed oak, shadier tree cover that reduced the grazing resources of large game animals such as deer and wild cattle. Much of the indigenous Mesolithic populations were settled by coasts, lakes, and rivers on ecotones, where they could exploit several ecological zones from summer and winter camps. The first European farmers settled on the mostly loess soils of central Europe, which were lightly wooded, fertile, and easily tilled with simple digging sticks and hoes (Starling, 1985).

**Bandkeramik
7300 B.P.**

No one questions that there was a directional movement of farming from the southeast to northwest (Ammerman and Cavalli-Sforza, 1973; J. G. D. Clark, 1952; Dennell, 1983). This is a far cry from thinking in terms of a wave of colonists, eager for new land, who poured into Europe. In fact, the first farming societies had population densities that were considerably lower than the carrying capacity of their lands. Furthermore, there is good reason to believe that indigenous Mesolithic peoples were important players in the adoption of the new economies. Indeed, European farmers are remarkable for the ways in which they adapted to the challenging and varied environments of temperate Europe. Here, as in areas such as the Near East, China, and the Americas, early farming was a matter of trial and error, of success and sometimes failure.

Recent excavations have also raised the possibility that some animals and plants were actually domesticated in Europe and not introduced from the Near East. The natural ranges of sheep and such plants as barley, einkorn, and some legumes may have once extended into southeast Europe (Dennell, 1983). Only emmer and bread wheat were certainly domesticated in the Near East. There is a real possibility, then, that hunter-gatherer societies in southeast Europe developed food production on their own, in response to such stresses as population pressure or environmental change—the exact stresses are still a mystery (G. Barker, 1985).

Graham Barker (1985) proposes a general scenario: In Greece, farming villages were well established by 8000 years ago and were based on sheep husbandry and the cultivation of crops sown each fall. North of Greece, the expansion of farming activity appears to coincide with a cycle of higher rainfall and warmer winters about 7500 years ago, which made Mediterranean styles of farming viable in the southern Balkans and somewhat different forms of agriculture possible to the north, in the Danube Basin.

6500 years ago

About 6500 years ago, farming based on cattle herding combined with spring-sown crops developed during a period of wetter conditions over enormous areas of continental Europe, especially on optimum loess soils. This agricultural system was perfectly adapted to such conditions, whereas stock-herding assumed much greater importance in nearby, more low-lying regions. At the same time, hunter-gatherer societies continued to flourish for at least another millennium in areas that were marginal for cultivation or herding. Eventually, distinctive local farming adaptations replaced hunting and gathering in southern Scandinavia and lowland Britain as well as along the Atlantic Coast and at higher altitudes. Only in the farthest north did hunting, foraging, and fishing remain dominant subsistence strategies, areas that were vulnerable to minor climatic change.

Contrary to what Ammerman and Cavalli-Sforza (1973) claim, very complete radiocarbon chronologies characterize the spread of farming in Europe as a stop-and-start process. There were major expansions and then long pauses, not gradual waves of advance. Barker (1985) believes that the expansions coincided with climatic changes that affected local landscapes and made farming viable in new areas. In short, the spread of farming was a complex process that involved major cultural change over many centuries.

The best-known early European farming culture is called the Bandkeramik complex (or sometimes the Danubian), so named after its distinctive, linear-decorated pottery (Figure 11.3). Its first colonization of the Middle Danube was on a small scale about 7300 years ago. It appears that small groups of people migrated along river valleys, avoiding areas where Mesolithic folk lived. Their farming territories were widely spaced and apparently very small, perhaps on the order of about 500 acres (202 ha), of which about a third to a tenth was in cultivation at one time (Dennell, 1983; Howell, 1987). The people lived in hamlets made up of individual farmsteads, separated by about 100-yard (90-m) intervals. Individual houses were rectangular, from 18 to 46 feet (5.4 to 14.02 m) long, made of timber and thatch, presumably sheltering families, their grain, and their animals (Champion et al., 1984). Population estimates of between 40 and 60 people per village seem reasonable, with a new settlement being founded as the population expanded (F. Hammond, 1981).

The Bandkeramik people cultivated barley, einkorn, emmer wheat, and minor crops including flax. These they grew by using systems of crop rotation and fallowing, which enabled the farmers to remain in the same place for long periods of time,

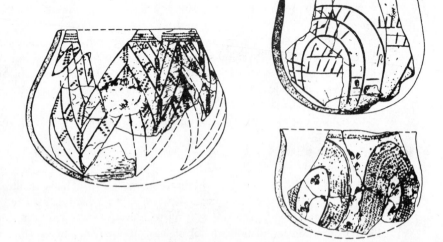

FIGURE 11.3   Danubian *Linearbandkeramik* (linear pottery) from Sittard, Holland, with characteristic line decoration (one-fourth actual size).

sometimes even growing hedges to delineate their field and to fence in their animals. Cattle were important in Bandkeramik life, as were sheep, goats, and dogs. Population growth after first settlement was slow. As each settlement grew, companion villages were founded nearby, gradually filling in the gaps between widely spaced neighboring communities. Within four or five centuries, population densities in parts of Germany rose from 1 per 386 square miles (1000 sq. km) to 1 per 46 square miles (120 sq. km) (Milisauskas and Kruk, 1989).

6000 B.P.   By 6000 years ago, cereal crops and domesticated animals were widely used in southeast and central Europe, and perhaps also in southern France. These farming communities were surrounded by scattered hunter-gatherer societies. The Bandkeramik people had spread far west to southern Holland, where they had settled by 6800 years ago, and east to the Vistula River and the Upper Dniester. In the prime agricultural areas, the people relied heavily on their cattle, sheep, and pigs. They may have moved their herds onto the northern European plain for part of the year. The Brzesc Kujawski site in southern Poland was inhabited by summer cattle herders, who also gathered wild vegetable foods and caught perch in northern streams (Grygiel and Bogucki, 1986; Bogucki, 1988). Eventually farmers settled on heavier soils. We find regional variations of Danubian culture in many parts of central Europe. Some farmers had to rely more on hunting and gathering because the soils of their gardens did not yield enough food to support their families. Defensive earthworks appeared later, as if vigorous competition for land had caused intertribal stress.

FRONTIERS AND TRANSITIONS

The Bandkeramik expansion created a "frontier" in many parts of Europe between farming communities and Mesolithic groups. It would be a mistake to think of this as a rigid boundary between different peoples, for both hunter-gatherer and farming societies have a tendency to stay within their own territories and to continue the way of life with which they are familiar (Dennell, 1983). By the same token, however, the peoples who lived on either side of the frontier inhabited a far from closed world. They knew of one another's presence, traded with one another, and interacted through an intricate web of contacts that were beneficial to both sides. There can be no doubt that Mesolithic people were well aware of cereal crops and domesticated animals. In many cases, they saw no advantage in adopting a new way of life that involved a great deal more work with few significant changes in the diet.

More likely, as Robin Dennell (1983) has argued, they incorporated some aspects of Neolithic culture into their lives, those that gave them immediate advantage. These could have included clay vessels for storage and cooking, perhaps status items acquired by trade that were soon copied by local women. Cereal crops and sheep may have been valuable simply because they solved problems of winter food supplies. Stored nuts, wild cereal grains, and dried deer meat or fish may have been Mesolithic winter staples. Sheep have lower feeding requirements than deer, have higher reproductive and growing rates, and can be used to keep woodland open for cereal growth. It would have been easy for Mesolithic people to graft sheep and domestic cereals onto their existing hunting and gathering practices. Dennell (1983) believes that these processes of assimilation caused farming to spread over much of temperate Europe after 8000 years ago and continue until as late as 5500 years ago, when many Scandinavian groups finally adopted food production.

Marek Zvelebil and Peter Rowley-Conwy (1984) take the argument a stage further, distinguishing three transition phases from hunting and gathering to farming:

- An "availability phase," when farming is known to Mesolithic peoples and there is some exchange of materials and information. Both farmers and hunter-gatherers are still independent units.

- A "substitution phase" that has two forms: (1) Farmers move into and settle hunter-gatherer territory in competition with the indigenous residents, and (2) hunter-gatherers add cultivation or animal husbandry to their range of subsistence activities. During this phase, there is competition for land, food, and raw materials, and perhaps social competition as well.

- A "consolidation phase," when food production becomes extensive and widespread, with hunting and gathering becoming subsistence strategies in emergencies. Farmers have now occupied the best soils and are using secondary areas with more intensive farming methods. By this time, the frontier has vanished.

The Zvelebil-Rowley-Conwy model serves as a descriptive device for analyzing the spread of food production into west and central Europe, but more data are needed to bolster it.

SOCIAL CHANGES, LINEAGES, AND THE INDIVIDUAL: 5500 TO 4400 YEARS AGO

Bandkeramik settlement was limited to very specific parts of the landscape—the edges of plateaus overlooking medium-sized streams in areas of loess soils (Howell, 1987). The people deliberately selected places where damp lowland pasture coincided with tracts of light, friable upland soils. They were cultivating fertile soils, land where hoe-using farmers could grow emmer wheat and other crops year after year, fertilizing their fields with cattle dung and domestic waste. Cattle were an important element in Bandkeramik economy, pointing to a "pioneer" economy introduced from southeast Europe rather than an indigenous farming culture that made full use of local plants and game animals.

The Bandkeramik people built large, permanent timber houses, investments in time and labor that would have been totally uneconomic if they had been engaged in slash-and-burn agriculture and had shifted their villages regularly (Figure 11.4). Bandkeramik sites formed clusters of settlements, separated from one another by distances of 12.4 or 18.6 miles (20 or 30 km). Up to a dozen or more houses stood in each settlement; the houses were apparently rebuilt in much the same place again and again. Bandkeramik settlements were occupied over long periods of time, so that

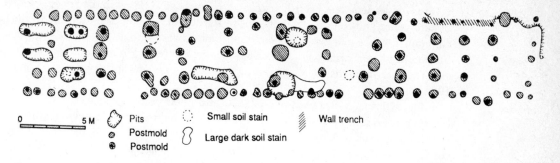

FIGURE 11.4   Plan of a Bandkeramik long house from Olszanica, Poland, with wall trenches, postholes, pits, and other features.

a basic site, and the social structure within it, was maintained over many generations. There was continuity of residence location and inheritance from one generation to the next. In some areas, settlements were closely packed within small areas, each hamlet owning a territory of 37 acres (15 ha) or so—not because land was in short supply but because factors such as trade and local outcrops of flint and other materials may have played a role.

All of these characteristics point to farming societies that were producing food at the household level but with cooperation between different lineages at the settlement level—to build houses, erect enclosures, and herd cattle (for discussion, see J. Thomas, 1987). The first settlement in an area was, perhaps, the senior one, the place where the elder of the senior lineage lived, where the group's cemeteries and ritual enclosures were to be found. In the cemeteries, there were two general distinctions among grave goods: between graves of males and females and those of young and old. Political power and social authority may have been in the hands of a group of older men, who controlled cattle ownership and the exchange of cattle and other exotic commodities with other settlements. In Bandkeramik society, then, a complex network of social relations controlled productivity. Lineages within society formed the links between people and the lands of their ancestors.

Some early Bandkeramik settlements in Belgium dating to about 6300 to 6000 years ago show evidence of substantial fortifications, which may have been erected for short-term protection against local hunter-gatherer bands trying to recover territory taken from them by the farmers (Keeley and Cahen, 1989). These fortifications did not last long, as if resistance was short-lived. About 5500 years ago, Bandkeramik settlements became more clustered and turned into villages. Many were protected by earthen enclosures. Divergent pottery styles hint that there were well-defined territories for different settlement clusters (J. Thomas, 1987). This was a time when more elaborate burial customs developed throughout Europe as ancestor cults became more complex.

In western Europe, communal tombs came into fashion, among them the celebrated megaliths, sepulchers fashioned from large boulders and buried under earthen mounds (see page 345). Such corporate burial places may have had locations where

5500 B.P.

revered kin leaders were buried; people with genealogical ties with the ancestors were of paramount and collective importance to a group of farming communities. In time, communal tombs may have become important power symbols among local groups, linked with their neighbors and others by both lasting kin ties and burgeoning exchange networks that were expanding throughout Europe at this time (J. Thomas, 1987).

4800 B.P.   Somewhat later, between about 4800 and 4400 years ago, another change in burial customs took hold throughout Europe. For the first time, individual graves as well as communal sepulchers appeared. S. J. Shennan (1982) has argued that group-based ideologies were replaced by new beliefs that reinforced individual power and prestige. It would have been very hard for a single elder to preempt political and economic authority in Bandkeramik society. There were simply too many kin ties and reciprocal obligations to overcome, as well as the collective bond with the ancestors. By being buried separately, in a burial adorned with elaborate grave furniture, a prominent elder could take on the role of sole male ancestor, the fountain of authority over land ownership, a role now assumed by his successor. Inheritance of land and wealth was now legitimized.

This is, of course, a speculative scenario but one supported by telling clues. There are many cases in which men and women were buried together in a single grave. This practice, argue some archaeologists, indicates monogamous marriages rather than the polygamous ones of lineage-based Bandkeramik society. The dominance of male burials from this period suggests that men were of great importance in establishing descent and rights of inheritance. Many individual graves were dug into older communal monuments, perhaps to reinforce the idea that individual ancestors were more important than collective ones. The rich grave goods found in such burials reveal new emphases in society: Many weapons such as daggers and swords appear, as well as battle axes, fine copper ornaments, and drinking cups. Everything points to the emergence of individuals who thought of themselves as warriors. Personal achievement and prestige were associated with males, who were involved in expanding exchange networks that handled luxury goods such as amber, gold ornaments, and weapons. These were the symbols of prestige, the means of cementing individual relationships, political links, and reciprocal obligations.

There are striking differences in the people buried, too. Bandkeramik farmers lavished their finest goods on older individuals. The later individual burials are those of men in their prime, indicating that personal achievement was the avenue to power and prestige.

THE INTRODUCTION OF THE PLOW

Andrew Sherratt (1981) believes that the introduction of plow agriculture was a seminal development in Europe. Plows are known to have been used as early as 5600 years ago, but Sherratt says they came into far more widespread and intensive use about 4600 years ago, when a number of other innovations or products reached Europe from the Near East. These included sheep shearing, milking, horse riding, and the use of oxen for traction. He goes so far as to argue for a "secondary products revolution," which transformed both settlement patterns and social organization throughout Europe.

Plow agriculture allows fewer people to work an acre of land; thus more land would be cleared, making an individual's fields more widely scattered, sometimes close to the outer limits of daily walking. The result was a much more dispersed settlement pattern, with a rapid expansion onto heavier soils and hitherto uncultivated areas around 4600 years ago. With much more acreage to clear and the technology to do it, the farmers of 4500 years ago were less tied to ancestral lands and the realities of household production and the kin ties these imply. Fewer people worked in the field, creating "unproductive" individuals in greater numbers, and there were compelling needs for social change. So, in place of the kin-based society arose a new social order in which individual success, prestige, and inheritance of land were the norm—with momentous consequences for the Europeans.

RUSSIAN PLAINS FARMERS: TRIPOLYE

While the Bandkeramik complex was developing in central Europe, a mosaic of different subsistence patterns emerged on the Russian plains to the east between 8000 and 6500 years ago (Dolukhanov, 1986; Telegin, 1987). The areas best suited for farming, such as intermountain basins, were settled by agricultural peoples, while hunter-gatherers continued to exploit the river basins, such as those of the Bug and Dniester rivers. The farmers and foragers interacted with one another, living in

6500 B.P. complementary environments, where one did not threaten the other. By 6500 years ago, Bandkeramik peoples had moved as far east as the Ukraine, bringing a mixed farming economy with them. They settled on the higher terraces of major rivers, still interacting with Mesolithic folk in the valley bottoms. Both Mesolithic and Neolithic peoples maintained their own identities. Farming reached its greatest extent in the

Tripolye forest-steppe regions of west Russia with the Tripolye culture some 6000 years ago
6000 B.P. (Figure 11.5). Soon after this, the farmers finally submerged the Mesolithic foragers of the valleys, perhaps because they relied extensively on cattle, whose grazing demands may have competed with hunter-gatherers' foraging needs. Some 4800 years
4800 B.P. ago, the climate deteriorated, making cultivation less viable. At this point balanced economies emerged, relying on stockbreeding on the steppe and farming in the forest-steppe, a balanced dynamic that survived into recent times, with important historical consequences.

MEDITERRANEAN AND WESTERN EUROPE

New artifacts, such as pottery, and food sources, such as sheep, were added to hunter-gatherer adaptations as farming took hold in central Europe and farther afield. This transitional phase lasted for centuries throughout Europe. In many areas the new items added to existing practices, but they did little to change the fundamental structure of Mesolithic society or lifeways. The full-scale adoption of farming economies in areas such as west Russia took a long time to achieve,

FIGURE 11.5   A Tripolye culture village.

whereas in other areas, such as Britain, a full changeover occurred within five centuries or so.

In the Iron Gates region of the Danube Valley, coastal Yugoslavia, central Italy, and southern France, pottery, cereal crops, and sheep appeared, but there was little immediate change in daily life. Many sites where such artifacts occur are in the same type of setting as Mesolithic settlements, where hunting continued for centuries, even millennia. Sheep were in use in southern France in the early Holocene, but the people were still hunter-gatherers. In the Mediterranean Basin, the long-term changes were an expansion in the use of obsidian and much wider ranging trade in this material after 7000 years ago. Obsidian was found on three Mediterranean islands, including Sardinia, and was now regularly traded to neighboring islands and the mainland. This trade was part of a widespread network of contacts, linked partly by sea, that carried seashells, exotic rocks, and later copper ore the length and breadth of the Mediterranean.

This trade also coincided in general terms with the manufacture of distinctive pottery styles decorated with impressions of seashells, among them the cockleshell, *Cardium* (Figure 11.6). This motif has given rise to the term *Cardial ware* to describe a range of indigenously developed pottery styles that mark the first use of clay vessels by Western peoples. Like sheep and goats and perhaps cereal crops, pottery was adopted long before fully fledged farming economies emerged in the western Mediterranean and west Europe (Whittle, 1985).

The decisive shift from hunting and gathering in the West took place in the sixth millennium before Christ, with sheep and goats being acquired by trade, exchange, or theft considerably earlier, cereal crops arriving somewhat later.

By 6000 years ago, a series of fishing villages was thriving on the shores of the Swiss lakes (Muller-Beck, 1961). They were occupied by cattle and sheep farmers who

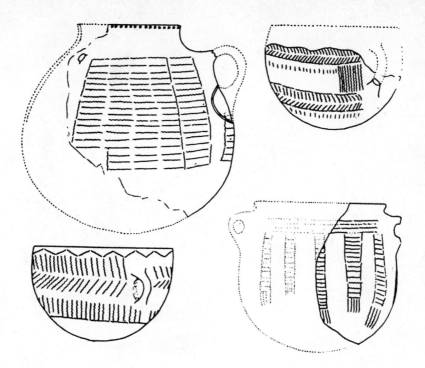

FIGURE 11.6   Cardium-shell-impressed pottery from southern France (one-fourth actual size).

cultivated barley and wheat as well as many minor crops, including cider apples and flax (used for textiles) (Figure 11.7). Their houses were built on the damp ground between the lake reed beds and the scrub brush of the valley behind. The first dwellings were small rectangular huts, but they eventually gave way to larger, two-room houses. Some villages grew to include between 24 and 75 houses clustered on the lakeshore, a density of population much the same as that of modern Swiss villages, which have approximately 30 households.

In the extreme northwest, food production was adopted comparatively late. From 8000 years ago through 6000 years ago, the newly isolated Mesolithic peoples of Britain developed with little or no significant contact with the continent. The earliest traces of pottery and forest clearance appeared soon after 6000 years ago, with well-documented cereal agriculture by 6300 years ago. The same processes may have operated here as in west Europe. Robin Dennell (1983) theorizes that European farmers did not cross the channel and settle in Britain. Rather, Mesolithic peoples experienced population pressure about 6000 years ago, perhaps as a result of forest expansion due to warmer climate and also because of population growth. Hunting became more difficult, so the people began clearing woodland to provide more animal forage and plant foods and to make hunting more predictable. The people also increased their exploitation of marine resources, and seafaring techniques developed, leading to contacts with other coastal communities in Britain and on the continent.

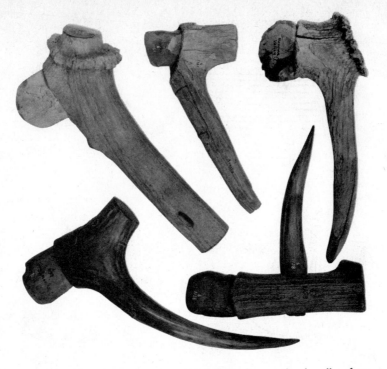

FIGURE 11.7   Sample prehistoric stone axes mounted in deer antler handles from the Swiss lake dwellings, typical of those used by early farmers in Europe.

Eventually, Mesolithic populations in Britain became aware of new food resources like domestic cereals and sheep and acquired them. Ample open grassland was available for herding and cultivation in southern Britain. Within five centuries or so Mesolithic populations had transformed themselves into farmers with their own distinctive cultural traditions. Somewhat similar processes probably led to the adoption of agriculture and stock rearing among Mesolithic Scandinavians.

THE MEGALITHS

Early European farming societies were basically egalitarian, with the family as the basic productive unit at the center of a web of intricate kin ties and reciprocal social relationships that linked communities near and far and tied people to the land of their ancestors. There was probably equal access to resources, with sufficient food being produced to feed individual families. In a real sense, the subsistence farming economy *was* society (Champion et al., 1984). In general, early Neolithic burials in Europe do not reflect any social differentiation between individuals.

There are signs of variation, notably in the intensity of trading activities through barter networks and in burial customs. A slow process of social change can be documented throughout Europe after 6000 years ago, moving toward greater emphasis on craft specialization and burial ritual and the emergence of regional trading centers that controlled exchange networks, and perhaps ritual as well. The famous megalithic tombs of the Mediterranean and west Europe are one symbol of this trend toward social change.

As early as 6000 years ago, some French farmers were building large communal stone tombs, known to archaeologists as *megaliths* ("large stone" in Greek) (Figure 11.8). Megaliths are found as far north as Scandinavia, in Britain, Ireland, France, Spain, the western Mediterranean, Corsica, and Malta. For years, scholars thought that megaliths had originated in the eastern Mediterranean approximately 4500 years ago and spread westward into Spain with colonists from the Aegean, who had carried a custom of collective burial and their religion with them. Megalithic tombs were believed to have then been built in west Europe, witnesses to a lost faith perhaps spread by pilgrims, missionaries, or merchants. With their massive stones and large burial chambers, megaliths remain one of the mysteries of European prehistory (Daniel, 1973; C. Renfrew, 1973).

This popular and widely accepted hypothesis was badly weakened by C14 dates from France that turned out to be earlier than others from west Europe. Furthermore, new calibrated dates have placed Spanish megalithic sites and their associated culture as early as approximately 6000 years ago, much earlier than their alleged prototypes in the Aegean. Thus, megaliths were being built in west Europe at least a millennium

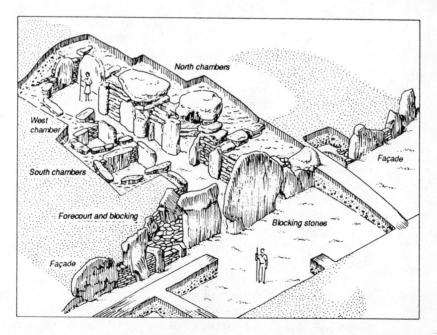

FIGURE 11.8   Interior of a megalithic chamber tomb in West Kennet, England, C14 dated to approximately 5500 years ago (Piggott, 1965).

before massive funerary architecture became fashionable in the eastern Mediterranean. This remarkable freestanding architecture is a unique local European creation.

What exactly were megaliths? Were they the surviving remains of a powerful religious cult that swept west Europe, or did they symbolize the emergence of new, more sophisticated political and social structures in the West? Colin Renfrew (1983) has argued that the tradition of communal burial developed in very early west European farming societies and that it is manifested by the famous long barrows of southern Britain (Figure 11.8), many of which had stone boulder, megalithic interiors. The long barrows were fairly small structures, requiring not more than about 5000 to 10,000 worker-hours to build (a figure equivalent to 20 men taking 50 days). Between 6000 and 5500 years ago, these barrows were associated with more elaborate monuments, among them enclosed earthworks (often called "causewayed camps"), which are known to have been protected by timber palisades. Recent excavations have shown that these camps were littered with human bones, many of them skeletons from which the flesh had weathered in the open. Perhaps these camps were places where the dead were exposed for months before their bones were deposited in nearby communal burials.

As time went on, the argument goes, burial ceremonies revolved around even larger monuments, the so-called henges, stone- and wood-built circles of which Stonehenge in southern Britain is the most famous (Figure 20.6). In this sense, megaliths of all types formed a kind of settlement hierarchy on the prehistoric landscape, a hierarchy that may have reflected profound changes in European society.

Another ingenious theory argues that megalithic monuments appeared in west Europe at just the moment when farming took hold all across Europe. This final colonization must have had a major impact on the stable Mesolithic societies that were exploiting coastal resources along the Atlantic Ocean and North Sea shores from the Bay of Biscay in France to the Baltic. Indeed, Mesolithic stone tools have been found in association with some French megaliths. Ian Kinnes (1982) believes that megaliths first appeared in the margins of Neolithic society, along the Atlantic Coast, where competition with Mesolithic groups may have been most acute. Perhaps, he believes, the megaliths served as territorial markers, signs of ancestral ownership of the surrounding land.

Colin Renfrew and others have called megaliths the "tombs of the living," lasting, humanly made symbols of the continuity of human life as well as symbols of the continuity of ownership of land from one generation to the next. The annual round of religious rituals at places like Stonehenge reinforced this continuity, and at a time when population densities were rising sharply, the megaliths associated with them became important symbols of political and social continuity. They also reinforced the political, economic, and spiritual power of those who supervised the building and worship at places such as Stonehenge (Figure 20.6). That such supervision was necessary is certain, for it has been estimated that Stonehenge required at least 30,000 worker-hours to complete. So the appearance of megaliths and the hierarchy of more elaborate stone and wooden monuments associated with them may have foreshadowed profound social changes in prehistoric Europe that came with the increasing use of bronze and other metals (Chippindale, 1983).

A complex set of processes governed the emergence of food production in temperate Europe, processes only rarely involving the movement of entire populations from one region to the next. Here, as in other parts of the world, one should think of agriculture not as a miracle invention or in terms of conquest but as yet another instance of how readily hunter-gatherers adapted to new opportunities and conditions. As is so often the case in prehistory, continuity was as important as change, but this continuity was born of inherent flexibility, an ability to adapt to new circumstances.

GUIDE TO FURTHER READING

Barker, Graham. 1985. *Prehistoric Farming in Europe.* Cambridge, Eng.: Cambridge University Press.
> *An analysis, aimed at specialists, of the spread of farming into temperate Europe.*

Champion, T. G., et al. 1984. *Prehistoric Europe.* New York: Academic Press.
> *An up-to-date summary of European prehistory, with a major emphasis on trade, subsistence, and social organization.*

Clark, J. G. D. 1952. *Prehistoric Europe: The Economic Basis.* Palo Alto, CA: Stanford University Press.
> *The classic essay on prehistoric European economic life. Still of immense value to the general reader.*

Dennell, Robin C. 1983. *European Economic Prehistory: A New Approach.* New York: Academic Press.
> *An enjoyable essay on European prehistory that formed my ideas on this chapter. Strongly recommended for newcomers to the subject.*

Renfrew, Colin. 1973. *Before Civilization.* New York: Knopf.
> *A well-written essay on recent advances in European prehistory that concentrates on the calibration of radiocarbon dating. Essential reading for any more-than-casual student of Old World archaeology.*

Trump, David. 1980. *The Prehistory of the Mediterranean.* New Haven, CT: Yale University Press.
> *A fundamental source on a key area of the world. For the informed reader.*

Whittle, Alastair. 1985. *Neolithic Europe: A Survey.* Cambridge, Eng.: Cambridge University Press.
> *A summary of the European Neolithic for the more advanced reader.*

Zvelebil, Marek, ed. 1986. *Hunters in Transition.* Cambridge, Eng.: Cambridge University Press.
> *A volume of articles that describes basic Mesolithic theory and analyzes the Neolithic transition in various parts of Europe.*

CHAPTER 12 EARLY FARMERS OF AFRICA

Preview

- Some archaeologists believe that agriculture and animal domestication first took hold in the eastern Sahara about 10,000 years ago among people who left the Nile Valley after catastrophic flooding some 12,000 years ago. Increasing aridity about 7000 years ago then caused some of these nomadic cattle herders and farmers to settle in the Nile Valley, where food production was well established by 7000 years ago.

- The earliest Egyptian farmers probably had little need for irrigation agriculture, the introduction of which appears to have coincided with the political unification of Egypt approximately 5000 years ago.

- The Sahara was sufficiently well watered to support cattle-herding peoples from approximately 7500 to 5000 years ago. With the desiccation of the desert, Saharan peoples moved southward into sub-Saharan Africa, where they domesticated summer rainfall crops like sorghum and millet.

- Cattle-herding people were living in East Africa by 5000 years ago, and cattle may have been domesticated there much earlier. Agriculture and domesticated animals did not spread to tropical Africa as a whole until the advent of ironworking, approximately 2000 years ago.

Like the Tigris and Euphrates in Mesopotamia, the lower reaches of the Nile River flow through wide areas of rich, easily cultivable floodplain soil (see Figure 10.1). This context gave the Nile Valley the same potential of becoming a center of early agriculture and civilization as Iraq. The Nile floodplain is wider, with more predictable annual floodwaters, which were easier to control than those of the twin rivers. The Egyptians could water their highly productive fields very easily by modifying natural basins to retain floodwater (Aldred, 1986; Fedden, 1977; Trigger et al., 1983). The Nile Valley was always an isolated oasis, a slash of green, fertile land flowing between desert bastions (Figure 12.1). There were intervals of higher rainfall, however, one of them between 11,000 and 8000 years ago, when there was some runoff at the edges of the valley. This would have made it possible for Neolithic farmers to cultivate the margins of the gullies leading down from the desert. The Nile Valley floor itself consisted for the most part of seasonally flooded natural basins that supported grass and brushland. People lived on higher levees along the river, where trees grew and settlements escaped the annual inundation.

HUNTER-GATHERERS ON THE NILE

During the last millennia of the Ice Age, the Nile Valley was a rich, diverse habitat, abounding in game of all sizes and in wild vegetable foods. Fish and waterfowl added to the bounty of resources. From about 15,000 years ago until perhaps as late as 6500 years ago, a diverse population of hunter-gatherers exploited these resources. They are grouped under the name *Qadan culture* by archaeologists (J. D. Clark, 1971). The Qadan is best known from microlithic tools found on riverside campsites near the Nile. In the earlier stages of the Qadan, fishing and big-game hunting were important, but large numbers of grindstones and grinding equipment came from a few localities, which seems to show that gathering wild grains was significant to at least part of the economy. Some Qadan settlements were probably large and occupied for long periods. The dead were buried in cemeteries, in shallow pits covered with stone slabs. Some pits held two bodies. In six instances, small stone tools were embedded in the bones of these Qadan people, who must have met a violent end (Wendorf, 1968).

Qadan culture
15,000 to 6500
B.P.

Other distinct cultural traditions are known to have prospered in the Nile Valley at this time (Hassan, 1988). Around Kom Ombo, upstream of Qadan country, Stone Age hunter-gatherers lived on the banks of lagoons and flood channels of the Nile, seeking game in the riverside woodlands and on the plains overlooking the valley. They fished for catfish and perch in the swamps. Here, too, wild grasses were important in the economy from approximately 14,000 years ago (Wendorf and Schild, 1980).

AGRICULTURAL ORIGINS ON THE NILE

The Nile Valley is unusual in that its water supplies depend not on local rainfall but on annual floods from far upstream in Ethiopia. Thus, fluctuations in these inunda-

FIGURE 12.1   The Nile, close to the First Cataract.

12,000 B.P.

tions had a profound effect on the pattern of Holocene settlement along the Nile. A series of catastrophic floods about 12,000 years ago apparently brought an intensification of hunting, gathering, and fishing in the valley to a halt, delaying the development of food production along the Nile for as long as 2000 years.

For years, people assumed that cereal crops and domesticated animals were introduced into the Nile Valley from southwest Asia sometime after 10,000 years ago (Childe, 1952). In recent years, this viewpoint has been rejected. Fekri Hassan (1986) has spent many years studying climatic change in the Nile Valley and eastern Sahara. He believes that food production began very early in, of all places, the eastern Sahara Desert. During the early Holocene, he argues, the Sahara was wetter than today, and the catastrophic Nile floods caused people living in the river valley to spill over onto the harsh, poorly watered desert plains. Those who remained alongside the Nile probably took advantage of the fish resources of the great river, whereas those who left the valley followed game animals onto the stunted grassland plains of the Sahara with no idea of the major climatic fluctuations that were to follow.

The areas that are now desert were, like all arid regions, very susceptible to cycles of higher and lower rainfall, resulting in major, sudden changes in distributions of plants and animals. Hassan argues that these shifts in the Saharan environment led the people who preyed on the sparse desert fauna to manage the wild resources they hunted and gathered, especially wild oxen, which must have regular water supplies to survive. The human population was never large, and the people probably lived in small bands, subsisting off a wide variety of plant and game resources, at the same time engaging in some small-scale cattle herding. The very flexibility and mobility of hunter-gatherer life in these marginal lands probably made pastoralism adaptive. The people may have extended the distributions of stands of wild cereal grasses by deliberate cultivation as well. It is thought that some cattle bones found in the Egyptian part of the eastern Sahara are from domesticated beasts dating to between 10,000 and 8000 years ago, a date for domesticated cattle far earlier than that from Greece (Chapter 10). Domesticated barley is known from the Nabta Playa site in the Western Desert and dates to about 8000 years ago. These cultivators and their neighbors at Bir Kiseiba to the west were living in large settlements with houses set in rows or in an arc. Perhaps as many as 14 families lived in these villages, dwelling in low pit houses sunk into the ground (Wendorf et al., 1984).

Nabta Playa
8000 B.P.

Further north, in the Fayyum depression west of the Nile, small fishing camps flourished along the water's edge at the time of Bir Kiseiba and Nabta (Wenke et al., 1988). Unlike their relatives far to the south, they did not use cereals. For reasons that are still not understood, the Fayyum was abandoned after about 8000 years ago. Then, about 6350 years ago, the lake shores were home to people living in short-term seasonal camps that moved as the lake level fluctuated. These people cultivated wheat and barley, locating their gardens on patches of fertile soil whose distribution changed as the lake did. They also herded cattle, sheep, and goats, but fish were overwhelmingly important in their diet. Unlike their contemporaries in the Near East, the Fayyum people never built permanent villages, for their environment was too unpredictable to allow complete dependence on agriculture. Considerable debate surrounds the Fayyum discoveries, which have long been hailed as evidence for the earliest farming in the Nile area (Caton-Thompson and Gardner, 1934). In fact, this lake-filled depression may have supported groups who only partially adopted the new lifeways because their environment was too unpredictable. In fact, dozens of farming villages may have flourished in the fertile Nile Valley as early as 7000 years ago if not earlier, settlements that are now inaccessible beneath deep alluvial deposits laid down by thousands of years of river floods.

Fayyum
6350 B.P.

Fekri Hassan believes that agriculture was introduced to already preadapted hunter-gatherer groups in the Nile Valley as the climate grew progressively drier after 7000 years ago (J. D. Clark, 1971; Hassan, 1986). The earliest dated farming settlements from the Nile Valley, both from Egypt and the Sudan, date to between 6300 and 5300 years ago. Hassan believes that the nomadic peoples of the desert now included the fertile river valley in their wanderings, moving in and out of the desert as conditions warranted, as they do in the Sahel at the southern fringes of the Sahara today. These movements, he believes, were especially significant after 4500 years ago, when conditions became very arid indeed. This was also a time of exceptionally low Nile floods, so the sparse agricultural sites dating from early farming times are probably buried under many feet of later river alluvium. Hassan argues that irregular population movements involving small numbers of people continued for thousands of years and came into the valley from many desert regions. The result was considera-

7000 B.P.

6300 B.P.

ble cultural diversity within the Nile Valley, caused by both immigration and fusion with existing populations.

Up to about 7000 years ago, the inhabitants of the Nile Valley hunted, foraged, and exploited the rich aquatic resources of the great river. Then an arid cycle lowered river levels significantly, which may have affected the fisheries and the productivity of wild plant foods. At the same time, desert peoples with cattle and small stock (goats and sheep) moved away from the deserts into the narrow valley. The resulting demographic and cultural merger may have introduced a new way of life to the Nile and led subsequently to the rise of ancient Egyptian civilization.

Many of the new floodplain settlements may have been like the village of Merimda Beni Salama near the Nile Delta. There a cluster of oval houses and shelters was built half underground and roofed with mud and sticks (Hoffman, 1979). An occupation mound 7 feet (2 m) high accumulated over 600 years from approximately 5900 B.P. Simple pottery, stone axes, flint arrowheads, and knives were in use. Agriculture and the cultivation of cereal crops are evidenced by grains stored in clay pots, baskets, and pits. Dogs, cattle, sheep or goats, and pigs were kept. Farming at a subsistence level was characteristic of large areas of the Nile floodplain for thousands of years (Hassan, 1988).

Merimda
c. 5900 B.P.

Other farmers who flourished along the Upper Nile are known to us mainly from cemetery burials. Like their northern neighbors, they used bows and arrows in the chase, many tipped with finely flaked arrowheads. Emmer wheat and barley were cultivated, and cattle and small stock provided much of the meat. Settlements here were typified by mud-brick and transient architecture. The dead, however, were buried with some ceremony—in linen shrouds and covered with skins. The women wore ivory combs and plaited their hair. This culture, named the *Badarian* after a village where the first settlements were found, is thought to have been broadly contemporary with Merimda (Butzer, 1976; Hassan, 1988; Hays, 1984).

Badarian culture
5700 B.P.

The early farming communities of the Nile continued to use the forested riverbanks for settlement (Butzer, 1976). Animals grazed in the flat grasslands of the plain for most of the year, and crops were planted on wet basin soils as the waters receded. Game was still abundant in the Nile Valley 6000 years ago; even so, the people ventured to the edge of the deserts in search of gazelles and other small animals. They buried their dead in cemeteries overlooking the Nile, where the graves would not take up valuable agricultural land.

By 5500 years ago, the inhabitants of the Nile Valley were living almost entirely off agriculture, with hunting playing a negligible role in daily life. Four hundred years later, Egypt was unified into a single state. The density of population was probably low enough so that the people had no need of either government or government-regulated irrigation canals. They made use of natural floods and drainage basins to grow their crops. One authority has estimated that an average Nile flood would have allowed early Egyptian farmers to harvest grain over perhaps two-thirds of the floodplain of the Nile (Hamden, 1961). The first appearance of irrigation seems to have coincided with the unification of Egypt and is described in Chapter 17.

THE SAHARA

Many people think of the Sahara as a vast sand sea, one of the most desolate places on earth. In fact the Sahara is a highly diverse, albeit dry, region that has undergone major climatic changes during the past 12,000 years (McIntosh and McIntosh, 1988). Before 8000 years ago, there were shallow lakes in the central and southern Sahara that supported hippopotamuses and many species of fish. Many prehistoric hunting camps have been found on these long-dry lakes (A. B. Smith, 1984). Similar hunter-gatherer groups flourished along the Nile in the Sudan (J. D. Clark and Brandt, 1984).

After a short drying period around 7000 years ago, climatic conditions in the central and southern Sahara improved (Rognon, 1981). The lakes expanded and filled again. This time cattle herders camped by their shores. The earliest cattle bones come from a cave in southwest Libya dated to about 5000 B.P., but they may be as much as 7000 years old. Pastoralists were widespread in the central and southern Sahara during the fourth millennium B.C., and it seems certain that they were using wild cereal grasses and perhaps cultivating such tropical crops as sorghum. Opinions vary concerning how domestic animals reached the Sahara. The most common hypothesis has goats and sheep being introduced to North Africa about 8000 years ago, with cattle domestication about a millennium later. It is thought that wild cattle in the Sahara were the source of local domestication.

The cattle herders had only a few possessions, unsophisticated round-based pots and flaked and polished adzes. They also hunted with bow and arrow. The Saharan people left a remarkable record of their lives on the walls of caves deep in the desert. Wild animals, cattle, goats, humans, and scenes of daily life are preserved in a complicated jumble of artistic endeavor extending back perhaps to 7000 years ago (Lhote, 1959). The widespread distribution of pastoral sites of this period suggests that the Saharans were ranging their herds over widely separated summer and winter grazing grounds.

About 5500 years ago, climatic conditions deteriorated. The Sahara slowly became drier and lakes vanished. Rainfall rose in the interior of west Africa, and the northern limit of the tsetse fly belt moved south (this insect is endemic to much of tropical Africa and is fatal to cattle). So the herders shifted south, following the major river systems into savanna regions. By this time, the Saharan people were probably using domestic crops, experimenting with such summer rainfall crops as sorghum and millet as they moved out of areas where they could grow wheat, barley, and other Mediterranean crops (for a full discussion, see J. D. Clark, 1984; McIntosh and McIntosh, 1988).

SUB-SAHARAN AFRICA

At the end of Pleistocene times, the indigenous inhabitants of sub-Saharan Africa were already adapted to many kinds of specialized environment. Some lived by intensive fishing, others by gathering or hunting, depending on their environment. In a primitive way the techniques of food production may have already been employed on the fringes of the rain forests of west and central Africa, where the common use of such root plants as the African yam led people to recognize the advantages of growing their own food (J. D. Clark, 1984; M. Harris, 1968). Certainly the yam can easily be germinated by replanting its top. This primitive

Vegeculture (plant manipulation)

form of "vegeculture" may have been the economic tradition onto which the cultivation of summer rainfall cereal crops was grafted as it came into use south of the grassland areas on the Sahara's southern borders (Harlan et al., 1976; McIntosh and McIntosh, 1981).

The East African highlands are ideal cattle country and the home of such famous cattle-herding peoples as the Masai today. They were inhabited by scattered bands of hunter-gatherers living around mountains near the plains until about 5300 years ago, when the first cattle herders appeared. Their emergence may be connected with shifts in climatic zones that opened up the highlands to pastoral peoples for the first time (Ambrose, 1984). These cattle people may have moved between fixed settlements during the wet and dry seasons, living off hunting in the dry months and their own livestock and agriculture during the rains (Bower, 1984).

Stone Age cattle herds appeared in other parts of sub-Saharan Africa as well, in the grasslands south of the Sahara in west Africa and even at the extreme southern tip of Africa. These Khoikhoi people were still flourishing when Portuguese explorer Bartolomeu Dias rounded the Cape of Good Hope in A.D. 1488. The explorers who had dealings with them commented on their simple material culture and constantly nomadic lifeway, which was finely attuned to the seasonal Cape environment. They are known to have lived on the Cape for at least 2000 years (Elphick, 1977; R. Klein, 1984). It is not known how they reached their homeland. The Khoikhoi did not long survive European settlement in the seventeenth century, and their lifeway is extinct today.

A.D. 100

Approximately 2000 years ago, with the arrival of ironworking, the practices of producing food and keeping domestic animals spread throughout the African continent (Phillipson, 1977). For thousands of years after the Near East had started to enjoy literate civilization, San hunter-gatherers continued to flourish on the rich savanna woodlands of east and southern Africa. Their environment was so rich that they had no incentive to take up the new economies, even if they were aware of them. Agriculture finally came to the savanna when widespread forest clearance was made easier by iron tools and tougher working edges, starting approximately 2000 years ago.

GUIDE TO FURTHER READING

Butzer, Karl. 1976. *Early Hydraulic Civilization in Egypt.* Chicago: University of Chicago Press.

A fundamental source on ancient Egyptian irrigation that has great relevance to this chapter.

Clark, J. Desmond, and Brandt, Steven A., eds. 1984. *From Hunters to Farmers.* Berkeley: University of California Press.
> *A set of scholarly essays summarizing recent evidence for early agriculture in Africa. Excellent for specialists, and definitive.*

Hassan, Fekri. 1988. "The Predynastic of Egypt." *Journal of World Prehistory* 2 (2):135–186.
> *A definitive critical summary of early agricultural and later societies on the Nile. For the advanced reader.*

Hoffman, Michael A. 1979. *Egypt Before the Pharaohs.* New York: Knopf.
> *A fascinating study of prehistoric Egypt that not only recounts key discoveries but also recalls the archaeologists who made them. The first detailed account of this subject for many years, written for the general reader.*

Oliver, Roland, and Fagan, Brian M. 1975. *Africa in the Iron Age.* Cambridge, Eng.: Cambridge University Press.
> *A general history of Africa from approximately 500 B.C. that covers much of the material in this chapter in a wider historical context.*

Chronological Table G

C14 Years A.D./B.P.	SOUTHEAST ASIA	CHINA — South	CHINA — North	PACIFIC
	Chapter 18 ↑			European contact
1,000				Society Islands Tahiti Hawaii New Zealand Marquesas Easter Island
A.D. 1		Chapter 19 ↑		Lapita ware
3,000 B.P.	Khok Phanom Di Banyan Valley Cave Non Nok Tha			
4,000				
5,000			LONGSHANOID	Pre-Lapita occupation of Bismarck Archipelago
6,000		QINGLIANGING	YANGSHAO	Highly developed agricultural systems
7,000		Ta-p'en-k'eng Ma-xia-pang Ho-mu-tu	Cord-decorated pottery and early farming	Kuk Basin
8,000		?Early food production		
9,000	Spirit Cave	PENGTOUSHAN		?Forest clearance in New Guinea
10,000				Jomon (Japan)
11,000				
		Chapter 13 ↑		

356

CHAPTER 13

ASIA
RICE, ROOTS, AND
OCEAN VOYAGERS

Preview

- Southeast Asia is widely believed to have been an early center of root crop domestication. The archaeological evidence from Spirit Cave, Thailand, shows that people were hunting and gathering a broad spectrum of animal and vegetable foods 11,000 years ago.

- Rice was, and still is, a key crop in Asia. Its origins are still not certain. The earliest recorded date for domesticated rice in southern China is from the Pengtoushan site in the Middle Yangtze Valley, which dates to between 9000 and 7500 years ago. The widespread dispersal of rice cultivation in China probably dates to after 5000 years ago.

- The human settlement of the Pacific was dependent on Asian root crops. The Kuk Basin in New Guinea has yielded traces of forest clearance and drainage as early as 9000 years ago, with the cultivation of taro and yams probably beginning as early as 6000 years ago.

- The Bismarck Archipelago was occupied continuously from the late Ice Age into postglacial times. Long distance, open-water trading was commonplace in the region by 4900 years ago, and the Lapita Cultural Complex there appears by 3600 B.P.

- The first settlement of Fiji and west Polynesia resulted from the development of double-hulled, oceangoing canoes and took place as far-flung trading networks developed through island Southeast Asia. First settlement may have occurred as early as 4000 years ago. Expansion is marked by the widespread Lapita Cultural Complex, which occurs as far east as Fiji and Tonga in western Polynesia.

- Polynesia was settled within the last 2500 years: the Marquesas were colonized approximately A.D. 400, Hawaii some 1350 years ago, and Easter Island approximately A.D. 500. The Polynesians were technologically in the Stone Age, but they developed powerful chiefdoms that were at the height of their power when the first Europeans arrived in the eighteenth century.

- New Zealand was first colonized by Polynesians in A.D. 900 or so, but the introduction of the sweet potato led to rapid population buildup that coincided with the emergence of Maori culture approximately 600 years ago. The Maori developed a warlike society with constant competition for prime agricultural land.

Chronological
Table G

Fifteen thousand years ago much of Southeast Asia was inhabited by hunter-gatherers whose stone toolkits reveal remarkable uniformity over large areas of the mainland and islands (Bellwood, 1985; Higham, 1989). These stone assemblages do not necessarily reflect a stagnation of cultural innovation or a simple lifeway. Rather, it seems certain that the people were exploiting a broad range of game and vegetable foods.

15,000 to 8000
B.P.

Very few scientific excavations have been made on sites that cover the period 15,000 to 8000 years ago, when food production may have begun in this region (Gorman, 1969, 1971). The controversies about early food production in Southeast Asia surround two questions:

- When did people first start to cultivate root crops?

- What are the origins of rice cultivation (rice being the vital staple cereal crop in much of Asia throughout later prehistory)?

EARLY FOOD PRODUCTION IN THAILAND

As Carl Sauer has pointed out (1952), the domestication of root crops is difficult to identify in the archaeological record at the best of times. The only way that one can deduce cultivation is by examination of vegetable remains found in excavations, comparing these finds with the modern flora and extrapolating modern uses of the flora into the past (on the assumption that use patterns have not changed).

Spirit Cave
11,000 to 9000
B.P.

Chester Gorman's excavations at Spirit Cave in northeast Thailand took him to a limestone cave overlooking a small stream (Figure 13.1). He found that the lowest levels of the site were formed more than 11,000 years ago (for a summary, see Bellwood, 1985). What he called Hoabhinian tools, including small flakes and chop-

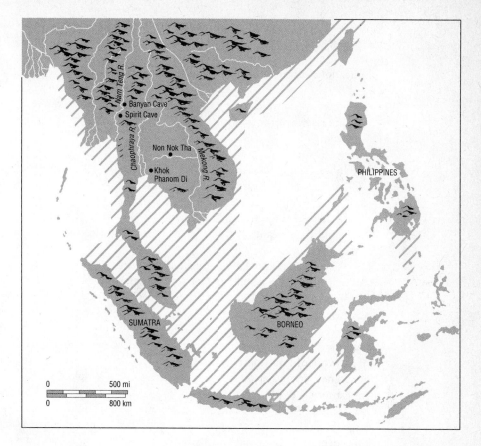

FIGURE 13.1   Southeast Asian sites mentioned in this chapter. Shaded areas show the extent of low sea levels during the Weichsel glaciation.

pers, came from these horizons, and it was clear that such tools were used for a long time. Gorman was able to identify quantities of seeds from the Hoabhinian levels. When botanists examined these finds, they found that the people had exploited almonds, betel nuts, broad beans, gourds, water chestnuts, peppers, and cucumbers. Douglas Yen (1977) of the Bishop Museum in Honolulu visited the area and collected modern floral specimens for comparative purposes. He even ate some of the wild foods himself. He noted that there were at least eight wild species of yam in the area and that the seeds found in Spirit Cave were from plants that can be collected in the wild and have a variety of dietary, medicinal, and other uses. The botanists had great difficulty in establishing whether the Spirit Cave seeds were domesticated or wild and in fact have produced no definite grounds for calling them deliberately planted.

The Spirit Cave finds provide no firm evidence for domestication of plants as early as 11,000 years ago, but despite the uncertainty of the botanical evidence,

William Solheim (1971) and others have claimed that Southeast Asia was a major center of early plant and animal domestication. There is certainly insufficient evidence from the few excavations in the area to make such a claim. However, there are indications of the following:

- There was a wide variety of yams and other potential domesticates in Thailand and elsewhere; these were exploited by hunter-gatherers at the end of the Pleistocene.

- In the case of yams, there were enough species present for people under demographic or other stress to experiment with hybridization if they wished.

- In view of these two factors, there is no reason to doubt that food production could have begun in this area quite independently from other regions.

As we have pointed out before, yam planting is very simple, and hunter-gatherers are well aware that deliberate cultivation is possible. The problem is to identify the factors that led people to deliberate experimentation with various plants. In the absence of firm archaeological evidence, we can speculate that primitive shifting agriculture, with a combination of diverse crops and some animal herding, may have had its origins in a broad spectrum of hunting and gathering, as it did in other regions of the world. In the final analysis, all that is needed for a culture to make the transition are some clearings at the edge of the forest and a simple digging stick, already used for gathering, to plant the crop (Yen, 1977). Charles Higham, who studied the animal bones from Spirit Cave and other localities in northern Thailand, argues that the large range of species found in the sites indicates a broadly based hunting economy that focused on deer, pigs, and arboreal creatures such as monkeys (Higham, 1972). The case for indigenous development of agriculture and animal domestication in Southeast Asia is still unproven.

RICE CULTIVATION

Rice is one of the world's staple crops, yet surprisingly little is known about its origins (Bellwood, 1985). It was certainly one of the earliest plants to be domesticated in the northern parts of Southeast Asia and southern China. Botanists believe that the rices and Asian millets ancestral to the present domesticated species radiated from perennial ancestors around the eastern borders of the Himalaya Mountains at the end of the Ice Age (R. White, 1982). There is fairly general agreement that the wild annual ancestor of modern cultivated rice was first domesticated somewhere between northeast India, northern Southeast Asia, and southern China (Chang, 1986). The initial cultivation of rice is thought to have taken place in an alluvial swamp area, where there was plenty of water to stimulate cereal growth. Perhaps this cultivation occurred under conditions in which seasonal flooding made field preparation a far from burdensome task (Bellwood, 1985). Such conditions could have been found on the

Ganges Plain in India, in northern Thailand, and in China's middle Yangtze Valley, where the earliest records of cultivated rices are found, outside the modern range of wild rice, as early as 9000 years ago.

Peter Bellwood (1985) hypothesizes that a sedentary lifeway based on the gathering of wild rice developed in areas like this at the beginning of the Holocene, with systematic cultivation resulting from a response to population growth, climatic change, or some other stress. Kwang-Chih Chang (1986) believes that truly domesticated rice first developed in southern China, where cooler weather and a shorter growing season exerted greater selection pressure on the early cultivated cereals and made them more dependent on human care. These ideas are based on the most inadequate of evidence, and we may learn that rice was domesticated in several different areas by 7000 years ago, perhaps considerably earlier.

By 8500 years ago, people were moving from the hills onto river plains and into lowland areas. River plains were the best places for the intensive cultivation and simple irrigation needed to grow rice. Crop yields, far superior to those from small highland root crop gardens, were ample and easily obtained. Whether this supposed population movement was associated with the beginnings of rice cultivation is a matter of conjecture.

Archaeological evidence for early rice cultivation in Southeast Asia is still very sketchy. The material culture of the Spirit Cave people shows a distinct change after about 9000 years ago. From then until approximately 7600 years ago, the inhabitants began to use adzes, pottery, and slate knives. The knives strongly resemble later artifacts used for rice cultivation in parts of Indonesia and could be interpreted as a suggestion that cereals were cultivated near the site—but this is pure speculation.

Khok Phanom Di

4000 to 3400 B.P.

Charles Higham (1984a; 1989) has excavated an early rice farming community at Khok Phanom Di in Thailand, a settlement that was close to coastal mangrove swamps between 4000 and 3400 years ago but is now over 12 miles (19.3 km) from the seashore. The site covers 12.3 acres (5 ha), is 39 feet (12 m) deep, and contains rice specimens and other evidence of agriculture. Higham hypothesizes that the inhabitants of the coastal plains took up wild rice cultivation as sea levels rose, inundating the game and woodland resources of the fertile shoreline. Other rice specimens come from Banyan Valley Cave in northern Thailand and Non Nok Tha, a low mound on a Mekong River tributary in the same general area (Bayard, 1970, 1972). Gorman (1969, 1971) found rice husks in Banyan levels dating to between 7500 B.P. and A.D. 800, none of which the botanical experts could positively identify as fully domesticated. Experiments with milling stones showed that the husks had been ground by a quite different method from that used by modern rice farmers in the area. Douglas Yen (1977), whose studies of rice can surely be described as comprehensive, speculates that the Banyan finds are the result of a form of gathering plus selective cultivation of wild rice—a stage in the gradual domestication of the cereal. There are many wild species in the region, several of which could have been candidates for cultivation.

Non Nok Tha may have been occupied before 5000 to 4000 years ago, but it was abandoned at some time before 2000 years ago. (The chronology is controver-

Non Nok Tha

5000 B.P. to A.D. 1

sial.) The excavators found traces of rice in the form of grain impressions on clay pots in the lowest levels. They point out that the site dates to the time when the lowlands were already settled, which means that the rice was probably cultivated. Bones of domesticated cattle came from the same site. The inhabitants were sedentary farmers depending on rice and cattle for most of their diet. Hunting and gathering were less important than in earlier millennia, when highland sites were occupied all year.

Rice cultivation has become the major cereal crop agriculture of the world, but its origins are still uncertain. Southeast Asia did not suffer from the drastic climatic changes of northern latitudes. No prolonged droughts or major vegetational changes altered the pattern of human settlement in this region. Only dramatic rises in low sea levels altered the geography and environment of Southeast Asia, creating islands from dry land and reducing the amount of coastal floodplain available to hunters and gatherers. Conceivably, these major changes in coastline and available land surface were among many factors that moved the inhabitants of Southeast Asia to experiment with plants and domestic animals.

EARLY FARMING IN CHINA

"In the wealth of its species and in the extent of the genus and species potential of its cultivated plants, China is conspicuous among other centers of origin of plant forms." Thus wrote the great Russian botanist N. I. Vavilov 40 years ago (Vavilov, 1951). Early agriculture occurred in at least six different regions of China, three of them—the southern and eastern coastal areas and the north—of major importance (Keightley, 1983).

Southern and Eastern China

No one knows when agriculture first began in southern China, but Chang (1986) hypothesizes that it may have begun as early as 12,000 years ago with the cultivation of roots and tubers. It is possible that the many ways of exploiting wild vegetable foods in Southeast Asia may have been practiced in southern China too.

For much of postglacial times, the Chinese environment was warmer and wetter than today. These conditions meant that forests were widespread at lower elevations. Lakes were larger, and many waterside locations offered environments with plentiful animal and plant resources (for details, see Chang, 1986). These local areas of rich diversity were probably a key to early experiments with food production, just as they were elsewhere in the world.

10,000 B.P.

Some ill-defined Upper Paleolithic stone industries record the presence of hunter-gatherer societies throughout China immediately before 10,000 years ago; these peoples were probably the first to experiment with cultivation and animal domestication. Unfortunately, their lifeways are virtually unknown.

Early food production developed in many regions of eastern and southern China, regions that were to interact with one another throughout later prehistory. Some cave sites are said to contain evidence of food production as early as 9500 to 8000 years ago (Pearson et al., 1986), while the Pengtoushan site in the Middle Yangtze Valley dates to between 9000 and 7500 years ago. The Pengtoushan excavations have yielded what are at present the earliest domesticated rice grains in the world. Wild rice does occur in the Yangtze Valley, and it may be that the deliberate growing of rice resulted from a desire to provide larger natural crop yields, just as happened with native plants in areas such as Mexico and Peru. This is not to say, of course, that the Middle Yangtze Valley was the cradle of rice agriculture, which probably arose in many areas of southern China at about the same time (Yan Wenming, 1990).

**Pengtoushan
9000 to 7500
B.P.**

The Lake T'ai-hu region of the lower Yangtze Valley east of Shanghai is another area of early agriculture, a lacustrine environment with a wealth of plant and aquatic resources and abundant freshwater vegetation that could be exploited and deliberately cultivated as well. More than 100 early farming sites are known from this region, of which at least 20 have been excavated. Wang Tsun-kuo divides the Lake T'ai-hu sites into three phases, the earliest two dating to between about 7000 and 5000 years ago (for full discussion, see Chang, 1986).

**7000 to 5000
B.P.**

The earliest Lake T'ai-hu "Ma-xia-pang" sites occur on slightly higher ground or artificial mounds near rivers and ponds. The people lived in rectangular houses built of timber with carefully fashioned mortise and tenon joints and sand, shell, or clay floors. The people grew rice and a plant named the water caltrop as well as bottle gourds. They used domesticated dogs, water buffalo, and pigs, hunting a wide variety of mammals, birds, and fish. Wood, bamboo, antler, and bone served to manufacture arrowheads, trowels, needles, and many other artifacts. Stone-bladed adzes and axes were used for woodworking, and animal-shoulder-bladed hoes turned the soil. The people were skilled potters and expert farmers, whose economy depended heavily on raising annual crops of sun-loving aquatic plants that grow naturally in marshes and lakes. These crops, species like lotus seed and water chestnut, were raised in rotation with rice. Later phases of this distinctive and well-established farming culture witnessed much greater sophistication in pottery forms and considerable elaboration of material culture.

Parallel farming cultures are known from other parts of southern China, where rice cultivation was well established at least 7000 years ago. One such contemporary culture was the Ho-mu-tu, south of Shanghai, dating to about the same period as Ma-xia-pang. Ho-mu-tu itself lies in a marshy area and was once surrounded by forests and ponds and a great diversity of natural resources. Four cultural layers have been radiocarbon dated to between about 7000 and 6000 years ago, all of them from wooden pile dwellings on the damp shores of a lake. This remarkable site has yielded beautifully mortise-and-tenon-joined building planks, bone hoes, and coarse black pots decorated with cord impressions. This is ideal rice-growing country, and it was hardly surprising to find abundant rice in the site as well as the remains of bottle gourds and numerous wild vegetable foods. The Ho-mu-tu people were skilled hunters who kept water buffalo, pigs, and dogs. Ho-mu-tu was roughly contemporary with

**Ho-mu-tu
c. 7000 to 6000
B.P.**

Khok Phanom Di in Thailand, and the cord-decorated pottery made by the Ho-mu-tu people is widespread in southern China as well as in Taiwan, Southeast Asia, and Japan.

Many other early farming traditions are known to have emerged in southern China after 7000 years ago (for details, see Chang, 1986). Much of the earliest agricultural development may be associated with the widely distributed cord-decorated pottery traditions found in Ho-mu-tu and other mainland sites. Offshore, the Ta-p'en-k'eng culture of Taiwan is one of the better known of early farming traditions, a culture of people who lived close to lakes and rivers. As early as 7000 years ago, the Ta-p'en-k'eng people were engaged in intensive fishing and shellfish collecting, and hunting and foraging. Chang (1986) believes they may have been gardening as well. It is likely that this is only one of many cord-decorated cultural traditions that flourished over this vast area in the millennia after the first development of agriculture.

Ta-p'en-k'eng
7000 B.P.

By 5000 years ago, much more sophisticated agricultural societies were flourishing on the Yangtze River and farther afield (Chang, 1986). The archaeology of these traditions is known primarily from cemetery excavations that show slow changes in grave goods (R. Pearson, 1981). The earliest graves indicate few social differentiations, but later sepulchers show not only a much wider variety of artifacts—pottery, bone and stone tools, jade objects, and other ornaments—but also an increase in the number of elaborately adorned burials. Richard Pearson, who has analyzed several cemeteries, argues that they demonstrate an increase in the concentration of wealth, a trend toward ranked societies, and a shift in the relative importance of males at the expense of females; the last trend may be associated with the development of more intensive agriculture, an activity in which males are valued for their major roles in cultivation and production of food and manual labor is carried out by women, when land is plentiful and shifting cultivation is the rule of the day.

Northern China

The earliest farming traditions of the south are represented by the widespread cord-decorated pottery cultures that date to before 7000 years ago. Another set of early farming traditions emerged in the north, either independently or as a result of interaction with the south (Chang, 1986).

Northern Chinese agriculture has one great contrast with that of the south: It is based heavily on cereals and seeded plants. The first northern agricultural communities were sited in the central regions of the Yellow River Valley (Figure 13.2). The area is a small basin, forming a border between the wooded western highlands and the swampy lowlands to the east. Pollen analysis has provided evidence for a prolonged period of warmer climate from approximately 8000 to 4000 years ago, when favorable rainfall patterns and greater warmth made this nuclear area a fine place for agriculture (Ho, 1969).

During the glaciations of the Pleistocene, loess soils were formed over a wide

FIGURE 13.2   Early Chinese farming cultures, with names of three major local variants. Yangshao sites occur both within the northern shaded area and outside it. Southern sites of corded pottery are found in the Kwangtung, Fukien, and Taiwan areas.

area of the north. The fine, soft-textured earth was both homogeneous and porous and could be tilled by simple digging sticks. Because of the concentrated summer rainfall, cereal crops, the key to agriculture in this region, could be grown successfully. The indigenous plants available for domestication included the wild ancestors of foxtail millet, broom-corn millet, sorghum, hemp, and the mulberry.

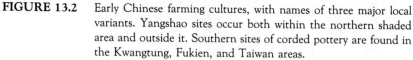

Ancient Chinese farmers developed their own cultivation techniques, which persisted for thousands of years before irrigation was developed. Although irrigation gradually became the basis of the agricultural economies of Egypt, the Indus Valley, and Mesopotamia, it was not important in northern China until much later (Ho, 1969).

The earliest millennia of northern Chinese agriculture are still a blank on the archaeological map. Two hypotheses are possible. We can assume that the inhabitants of the Yellow River region passed through a long phase of experimental cultivation and intensive exploitation of the indigenous flora before developing their own distinctive agricultural techniques, or we can assume that food production was developed farther south in China and adopted later in the north. Neither hypothesis can be tested with the available evidence. It is known that early farming villages were associated with coarse, cord-marked pottery found on the banks of the Yellow River in western Henan province. Perhaps these vessels are related to the cord-decorated pottery traditions of southern China, Southeast Asia, and Taiwan.

**Early farming
7000 B.P. and
earlier**

The earliest farming villages in central and northern China date to as early as 7000 years ago (see Figure 13.2) (Chang, 1986). Many settlements consisted of semi-subterranean houses with large storage pits. Their owners grew foxtail millet and kept dogs and pigs. By far the best known of China's early farming cultures is the Yangshao, which flourished over much of the Yellow River Basin, an area as large as the early centers of agriculture in Egypt or Mesopotamia, from before 7000 years ago to about 5200 years ago.

**Yangshao
7000 to 5200
B.P.**

Each Yangshao village was a self-contained community, usually built on a ridge overlooking fertile river valleys, situated to avoid flooding or to allow maximal use of floodplain soils (Figure 13.3). Using hoes and digging sticks, the farmers cultivated foxtail millet as a staple, mainly in riverside gardens that were flooded every spring. Hunting, foraging, and fishing were still important, and the people moved their villages when local soils became exhausted. Yangshao culture evolved over many centuries. By 5000 years ago, it boasted of a characteristic, and thoroughly Chinese, culture, with its own naturalistic art style (Figure 13.4), and expert potters who made cooking pots for steaming food, the basis of much Chinese cuisine to this day. The Chinese language may have its roots in Yangshao as well.

FIGURE 13.3   Reconstruction of Yangshao huts from Ban-p'o-ts'un, China.

FIGURE 13.4   Yangshao pottery from Ban-po, China (approximately one-fourth actual size). The fish motifs often used to decorate Yangshao pottery can be clearly seen (other motifs are drawn separately).

Over the centuries, the distribution of Yangshao culture expanded as new villages split off from older communities and brought new land under cultivation. Yangshao and other settlements tended to follow a pattern of river valleys and sea coasts, as many regional variations of peasant farming culture developed throughout China (Figure 13.5). Agriculture developed over wide areas at about the same time, with people adapting their crops and farming techniques to local conditions. In time, the success of the new economies led to local population increases, more complex cultures, and the concentration of wealth in privileged hands.

Longshanoid
5800 B.P.

By 5000 years ago, "Longshanoid" farming cultures flourished throughout much of northern China, based on larger, more permanent, and often earthen-walled settlements. Longshanoid cultures were based in part on irrigation and rice cultivation, for the new tropical crop had been introduced from the lush water meadows of the south, reducing dependence on dry agriculture. These much more elaborate, and wealthier, farming cultures were among the roots of Chinese civilization (Figure 13.6). (For Korea, see Nelson, 1990.)

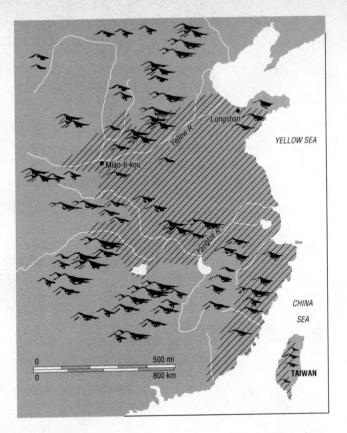

FIGURE 13.5 Approximate distribution of later farming cultures in China (cross-hatched area).

FIGURE 13.6 Some typical Longshanoid vessels used for cooking and other purposes, from Miao-ti-kou, China (scale not recorded).

JOMON AND EARLY AGRICULTURE IN JAPAN

Throughout east Asia, later Stone Age cultures were characterized by a wider variety of adaptations and a great diversity of blade tools, including projectile heads and scrapers. This diversity is well documented in Japan, where by 12,000 years ago, sea levels were rising and the landmass area available to hunter-gatherers shrank considerably. In postglacial times, many Asian groups settled by coastlines and lakeshores, just as they did in Europe. They began exploiting a wide range of land and maritime resources in many different climatic zones. In some areas where resources were concentrated, people began to adopt more sedentary settlement patterns and live in well-defined territories. In Japan, for example, shellfish collecting provided a relatively stable subsistence base for the Jomon people. As early as 12,500 years ago, they made clay vessels, which they used for steaming mollusks and making vegetable foods palatable (Ikawa-Smith, 1980). These are some of the earliest clay pots ever made, but the same cultural development may have taken hold elsewhere as Stone Age people adapted to radically new environmental conditions and exploited an even wider resource base. As postglacial times continued, the people turned to another logical adaptive strategy, deliberate growing of crops and taming of animals to ensure more reliable food supplies.

Jomon tradition 12,500 to 2300 B.P.

More than 10,000 Jomon sites are known, most of them from Honshu in central Japan. All are linked by a common cultural tradition that lasted for thousands of years, but there were probably different ethnic groups, who perhaps spoke different languages and adapted to diverse environments. The Jomon people hunted deer and other game with bows and arrows, collected thousands of shellfish, mainly in the spring, and fished much of the year. At first they caught all types of fish, but as time went on they concentrated on a few carefully selected species, inshore and lake fish as well as deep-water forms such as the bonito and tuna. Above all their diet depended heavily on wild vegetable foods such as acorns, nuts, and edible seeds. They lived in relatively sedentary settlements, perhaps because of carefully scheduled seasonal hunting, gathering, and fishing activities. Some believe that they supplemented these activities with cultivation of root crops and cereals or simply by careful management of nut trees. The evidence for agriculture is still sketchy, but it seems possible that the Jomon people flourished by developing an elaborate technology for processing and storing huge stocks of nuts, an activity they may have combined with cultivation of milletlike plants.

The Jomon tradition lasted from as early as 12,000 years ago until as late as 2300 years ago. During this period, the focus of settlement shifted from the coasts to central Honshu and to the northern shores of Japan. By 7000 years ago, the inhabitants of Honshu were enjoying an elaborate material culture, including finely made ritual clay pots adorned with intricate decorations (Figure 13.7). The people often lived not in the caves and simple pit houses of earlier times but in large clusters of wooden houses with elaborate hearths. After 5000 years ago, the climate began to cool, overpopulation may have strained the carrying capacity of arable land, and

FIGURE 13.7   Jomon gray-bodied molded jar, of conical form with loop handles and decorated with combwork.

clearance of natural vegetation affected hunting activities. Hence, the population declined and the major centers of Jomon occupation moved toward the coasts. In the south, the inhabitants of Kyushu took up rice and barley cultivation after 3000 years ago (for a lengthy discussion, see Akazawa, 1982).

Yayoi
2300 B.P.
Unification
A.D. 600

    The basis for what was to become traditional Japanese society was formed during the Yayoi period, which began after 2300 years ago, when new crops and technologies spread through the islands. Japan was unified into a single state in approximately A.D. 600, by which time complex, stratified societies were commonplace throughout the archipelago.

RICE AND ROOT CULTIVATION IN ISLAND
SOUTHEAST ASIA

Offshore from mainland Asia one enters what archaeologist Peter Bellwood (1985) has called "a totally different Neolithic world." He believes that swamp cultivation of rice was introduced from the north, where it took hold considerably earlier. Rice agriculture dates to around 5500 years ago on Taiwan, perhaps earlier, and only dates back to about 3700 years ago in the Philippines, although agriculture may be as early

5000 B.P.

as 5000 years ago there and on Sulawasi (for detailed discussion, see Spriggs, 1989).

Farmers were living on East Timor before 4100 years ago and offshore in the Bismarck Archipelago by 3900 to 3500 years ago.

4000 B.P.

This initial farming settlement is marked by a relatively homogeneous Neolithic culture of farmers who settled mainly by coasts and rivers. Canoes played a major role in intervillage exchange, which persisted for 2000 years. These constant exchanges meant that such items as clay vessels, adzes, and axes were fairly standardized over large areas, and communities as far separated as Taiwan and Manus enjoyed the same general economy, material culture, and social organization. The same exchange networks not only carried New Britain obsidian over hundreds of miles but also introduced metal, which spread rapidly through the region from the mainland before 3000 years ago.

This culture does not appear to have penetrated highland New Guinea, where agriculture developed quite independently. Here hunter-gatherers lived in damp, often densely forested environments, where the cultivation of root crops like taro and yams and fruit trees such as bananas required less forest clearance. Agricultural systems of this type, widespread in parts of Indonesia and in island Melanesia, spread widely after 4500 years ago.

Archaeologists Jack Golson, Peter White, and others have researched early agriculture in the New Guinea highlands, using both pollen analysis and the study of old irrigation channels to amplify the archaeological record (Allen, 1969; Golson, 1977).

Kuk Basin
9000 B.P.

There are traces, at approximately 9000 years ago, of deliberate diversion of river water in the Kuk Basin, which have been interpreted to mean that the people were cultivating taro or yams at a very early date. The evidence is still uncertain, although signs of increased erosion in the area may be the result of forest clearance for taro or yam gardens or possibly for the deliberate growing of indigenous New Guinea plants (White and O'Connell, 1982).

6000 B.P.

By 6000 to 5500 years ago, much more organized agricultural works were found in the Kuk Basin. There is pollen evidence for quite extensive forest clearance in the general area. These works may have been created for yam and taro crops, while indigenous plants were grown on the better-drained soils between the channel banks.

4000 B.P.
2500 B.P.

After 4000 years ago, the first highly developed drainage systems occurred in the area, a sign that people were farming much more intensively. After 2500 years ago, the people depended more and more heavily on dry and wet agriculture, for the forest resources they had relied on were replaced by an environment that had been altered permanently by human activity. A slow population growth resulted eventually in the taking up of uncleared land. After that was exhausted, the only option was to shorten the fallow periods on cleared gardens—something that, if taro was the crop, would have resulted in lower crop yields.

The archaeological investigations and pollen analysis of Golson (1977) and others have produced firm evidence for sedentism, forest clearance, stone agricultural tools, and water-control techniques in the New Guinea highlands by 6000 to 5000 years ago. What is uncertain, however, is the means by which food production began in New Guinea. Was it developed locally with introduced plants after the local hunter-gatherers had manipulated indigenous plants for centuries? Or did the people manipulate local plants as a result of adopting a few introduced crops first? Whatever the answer, it appears that the New Guinea highlands were an area where people created an artificial garden environment as a result of a long period of experimentation, in which they were raising plants *within* their natural environment. By exploiting a wide range of tropical animals and plants, the people became more sedentary and later started to plant small plots of root crops; ultimately, they would have intensified their food production until they modified their environment beyond recognition. This hypothetical model for early agriculture in New Guinea may serve as a possible model for other tropical areas in Asia as well.

AGRICULTURE IN THE PACIFIC ISLANDS

The origins of the peoples of the Pacific islands have fascinated scientists since the eighteenth century (Figure 13.8), but most authorities now look to Southeast Asia for the origins of the Melanesians and Polynesians. They point out that settlement

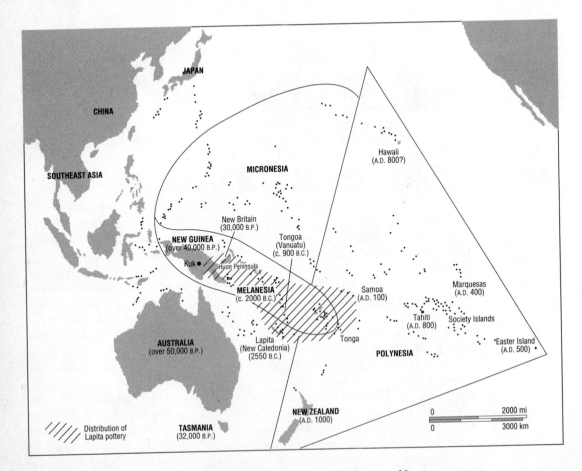

FIGURE 13.8   Map of Pacific sites. Cross-hatching shows distribution of Lapita pottery.

of the offshore islands depended on the successful cultivation of root crops such as taro and yam, as well as breadfruit, coconuts, and sugarcane. Chickens, dogs, and pigs were also valued as food and were domesticated in Asia before being introduced to the Pacific. Why did these foods have to be established in the diets and farming repertoires of the island settlers? Small animals such as pigs and chickens could readily have been carried from island to island in canoes, as could easily germinating root plants such as the yam. Both food sources allowed a sizable population to spread to many hundreds of small islands separated by miles of open water.

The first settlement of the Pacific islands is closely connected to the early cultivation of yams, and especially of taro. As we pointed out earlier in this chapter, taro and yams were probably domesticated in Southeast Asia before the development of rice cultivation, but exactly when and where they were first grown is unknown. In all probability, there were several centers of early domestication within Southeast Asia as early as 40,000 years ago, as early seafarers settled not only New Guinea but also close island chains like the Solomons and perhaps the Bismarck Archipelago as early as 31,000 years ago (Chapter 8). Beyond the Solomons and further offshore was a biologically more impoverished world that awaited domesticated crops and animals and more developed seafaring and navigational techniques before human colonization.

THE LAPITA CULTURAL COMPLEX AND THE SETTLEMENT OF MELANESIA AND WESTERN POLYNESIA

The first settlement of offshore Melanesia from the Bismarck Archipelago eastward as far as Tonga and Samoa was one of the most dramatic human expansions in all prehistory (Bellwood and Koon, 1989; Terrell, 1989), covering a distance of 3100 miles (5000 km) of island chains and open ocean during a period of six centuries from about 3600 to 3000 years ago. This was human settlement that followed on the domestication of plants and animals and the development of new maritime technologies, presumably including oceangoing, double-hulled sailing canoes. In archaeological terms, this development is associated with the highly distinctive Lapita Cultural Complex, named after a site on New Caledonia Island. Most experts agree that the Lapita people were Australonesian-speakers, who traded widely through the southwestern Pacific. Their settlements are marked by characteristic stamp-decorated pottery, often adorned with elaborate designs (Figure 13.9).

The original homeland of the Lapita people is a matter of considerable debate. One school of thought considers them to have originated in western Melanesia, whereas others believe they arrived in the islands from the Southeast Asian mainland (Kirch, 1988; White et al., 1988). The issue is unresolved, but it is clear that there was widespread trade in New Britain obsidian that traveled far and wide through the Southeast Asian islands, through exchange networks that carried the same toolmak-

FIGURE 13.9   Lapita pottery from Melanesia.

ing stone as far west as farming settlements on the eastern coast of Malaysia (Bellwood and Koon, 1989). That is not to say, of course, that Lapita canoes traveled all the way to Malaysia. Rather, there was what Peter Bellwood calls a "linked chain" of exchange networks over more than 5000 miles (8100 km) through the Southeast Asian islands deep into the central Pacific over 3000 years ago. People living in small island environments usually depend on their neighbors for many important commodities, an interdependency that was reflected in complex exchange networks spanning many miles of open ocean. The commodities carried in canoes ranged from foodstuffs to manufactured items and may have included ceremonial objects as well. The social and economic complexities of Melanesian trading systems have long excited anthropologists, starting with Bronislaw Malinowski's (1922) famous fieldwork on the celebrated *kula* ring of the Trobriand Islanders that circulated shell necklaces and bracelets from island to island in complex circles. The *kula* ring with its elaborate ceremonial is just one of many related exchange trading systems that linked all parts of coastal New Guinea and much of Melanesia. These networks are reciprocal and self-perpetuating and have their ancestry in much earlier exchange patterns that began, albeit in a more simple form, among Lapita peoples (Allen and White, 1989).

Bismarck
Archipelago
11,400 to 3500
B.P.

The Lapita homeland is thought by some to have been in the Bismarck Archipelago area, which was inhabited during the late Ice Age (Chapter 8) and as far back as about 11,400 years ago in post-Ice Age times on New Britain (Gosden et al., 1989). There is clear evidence for open-water voyaging as far as Manus Island, an island where obsidian is to be found, some 124 straight-line miles (200 km) offshore by 4900 years ago. An Australian research team has identified widespread human occupation through the Bismarck Archipelago before Lapita pottery appeared about 3500 years ago, and it may be that some, if not most, elements of the Lapita Cultural Complex came from local roots. By identifying the sources of island obsidians and pottery clays, the Australians have been able to show that local trading patterns changed constantly during pre-Lapita times and throughout the Lapita occupation of the archipelago. Clearly, both these cultures were dynamic, ever-changing systems.

These excavations show that there is a very long history of human occupation indeed in the Bismarck Archipelago, one that stretches back far into the Ice Age. Throughout most of this long period, obsidian was moved through the islands and far beyond them toward Southeast Asia. The region was never isolated from the outside world, but its inhabitants were part of a vast network of interconnections that linked the entire western Pacific and island Southeast Asia over a period of at least 1500 years. It was not until sometime after Christ that these broad links vanish, to be replaced by more local cultural developments.

It is very difficult to define the Lapita Cultural Complex (Terrell, 1989). It was either a migration of new peoples from Southeast Asia into the islands, as was once thought, or a vast exchange system that linked island after island through reciprocal trading between kinspeople. Archaeologically, we know that Lapita pottery from the Santa Cruz Islands, decorated with stamped designs and made of clay tempered with shell, is found as far east as Vanuatu, Fiji, Tonga, and Samoa. We know it dates generally to the last thousand years before Christ but seems to have gone out of fashion approximately 1800 years ago (Kirch, 1982). To associate this pottery distribution with a migrating ethnic group is to oversimplify a very complex picture of long-distance exchange, ocean voyaging, and island settlement.

Lapita
3600 to 3000
B.P.

Clearly, one catalyst for this expansion was the development of the oceangoing, double-hulled canoe. This canoe was the means by which efficient exchange networks were maintained from island to island over distances up to 372 miles (600 km) far out into the Pacific, into western Polynesia. The rapid expansion from island to island that carried Lapita pottery far offshore developed among societies living in an island environment that extended from the Southeast Asian mainland far southwestward. The inhabitants of this vast archipelago lived on relatively benign coasts and maintained contacts with one another that extended over hundreds of miles. That there was some standardization of artifacts and culture among them after 4000 years ago is hardly surprising. It is only when one reaches off-lying islands such as Fiji and Tonga that one can legitimately think in terms of Lapita "settlers," who were the first human settlers of the Pacific. Here, open-water distances are much longer, involving, for example, voyages of nearly 600 open-water miles (592 km). Here, two-way voyages were rare, if they ever occurred at all. Occasional one-way trips may have settled Fiji, but the barrier to regular exchange was a formidable one (Green, 1969). In Fiji, Samoa, and Tonga, the first settlers carried Lapita artifacts with them, but subsequent cultural development proceeded along local lines.

LONG-DISTANCE VOYAGING IN THE PACIFIC

From Melanesia, canoes voyaged through western Polynesia, taking the plants and domesticated animals of their homelands with them. As distances grew longer, so did the navigational challenges, challenges so formidable that many early scholars argued that the Polynesian islands were settled by accidental voyages (Sharp, 1957). Some compelling studies of Polynesian navigation and voyaging by both anthropologists and small-boat sailors have dispelled any lingering doubts about the navigational abilities of the early Polynesians.

Nearly all the long trips attributed to the Polynesians were from north to south, which involved simple dead-reckoning calculations and an elementary way of measuring latitude from the stars. Anthropologist Ben Finney (1967) made detailed studies of Polynesian canoes and navigational techniques; his findings support a notion of deliberate one-way voyages, sparked as much by necessity—drought or warfare—as by restless adventure. Evidence for the carrying of women, animals of both sexes, and plants for propagation, however, shows that colonization was the deliberate aim.

Amateur sailor David Lewis (1972) completed a remarkable study of Polynesian navigation, voyaging under prehistoric conditions and accumulating navigators' lore from surviving practitioners of the art. He found that navigators were a respected and close-knit group. Young apprentices learned their skills over many years of making passages and from orally transmitted knowledge about the stars and the oceans accumulated by generations of navigators. The navigational techniques used the angles of rising and setting stars, the trend of ocean swells, and the myriad inconspicuous phenomena that indicate the general direction and distance of small islands. The navigators were perfectly capable of voyaging over long stretches of open water, and their geographic knowledge was astonishing. They had no need for the compass or other modern aids, and their landfalls were accurate. Lewis's findings confirm those of Finney and others who believe that deliberate voyages colonized even remote islands.

Eastern Polynesia
150 B.C. to A.D. 800

From Melanesia, canoes voyaged to Micronesia and Polynesia, taking the plants and domestic animals of their home islands with them. The antiquity of human settlement in Micronesia and eastern Polynesia is approximately 2000 years (Jennings, 1979; Kirch, 1982). It is thought that the Polynesians originated in the Fiji area before the great elaboration of Melanesian culture after A.D. 1. After a lengthy period of adaptation in western Polynesia, small groups began to settle the more remote islands. The Marquesas were settled by A.D. 400 and the Society Islands and Tahiti by A.D.

800 (Oliver, 1977). The first canoes arrived in Hawaii some 1350 years ago and on Easter Island by A.D. 500 (Emory, 1972; Kirch, 1985). The human settlement of Polynesia seems to have taken approximately 2500 years from its beginnings by people who were still, technologically speaking, in the Stone Age. They relied heavily on stone axes and adzes and an elaborate array of bone and shell fish hooks (Figure 13.10). The crops the people planted varied from island to island, but breadfruit, taro, coconut, yams, and bananas were the staples. The food surpluses generated on the larger islands were used as a form of wealth. (For a valuable discussion of the colonization process, see Kirch, 1982, 1984, 1986.)

When the French and British visited Tahiti in the eighteenth century, they chanced upon the center of a vigorous eastern Polynesian society (Oliver, 1977). The islands were ruled by a powerful hierarchy of chiefs and nobles, many of them descendants of the canoe crews who had settled the archipelago. The chiefs acquired prestige by controlling and redistributing wealth and food supplies. Their formidable religious and social powers led them to warfare and to the undertaking

FIGURE 13.10   Bone fish hooks from Polynesia.

**FIGURE
13.11**
A *marae* on Tahiti.

of elaborate agricultural projects and the erection of monumental shrines and temples of stone: The famous *maraes* of Tahiti are typical examples (Figure 13.11). On remote Easter Island the people erected vast statues up to 32 feet (9.8 m) high. They are thought to be images of deified ancestors associated with different kin groups.

The full diversity of Polynesian culture is still imperfectly understood, for archaeological research has hardly begun in the South Seas, but it is certain that the Polynesians were making ocean voyages on a large scale at a time when the Greeks and Romans were little more than coastal navigators.

Settlement of New Zealand

New Zealand is the largest and among the most remote of all of the Pacific islands; it is actually two large islands. It has a temperate climate, not the tropical warmth enjoyed by most Polynesians. Despite this ecological difference, New Zealand was first settled by Polynesians who voyaged southward in comparatively recent times and settled on the North Island. Maori legends tell of a migration from Polynesia in the mid-fourteenth century A.D. Settlers including Toi Ete'hutai, who came to New Zealand in search of two grandsons blown away from Tahiti during a canoe race, may have arrived 400 years before. The earliest C14 dates for New Zealand archaeological sites are a matter of controversy but they are within the present millennium (Bellwood, 1979; Davidson, 1985).

First settlement
? A.D. 900

The temperate climate of the North Island formed a southern frontier for most of the basic food plants of Polynesia. The yam and gourd can be grown only there, but the sweet potato can be cultivated in the northern part of the South Island if adequate winter storage pits are used. The Polynesian coconut never grew in New Zealand. The earliest settlers relied heavily on hunting, fishing, and gathering. Even later, though some peoples specialized in food production, others did not, especially on the South Island, where many settlements were close to abundant ocean resources (Prickett, 1983).

The first settlers found great flocks of flightless Moa birds, cumbersome and helpless in the face of systematic hunting. They hunted the Moa into extinction within a few centuries. Fish, fern roots, and shellfish were important throughout New Zealand's short prehistory. The introduction of the sweet potato made a dramatic difference to the New Zealanders, for the tubers, if carefully protected from cold, could be eaten in the winter months, and some could be kept for the next year's planting. Sweet potatoes have a large crop yield and are thought to have contributed to a rapid population buildup, especially on the North Island. This, in turn, led to competition among groups for suitable agricultural land to grow the new staple (Davidson, 1985).

Maori
A.D. 1400

When the Moa became extinct, the Maori had few meat supplies except birds, dogs, and rats. Their only other meat source was human flesh. The archaeological record of Maori culture from approximately A.D. 1400 onward shows not only population growth but also an increasing emphasis on warfare, evidenced by the appearance of numerous fortified encampments, or *pa's,* protected with earthen banks. The distribution of *pa's* coincides to a large extent with the best sweet potato lands (Bellwood, 1970; Groube, 1970). In the course of a few centuries, warfare became a key element in Maori culture, to the extent that it was institutionalized and an important factor in maintaining cohesion and leadership in Maori society. The booty of war was not only *kumara* (sweet potato) but also the flesh of captives, which became a limited part of the Maori diet.

Maori warfare, mainly confined to the North Island, where more than 5000 *pa's* have been found, was seasonal and closely connected with the planting and harvest of sweet potatoes, when everyone was busy in the gardens. Military campaigns were short and intense, very often launched from the sea in war canoes up to 78.7 feet (24 m) or more in length (Figure 13.12). These elaborately carved vessels could hold as many as 150 men on a short expedition. So formidable was the reputation of the Maori that European ships avoided New Zealand ports for years before permanent white settlement was achieved. The last Maori war ended in 1872, by which time the indigenous population had been decimated by disease, warfare, and European contact.

**FIGURE
13.12**   Maori war canoe recorded by Captain Cook in the eighteenth century.

GUIDE TO FURTHER READING

Bellwood, Peter. 1986. *The Prehistory of the Indo-Malaysian Archipelago.* Sydney: Academic Press.
  A valuable summary of Southeast Asian mainland prehistory.

———. 1987. *The Polynesians.* London: Thames and Hudson.
  A synthesis of what we know about Polynesian prehistory. Excellent illustrations.

Chang, Kwang-Chih. 1986. *The Archaeology of Ancient China,* 4th ed. New Haven, CT: Yale University Press.
  The definitive account of Chinese prehistory in the English language. A highly technical work truly designed for the advanced student or professional archaeologist.

Davidson, Janet. 1985. "New Zealand Prehistory," *Advances in World Archaeology* 4:239–292.
  An exemplary article on general trends in New Zealand prehistory with a very complete bibliography.

Jennings, Jesse D., ed. 1979. *The Prehistory of Polynesia.* Cambridge, MA: Harvard University Press.
  A series of essays that provides a state-of-the-art summary of Pacific prehistory.

Kirch, Patrick V. 1984. *The Evolution of the Polynesian Kingdoms.* Cambridge, Eng.:
Cambridge University Press.
   A splendid analysis of this important development in Polynesian prehistory.

Lewis, David. 1972. *We the Navigators.* Honolulu: University of Hawaii Press.
   *An account of traditional Polynesian navigational methods based on both local lore
   and experiments navigating a yacht without a compass and sextant. What makes
   this book fascinating is that the author is a practical sailor himself.*

Chronological Table H

C14 Years A.D./B.P.	ANDES	MESOAMERICA	NORTH AMERICA West	NORTH AMERICA East
Modern Times			European contact	
1,000			HOHOKAM ANASAZI MOGOLLON	MISSISSIPPIAN HOPEWELL
A.D. 1	Chapter 23			ADENA
3,000 B.P.	Intensification of agriculture El Paraíso Playa Culebras Maize appears	Chapter 22	Experimentation with maize Manipulation of food plants	POVERTY POINT
4,000	Huaca Prieta			
5,000	Paloma Chilca			
6,000				
7,000	Puente	TEHUACÁN	COCHISE CULTURE	
8,000	Pikimachay			ARCHAIC CULTURES
9,000				
10,000		Guilá Naquitz		
11,000	Early hunter-gatherers	Chapter 7	CLOVIS	

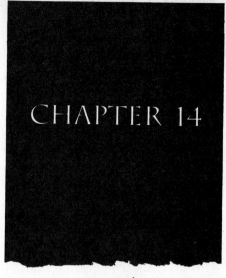

CHAPTER 14

THE STORY OF MAIZE

EARLY FARMING SOCIETIES IN THE AMERICAS

Preview

- New World agriculture was based on crops quite different from those grown in the Old World. The root crops included manioc and sweet potato, and maize was the most important staple cereal. Domesticated animals included the llama, turkey, and guinea pig.

- Kent Flannery's excavations at Guilá Naquitz in the valley of Oaxaca have produced models suggesting that agriculture may have developed among hunter-gatherer societies who were coping with consant environmental change and unpredictable population shifts. What began as wet-year strategies eventually became permanent shifts in subsistence activities, and more sedentary peoples grew crops on alluvial soils that were now more productive (see also Chapter 9).

- Domesticated maize probably evolved from a native grass named teosinte and has been identified in the Tehuacán Valley of southern Mexico as early as 7000 years ago. Maize agriculture spread from southern Mexico and Guatemala thousands of miles to the north and south. A long tradition of fishing and gathering in coastal Peru gave way to food production in some areas by approximately 5000 years ago. The Ayacucho area of the Andes provides evidence for food production in the highlands of Peru by 5500 years ago.

- Maize agriculture reached the North American Southwest by approximately 2500 years ago. By 2300 years ago, sedentary villages and a much greater dependence on farming were characteristic of the Southwest, leading to the emergence of Hohokam, Mogollon, and Anasazi cultural traditions (Birdsell, 1977). Hohokam and Anasazi are thought to be ancestral to American Indian groups still living in the Southwest.

- Gourds were cultivated in the midwestern parts of North America by 7000 years ago. Subsequently, many groups domesticated native plants, such as sunflowers and sumpweed.

- Maize and bean agriculture were late developments, taking hold after A.D. 900.

- After 3000 years ago, a series of powerful chiefdoms emerged in the East and Midwest, peoples among whom elaborate burial customs and the building of burial mounds and earthworks were commonplace. The Adena tradition emerged about 2700 years ago and was overlapped by the Hopewell in approximately A.D. 200. Both traditions depended on long-distance trade in essential commodities and cult objects for much of their prosperity. A preoccupation with death and status was at the focus of Hopewell life, for their burials show extraordinary lavishness.

- Twelve hundred years ago the center of economic, religious, and political power shifted to the Mississippi Valley with the emergence of the Mississippian tradition. The Mississippian had powerful religious and secular leaders; it survived in a modified form until European contact in the sixteenth century.

Chronological
Table H

The American Indians domesticated an impressive range of native New World plants, some of which—like maize, potatoes, and tobacco—were rapidly adopted by European farmers after contact.

The most important staple crop was Indian corn, properly called maize, the only significant wild grass in the New World to be fully domesticated. It remains the most important food crop in the Americas, being used in more than 150 varieties as both food and cattle fodder. Root crops formed another substantial food source, especially in South America, and included manioc, sweet potatoes, and white potatoes. Chili peppers were grown as hot seasoning; amaranth, sunflowers, cacao, peanuts, and several types of bean were also significant crops. Some crops, such as cotton and gourds, are common to both Old and New Worlds but were probably domesticated separately (see Pickersgill, 1972).

In contrast to Old World farmers, the Indians had few domesticated animals, including the llama of the Andes and alpacas, which provided wool. Dogs appeared in the Americas, and the raucous and unruly turkey and the muscovy duck were domesticated.

Most archaeologists now agree that there were two major centers of plant domestication in the Americas: Mesoamerica for maize, beans, squash, and sweet potatoes, and the highlands of the central Andes for root crops. There were also four major areas of later cultivation activity: tropical (northern) South America, the Andean area, Mesoamerica, and eastern North America.

THE ORIGINS OF PLANT DOMESTICATION
IN MESOAMERICA

In Chapter 9, we described the sophisticated model, which chronicles the shift from hunting and foraging to agriculture in the valley of Oaxaca, a model derived from Kent Flannery's excavations at the Guilá Naquitz rock shelter (Flannery et al., 1986). Flannery established that the changeover took a very long time indeed, and he believes it was the result of strategies designed to cope with continuous short-term climatic fluctuations and constant population shifts. This model, based as it is on only one excavation, seems to agree well with what we know about the gradual adoption of agriculture elsewhere in the Tehuacán Valley (see later) and other locations. It provides a working scenario for the beginnings of farming over a wide area of Mesoamerica.

Flannery believes that the gourds, members of the Cucurbitaceae family, were the first plants domesticated in the Americas, not only pumpkins and squashes but also the bottle gourd, an invaluable container for holding liquids both before and after its domestication. The latter may be of African origin, where it is widely used as a fishing net float. Perhaps, argue some experts, it floated across the Atlantic and washed up on American shores, possibly even before European settlement. At any rate, the seeds would provide hunter-gatherers with an easy source of water containers, a preadaptation that might have led to the cultivation of wild squashes and other cucurbits. They were certainly in use in Mesoamerica as early as 7000 years ago.

Wild ancestors of beans occur in Mesoamerica, and small, wild runner beans were collected at Guilá Naquitz as early as 9000 to 7500 years ago. As is well known, maize, beans, and squash, which can be grown in the same garden, are a classic triumvirate of food crops in the Americas. Initially, this association probably occurred in the wild, for runner beans and squashes grow naturally around the stalks and bases of teosinte, thought to be the ancestor of maize. In the end, humans disturbed the land by clearing it, observed the association of teosinte, beans, and squash, and domesticated the three in combination.

Of these three crops, by far the most complex and most debated is *Zea mays*, maize.

MESOAMERICA: TEHUACÁN AND THE
ORIGINS OF MAIZE AGRICULTURE

Maize was the staff of life for many native Americans when Christopher Columbus landed in the New World. It was cultivated over an enormous area of the Americas, from Argentina and Chile northward to Canada, from sea level to high in the Andes, in low-lying swampy environments and in arid lands. Hundreds of races of domesticated maize evolved over the millennia, each a special adaptation to local environmental conditions.

The origins of domesticated maize are still the subject of great controversy, which centers on the relationship between a wild grass named teosinte (*Zea mexicana*), which grows over much of Mesoamerica, and early strains of domesticated maize (for a comprehensive review, see Galinat, 1985). The botanist George Beadle (1981) concludes that "it now seems quite likely that a teosinte of some 8,000 to 15,000 years ago was the direct ancestor of modern corn and was transformed into a primitive corn through human selection." According to Beadle, there was a mutation in the tunicate gene in an ancestral form of teosinte that converted the hard fruit cases of the grass into shallow, softer cupules that carried elongated glumes, which enclosed and protected the kernels. This change made wild teosinte much easier to thresh (Galinat, 1985). The transformation to a domesticated form of early maize may have taken place simultaneously in many areas and may have occurred within a very short time, perhaps only a century.

There are impressive grounds for considering teosinte the wild ancestor of maize. A perennial teosinte found in Mexico in recent years has been crossbred with maize. Experiments have shown that teosinte can be "popped" in a fire, on a hot rock, or on heated sand, just like the popcorn we consume at the movies. Dry teosinte seeds also can be cracked with even a simple grindstone, or softened before eating by being soaked in water.

The hypothetical scenario for maize domestication goes as follows (Figure 14.1) (Galinat, 1985). The process may have started as an unintentional byproduct of gathering wild teosinte, for gathering would lead to selective pressure for harvestable types of the grass, with their spikes condensed into fascicles. Such condensation made it harder for the seeds to scatter. In time, this form of teosinte would become established by campsites and in abandoned middens. These colonies would automatically diverge toward greater domestic kinds of variation, from which human beings could select the most useful types. In time, too, humans would remove weeds from these teosinte stands, then start deliberately planting the more useful types. Thus the female teosinte spike became canalized down a pathway leading toward maize. Cultivation and fertilization of semiwild grass populations were followed by attempts to sow selected seed from the most desirable types. At first the planted teosinte was no more productive than wild forms, but it was easier to harvest, a critical stage in the process of domestication. When people began selective harvesting and planting of transitional forms of teosinte, the grass's reproductive strategy changed to dependency on human intervention. A genetic revolution followed, in which attributes that made harvesting easier and favored teosinte's use as a human food had a selective advantage.

There is no archaeological evidence for transitional forms of teosinte, perhaps because the domestication process was very rapid. Some of the oldest maize cobs discovered in archaeological sites, as well as ancient teosinte grasses, do bear marks of earlier transformations. One maize cob from Tehuacán Valley in Mexico dating to about 7000 years ago appears to show some intermediate features between teosinte and maize, but it may be a degenerate form. The earliest known archaeological occurrence of condensed teosinte comes from Tlapacoya in the valley of Mexico and dates to about the same time (Galinat, 1985).

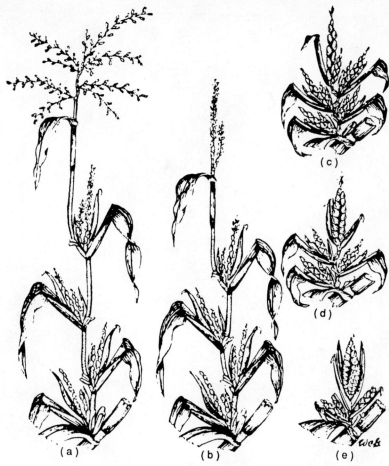

FIGURE 14.1   The various stages in an apparent transformation from teosinte to maize. The earliest teosinte form is (a), the stabilized maize phenotype (e). The harvesting process increased condensation of teosinte branches and led to the husks becoming the enclosures for corn ears. (After Galinat, 1985.)

Traces of early experimentation with the deliberate cultivation of crops such as maize and squash have come from regions in Mexico, notably from Sierra Madre, Sierra de Tamaulipas, and the Tehuacán Valley (Figure 14.2). The dry, highland Tehuacán Valley in southern Mexico has many caves and open sites and is sufficiently arid to preserve seeds and organic finds in archaeological deposits. This was the valley that Richard MacNeish (1970, 1978) chose as a promising area in which to seek the origins of domesticated maize. MacNeish soon found domestic maize cobs dating back to approximately 5000 years ago, but not until he began digging in the small Coxcatlán rock shelter did he find maize that even vaguely resembled what at that time was considered the hypothetical ancestor of maize. Coxcatlán contains 28 occupation levels, the earliest of which dates to approximately 12,000 years ago.

FIGURE 14.2   Archaeological sites and culture areas mentioned in this chapter. (After Meggers, 1973.)

MacNeish eventually excavated 12 sites in Tehuacán, which revealed a wealth of information about the inhabitants of the valley through nearly 12,000 years of prehistory.

MacNeish found that the earliest Tehuacán people lived mainly by hunting horses, deer, and other mammals and also by collecting wild vegetable foods (Mac-Neish, 1978). These hunters used stone-tipped lances in the chase. They also hunted

12,000 to 9000
B.P.

large numbers of jackrabbits, probably in organized drives. MacNeish estimates that 50 to 60 percent of the people's food came from game 12,000 years ago, and only 30 to 40 percent 9000 years ago. Hunting seems to have been the major activity year-round (Table 14.1).

After 10,000 years ago, the game population declined, and the people turned more and more to wild plant foods. Instead of hunting year-round, the Tehuacán bands scheduled their food gathering on a seasonal basis and were able to exploit the vegetable and other foods in their environment very intensively. The dietary scenario has been reconstructed by using carbon and nitrogen isotope ratios in bone collagen from people who lived in the Tehuacán Valley after 8000 years ago (Farnsworth et al., 1985). By at least 6500 years ago, about 90 percent of the Tehuacano diet consisted of tropical grasses such as *Setaria,* and such plants as cacti and maguey. So much grain was necessary that cultivation or domestication must have been essential by this time.

Crop yields grew after 6000 years ago, and the people grew foods that when stored would tide them over lean months: beans, amaranth, gourds, and maize. The

Table 14.1 MacNeish's Sequence for Tehuacán Summarized, Modified to Accommodate Carbon Isotope Reconstructions of the Diet.

Years	Phase	Characteristics
A.D. 750 to 1531	VENTA SALADA	Spanish contact: A.D. 1531.
100 B.C. to A.D. 750	PALO BLANCO	Village life.
800 to 100 B.C.	SANTA MARIA	Village life.
3,450 to 2,800	AJALPAN	Establishment of village life. Single-season economy with spring and summer agriculture.
4,250 to 3,450	PURRON	Hamlet villages and appearance of pottery. Agriculture important but few details known.
5,350 to 4,250	ABEJAS	Seasonal economy, with hunting important in the winter, collecting in spring, simple agriculture in summer and fall. Some year-round settlements; small food surpluses.
6,950 to 5,350	COXCATLAN	Seasonal scheduling of hunting and gathering. Planting of domesticates in spring and summer. Very limited food surpluses. Maize cultivated and a major element in the diet.
8,950 to 6,950	EL RIEGO	Foraging of tropical grasses increasingly imported. Seed planting appeared late in phase during summers. Food storage more important.
11,950 to 8,950	AJUEREADO	Lance ambushing of game important. Rabbit drives and small game significant. Less gathering than in later phases? Seasonal camps; no food storage.
Before 12,000	Hunter-gatherers	

Note: For full details, see Richard MacNeish, *The Science of Archaeology* (North Scituate, MA: Duxbury Press, 1978).

people lived in larger and more permanent settlements, grinding their maize into quite well-made grindstones (metates). The maize itself was smaller than modern strains and probably much like teosinte (Figure 14.1).

By this time, the scheduled gathering and nomadic settlement patterns of earlier times had been replaced by more sedentary villages; these were small hamlets that were moved very rarely and depended on agricultural systems that planted crops in fields. The villages were located near fertile flatlands and consisted of pit houses with brush roofs. Their ample storage facilities helped the people live through the lean months (Flannery, 1976).

The sequence of events at Tehuacán is by no means unique, for other peoples were also experimenting with cultivation. Different hybrid forms of maize are found in Tehuacán sites; these were not developed locally and can have been introduced only from outside. Dry caves elsewhere in northern Mesoamerica show that other cultures paralleled the cultural events in Tehuacán. On the other hand, the highland lakes of the valley of Mexico and elsewhere may well have supported sedentary communities subsisting on fish and wild vegetable foods as well as experimenting with amaranth, corn, and other crops as early as the sixth millennium B.C. (Niederberger, 1979).

If Kent Flannery's hypothesis is correct (Flannery et al., 1986), plant domestication in Mesoamerica was not so much an invention in one small area as a shift in ecological adaptation deliberately chosen by peoples living where economic strategies necessitated intensive exploitation of plant foods. It appears that the evidence from both Tehuacán and Guilá Naquitz bears out this hypothesis.

Earlier theories of the origins of maize assumed that it was domesticated in many areas of the Americas from six or more presumed wild races. Modern pollen studies have shown convincingly that there was never a wild *Zea* with a wide range that extended outside southern Mexico and Guatemala. Apparently, a primitive form of domesticated eight-rowed maize (*Maiz de ocho*) with soft glumes represented at Tehuacán was the common ancestral corn that spread thousands of miles from its original homeland after 7000 years ago. Subsequent derivatives of this basic maize developed in many different North and South American environments, as well as in Mesoamerica (Galinat, 1985).

EARLY FOOD PRODUCTION IN THE ANDES

The Highlands

The great eighteenth-century German naturalist Alexander von Humboldt was the first European scientist to explore the high Andes. He marveled at the great variety of wild plants and animals that thrived in the harsh and varied landscape of high peaks and mountain valleys. Only a handful of these many species had been tamed by the farmers living in the foothills of the great mountains. They lived in horizontal environmental zones stacked one above the other on the sides of deep valleys. Humboldt observed how the ever-growing human populations moved upward and outward into much harsher and more marginal environments. As they did so, they tried to encourage animals and plants living in one zone to adapt to another, to extend their range into unoccupied land. By seeding beans and cereal and transplanting roots and fruit trees, they struggled constantly to maintain a foothold outside natural faunal and floral ranges. The same upward assault continues to this day in the Andes, a quiet battle waged with robust root crops and hardy cereal strains. It seems that much the same struggle went on in early prehistory, too (Moseley, 1991).

According to veteran archaeologist Richard MacNeish, the finds from Pikimachay Cave high in the Andes show that the few inhabitants of this and other sites at the end of the Ice Age had several subsistence options. They could hunt various sizes of mammal, including the giant sloth and varied small creatures, or concentrate on foraging for plant foods (MacNeish, 1978; MacNeish et al., 1980; Moseley, 1978). Their options were exercised by priority rather than by season, the idea being that

11,000 B.P. one acquired food with the minimum effort. Approximately 11,000 years ago, however, the subsistence strategies changed. There is reason to believe that seasonal exploitation had replaced other options, with hunting, trapping, and plant collecting at high altitudes important in the dry season. During the wetter months, collecting and possibly penning small game, as well as seed collecting, were dominant activities.

About 12,000 years ago, small groups of hunter-gatherers began using Guitarrero Cave, 1.5 miles (2.5 km) above sea level in the Peruvian Andes (Lynch, 1980) (Figure 14.3). They relied on a technology that made heavy use of hemplike fibers and wood, the former to make cordage, nets, and simple textiles. In 10,000-year-old levels, Thomas Lynch, the excavator, recovered local wild fruit and tubers, a few specimens

FIGURE 14.3   Guitarrero Cave, looking toward the Andes.

of common beans and lima beans, and a single chili pepper. Neither of the beans nor the pepper grew wild in the area, the lima being a native of the rain forests east of the Andes. It is possible that people living in these forests first domesticated the lima, and later, domesticated beans spread into drier terrain across the mountains. Perhaps the people who grew beans at Guitarrero tended small gardens close to the nearby river, leaving the plants to fend for themselves while they hunted and foraged elsewhere.

This pattern of early plant tending persisted in the Andes for many centuries. Gourds, potato, and ulluco were probably grown by 10,000 to 9000 years ago in the same area but, like beans, served as a supplementary food and as a means of expanding into hitherto marginal areas. It was many thousands of years before these plants became the economic staple.

7000 to 6500 B.P.

After 7000 to 6500 years ago, the archaeological evidence becomes more abundant. In the Ayacucho-Huanta region 25 dry- and wet-season camps have been found, which provide signs of continued exploitation of wild vegetables as well as game during the dry season. The Pikimachay Cave levels of this period yielded wet-season living floors. There, wild seeds are abundant, along with remains of gourds and seeds of domesticated quinoa and squash. Game remains are very rare, as if a vegetable diet, whether wild or domesticated, was of prime importance during the wet months. Another wet-season locality, Puente Cave, yielded a few bones of tame guinea pigs as well as the remains of many small wild mammals. Grinding stones and other artifacts used for plant collecting, or perhaps incipient agriculture, are also common at Puente. Throughout this period, many wet-season camps became larger and more stable, with their use extending over longer periods of the year.

Pikimachay

Puente

6000 B.P.

After 6000 years ago, the Ayacucho peoples relied more on food production. The potato was cultivated; hoes appeared, as well as domesticated corn, squashes, common beans, and other crops. Guinea pigs were certainly tamed, and llama were domesticated in central Peru by at least 5500 years ago. By this time, too, there was more interaction between coast and interior, trade in raw materials, and some interchange of domesticates. MacNeish believes corn spread from the north, ultimately from Mesoamerica, into Ayacucho. Root crop agriculture may have diffused from highland Peru into the lowlands, too.

5500 B.P.

The Ayacucho sequence is illustrative of the complex adaptive shifts that took place in many parts of South America after 7000 years ago. In both highlands and lowlands, the beginnings of agriculture were a gradual adjustment, with food production gradually supplanting gathering as the major subsistence activity.

The Coast

On the Peruvian coast, the gathering of vegetable foods and fishing were supplemented by irrigation farming as early as 5000 years ago, while the highland peoples were cultivating a variety of crops by the same time, crops that amplified the horizontally stacked natural resources of their mountain homeland.

Peruvian coast

The Peruvian coast forms a narrow shelf at the foot of the Andes, crossed by small river valleys descending from the mountains to the sea. These valleys are oases in the desert plain, with deep, rich soils, blooming vegetation, and plentiful water. For thousands of years Peruvians have cultivated these valley floors, building their settlements, pyramids, and palaces at the edges of their agricultural land. Because conditions for preservation in this arid country are exceptional, the archaeological record often is quite complete. The coast itself forms a series of related microenvironments, such as rocky bars where shellfish are abundant, places where seasonal vegetable foods nourished by damp fogs are common, and the floors or sides of river valleys flow into the Pacific. One would assume that a combination of these microenvironments would provide a rich and uniform constellation of food resources that could normally be exploited with ease from relatively sedentary base camps (Moseley, 1975b). However, the bountiful maritime environment occasionally is disrupted by a warm countercurrent known as El Niño, which can flow for as long as 12 months. El Niño occurs at highly irregular intervals, perhaps every 6 years and sometimes much longer. It reduces marine upwelling so much that the fish migrate elsewhere, and thus one of the coastal peoples' staple diet sources is greatly reduced. This phenomenon is so unpredictable that the people could not store food against its arrival; they also could not move from the coast, and they did not have the offshore vessels needed for deep-water fishing. Their only strategy, other than moving or starving, was to limit their population densities to the lowest levels of available natural resources until such time as they developed alternative food sources, such as maize grown by intensive irrigation agriculture (Raymond, 1981; Yesner, 1980).

7000 B.P.

The archaeological evidence for the Peruvian coast is incomplete for the period immediately preceding early food production. During the dry winter months the inhabitants collected shellfish and other marine resources, and hunting and vegetable foods were more important in the summer. After 7000 years ago, however, more efficient collecting strategies came into use, with greater attention to exploiting maximally natural food sources. Fishing, in particular, became more important.

6200 to 4500 B.P.

Between approximately 6200 and 4500 years ago, Peruvian coastal peoples depended on marine resources—fish, sea birds, and mollusks—for much of their diet. During the warmest and driest period after the Pleistocene, the coastal peoples moved closer to the shore, dwelling in larger and more stable settlements. Along with the shift to more lasting coastal dwelling came the development of sophisticated equipment for deep-sea fishing. As early as 7500 years ago, the coastal peoples were manipulating plants for their own purposes. The Paloma site on the central coast was occupied more than 7500 years ago, a settled community with numerous simple huts and grass-lined pits where the inhabitants stored food for the occasional lean year. The people relied heavily on fishing and gathering but also manipulated some plant species, including tuberous begonias, gourds, squashes, peppers, and possibly peanuts. They may also have kept llamas, the same species used much later by the Incas for carrying loads in the Andes (Benfer, 1982).

Paloma
7500 to 4500 B.P.

Chilca
5800 to 4650 B.P.

A later coastal settlement that perpetuated the same subsistence pattern flourished at Chilca, 45 miles (72 km) south of present-day Lima. Frederic Engel (1966a) excavated refuse heaps there and C14 dated the earlier Chilca occupation to between 5800 and 4650 years ago. When the site was in use, it probably lay near a reedy marsh, which provided both matting and building materials as well as sites for small gardens. The Chilca people lived on sea mollusks, fish, and sea lions; they apparently hunted few land mammals. They cultivated jack and lima beans, gourds, and squashes, probably relying on river floods as well as rainfall for their simple agriculture.

One remarkable Chilca house was uncovered: A circular structure, it had a domelike frame of canes bound with rope and covered with bundles of grass (Figure 14.4); the interior was braced with bones from stranded whales. Seven burials had been deposited in the house before it was intentionally collapsed on top of them. The skeletons were wrapped in mats and all buried at the same time, perhaps because of an epidemic.

The new emphasis on fish, increased use of flour ground from wild grass seed, and availability of cultivated squashes provided new sources of nutrition for some coastal groups. This supply may ultimately have set off a sustained period of population growth. Certainly the succeeding millennia saw many permanent settlements established near the ocean; the people combined agriculture with fishing and mollusk

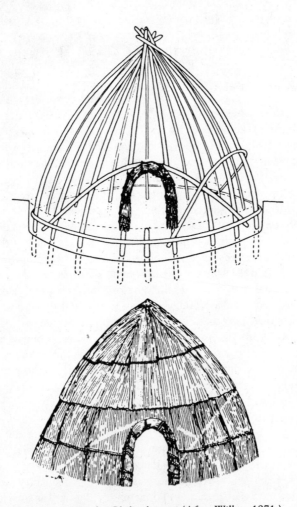

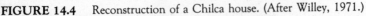

FIGURE 14.4   Reconstruction of a Chilca house. (After Willey, 1971.)

4500 B.P. gathering. Domesticated cotton first appeared around 4500 years ago. Squashes, peppers, lima beans, and other crops remained staple foods until recent times. Maize and other basic foods were still unknown. Agriculture remained a secondary activity much later than it did in Mesoamerica.

Huaca Prieta One later site is Huaca Prieta, a sedentary village that housed several hundred
4500 to 3800 people on the north coast of Peru between 4500 and 3800 years ago (Banks, 1977;
B.P. Hyslop et al., 1987). The vast refuse mound there contains small one- or two-room houses built partially into the ground and roofed with timber or whalebone beams. The inhabitants were remarkably skillful cotton weavers who devised a sophisticated art style with animal, human, and geometric designs.

Playa Culebras Maize made its first appearance on the coast at Playa Culebras, another important and contemporary settlement south of Huaca Prieta (Engel, 1957; Moseley, 1991). The new crop was soon grown on a considerable scale in large irrigation systems in coastal river valleys. Irrigation required considerable organization and deployment of people to dig and maintain canals, communal work on a scale that could only be organized by a system of taxation by labor, such as was commonplace in the Andes in later millennia. Much higher crop yields resulted as the focus of coastal population moved inland and local kin leaders and priests assumed much more prominent roles in society. These social changes were reflected in more permanent housing and in large ceremonial pyramids and other public buildings. A complex of stone and mud mortar platforms lies at El Paraíso on the floodplain of the Chillón Valley, some distance from the sea. At least one mound had complexes of connected rooms built in successive stages. Settlements such as El Paraíso obviously depended more on agriculture than had earlier sites. By the time the temple com-
4300 to 3800 plexes were built there, after 3800 years ago, loom-woven textiles and pottery had
B.P. come into widespread use (Figure 14.5). All the major food plants that formed the basis of later Peruvian civilization were employed.

EARLY FARMERS IN SOUTHWESTERN
NORTH AMERICA

Eleven thousand years ago the Southwest United States was populated by hunter-gatherers whose culture was adapted to desert living (Cordell, 1984a, b; Lipe, 1978).
Cochise A distinctive foraging culture, the Cochise, flourished in southeast Arizona and
11,000 to 3000 southwest New Mexico from about this time. The Cochise people gathered many
B.P. plant foods, including yucca seeds, cacti, and sunflower seeds. They used small milling stones, basketry, cordage, nets, and spear-throwers. Many features of their material culture survived into later times, when cultivated plants were introduced into the Southwest.

The earliest Mesoamerican crops to cross the Rio Grande were maize, beans, and squash, which were probably cultivated for some time in northern Mexico before they reached the Southwest. The maize farmers of northern Mexico must have had sporadic contact with Archaic hunter-gatherers living in the deserts to the north, so it would have been easy for knowledge of plants, even gifts of seeds or seedlings, to

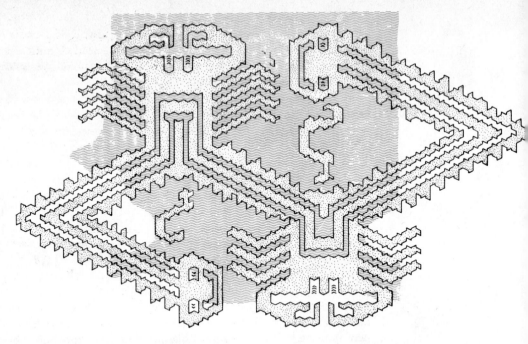

FIGURE 14.5   A double-headed snakelike figure with appended rock crabs revealed by plotting the warp movements in a preceramic twined cotton fabric from Huaca Prieta, Peru. The original length was approximately 16 inches (14 cm). The shaded area indicates the surviving textile. Double-headed motifs have persisted through more than 3000 years of Peruvian art. (Courtesy of Junius Bird.)

pass from south to north. Probably, the opportunity for adopting crops was there long before anyone thought it worth doing so.

Between about 2500 and 100 B.C., the southwestern climate was relatively stable, perhaps somewhat wetter than today. However, it was an environment where hunting and gathering were high-risk occupations, mainly because rainfall patterns were always unpredictable. Despite generally low population densities, local populations may have occasionally risen to saturation point, causing food shortages. Domesticated plants like maize and beans had one major advantage: They might have low yields, but they were predictable. Cultivators of the new crops could control their location and their availability at different seasons by storing them carefully. Perhaps people living in the southern deserts of the Southwest began growing maize because it gave them food supplies to tide them over the lean months until spring. Further north, in the uplands, growing crops would have enabled hunter-gatherer peoples to exercise more effective control over their environment. In the final analysis, it was probably a combination of rising populations and food shortages that caused the adoption of low-yielding forms of maize. One could argue, indeed, that the people accepted the new crops not because they wanted to become farmers but so they could be more effective foragers (Wills, 1989).

The hardy, low-yielding maize that first entered the Southwest was the so-called

Chapalote form, a small popcorn of great genetic diversity. It may have arrived during a period of higher rainfall between 1500 and 1000 B.C. It was soon introgressed with the indigenous, wild teosinte, creating a highly varied, more productive hybrid maize with larger cobs and more kernel rows.

However, a radically different maize, Maize de Ocho, was the key to new cultural developments in the Southwest. Maize de Ocho, with its large, more productive, flowery kernels, may have evolved from earlier, highly variable Chapalote maize. It may have resulted from a selection for a large kerneled corn that was easier to grind and flowered earlier, both important attributes in the hot and arid Southwest. Here, growing seasons are often restricted by the irregular timing and distribution of rainfall, leaving little time for kernels to fill out. These characteristics of Maize de Ocho were highly adaptive in North America, with its short growing seasons and very diverse, temperate environments.

Archaeologists Steadman Upham and Richard MacNeish have found Maize de Ocho in rock shelters in southern New Mexico dating to about 1225 B.C. (Upham et al., 1987). It spread widely through the Southwest in later centuries, as did other maize forms. Southwestern farmers experimented with the new crop at many elevations. After 500 B.C., they combined maize with beans, for these legumes when underplanted with corn return vital nitrogen to the soil, nitrogen that is depleted by maize. By planting the two crops together, the southwestern farmer could maintain the fertility of the soil for longer periods of time.

In the Southwest, as in the Andes, the farmers were working close to the limits of corn's range. Maize is intolerant of too-short growing seasons, weak soil conditions, and such hazards as crop disease and strong winds. Most important were adequate soil moisture and water supplies. By careful seed selection, the farmers developed higher-elevation varieties with elongated cobs, distinctive root structures, and seeds that could be planted at considerable depths, where they could be nourished by retained ground moisture. The farmers became experts at soil selection, favoring those with good moisture-retaining properties in north- and east-facing slopes that receive little direct sunlight. They also favored floodplains and canyon mouths, where the soil was naturally irrigated. They would divert water from seasonal streams, springs, or rainfall runoff to irrigate their lands. As with hunting and foraging, risk management was vital, so the cultivators widely dispersed their gardens to minimize the danger of local drought or flood. Over the centuries, a great diversity of highly effective dry-climate agricultural techniques

developed throughout the Southwest. Between A.D. 300 and 500, another complex of domestic tropical plants, including pigweed, cotton, and several varieties of beans, arrived in the region. These tended to require more irrigation and were confined to the hot regions of the south, where the irrigation-experienced Hohokam adopted them.

The appearance of maize did not trigger a dramatic revolution in southwestern life. The earlier corns were not that productive and could be planted fairly casually. Under these circumstances, their yields were probably less than those of good piñon nut harvests. Eventually, however, they became of staple importance to many southwestern peoples, who were now living in more permanent villages and in more restricted territories. As life became more sedentary, the people invested more time and energy in their crops, which provided protection from shortages of wild plant foods in their smaller territories.

2300 B.P.

By 2300 years ago, experimentation and new hybrid varieties of maize introduced from the south had led to sedentary villages and much greater dependence on farming. The cultural changes of the period culminated in the great southwestern archaeological traditions: Hohokam, Mogollon, and Anasazi (Cordell, 1984b).

Hohokam
?2300 B.P. to
A.D. 1500

The Hohokam tradition has long been thought to have originated in the Cochise. No one knows exactly when the tradition emerged, but it was probably in the first five centuries of the Christian era. However, Emil Haury, who dug the important Snaketown site in the Gila River Valley, believes that the Hohokam people were immigrants from northern Mexico who brought their pottery and extensive irrigation agriculture with them (Haury, 1976). Under this scenario, the newcomers soon influenced the lifeway of the local people, and a desert adaptation of Hohokam resulted. Recent research tends to discount the migration theory. Reexamination of the Snaketown data and further fieldwork suggest that the Hohokam enjoyed complex trading and ceremonial relationships with peoples living all over the Southwest and northern Mexico. As time went on, this trade expanded, perhaps within the context of a common ceremonial system centered on the ball courts and other ceremonial structures at Snaketown and other focal points. In all probability, the Hohokam was an indigenous culture, one that acquired much greater social complexity through time (for a discussion, see Fish and Fish, 1977; Wilcox, 1980, 1985).

Hohokam subsistence was based on maize, beans, cucurbits, cotton, and other crops, as well as on gathering. The people planted their crops to coincide with the semiannual rainfall and flooding patterns. Where they could, they practiced irrigation from flowing streams; otherwise they cultivated floodplains and caught runoff from local storms with dams, terraces, and other devices. Hohokam people occupied much of what is now Arizona. Their cultural heirs are the Pima and Papago Indians of today (Figure 14.6).

Hohokam culture evolved slowly over as long as 2000 years. There are at least five stages of the culture, culminating in a classic period from approximately 850 to 500 years ago, when large pueblos (communal villages) were built and canal irrigation was especially important. At this time and somewhat earlier, Mexican influences can be detected. These include new varieties of maize, the appearance of platform mounds and ball or dance courts at Snaketown and elsewhere, and imports such as copper bells. Does this mean that Mexican immigrants transformed Hohokam culture, or were there internal factors that caused greater elaboration of local society at the same time as some ideas arrived from Mexico? Archaeologists remain divided on this point.

Originally, anthropologists believed the Mexican influence was transitory and weak, but excavations at a prehistoric town named Casas Grande in northern Chihuahua, Mexico, have changed their minds (Di Peso et al., 1974). (This site should not be confused with Casa Grande, Arizona.) At the height of its prosperity, around A.D. 1400, Casas Grande boasted approximately 1600 rooms and housed more than 2200 people. The dig showed that its inhabitants exchanged turquoise and painted pottery from the Southwest for marine shells and exotic bird feathers from Mexico. Local traditions connect Casas Grande with a settlement named Paquimé, which was more of a Mexican town than an Indian pueblo. The archaeologists argue

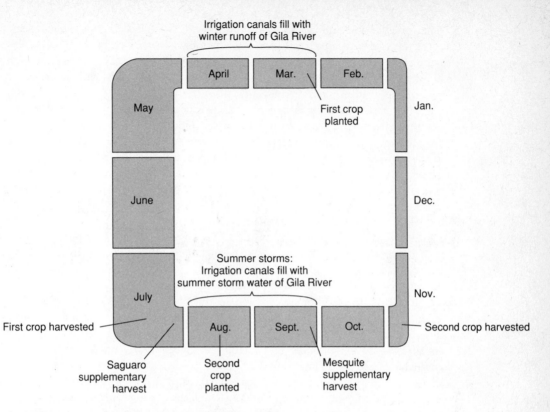

FIGURE 14.6   A scheduled agricultural round. Diagram showing how the Pima Indians of the Southwest, descendants of the Hohokam, schedule their plantings and harvests around rainfall seasons. The Hohokam probably relied on a similar annual round. The thickness of the shaded area reflects the relative plenty of food resources. (From Jesse D. Jennings, *Ancient Native Americans,* New York: Freeman, 1978, p. 349.)

that Paquimé was founded by Mexican traders from the south, possibly itinerant merchants known to the Aztec as *pochteca,* who often served as spies. Perhaps, too, contacts between the Hohokam and Mexican civilization were far more regular than once was suspected.

Mogollon
2300 to 1700
B.P.

The Mogollon tradition emerged from Archaic roots between 2300 and 1700 years ago and disappeared as a separate entity between 1100 and 500 years ago, when it became part of Anasazi (Haury, 1936; Lipe, 1978). The Mogollon is well known from dry caves in New Mexico as an agricultural tradition in which hunting and gathering in the highlands were always important. Mogollon agriculture depended on direct rainfall, with only very limited use of irrigation. The people lived in small villages of pit dwellings with timber frames and mat or brush roofs. Their material culture was utilitarian and included milling stones, digging sticks, bows and arrows, fine baskets, and characteristic brown-and-red pottery.

At least six regional variants of Mogollon are known, and there were five chronological stages, the fifth ending approximately 500 years ago. Early Mogollon villages often were located on high promontories close to more fertile lands. The settlement pattern varied from area to area but had a tendency toward larger sites and increased populations throughout the life of the tradition. By A.D. 1500, pueblos of several hundred rooms had developed in some areas, but by this time Mogollon had become part of the western pueblo Anasazi tradition.

Anasazi

Last 2000 years

The Anasazi tradition is, in general terms, ancestral to the cultures of the modern Pueblo Indians—the Hopi, Zuni, and others (Judd, 1954, 1964; Zubrow, 1971). Its emergence is conventionally dated to 2000 years ago, but this is a purely arbitrary date, for Anasazi's roots lie in Archaic cultures that flourished for a long time before. The Anasazi people made heavy use of wild vegetable foods, even after they took up maize agriculture seriously, after A.D. 400. Most of their farming depended on dry agriculture and seasonal rainfall, although they, like the Hohokam, used irrigation techniques when practicable. They made use of flood areas, where the soil would remain damp for weeks after sudden storms. Moisture in the flooded soil could be used to germinate seeds in the spring and to bring ripening crops to fruition after later rains. However, this is a very high-risk type of agriculture, and the Anasazi relied on wild resources to carry them through lean years.

The Anasazi tradition is centered in the "Four Corners" area, where Utah, Arizona, Colorado, and New Mexico meet. Anasazi chronology is well established thanks to the use of dendrochronology on beams from abandoned pueblos. There are at least six Basketmaker and Pueblo subdivisions of Anasazi; each marked a gradual increase in the importance of agriculture and the emergence of some larger sites with *kivas,* ceremonial sweathouses. Pueblos, which are complexes of adjoining rooms, occurred more frequently after A.D. 900; the population congregated in fewer but larger pueblos after A.D. 1180. These were located in densely populated areas, some of them moved from the open to under cliff overhangs, the so-called cliff dwellings. Some of the features of these sites, such as turrets and loopholed walls, appear to be defensive.

At the same time people concentrated in larger sites, there was depopulation of many areas of the northern Southwest. The reasons for these changes are imperfectly understood. In some areas, such as Chaco Canyon, New Mexico, the concentrated populations enjoyed roads, extensive irrigation systems, and more elaborate social and political organizations as well as trading connections with widespread areas of the Southwest, but most pueblos seem to have been more egalitarian in their organization and relatively self-sufficient. It may be that the changes generated by the developments in Chaco and elsewhere caused people to congregate more closely. Alternatively, it has been argued that some climatic and environmental changes, as yet little understood, may have caused major shifts in the settlement pattern. More likely, a combination of environmental, societal, and adaptive changes set in motion a period of turbulence and culture change.

By approximately A.D. 500, the basic Anasazi settlement pattern had evolved, and above-the-ground houses were being substituted for the pit dwellings of earlier centuries. The pit dwellings developed into kivas, subterranean ceremonial structures that existed in every large village. Large settlements of contiguous dwellings became the rule after A.D. 800, with clusters of "rooms" serving as homes for separate families or lineages. Large settlements such as Pueblo Bonito developed around A.D. 1100; this was a huge D-shaped complex of 800 rooms rising several stories around the rim of the arc (Figure 14.7). The room complexes surrounded courts, with the highest stories at the back. They formed a blank wall; a line of one-story rooms cut off the fourth side. Within the court lay the kivas, always one great kiva and usually several smaller ones. The great kivas were up to 60 feet (18.2 m) in diameter, with wide masonry benches encircling the interior. The roof was supported by four large pillars near the center, where a raised hearth lay. Two subterranean, masonry-lined rooms were situated on either side of the fireplace. A staircase leading from the floor of the kiva to the large room above it gave access to the sacred precinct.

The period between A.D. 1000 and 1300 was one of consolidation of population into a few more congested settlements, where more elaborate social organizations may have developed. The pueblos were probably communities run for the collective good,

FIGURE 14.7   Pueblo Bonito, New Mexico, dated by dendrochronology to A.D. 919–1130. The round structures are kivas.

with at least some ranking of society under a chieftain. In modern Hopi society, clan superiority and kinship lineages played an important role in the election of chieftains. Thrust into close intimacy by the nature of pueblo architecture, the people developed well-integrated religious and ceremonial structures to counteract the tensions of close living.

The Anasazi enjoyed a relatively elaborate material culture at the height of their prosperity; at this time they were making distinctive black-and-white pottery, well-formed baskets, and fine sandals. However, their architecture was neither very sophisticated nor particularly innovative. Rocks and baked mud were formed into boxlike rooms; a roof of mud rested on horizontal timbers. Room after room was added as the need arose, using local materials and a simple architectural style entirely appropriate for its environment.

The southwestern farmer won success by skillfully using scarce water resources and bringing together soil and water by means of dams, floodwater irrigation, and other systems for distributing runoff. Planting techniques were carefully adapted to desert conditions, and myriad tiny gardens supplied food for each family or lineage. This successful adaptation is also reflected in the architecture.

PREAGRICULTURAL AND AGRICULTURAL SOCIETIES IN EASTERN NORTH AMERICA

The Archaic hunter-gatherer traditions of eastern North America enjoyed many regional variations in material culture; these occurred because the people concentrated on different, locally abundant food sources (Fagan, 1991a; B. D. Smith, 1986; Yerkes, 1988). In general, however, the lifeway was similar among them: a seasonal one, based on a very broad spectrum of game and vegetable foods (Brose, 1980). As long as the population density was low, every band could react relatively easily to changes in local conditions. Since many of their favorite vegetable foods were subject to cycles of lean and abundant years, a flexibility in choice and movement was essential. However, as population grew slowly throughout the Archaic, this flexibility was increasingly restricted and the people tended to specialize in local resources that were available most of the year. They developed better storage techniques and fostered closer contacts with their neighbors through exchange networks that handled foodstuffs and other commodities. The development of these types of response may have required more complex social organization than the simple band structure of earlier times, and it is no coincidence that burial patterns during the late Archaic, approximately 3700 years ago, reflect greater differentiation in social status. Cemeteries may also have served as territorial markers (Yerkes, 1988).

Transitional period
5000 to 2000 B.P.

Under these circumstances, perhaps it was inevitable that late Archaic peoples in the eastern woodlands turned to the deliberate cultivation of food plants to supplement wild plant yields. They did so quite independently of other centers of plant domestication (B. Smith, 1987), starting with an indigenous, thin-walled gourd, fragments of which occur as early as 7150 years ago at Koster, Illinois. By 4000 years ago, marsh elder was being planted, soon followed by other native plants such as sumpweed and goosefoot. Sunflowers were probably domesticated by 3500 years ago. Most of these species flourished in river valleys, where there were many and diverse wild vegetable foods, and they may have first been cultivated to supplement natural stands. Sumpweed was widely cultivated in the Midwest in the first millennium B.C., and sunflowers were prized for their edible seeds and oil by the same period. Several species were grown outside their natural ranges, but it seems likely that domestication of these native plants first took hold in locations like the lower Mississippi River Delta, where wild ancestors of these species grow in abundance (Ford, 1985). It is significant that none of the domesticates required the kind of wholesale adaptive shift in year-round routine that maize cultivation demanded of its practitioners. Maize and bean agriculture did not flourish in the eastern woodlands until much later in prehistory (Stoltman, 1978).

4000 B.P.

After 4000 years ago, we find increasing signs of preoccupation with burial and with life after death, a new ideological foundation for local society in the East. These burial cults shared many practices, among them cremation, the deposition of exotic objects with the dead, and the custom of building burial mounds.

More intensive exploitation of food resources, greater sedentism, regular social interaction and exchange, a degree of social ranking, increased ceremonialism—these were the culminating elements in late Archaic life in eastern North America. While most groups still lived in temporary encampments or even sizable base camps used for most, if not all, of the year, the Poverty Point culture of the lower Mississippi Valley and adjacent Gulf Coast offers a dramatic contrast.

Poverty Point

1450 to 1100 B.C.

The earliest Poverty Point sites date to about 3600 years ago, forming the oldest component in a cultural sequence that lasted for 1000 years. Poverty Point itself is the nexus of the culture and stands on Macon Ridge overlooking the Mississippi floodplain, near the confluence of six rivers (Figure 14.8). This was a strategic point from which to trade upstream and downstream, to receive and exchange raw materials and finished products. Some of the exotic materials at Poverty Point came from as far as 600 miles (1960 km) away. The leaders of Poverty Point not only exchanged materials with peoples far away but also redistributed them to regional centers in their own culture area.

Poverty Point, with its great earthworks, is a remarkable contrast to the humble base camps elsewhere in the East. Six concentric semicircular earthen ridges are divided into segments. They average about 82.0 feet (25 m) wide and 9.8 feet (3 m) high and are set about 131 feet (40 m) apart. Their significance is a complete mystery, beyond a suspicion that they were connected with astronomical observations. To the west lies an artificial mound more than 66 feet (20 m) high and more than 660 feet (200 m) long. A person standing on this mound can sight the vernal and autumnal equinoxes directly across the center of the earthworks to the east. These are the points where the sun rises on the first days of spring and fall. Built between 3000 and 2600 years ago, Poverty Point took more than 1,236,007 cubic feet (35,000 cu. m) of basket-loaded soil, a task that would have taken 1350 adults laboring 70 days a year 3 years to complete. Estimates of Poverty Point's population are hard to come by, but even a population of 1000 people makes the site unique for the period. At present, the significance of this extraordinary site and associated culture is little understood (C. H. Webb, 1968).

The Poverty Point culture went into decline approximately 2700 years ago, just

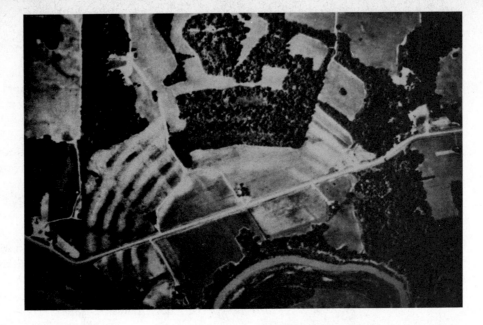

FIGURE 14.8 Poverty Point, Louisiana. *Top:* Aerial view of the site taken about 40 years ago, showing the six concentric earth ridges. The ridges and intervening hollows (swales) show up as light and dark stripes in the fields. Mound A, covered with trees, is at center left. The white, straight line running diagonally across the picture is a modern road. *Right:* The south side of Mound A. The steps lead to the summit, which is now 70 feet (21.3 m) above the surrounding terrain.

as mound building reached new heights in the Ohio Valley, to the northeast (Otto, 1979).

Adena

Adena
**2500 B.P. to
A.D. 400**

By 2700 years ago, the people of eastern North America enjoyed a tradition of long-distance trading that had flourished for centuries. The trade carried not only prosaic commodities such as stone ax blades but also large quantities of prestigious imports such as conch shells and copper artifacts, most of which were deposited in the graves of their owners. These exotic objects may have been status symbols, indicating some social differentiation within groups. As far as is known, these artifacts were buried with their owners at death, and the special status associated with them was not passed on from one generation to the next (Yerkes, 1988).

Between 2500 B.P. and about A.D. 400, the Adena culture flourished in the Ohio Valley. The people lived in seasonal camps, relying not only on hunting and gathering, but on the cultivation of squash and local starchy and oily plants (Figure 14.9). Major camps lay close to ceremonial burial mounds. The construction of even the largest mounds involved relatively few people. This mound building and other earthwork construction may have reflected a strengthening of group identity and the establishment of social and territorial boundaries, which were often marked by cemeteries (Yerkes, 1988). At the same time, the Adena people developed large

0   8 ft
0   2.5 M

FIGURE 14.9   Reconstruction of an Adena ceremonial structure from the posthole pattern shown at left.

exchange networks that extended over enormous distances, the prototypes of even more elaborate trade routes in later centuries. It was powerful loyalties to local lineages that caused the people to commemorate their dead not only with imposing burial mounds but with extensive earthworks as well.

Adena earthworks follow the contours of flat-topped hills and form circles, squares, and other shapes, enclosing areas perhaps as much as 350 feet (105 m) in diameter. The earth used to make the enclosures came from just inside the walls, giving a false impression of an interior moat. These were probably ceremonial compounds rather than defensive earthworks. The Adena people built large burial mounds, some placed inside enclosures, others standing independently outside. Most are communal rather than individual graves. The most important people lie in log-lined tombs. Their corpses are smeared with red ocher or graphite. Nearby lie ceremonial soapstone pipes and tablets engraved with curving designs or birds of prey. Some prestigious individuals were buried inside enclosures or mortuary structures, which were burned down as part of the funeral rites. Occasionally, the burial chamber was left open so that bodies could be added later. Dozens of people from miles around piled basketfuls of earth to form an imposing burial mound for a single ruler. More often, the mounds were piled up gradually over the years, as layers of bodies were added. However, the vast majority of less important Adena people were cremated: Only their ashes were placed inside the burial mound.

Hopewell

Hopewell
c. 250 B.C. to
c. A.D. 400

The Hopewell tradition, a later elaboration of Adena, first appeared in Illinois approximately 2200 years ago. Its religious cults were such a success that they spread rapidly from their heartland as far as upper Wisconsin and Louisiana and deep into Ohio and New York State. For nearly 1000 years, the Midwest experienced a dramatic flowering of artistic traditions and of long-distance trade that brought copper from the upper Great Lakes region, obsidian from Yellowstone, and mica from the southern Appalachians. Some archaeologists call this the Hopewell Interaction Sphere (Caldwell, 1958). The Hopewell people themselves lived in relatively small settlements and used only stone artifacts to plant, hunt game, and fish. They wore leather and woven clothes of pliable fibers. Much wealth and creative skill were lavished on a few individuals and on their life after death. At first glance, the exotic artifacts and ritual traditions of the Hopewell seem completely alien to the indigenous culture of the area, but a closer look reveals the links between the underlying traditions and the magnificent art created by Hopewell artisans. Their manufactures were traded from hand to hand throughout Hopewell territory in a vast network of gift-giving transactions that linked kin leaders with lasting, important obligations to one another (Brose and Greber, 1979).

The cult objects associated with this trade are found in dozens of Hopewell burial mounds and tell us something of the rank and social roles of the people with whom they are buried. Some of the exotic grave goods, such as pipe bowls or axes, were buried as gifts from living clan members to a dead leader. Others were personal possessions, cherished weapons, or sometimes symbols of status or wealth. Hopewell graves contain soapstone pipe bowls in the form of beavers, frogs, birds, bears, and even humans. Skilled smiths fashioned thin copper sheets into head and breast ornaments that bear elaborate repoussé animal motifs (Figure 14.10). There were copper axes and arrowheads, trinkets, and beads. A few specialists cut mica sheets into striking lustrous silhouettes of human figures, bird talons, and abstract designs. Most of these artifacts were manufactured by a few artisans, perhaps produced in workshops within large earthwork complexes, themselves close to major sources of important raw materials. Some elaborate artifacts may also have been manufactured at special "mortuary camps" for use in the graves of high status individuals (Baby and Langlois, 1979; Cinadr and Genheimer, 1983; Yerkes, 1988). The same prestigious objects may have been distributed via the trade networks that carried foodstuffs and tools throughout Hopewell territory. Many of them show surprisingly little wear, as if they were soon buried with their owners.

Hopewell burial mounds are much more elaborate than their Adena predecessors. For example, Cook's Mound in Louisiana rises 40 feet (12 m) and is more than 100 feet (30 m) across. Its builders followed the established custom when they buried 168 bodies within an extensive earthen platform. Then they placed a further 214 corpses on the platform before covering the entire sepulcher with a large mound. Another Hopewell burial mound complex in Ohio, appropriately named Mound City, contains no fewer than 24 mounds inside an enclosure covering 13 acres (5.2 ha). The Newark, Ohio, Hopewell earthworks cover 4 square miles (1040 ha).

The decline of the Hopewell culture after A.D. 400 is still imperfectly understood,

 FIGURE 14.10   Hopewell artifacts: (a) raven or crow in beaten copper; (b) bird claw in mica; (c) soapstone frog.

but it is possible that a rapid and dramatic population increase strained the limits of the economic system, causing competition between trading networks and rupturing long-established economic and political relationships. It is possible, too, that as agriculture became more efficient and spread to other groups there was an increase in population and in the number of settlements, so much so that there was greater competition for land. This in turn would have led to the development of local rule by chieftains who could have challenged the overbearing powers of those who controlled the centuries-old burial cults (Dragoo, 1976). In contrast, David Braun argues (1988) for much more regional integration, because of larger, more sedentary communities and changing settlement patterns and growing populations that dispersed people from major river valleys into outlying watersheds. We do not know why the center of religious and political power had spread southward from the Ohio Valley into the lower Mississippi bottomlands by A.D. 800, but the shift may be connected with the realization that maize offered great potential as a food staple.

Maize may have spread from the Southwest in forms preadapted to high altitudes and lower temperatures along riverine areas toward the Northeast. Midwestern twelve-row or Chapalote maize was known to southeastern populations by the late first millennium A.D., but it was some time before its dietary staple potential was realized in the Late Woodland and Mississippian cultures of the Midwest (B. D. Smith, 1986; Yerkes, 1988). The lush floodplain of the lower Mississippi was ideal for cultivating high-yeilding maize strains and also for growing beans. Beans arrived after the full potential of maize agriculture was realized. They had not only the advantage of a high protein value but also the asset of compensating for the amino-acid deficiencies of corn. The new agriculture adaptations were a considerable success.

Mississippian

A.D. 1 to 450   Between A.D. 1 and about 450, two important cultural developments emerged in the Southeast. First, mortuary customs became far more elaborate. Second, there are signs that some individuals had achieved greater social and political importance among what had been relatively egalitarian societies. These four and one-half centuries saw the construction of hundreds of low, oval, or circular burial mounds throughout much of the Southeast. The burials within them vary considerably in their elaborations, a reflection of the increased social complexity that accompanied accelerating population growth, intercommunity exchange, and more intensive cultivation of native plants and later maize between A.D. 450 and 800. These developments were to culminate in a series of remarkable riverine cultures after A.D. 900, in the great Mississippian tradition of the South and southern Midwest.

The Mississippian's ultimate roots lay in much earlier Archaic and woodland cultures that flourished long before maize agriculture became widespread in the great river valleys of eastern North America (for an example, see Milanich et al., 1984; see also B. D. Smith, 1986; Steponaitis, 1986; Yerkes, 1988). But it was the widespread cultivation of maize and beans that helped foster higher population densities and the more complex social and political organization of the centuries immediately before

European contact in the sixteenth century. Most likely, the shift to maize agriculture was the result of stress largely precipitated by population pressure or the demands of elites (Steponaitis, 1986). Such stress could easily occur even if plenty of land was available because the start-up labor needed to create maize gardens was much larger than that for native plants. Begun initially to create more supplemental foods, the new agriculture transformed valley landscapes in such ways that hunting and foraging soon provided less food for energy expended than maize cultivation. Within a short time, an entirely new economic pattern came into being.

Mississippian
A.D. 800 to 1580

Between A.D. 800 and 1000, there were significant changes in subsistence, material culture, and settlement patterns over much of the South and Southeast (Yerkes, 1988). Maize and bean agriculture now transformed many valley landscapes. Many of the cultural changes of these centuries, including new pottery forms, platform mounds, and substantial rectangular houses, may reflect the adoption of maize not only as a crop to be eaten at once, but one to be stored for use throughout the year. Settlements were sometimes palisaded, perhaps for defense, and more formal layouts included grouping houses around open plazas and mounds. Society itself was changing, perhaps becoming more hierarchical as a powerful elite gradually emerged, based on larger communities with burial mounds and other symbols of religious and political power. Regional Mississippian societies developed in river valleys large and small over a large area at about the same time and interacted with one another for several centuries. Many Mississippian societies flourished on river valley soils fertilized by water-borne nutrients. It has always been assumed that this distribution occurred because of the availability of easily tilled soils. In fact, we know now that this restricted distribution was the result of the complex adaptation that the people developed in an area with well-defined bands of arable soils fertilized by spring floods just before planting season. They lived in valleys with many lakes and swamps, where fish trapped by receding floods were plentiful and migrating waterfowl paused to rest in spring and fall. The Mississippian people not only grew maize, squashes, and beans but they also relied heavily on seasonal crops of nuts, fruits, berries, and seed-bearing plants. They hunted deer, raccoon, and turkey, and took thousands of migratory waterfowl in spring and fall. Fish and waterfowl may have constituted up to 50 percent of the diet of the villagers living within the meander zones of the floodplain (Nassaney, 1987). Bruce Smith (1978a) defines the Mississippian as a society that "had a ranked form of social organization, and had developed a specific complex adaptation to linear, environmentally circumscribed floodplain habitat zones" in the eastern deciduous woodlands. This definition reflects the great variation in social complexity, with great centers like Cahokia in the so-called American Bottom near St. Louis at one end of the spectrum (Figure 14.11) and hundreds of small local centers and minor chiefdoms at the other (Fowler, 1978). Mississippian populations lived under a variety of circumstances. Some groups flourished in small, dispersed homesteads, while others lived in compact villages often best described as towns; in locations like Cahokia, tens of thousands of people lived.

Cahokia

By A.D. 900, some Mississippian centers presided over what might even be described as forms of state-organized society, while complex chiefdom is probably a more appropriate description for others. Larger Mississippian communities housed thousands of people and were fortified with defensive palisades. The largest Mississip-

FIGURE 14.11   The central portion of Cahokia Mounds as it may have appeared around A.D. 1150, at its peak.

pian center was Cahokia, on the east bank of the river at St. Louis (Figure 14.11) (M. D. Fowler, 1969, 1978). Cahokia once contained more than 100 earthen mounds and catered to a population of at least 30,000 to 35,000 people. It was a great ceremonial center; its mounds and plazas dominated the countryside for miles. Monk's Mound at the center of Cahokia rises 102 feet (32 m) above the floodplain and covers 16 acres (6.4 ha) (Figure 14.12). This gigantic mound is as tall as a ten-story building and was erected in at least four stages between the ninth and eleventh centuries A.D. Millions of basketloads of soil deposited by thousands of people went into this monumental earthwork. On the summit stood a thatched temple at the east end of an enormous central plaza. Around the plaza rose other mounds, temples, warehouses, administrative buildings, and the homes of nobles. The entire "downtown" area covered more than 200 acres (80.1 ha) and was fortified by a log fence with gates and watchtowers. Numerous mounds and lesser communities lay outside the walled interior core of Cahokia, each with its own plazas and burial mounds. The pole-and-thatch houses of the residential areas extended over 2000 acres (809 ha), the clusters of houses being separated by several acres of land. There is every reason to believe that Cahokia was planned and controlled by a powerful central authority and that there were many craft specialists.

Cahokia was by no means unique. It lay in the north of Mississippian territory, and its southern rival was Moundville in Alabama. Dozens of small centers and towns sprang up between the two. More than just sacred places for annual ceremonies of

FIGURE
14.12

Aerial view of Monk's Mound, Cahokia, Illinois, taken in 1983. (Courtesy Cahokia Mounds State Historic Site.)

planting and harvest, the centers were markets and focal points of powerful chief-doms. Cahokia owed some of its importance to the manufacture and trading of local salt and chert, a fine-grained rock used to make hoes and other tools. Above all, Cahokia and its neighbors were the places where the Mississippian leaders displayed their political and religious power.

We know little about how Mississippian society functioned, but it seems likely that the floodplain was ruled as a series of powerful chiefdoms, or even small states, by an elite group of priests and rulers who lived somewhat separated from the rest of the population. The chieftains controlled most long-distance trade and were the living intermediaries between the ancestors and the gods. As in the Hopewell culture, high-ranking individuals went to the next world in richly decorated graves, with clusters of ritual objects of different styles that symbolized various clans and tribes.

Excavations at one burial mound revealed at least six different burial events that involved 261 people, including 4 mutilated men and 118 women, who were probably retainers sacrificed to accompany a chief in the afterlife. One such chief lay on a layer of thousands of shell beads, surrounded by grave offerings from as far afield as Wisconsin and Tennessee (Yerkes, 1988).

Cahokia and other, larger Mississippian communities enjoyed a more or less standardized layout. Their inhabitants built platformlike mounds and capped them with temples or the houses of important individuals. These mounds were grouped around an open plaza, while most people lived in humbler, thatched dwellings clustered nearby. Hardly surprisingly, many scholars have pointed to these large earthworks, the plazas, and the platform mounds, and assumed they were the result of cultural influence from Mexican civilizations far to the south. As we shall see in Chapter 22, Mesoamerican civilizations relied on an intricate, intensely symbolic, and highly complex religious cosmology, commemorated with elaborate public ceremonies centered around large pyramids and plazas.

Southern

Mississippian graves and mound centers contain finely made pottery and other artifacts that bear elaborate decoration and distinctive artistic motifs. These artifacts include axes with head and shaft carved from a single piece of stone, copper pendants adorned with circles and weeping eyes, shell disks engraved with woodpeckers and rattlesnakes, elaborately decorated clay pots, and engraved shell cups adorned with male figures in ceremonial dress. The themes and motifs on these objects have many common features throughout the South and Southeast, so much so that they have been thought to link a vast area as far inland as the borders of the Ohio Valley to a common set of ritual beliefs and an art style that has been called the "Southern Cult" or "Southeastern Ceremonial Complex" (Galloway, 1989). Some of these motifs, such as the persistent use of bird symbolism and a "weeping eye" theme, were thought to display Mexican influence.

The term *Southern Cult* was coined in the 1930s, when many fewer Mississippian ceremonial objects were known, and those from larger centers. Today, we know that only a few distinctive stylistic elements were widely used. These include striped poles and fringed aprons on some human figures. As Jon Muller (1989) has pointed out, there are so many differences and similarities among local Mississippian art traditions that it is more economical to attribute the varied regional art styles of the Southern Cult to centuries of intensive exchange among hundreds of different local communities. In time, there was a degree of standardization in art traditions over a wide area, reflecting also a complex, highly variable set of religious mechanisms that supported the authority of local leaders. Undoubtedly, some of the ceremonial artifacts associated with the cult served as badges of rank and status. Far from having Mexican ancestry, the religious beliefs behind Mississippian society had their roots in far earlier indigenous beliefs. Any Mexican connections with Mississippian culture are now discounted. It was an entirely local efflorescence, born of centuries of vigorous cultural evolution in an area of exceptional resource diversity and potential.

Cahokia, Moundville, and other great Mississippian centers were past the height of their powers by the time European traders and explorers reached the Mississippi Valley. Cahokia was abandoned by 1500, even if Moundville was still an important center. Numerous chiefdoms still flourished in the mid-South and Southeast right up

A.D. 1500

to European contact and beyond, some of which, like the kingdom of Coosa, were visited by conquistador Hernando de Soto during his journey across the Southeast in 1540–1542 (M. Smith, 1987). There are grounds to suspect, however, that small-pox and other diseases had spread among the peoples of the interior before the arrival of the Spaniards, decimating and weakening Mississippian society (Ramenovsky, 1987).

A.D. 1720   In the year 1720, French explorer Le Page du Pratz spent some time among the Natchez people of the Mississippi Valley. He found himself in a rigidly stratified society, divided into nobles and commoners and headed by a chieftain known as the Great Sun, who lived in a village of nine houses and a temple built on the summit of an earthen mound. Pratz witnessed the funeral of the Great Sun. His wives, relatives, and servants were drugged, then clubbed to accompany him in death (Swanton, 1911). Pratz was the first and only European to witness a Mississippian funeral, for epidemics of smallpox and other exotic diseases had already caused the fabric of this most complex of North American societies to fall apart. Within two centuries of De Soto, the last vestiges of Mississippian society had been submerged.

GUIDE TO FURTHER READING

Cordell, Linda S. 1984. *Prehistory of the Southwest.* Orlando, FL: Academic Press.
A definitive, closely argued synthesis of southwestern archaeology.

Fagan, Brian M. 1991. *Ancient North America.* New York: Thames and Hudson.
A general account of North American archaeology with a long summary of south-western and eastern woodlands prehistory. Heavily referenced and aimed at the beginning reader.

Jennings, Jesse D., ed. 1978. *Ancient Native Americans.* New York: Freeman.
A volume of essays that summarizes the culture history of the Americas. Some chapters have a stronger theoretical background than others.

Keatinge, Richard, ed. 1988. *Peruvian Prehistory.* Cambridge, Eng.: Cambridge University Press.
Useful essays on Andean archaeology for more specialist readers.

MacNeish, Richard. 1978. *The Science of Archaeology.* North Scituate, MA: Duxbury Press.
An account of MacNeish's research in Mexico and Peru that summarizes the work and contains much common-sense advice about contemporary archaeology.

Moseley, Michael E. 1975. *The Maritime Foundations of Andean Civilization.* Menlo Park, CA: Cummings.
A clearly written, informative essay on the origins of food production and civilization in Peru that was an important basis for this chapter.

Smith, Bruce D. 1986. "The Archaeology of the Southeastern United States: From Dalton to De Soto. 10,500–500 B.P." *Advances in World Archaeology* 5 (1):1–92.
Comprehensive, critical synthesis that is fundamental to understanding southeastern archaeology.

Yerkes, Richard. 1988. "The Woodland and Mississippian Traditions in the Prehistory of Midwestern North America." *Journal of World Prehistory* 2(3): 307–358.
A useful account of later cultural developments in the Midwest.

PART V

OLD WORLD CIVILIZATIONS

(5000 YEARS AGO TO
MODERN TIMES)

The great tide of civilization has long since ebbed, leaving these scattered wrecks on the solitary shore. Are those waters to flow again, bringing back the seeds of knowledge and of wealth that they have wafted to the West? We wanderers were seeking what they had left behind, as children gather up the coloured shells on the deserted sands.

Austen Henry
Layard

AS IN PART IV, A DISCUSSION OF THE THEORETICAL BACK-GROUND AND THE MAJOR CONTROVERSIES PRECEDES THE NARRATIVE PREHISTORY. PART V DEALS WITH THE BEGIN-NINGS OF COMPLEX STATES AND URBAN CIVILIZATION. THESE CHAPTERS PRESENT AN UNCONVENTIONAL AC-COUNT OF EARLY CIVILIZATION IN THAT THEY DEAL WITH LESSER KNOWN PARTS OF THE WORLD, SUCH AS AFRICA AND SOUTHEAST ASIA, AS WELL AS THE NEAR EAST. RE-SEARCH IN AFRICA AND ASIA HAS HARDLY BEGUN; FU-TURE EXCAVATIONS IN THESE REGIONS ARE LIKELY TO THROW SIGNIFICANT NEW LIGHT ON SUCH MUCH-DE-BATED ISSUES AS THE IMPORTANCE OF CEREMONIAL CEN-TERS AND LONG-DISTANCE TRADE IN THE EMERGENCE OF COMPLEX SOCIETIES. ONCE AGAIN, THE READER IS URGED TO START WITH THE THEORETICAL BACKGROUND BEFORE EMBARKING ON THE NARRATIVE CULTURAL HISTORY.

CHAPTER 15   THE DEVELOPMENT OF CIVILIZATION

Preview

- V. Gordon Childe's pioneer definition of the urban revolution was widely accepted; it centered on the development of the city, metallurgy, food surpluses, writing, and a unifying religious force. Unfortunately, his criteria are not universal enough to be generally applicable.

- Evolutionary models of the development of sociopolitical units give us a framework for looking at the mechanisms that led to the emergence of urban societies.

- We summarize various commonly held theories about how complex societies began, describing the major potential causes for civilization: ecological stress, population stress, technological change, irrigation agriculture, and the notion of the hydraulic civilization. Exchange networks, religion, ceremony, and warfare have all been espoused as potential factors and have been approached both structurally and ecologically.

- Kent Flannery has used an ecologically based systems approach to early civilization, arguing that the emergence of complex societies was a gradual process caused by many interacting factors. One must look at the processes and mechanisms by which the necessary changes took place. The ultimate objective is to establish the set of rules by which a complex state could have come into being. Religious and informational factors seem to have been key ele-

417

ments in the regulation of environmental and economic variables in early civilization.

- Elizabeth Brumfiel argues for a social or "structural" approach to the origins of states. She believes that the social structure of a society ultimately determines its transformation over time. Pressures for state formation are triggered in some social and cultural systems but not in others. The search for causes therefore involves identifying the structures that lead to state formation and the conditions that determine their distribution in time and space. This process means focusing on ecological variables and the obstacles and opportunities they present to individuals pursuing political goals in different societies. In other words, how is ecological opportunity or necessity translated into political change?

CIVILIZATION

Civilization

Everyone who has studied the prehistory of human society agrees that the emergence of civilization in different parts of the world was a major event in human adaptation. The word *civilization* has a ready, everyday meaning. It implies "civility," a measure of decency in the behavior of the individual in a civilization. Such definitions inevitably reflect ethnocentrism or value judgments because what is "civilized" behavior in one civilization might be antisocial or baffling in another. These simplistic understandings are of no use to students of prehistoric civilizations seeking basic definitions and cultural processes.

The generally agreed-upon, special attributes that separate civilizations from other societies can be listed as follows:

- Urbanized societies, based on cities, with large, very complex social organizations. The early civilization was invariably based on a specific territory such as, the Nile Valley, as opposed to smaller areas owned by individual kin groups.

- Symbiotic economies based on the centralized accumulation of capital and social status through tribute and taxation. This type of economy allows the support of hundreds, often thousands, of nonfood producers such as smiths and priests. Long-distance trade and the division of labor, as well as craft specialization, are often characteristic of early civilizations.

- Advances toward record keeping, science and mathematics, and some form of written script.

- Impressive public buildings and monumental architecture.

These attributes are by no means common to all early civilizations, for they take different forms in each.

CITIES

Archaeological research into early civilization concentrates on the origin and development of the city. Today the city is the primary human settlement type throughout the world, and it has become so since the industrial revolution altered the economic face of the globe. The earliest cities assumed many forms, from the compact, walled settlement of Mesopotamia to the Mesoamerican ceremonial center, with a core population in its precincts and a scattered rural population in villages arranged over the surrounding landscape. The cities of the Harappan civilization of the Indus were carefully planned communities with regular streets and assigned quarters for different living groups. The palaces of the Minoans and Mycenaeans functioned as secular economic and trading centers for scattered village populations nearby.

City   A *city* is best defined by its population, which is generally larger and denser than that of a town or village. A good and generally used rule of thumb is a lower limit of 5000 people for a city. However, numbers are not a sufficient determinant: Many people can congregate in a limited area and still not possess the compact diversity of population that enables the economic and organizational complexity of a city to develop. It is this complexity that distinguishes the city from other settlement types. Most cities have a complexity in both organization and nonagricultural activities that is supported by large food surpluses. Further, the city is a functioning part of a complex system of different settlements that rely on its many services and facilities.

AN URBAN REVOLUTION?

Since archaeological research into early civilization has concentrated on excavations of ancient cities and ceremonial centers, it was perhaps inevitable that the first attempts to explain the origins of civilization focused on the city and its implications.

Early scholars who debated the origins of civilization were concerned with the cultural evolution of humankind from a state of savagery toward the full realization of human potential. This, in their Victorian eyes, was civilization. They considered that their civilization had originated in ancient Egypt and that bold mariners had spread its ideas all over the globe. These simplistic hypotheses collapsed in the face of new archaeological discoveries in Mesopotamia and the Nile Valley in the early decades of this century. With the discovery of Sumerian sites and early Egyptian farming villages, scholars came to realize that early civilization had developed over a wide area and a considerable span of time.

The first relatively sophisticated theories about the origins of urban civilization were formulated by V. Gordon Childe, of Neolithic Revolution fame (Chapter 2). Urban revolution   Childe claimed that his Neolithic Revolution was followed by an Urban Revolution, when the development of metallurgy created a new class of full-time specialists and changed the rules of human social organization (Childe, 1936, 1956). He argued that the new specialists were fed by food surpluses raised by the peasant farmers. The products of the craftsworkers had to be distributed, and raw materials had to be obtained from outside sources. Both needs reduced the self-reliance of peasant societies. Agricultural techniques became more sophisticated as a higher yield of food per capita was needed to support the nonagricultural population. Irrigation increased productivity, leading to centralized control of food supplies, production, and distribution. Taxation and tribute led to the accumulation of capital. A new class-stratified society, based on economic classes rather than kin, came into being. Writing was essential for keeping records and for developing exact and predictive sciences. Transportation by water and land was part of the new order. A unifying religious force dominated urban life as priest-kings and despots rose to power. Monumental architecture testified to their activities.

The notion of an Urban Revolution dominated archaeological and historical literature for years, but this hypothesis has flaws as an all-embracing definition of civilization and a description of its development. Childe's criteria are far from universal. Some highly effective and lasting civilizations, such as those of the Minoans and the Mycenaeans, never had cities (Redman, 1978; C. Renfrew, 1973). The Maya built elaborate ceremonial and religious centers with semiurban populations concentrated around them, surrounded by a more scattered rural population clustered for the most part in small villages. Writing was absent from the Inca civilization of Peru. Some craft specialization and religious structure are typical of most civilizations, but it cannot be said that these form the basis for an overall definition of civilization.

LATER THEORIES ABOUT THE ORIGINS OF STATES

Adams: social organization

American archaeologist Robert Adams (1966) stresses the development of social organization and craft specialization during the urban revolution. He raises objections to the Childe hypothesis, arguing that the name implies undue emphasis on the city at the expense of social change, that is, the development of social classes and political institutions. Many of Childe's criteria, like the evolution of the mathematical sciences, have the disadvantage of not being readily preserved in the archaeological record. Furthermore, Childe's urban revolution was identified by lists of traits, although the name implies emphasis on the *processes* of culture change. Childe believed technological innovations and subsistence patterns were at the core of the urban revolution. Adams directed his work toward changes in social organization; he describes early Mesopotamia and central Mexico as following "a fundamental course of development in which corporate kin groups, originally preponderating in the control of land, were gradually supplemented by the growth of private estates in the hands of urban elites." The eventual result was a stratified form of social organization rigidly divided along class lines (Service, 1962, 1975).

By the time Adams was criticizing Childe's Urban Revolution, people were beginning to investigate the many interacting factors that led to the emergence of complex states. Everyone agreed that complex societies appeared during a period of major economic and social change, but different scholars emphasized various possible factors that contributed to the rise of civilization. These factors include ecology, population growth, technology, irrigation, trade, religious beliefs, and even warfare.

Ecology

Many have said that the exceptional fertility of the Mesopotamian floodplain and the Nile Valley was a primary reason for the emergence of the cities and states in these regions. The fertility and benign climate led to the food surpluses that were capable of supporting the craftsworkers and other specialists who formed the complex fabric of civilization (Wheatley, 1971). This notion was the foundation of what was known in the 1920s and 1930s as the Fertile Crescent theory.

Social surplus

Reality, of course, is much more complicated. The true surplus was probably one of capacities, a *social surplus*, which is one that consciously reallocates goods or services. A social surplus is created by a society's deliberate action through some form of government force. In a sense this is a taxation authority, a person or organization that wrests surplus grain or other products from those who grow or produce them. Another problem with the Fertile Crescent theory is that the environments of all the major centers of early civilizations are far too diverse—in altitude above sea level, for example—for any assemblage of environmental conditions to be set forth as the requisites for civilization's start.

The earliest civilizations in Egypt and Mesopotamia were certainly based on complex subsistence patterns (Hassan, 1988), patterns that involved integrating several ecological zones. Complex subsistence patterns like these were almost certainly active in Mesoamerica and Southeast Asia, to say nothing of Egypt, although the evidence is very incomplete. Even in the best-documented areas, evidence comes from later, well-documented periods, and we can only surmise that complexities were similar in earlier times. Several ecological zones became integrated, each producing a different food as a main product. A localized center of power could control different ecological zones and the products from them, a more deliberate hedge against famine that was indispensable for planning food surpluses. This is not at all the same as saying that favorable ecological conditions caused trade and redistributive mechanisms, and therefore some form of centralized authority, to develop. Rather, ecology was only one component in a close network of the many changes that led to civilization.

Population Growth

Malthus and Boserup

Thomas Henry Malthus argued as long ago as 1798 that human reproductive capacity far exceeds the available food supply. Many people have argued that new and more intensive agricultural methods created food surpluses. These in turn led to population growth; more leisure time; and new social, political, and religious institutions, as well as the arts.

Ester Boserup, among others, has criticized this point of view. She feels that population growth provided the incentive for irrigation and intensive agriculture (Spooner, 1972). Her theories have convinced others that social evolution was caused by population growth. No one has explained, though, why the original populations should have started to grow. By no means do all farming populations, especially those using slash-and-burn cultivation, live at the maximum density that can be supported by the available agricultural land; population often is regulated artificially. Claiming that population growth explains how states were formed necessitates finding out why such decisions would have been made.

Slash-and-burn, or *swidden,* agriculture, with its shifting cultivation, is very delicately balanced with the rest of its ecosystem. Populations are dispersed and have relatively little flexibility in movement or growth because the land has low carrying capacity and relatively few ecological niches to carry edible crops (Allan, 1965). More lasting field agriculture, like that in Mesopotamia, is far more intensive and exploits much more of the environment in an ordered and systematic way. The more specialized ecosystem created by these efforts supports more concentrated populations. It creates conditions in which more settlements per square mile can exist on foods whose annual yields are at least roughly predictable.

Most significant concentrations of settlements that might be called prototypes for urban complexes developed in regions like Egypt and Mesopotamia where permanent field agriculture flourished. However, unlike the period immediately after food production began, there is no evidence for a major jump in population immediately before civilization appeared. Also, a dense population does not seem to have been a precondition for a complex society or redistribution centers for trade. We have no reason to believe that a critical population density was a prerequisite for urban life.

Technology

In Mesopotamia, again our best-documented area, agricultural technology did not advance until long after civilization began. The technological innovations that did appear (the wheel, for example) were of more benefit to transportation than to production. Copper and other exotic materials were at first used for small-scale production of cult objects and jewelry. Not until several centuries after civilization started were copper and bronze more abundant, with demand for transportation and military needs burgeoning. Then we see an advance in technology or an increase in craftspeople. Technology did evolve, but only in response to developing markets, new demands, and the expanded needs of the elite.

Irrigation

Most scholars now agree that three elements on Childe's list seem to have been of great importance in the growth of all the world's civilizations. The first was the creation of food surpluses, used to support new economic classes whose members were not directly engaged in food production. Agriculture as a way of life immediately necessitates storing crops to support the community during the lean times of the year. A surplus above this level of production was created by both increased agricultural efficiency and social and cultural changes. Specialist craftsworkers, priests, and traders were among the new classes of society that came into being as a result.

Second, agricultural economies may have tended to concentrate on fewer, more productive crops, but they remained diversified so that the ultimate subsistence base was still relatively wide. The ancient Egyptians relied on husbandry, especially in the Nile Delta. The diversity of food resources not only protected the people against the dangers of famine but also stimulated the development of trade and exchange mechanisms for food and other products and the growth of distributive organizations that encouraged centralized authority.

The third significant development was intensive land use, which probably increased agricultural output. Intensive agriculture usually implies irrigation, often hailed as one fundamental reason for a civilization's inception. Archaeologists have long debated how significant irrigation was in getting urban life started. Julian Steward and Karl Wittfogel argue that irrigation was connected with development of stratified societies (Steward et al., 1955; Wittfogel, 1957). The state bureaucracy had a monopoly on hydraulic facilities and created the hydraulic state; in other words, the social requirements of irrigation led to the development of states and urban societies. Robert Adams (1966) takes a contrary view. He feels that the introduction of great irrigation works was more a consequence of dynastic state organizations, however much the requirement of large-scale irrigation subsequently may have influenced the development of bureaucracies.

Irrigation and the hydraulic state

Early irrigation in Mesopotamia was conducted on a small scale (R. M. Adams, 1966, 1981; Adams and Nissen, 1972). Natural channels were periodically cleaned and straightened; only small artificial feeder canals were built. Maximum use was made of the natural hydrology of the rivers. Most settlement was confined to the immediate vicinity of major watercourses. Irrigation was organized by individual small communities. Large-scale artificial canalization did not take place until long after urban life appeared. The same is true of ancient Egypt, where construction of large artificial canals seems to have been the culmination of long evolution of intensive agriculture (Kemp, 1989).

Building and maintaining small canals requires neither elaborate social organization nor population resources larger than those of one or several communities. Large-scale irrigation requires technical and social resources of a quite different order. Huge labor forces must be mobilized, organized, and fed. Maintenance and supervision require constant attention, as do water distribution and resolution of disputes over water rights. Because those living downstream are at the mercy of those upstream, large irrigation works are viable only as long as all who enjoy them remain within the same political unit. A formal state structure with an administrative elite is essential.

Growth of Trade

The origins and evolution of complex societies in human prehistory have long been linked to burgeoning trade in essential raw materials such as copper and iron ore or in luxuries of all types. However, claiming that a dramatic increase in trading was a primary cause of civilization grossly oversimplifies a complicated proceeding. Trade is two things: a helpful indicator of new social developments and a factor in the rise of civilization. Many commodities and goods are preserved in the archaeological record, including gold and glass beads, seashells, and obsidian mirrors. These finds have enabled archaeologists to trace trade routes through the Near East, Europe, and other regions. With the many analytic methods for looking at the sources of obsidian, stone ax blanks, and metals, people now realize that prehistoric trade was much more than a few itinerant tradespeople passing objects from village to village (Sabloff and Lamberg-Karlovsky, 1975).

Trade and exchange networks

Trade as an institution could have begun when people sought to acquire goods from a distance for prestige and individual profit. The decision to acquire any commodity from afar depends both on how urgent the need for it is and on the difficulties in acquiring and transporting it. Much early trade was based on obtaining specific commodities, such as copper ore or salt, that had peculiar and characteristic problems of acquisition and transport. There was no such thing as trading in general. Trade in any one commodity was almost a special branch on its own. Clearly such items as cattle or slaves are more easily transported than tons of iron ore or cakes of salt; the former move on their own, but metals require human or animal carriers or wheeled carts. To ignore these differences is to oversimplify the study of prehistoric trade.

In more complex societies, the ruler and his immediate followers were generally entitled to trade and to initiate the steps leading to acquisition of goods from a distance. The king might employ merchants or traders to do the work for him, but the trade was in his name. The lower-class traders of Mesopotamian society were more menial and were often bound by guilds or castes. These were carriers, loan administrators, dealers—people who kept the machinery of trade going. Both the royal merchant and the lower-class trader were distinct from peoples such as the Phoenicians, who relied on trade as a continuous activity and a major form of livelihood.

Trade before markets were developed can never be looked at as the one cause of civilization or even as a unifying factor. It was far more than just a demand for obsidian or copper, for the causes of trading were infinitely varied and the policing of trade routes was a complex and unending task. It is significant that most early Mesopotamian and Egyptian trade was based on rivers, where bulk transportation was easier. When the great caravan routes opened, the political and military issues—tribute, control of trade routes, and tolls—became paramount. The caravan predates the great empires, a form of organized trading that kept to carefully defined routes set up and armed by state authorities for their specific tasks. The travelers were bent only on delivering and exchanging imports and exports. These caravans were a far cry from the huge economic complex that accompanied Alexander the Great's army across Asia or the Grand Mogul's annual summer progress from the heat of Delhi in India to the mountains, moving half a million people including the entire Delhi bazaar.

Markets represent a more complex form of trading. The market encourages people to develop one place for trading at the relatively stable, almost fixed prices for staple commodities. This does not, however, mean regulated prices. The trade market is a network of market sites (marketplaces) at which the exchange of commodities, especially the *mechanisms* of the exchange relationship, from an area where supplies are abundant to one where demand for the same materials is high is regulated to some degree.

This emphasis on mechanisms led C. C. Lamberg-Karlovsky (Sabloff and Lamberg-Karlovsky, 1975), William Rathje, and others to study market networks and the mechanisms by which supplies are channeled along well-defined routes; how profits are regulated and fed back to the source, providing further incentive for more supplies; and so on. There may or may not be a marketplace; the focus of the trading system and the mechanisms by which trade interacts with other parts of the culture are formed by the state of affairs surrounding the trade. Taking a systems approach to trading activity means regarding archaeological finds as the material expressions of interdependent factors. These include the need for goods, which prompts a search for supplies, themselves the product of production above local needs, created to satisfy external demands. Other variables are the logistics of transportation and the extent of the trading network, as well as the social and political environments. With all these variables, no one aspect of trade is an overriding cause of culture change or of evolution in trading practices. Hitherto, archaeologists have concentrated on trade in the context of objects or as an abstraction—trade as a cause of civilization—but have had no profound knowledge about even one trading network from which to build more theoretical abstractions.

Systems
approach

The reality is that long-distance trade was carefully melded with fluctuating demands and availabilities of supplies. It is not enough to think of trade in terms of the distribution of exports and imports (Kohl, 1978). Any study of prehistoric trade must consider also the production and consumption of the goods involved. Were they essential raw materials or exotic luxuries, finished manufactures or ax blanks that were completed at their destination? Was the trade continuous or seasonal, carried on by specialist traders, only by the wealthy, or by everyone? Changes in the volume and nature of trade can influence and modify not only production in a society but its social and economic structures as well. For example, we know that the Aztec merchant could purchase the title *Lord*, presumably as a measure of his status as a successful trader. There was room for private dealing, specialist merchants, commodities markets, perhaps even smuggling and tax evasion. Archaeologists cannot understand a trading network without analyzing the social and economic structures of each society participating in the exchange, for in many cases they became interdependent, often without realizing that they were. Until there is much more systematic study of the data for early trade, no one will fully understand trade's influence on nascent civilization anywhere.

Warfare

Carneiro:
"coercive theory"

Robert Carneiro (1970) has suggested a "coercive theory" of state origins. Based on the archaeology of Peruvian coastal valleys, it argues that areas such as these valleys, where the amount of agricultural land is very limited and circumscribed by desert, are the ones where states may well form through a predictable series of events. Carneiro's scenario begins with autonomous farming villages scattered over the valley landscape. As the population grows and more land is taken up, the communities start fighting and raiding one another's fields as they compete for limited acreage. Soon some village leaders emerge as successful warlords, become chieftains, and preside over larger tribal politics. The valley population continues to grow and warfare continues to intensify until the entire region falls under the sway of one warrior-ruler, who presides over a single state centered within the valley. Then this ambitious ruler and his successors start raiding neighboring valleys. Eventually a powerful state emerges and rules over several valleys, which creates much larger civilizations.

The Carneiro hypothesis is difficult to test, but an attempt to do so in the Santa Valley, Peru, has produced an interesting picture of changing settlement patterns. Suffice it to say here that there are no signs of the kinds of dispersed, autonomous village that Carneiro's scenario begins with. The processes that shaped the emergence of state societies in the Santa Valley appear to have been much more complex and multifaceted than just tribal warfare. David Wilson (1983) points out that the only "coercive" processes came in about A.D. 400, when the Moche people carved out a multivalley state by military conquest of neighboring valleys. Their conquest took place long after complex, irrigation-based societies flourished in the Santa Valley. As with irrigation hypotheses, reality is much more complex than the straightforward scenario Carneiro developed.

There is an attractive simplicity to the idea that the early town or city was a mighty fortress to which the surrounding tribes could run in times of stress. This has been the argument for the massive stone walls and tower that protected early Jericho (Chapter 10), for example. Thus, goes the argument, the groups that flocked within the walls came to depend on one another and their city as a fundamental part of society. However, warfare can be rejected as a primary cause of civilization without much discussion since large military conflicts appear to have been a result of civilization, not a direct cause of it. For one thing, the earliest ceremonial centers apparently were not fortified. For another, in earlier times the diffuse social organization of village communities had not yet led to the institutional warfare that resulted from the concentration of wealth and power in monopolistic hands. Only when absolute and secular monarchs came to power did warfare become endemic, with raiding and military campaigns designed to gain control of important resources or to solve political questions. This type of warfare is a far cry from the tribal conflict common to many peasant societies. It presupposes authority.

THE CEREMONIAL CENTER

The nucleus of the first cities was a complex of public buildings that fulfilled both secular and religious functions (Eliade, 1954, 1959). These centers were either very compact, like the Mesopotamian *ziggurat,* or dispersed, like Mayan examples. Those of the Mesopotamians and Chinese were relatively compact, with a reasonably dense population around them. Many Maya centers, such as Tikal in Guatemala, were huge urban complexes, with dense city and rural populations (N. Hammond, 1982). The priestly elite and rulers who lived at the center were surrounded by retainers and craftsworkers. The rural population in the environs was probably bound to the center both economically and by kinship ties. The ceremonial functions of the center were of fundamental importance in validating these links. As such a center became a focus for a group of independent settlements, it supplied reassurance, or what Chinese historian Paul Wheatley (1971) calls "cosmic certainty." It was "the sanctified terrain where [the common people were] guaranteed the seasonal renewal of cyclic time, and where the splendor, potency, and wealth of their rulers symbolized the well-being of the whole community." The rural population felt no alienation from those who lived at the center; the distinction was between the ruler and the ruled.

Eliade and the ceremonial center

This classic interpretation of the ceremonial center is long established, notably in writings by Mircea Eliade (1959). To this school of thought, the ceremonial center was not a prime mover of civilization but an instrument of "orthogenetic transformation." The religious and moral models of society provided a sacred canon circumscribing economic institutions and laying out the social order. It ensured the continuity of cultural traditions and was recited in temples, where the word of the gods rang out in reassuring chants passed from generation to generation. The ceremonial center was a tangible expression of this continuity.

Eventually the ceremonial center was taken over by the rising secular kings, who were sometimes installed by force. As the kingship's power grew, the ceremonial center's political power declined, although its religious functions were faithfully retained. In Mesopotamia, church and state separated when the power of the temple ruler, or *en*, was restricted to religious matters after 5000 years ago. The *lugal*, or king, assumed the secular and often militaristic leadership of the state (Kramer, 1963).

We can detect secularization of the ceremonial center in the appearance of the palace, where the secular king resided. The king himself might have enthusiastically believed in the state faith, but his functions were almost entirely secular, even if he used religion to justify his actions. He might have assumed a divine role himself. When the palace appears, we find the royal tombs standing as garish and splendid monuments to the awesome political and social power behind them.

With the changeover from hunting and gathering to food production, the relationship between people and their land changed fundamentally. Complex issues of land ownership—of inheritance of gardens from one generation to the next or of field boundaries—changed political and social institutions and the religious beliefs associated with them. In many societies, the relationship between the living and the dead, the ancestors, played a major role in ceremonies that interceded with the spiritual world for fertile soils and good crops. There are clear signs of ancestor cults in early Jericho and other farming settlements at 'Ain Ghazal (Chapter 10), and shrines and sacred places occur at Jericho; Çatal Hüyük; and Las Haldas, Peru (Wheatley, 1971). These religious shrines were predecessors of the great ceremonial centers of Mesopotamia and Egypt, Mesoamerica, and Peru. In each part of the world where civilization appeared, ceremonial centers were preceded by inconspicuous prototypes tended by priests or cult leaders. These people must have been among the first to be freed of the burden of having to produce food, supported by the communities they served. In every region the ceremonial center was the initial focus of power, exchange, and authority, an authority vested in religious symbolism and organized priesthoods.

It is no coincidence that the Mesopotamians' earliest recorded gods were those of harvest and fertility, or that in Mexico Tlaloc was the god of rain and life itself. These preoccupations may have become the focus of new and communal belief systems. Those who served the deities of fertility thus became people of authority, the individuals who controlled economic surpluses, offerings, and the redistribution of goods. The temple became a new instrument for organizing fresh political, social, and religious structures.

As society grew more complex, more sophisticated ethics and beliefs provided a means for sanctioning the society's new goals. The temple was an instrument for disseminating these new beliefs, a means for the new leaders to justify their acts and develop coherent policies. Symbolic statements describing society served as models not only for behavior and belief but also for the ceremonial centers that perpetuated and formulated them.

SYSTEMS AND CIVILIZATIONS

Everyone seems to agree that urban life and civilization came into existence gradually during a period of major social and economic change. The earlier linear explanations invoking irrigation, trade, or religion as a major integrative force are inadequate for our purposes.

Adams: multiple
causes

Robert Adams has been a pioneer in looking at multiple causes of state formation. In 1966 he argued that irrigation agriculture, increased warfare, and "local resource variability" were three factors vital in newly appearing civilizations. Each affected society and one another with positive feedback, helping to reinforce one another. The creation of food surpluses and the emergence of a stratified society were critical developments. Irrigation agriculture and more intensive horticulture could feed a bigger population. Larger populations and increased sedentariness, as well as trade with regular centers for redistributing goods, were all pressures for greater production and increased surpluses, actively fostered by dominant groups in society. The greatly enlarged surpluses enabled those who controlled them to employ large numbers of craftsworkers and other specialists who did not themselves grow crops.

Adams develops his thesis further by arguing that some societies were better able to transform themselves into states because of the favorable variety of resources on which they could draw. Higher production and increased populations led to monopolies over strategic resources. These communities eventually were more powerful than their neighbors, expanding their territories by military campaigns and efficiently exploiting their advantages over other peoples. Such cities became the early centers of religious activities, technological and artistic innovations, and the development of writing (Figure 15.1).

Flannery: systems

Kent V. Flannery (1972) has a more complex and somewhat abstract scheme, further explaining the state's origins. He and others see the state as a very complicated living system, the complexity of which can theoretically be measured by the internal differentiation and specialization of its subsystems, such as those for agriculture, technology, religious beliefs, and so on. The ways these subsystems are linked, as well as the controls that society imposes on the system as a whole, are vital. Archaeologists who think this way make a fundamental distinction among the following:

- The *processes* of culture change, the succession of changes by which the early states developed their new complexity.

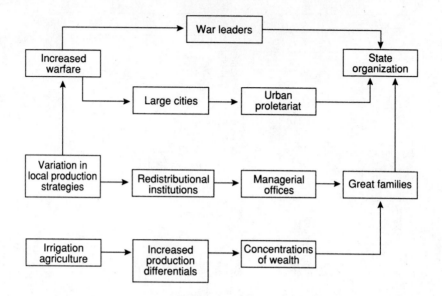

FIGURE 15.1   Hypothetical model of the state's beginnings. (Compiled from R. M. Adams, 1966.) Compare with Figure 15.2.

- The *mechanisms,* the actual ways in which the processes of increasing complexity occurred.

- The socioenvironmental *stresses* that select for these mechanisms. Socioenvironmental stresses can include food shortages, warfare, and population growth and are by no means common to all states.

"An explanation of the rise of the state then centers on the ways in which the processes . . . took place," writes Flannery.

A series of subsystems operate in human cultural systems, subsystems that interact with one another, just as the cultural system as a whole interacts with the natural environment. Each subsystem is regulated by a control apparatus that keeps all the variables in a system within bounds so that the survival of the system as a whole is not threatened. This apparatus of social control is vital, for it balances subsistence needs with religious, political, social, and other ideological values. There is a well-defined hierarchy of regulation and policy, ranging from those decisions under the control of individuals to institutions within society with specialized functions (such as the priesthood) on up to the basic, highest-order propositions, those of societal policy. These abstract standards or values lie at the heart of any society's regulation of its cultural system. Not only crops and domesticated animals but also all sorts of subtle relationships and regulatory measures make up the basis of a civilization (see Figure 15.2 for an example from Mesopotamia).

The management and regulation of a state is a far more elaborate and centralized undertaking than that of a hunter-gatherer band or a small chiefdom. Indeed, the

Control
apparatus

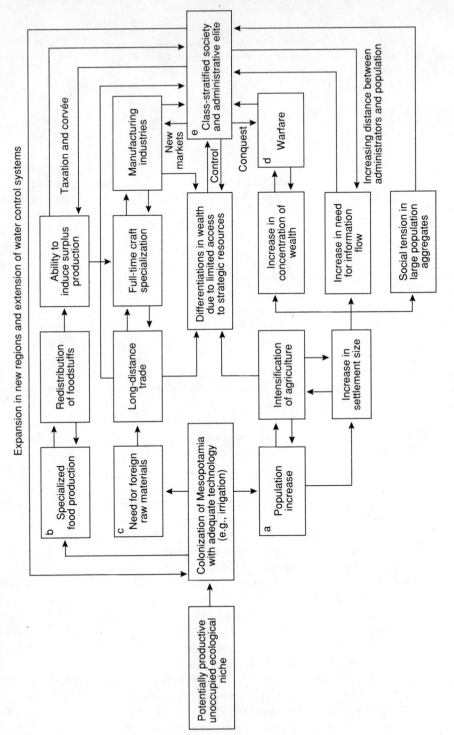

FIGURE 15.2   A systems diagram showing the interrelationships between cultural and environmental variables that led to increased stratification of class structure in early Mesopotamian urban society. (Developed by Redman, 1978.)

most striking difference between states and less complicated societies is the degree of complexity in their ways of reaching decisions and their hierarchic organizations, not in their subsistence activities. Any living system is subjected to stress when one of its many variables exceeds the range of deviation that the system allows it. The stress may make the system evolve new institutions or policies. Such coping mechanisms may be triggered by warfare, population pressure, trade, environmental change, or other variables. These variables create what Flannery calls an "adaptive milieu" for evolutionary change. His specific mechanisms include "promotion" and "linearization," when an institution in a society may assume new powers or some aspect of life may become too complex for a few people to administer. Both mechanisms lead to greater centralization, caused by selective pressures on the variables that produced the coping mechanisms.

The ultimate objective of a systems analysis of how a civilization began could be the establishment of rules by which the origins could be simulated, but such rules are a goal for the future. Flannery lists 15 beginning rules that could affect the cultural evolution of a simple human population forming part of a regional ecosystem (for this list, see Flannery, 1972). These rules can lead to new models for understanding the cultural evolution of civilization. Such models are certain to be most complex. We now must be specific about the links between subsystems—distinguishing between the mechanisms and processes and the socioenvironmental pressures that are peculiar to each civilization and have, until now, been the means by which we have sought to explain the origins of civilization (Redman, 1978). Religion and control of information now appear to be key elements in the regulation of environmental and economic variables in early civilizations and, indeed, in any human society.

Flannery's ecologically based theories have enjoyed a relatively long life compared with some other hypotheses, but they face the objection that testing multicausal models is very difficult indeed. William Sanders and David Webster (1978) point out that Flannery's approach relies heavily on cultural evolution and invokes a number of universal processes that affected the formation of complex societies (see also Binford, 1983), when in fact the environment in Mexico and other centers of early state formation was much more complex and variable. In their classic study of the basin of Mexico, Sanders and others (1979) show how the Aztec created and organized huge agricultural systems that spread over the shallow waters of the basin's lakes. The variability of the basin environment meant that the Aztecs had to exploit every environmental opportunity afforded them. Thus, he argues, the state organized large-scale agriculture to support a population of up to 250,000 just in and close around the Aztec capital, Tenochtitlán.

ECOLOGICAL AND STRUCTURAL
APPROACHES

Two theoretical approaches to the emergence of states have dominated archaeological thinking in recent years (Brumfiel, 1983). The first originates in the pioneer work of Julian Steward in the 1950s, relating state formation to the challenges offered by the local environment. Population growth and pressure are thought to be the dynamics that fuel the process of state formation. The initial stages of state formation are claimed to be accelerated by the ecological benefits the people accrue from a more centralized (state) organization. The second approach argues that states came into being as a result of certain social and cultural conditions. This "structural" approach, which owes much to Karl Marx and Friedrich Engels, argues that even societies with stable populations and balanced relationships with their environments possess an internal dynamic that fuels their progress toward greater social complexity. In other words, social components of society are more important than general conditions within a human population as a whole.

Ecological approach

The ecological approach to state formation has focused attention on the effectiveness of centralized organization as a way of solving social and environmental problems. A powerful leader has the information about state-held resources at his or her disposal to make decisions along with the ability to command people's labor and to collect and redistribute the results of that labor. Thus, goes the argument, states arise in social and environmental contexts in which centralized management solves problems effectively.

Centralized organization was at the core of Wittfogel's (1957) arguments for hydraulic civilizations, but as we have seen, his theories proved invalid when it was shown that large-scale irrigation developed in Egypt and Mesopotamia long after urban civilizations had emerged. Management has been the focus of many other theories, too—theories that invoke the need to distribute food within a region; to organize the procurement of metals, salt, or other essentials from outside; to maintain defense or conduct wars of conquest (Carneiro, 1970); or to perform a multitude of interlocking functions (Flannery, 1972). Kent Flannery's systems approach to state formation epitomizes the management view, for it argues that effective leadership endowed emerging states in many parts of the world with the ability to deal with a great diversity of ecological and population problems.

Flannery's hypotheses have been elaborated even further because we must account for one unquestionable fact. Complex states arose only in a few locations at certain moments; state formation is not a universal phenomenon. Those who espouse the ecological approach have focused on the complex interactions between population growth and the local environment. For example, William Sanders and Barbara Price (1968) argue that, in the Valley of Mexico, rapid population growth caused serious problems for small-scale societies after centuries of relatively egalitarian political organization. States emerged because they were beneficial as a way of organizing both increased food supplies through intensified agriculture and trade and external relations with neighbors. Thus, states would emerge only in certain environmental settings, those with especially severe population problems or shortages of agricultural land. Effective, centralized management of food production, through state-organized irrigation systems and other means, and of trade could bring ecological imbalance under control within a short time.

The ecological approach has problems. How, for example, does one tell which environments would foster state formation? Fertile floodplains like Mesopotamia? Coastal river valleys like those in Peru? Or areas where land is in short supply (also coastal Peru)? States have arisen in regions where there are few geographic constraints, like the Maya lowlands of Mesoamerica, and in the Nile Valley. Further, civilizations have arisen without any sign of rapid population growth, in Iran and other parts of the Near East. Although agricultural intensification often accompanied state formation, it occurred in many forms—in the adoption of swamp garden agriculture (Maya lowlands), in the diversion of river water into flood basins (Egypt), and by exploitation of different ecological zones (Aegean). The classic models, like Flannery's, of the origins of state-organized societies rely on positive feedback between population growth and recurring population pressure to maintain the cultural system in a state of evolutionary change, or on some other device. These models result invariably in complex feedback diagrams, which are fine in general theory but very difficult to document with archaeological data (for a full critique, see Brumfiel, 1983).

Brumfiel: structural approach

Elizabeth Brumfiel (1983) names the "social" approach to the origins of the state the "structural approach." Under this rubric, the social structure of a society ultimately determines its transformation over time. Perhaps the most commonly invoked structure is that of social conflict, first espoused by Marx and Engels more than a century ago. They believed that new technological innovations like metallurgy led to new economic institutions like slavery that divided society into ranked classes. The state, with its special mechanisms for maintaining law and order, came into being as a way of reducing social conflict. Although Engels was obviously wrong in invoking technological innovation as a catalyst for civilization, some anthropologists believe that the state did develop as a means of suppressing conflict between social classes. However, Elman Service (1975) among others argues that Engels was entirely wrong. Social inequality, or social ranking, evolved as a result of the intensification of social institutions like tribute and taxation of goods and labor that were commonplace in chiefdoms, societies less developed than states. In other words, social inequality was already in existence.

Service (1975) also points out that there is no evidence for class conflict wars in early civilizations, as Engels would have had us believe. Service believes that there were political reasons for state formation. Many early chieftains, even if they were perceived as having divine powers, were in insecure positions. Thus, he argues, they secured permanent dominance by developing new political structures to bolster their authority. Brumfiel (1983) notes that "if, in certain types of political systems, threats to the leader's status are regularly generated," then one might be able to formulate an alternative to the Marxist social conflict theories, a theory "that explains the state as a consequence of conflicts resulting from political, rather than economic, structures."

We know that many historic chiefdoms were politically insecure, faced with constant rebellions and threats to their authority. Tahitian chiefs faced competition for power and prestige (D. Oliver, 1977), as did Hawaiian rulers. They achieved power by a combination of aggressive warfare, trading, and control of irrigated lands (Earle, 1978). Thus, argues Brumfiel (1983), the structure of societies where political systems involve weak, permanent leadership can lead to social conflict that has both a political and an economic basis. "The process of state formation might be nothing more (or less) than a series of effective strategies designed and implemented by beleaguered rulers to survive . . . challenges to power," she writes. At first, the strategies used to maintain power might vary greatly, encompassing everything from politically motivated marriage alliances with neighbors to regional trade or outright wars of conquest. As time goes on, the rulers' options would widen since they would be less constrained by the realities of their own insecurity and local conditions. However, in many cases the limited potential of the underlying agricultural system or the realities of the environment, which might limit communication or trade (as happened in Hawaii), may profoundly affect the prospects for state formation. Environmental factors play an important role in structural models of state formation, just as they do in ecological ones.

The crux of the Brumfiel argument is simple: that pressures for state formation are triggered in some social and cultural systems but not in others, hence the historical distribution of early states in the world. Thus, a search for the causes of state formation involves identifying the structures that lead to state formation and the conditions that determine their distribution in time and space. In particular, we need to focus on population ecology, on how "ecological variables present obstacles and opportunities to individuals pursuing their political goals in various structural contexts" (Brumfiel, 1983).

Brumfiel supports her structural model with an analysis of Aztec state formation in the Valley of Mexico (for a description of Aztec civilization, see Fagan, 1984a). Aztec civilization had roots in a millennium of earlier states, but the stages of its emergence are instructive. She hypothesizes that the Aztec state came into being in four "logically discrete" steps, each made possible by the structural changes that preceded it:

1. Competition intensified between petty kingdoms in the valley. This intensification crystallized in the famous Triple Alliance, formed in A.D. 1434 by the rulers of Aztec Tenochtitlán, Texcoco, and Tlacopán.

2. The emerging rulers centralized their power by organizational reforms that reduced the power of subordinate rulers and the nobility, thereby eliminating much of the competition for political leadership.

3. The Triple Alliance further consolidated its power by undertaking ambitious public works in the Valley of Mexico, not only wars of conquest but temple building, causeway and canal construction, and massive swamp agriculture.

4. The final development was the emergence of a complex bureaucracy that oversaw the affairs of state, with specialized administrative personnel and several levels of decision making.

By the time of the Spanish conquest, in 1519–1521, the population of the Valley of Mexico was about four times that of earlier periods; the state was performing many of the ecological functions that one might expect of powerful bureaucratic and political systems (Brumfiel, 1983; Sanders, Parsons, and Santley, 1979). This structural model directs attention away from purely ecological factors to the specific problem of what implications ecological variables have for prestate political orders. In other words, the question that still faces students of state formation is how ecological opportunity or necessity is translated into political change. What were the goals of the political actors, who were pursuing their individual goals while states were coming into being? Which ecological variables were obstacles? Which were opportunities? Until we have the answers to these questions, it will be difficult to develop any general theories of state formation.

THE COLLAPSE OF CIVILIZATIONS

The great British historian Arnold Toynbee (1962) is only one of many scholars who have written about cycles of history. Toynbee was referring to civilizations that rise to power, enjoy a period of prosperity, and then suddenly decline. Eventually, another civilization arises to take its place, which in turn goes through the same cycle of rise and fall. The cyclical view of history has recently enjoyed a new popularity in the hands of David Kennedy, whose *Rise and Fall of the Great Powers* (1987) has been required reading for policymakers in Washington, D.C. The record of early civilizations could easily be interpreted in cyclical terms, for states have risen and then collapsed with bewildering rapidity in all parts of the world within the last 5000 years. In Mesopotamia, for example, Sargon of Akkad used military force and trading acumen to establish his rule over Mesopotamia about 4350 years ago. This empire lasted a mere two centuries before it collapsed in the face of widespread rebellion. Half a century later, the III Dynasty kings of Ur created an enormous bureaucratically controlled empire that extended far to the north and northwest of Mesopotamia. It, too, collapsed rapidly, with disastrous results (Chapter 16). Later, Assyrians, Persians, Parthans, and Islamic rulers all created empires that encompassed Mesopotamia. Finally, between the seventh and tenth centuries A.D., the agricultural economy in the early heartland of civilization collapsed. Within five centuries, the occupied area of the alluvial lowlands between the Tigris and Euphrates shrank to only 6 percent of its former size. The rest became desert.

A similar history of remarkable volatility can be found in Mesoamerica and Peru (Chapters 22 and 23). In the Mesoamerican highlands, for example, the great city of Teotihuacán flourished between about 200 B.C. and A.D. 700. In A.D. 600, it had a population of more than 125,000 people and was the sixth-largest city in the world. For 600 years or so, more than 85 percent of the population of the eastern and northern Valley of Mexico lived in or close to Teotihuacán. Then in about A.D. 700, the city collapsed. Within half a century, the population declined to a fourth of its former size. The lowland Maya, Monte Albán, and the Toltecs were other Mesoamerican civilizations that collapsed with extraordinary rapidity.

Few archaeologists, preoccupied as they are with the rise of civilizations, have ever paused to study their collapse. Only the collapse of the classic Maya has received serious attention (Chapter 22), yet "collapse is recurrent in human history, it is global in its occurrence, and it affects the spectrum of societies from simple foragers to great empires" (Tainter, 1988). When a complex society collapses, it suddenly becomes smaller, simpler, and often more egalitarian. Population densities fall; trade and economic activity dries up; information flow declines; and as Tainter puts it, "for those who are left the known world shrinks." What were the conditions under which early civilizations collapsed? Was it the result of food shortages, a catastrophic event, social conflict, or warfare? (For a summary of the many theories, see Tainter, 1988.)

Joseph Tainter, one of the few archaeologists to study collapse, points out that an initial investment in a society in growing complexity is a rational way of trying to solve the needs of the moment. At first the strategy works. Agricultural production increases through more intensive farming methods; an emerging bureaucracy works well; expanding trade networks bring wealth to the new elite, who use their authority and economic clout to undertake great public works, such as pyramids and temples, that validate their spiritual authority and divine associations. Maya civilization prospered greatly in the Mesoamerican lowlands for many centuries until a point of diminishing return was reached.

As the most costly solutions to society's needs are exhausted, so does it become more and more imperative that new organizational and economic answers be found, which may have much lower yields and cost a great deal more. As these stresses develop, argues Tainter, a complex society such as that of the Maya is increasingly vulnerable to collapse. There are few reserves to carry society through famines, floods, or other natural disasters. Eventually, collapse ensues, especially when important segments of the society perceive that centralization and social complexity simply do not work any more and that they are better off on their own. The trend toward decentralization, toward collapse, becomes compelling. Tainter calls collapse not a catastrophe but a rational process that occurs when increasing stress requires some organizational change. The population declines and other catastrophic effects that either just preceded, accompanied, or followed collapse may have been traumatic at the time, but they can be looked at as part of what Tainter calls an "economizing process."

There is, of course, more to collapse than merely an "economizing process." Complete collapse can only occur in circumstances in which there is a power vacuum. In many cases, there may be a powerful neighbor waiting in the wings. The Ottoman Empire headed by the Sultan of Turkey was a dominant force in Near Eastern politics for centuries after the fifteenth century. The empire never collapsed; it simply declined, finally to vanish in the morass of World War I. Victorian statesmen called it "the sick man of Europe." Over many generations, the Ottomans lost territory to eager competitors. In earlier times, numerous small city-states or polities traded and competed with one another within a small area. Sumerian city-states in Mesopotamia, Mycenaean palace-kingdoms in Greece and the Aegean, the Maya in Mesoamerica— all lived in close interdependence, in a state that Colin Renfrew and Simon Shennan (1982) have called "peer-polity interaction." These situations are often competitive, maintained by trade, warfare, and constant diplomacy. Under these circumstances, to collapse is an invitation to be dominated by one's competitors, so complexity is maintained at almost any cost. It is interesting to note that both Mayan and Mycenaean states existed as peer polities for centuries, then all collapsed within a brief time of one another. There is only loss of complexity when every polity in the interacting cluster collapses at the same time. As Colin Renfrew puts it, "The specific state is legitimized in the eyes of its citizens by the existence of other states which patently do function along comparable lines."

The collapse of early civilizations may, then, be closely connected to declining returns from social complexity.

GUIDE TO FURTHER READING

Adams, Robert M. 1966. *The Evolution of Urban Society.* Chicago: Aldine.
   An essay on the origins of civilization that stresses social and economic change, based on the author's fieldwork in Mesopotamia and comparative data from the New World.

Brumfiel, Elizabeth. 1983. "Aztec State Making: Ecology, Structure, and the Origin of the State." *American Anthropologist* 85 (2):261–284.
   A lucid and provocative analysis of the origins of states that uses the Aztec as a model. Represents much current thinking on the subject.

Childe, V. Gordon. 1936. *Man Makes Himself.* London: Watts.
   Perhaps the classic exposition of the revolution theory of civilization by a master at eloquent writing. Outdated but seminal.

Flannery, Kent V. 1972. "The Cultural Evolution of Civilizations." *Annual Review of Ecology and Systematics.* Palo Alto, CA: Annual Reviews, pp. 399–426.
   A masterly summary of the systems approach to early civilization that demonstrates the complexities of explaining the past.

Redman, Charles L. 1978. *The Rise of Civilization: From Early Farmers to Urban Society in the Ancient Near East.* San Francisco: Freeman.
   A book that covers all the theories of the 1960s and 1970s about the origins of civilization and the key sites and concepts for the advanced student. Strongly recommended as a follow-up to this volume.

Sanders, William T., Parsons, Jeffrey R., and Santley, Robert S. 1979. *The Basin of Mexico: Ecological Processes in the Evolution of a Civilization.* New York: Academic Press.
   An exemplary area study of highland Mesoamerican civilization that is crammed with wisdom about the study of complex societies. Also an unusually thorough archaeological study. Technical, but strongly recommended.

Years A.D./B.P.	Egypt/Nile	Sub-Saharan Africa	Southeast Asia
1950			
			Historic times
		European contact	
			Angkor
		Zimbabwe	
	Turkish Empire		
A.D. 1000		Emergence of West African states	
	Islamic rule		Mekong Delta states
		Bantu diaspora	
A.D. 1			
	MEROE	Ironworking in tropical Africa	Indigenous states?
	Late period of Egyptian civilization		
	Chapter 12	Chapter 12	Chapter 13

438

Years B.C.	Indus/Baluchistan	Iranian Plateau	Susa	Mesopotamia	Levant	Egypt	Anatolia	Aegean

2000 B.C.

PERSIANS
BABYLON
LATE PERIOD
CLASSICAL GREECE

KING DARIUS'S INVASION OF INDIA

3000

Ironworking
Painted gray wares

ARYANS

ISRAEL
Ugarit
ASSYRIAN EMPIRE MITANNI

SEA PEOPLES
HITTITES
MYCENAE-ANS

NEW KINGDOM

THERA
MINOANS

HAMMURABI
III DYNASTY UR
SARGON
LUGALZAGESI

MIDDLE KINGDOM

Kanesh

4000

MATURE HARAPPAN
KULLI

Alaca
Huyuk
Hissarlik

OLD KINGDOM

SUMERIAN CIVILIZATION

EARLY HARAPPAN SHARI-I-SHOKHTA ELAMITE KINGDOM

Tepe Yahya *Susa*

5000

Mehrgarh

Uruk

UNIFICATION

Village settlements Village settlements

Village settlements Village settlements

'Ubaid

Chapter 12 Chapter 11

6000

Chapter 10

439

CHAPTER 16 · MESOPOTAMIA AND THE FIRST CITIES

Preview

- Approximately 8000 years ago highland peoples began to settle in northern Mesopotamia in areas where agriculture was possible through the use of seasonal rainfall. These Hassuna people lived in close contact with other societies downstream that developed irrigation agriculture.

- Approximately 7500 years ago Halafian painted wares appeared over a wide area of upland northern Mesopotamia and Anatolia; they are thought to have coincided with the emergence of chiefdoms in this area. Two hundred years later the first farmers settled in the Mesopotamian delta.

- The first inhabitants of the delta practiced small-scale irrigation and lived in groups of communities linked by trade networks. In time, some, like Eridu, became ceremonial centers and towns. By 6500 years ago, the population of the emerging city of Eridu may have been as large as 5000 people.

- A rapid evolution to urban life ensued—marked by rapid population growth, congregation of people in small cities, and development of long-distance trade. The emerging city of Uruk and its satellite villages epitomize the period between 5600 and 5000 years ago, when its temple (*ziggurat*) was the center of ritual and economic life. This new urban society was organized in distinctive, stratified social classes.

- Writing developed around 5400 years ago as a recording system for long-distance business transactions. It is thought to have evolved from a system of clay tokens that had been in use for several thousand years. Copper metallurgy developed at about the same time on the highlands and soon came into widespread use.

- By 4900 years ago, Sumerian civilization was in full swing. As such, it did not flourish in isolation, for it was part of what we call a "nascent world system," which linked polities as far afield as the Iranian Plateau and the Indus in the east with the Mediterranean and the Nile Valley in the west. This interdependence was fostered by regular exchange and organized trade.

- Mesopotamia never achieved political unification under the Sumerians. Rather, dozens of city-states vied for political and economic supremacy and competed with other societies in northern Mesopotamia and close to the Zagros Mountains.

- Sumerian civilization flourished until about 4000 years ago, when it was eclipsed by Akkadian and then Babylonian power. In the late second millennium B.C. the city of Assur in the north nurtured the Assyrian Empire, which was extended by vigorous and despotic kings during the first half of the succeeding millennium. The Assyrian Empire at one time stretched from the Mediterranean to the Persian Gulf.

- The Assyrian Empire fell in 612 B.C., and the power vacuum was filled by the Babylonians under the rule of Nebuchadnezzar. Babylon fell to Cyrus of Persia in 534 B.C., and Mesopotamia became part of the Persian Empire.

Chronological
Table I

The delta regions and floodplain between the Tigris and Euphrates rivers form a hot, low-lying environment, much of it inhospitable sand, swamp, and dry mud flats. Yet this region, Mesopotamia (Greek for "land between the rivers"), was the cradle of the world's earliest urban civilization (Fagan, 1979; Lloyd, 1980). From north to south, Mesopotamia is approximately 600 miles (965 km) long and 250 miles (402 km) wide. (Figure 16.1 shows its location.) The plains are subject to long, intensely hot summers and harsh, cold winters. Before 7500 years ago, the floodplain may have been uninhabited except for a few nomadic groups. Dry agriculture, which relies on seasonal rainfall, was totally impracticable, and the plants and animals of the highlands around Mesopotamia were unable to tolerate the climatic extremes of the delta.

There are few permanent water supplies away from the great rivers and their tributaries. However, once watered, the soils of Mesopotamia proved both fertile and potentially highly productive. The agricultural potential of the areas close to rivers and streams could be realized for the first time. By 7000 years ago and perhaps earlier, village farmers were diverting the waters of the rivers. Within 2000 years the urban civilization of the Sumerians was flourishing in Mesopotamia.

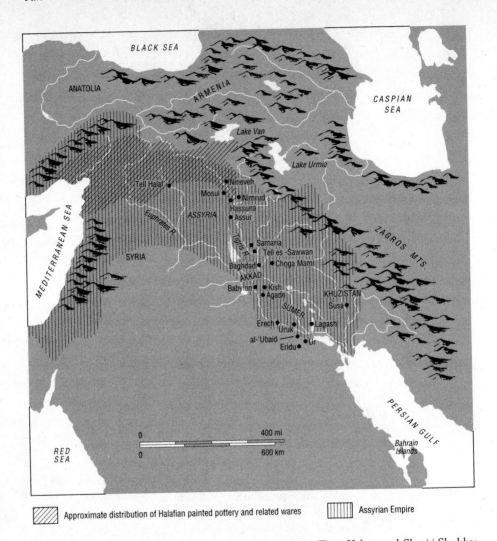

Approximate distribution of Halafian painted pottery and related wares   Assyrian Empire

FIGURE 16.1   Sites and culture distributions mentioned in this chapter. (Tepe Yahya and Shari-i-Shokhta lie to the east of the map.)

UPLAND VILLAGES

With continued improvement in the effectiveness of agriculture and development of such technological innovations as pottery, the village communities of the Zagros foothills, east of Mesopotamia, achieved a more efficient subsistence base, which fed a gradually increasing farming population. These technological and economic changes were far from spectacular: By at least 8000 years ago, farmers were living on the Assyrian plains, at first in areas where they could rely on seasonal rainfall to water their crops; later they settled by the rivers, with animals and crops that could tolerate the climate of the lowlands. There they developed simple irrigation methods to bring water to their fields.

The first farmers to settle in Assyria were scattered over the undulating plains in small village settlements like Tell Magzaliyah. Umm Dabaghiyah (Kirkbride, 1975; Lloyd, 1983; Oates and Oates, 1976; Redman, 1978) was a settlement of Onager hunters who traded processed hides. It contained a few huts and storage bins made of packed mud. Commonly the houses, which were probably entered from the roof, consisted of two or three rooms with small doors. Ovens and chimneys were integral parts of the houses. The successive occupation layers of these sites are filled with handmade pottery of coarse clay painted or incised with dots, circles, and other designs (Figure 16.2). Such wares—named Hassunan pottery, after Hassuna, the first village of this type excavated—are found over a wide area of the north, from the upper Tigris Valley to the plains west of the modern city of Mosul.

The regions between Mosul in the north and Baghdad in the south were inhabited by irrigation farmers by at least 7500 years ago. We know this from discoveries of villages in the region of Samarra, on the fringes of the Mesopotamian delta. Samarran culture painted pottery (Figure 16.2), which comes from such sites as Tell es-Sawwan and Choga Mami, reveals early farming villages situated in areas where irrigation agriculture was the only viable means of food production (Oates, 1973). The Samarran sites near Choga Mami are situated along low ridges parallel to nearby hills, where irrigation could be practiced with the least effort. Traces of canals are found at Choga Mami, as are wheat, barley, and linseed, a crop that can be grown in this area only when irrigation is used. Choga Mami itself lies between two rivers, where floodwaters could be diverted across the fields and then drained away to prevent salt buildup. This is a relatively easy form of irrigation to adopt. Presumably, later refinements in technology enabled other farming settlements to move away from naturally flooded areas into regions where more extensive irrigation was necessary. There is every indication that the Samarrans were advanced farmers who lived in substantial villages, which in the case of Choga Mami, may have covered up to 14.8 acres (6 ha) and housed more than 1000 souls. The other excavated Samarran village, Tell es-Sawwan, was surrounded by a ditch and a wall, as if defense was a major consideration.

The Samarrans occupied relatively low-lying territory between the arid delta of the south and the dry agriculture areas of the Hassunans to the north. Their newly developed irrigation techniques and heat-tolerant strains of wheat and barley enabled them to settle in areas that were hitherto inaccessible. Their sedentary and permanent settlements and great reliance on agriculture allowed them to forge community and external social and economic bonds that provided a catalyst for more complex societies to develop in future millennia.

Approximately 7500 years ago, many village farmers in the Near East began to make a characteristic style of painted pottery, abandoning the monochrome wares they had made before. The new fashion spread from southwest Turkey around the shores of Lake Van, famous for its obsidian, and as far east as the Zagros Mountains. The most brilliantly painted pottery was made in northern Iraq by the inhabitants of Tell Halaf, whose enormous kilns produced bowls, dishes, and flasks adorned with

Hassuna
8000 B.P.

Samarra
7500 B.P.

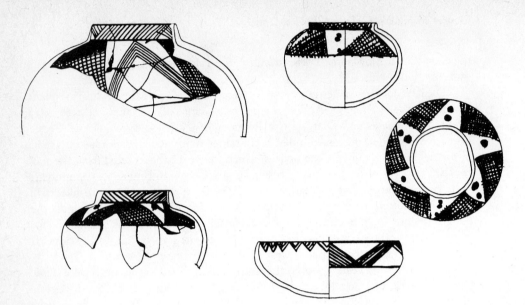

(a)

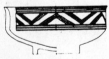

(b)

FIGURE 16.3   Halafian vessel from Iraq.

Halafian
7500 B.P.

elaborate, stylized patterns and representations of people and animals (Figure 16.3). The Halafian cultural tradition flourished in what had once been Hassunan territory, and the people maintained regular contact with the Samarrans to the south.

The Halafians still lived in much the same ways as their predecessors and made no startling agricultural or technological innovations. They developed new contacts between villages hundreds of miles apart, trading such commodities as obsidian, semiprecious stones, and other luxury items including painted pots with motifs that are standardized over large distances. Neutron activation and other chemical studies of pottery clays have shown that Halafian painted pots made at a so-far unidentified location were traded to settlements like Mersin and Choga Mami, about 600 miles (965 km) apart. Yet in the Chaga Bazar area, most of the fine pottery found in the villages of the surrounding hinterland were produced in the main settlement. It is as if production and distribution of some items favored by elite members of society were concentrated at key trade centers along water routes. In the Khabur area, the same clay studies hint that both major and minor Halafian settlements produced the goods consumed in their own hinterlands, while restricting access of nearby subordinate villages to this higher-level trade. This may be a sign that important chiefdoms had evolved among Halafian communities in the region. As with the Hopewell in North America, these new elite groups required greater communication and the sharing of status goods such as painted pottery to reinforce their authority (Redman, 1978).

FIGURE 16.2   Early Mesopotamian painted pottery: (a) vessels from Hassuna; (b) Samarra-type vessels from Hassuna.

SETTLEMENT OF THE LOWLANDS

Before 7300 years ago, the first farmers to settle in the lowlands of the south moved into the land between the Tigris and Euphrates. These first communities are little known but were located in clusters along the Euphrates channels. The largest of these clusters consisted of small rural communities located around a larger town that covered about 28 acres (10 ha) and housed perhaps between 2500 and 4000 people. The fields around these settlements were watered by small canals up to 3 miles (5 km) long. The farmers grew barley and dates and herded cattle, sheep, and goats (Wright and Pollack, 1986). Simple irrigation works made it possible for people to grow vegetables as well as cereal crops. Fish and waterfowl were important dietary supplements. These clusters of settlements are subsumed under the term 'Ubaid, after a small site of that name near Ur-of-the-Chaldees.

We do not know anything about how the first inhabitants of the Mesopotamian floodplain acquired or developed the skills needed to survive in their harsh environment. Interdependence among members of the community was essential because raw materials suitable for building houses had to be improvised from the plentiful sand, clay, palm trees, and reeds between the rivers. Digging even the smallest canal required at least a little political and social leadership. The annual backbreaking task of clearing silt from clogged river courses and canals can have been achieved only by communal effort. As both Robert Adams (1966) and Kent Flannery (1972) point out, the relationship between developing a stratified society and creating food surpluses is close. Distinctive social changes came from the more efficient systems for producing food that were essential in the delta. As food surpluses grew and the specialized agricultural economies of these 'Ubaid villages became successful, the trend toward sedentary settlement and higher population densities increased. Expanded trade networks and the redistribution of surpluses and trade goods also affected society, with dominant groups of 'Ubaid people becoming more active in producing surpluses, which eventually supported more and more people who were not farmers.

'Ubaid settlements display considerable variation. The earliest known community is Tell al 'Ouelli, near Larsa, which dates to before 7300 years ago (Forest, 1986). Some of the larger settlements had substantial buildings, alleyways, and courtyards, but rural settlements like al-'Ubaid itself consisted of mud brick and reed huts with roofs formed of bent sticks (R. M. Adams, 1981; Adams and Nissen, 1972; Redman, 1978). Al-'Ubaid and similar small clusters of hamlets shared ceremonial centers and were linked by kin and clan ties, with one clan authority overseeing the villagers' affairs and, probably, the irrigation schemes that connected them. In time, the small village ceremonial centers grew, as did the one at Eridu (first settled around 6750 years ago, when the Tell Halaf peoples were still making their painted pottery in the north). Except at the very end of 'Ubaid times, there are no signs of social ranking in cemeteries or of any great differences in wealth between different individuals.

Eridu consisted of a mud-brick temple with fairly substantial mud-brick houses around it, often with a rectangular floor plan. The craftsworkers lived a short distance from the elite clustered around the temple, and still farther away were the dwellings of the farmers, who grew the crops that supported everyone. By 6500 years ago, the Eridu temple had grown large, containing altars and offering places and a central

'Ubaid Period
?8000 to 5600
B.P.

6350 B.P.

room bounded by rows of smaller compartments. It has been estimated that the population of Eridu was as high as 5000 at this time, but exact computations are impossible.

URUK—THE MESOPOTAMIAN CITY

Uruk
5600 to 4800
B.P.

As Mesopotamian society grew in complexity, so did the need for social, political, and religious institutions that would provide an integrative function for everyone (Nissen, 1988). The ancient city of Uruk epitomizes cultural developments just before and during the early stages of Sumerian civilization. Archaeologically, we know most, of course, about the later stages of the city. During early Dynastic times, about 4800 years ago, the city core covered an estimated 617 acres (250 ha), with more people living in the hinterland. Anyone approaching Uruk in those days could see the great ziggurat, the stepped temple pyramid, for miles (Figure 16.4). Built with enormous expenditure of work as a community project, the ziggurat complex and its satellite temples were the center of Uruk life. The temples were not only storehouses and places of worship but also redistribution centers for surplus food. Hundreds of craftsworkers labored for the temple as stonemasons, copperworkers, weavers, and dozens of other specialized tasks. None of these people tilled the ground or worked on irrigation; they formed a distinctive class in a well-stratified society (Lloyd, 1983). In its earliest manifestations, between 5600 and 5000 years ago, Uruk was a nascent city on a much smaller scale but a settlement that was growing rapidly, many surrounding villages becoming part of the dense urban landscape. An earlier and smaller ziggurat towered over the city, which formed the core for the later monumental structure of early Dynastic times.

Even as early as 5000 years ago, the entire life of Uruk and its connections with cities, towns, merchants, and mines hundreds of miles away revolved around the temple. The ruler of Uruk and the keeper of the temple was the *en,* both the secular and religious leader. His wishes and policies were carried out by his priests and by a complex hierarchy of bureaucrats, wealthy landowners, and merchants. Tradespeople and craftsworkers were a more lowly segment of society, and under them were the thousands of fisherfolk, peasants, sailors, and slaves that formed the bulk of Uruk's burgeoning population.

In its early Dynastic heyday, Uruk was far more than a city. Satellite villages extended out at least 6 miles (10 km), each with its own irrigation system, but population densities around the city were lower than they were in earlier times. All provided food for those in the city, whether grain, fish, or meat. Each settlement depended on the others for survival, at first because each provided things essential for a well-balanced existence; later they needed protection from outsiders who would have plundered their goods. The Mesopotamian city had developed an elaborate system of management with a well-defined hierarchy of rulers and priests, landowners and bureaucrats, traders and peasants. This system organized and regulated society, meted out reward and punishment, and made policy decisions for the thousands of people who lived under it.

The city was a hallmark of early Mesopotamian civilization, but each urban

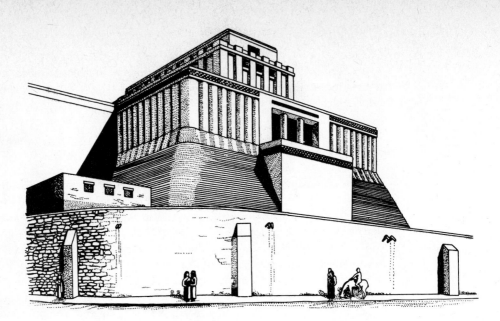

FIGURE 16.4 *Above:* Reconstruction of an Uruk temple at Eridu. Notice the great platform supporting the temple and the drainage pipes in the walls. *Below:* A photograph of the great ziggurat (temple mound) of Ur, built approximately 4000 years ago.

center had different settlement characteristics and histories. Archaeological surveys record the remarkable fact that over 80 percent of the Sumerian population lived in settlements covering at least 25 acres (10 ha), in a form of "hyperurbanism" in the third millennium B.C., a figure that declined steadily to just over 50 percent by 2000 B.C. (Adams, 1981).

By 5400 years ago, the first signs of writing appear. One theory has it that the Sumerians' commercial transactions were so complex that the possibilities for thievery and accounting mistakes were endless. It was impossible to keep all the details in one's head. Many people used marked clay tokens, which they carried around on strings. Eventually some clever officials made small clay tablets and scratched them with incised signs that depicted familiar objects such as pots or animals (Schmandt-Besserat, 1978). From there it was a short step to more simplified, conventionalized, wedge-shaped (cuneiform) signs that were modeled closer and closer to phonetic syllables and spoken language (Figure 16.5). In fact, the earliest economic texts deal with internal administrative matters, usually small numbers and inventories, not with external trade. The new script was also commonly used for compiling lists of all kinds—of occupations, places, things in the world, and so on—a common application of writing systems all over the globe, for example, as among the Mycenaeans of Greece (Chapter 20).

At first, specially trained scribes used cuneiform to record inventories and administrative and commercial transactions. Over more than 1000 years, they gradually began to explore the limitless opportunities afforded by the ability to express oneself in writing. Kings used tablets to trumpet their victories and political triumphs. Fathers chided errant sons, and lawyers recorded complicated land transactions. Sumerian poetry includes love stories, great epics, hymns to the gods, and tragic laments bemoaning the destruction of city after city (Kramer, 1963). Temple records and accounts tell us much not only of economic and social organization but also of Mesopotamian folklore and religion.

On the plateau to the north, copper tools and ornaments had been in use for centuries, first appearing as early as the fifth or sixth millennium B.C. (for chronology, see Hassan, 1987). Although many peasant societies were aware of the properties of native copper, and both the early Egyptians and American Indians made hammered ornaments from it, the softness of the metal limits the uses to which it can be put. Eventually, though, people familiar with the kiln firing of pottery developed techniques for smelting copper ore. Copper is fine and lustrous and makes admirable ornaments. At first, it was a high-status metal, valued for its prestige. Copper was in widespread use for ornamentation in Iran during the fourth millennium and was imported into southern Mesopotamia as early as 5500 years ago, perhaps earlier. It enjoyed high status, for utilitarian implements like stone-bladed sickles remained in use throughout the third millennium. Eventually, during the early second millennium, alloying with lead or tin came into widespread use, as metalsmiths learned how to produce bronze and other forms of tougher metal. Once alloying was understood, copper assumed a more important place in agriculture and warfare (Moorey, 1982). The later development of bronze weapons can be linked to the rise of warfare as a method of attaining political ends, for cities like Eridu and Uruk were not isolated from other centers. Indeed they were only too aware of their neighbors. The city-

Earliest pictographs (3000 B.C.)	Denotation of pictographs	Pictographs in rotated position	Cuneiform signs c. 1900 B.C.	Basic logographic values	
				Reading	Meaning
	Head and body of man			lu	Man
	Head with mouth indicated			ka	Mouth
	Bowl of food			ninda	Food, bread
	Mouth + food			kú	To eat
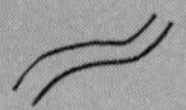	Stream of water	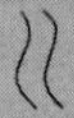		a	Water
	Mouth + water			nag	To drink
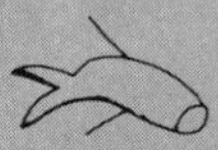	Fish			kua	Fish
	Bird			mušen	Bird
	Head of an ass			anše	Ass
	Ear of barley			še	Barley

FIGURE 16.5 Development of Sumerian writing, from a pictographic script to a cuneiform script and then to a phonetic system. The word *cuneiform* is derived from the Latin word *cuneus*, meaning "a wedge," after the characteristic impression of the script.

states of Lagash and Umma were uneasy neighbors and engaged in a tendentious border dispute that dragged on for three or four centuries (Cooper, 1983). Cities soon had walls, a sure sign that they needed protection against marauders. Earlier cylinder seals bear scenes with prisoners of war.

By this time, too, there were southern Mesopotamian "colonies" in what is now northern Iraq, at Susa across the Tigris, in the Zagros, and elsewhere on the northern and northeastern peripheries of the lowlands. Some of these colonies were entire transplanted communities; others are represented by characteristic Uruk-style artifacts far from their homelands. Artifacts and artistic styles characteristic of Uruk and also Susa have come from the Nile Delta during the centuries when long-distance caravan trade was expanding rapidly in Egypt and across the Sinai.

A NASCENT "WORLD SYSTEM" APPEARS: SUMERIAN TRADE

With the emergence of the Sumerian civilization about 5200 years ago, we have entered a new era in human experience, one in which the economic, political, and social mechanisms created by humans begin to affect the lives of cities, towns, and villages located hundreds, if not thousands, of miles apart. No human society created by *Homo sapiens sapiens* has ever flourished in complete isolation, and as we saw in Chapter 6, regular interaction and exchange between neighboring hunter-gatherer groups assumed ever-greater importance in the late Ice Age and early Holocene. In the Near East, after 10,000 years ago, long-distance exchanges in such vital commodities as obsidian, to say nothing of luxury goods like seashells, reached considerable proportions and extended over much of Anatolia and the Levant and even further afield. The real launching point in long-distance exchange and organized trade took place during the fourth millennium B.C., the first millennium in prehistory when the history of an individual society can only be understood against a background of much broader regional developments. In a real sense, a rapidly evolving "world system" linked hundreds of Near Eastern societies all the way from eastern Iran and the Indus Valley in Pakistan to Mesopotamia, the Levant, Anatolia, and the Nile Valley with ever-changing cultural tentacles. In the third millennium B.C. this system not only embraced the Near East but also extended to Cyprus, the Aegean, and mainland Greece.

This nascent world system developed as a result of insatiable demands for nonlocal raw materials in different ecological regions where societies were developing along very similar general evolutionary tracks toward greater complexity. The broad, and apparently linear, cultural sequence in southern Mesopotamia just described can be matched by equivalent developments in northern Mesopotamia and east of the Tigris. In each area, these developments and many technological innovations were triggered not only by basic economic needs but also by the competitive instincts of newly urbanized elites, who used lavish display and exotic luxuries to reaffirm their social prestige and authority.

Sumerian civilization is a mirror of this developing regional interdependence.

The Sumerians lived in a treeless, lowland environment with fertile soils but no metal, little timber, and no semiprecious stones. They obtained these commodities by trading with areas where such items were in abundance, perhaps initially on a village-by-village basis and later in far more organized fashions. Much of this trade was in the hands of temple organizations, for the temples served as centralized storehouses, and many luxury goods were used to embellish public buildings. Trading was an integral part of Sumerian life, a multifaceted activity absorbing the energies of many people. Food and many basic commodities were redistributed by different institutions for specific purposes. For example, temples would distribute food rations to those who labored for them. Petty officials were allocated land for their services. Raw materials were obtained from the highlands and the Iranian Plateau to the east for the manufacture of weapons, ornaments, and prestigious luxuries.

The increased tempo of interregional exchange is reflected in increased wealth in archaeological sites both within Sumer and outside its boundaries. Metal tools became much more common, and domestic tools as well as weapons proliferated Metallurgy benefited from important technological innovations carried along trade routes, among them the development of alloying copper with tin to make bronze. This produced tougher-edged, more durable artifacts that could be used for more arduous, day-to-day tasks. One resulting innovation was the metal- and wood-tipped plow, an implement dragged by oxen that was capable of digging a far deeper furrow than the simple hoes and digging sticks of earlier times. The plow, which incidentally was never developed in the Americas, was developed as irrigation agriculture assumed greater importance in Sumer, and the combined innovations increased agricultural yields dramatically. These yields not only supported larger urban and rural populations but also provided a means for the rulers of city-states both in Sumer and further afield to exercise more control over food surpluses and over the wealth obtained by long-distance exchange. Soon, Sumerian rulers became more despotic, controlling their subjects by military strength, religious acumen, and economic incentive (Adams, 1966).

Lowland Mesopotamia lacked the mineral and stone resources that were plentiful in distant, more highland environments in Anatolia to the northwest and on the Iranian Plateau to the east. By the same token, the Sumerians controlled not only large surpluses of grain that could be moved in ships but also a flourishing industry in textiles and other luxuries. Demand rose steadily for raw materials, which arrived in Sumerian cities along southern Mesopotamian waterways, especially up the placid Euphrates, easily navigable for long distances. This great river transmitted raw materials from the north and trade goods from the Persian Gulf to the Mediterranean. From the rivers and cities, intricate, centuries-old exchange networks and sometimes formal caravan routes carried metals, timber, skins, ivory, and precious stones over enormous distances and often rugged terrain. Even as early as Sumerian times, caravans of pack animals (in later times, often black asses) joined Anatolia to the Euphrates, the Levant to Mesopotamia, and Mesopotamia to isolated towns on the Iranian Plateau. An intricate and ever-changing system of political alliances and individual obligations of friendship linked community with community and city-state with city-state. In time, financial and logistical checks and balances were maintained by an administrative system based in the temples to bring order to what had begun as informal bartering. Specialized merchants began to handle such commodites as copper and lapis lazuli. There was wholesaling and contracting, loans were floated, and individual profit was a prime motivation. Increasingly, every city-state, and indeed entire civilizations, came to depend on what we have called a nascent world system, not so much for political stability but for survival. Reliable, long-term interdependency became a vital factor in the history of Near Eastern states at least as early as 5000 years ago.

EXCHANGE ON THE IRANIAN PLATEAU

5500 B.P.

The rise of urbanization in Sumer was by no means a unique phenomenon, for cities came into being upstream of the lowlands by 5500 years ago in areas where only dry farming was possible (Weiss, 1986). Cultural developments remarkably parallel to those in Sumer unfolded in the area between the Zagros foothills and the Tigris and Euphrates (Lamberg-Karlovsky, 1978; Wright and Johnson, 1978). These developments did not occur in isolation, for even as early as 5000 years ago there was regular interaction between the two regions.

8000 B.P.

During the sixth and early fifth millennia B.C., small farming villages flourished in the heart of Khuzistan. The people were irrigation farmers who herded goats, sheep, and cattle as well. So many of their sites are known that it seems certain that areas such as the Deh Luran Plain were intensively settled by this time. During the next thousand years or so, Khuzistan was still densely populated, and village settlements grew larger and larger. It was about this time that the famous archaeological site of Susa began to achieve special prominence.

Susa

The earliest occupation levels at Susa are broadly contemporary with the late 'Ubaid occupation of Mesopotamia. The first village on the site was 61.7 to 74.0 acres (25 to 30 ha) in area and was inhabited by metal-using farmers. Strong Mesopotamian influence can be detected in slightly later levels at Susa, as if there was at least some colonization of Khuzistan by Uruk people from the delta toward the end of the fourth millennium B.C.

Proto-Elamites
5200 B.P.

Approximately 5200 years ago, a distinctive cultural tradition known as the *Proto-Elamite* (Elamite is a language) appeared at Susa and elsewhere in Khuzistan. The Proto-Elamite state seems to have evolved in what is now southwest Iran, but within a short time its distinctive tablets, seals, and ceramic types came to be found in widely scattered sites on the Iranian highlands. Their clay tablets have turned up in settlements in every corner of the Iranian Plateau, in central Iran, and on the borders of Afghanistan. Susa itself grew into a great city, where the trade routes between Mesopotamia and the east converged. The Elamite state emerged in all its

Elamites
5000 B.P.

complexity after 5000 years ago and came under the rule of Akkadian kings from central Mesopotamia for a while, but by 4000 years ago the Elamites were strong enough to attack and destroy Ur of the Chaldees in Sumer. The Elamites' power and importance depended on their geographic position at the center of a network of trade routes that led to the Iranian Plateau, to the Persian Gulf, and to most city-states in the lowlands.

From as early as 7000 years ago, raw materials from the Iranian Plateau were traded to the lowlands. As the volume of the plateau trade increased, Susa was in an increasingly strategic position to control access routes. Proto-Elamite developments at Susa followed on the Uruk episode at the site and can be seen as a local response to the Uruk domination of lowland Khuzistan, even if the same administrative devices such as writing and cylinder seals were retained in local forms.

On the resource-rich Iranian Plateau, long-distance exchange joined widely separated communities in what has been called an "interaction sphere," which linked most of the southern part of the region for many centuries. These long-lived networks are little studied but may have linked major centers near key sources of such commodities as lapis lazuli, turquoise, chlorite, and other materials. Each center became a locus for the manufacture and exchange of prestigious objects made of these commodities, maintaining contacts with remote areas such as Sumer and Elam.

Tepe Yahya
5400 to 5200
B.P.

One such center was Tepe Yahya, which was a prosperous rural community between 5400 and 5200 years ago (Lamberg-Karlovsky, 1973, 1978). The inhabitants exploited local sources of chlorite (steatite). After 5200 years ago, Tepe Yahya grew and was engaged in much more intensive trading activities. Eventually, it became an important political and administrative center that manufactured and traded carved chlorite bowls. The bowls produced at Tepe Yahya and elsewhere were definitely luxury items, so highly prized in Mesopotamia that they may have caused keen competition among those rich enough to afford them (Kohl, 1975). Chlorite tools and ornaments were so popular that they occur over a very wide area of the Iranian Plateau as well as on islands in the Persian Gulf and at Mohenjo-daro, one of the major cities of the Harappan civilization of the Indus Valley (Chapter 18).

The plateau trading networks also extended to the important settlement of Shari-i-Shokhta, which stood by the shores of Lake Helmand south of the Hindu Kush in east Iran. An extensive trade in turquoise and lapis lazuli flourished there after 4800 years ago. The lapis came from the distant Hindu Kush embedded in limestone. Shari-i-Shokhta's artisans chipped away the limestone and turned the semiprecious stone into beads. The beads and lumps of raw lapis were then traded across the desert to Mesopotamia and also north into southern Turkmenia, probably in exchange for textiles (Tosi, 1983).

The plateau trade handled the work of local artisans but was ultimately founded on the movement of a number of vital, staple commodities, among them textiles and timber (Possehl, 1986). The nature of this trade is the subject of some controversy. Some scholars believe that the commerce was based on markets and in the hands of traders controlled by Sumer and Elam, who could affect the trade by simple application of the laws of supply and demand (Kohl, 1978). Another viewpoint suggests that the trade itself may have been in the hands of entrepreneurs, but the areas of high demand for its products were both local and at a distance in Mesopotamia and Elam. Although some of the commodities found on the Iranian Plateau may have been transported in large quantities, much exchange proceeded in more informal ways, through occasional purchases, gift exchanges, tribute, booty-taking, and individual initiative. It was not until the third millennium that much larger-scale, highly organized trade became the rule rather than the exception. The Iranian Plateau trade may have developed as an indigenous exchange system, which later spilled over to the west in response to demands from the lowlands. However, this latter trade was a question of people getting what they could get rather than a high degree of organization. In other words, supplies were irregular rather than predictable, in sharp contrast to the much more highly organized regional trade organizations that evolved after 4000 years ago (Possehl, 1986).

Whatever the mechanisms of the Iranian trade, it is clear that an extensive network of interdependence was linking widely separated city-states and polities all over the Near East by 4500 years ago. This network of interdependence and interaction was highly flexible but continued to develop over many centuries, as different city-states and larger states vied with one another to control and administer ever-larger kingdoms.

THE WIDENING OF POLITICAL AUTHORITY

By 4800 years ago, Mesopotamia held several important city-states, each headed by rulers who vied with the others for status and prestige. The Sumerians were in contact with other states and urban centers in northern Mesopotamia and across the rivers in Elam and further afield to the east. They maintained regular contacts with Anatolia, the Levant, and sporadically with the Nile Valley. Political authority was still most effective at the city level, with temple priests as the primary controllers of trade, economic life, and political matters. Inevitably, as society became more complex, the priests were increasingly concerned with secular matters, such as the organization of irrigation systems that expanded as population densities rose and more and more prime agricultural land was cultivated. As the Mesopotamian delta became an environment increasingly controlled by human activities, the people began to concentrate in larger cities under secular leaders, abandoning many smaller towns. At the same time, the volume of long-distance trade rose dramatically, to the point, some experts believe, that Sumerian rulers made a conscious decision to develop a formal maritime trade through the Persian Gulf with areas to the east such as the Indus Valley (Possehl, 1986) (Chapter 18).

In political terms, the population shifts of the third millennium B.C. may also reflect a much greater concern with defense, for both Sumerian tablets and the archaeological record tell of warfare and constant bickering between neighbors. Competition over natural resources intensified as each state raised an army to defend its water rights, trade routes, and city walls. The onerous tasks of defense and military organization passed to despotic secular kings supposedly appointed by the gods. As the wealth and power of the cities increased, so did internecine strife. Such states as Erech, Kish, and Ur had periods of political strength and prosperity when they dominated their neighbors. Then, just as swiftly, the tide of their fortunes would change and they would sink into obscurity. There was a constant threat from nomadic peoples of the surrounding mountains and deserts, who encroached constantly on settled Sumerian lands. At times, they disrupted city life so completely that any form of travel became an impossibility.

Some Sumerian cities nurtured powerful and wealthy leaders. When Sir Leonard Woolley (1934) excavated a royal cemetery in Ur of the Chaldees (Figure 16.6), he found a series of kings and queens who had been buried in huge graves with their

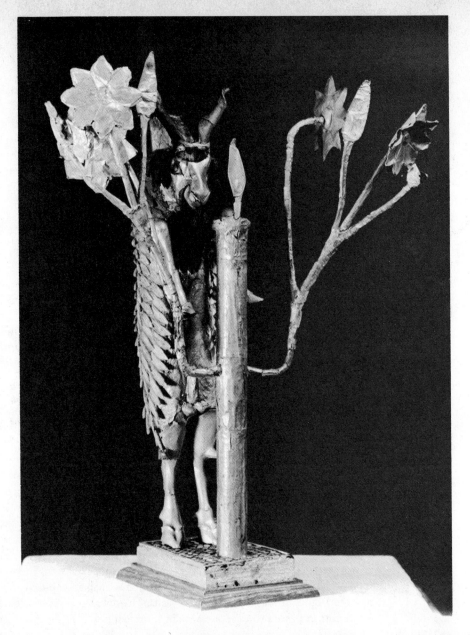

FIGURE 16.6 A famous ornament from the Royal Cemetery at Ur of the Chaldees, entitled *Ram in the Thicket*. The wood figure was covered with gold leaf and lapis lazuli, the belly in silver leaf, and the fleece in shell.

entire retinue of followers. One tomb contained the remains of 59 people who were poisoned to accompany the king, even courtiers and soldiers as well as serving women. Each wore his or her official dress and insignia and had lain down to die in the correct order of precedence, having taken poison.

Inevitably, the ambitions of some of these powerful and proud Sumerian rulers led them to entertain bolder visions than merely the control of a few city-states in the lowlands. They were well aware that they lived in a wider world of prosperous and not-so-prosperous neighbors, in a world in which control of lucrative sources of raw materials and trade routes was the secret of vast political power. The first recorded success at such an endeavor was that of Lugalzagesi (c. 4360–4335 years ago). Not content with the control of Uruk, Ur, Lagash, and several other cities, he boasted of overseeing the entire area from the Persian Gulf to the Mediterranean. The god Enlil, king of the lands, "made the people lie down in peaceful pastures like cattle and supplied Sumer with water bringing joyful abundance" (Kramer, 1963). Lugal-zagesi's boasts must be taken with a large pinch of historical salt and must be judged not in terms of conquering armies but in the context of a nascent world system of interaction and trading, which carried Sumerian political and religious ideas as far as the shores of the Mediterranean. The tenuous and sometimes more regular contacts maintained by Mesopotamia with dozens of city-states in Anatolia and the Levant foreshadow the constant political and economic rivalry that was to dominate Near Eastern history during the second millennium B.C., rivalry over control of the Levant. Here two oceans and three continents meet. The Levant had no natural harbors, so the control of its overland routes was the key to dominating a vast area of the known world, resource-rich Anatolia and grain-rich Egypt. As we shall see in Chapter 20, the history of this region was bound inextricably to the fortunes of the larger powers that surrounded it.

Lugalzagesi

4360 to 4335 B.P.

AKKADIANS AND ASSYRIANS

While Sumerian civilization prospered, urban centers waxed and waned in neighboring areas. In these regions, too, lived rulers with wider ambitions, who had a vision of a larger role.

Akkadians and Ur

By 4500 years ago, Akkadian cities to the north of Sumer began to compete with lowland cities for trade and prestige. Approximately 4370 years ago, a Semitic-speaking leader, Sargon, founded a ruling dynasty at the town of Agade, south of Babylon. By skillful commercial ventures and judicious military campaigns, his northern dynasty soon established its rule over a much larger kingdom that included both Sumer and northern Mesopotamia. After a short period of economic prosperity, the Akkadians were toppled by desert nomads. Forty years of political instability ensued before the powerful III Dynasty kings of Ur took control of Sumer and Akkad and created an empire that extended far to the north. Sargon had forged an empire by

Sargon

4370 B.P.

4300 B.P.

military conquest but had never followed up his victories with proper administrative governance. The kings of Ur were a new breed of ruler, who placed great emphasis on consolidating their new empire into a powerful and well-organized bureaucracy. We know much of this kingdom from thousands of administrative tablets from III Dynasty levels at Ur (Steinkeller, 1989). With the Akkadian and Ur empires was forged a persistent tradition of Mesopotamian civilization—the combination of trade, conquest, ruthless administration, and tribute to forge large, poorly integrated, and highly volatile empires that sought to rule an enormous territory between the Mediterranean and the Persian Gulf.

Babylon

**Hammurabi
3790 B.P.**

Ur in turn gave way to Babylon and its Semitic rulers by 3990 years ago. Babylon's early greatness culminated in the reign of the great king Hammurabi 3790 years ago. He integrated the smaller kingdoms of Mesopotamia for a short period, but his empire declined after his death as Babylonian trade to the Persian Gulf collapsed and trade ties to Assur in the north and for Mediterranean copper in the west were strengthened.

The Assyrians

By this time, the various masters of Mesopotamia were major players in a much wider eastern Mediterranean world (Chapter 20). They vied with the Hittites of Anatolia, with Mitanni on the Euphrates, and with the Egyptians for control of the Levant. Perhaps the most successful of them were the Assyrians, who rose to prominence in the mid-fourteenth-century B.C. as Babylon declined.

Assur on the Tigris had been a major force in Near Eastern trade since Sumerian times (Postgate, 1977). The merchants of Assur traded far to the east and west and controlled the trade down the Tigris to Babylon and beyond. The city came into great prominence during the reign of King Assur-uballit (1365–1330 B.C.). He created a great state through ruthless and efficient conquest and political maneuvering that maintained diplomatic relations with the pharaohs of Egypt, with the Hittite and Mitanni kingdoms of Anatolia (Chapter 20), and with Babylonia. His power was based on control of trade routes and the rich cereal-growing lands of northern Iraq, as well as on military prowess. His armies swept everything before them and occupied Babylonia for a while. The empire collapsed soon after the king's death.

**Assyrian Empire
c. 1350 to 612
B.C.**

A second imperial expansion occurred in the ninth century B.C. under Assyrian monarchs based in northern Iraq, who expanded their domains with annual campaigns of military conquest. These were absolute despots, vain and grandiloquent men, who boasted of their conquests on their palace walls. When King Assurnasirpal completed his palace at Nimrud he threw a party for the 16,000 inhabitants of the city, 1500 royal officials, "47,074 men and women from the length of my country," and 5000 foreign envoys (Postgate, 1977). The king fed this throng of more than 69,000 people for ten days, during which time his guests ate 14,000 sheep and consumed more than 10,000 skins of wine. Following a succession crisis, the Assyrian Empire collapsed but was revived in a more bureaucratically efficient form by King Tiglathpileser III. The last of the great Assyrian kings was Assurbanipal, who died in approximately 630 B.C. When he died, the Assyrian Empire entered a period of political chaos. The Babylonians achieved independence, and Assyrian power finally was broken in 612 B.C. when Nineveh was sacked by the Persians and Babylonians. For 43 years, the mighty King Nebuchadnezzar ruled over Mesopotamia and turned his capital into one of the showpieces of the ancient world. His double-walled city was adorned by magnificent mud-brick palaces with elaborate hanging gardens, a great processional way, and a huge ziggurat. It was to Babylon that a large contingent of Jews were taken as captives after Nebuchadnezzar's armies sacked Jerusalem, an exile immortalized by the lament "By the waters of Babylon we sat down and wept" (Psalm 137:1).

Cyrus
539 B.C.

The Babylonian Empire did not long survive the death of Nebuchadnezzar in 556 B.C. His successors were weak men who were unable to resist the external forces that now pressed on Mesopotamia. The armies of Cyrus the Great of Persia took Babylon virtually without resistance in 539 B.C., and Mesopotamia became part of an empire even larger than that of the Assyrians. By this time, the effects of constant political instability and bad agricultural management were beginning to make themselves felt. The Mesopotamian delta was a totally artificial environment by 4000 years ago, and poor drainage and badly maintained irrigation works in later centuries led to inexorable rises in the salt content of the soil and to drastic falls in crop yields in some areas. Nothing could be done to reverse this trend until modern soil science and irrigation techniques could be imported to the delta at vast expense.

GUIDE TO FURTHER READING

Fagan, Brian M. 1979. *Return to Babylon*. Boston: Little, Brown.
   A history of archaeological research in Mesopotamia that starts with the first Arab geographers and ends with modern excavations.

Kramer, Samuel. 1963. *The Sumerians*. Chicago: University of Chicago Press.
   The classic account of Sumerian civilization, written by one of the foremost experts on Sumerian cuneiform tablets and literature. A model of what such books should be.

Lloyd, Seton. 1983. *The Archaeology of Mesopotamia*, 2d ed. 1983. London: Thames and Hudson.
   A synthesis of Iraqi archaeology that concentrates mainly on the early civilizations. Strong on archaeological data, well illustrated, and informative on architecture.

Nissen, Hans J. 1988. *The Early History of the Ancient Near East, 9000 to 2000 B.C.* Chicago: University of Chicago Press.
   An up-to-date, useful introduction to Mesopotamian history and archaeology for beginning students.

Oates, David, and Oates, Joan. 1976. *The Rise of Civilization.* Oxford, Eng.: Elsevier Phaidon.

Postgate, Nicholas. 1977. *The First Empires.* Oxford, Eng.: Elsevier Phaidon.
    Oates and Postgate are two volumes in the Making of the Past series that describe for the lay reader the cultures and civilizations discussed in this chapter in more detail than is possible here. Recommended for paper writers.

CHAPTER 17   PHARAOHS AND AFRICAN CHIEFS

Preview

- Egyptian pre-Dynastic people lived at a time of gradual population growth and enrichment of the native culture, probably as a result of expanded trading contacts. The number of luxury goods increased, metallurgy was introduced from Mesopotamia, and social structure seems to have become more elaborate.

- The acquisition of writing by the Egyptians probably was one of the catalytic events that led to the unification of Egypt and the emergence of civilization there. The process of unification culminated under the pharaoh Narmer approximately 5000 years ago.

- Ancient Egyptian civilization is divided into four main periods: the Old, Middle, New, and Late Kingdoms, the earlier of which were separated by brief intermediate periods of political chaos.

- The Old Kingdom is notable for its despotic pharaohs and the frenzy of pyramid construction, an activity that may be connected with pragmatic notions of fostering national unity.

- The Middle Kingdom saw a shift of political and religious power to Thebes and Upper Egypt.

- New Kingdom pharaohs made Egypt an imperial power with strong interests in Asia and Nubia. These pharaohs were buried in the Valley of Kings near

461

Thebes. The cult of Amun was all-powerful, except for a brief interlude when the heretic pharaoh Akhenaten introduced the worship of the sun god Aten.

- Ancient Egyptian civilization began to decline after 3100 years ago, and the Nile eventually came under the rule of the Assyrians, then the Persians, and finally the Greek pharaohs, the Ptolemies.

- Egypt had few contacts with sub-Saharan Africa, which was widely settled by tropical farmers approximately 2000 years ago. The diffusion of farming coincided with both the introduction of ironworking and the spread of the Bantu-speaking peoples from West Africa over much of east, central, and southern Africa.

- Indigenous African states developed on the southern fringes of the Sahara Desert at the end of the first millennium A.D., owing their initial prosperity to the gold trade across the desert.

- The later prehistory of Africa is marked by continued contacts between Africans and societies living outside the continent. Complex states like that of the Karanga of southern Africa emerged in the last thousand years, several of them trading actively with foreign merchants and voyagers until Africa came into the purview of written history in recent times.

By 5600 years ago, the average Egyptian probably lived much as Upper Nile villagers do today (Hassan, 1988; Johnson, 1978). Wheat and barley were cultivated in riverside gardens and supplemented by intensive gathering of wild vegetable foods. Cattle, goats, sheep, and pigs were herded. The meat from the herds was supplemented by the rich Nile game population and by fishing. These Amratian (or pre-Dynastic) people were the successors of the Badarians (Chapter 12) (Hassan, 1988; Hoffman, 1979; Trigger et al., 1983). Amratians derive their name from the archaeological site in Upper Egypt, El Amra. Amratian settlements apparently had a material culture somewhat similar to that which flourished in earlier centuries on the same sites of the Nile floodplain (Figure 17.1). The human population of the valley was growing slowly, and there was some cultural fusion and increased interaction between more closely spaced settlements along the river, a natural highway for hundreds of miles. Pottery was still being made, but elegant stone vessels in alabaster and basalt also were used, probably shaped by specialist craftsworkers and traded widely throughout the valley. Amratian flint workers created magnificent knives and daggers, which also were prized possessions. A gradual enrichment of pre-Dynastic culture can be discerned over the centuries, resulting in part from the introduction of coppersmithing from Asia. Soon metalworkers were making pins, flat axes, and daggers of the new material. The Amratians began to import copper from Sinai, and lead and silver came from Asia. The proportion of luxury goods to functional goods rose steadily; one of the locally manufactured items was *faience,* a form of glass widely traded in prehistoric times. Amratian settlements slowly became larger, and social structure became more

Amratian
5600 B.P.

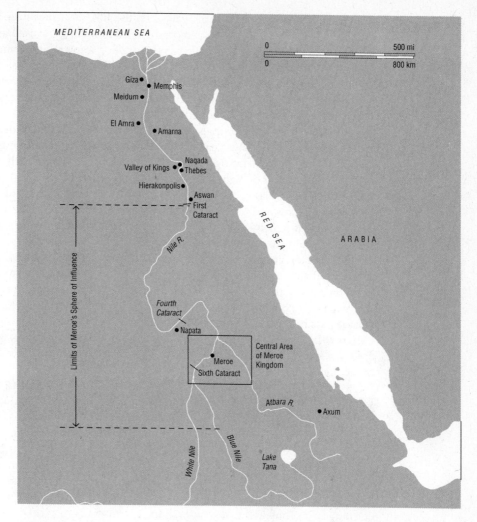

FIGURE 17.1   The Nile Valley.

elaborate. The archaeological record contains some signs of social classes, in the form of graves of varying opulence.

EL-OMARI AND MAADI: TRADE ON THE NILE

There are signs to show that the earlier barter networks that linked Nile communities may have given way by about 5200 years ago to more formalized trade (Hassan, 1988). This change was linked with not only increasing craft specialization but also major social and political changes in the valley. At the El-Omari sites near Helwan in the Nile Delta, one location contains more than 100 dwellings, as well as the burial of a chief or ruler holding a well-made wooden staff or scepter. This remarkable object, pointed at one end, flat at the other, foreshadows the ceremonial staffs carried by later Egyptian pharaohs and gods. There are many imports in the El-Omari settlements, among them seashells, ostrich eggshells, mother of pearl, and necklaces and pendants fabricated from Red Sea gastropods.

In contrast to simpler burials of earlier centuries, the El-Omari dead were buried in cemeteries outside the settlement, the body wrapped in a mat or coarse fabric and placed on its left side, facing south. One cemetery associated with a small village contained the burials of higher-status individuals, graves covered with stone mounds. Interestingly, the village contained many cellarlike storage areas that held large numbers of stone tools and roughs for such implements as knife blades and arrowheads. The settlement may have belonged to traders, who apparently maintained contacts with the Levant (Rizkana and Seeher, 1985).

The Maadi site on the outskirts of Cairo was an important trading center in about 3650 B.C., a place with large, roofed oval or rectangular cellars up to 13 feet (4 m) long and 3 to 7 feet (1 to 2.1 m) deep. They contained jars, grains, animal and fish bones, stone vases, beads, and lumps of imported asphalt. Rows of large clay storage pots held grain, cooked meat, dried fish, flint tools, spindle whorls, and other objects. Maadi was an important link in a major trade network that brought commodities from the Levant and perhaps even from Mesopotamia to the Nile, probably by donkey caravan (Caneva et al., 1987).

At this time, many Egyptians still lived in dispersed settlements, with the occasional larger community housing up to 2500 people. Only a few of these small towns were of more than local importance, and then only for their sacred shrines and important deities. These settlements probably contained many farmers as well as nonfood producers, for the configuration of the narrow floodplain probably inhibited the formation of large cities. By about 3600 B.C., a network of larger, sedentary settlements, with a subsistence based firmly on cereal agriculture and more formal trade networks, were the foundation for the rise of a powerful elite and a funerary cult that was an integral part of a symbolic transformation at the center of Egyptian kingship (Hassan, 1988). The elite lived in great splendor and were buried with an elaborate panoply of worldly goods, which served to legitimize their authority.

WRITING

The increased volume of trade during late pre-Dynastic times is reflected in the importation of not only copper but also other exotic items that occur in profusion in sites of about 5500 years ago. Some of these objects are of unmistakable west Asian or Mesopotamian origin. The Nagada site, for example, yielded a cylinder seal of Mesopotamian form. Some pots bear depictions of Mesopotamian boat designs and of fabulous animals and creatures with intertwined necks and other motifs that derive from Asia.

The same trade brought another innovation: the art of writing, which became fully developed in Egypt. Hieroglyphs (Greek for "sacred carving") are commonly thought to be a form of picture writing. In fact they constitute a combination of pictographic (picture) and phonetic (representing vocal sounds) script, which was not only written on papyrus but also carved on public buildings or painted on clay or wood. It seems likely that writing was first developed in Mesopotamia and that Egyptian priests developed their own script, which was easier to produce with papyrus reed paper and ink rather than on clay. Doubtless, early hieroglyphs played an important role in trade and record keeping, but they may also have evolved as a way of conveying the meanings of funerary rituals on painted pots deposited with the dead (Hassan, 1988).

Ultimately, Egyptian scribes developed a cursive (running-on) hieroglyphic script that was a form of handwriting and was much easier to use on documents and other, less formal communications. Only the consonants were written in all forms of hieroglyphs; the vowel sounds were omitted, although both were pronounced. With practice, reading this form of script is easy enough, and a smpl tst 'f ths srt shld shw ths qt wll (Figure 17.2) (Diringer, 1962; Pope, 1973).

UNIFICATION AND THE RISE OF THE EGYPTIAN STATE

The acquisition of writing, with all its organizational possibilities, was one of the catalysts for the unification of all Egypt into a single political entity. This moment of unification cannot be pinned to a precise date. As we saw in Chapter 15, many causes contributed to the rise of state-organized societies. Fekri Hassan (1988) hypothesizes that the social ecology of Nile agriculture played an important role in the initial stages of the process. Neighboring communities pooled their efforts to

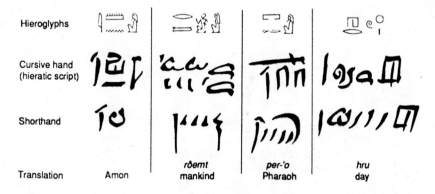

Hieroglyphs			
Cursive hand (hieratic script)			
Shorthand			
Translation	Amon	rŏemt mankind	per-'o Pharaoh	hru day

FIGURE 17.2   Egyptian writing is referred to as hieroglyphs, the familiar symbols that appear on formal inscriptions and on tomb walls. In fact, Egyptian scribes developed cursive hands used in everyday life. These examples show formal hieroglyphic script *(top line)* and below it both the cursive style and the scribe's shorthand, which was used for rapid writing.

minimize the effects of catastrophic fluctuations in the annual Nile flood. In time, local chiefs emerged as key players in these cooperative ventures. As the economic unit grew larger over the generations, regional political structures came into being. These leaders sought to legitimize their positions with fine possessions and elaborate funerary rites. Unification was the culmination of local social and political developments that resulted from centuries of gradual change in economic and social life. Pre-Dynastic villages were autonomous units, each with its local deities. During the fourth millennium B.C., the more important villages became the focal points of different territories, which in Dynastic times became the *nomes,* or provinces, through which the pharaohs administered Egypt. The nomarchs (provincial leaders) were responsible for the gradual coalescence of Egypt into larger political and social units. Their deeds are recorded on ceremonial palettes that were used for moistening eye powder. Some of these palettes show alliances of local leaders dismantling conquered villages. Others commemorate the administrative skills of leaders who brought their villages through drought years by skillful management. The unification of Egypt was a gradual process of both voluntary and involuntary amalgamation. Voluntary unification resulted from common needs and economic advantage. Perhaps it was only in the final stages of unification that military force came into play to bring larger and larger political units under single rulers (Hoffman, 1979).

There is little archaeological evidence that documents the long process of unification. Michael Hoffman and a team of Egyptologists (1982) have investigated ancient Nekhen, a city called Hierakonpolis, "City of the Falcon," by the Greeks. Pre-Dynastic settlements and cemeteries surround the town. Some 5800 years ago, Nekhen was a village inhabited by a few hundred people. During the next three centuries the population mushroomed to perhaps as many as 10,500. People lived in closely clustered mud-brick and plaster dwellings, the more important artisans and traders in larger houses with separate compounds. For the first time, there are signs of social differentiation in Egyptian society. The Abu Suffian cemetery near Nekhen housed important citizens, many of them prosperous traders who had profited from locally made, fine-quality "Plum Red" pottery, which was used to adorn tombs up and down the river. These people became powerful members of the community, with widespread contacts with settlements near and far.

About 5500 years ago, the fragile ecological balance of desert and grassland collapsed, perhaps as a result of overgrazing by goats and sheep and intensive pottery firing by local artisans. Hoffman believes that some of the local leaders profited from the disaster by using their wealth to foster irrigation agriculture and settlement closer to the Nile. Their venture was successful and yielded large grain surpluses under the control of the new elite. They used their wealth to increase trade, erect public buildings like temples, and invest in imposing sepulchers. The ambitious leaders of Nekhen were buried in the same Abu Suffian cemetery, which straddled a dry gulch, their graves laid out on either side of the wadi in what Hoffman believes is a symbolic map of a unified Upper and Lower Egypt.

Egypt was finally unified under the pharaoh Narmer at Hierakonpolis about 5050 years ago. In economic terms, the unification may have involved some intensification of agriculture as population densities rose; but as Karl Butzer (1976) has pointed out, the technology for lifting water was so rudimentary that the early

Nekhen

3500 B.C.

3050 B.C.

rulers of Egypt were unable to organize any elaborate forms of irrigation. In all probability, most ancient Egyptian agriculture involved irrigation schemes on a modest scale that merely extended the distribution of seasonal floodwaters from natural flood basins. Still, even these efforts must have required a considerable degree of administrative organization. Also, with a centralized form of administration, the divine leader, the pharaoh himself, was responsible for the success of the harvest. Since the Nile flood fluctuated considerably in cycles of abundant and lean years, and the pharaohs could do little to control the success or failure of irrigation without much more elaborate technology than they possessed, their political position could, theoretically at any rate, be threatened by famine years. If the divine leader could not provide, who could? Perhaps a different leader. Small wonder that some periods of political instability, which may have coincided with poor flood years, saw rapid successions of ineffective pharaohs.

Karl Butzer (1981) has pointed out that civilizations can be regarded as ecosystems that emerge in response to sets of ecological opportunities. Over time, a variety of social and environmental adjustments are inevitable, some of them successful, leading to population growth, and others unsuccessful, so that the population shrinks. These demographic adjustments are commonly associated with ups and downs of political power. The political structures of, say, ancient Egyptian civilization are not nearly as durable as the basic adaptive system they purport to control or the cultural identity of which they were once part. Butzer draws an analogy with the ecological concept of trophic levels among biotic communities, in which organisms with similar feeding habits, such as herbivores and carnivores, define successive tiers interlinked in a vertical chain. Likewise, he hypothesizes, an efficient social hierarchy comprises several levels arranged in what he calls a "low-angle pyramid, supported by a broad base of farmers and linked to the peak of the pyramid by a middle-level bureaucracy. The vertical structures channel food and information through the system, and an efficient energy flow allows each trophic level to flourish in a steady state." In this model, a flatter pyramid with little vertical structure would provide less information flow and limit the potential productivity of the lower levels. Butzer's pyramid would allow growth at the lower levels, with new technologies or organizational devices favoring expanded energy generation. A steep, top-heavy pyramid laden with nobles and bureaucrats places excessive burdens on the lowest levels, so much so that external and internal forces can undermine the stability of society.

This model, when applied to the long history of ancient Egyptian civilization, shows how the Egyptians persisted in adjusting to a floodplain environment for thousands of years. They overcame external and internal crises by reorganizing their state and economic structure. The key variables were the fluctuations of the Nile itself, occasional foreign intervention, the character of the pharaohs' leadership, and a progressively pathological society of elite nonproducers who persisted in exploiting the common farmer, a process that led to eventual social collapse. However, through all these variables the essential components of the sociopolitical system survived more or less intact, right up to the nineteenth century A.D. Indeed, the visitor to rural Egypt can still see farming villages functioning much as they did in ancient Egyptian times.

PYRAMIDS AND THE OLD KINGDOM: 5050
TO 4131 YEARS AGO

Archaic and Old
Kingdoms
**5050 to 4131
B.P.**

Egyptologists conventionally divide Ancient Egyptian civilization into four broad periods, separated by at least two intermediate periods that were intervals of political change and instability (Table 17.1). The most striking feature of ancient Egyptian civilization is its conservatism. Many of the artistic, religious, and technological features of early Egyptian civilization survived intact into Roman times. The political and religious powers of the pharaohs changed somewhat through time, as later rulers became more imperialistic in their ambitions or different gods assumed political supremacy, but the essential continuity was there in the form of a civilization whose

Table 17.1 A Much Simplified Chronology of Ancient Egyptian Civilization.

Years B.C./B.P.	Period	Characteristics
30 B.C.	Roman occupation	Egypt an imperial province of Rome
332 to 30	Ptolemaic period	The Ptolemies bring Greek influence to Egypt, beginning with conquest of Egypt by Alexander the Great in 332 B.C.
1085 to 332	Late period	Gradual decline in pharaonic authority, culminating in Persian rule (525 to 404 and 343 to 332 B.C.)
3517 to 3035 B.P.	New Kingdom	Great imperial period of Egyptian history, with pharaohs buried in Valley of Kings; pharaohs include Rameses II, Seti I, and Tutankhamun, as well as Akhenaten, the heretic ruler
3736 to 3517	Second Intermediate period	Hyksos rulers in the delta
3941 to 3736	Middle Kingdom	Thebes achieves prominence, also the priesthood of Amun
c. 4131 to 4123	First Intermediate period	Political chaos and disunity
4636 to 4131	Old Kingdom	Despotic pharaohs build the pyramids and favor conspicuous funerary monuments; institutions, economic strategies, and artistic traditions of ancient Egypt established
5050 to 4036	Archaic period	Consolidation of state (treated as part of Old Kingdom in this book)
5050	Unification of Egypt under Narmer-Menes	

life was governed by the unchanging environment of the Nile Valley, with its annual floods, narrow floodplain, and surrounding desert.

The Old Kingdom (c. 4636 to 4131 years ago) saw four dynasties of pharaohs governing Egypt from a royal capital at Memphis near Cairo. Apparently the country's resources were well organized and controlled by a centralized government. Some of the pharaohs had reputations as cruel despots, notably Cheops and Chephren, who built the pyramids of Giza. The building of pyramids is regarded as the mark of the Old Kingdom pharaohs (Edwards, 1973; Mendelssohn, 1974). The first royal pyramid was built by Djoser approximately 4680 years ago; it was a six-step pyramid that was surrounded by a veritable town of buildings and shrines. The step pyramid is a somewhat hesitant structure, its architectural roots in earlier stone-built tombs, but the great pyramids built over the next century show increasing confidence, culminating in the brilliant assurance of the pyramids of Giza, with their perfect pyramid shape (Figure 17.3). The largest of these, the Great Pyramid, covers 13.1

FIGURE 17.3   The pyramids of Giza.

acres (5.3 ha) and is 481 feet (146 m) high. It dates to the IV Dynasty reign of Cheops, approximately 4600 years ago. Just under two centuries later, the pharaohs stopped building huge pyramids and diverted their organizational talents to other public works.

There is something megalomaniacal about the pyramids, built as they were with an enormous expenditure of labor and energy. They reflect the culmination of centuries of gradual evolution of the Egyptian state, during which the complexity of the state and the authority of the bureaucracy grew hand in hand. The pyramids were the houses and tombs for the pharaohs in eternity, symbols of the permanence of Egyptian civilization. They reflect the importance that the Egyptians placed on the life of the pharaoh in the afterworld and in the notion of resurrection, a central belief in their religion for thousands of years.

Kurt Mendelssohn (1974) has argued that the pyramids were built over a relatively short period of time, during which the architects experimented with the pyramid shape. At least one pyramid collapsed during construction, before the builders mastered the correct 52° angles of the Great Pyramid. Every flood season, when agriculture was at a standstill, the pharaohs organized thousands of peasants into construction teams who quarried, transported, and laid the dressed stones of the pyramids. The permanent (year-round) labor force comprised relatively few, mainly skilled artisans, the fruit of whose work was placed in position on the main structure once a year. As far as is known, the peasants were paid volunteers, fed by the state bureaucracy, whose loyalty to the divine pharaoh provided the motivation for the work. Mendelssohn feels the construction of the pyramids was a practical administrative device designed to organize and institutionalize the state. As construction proceeded from one generation to the next, the villagers became dependent on the central administration for food for three months a year, food obtained from surpluses contributed by the villages themselves in the form of taxation. After a while the pyramids fulfilled their purpose, and the state-directed labor forces could be diverted to other, less conspicuous state works. A new form of state organization had been created, one that both fostered and exploited the interdependence of Egyptian villages.

The Egyptian State

Egypt was the first state of its size in history (Kemp, 1989). The pharaohs ruled by their own word, following no written laws, unlike the legislators of Mesopotamian city-states. The pharaoh had power over the Nile flood, rainfall, and all people, including foreigners. He was a god in his own right, respected by all people as a tangible divinity whose being was the personification of *Ma'at*, or "rightness." *Ma'at* was far more than just rightness; it was a "right order" and stood for order and justice. The pharaoh embodied *ma'at* and dispensed justice. *Ma'at* was pharaonic status and eternity itself—the very embodiment of the Egyptian state (Morenz, 1973).

The pharaoh's pronouncements were law, regulated by a massive background of precedent set by earlier pharaohs. Egyptian rulers lived a strictly ordered life. As one Greek writer tells us, "For there was a set time not only for his holding audience or rendering judgment, but even for his taking a walk, bathing, and sleeping with his wife; in short, every act of his life" (Aldred, 1986).

A massive, hereditary bureaucracy effectively ruled the kingdom, with rows of officials forming veritable dynasties. Their records tell us that much official energy was devoted to tax collection, harvest yields, and administration of irrigation (Figure 17.4). An army of 20,000 men, many of them mercenaries, was maintained at the height of Egypt's prosperity. The Egyptian Empire was a literate one; that is, trained scribes who could read and write were an integral part of the state government. Special schools trained writers for careers in the army, the palace, the treasury, and numerous other callings (Aldred, 1986; Kemp, 1989).

Despite the number of scribes and minor clerics, a vast gulf separated one who could read and write from the uneducated peasant worker. The life of an Egyptian

FIGURE 17.4   A tomb painting from the tomb of Menena at Thebes showing the harvesting and measuring of fields near the Nile.

peasant, given good harvests, was easier than that of a Greek or a Syrian farmer, although the state required occasional bouts of forced labor to clear irrigation canals or to haul stone, both tasks being essential to maintain Egyptian agriculture. Minor craftsworkers and unskilled laborers lived more regimented lives, working on temples and pharaohs' tombs (Steindorff and Steele, 1954). Many were organized in shifts under foremen. There were strikes, and absenteeism was common. A scale of rations and daily work was imposed. Like many early states, however, the Egyptians depended on slave labor for some public works and much domestic service, but foreign serfs and war prisoners could wield much influence in public affairs. They were allowed to rent and cultivate land.

THE FIRST INTERMEDIATE PERIOD AND MIDDLE KINGDOM: 4131 TO 3736 YEARS AGO

First
Intermediate
period
4131 to 4123
B.P.

Middle Kingdom
3941 to 3736
B.P.

The Old Kingdom ended with the death of Pepi II approximately 4200 years ago (Wilson, 1951). By this time the authority of the monarchy had been weakened by constant expenditure on lavish public works and, perhaps, by a cycle of bad harvest years, which undermined the people's confidence in the abilities of the rulers to provide for them. A period of political instability now known as the First Intermediate ensued, during which there were Asian incursions into the fertile delta country and Egypt was ruled by the local monarchs, even though there was nominal allegiance to a central government.

Approximately 4133 years ago, the city of Thebes in Upper Egypt became the center of rebel movements that eventually took over the country under pharaoh Mentuhotep II 3990 years ago. The Middle Kingdom pharaohs who followed were mostly energetic rulers who extended trading contacts throughout the Near East and conquered the desert lands of Nubia south of the First Cataract (see Figure 17.1). The pharaohs became somewhat less despotic and considered themselves more like shepherds of the people, who had some concern for the common welfare. It was during the Middle Kingdom that the city of Thebes came into prominence, especially as a center for the worship of the sun god Amun.

THE SECOND INTERMEDIATE PERIOD: 3736 TO 3517 YEARS AGO

Second
Intermediate
period
3736 to 3517
B.P.

The Middle Kingdom lasted until approximately 3736 years ago, when another period of political instability and economic disorder ensued. Disputes over the royal succession at Thebes led to procession of pharaohs who reigned for short periods. Pharaonic control of the Nile Valley as a whole weakened, and Asian intruders managed to penetrate the fertile lands of the delta downstream. Their leaders became known as the Hyksos and formed two dynasties that ruled over much of Egypt between 3625 and 3517 years ago. They probably were nomadic chiefs from the desert, who brought the horse and chariot to Egypt for the first time.

The Hyksos had little control over Upper Egypt, where the pharaohs of Thebes quarreled among themselves. Eventually, though, the Thebans came to realize that they could never control the whole of the country again unless they threw out the Hyksos and paid careful attention to the political realities of Asia. From this point on, the Egyptian pharaohs took an active interest in their Asian neighbors, and there was a constant flow of people and ideas with other nations.

THE NEW KINGDOM: 3517 TO 3085 YEARS AGO

New Kingdom
3517 to 3085
B.P.

The New Kingdom began when a series of Theban pharaohs fought and won a war of independence from the Hyksos. It was Ahmose the Liberator who finally overcame the foreigners and established a firm hold on Egypt from the delta to Nubia. He was the first of a series of great rulers whose names have become symbolic of the power of ancient Egypt: Tutmosis, Amenophis, Seti, and Rameses. Rameses, the greatest of Egypt's pharaohs, extended the Egyptian Empire far beyond the narrow confines of the Nile Valley, deep into Nubia and into the Levant. By this time, political events in the Near East involved a delicate balance of diplomatic and military power between the Hittites in Anatolia to the north (Chapter 20) and the Mesopotamians to the east (Chapter 16). All three powers sought to control the lucrative trade and trade routes of the eastern Mediterranean (Chapter 20), and the famous Amarna archives chronicle some of the complex diplomatic maneuvering that went on. In the end, it was Egypt that lost out in the balance of power; its influence steadily declined and was eventually confined to the southern Levant.

Egypt may have been a major player on the world stage during the New Kingdom, but the spiritual center of the empire was at Thebes, where the priests of the great temples of Luxor and Karnak were a potent political force in the affairs of state.

Karl Butzer (1981) argues that episodes of rapid growth in ancient Egyptian civilization were made possible by a series of important innovations. One was improved irrigation organization in the Old Kingdom, after 4800 years ago. This allowed the development of the delta regions of Lower Egypt, once the bureaucratic structure to organize the work was in place. During the Middle Kingdom, the pharaohs responded to several centuries of repeated low floods by placing closer government controls over food distribution and moving large numbers of people out of the valley into such areas as the Fayyum Depression, where they organized huge drainage and irrigation works. The New Kingdom saw the introduction of the *shaduf*, a bucket-and-lever lifting device that raised water a yard or so from wells or ditches to gardens and estates. One result of this innovation was a shift of population from the narrow valley to the broad delta. The culmination of agricultural productivity came in the last few centuries B.C., when the last pharaohs undertook the complete drainage of the Fayyum, introduced summer crops such as sorghum, and encouraged the development of the animal-drawn waterwheel, known as the *saqiya*. The impact of all these innovations was to increase both the productivity of the state and the size of the labor force. It is probable that the population of ancient Egypt rose from less than a million 5000 years ago to approximately 5 million by 3500 years ago. These innovations were to continue to support Egyptian agriculture right up to the building of the High Dam at Aswan in the twentieth century A.D. (Fedden, 1977).

The New Kingdom pharaohs adopted new burial customs and abandoned conspicuous sepulchers. Their mummies were buried in the desolate Valley of Kings on the west bank of the Nile at Thebes (El Mahdy, 1989; Romer, 1981). An entire community of workers did nothing but prepare the rock-cut tombs of the pharaohs, their queens, and privileged nobles. To date, only one undisturbed royal tomb has come to light in the Valley of Kings, that of the pharaoh Tutankhamun, who died 3296 years ago (H. Carter, 1923; Desroches-Noblecourt, 1963). The world was astounded when Howard Carter and Lord Carnarvon discovered and cleared the tomb of the young pharaoh in the 1920s (Figure 17.5). It gives us an impression of the incredible wealth of the New Kingdom pharaohs' courts.

Tutankhamun died in his late teens but was responsible for restoring the religious order after a curious interlude of chaos during the reign of Akhenaten (3313–3300 B.P.) (Aldred, 1986). Like many pharaohs before him, Akhenaten had been

FIGURE 17.5   The antechamber of Tutankhamun's tomb, stacked with priceless royal possessions. Tutankhamun's chariots lie against the left wall; two animal-head funerary beds, stools, storage chests filled with possessions, and other items are to the right.

worried about the overriding power of the priests of Amun at Thebes, so he espoused the worship of the god Aten, the life-giving disk of the sun. Akhenaten took up the new religion with fanatical zeal and even founded a new capital downstream of Thebes called Akhetaten, near the modern village of el-Amarna. After his death 3300 years ago, the regents for Tutankhamun worked hard to restore the power and prestige of Amun, a move apparently supported by the mass of the people, for Akhenaten had produced no viable alternatives to the established political and religious institutions he had abolished.

THE LATE PERIOD: 1085 TO 332 B.C.

Late Period
1085 to 332
B.C.

With the death of Rameses III in 1085 B.C., Egypt entered a period of political weakness, when local rulers exercised varying control over the Nile. The pharaohs were threatened by Nubian rulers, who actually ruled over Egypt for a short time in the eighth century B.C. The Assyrians were a constant hazard after 725 B.C. and occupied parts of the country and looted Thebes in 665. After the eclipse of Assyria, the Egyptians enjoyed a few centuries of independence before being conquered by the Persians in 343 B.C. and Alexander the Great in 332 B.C. He in turn was succeeded

Ptolemies
332 to 30 B.C.

by the Ptolemies, pharaohs of Greek ancestry, who ruled Egypt until Roman times. It was they who brought much of Egyptian lore and learning into the mainstream of emerging Greek civilization and ensured that the Land of the Pharaohs made a critical contribution to Western civilization.

THE EMERGENCE OF AFRICAN STATES

What were Egypt's relationships with the vast African continent that bordered the Nile? Its influence on southern and Saharan neighbors was surprisingly small, for Egypt's ties were closer to the Mediterranean world than to sub-Saharan Africa. The pharaohs exercised political control only as far south as the First Cataract, near today's Aswan Dam, but the areas to the south were an important source of ivory for ornaments and of slaves for the divine rulers.

Meroe

900 B.C.

Approximately 900 B.C., an unknown governor of the southernmost part of Egypt founded his own dynasty and ruled a string of small settlements extending far south into the area that is now the Sudan. His capital at Napata began to decline because the fragile grasslands by the Nile were overgrazed. The inhabitants moved south and founded a town called Meroe on a fertile floodplain between the Nile and Atbara rivers. There they built their own thriving urban civilization, which was in contact with peoples living far to the west on the southern edge of the Sahara (Shinnie, 1967).

590 B.C.

Meroe's inhabitants kept at least sporadic contacts with the classical world. They gained prosperity from extensive trading in such items as copper, gold, iron, ivory, and slaves. Some of Meroe's prosperity may have been based on ironworking, for deposits of this vital material were abundant near Napata. Iron artifacts are, however, fairly rare in the city itself.

In the early centuries after Christ, the empire declined, following raids from the kingdom of Axum, centered on the Ethiopian highlands (Oliver and Fage, 1963). Meroe was abandoned, and the stratified society that had ruled it collapsed. A scattered rural population continued to live along the banks of the Nile. The fertile grasslands that had surrounded Meroe were now overgrazed, and the increasingly arid countryside made urban life difficult. A dispersed settlement pattern replaced the centralized city style of Meroe's heyday. Chiefdoms replaced divine kings.

A.D. 300

North Africa

The North African coast had long been a staging post for maritime traders from the eastern Mediterranean. During the first millennium B.C., the Phoenicians set up port-colonies (N. K. Sanders, 1977). The colonists came into contact with well-established barter networks that crisscrossed the Sahara (Bovill, 1968). The desert is rich in salt deposits that were controlled by the nomadic peoples who lived there. They came in touch with black tribes living to the south of the desert, who bartered salt for copper, ivory, gold, and the other raw materials that Africa has traditionally given to the world. Soon, long trading routes connected North Africa with tropical regions, well-trodden highways that provided much of the Greek and Roman wealth during the height of their civilizations.

Most of the Saharan trade was in the hands of nomadic tribes, middle agents between sub-Saharan Africa and the bustling markets of the Mediterranean. In Roman times the camel was introduced to the Sahara. These "ships of the desert" enabled merchants to organize sizable camel caravans that crossed the Sahara like clockwork, from the North African coast to West Africa; the caravans increased direct contact between the Mediterranean world and West Africa and built a much greater volume of trade.

A.D. 350

Ironworking and African States

Ironworking had reached West Africa by the fourth century B.C., perhaps by the Saharan trade routes (McIntosh and McIntosh, 1988). The new metallurgy, unlike that of copper, spread rapidly over sub-Saharan Africa in a few centuries. Its spread was connected in part with the dispersal of Bantu-speaking peoples over much of east, central, and southern Africa. Bantu languages are now spoken by many inhabitants of tropical Africa. The original area of Bantu tongues may have been north of the Zaire forest (Oliver and Fagan, 1975).

300 B.C.

This spread of new language coincides with the arrival of negroid (a racial term) peoples both in the Zaire forest and on the savanna woodlands to the east and south of it. Ironworking farmers were living near the great East African lakes by the third century A.D., by the banks of the Zambezi River at approximately the

A.D. 250

same time, and crossing the Limpopo into South Africa during the first millennium A.D. They introduced farming and domestic animals into wide areas of Africa, absorbing, eliminating, or pushing out the indigenous hunter-gatherers (Phillipson, 1977).

The Bantu farmers used shifting agriculture and careful soil selection to produce a diet of sorghum, millet, and other cereal crops. They kept cattle and sheep or goats and relied on hunting and gathering for much of their diet. Their architectural styles and pottery have a clear but indirect relationship with those of many present-day, rural, black Africans.

West African States

The past 1000 years have seen the proliferation of prosperous African states ruled by leaders whose power was based on religious authority, entrepreneurial skill, and control of vital raw materials (Connah, 1987; McIntosh and McIntosh, 1981). The West African states at the southern edges of the Sahara, such as Ghana, Mali, and Songhay, based their prosperity on the gold trade with North Africa (Figure 17.6). The Saharan trade passed into Islamic hands at the ends of the first millennium A.D., and Arab authors began describing the remarkable African kingdoms flourishing south of the desert. The geographer al-Bakri drew a vivid picture of the kingdom of Ghana, whose gold was well known in northern latitudes by the eleventh century. "It is said," he wrote, "that the king owns a nugget as large as a big stone."

Ghana

The Kingdom of Ghana straddled the northern borders of the gold-bearing river valleys of the upper Niger and Senegal (Levetzion, 1973). No one knows when it first came into being, but the kingdom was described by Arab writers in the eighth century A.D. The Ghanians' prosperity depended on the gold trade and the constant demand for ivory in the north. Kola nuts (used as a stimulant), slaves, and swords also crossed the desert, but gold, ivory, and salt were the foundations of their power. Islam was brought to Ghana sometime in the late first millennium and linked the kingdom more closely to the desert trade. The king of Ghana was a powerful ruler, who, wrote al-Bakri, "can put 200,000 men in the field, more than 40,000 of whom were bowmen."

Ghana was a prime target for Islamic reform movements, whose desert leaders longingly eyed the power and wealth of their southern neighbor. One such group, the Almoravids, attacked Ghana in approximately A.D. 1062, but it was 14 years before the invaders captured the Ghanian capital. The power of Ghana was fatally weakened, and the kingdom disintegrated into a series of minor chiefdoms, somewhat, perhaps, as many early Egyptian polities had done in the centuries preceding unification in 3250 B.C.

A.D. 1062

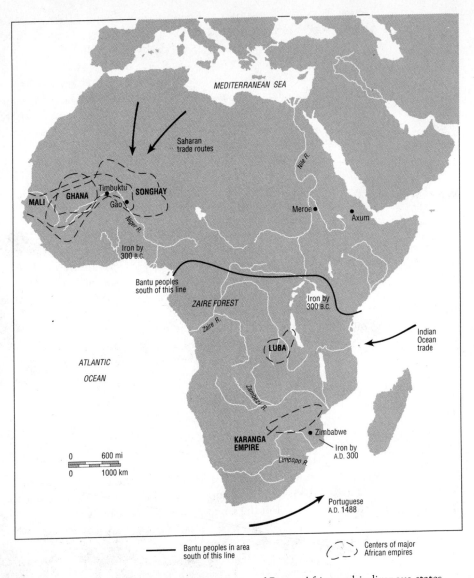

Bantu peoples in area south of this line

Centers of major African empires

FIGURE 17.6   Map of later African prehistory, showing extent of Bantu Africa and indigenous states.

Mali

A.D. 1230

The kingdom of Mali appeared two centuries later, after many tribal squabbles (Levetzion, 1973). A group of Kangaba people under the leadership of Sundiata came into prominence in approximately A.D. 1230 and annexed their neighbors' lands. Sundiata built his new capital at Mali on the Niger River. He founded a vast empire that a century later extended over most of sub-Saharan West Africa. The fame of the Mali kings spread all over the Muslim world. Timbuktu became a widely known center of Islamic scholarship. Malian gold was valued everywhere. When the king of Mali went on a pilgrimage to Mecca in A.D. 1324, the price of gold in Egypt was reduced sharply by the king's liberal spending. Mali appeared on the earliest European maps of West Africa as the outside frontier of the literate world. It was a major source of gold, ivory, and other exotic commodities for Europe and North Africa. Before Columbus discovered the Americas, the West African mines provided most of Europe's gold reserves and royal wealth.

The key to Mali's prosperity and political stability was the unifying effect of Islam, which overcame much factionalism and tribal rivalries. Mali's Islamic rulers governed with supreme powers granted by Allah and ruled their conquered provinces with carefully selected religious appointees, or even with politically astute slaves, chosen for their loyalty and political acumen. Islam provided a reservoir of thoroughly trained, literate administrators, who believed that political stability resulted from efficient governance and sound trading practices.

Songhay

A.D. 1325

In approximately A.D. 1325, the greatest of the kings of Mali, Mansa Musa, brought the important trading center of Gao on the Niger under his sway (Hunwick, 1971). Gao was the capital of the Dia kings, who shook off Mali's yoke in approximately A.D. 1340 and founded the kingdom of Songhay. Their state prospered increasingly as Mali's power weakened. The great chieftain Sonni Ali led the Songhay to new

A.D. 1464 to 1492

conquests between A.D. 1464 and 1492, expanding the frontiers of his empire deep into Mali country and far north into the Sahara. He monopolized much of the Saharan trade, seeking to impose law and order with his vast armies to increase the

A.D. 1550

volume of trade that passed through Songhay hands. Sonni Ali was followed by other competent rulers who further expanded Songhay. Its collapse came in the sixteenth century.

Karanga and Zimbabwe

Powerful kingdoms also developed in central and southern Africa. The Luba kingdom of the Congo and the Karanga Empire between the Zambezi and Limpopo rivers were led by powerful chiefs, priests, and ivory traders, who also handled such diverse raw materials as copper, gold, seashells, cloth, and porcelain. Their power came from highly centralized political organizations and effective religious powers, which channeled some of their subjects' energies into exploiting raw materials and long-distance trade.

The Karanga peoples lived where the nation of Zimbabwe is today and developed a remarkable kingdom that built its viability on trade in gold, copper, and ivory and on its leaders' religious acumen (Garlake, 1973). The Karanga leaders founded their power on their roles as intermediaries between the people and their ancestral spirits, upon whom the people believed the welfare of the nation de-

A.D. 1000

pended. Approximately A.D. 1000, the Karanga began to build stone structures, the most famous of which is Zimbabwe, built at the foot of a sacred hill. Zimbabwe became an important commercial and religious center. Its chiefs lived in seclusion on the sacred hill, known to archaeologists as "the Acropolis." In the valley below sprawled a complex of homesteads and stone enclosures, which were dominated in later centuries by the high, freestanding stone walls of the Great Enclosure, or Temple (Figure 17.7).

At least five stages of occupation have been recognized at Zimbabwe, the first of them dating to the fourth century A.D., when a group of farmers camped at the site but built no stone walls. They were followed by later occupants, who constructed the Great Enclosure in stages and built retaining walls on the Acropolis. The heyday of Zimbabwe was between A.D. 1350 and 1450, when imported cloth, china, glass, and porcelain were traded to the site. Gold ornaments, copper, ivory, and elaborate iron tools were in common use.

Part of Zimbabwe's subsistence base consisted of farming, but cattle herding assumed considerable importance on the open savanna between the Zambezi and Limpopo rivers. The site was abandoned sometime after A.D. 1450, partly because of changing political conditions, but also because of overgrazing of only moderately nutritious grazing grass.

A.D. 1350 to 1450

FIGURE 17.7   The Zimbabwe ruins, an important trading and religious center of the Karanga peoples of south central Africa in the second millennium A.D. Most of the Great Enclosure, or Temple, was built by A.D. 1500.

Foreign Traders

A.D. 1488

A.D. 1850

Most of African history is about exploitation of its peoples and raw materials by foreign traders and explorers. The East African coast was visited by Arabs and Indian merchants who used the monsoon winds of the Indian Ocean to sail to Africa and back within 12 months on prosperous trading ventures. The Portuguese skirted Africa's western and southeastern coasts in the fifteenth century and rounded the Cape of Good Hope in 1488, establishing precarious colonies ruled from Portugal to exploit raw materials (Alpers, 1975). However, some parts of Africa had no contact with the outside world until Victorian explorers and missionaries met remote and exotic peoples as they strove toward elusive goals, including such prizes as the source of the Nile (see Brodie, 1957).

GUIDE TO FURTHER READING

Aldred, Cyril. 1986. *The Egyptians,* 2d ed. New York: Thames and Hudson.
  A superb short essay on ancient Egyptian civilization that is especially good on daily life and society. Exceptional illustrations.

Connah, Graham. 1987. *African Civilizations.* Cambridge, Eng.: Cambridge University Press.
  A general account of early sub-Saharan African states for the beginning reader.

Fagan, Brian M. 1975. *The Rape of the Nile.* New York: Scribner's.
  A history of Egyptology, complete with tomb robbers, travelers, and the most flamboyant of archaeologists. Concentrates on Giovanni Belzoni, circus performer and grave robber extraordinaire.

Fedden, Robin. 1977. *Egypt.* London: Murray.
  The best book ever written on ancient and modern Egypt for the casual tourist. Gives a striking impression of modern Egyptian life and also of Islamic architecture and the Egyptian personality.

Kemp, Barry. 1989. *Ancient Egypt: The Anatomy of a Civilization.* London: Routledge.
  Quite simply, the best book on ancient Egyptian civilization ever written. Destined to become a classic for its elegant exposition and beautiful line drawings.

Romer, John. 1981. *The Valley of Kings.* New York: Morrow.
  A description in exhaustive detail of centuries of excavations in the royal burial grounds near Thebes. Shows vividly how modern Egyptology is as much detective work as it is excavation.

Trigger, Bruce C., et al. 1983. *Ancient Egypt: A Social History.* Cambridge, Eng.: Cambridge University Press.
  A series of authoritative essays on the changing face of ancient Egyptian society. Deservedly a popular college text.

CHAPTER 18 KULLI, HARAPPA, AND SOUTHEAST ASIA

Preview

- State-organized societies in the Indian subcontinent developed from indigenous roots about 4600 years ago. The Harappan civilization of the lowland Indus Valley developed as the result of a major shift in Sumerian long-distance trade patterns and long-term interactions between the Harappan culture of the lowlands and the Kulli Complex of the Baluchistan highlands.

- Harappan civilization displayed great internal variability, and survived as a series of flourishing rural communities long after the collapse of the great cities about 3700 years ago.

- Harappa and Mohenjo-daro were the largest cities, each laid out with a careful design dominated by a great citadel. It is assumed that society was ruled by priest-kings, who controlled both religious and economic life.

- After 3900 years, the major Harappan cities went into decline, but Harappan society flourished in rural, village-based settings for a considerable time.

- The period between the end of the Harappa culture and the beginnings of ironworking is obscure. Ironworking in India, by comparison, is associated with the period of painted gray wares, beginning around 3100 years ago and thriving when the subcontinent was occupied by the Persian King Darius, in 516 B.C.

- Southeast Asian peoples had developed bronze working by at least 3500 years ago, possibly very much earlier. The process of local state formation began around the same time, but the first historical records of complex states date to the third century A.D.

- Later Southeast Asian prehistory was dominated by the changing fortunes of various empires ruled by divine kings who espoused a strongly centralized economic system, as secular and religious concerns were molded together in a single type of complex society.

Water has always played an important role in Indian life and thought, for India's great rivers are the perennial gift of the snow-clad Himalayas. The Indus River, on the banks of which Indian civilization began, rises in southern Tibet and then descends 1000 miles (1609 km) through Kashmir before debouching onto the Pakistani plains (Figure 18.1). The Indus floodplain landscape now is almost entirely humanly made, a network of irrigation canals and flood embankments used to control the inundation that reaches the plains between June and September of each year. The people plant their wheat and barley on the fertile alluvial plains as the floods recede, then harvest them the following spring. They use the flood-borne silts as a natural fertilizer. The soils are soft enough to be cultivated without the aid of metal artifacts. Five thousand years ago, the Indus farmers were making use of the same flood cycle to irrigate their fields.

THE ROOTS OF INDIAN CIVILIZATION

As in other parts of the world, it seems that the roots of south Asian farming and later civilization were almost entirely indigenous. Most authorities on south Asian archaeology agree that humped cattle, buffalo, and pig were domesticated there from local wild populations (Sharma et al., 1980). Perhaps sheep and goats were also. The earliest dates for domesticated animals are in the 6500- to 6000-year range, from sites near Quetta in Baluchistan and Rajastan in northwest India. However, it seems likely that farmers and herders have lived in these areas for much longer, for palynologists have found evidence for recurrent fires in the desert savanna of Rajastan starting approximately 10,000 years ago (Jacobson, 1979). These may signal repeated clearance of sour grass to allow lush grazing for cattle, a practice followed in the area to this day. The farmers eventually domesticated not only indigenous Indian cultigens such as rice and dwarf wheat but also peas, barley, lentils, and other west Asian species, but the dates of early domestication are still unknown. In the millennia before the emergence of urban civilization in India, dozens of regional variations of farming culture flourished throughout India and Pakistan; these peasant cultures still are little understood (Allchin and Allchin, 1983; Possehl, 1982).

Mehrgarh
8000 to 5000
B.P.

French and Pakistani archaeologists are excavating a series of agricultural settlements at Mehrgarh south of Quetta, 125 miles (201 km) west of the Indus River (Jarrige and Meadow, 1979). They have found traces of farmers who had settled in the area before 8000 years ago. By 7000 years ago, the Mehrgarh people lived in

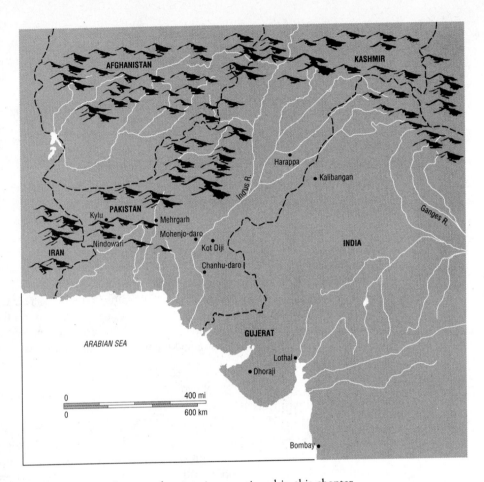

FIGURE 18.1   The Harappan civilization, showing sites mentioned in this chapter.

sizable, permanent houses of mud brick, a building material used not only by the Harappan civilization in later times but also by Indus people to this day. They possessed copper tools and imported turquoise from Iran and shells from the Arabian coast. Living as they did on a direct trade route from the Indus Valley to the Iranian Highlands, the Mehrgarh people learned of the unique qualities of a new Indian-domesticated crop: cotton. This white, fluffy flower turned out to be a priceless asset, for it could be woven into fine cloth not only for convenient domestic use in a hot climate but also for export to people looking for a light, hard-wearing textile. Cotton was to become a staple of Indian trade for the rest of recorded history.

The Mehrgarh sites include the Nausharo mound, which dates from about 5000 to 2500 years ago, about the time when the mature Harappan civilization developed in the lowlands of the Indus Valley. The alluvial plains themselves were settled as early as the fourth millennium B.C. Scattered across a vast area of the plains are hundreds of pre-Harappan settlements, many of them boasting fortifications, metallurgy, and

Kot Diji

planned streets. There are clear signs that many villages and small towns practiced intensive agriculture and were built above the highest flood level but as close to the river as possible. Typical of these settlements is Kot Diji on the left bank of the Indus approximately 20 miles (33.3 km) from the river (Jacobson, 1979; Mughal, 1974). In the early third millennium B.C., the inhabitants were forced to pile boulders to protect themselves against the inundation. They ended up erecting a massive defensive wall that served as both a flood dike and a fortress. The stone and mud-brick houses of the village were clustered inside the wall. Nevertheless, Kot Diji was attacked and burned at least twice. The same fate must have awaited many other settlements that became involved in quarrels between ambitious local chieftains vying for control of smaller communities and prime agricultural lands. The increased competition is hardly surprising, for between 5000 and 4500 years ago farming had changed the natural ecology of the Indus Valley beyond all recognition (Agrawal, 1982).

Botanists have chronicled these ecological changes by using the minute pollen grains embedded in the Indus Valley soils. They found that the natural tree and grass cover on the floodplain increased between 4400 and 3000 B.P., perhaps as a result of a period of higher rainfall that lasted at least 2000 years. This thicker tree cover became established just as the farming population was taking advantage of good rains and expanding agricultural production. The pollen counts show not only more trees but also dramatic rises in the proportions of cereal grains and cultivated weeds at the expense of the natural vegetation. A complex multiplier effect then linked rapidly rising village populations with corresponding increases in agricultural production, leading to drastic consequences for the plains environment. As the valley population rose, so did pressure on the land. The farmers cleared and burned off more and more riverine forest and grazed ever-growing herds of goats and sheep on watershed meadows. Acres of forest were burned to bake bricks for the houses of growing villages and newly founded cities. Mile after mile of the plains were denuded of natural vegetation, with disastrous consequences for erosion control and the flood-plain environment. Deprived of natural controls, the rising floodwaters swept over the plains, carrying everything with them. Confronted with what may have seemed like the wrath of the gods, the people had only one defense—cooperative flood-works and irrigation agriculture that fed more mouths and provided at least a degree of security from the vagaries of the elements. The obvious leaders of these new communal efforts were the chieftains, priests, and kin leaders, who acted as intermediaries between the people and the gods. The religious philosophy and motivation that provided the catalyst for these efforts was a simple one, a pervasive belief that humans are part of an ordered cosmos that can be maintained only by unremitting toil and a subordination of individual ambition to the common good.

HIGHLANDS AND LOWLANDS:
THE KULLI COMPLEX

This scenario fits the few archaeological facts available from the lowlands. In archaeological terms, the early stages of the Harappan civilization date to between 5200 and

4600 years ago. The people lived in small villages covering only a few acres, and there are no signs of social ranking (Possehl, 1980). Their environment was like that of Mesopotamia, low lying, hot, and with fertile soils but no metals. Thus, its inhabitants could not flourish in isolation. Long before the rise of Harappan civilization in the valley, the peoples of the lowlands interacted constantly with their neighbors to the north and west, especially in the highlands of southern Baluchistan in western Pakistan. Metals, semiprecious stones, and timber came from the highlands, where people depended for their subsistence on dry agriculture and sheep herding. Over the millennia, the relationship between lowlands and highlands was fostered not only by regular exchange of foods and other commodities but also by seasonal population movements that brought enormous herds of goats and sheep down from mountain summer pastures in Baluchistan to the lowlands during the harsh winters in the west. In a real sense, economic and social development in both regions developed along parallel if somewhat diverse tracks.

In Baluchistan, a complex of large and small centers subsumed under the *Kulli Complex* evolved during the third millennium B.C. The largest of these settlements was Nindowari, a major center dominated by a sizable monumental structure and massive public buildings. Nindowari was occupied between about 4600 and 4200 years ago, contemporary with that of mature Harappan civilization in the Indus lowlands. Harappan seals and other artifacts occur at Nindowari, and there are signs that Kulli communities were heavily involved in regular exchange with the lowlands to the east. Kulli, too, lay on the borders of eastern Iran, with its intricate exchange networks that reached far to the west toward Mesopotamia (Chapter 16), but it is uncertain how many of its products flowed to the east. For centuries, the Kulli communities of the highlands were specialized partners of the Harappan civilization of the lowlands. This symbiosis between two regions may have been a major catalyst in the rise of complex societies in both regions, a symbiosis that was of vital importance not only in the Indus Valley but in distant Mesopotamia as well.

A RAPID TRANSITION

Early Harappan society was in sharp contrast to the complex, sometimes urban society that developed in the lowlands after about 4600 years ago. The transition from egalitarian to ranked society was an indigenous one, which took place with what Gregory Possehl (1986) calls "a veritable paroxysm of change." There was a short period of explosive growth over a period of one or two centuries ending about 4500 years ago. This contrasts dramatically with the long period of increasing social, political, and economic complexity in Egypt and Mesopotamia.

Gregory Possehl (1986) believes that this growth may have coincided with a major shift in Sumerian trade patterns. As we saw in Chapter 16, the Sumerians obtained many exotic objects and basic raw materials from the Iranian Plateau before 4600 years ago. Judging from historical records, they experienced considerable frustration in their transactions with these exchange networks. After 4600 years ago, they reorganized their trade in luxuries and raw materials and then obtained many of their needs by sea from three foreign states—Dilmun, known to be located on the island of Bahrein in the Persian Gulf; Magan, a port further east; and Meluhha, even further away, a place where ivory, oils, furniture, gold, silver, and carnelian, among other commodities, were to be obtained. The Mesopotamians exchanged these goods for wool, cloth, leather, oil, cereals, and cedarwood. The location of Meluhha is unknown, but Possehl believes it may be the Indus Valley region. About 4350 years ago, King Sargon of Agade boasted that ships from all these locations were moored at his city. There are even records of villages of Meluhhans near Lagash and elsewhere in Mesopotamia. This was a highly organized mercantile trade conducted by specialized merchants, a trade quite different than that of the exchange networks on the highlands far inland.

The sea trade increased the volume of Sumerian imports and exports dramatically. One shipment of 13,000 pounds (5900 kg) of copper is recorded, and the entire enterprise was very different from the basically noncommercial exchange systems of the Iranian Plateau. The trade was under Mesopotamian control, much of it conducted through Dilmun and, in Possehl's (1986) view, it had a major impact on the growth of Harappan civilization. Interestingly, its beginnings coincide with the growth of urban centers in the Indus Valley.

A dramatic increase in long-distance trade may well have been the context in which Harappan civilization developed. It is clear that the lowlands were not the source of many of the products shipped to Sumer. Metals, semiprecious stones, and timber came from the highlands to the north and west. It was here that the long-term symbiosis between the highlands and lowlands came into play, for it was this long-term relationship between two separately developing but contiguous regions that made the Harappans' trade with Mesopotamia a practical reality.

THE HARAPPAN CIVILIZATION

4700 B.P.

By 4700 years ago, the Indus people had mastered the basic problems of irrigation and flood control, partly by using millions of fired bricks made of river alluvium, baked with firewood cut from the riverine forests. Like the Sumerians, they adopted the city as a means of organizing and controlling their civilization. We know of at least five major Harappan cities: Harappa, after which the civilization is known, Mohenjo-daro, Kalibangan, Chanhu-daro, and the recently discovered Dhoraji in Gujerat (Allchin and Allchin, 1983; Possehl, 1982). Harappa and Mohenjo-daro were built on artificial mounds above the floods at the cost of Herculean efforts. Mohenjo-daro was rebuilt at least nine times, sometimes as a result of disastrous inundations. Yet on each occasion the builders followed a gridlike street pattern that was set by the first city rulers and followed until the end. Sir Mortimer Wheeler (1962, 1968) characterizes both cities as giving an impression of "middle-class prosperity with zealous municipal supervision." The two cities are so similar that they might have been designed by the same architect.

A high citadel lies at the west end of each city, dominating the streets below.

Here lived the rulers, protected by great fortifications and flood-works. Harappa's citadel is 460 yards (414 m) long and 215 yards (194 m) wide, surrounded by a forbidding brick wall at least 45 feet (13.5 m) high. Mohenjo-daro's towering citadel rises 40 feet (12 m) above the plain and is protected by massive flood embankments and a vast perimeter wall with towers. The public buildings on the summit include a pillared hall almost 90 feet (27 m) square, perhaps the precinct where the rulers gave audience to petitioners and visiting officials. Everything is utilitarian, efficient, and unostentatious, for there are no spectacular temples or richly adorned shrines. Religious life was centered on a great lustral bath made of bitumen-sealed brickwork and fed by a well. An imposing colonnade surrounded the pool, which was approached by sets of steps at both ends. We cannot be sure of the exact use of the great bath, but perhaps it was where the devout carried out their ceremonial bathing rituals.

The rulers of each city looked down on the north-south street grid laid out in city blocks. The widest east-west thoroughfares at Mohenjo-daro were only 30 feet (9 m) wide, the cross streets only half as wide and unpaved (Figure 18.2). Hundreds of drab, standardized houses presented a blind brick façade to the streets and alleys they lined. The more spacious dwellings, perhaps those of the nobility and merchants, were laid out around a central courtyard where guests may have been received, where food was prepared, and where servants probably lounged. Staircases and thick ground walls indicate that some houses had two or even three stories, with wooden balconies overlooking the courtyard rather than the street, as was the case at Sumerian Ur. The larger residences owned a well and had bathrooms and toilets that may have been joined to an elaborate system of public drains.

The organizing tentacles of the government extended to every detail of city life. Some areas of Harappa and Mohenjo-daro were designated as bazaars, complete with shops (Fairservis, 1976). Archaeologists have inventoried the finds from artisans' quarters where bead makers, coppersmiths, cotton weavers, and other specialists manufactured and sold their wares. The potters' workshops were filled with painted pots decorated with animal figures and everyday plain, wheel-made vessels manufactured not only in the cities but also in villages for hundreds of miles around. There were water jars and cooking bowls, storage pots, and drinking vessels. Metalworkers cast simple axes in open molds and manufactured chisels, knives, razors, spears, and fish hooks. Only a few expert artisans made more elaborate objects, such as small figurines or a piece as complicated as a canopied cart. They would make a wax model of the cart and encase it in clay, which was fired to melt the wax. Then molten copper or bronze was poured into the mold. This "lost-wax" method is still employed by Indian artists.

The technologies used in Harappan cities were developed centuries earlier in small villages and transferred to the cities without change. One of the most developed manufactures was the seal, made from steatite and other soft rocks. Seal workshops have yielded not only finished specimens, hardened in a furnace, but also the blocks of steatite from which square seals were cut as intaglios. For hours, the seal makers would crouch over the tiny squares, expertly cutting representations of animals in profile. They reserved some of their best efforts for religious scenes. Indian archaeolo-

FIGURE 18.2   A typical street in Mohenjo-daro, Pakistan, uncovered in Sir Mortimer Wheeler's excavations.

gists working at the Harappan town of Chanhu-daro south of Mohenjo-daro found a complete bead maker's shop that gave some idea of the labor needed to produce small ornaments. The bead makers prepared bars of agate and carnelian approximately 3 inches (7.6 cm) long that were then ground and polished into shorter, perforated cylinders and strung in necklaces. To experience the bead-making process, the archaeologists took a Harappan stone-tipped drill and some abrasive powder from the workshop and attempted to drill through one of the bead blanks. It took them 20 minutes to drill a small pit in the end of the bead. At that rate, it would have taken 24 hours to drill a single bead!

The overall impression of Harappan cities is faintly depressing. Perhaps the most striking memory of many visitors might have been the constant thump of grain pounders wielded by hundreds of menial workers laboring at the public granaries. The city authorities provided row after row of standardized, two-room houses for those who labored on this and the many other routine but essential tasks that kept this labor-intensive civilization running. With so many unskilled hands and abundant food supplies, there was no incentive for technological innovation, nor apparently did the religious philosophies of the time encourage culture change.

WHO WERE THE HARAPPANS?

Three-quarters of a century of excavations has revealed a highly varied, state-organized society that archaeologists have named the *Harappan* simply because they do not know what the Harappans called themselves. We do not even know the names of the rulers who controlled the major cities, like Harappa and Mohenjo-daro, nor do we have insights into the intricate ties that linked city with town and major centers with minor hamlets. This civilization was different from that of the predominantly urban Sumerians in Mesopotamia. There were only two major cities the size of Uruk in an area of more than 300,000 square miles (Possehl, 1980). It seems unlikely that there was the cultural and social uniformity that one finds in Sumer. Gregory Possehl makes an analogy with ancient Egypt. The Upper and Lower Nile were part of the same civilization, with many common institutions, but there were always administrative, cultural, and social differences between the two regions. The same may be true with the Harappan, with Mohenjo-daro in Sind and Harappa in the Punjab. The Indus Valley may have been a cultural focus of the Harappan civilization, but it was only one part of a much larger, very varied civilization, whose influences and ties extended not only over the lowlands of the Punjab and Sind but also from the highlands of Baluchistan to the deserts of Rajastan and from the Himalayan foothills to near Bombay. There was constant interaction throughout this vast area, with abundant evidence that contemporary, relatively complex societies were developing elsewhere at the same time, developments known from sites like Kulli in Baluchistan (Possehl, 1986). The relationships between highland areas like Baluchistan, with their cold winters, and the lowlands led to complicated seasonal population shifts that brought highlanders and their herds to the Indus lowlands. This classic transhumance pattern may have placed the Harappans and their highland neighbors within the same larger cultural system. A similar kind of relationship may have operated between the Indus Valley and Gujerat to the south. Possehl (1980) considers the Harappan civilization an "experiment in sociocultural organization which failed." It was a large system, but one that did not fully mature. Another expert, Walter Fairservis (1976), called it "more village-like than city-like in the western sense." He compared it to the latest stages of the 'Ubaid in Mesopotamia, just before the profound changes of the Uruk period: "For all its sophistication, it lacked the dynamism that led to the innovation that was historical Sumeria."

The Harappan civilization was an important part of a vast network of regional interactions that functioned through trade routes that extended along the Arabian coast, into northern Afghanistan and Turkmenia, and onto the Iranian Plateau, through thousands of square miles of mountainous terrain rich in minerals and other natural resources. There were regular caravan routes that linked lowlands and highlands. These carried grain and textiles, carnelian beads, pearls, and sweet-smelling rosewood, luxuries exchanged for minerals and other raw materials. Much long-distance trade was conducted by deep-sea vessels cruising the shores of the Indian Ocean into the Persian Gulf. During the 1950s and 1960s, Indian archaeologists uncovered a Harappan-style coastal town on the Gulf of Cambay. This settlement may have served as a river port, perhaps one of several elsewhere on the Pakistani coast.

The anonymity of the Harappan leaders extends even to their appearance. These were no bombastic rulers, boasting of their achievements on grandiose palace walls. They left almost no portraits. One exception is a limestone figure from Mohenjo-daro that depicts a thick-lipped, bearded man staring at the world through slitted eyes. He seems to be withdrawn in meditation, perhaps detached from worldly affairs. The man wears an embroidered robe that was once inlaid with metal. The only clue to his status is that one shoulder is uncovered, a sign of reverence during the Buddha's lifetime more than 1000 years later. Could it be that the same convention applied in Harappan times and the portrait is that of a priest or a priest-king? Thus far, the evidence of archaeology reveals leadership by rulers who led unostentatious lives marked by a complete lack of priestly pomp or lavish public display. There is nothing of the ardent militarism of the Assyrian kings nor of the slavish glorification of the pharaohs.

The focus of Harappan civilization may have been on the irrigated lands of the Indus, where barley and wheat were cultivated in irrigated fields that lapped the city's suburbs, but most people were still village farmers practicing dry agriculture in and away from the valley. The lowland Harappans relied on rice, a crop first cultivated somewhere between India and Southeast Asia before 7000 years ago. They cultivated cotton and dates and kept cattle and water buffalo. Every farmer turned over a substantial portion of the annual harvest to the state, and indeed the authorities may have controlled the ownership of much of the land. The entire agricultural enterprise was a much larger-scale version of the communal village farming that originally had made colonization of the Indus Valley possible.

Both Harappa and Mohenjo-daro housed a comfortable and unpretentious middle class of merchants and petty officials who lived in stolid and standardized brick houses along the city streets. They wore finely woven, decorated cotton robes. Judging from clay figurines, the women wore short skirts and headdresses and perhaps longer robes (Figure 18.3). Dozens of shops sold wire neck bangles, necklaces, and pendants, but there is nothing of the elaboration found in Egyptian or Mycenaean palaces. The more prosperous city dwellers sometimes owned some ornate carved rosewood furniture, but the life-style was far from lavish.

The artisans—metalsmiths, potters, weavers, bead makers, seal carvers—formed a distinct class, as did the many petty bureaucrats and priests needed to run the multifarious affairs of government, each with his designated quarters. However, such people were a tiny minority compared with the vast mass of the populace: farmers, laborers, seafarers, and menial workers of every type. They lived in small urban dwellings or, more often, in the countryside and wore the simplest cotton loincloths or robes. To judge from modern Indian life, they had an extended family of several generations, which provided a network of kinship ties and other benefits such as communal ownership of property. Perhaps, too, the Harappan people were organized

FIGURE 18.3   Bronze figurine of a dancing girl from Mohenjo-daro, Pakistan, 4.3 inches (11 cm) high.

in a hierarchy of castes that restricted upward mobility and provided a wider identity outside the confines of the family.

Harappan Beliefs

Like the Sumerians, the Harappans lived in an environment that they modified for their own protection, one in which the annual floods meant a renewal of life and food for the coming year. Like the Mesopotamians, they seem to have believed that they lived in the valley to serve the gods, who caused crops to grow and soils to be fertile. The primeval roots of Indian religion may have been age-old fertility cults that served the same function as Inanna among the Sumerians and the mother goddess in many other Near Eastern civilizations—an assurance that life would continue. The only clues we have to the origins of Indian religion come from minute seal impressions and small clay figurines from Harappan villages and cities that depict a female deity with conspicuous breasts and sexual organs. We do not know her name, but she probably embodied earth and life-giving nature for the Indus people.

A seal from Mohenjo-daro bears a three-headed figure who sits in the yogic posture and wears a horned headdress. He is surrounded by a tiger, elephant, rhi-

noceros, water buffalo, and deer. Some archaeologists believe that the seal represents a forerunner of the great god Shiva in his role of Lord of the Beasts. Many
Harappan seals depict cattle, which may be symbols of Shiva, who was worshiped
in several forms. To judge from later beliefs, he may have had a dual role, serving
as a fertility god as well as a tamer or destroyer of wild beasts (Miller, 1985; Wolpert, 1977). Shiva gave life by planting the seed but also could destroy any creature, including human beings, at a flick of the finger. In part he may symbolize the
unpredictable dangers of flood and famine that could threaten a village or a city.
Harappa and Mohenjo-daro have yielded dozens of carved phallic symbols and
circular stones with round holes, which represent Shiva's consort Devi's teeming
womb. Perhaps these are simple prototypes of the Hindu *lingam* and *yoni* symbols
that are found in the temples of Shiva and Devi to this day. If the evidence of
figurines and seals is to be believed, the symbolism of early Indus religion bears
remarkable similarities to that of modern Hinduism. This similarity highlights the
deeply ingrained conservatism of Indian society from the very earliest moments of
Harappan civilization.

Writing and Weights

One reason we know so little about the Harappans is that their script still has not
been deciphered. Almost 400 different pictographic symbols have been identified
from their seals. Linguists do not even agree on the language in the script, let alone
the ultimate identity of the Harappans. Some authorities believe the seals served not
only as religious symbols but also as tags or labels written in Sumerian on bundles
of merchandise sent to distant Sumer. Some success has been attained with computer-
aided deciphering techniques, which have established the script as logo-syllabic; that
is, it is a mixture of sounds and words, just like Egyptian hieroglyphs (Fairservis,
1983).

Enough of the Indus script has been deciphered to show how many of the short
seal inscriptions designate the names of individuals and their ranks. It seems, too, that
some describe major figures of the Harappan cosmos and name the chiefs, as well as
identifying scribes and artisan leaders in society. There are certainly close links
between the Harappan script and later writings. Many of the Indus symbols are
similar to those on Brahmi documents from the Ganges Valley centuries later. Both
were written in what is called the *boustrophedon* style. This writing alternates lines
going from right to left and left to right. This style contrasts with English, which
progresses from left to right, and Arabic, which runs in the opposite direction. Many
signs and symbols used on Harappan seals are found on pottery and other objects
made as late as the ninth century B.C.

Even more striking evidence for cultural continuity comes from the humble
half-ounce weight. No government monopoly can survive without weights and measures, so the Harappan authorities developed a standard weight that was close to
one-half of a modern ounce. Later, Indian societies used a unit known as the *karsa*
for the same purpose. This weighed the equivalent of 32 *rattis*, seeds of the Gunja

creeper, a measure that could fluctuate slightly from year to year. Four karsas weighed almost exactly the same as the basic Harappan unit of a half ounce. Similar devices could be found in nineteenth-century bazaars.

The Decline of Harappan Civilization

The Harappan civilization reached its peak approximately 4000 years ago. Mohenjo-daro housed at least 40,000 people at the time and was at the apogee of its prosperity. By 3700 years ago, Harappa and Mohenjo-daro were in decline and soon abandoned. This decline may be associated with major changes in Indus flood levels, but there are no reasons to suppose there were catastrophic floods that destroyed the Harappan civilization, as has been suggested (Raikes, 1967). What is known is that the decline of the two great cities was followed by an explosion of village settlement in Gujerat to the south, as if the experiment in urban living was a failure. It may be that the shift from irrigation farming to dry agriculture, from major urban centers to a more rural settlement pattern, may be the result of major shifts in trading activities throughout northwestern Pakistan and neighboring areas. Some fundamental questions remain. How did the various regions affected by the Harappan civilization form a single, integrated system? What were the links between the Indus Valley core and the periphery? At present, we do not know (Possehl and Raval, 1989).

The rural components of Harappan culture continued to flourish in Gujerat and other areas for two centuries or more, until Aryan nomads swept down on the Indus Valley and the lowlands. By that time, the Harappans had passed on a priceless legacy of beliefs and philosophies that formed one of the mainstreams of all subsequent Indian history.

From the archaeological point of view, the period between the breakdown of the Harappan cities and the beginning of ironworking is the most obscure in India's later prehistory (Wolpert, 1977). Despite the abandonment of the cities, there were no major disruptions in economy or material culture. Iron tools appeared in India by 3100 years ago and are associated with painted gray wares, made on a wheel and adorned with simple, black-painted designs. The advent of iron tools enabled farmers to break up the hard, calcareous soils of the Ganges Plain, an area that was to become the heartland of later empires.

Meanwhile, King Darius of Persia invaded the subcontinent in 516 B.C. and incorporated part of India into the Persian Empire. Two centuries later, Alexander the Great ventured to the Indus River and brought Greek culture to the area. His incursion also provided a stimulus for cultural developments in the Ganges, which culminated in a nationalistic revolt headed by the priest Chandragupta. This leader founded an empire that linked the Indus and the Ganges in a single administrative unit that traded as far afield as Malaya and the Near East. The period between approximately 200 B.C. and A.D. 300 saw India linked with lands far to the east and west by regular trading routes that persisted more or less independently of political developments. By this time, the influence of Indian religion in the form of Buddhism and Hinduism was being felt over enormous areas of Asia.

Marginal notes:

Ironworking
Painted gray wares
3000 B.P.

516 B.C.

316 B.C.

SOUTHEAST ASIAN CIVILIZATIONS

The emergence of complex states in Southeast Asia (Figure 18.4) probably is closely connected with the spread of rice cultivation and bronze metallurgy. As we saw in Chapter 13, the early history of rice cultivation is inadequately documented, but we do know that the spread of rice agriculture throughout Southeast Asia may prove to be connected with farmers originating in what is now southern China. Pottery that

FIGURE 18.4   Southeast Asia.

shows the influence of their widespread traditions has been found in Thailand and possibly Malaya. The genesis of copper and bronze metallurgy in Southeast Asia is even less well documented. The Non Nok Tha cemetery yielded some bronze axes originally dated to about 4100 years ago (Bayard, 1977). However, the contexts from which the dates came have been a matter of controversy. Some authorities believe they date to no earlier than the second millennium B.C. (Higham, 1989; Higham and Kijngam, 1984; for more discussion, see Bayard, 1984).

Ban Chiang
4000 B.P.

More controversy surrounds the emergence of bronze working in Southeast Asia. Until recently, the Ban Chiang cemetery in northern Thailand was claimed as evidence for very early bronze working in the area, with burials dating to a long period between about 5600 years ago and A.D. 300 and bronze artifacts to at least 4000 years ago (Figure 18.5) (R. White, 1982). The radiocarbon dates from the burial pits have been questioned by archaeologists digging three other sites nearby (Higham, 1989). Recent excavations at the Non Pa Wai site in northeast Thailand dissected a large mound of copper smelting debris, dating the earliest levels of smelting activity there to some centuries before 4000 years ago (Pigott and Natapintu, 1990). A vigorous debate still surrounds the origins of bronze working in Thailand (see Bayard, 1984; Higham, 1989).

3500 B.P.

Charles Higham's shorter chronology receives important support from excavations in Vietnam's lower Red River Valley. There, bronze appeared by about 3500 years ago in sites of the late Phung Nguyen culture (Huyen, 1984). Unfortunately,

FIGURE 18.5   Excavation at Ban Chiang, Thailand, 1975.

only isolated radiocarbon dates are available, so the chronology is still loosely an-chored. Bronze metallurgy was also well established on the Vietnamese coast during the late second millennium B.C. One site near Ho Chi Minh City has yielded sand-stone molds and bronze artifacts identical to those found in northeast Thailand (Higham, 1989).

There are two possible interpretations of this dating evidence. The long time scale means that the Ban Chiang people worked bronze at least 1500 years earlier than people elsewhere in Southeast Asia. Proponents of the shorter chronology say that bronze working was present in coastal Vietnam and the Mekong Valley by 3500 years ago.

Dong Son
culture
300 B.C.

Vietnam's Dong Son culture represents the culmination of early bronze and ironworking in prehistoric times. Co Loa, near Hanoi, comprises three sets of ram-parts, with moats supplied with water by a tributary of the Red River. At Co Loa's greatest extent, the fortifications enclosed about 1482 acres (600 ha). By this time, rice cultivation was sufficiently productive to support a considerable population density, combined as it was with plow cultivation, double cropping, and water con-trol. According to Chinese records, local chieftains named Lac Lords, keepers of the drums, controlled the rights to rice land. The area was incorporated as a Chinese protectorate in 111 B.C., by which time the Dong Son rulers were in regular contact with Han China (Wheatley, 1979). From this point on, as in earlier times, much social change concerned the states and role of individuals rather than wider communities (Higham, 1989).

Foreign Influences

Although archaeological evidence is still largely lacking, it seems likely that state forms of society were evolving in Southeast Asia as early as 1800 years ago (Higham, 1989). What is uncertain is the extent to which foreign influences played a part in the dissemination of more complex state organizations. Much of our information on early Southeast Asian states comes from Chinese and Indian sources (Hall, 1985).

Trading Systems Established

For centuries Southeast Asia was dominated, at least tangentially, by two foreign presences. To the north the Chinese imposed their political will on the Lăc peoples on the Tong-king lowlands and extended their tribute systems into the Red River Valley. This was an arbitrary imposition of an entirely different economic system onto trading systems based on reciprocity. It was quite different from the cultural changes going on in the southerly parts of Southeast Asia.

A.D. 1

Approximately 2000 years ago, the busy sea-trading networks of Southeast Asia were being incorporated into the vast oceanic trade routes stretching from China in the east to the shores of the Red Sea and the east coast of Africa in the west. No one people controlled the whole of this vast trade. Most of the Indian Ocean commerce was in the hands of traders, who used monsoon winds to traverse the long sea-lanes from India to Africa and from Arabia to both continents. The trade carried raw materials and luxury goods such as glass beads and cloth. During the heyday of the Roman Empire, the Greeks and Egyptians of Alexandria took some interest in the Indian Ocean trade but rarely ventured farther than the Red Sea.

Beyond India, the trade was held by Indian merchants who penetrated deep into the numerous islands and channels of Southeast Asia. The traders themselves were an entirely maritime people, called *Mwani,* or *barbarians,* by the Chinese of the time. They spoke a polyglot of tongues and were of many lands, some Malays, some Indians, true wanderers who ventured as far east as the South China Sea. The Gulf of Tonkin and South China were served by *Jiwet,* Chinese mariners who brought luxuries to the coast, whence they were transported overland to the Chinese capital.

Indian merchants certainly were active on Southeast Asian coasts by the early centuries of the Christian era. They were trading with the tribal societies of both mainland and islands. Voyaging was then accelerated by changing circumstances. First came larger cargo vessels with a more efficient rig that enabled them to sail closer to the wind. No one knows how large these vessels were, but they must have been substantial. The Chinese are known to have transported horses by sea to Indonesia in the third century A.D., and the monk Fa Hsien recorded his sailing trip from Ceylon to China with 200 other passengers in A.D. 414.

Another factor influencing trade was a new demand for gold and other metals. The Emperor Vespasian had prohibited exporting metals from the Roman Empire in approximately A.D. 70, a move that turned Indian merchants' eyes to the southeast, particularly because the Siberian gold mines had been closed to them by nomadic raids on Asian caravans. Metals were not the only attraction; spices could be obtained in abundance. Trade was expanded entirely for commercial profit.

Religions Imported

Buddhism had made great strides in India since it appeared in the fourth century B.C. The older religion, Brahmanism, had placed severe and authoritarian restraints on foreign voyages, but Buddhism and Jainism, a form of Hinduism, rejected the notion of racial purity espoused by the predecessor religion. Travel was encouraged; the merchant became a respected part of Buddhist belief. As voyaging increased, especially from southern India to Southeast Asia, a strong cultural influence came to be felt. The tribal societies of Southeast Asia were introduced to many alien products and some of the foreigners' philosophical, social, and religious beliefs. In a few centuries, kingdoms appeared with governments run according to Hindu or Buddhist ideas of social order.

Chieftains Become Divine Kings

The initial but regular contacts between merchants and tribal societies were seasonal, dictated by the monsoon winds. The chieftains who represented the people of the tribes would have acted as intermediaries between the foreigners and the indigenous people. All exchanges and transactions having to do with the trade were channeled through them. Inevitably, argues Sinologist Paul Wheatley (1975), the chieftains learned a new way of seeing society and the world, perhaps assembling the collection of commodities for trade, acquiring organizational skills alien to their own societies. As principal beneficiaries of the trade, they would gain status, many more possessions, and therefore strong interest in seeing the trade maintained. However, the authority and powers needed to expand and maintain the commerce were not part of the kin-linked society in which the chieftains had lived all their lives. In time, they might come to feel closer sympathy with their visitors, the people who gave them their power and prestige. Philosophically they would come to feel closer to Indian models of authority and leadership. They would become familiar with the Brahman and Buddhist conceptions of divine kingship. There was even a brahmanic rite by which chieftains could be inducted into the ruling class, a group whose authority was vested in an assumption of divine kingship. Wheatley hypothesizes that regular trading contacts, combined with changes in beliefs about the legitimizing of authority, led to the birth of states in Southeast Asia.

Divine kingship was a cultural borrowing from India that revolutionized social and political organization in Southeast Asia. Numerous city-states arose in strategic parts of this huge region. Many were served by Brahman priests, who among other functions consecrated divine kings as they started their reigns. Some of these states became very powerful, with extensive trading connections and large Brahman communities. As early as the third century A.D., Chinese envoys to Southeast Asia reported on a state in the northern part of the Malay Peninsula that enjoyed regular trading contacts with Parthia and India as well as southern China.

Funan

c. A.D. 100 to 546

The Chinese visited many small Southeast Asian kingdoms that modified Indian civilization to their own purposes, but the most famous was Funan, a mercantile empire that extended along the Mekong Delta in Vietnam and some distance inland into Kampuchea (Higham, 1989). Funan appears in Chinese histories from approximately the third to seventh centuries A.D. but probably came into being in approximately A.D. 100. Most accounts of Funan extol its "port of a thousand rivers" and its rich trade in gold, silver, bronze, and spices. They tell of the Funan people, who built a drainage and irrigation system that rapidly transformed much of the delta from barren swamps into rich agricultural land. The development of these fields took the communal efforts of hundreds of people living off the fish that teemed in the bayous of the delta. Most Funans lived in large lake cities fortified with great earthworks and moats swarming with crocodiles. Each major settlement was a port connected to the ocean and its neighbors by a network of artificial canals.

Funan prospered greatly from the third to sixth centuries. The ports handled goods from all over the East, even horses brought by sea from central Asia. Large numbers of Chinese merchants and Indian artisans settled in the cities and worked with bronze, ivory, silver, gold, and even coral. They brought new skills with them that the local people copied. In the sixth century many more Indian Brahmans arrived in Funan. They brought the cult of Shiva, the god who was to become the focus of all subsequent Southeast Asian civilization. He appeared in the temples in the form of a *linga*, a phallic emblem of masculine creative power. The royal linga stood in a temple on the hill that symbolized the center of every capital. Shiva's omnipresent emblem soon was the focus of all Kampuchean civilization, surviving the fall of Funan in the sixth century.

The Rise of the God-Kings

Chenla
A.D. 611 to 802

Khmer
A.D. 802 to
1218

Funan was succeeded by the state of Chenla, the economic hub of which lay around the Great Lake in the central basin of Kampuchea (Briggs, 1951). Most of the year the lake is a shallow series of muddy pools some 40 miles (66.6 km) long, drained by the Tonle Sap River that runs into the Mekong. However, so much water floods into the Mekong Delta from July to January that the Tonle Sap's course is reversed and the pools become a vast lake, 80 to 100 miles (133 to 167 km) long, 15 to 30 miles (25 to 50 km) wide, and up to 50 feet (15.5 m) deep. Late in October the water starts receding, trapping millions of fish in the muddy bayous. The Great Lake provided such favorable opportunities for rice cultivation and fishing that its shores supported a far higher population density than even the irrigated delta downstream. This unique environment enabled the Chenla kings not only to embark on ambitious conquests but also to develop a new political concept of divine kingship that united their far-flung domains in a common purpose—the glorification of the god-king on earth. The earlier Khmer kings were unable to hold the kingdom together until a dynamic monarch named Jayavarman II was crowned in A.D. 802. He had spent some years in Java, where he had studied a new cult, the worship of the god-king. This *Devaraja* cult taught that the king did not rule by divine authority alone but that he was a god himself to be worshiped and obeyed without question. Jayavarman II adopted the teachings of this powerful cult to consolidate his vast kingdom. His subjects were taught to worship him as a god. All resources were devoted to the preservation of the cult of the god-king. Everyone, whether noble, high priest, or commoner, was expected to subordinate his or her ambitions to the need to perpetuate the existence of the king on earth and his identity with the god in this life and the next. The symbol of the king's authority was the royal linga (Briggs, 1951). Jayavarman II's new strategy was brilliantly successful. He reigned for 45 years, founded a dynasty that prospered for 600 years, and united the Khmer kingdoms into a colorful, spectacular empire that reached the height of its prosperity between A.D. 900 and 1200, shortly after his death.

Previous monarchs had encouraged the worship of Shiva in the form of this phallic image, but now Jayavarman II presented himself as the reincarnation of Shiva on earth. He was the *varman*, the protector, and his priests were the instruments of practical political power. The high priests were invariably energetic, imposing nobles, who presided over a highly disciplined hierarchy of religious functionaries. They supervised every aspect of Khmer life, from agriculture to warfare and the rituals of the state religion. The custom of building a new majestic and holy temple to house the royal linga of each king was the most important of all the religious rituals. As a result, most of the 30 monarchs who followed Jayavarman II left massive religious edifices to commemorate their reigns. These they built on temple mountains or artificial mounds in the center of their capitals, the hub of the Khmer universe.

Jayavarman II's new policies, based on the assumption that he had no living superior on earth, succeeded but only after several decades of brutal suppression and cruelty. The king played one prince off against another, planted spies everywhere, and executed everyone who stood in his way. His propaganda machine successfully convinced the masses that their individual welfare as well as that of the kingdom depended on the success of the new cult. For the next three centuries, each Khmer king ruled as "great master, king of kings." Inevitably, however, the despotism overwhelmed them. They surrounded themselves with a brilliant and powerful court that upheld their desire for supreme power, so much so that the kings lost touch with their subjects. Soon they were completely obsessed with life after death and their memorials on earth. Thousands of their subjects toiled to build fabulous temples and palaces such as Angkor Wat purely for the king's pleasure. When the people were admitted, they prostrated themselves not before the gods but before the god-king. The Khmer's unique form of divine kingship produced, instead of an austere civilization like that of the Indus, a society with a blind faith in powerful kings who carried the cult of wealth, luxury, and self-aggrandizement to amazing lengths.

Angkor Wat

Angkor Wat
A.D. 1200 to 1432

The Khmer kings who followed Jayavarman II indulged two passions: warfare and temple building. They surrounded themselves with artists, poets, and sculptors whose sole task was to embellish and adorn their magnificent capitals. Most of these capitals were built in a fertile area teeming with fish near the Tonle Sap, an area known as *Angkor*. Of all the edifices there, the most famous is Angkor Wat (Figure 18.6). This extraordinary shrine is a spectacle of beauty, wonder, and magnificence, the largest religious building in the world, greater even than Vatican City, 5000 feet (1500 m) by 4000 feet (1200 m) across. The central block measures 717 feet (215 m) by 620 feet (186 m) and rises more than 200 feet (60 m) above the forest. It dwarfs even the largest Sumerian ziggurat and makes Mohenjo-daro's citadel look like a village shrine. Angkor Wat took 40 years to build and finally was abandoned in 1432.

Angkor Wat is approached through an entrance gallery with a tower by a paved causeway 500 feet (150 m) long that is flanked with balustrades adorned with mythical, multiheaded snakes. It opens onto a cruciform terrace in front of a rectangular temple that rises in three imposing tiers to a central cluster of five towers. Each tower bears a lofty pinnacle that from afar looks like a giant lotus bud. The causeway leads across a huge moat 600 feet (180 m) wide enclosed by masonry walls 4 miles (6.4 km)

FIGURE 18.6   The temple at Angkor Wat.

in circumference. The engineers built the walls with a total error of less than an inch! The moat still is a beautiful sight, with floating water lilies, wild orchids, and other shimmering blooms. Angkor Wat was built in three great rising squares (Giteau, 1966). A central group of chambers and then long open galleries extend all around each square, with a double square of columns on their outer face. Each terrace is surrounded by a gallery interspersed with corner towers, pavilions, stairways, and other structures. On the highest terrace, the central tower is tied to axial pavilions by galleries supported by pillars that divide it into four paved courts. The towers themselves are without interior windows or staircases and are finished with superb lotus-bud cones.

Every detail of this extraordinary building reproduces part of the heavenly world in a terrestrial mode. The Khmer believed that the world consists of a central continent known as *Jambudvipa*, with the cosmic mountain *Meru* rising from its center. The gods lived at the summit of Meru, represented at Angkor Wat by the highest tower. The remaining four towers depict Meru's lesser peaks; the enclosure wall, the mountain at the edge of the world; and the surrounding moat, the ocean beyond. Angkor Wat was the culminating attempt of the Khmer to reproduce a monument to the Hindu gods: Shiva, the creator; Vishnu, the preserver of the universe; and Brahma, who raised the earth. Everything about Angkor Wat is on a massive and lavish scale, as if expense, time, and slave labor were of little importance.

The galleries of Angkor Wat are adorned with more than 4000 feet (1212 m) of polished sandstone bas-reliefs, each approximately 8 feet (2.42 m) high (Giteau,

1966). Some 2000 temple dancers wearing ropes of pearls dance in graceful, acrobatic poses along the galleries, walls, and pillars. These lovely, smiling, and often seductive creatures, naked to the waist, soften the dark gray edifice, stretching for hundreds of feet over the walls of the second and third terraces. Most of the bas-reliefs depict religious scenes, popular legends, and wars. Hundreds of soldiers mounted on elephants ride victorious over opposing armies, warriors fight from chariots, and fleets sail to battle. There are even armies of monkeys and men, and victory marches with bands and banners. The sculptures invoke the Hindu Trinity, gods, goddesses, and guardian deities. The god-king rides on a royal elephant surrounded by slaves and soldiers. He is depicted setting forth to fight Angkor's enemies with the blessings of his priests and is seen administering his domains and enjoying the triumphs of his reign.

After A.D. 1218 an exhausted nation built no more stone temples. The seem-
Angkor Wat taxed the resources of the kingdom so severely that civil war ensued. Undeterred, the rulers used thousands of prisoners of war to erect a huge new capital at Angkor Thom nearby. The sheer size of Angkor Thom is overwhelming. A dark and forbidding 8-mile (12.8-km) wall surrounds the capital. The five gateways rise 60 feet (18 m), and the formerly crocodile-filled moat is 540 feet (162 m) across. When visitors walked into the capital, they entered a symbolic Hindu world with the king's funerary temple at the center. Great triple-headed elephants guard the flanks of the gates, and four huge Buddha faces adorn the towers above the massive doorways. The Grand Plaza of Angkor Thom was the scene of ceremonies and contests, of vast military reviews and massed bands. Long bas-reliefs of animals and kings walking in procession above seas of snakes and fish lead to the plaza and look down on its wide spaces.

It is said that a million people once lived in or near Angkor Thom. The architectural and artistic legacy they left is mind-boggling, one so large that a single frieze of marching elephants extends over 1200 feet (360 m) of sculpted wall. The task of building the city beggared the state. The temple of the king's father contained no fewer than 430 images, with more than 20,000 in gold, silver, bronze, and stone in the wider precincts. Another inscription in the same temple records that 306,372 people from 13,500 villages worked for the shrine, consuming 38,000 tons of rice a year. An inscription in the nearby temple of Ta Prohm inventories a staff of 18 senior priests, 2740 minor functionaries, 615 female dancers, and a total of 66,625 "men and women who perform the service of the gods." The same temple owned gold and silver dishes, thousands of pearls, 876 Chinese veils, and 2387 sets of clothing for its statues. The result of the ruler's megalomaniacal orgy was a totally centripetal and macabre religious utopia in which every product, every person's labor, and every thought was directed to embellishing the hub of the universe and the men who enjoyed it (Wheatley, 1975).

After A.D. 1218 an exhausted nation built no more stone temples. The seemingly endless pool of prisoners of war dried up once the economy faltered, and there were no longer the resources to support the army or maintain the great irrigation works of Tonle Sap. The only way the Khmer could maintain their strange utopia was through oppression, promiscuous use of slave labor, and the blind obedience of their own subjects. Once the image of the divine king was challenged and the slaves ceased to serve, the empire was doomed. Angkor Thom fell to alien armies in approximately 1430, and the divine kings and their works were soon just a shadowy memory.

GUIDE TO FURTHER READING

Allchin, Bridget, and Allchin, Raymond. 1983. *The Rise of Civilization in India and Pakistan.* Cambridge, Eng.: Cambridge University Press.
   A summary account of the roots of the Indus civilization that is readable and well argued.

Fairservis, Walter A. 1976. *The Roots of Ancient India,* 2d ed. New York: Macmillan.
   A popular account of the Harappan that contains an excellent description of the cities.

Possehl, Gregory. 1986. *Kulli: The Exploration of Ancient Civilization in Asia.* Durham: North Carolina University Press.
   A wide-ranging analysis of the Kulli Complex, with provocative discussion of the Harappan civilization. A specialist monograph.

Wheeler, Sir Mortimer. 1962. *The Indus Civilization,* 2d ed. Cambridge, Eng.: Cambridge University Press.
   Wheeler's classic account is based on his Indus Valley excavations in the late 1940s. Somewhat outdated, but it reads well.

Wolpert, Stanley A. 1977. *A New History of India.* London: Oxford University Press.
   By far the most lucid account of Indian history for the beginner. A good synthesis of archaeology, legend, and documentary sources.

Southeast Asia is difficult to study in any depth, for books are few and far between. However, the following are suggested:

Briggs, L. Cabot. 1951. "The Ancient Khmer Empire." *Transactions of the American Philosophical Society,* 41.
   Perhaps the standard archaeological and historical source for specialists and lay readers alike. Highly technical but crammed with useful information, much of it from very obscure sources.

Giteau, M. 1966. *Khmer Sculpture and the Angkor Civilization.* London: Thames and Hudson.
   A wonderful lay reader's guide to the elaborate artistry and architecture of the Khmer. Lavishly illustrated.

Higham, Charles. 1989. *The Archaeology of Mainland Southeast Asia*. Cambridge, Eng.: Cambridge University Press.

   A comprehensive account of mainland Southeast Asia that melds archaeological and historical evidence. Up to date and authoritative.

White, Joyce C. 1982. *Ban Chiang: Discovery of a Lost Bronze Age Civilization*. Philadelphia: University of Pennsylvania Press.

   A brief but clearly written account of this remarkable site written to accompany a museum exhibition. Gives useful insight into Southeast Asian bronze working.

Chronological Table J

Calibrated Dates a.d./b.c./b.p.	C14 Years A.D./B.C./B.P.	Culture	Phase
		Historic times	
420–5 b.c.	A.D. 1		
	221 B.C.	Unification of China	
820–400 b.c.	2500 B.P.	ZHOU	
1530–905 b.c.	3000 B.P.	SHANG	Late Shang
		SHANG CIVILIZATION[a]	Middle Shang
			Early Shang
		XIA	
4830–4305 b.p.	4000 B.P.	LONGSHAN	
5950–5640 b.p.	5000 B.P.		
		Chapter 13 ↑	

[a]SHANG CIVILIZATION refers to a civilization that survived the changing of ruling dynasties.

CHAPTER 19 | SHANG CIVILIZATION IN EAST ASIA

Preview

- Early Chinese civilization emerged independent of state-organized societies in the West. By 4500 years ago, population densities were rising in farming communities throughout China, and there are signs of social differentiation in village cemeteries. Exchange networks linked thousands of small communities by 6000 years ago, spurring social and technological changes that included copper metallurgy and the widespread use of earthen fortifications. A new cosmology based on animals and the use of divination to communicate with the dead came into widespread use. These Longshan cultures are found in at least three major variants throughout China.

- The Shang civilization of the Yellow Valley is the best-known early Chinese state, flourishing from approximately 3766 to 3122 years ago. It probably was the dominant state among several throughout northern China. Shang origins are partly from Longshan roots and partly from influences that came to the Shang from the east.

- There were at least three stages of Shang civilization, associated with distinctive writing and bronze metallurgy. Shang society was organized along class lines, with the rulers and nobles living in segregated precincts whereas the mass of the people were scattered in townships and villages in the surrounding countryside.

- Shang civilization ended with the overthrow of the Shang dynasty by Zhou rulers, who reigned over a wide area of northern China from 3122 to 2221 years ago.

Chronological
Table J

The origins of Chinese civilization were known only from legend until the late 1920s, when Tung Tso-pin and, later, Li Chi began digging in the Anyang area of Henan province in northern China. Their excavations resulted in the discovery of the Shang civilization, which flourished in the Yellow Valley more than 3500 years ago (Chang, 1980, 1986; Keightley, 1983).

THE EMERGENCE OF
CHINESE CIVILIZATION

4500 B.P.

By 4500 years ago, agriculture had taken such hold in China that population densities rose throughout the country. The farmers took more and more land into cultivation until there was little new acreage available for planting. Some pollen analyses from northern villages show how the trees that once surrounded many settlements were felled as the fields lapped right up to the houses (Chang, 1986). This population growth also coincided with an expansion of wet rice farming in lowland areas, on moist floodplains, and in lush water meadows where irrigation was easy (Figure 19.1). Those villages fortunate enough to possess lands that could be irrigated, especially in the Yellow and Yangtze valleys, soon turned into much more permanent settlements, often protected with earthen walls to guard against floods and marauding neighbors. Even these larger communities were part of a self-regulating folk society in which kinship loyalties and the extended family were all-important and age was deeply revered. The family ancestors were the conduit to the gods who controlled the harmony of the world.

However, there are signs that a new order existed, for some settlements of 5000 years ago contain elaborate burials adorned with jade ornaments and ceremonial weapons. Village artisans created fine clay vessels exclusively for the use of these privileged people. These were important leaders who are known to have raided their neighbors, for the corpses of their enemies have been found deposited in village wells. In both the north and south, a few peasant villages became important centers ruled by new generations of kin leaders who became the nobles of more sophisticated societies. They probably were expert warriors and certainly were people of great spiritual authority, experts at predicting the future and communicating with the ancestors.

These developments would never have been possible without the unswerving conservatism of the country farmer. The village crops might change from cereals to rice, the fertility of the soils depend on radically different rainfall patterns, and building materials alter from brick and tile to bamboo, but what never varied was the unquestioning acceptance by the peasants of an emerging social order that imposed an almost alien, wealthy, privileged society. The viability of this aristocratic civilization depended on simple loyalties that persisted from the earliest centuries of

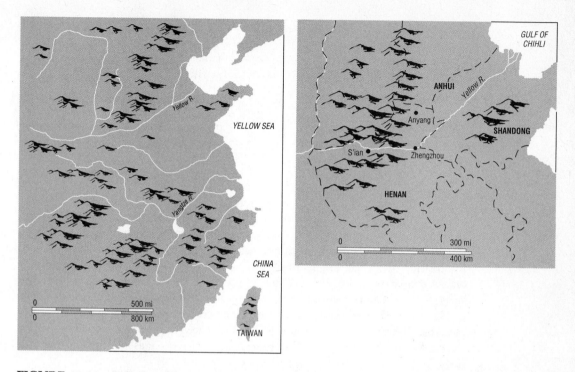

FIGURE 19.1   (*Left*) Distribution of farming cultures that immediately preceded Shang civilization in China (commonly called Longshan). Each cross-hatched area represents a different regional variant of Longshan (not discussed in detail in the text). Compare with the second map (*right*), which shows the approximate distribution of Shang culture about 3400 years ago. (Xiao-tun and other royal sites are close to Anyáng.)

farming life into modern times. Every Chinese noble, however unimportant, cashed in on this loyalty.

Longshan
?5000 B.P.

After about 6000 years ago, the several regional Longshan farming cultures of north and south China became interlinked in what Chang (1986) calls an "interaction sphere," trading raw materials, luxury goods, and other commodities over long distances. This interdependence spurred similar developments in more complex social organization as well as technological changes that spilled over from narrow territorial boundaries to affect much of China. These innovations included copper metallurgy, construction of stamped-earth town walls, and the first widespread use of earthen fortifications. There is far more evidence for warfare and violence, including the decapitation of prisoners. New, powerful rituals emerged, among them a cosmology based on animals and birds and the use of divination to communicate with the ancestors. These Longshan cultures, found in at least three major variants throughout China, show clear evidence of marked social stratification, with sharp economic and political distinctions between the elite and the mass of the common people.

These many changes were the result of constant interaction among many different farming societies, a kind of relationship among complex chiefdoms that inevitably drew them into a larger system (H. T. Wright, 1977). This interaction developed over a period of 2000 years after 6000 years ago, culminating in the emergence of Chinese civilization about 4000 years B.P. (for a full discussion, see Chang, 1986).

Shoulder Blades and Oracles

Longshan
?4700 B.P.

When archaeologists dug into a village named Longshan on the Yellow River in Shando province in 1930 to 1931, they found not only the remains of a farming village but also dozens of cracked ox shoulder blades that they identified as oracle bones used in divination ceremonies (Figure 19.2) (Keightley, 1983). The cracks were made by applying hot metal to the bone and then were interpreted as messages from the ancestors. None of the Longshan bones bore written inscriptions, but the hundreds of shoulder blades found in pits near Anyang farther upstream are a mine of information about the origins of Chinese civilization, a unique written archive of official deliberations by the very first kings of northern China. One scholar has suggested that Chinese writing may have originated from the need to interpret the cracks on the bones, with the new writing symbols resembling persistent crack patterns. Clearly some Chinese ideographs originated as pictograms, such as that for the hill, originally shown with three humps and now written as a horizontal line with three vertical strokes (Fitzgerald, 1978).

Perhaps as early as 4500 years ago, divination rituals were a vital part of village government. All official divinations were addressed to the royal ancestors, who acted as intermediaries between the living and the ultimate ancestor and supreme being, the ruler of heaven and the creator, Shang Di. This deity served as the ancestor not only of the royal line but also of the "multitude of the people." The king was the head of all family lines that radiated from his person to the nobility and then to the common people. These actual and imputed kinship ties were the core of early Chinese civilization, for they obligated the peasants to provide food and labor for their rulers.

In addition to shoulder blades from oxen and water buffalo, the diviners used tortoiseshell for their ceremonies. The term *scapulimancy,* meaning "shoulder blade divination," refers to the bones used most frequently in the ceremonies. The bones and shells were smoothed and cleaned and perhaps soaked in liquid to soften them. Rows of hollows were then produced on the underside to make the substance thinner and the surface more susceptible to being cracked. When a question was posed, the diviner would apply a metal point to the base of the hollow, causing the surface to crack. The response of the ancestors was "read" from the fissures. A skillful diviner could control the extent and direction of the cracks. Thus, divination provided an authoritative leader with a useful and highly effective way of giving advice; a leader could regard disagreement as treason.

Xia and Shang: ?4700 to 3100 B.P.

The obvious starting point in the study of Chinese civilization is Chinese legends, which tell us that the celebrated Yellow Emperor Huang Di founded civilization in

FIGURE 19.2 Shang oracle bones.

Xia and Shang
dynasties

**?4700 to 3100
B.P.**

the north approximately 4698 years ago. This great legendary warlord set the tone
for centuries of the repressive harsh government that was the hallmark of early
Chinese civilization. About 4200 years ago, a Xia ruler named Yu the Great gained
power through his military prowess and his knowledge of flood control, by which he
could protect the valley people from catastrophic inundations.

What exactly do these legends mean? Who were the Xia and the Shang? In all
probability they were dynasties of local rulers who achieved lasting prominence
among their many neighbors after generations of bitter strife (Chang, 1980, 1986).
Every chieftain lived in a walled town and enjoyed much the same level of material

prosperity, but each ruler came from a different lineage and was related to his competitors by intricate and closely woven allegiances and kin ties. Each dynasty assumed political dominance in the north in turn, but for all these political changes, Shang civilization itself continued more or less untouched, a loosely unified confederacy of competing small kingdoms that quarreled and warred incessantly.

The archaeological record reveals that Shang-type remains are stratified on top of Longshan occupation levels at many places in northern China, and they represent a dramatic increase in the complexity of material culture and social organization (Chang, 1986). The same trends toward increasing complexity are thought to have occurred elsewhere in China at approximately the same time, for literate states may have emerged from a Longshan base in the south and east as well. In form they probably resembled the Shang closely, but few details of the others are known. It seems likely that the Shang dynasty was dominant from approximately 3766 to 3122 years ago but that other states continued to grow at the same time. The larger area of Chinese civilization ultimately extended from the north into the middle and lower courses of the Yellow and Yangtze rivers. In this account, we concentrate on northern Chinese civilization simply because more is known about the archaeology of the Shang than about any other early Chinese state.

Shang
3766 to 3122
B.P.

Capitals and Sepulchers

The oracle bones and other historical sources provide only a sketchy outline of the early dynasties and the ways the Shang kings went about their business (Cheng Te kur, 1960). The bones inform us that they lived in at least seven capitals, situated near the middle reaches of the Yellow River in the modern provinces of Henan, Shandong, and Anhui (Keightley, 1978). The sites of all these towns are still uncertain, but approximately 3557 years ago the Shang kings moved their capital to a place named Ao, which archaeologists have found under the modern industrial city of Zhengzhou, some 95 miles (153 km) south of Anyang close to the Yellow River (Wheatley, 1971). Unfortunately, the royal compound lies underneath the modern downtown area, so only limited excavations have been possible. However, the diggers have found traces of a vast precinct surrounded by an earthen wall more than 33 feet (9.9 m) high, enclosing an area of 2 square miles (5.18 sq. km). It would have taken 10,000 workers laboring 330 days a year for no fewer than 18 years to erect the fortifications alone. This walled compound housed the rulers, the temples, and the nobles. Some foundations of their large houses and ancestral altars have come from excavations inside the compound. The residential quarters and craft workshops lay outside the Shang walls. These include two bronze factories, one of them covering more than an acre. The metalworkers lived in substantial houses near their furnaces. There were bone workshops, too, places where animal and human bones were fashioned into arrowheads, pins, and awls. Zhengzhou's potters lived in a satellite village close to the kilns, where they fired hundreds of fine vessels. The excavations revealed dozens of unfired and incomplete vessels.

Early Shang
?3750 to 3650
B.P.

Zhengzhou

Middle Shang
3650 to 3400
B.P.

Late Shang
3400 to 3100
B.P.

The capital moved to the Anyang area approximately 3400 years ago (the beginning of the Late Shang phase), where it remained until the fall of the Shang more than 250 years later. This new royal domain was known as *Yin* and may in fact have encompassed a network of compounds, palaces, villages, and cemeteries extending over an area some 120 square miles (310 sq. km) on the northern bank of the Yellow River. The core of this "capital" was near the hamlet of Xiao-tun, 1.5 miles (2.4 km) northwest of the modern city of Anyang. Years of excavations at Xiao-tun have revealed 53 rectangular foundations of stamped earth up to 120 feet (36 m) long, 65 feet (19.5 m) wide, and as much as 5 feet (1.5 m) high, many of them associated with sacrificial burials of both animals and humans (Chang, 1980, 1986). One group of 15 foundations on the north side of the excavated area supported timber houses with mud and stick walls, devoid of sacrificial victims. These are believed to be the royal residences that housed extended families of nobles living in large halls and smaller rooms closed off with doors (Figure 19.3). Twenty-one massive foundations on an elevated area in the center of the excavations formed two rows of temples associated with a series of five ceremonial gates. The builders buried animals, humans, and even chariots in this vicinity, perhaps to dedicate the temples. Nearby lay semisubterranean houses, where the royal servants and artisans lived. The service areas included bronze foundries, workshops, and pottery kilns.

The Shang Royal Burials

The Shang rulers at first buried their dead among the compound houses at Anyang but later moved their cemetery to a location just more than a mile northeast. Eleven royal graves from this cemetery were excavated during the 1930s (Chang, 1986). They were furnished on a lavish scale and date to between 3500 and 3200 years ago. The best-known grave is in the shape of a crosslike pit approximately 33 feet (9.9 m) deep with slightly sloping walls. Four ramps lead from the surface to each side of the pit (Chang, 1960). The coffin of the ruler, which was placed inside a wooden chamber erected in the burial pit, was accompanied by superb bronze vessels and shell, bone, and stone ornaments. One ceremonial halberd has an engraved jade blade set in a bronze shaft adorned with dragons and inlaid with malachite. The rulers were accompanied in death by slaves and sacrificial victims buried both in the chamber itself and on the approach ramps. Many were decapitated, so their bodies were found in one place and their heads in another.

The Shang kings surrounded their sepulchers with hundreds of lesser burials. No

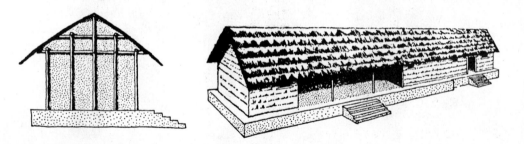

FIGURE 19.3   Reconstruction of a structure from the ceremonial area at Xiao-tun, Anyang, in Henan province.

fewer than 1221 small graves have been dug up nearby, many of them burials of between 2 and 11 people in a single tomb. Some of the skeletons are associated with pottery, weapons, or bronze vessels, but most are devoid of all adornment. In 1976 archaeologists uncovered nearly 200 of these graves. Most of them contained decapitated, dismembered, or mutilated bodies. Some of the victims had been bound before death. These can only have been sacrificial offerings consecrated when the kings and their relatives died.

The Bronze Smiths

The Shang people are justly famous for their bronze work, best known to us from ceremonial artifacts found in royal tombs. The prestigious metal was not gold, which was in short supply, but bronze. Most Shang bronzes are food or drinking vessels, some are weapons, a few are musical instruments, and many are chariot and horse fittings. Bronze working was the guarded monopoly of the rulers, a complex art that the Chinese developed quite independently from the West before 4000 years ago. Their smiths produced some of the most sophisticated and elegant bronze objects ever crafted (Figure 19.4).

The Shang people discovered bronze working on their own, perhaps as a result of their long experience with kiln-fired pottery baked at high temperatures (Barnard, 1961). The smaller objects, such as spear heads, arrowheads, and halberds, were made by pouring a mixture of copper and tin into a single- or two-piece mold. Much more complex procedures had to be employed to manufacture large ceremonial vessels.

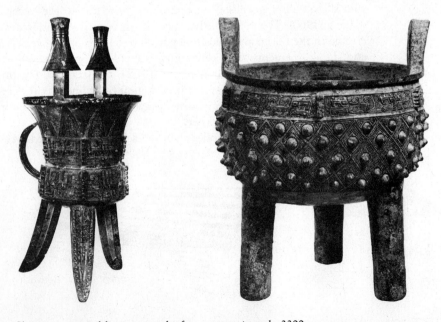

FIGURE 19.4   Shang ceremonial bronze vessels, from approximately 3300 years ago.

These elaborate display pieces were copies of clay prototypes carefully sculpted around a baked clay core and encased in a segmented mold. Once the clay version was completed, the baked outer mold was removed, the model broken away from the core, and the two parts reassembled to receive the molten bronze. This complex technique remained in use for at least five centuries. An alternative would have been the lost-wax method, in which a single-piece mold encases a wax mold that is heated and then poured out to be replaced with metal.

THE WARLORDS: 1122 TO 221 B.C.

Every early Chinese ruler stayed in power by virtue of a strong army. Shang society was organized on what might be called military lines, so that the royal standing army could be supplemented with thousands of conscripts on very short notice. The kings frequently were at war, protecting their frontiers, suppressing rebellious rivals, or raiding for as many as 30,000 sacrificial victims at one time. In a sense, every early Chinese state was an armed garrison that could call on armies of more than 10,000 men. The secret was a sophisticated, permanent military establishment and a kin organization through which people were obligated to serve the king when called upon. The same basic organization persisted long after the fall of the Shang dynasty in 1100 B.C.

The Anyang graves reveal that every foot soldier carried a set of weapons: a bow and arrows, halberd, shield, small knife, and sharpening stone. The bows were made of horn and ox sinew and were approximately a man's height. They propelled stone-, bone-, or bronze-tipped arrows equipped with feathers (Kiernan and Fairbank, 1974). The Shang soldiers used a small leather or basketry shield for chariot warfare and a longer one on foot, both painted with tiger designs. Most surviving Shang weapons come from sacrificial chariot burials, such as the one excavated near Anyang in 1973. The archaeologists did not uncover the wooden chariot itself but a cast of the wooden parts preserved in the soil (Figure 19.5). They brushed away the surrounding soil with great care until they reached the hardened particles of fine sand that had replaced the wooden structure of the buried chariot. They were able to photograph not only the "ghost" of the chariot but also the skeletons of the two horses. The charioteer had been killed at the funeral and his body placed behind the vehicle. The yokes of the chariot rested on the horses' necks. Even the reins were marked by lines of bronze roundels in the grave. The charioteer rode on a wicker and leather car measuring between 3 and 4 feet (0.9 and 1.2 m) across and borne on a stout axle and two spoked wheels with large hubs adorned with bronze caps. In all probability, the nailless chariot was held together with sinew lashings, adorned with bronze and turquoise ornaments, and perhaps painted in bright colors.

The Shang dynasty fell about 3100 years ago at the hands of the neighboring Zhou. The conquerors did not create a new civilization; rather, they took over the existing network of towns and officials and incorporated them into their own state organization, thus shifting the focus of political and economic power to the south and west, away from Anyang into the fertile Wei Valley near the modern city of S'ian. By this time, the influence of what may loosely be called Shang civilization extended

FIGURE 19.5   Chariot burial from the royal Shang tombs near Anyang. The wooden parts of the chariot were excavated by following discolorations made by the decaying wood in the ground.

far beyond the north, into the rice-growing areas of the south and along the eastern coasts. The Zhou divided their domains into various almost independent provinces, which warred with one another for centuries (Fitzgerald, 1978). It was not until 221 B.C. that the great emperor Xuang Ti unified China into a single empire. By Roman times, Chinese civilization had been flourishing for more than 2000 years, a distinctive and highly nationalistic culture that differed sharply from its Western contemporaries in its ability to assimilate conquerors and the conquered into its own traditions. In contrast, the Roman Empire was built on the groaning backs of slaves and collapsed into the Dark Ages when attacked by barbarian nomads. The ability of the Chinese people simply to assimilate these same nomadic conquerors explains why the essential fabric of their civilization survives to this day.

GUIDE TO FURTHER READING

Chang Kwang-Chih. 1980. *The Shang Civilization*. New Haven, CT: Yale University Press.

A detailed reconstruction of Shang civilization derived not only from archaeological data but also from a complicated palimpsest of legends, oracle bone inscriptions, and documentary records. An impressive, meticulous book that is an ultimate source on this remarkable society.

Chang Kwang-Chih. 1986. *The Archaeology of Ancient China*, 4th ed. New Haven, CT: Yale University Press.

The fundamental account of prehistoric China for all serious students, with the priceless advantage that it is regularly updated. Lavishly illustrated. Major emphasis on chronology and artifacts.

Fitzgerald, Patrick. 1978. *Ancient China*. Oxford, Eng.: Elsevier Phaidon.

A well-illustrated history (and prehistory) of China for the lay reader that concentrates on the period after the Shang dynasty. Clearly written and a good starting point.

Keightley, David N., ed. 1983. *The Origins of Chinese Civilization*. Berkeley and Los Angeles: University of California Press.

An up-to-date and authoritative description of early Chinese civilization, with a strong historical emphasis. Useful to read in conjunction with Chang's works.

Wheatley, Paul. 1971. *The Pivot of the Four Quarters*. Chicago: Aldine.

A learned book that will daunt many casual readers but is a crucial source for understanding early Chinese civilization. Concentrates on the early Chinese city.

Chronological Table K

	EASTERN MEDITERRANEAN	MEDITERRANEAN	TEMPERATE EUROPE	
A.D. 1	Trade with eastern	Roman Empire	LA TÈNE CULTURE	
500 B.C.	Mediterranean world	Rome founded Etruscans Carthaginians	HALLSTATT CULTURE	Heuneburg
3000 B.P.	Phoenician trade	VILLANOVAN CULTURE Phoenicians	URNFIELD CULTURES	Hascherkeller
3500	Aegean and eastern Mediterranean trade	METALWORKING CULTURES	Rapid expansion of bronze working Stonehenge	
4000	Rise of civilization			
4500			UNETICE CULTURE	
5000	Seafaring in the Aegean		KURGAN CULTURE Beakers Battle Axes	
6000				
	Obsidian trade		Varna Early copper working	
7000				
8000				

CHAPTER 20

ANATOLIA, GREECE, AND ITALY

Preview

- The eastern Mediterranean was linked by a vast nascent world system of exchange and trade routes that made many societies, large and small, economically interdependent. This system linked the Aegean with Anatolia and the eastern Mediterranean, and the entire region with Mesopotamia and the Nile.

- Small towns became important economic centers in parts of Anatolia as early as 7600 years ago. Communities like Çatal Hüyük failed to develop the necessary administrative and social mechanisms to cope with the increased complexity of the settlement and its trading activities. The town failed, and Anatolians of the fifth millennium B.C. reverted to village life.

- Small fortified villages flourished in the fourth millennium B.C. One of them, Troy I, dates to just after 5500 years ago. Troy II, founded approximately 4300 years ago, was a fortified town with more elaborate architecture and fine gold and bronze metallurgy. By this time the Anatolians were trading widely over the highlands and into the Aegean, and chieftaincies were scattered over mineral-rich areas. About 3900 years ago, the Assyrians set up a trading colony at Kanesh in central Anatolia.

- The Hittites originated in the north and assumed power in Anatolia approximately 3650 years ago. They held a vital place in contemporary history, for they played the Assyrians off against the Egyptians. Hittite power was based on diplomatic and trading skills until about 3200 years ago.

- About 3200 years ago, international trade in the eastern Mediterranean collapsed, and a period of confusion, partly the work of the Sea Peoples, ensued. The state of Israel was born during this interregnum, among agricultural and herding peoples on the Levant highlands.

- The Aegean and the Greek mainlands were settled by sedentary farming villages well before 7000 years ago. Painted pottery styles came into widespread use near that time.

- There were radical changes after 5500 years ago, when the cultivation of the olive and the vine became widespread and trading of minerals, stonewares, and other products expanded rapidly. Numerous small towns were flourishing throughout the Aegean and eastern Greece by 4500 years ago, linked by regular trading routes.

- The Minoan civilization of Crete developed as a result of these cultural routes approximately 4000 years ago and lasted until approximately 3400 years ago. The growth of this civilization is known from the ruins of the Palace of Knossos. The Minoans traded as far afield as Egypt and the eastern Mediterranean and were expert metalworkers and potters with a lively artistic tradition.

- Minoan power apparently was weakened by the great explosion of its satellite island, Thera, about 3500 years ago. The center of civilization passed to the mainland, where the Mycenaeans flourished until 3150 years ago. The Mycenaeans were able to develop some trading connections with temperate Europe as well as continue many Minoan trade routes. They were overthrown by Phrygian peoples at the end of the second millennium B.C.

- Trading activities continued to expand in the Aegean after the decline of Mycenae. Small city-states flourished, unifying only in the face of a common danger such as the Persian invasions of the fifth century B.C. The Athenians enjoyed a long period of supremacy among city-states, the period of classical Greek civilization in the fifth century B.C.

- Alexander the Great built an enormous empire across the Near East, of which Greece was part, in the late fourth century B.C. The Roman Empire, which followed, marks the entry of the entire Mediterranean area into historic times. Developed from Villanovan and Etruscan roots in Italy, Imperial Roman power was based on the ruins of Alexander's empire.

Chronological
Table K

This chapter covers an enormous area of the ancient world. It is concerned not only with the humble beginnings of state formation and complex societies in areas like Anatolia but also with the rapid growth of what we called a nascent world system over the mainland Near East and the entire eastern Mediterranean after about 4000 years ago. The societies described in this chapter cannot be considered in isolation, for they all played important parts in a much larger development—the growth of a truly international economic system that extended from Spain in the west to the distant Indus Valley in the east and lasted in various forms into historical times (Figure 20.1).

EARLY TOWNS IN ANATOLIA

Anatolia, with its rich obsidian and copper outcrops, was an early player in the great regional exchange networks that developed in the Near East as early as 9000 years ago (Chapter 10). At first, there were few large communities, but those that did flourish controlled trade over a large area around them. Çatal Hüyük in central Anatolia was one such community (Mellaart, 1967). This complex settlement was organized by creating ritual and other mechanisms that attempted to retain the close kinship ties of village life while adapting to the new complexities of long-distance trading and growing population. Unlike Mesopotamia, where new mechanisms and organizations evolved to handle social change, the system at Çatal Hüyük broke down. Anatolia's first and largest town was abandoned, and people went back to living in small villages (Mellaart, 1975; Redman, 1978).

The entire plateau of Anatolia seems to have experienced a subsequent gradual population increase after 5000 years ago, as long-distance trading with Mesopotamia in minerals and other materials increased. The evidence for the concentration of power and wealth in major Anatolian settlements is found after 5000

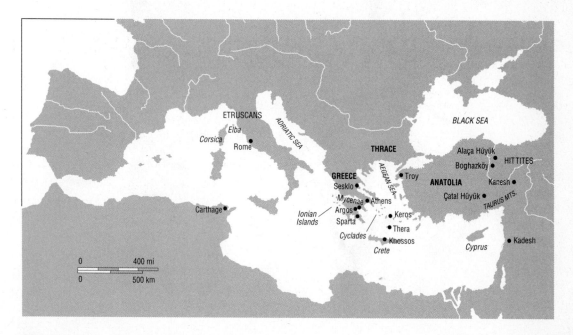

FIGURE 20.1   Sites and cultures mentioned in this chapter.

years ago in the walled fortresses of Hissarlik (Troy) and Kultepe (ancient Kanesh) (Blegen, 1971).

Troy I (Hissarlik)
5500 B.P.

Hissarlik was first occupied approximately 5500 years ago, when a small fortress was built on bedrock. Its foundations show that it contained a rectangular hall of a basic design that had been in use for centuries. The structure was to become the standard palace design of later centuries and perhaps a prototype for the classical Greek temple. Approximately 4300 years ago, a new settlement known to archaeologists as Troy II flourished at Hissarlik. This fortified town boasted more elaborate buildings and yielded valuable hoards of gold and bronze ornaments—a clear sign that the rulers of the settlement were supporting skilled craftspeople who designed and executed fine ornaments of rank.

Troy II
4300 B.P.

Alaça Hüyük
4000 B.P.

Thirteen royal tombs were found at the site of the town of Alaça Hüyük in central Anatolia, dating to about 4000 years ago. The tombs contain the bodies of men and their wives accompanied by domestic vessels, weapons, and many metal items (Piggott, 1965). The ornaments include copper figurines with gold breasts and finely wrought cast bronze stags inlaid with silver, which were perhaps mounted on the ends of poles (Figure 20.2).

4000 B.P.

Both the Alaça Hüyük and Hissarlik finds testify to the far-flung exchange networks that crisscrossed Anatolia by 4000 years ago. They were an important and

FIGURE 20.2   Bronze stag from Alaça Hüyük, inlaid with silver, and a figurine of a ruler.

emerging component in the nascent world system that brought copper, tin, and other raw materials from the highlands to the lowlands of Mesopotamia and textiles and other lowland products back in return. The coastal Levant and the island of Cyprus now emerged as major elements in the new trade networks, for maritime trade, using simple coastal vessels, was assuming considerable importance along the Turkish coast and among the Aegean Islands, where a trade in obsidian, timber, pottery, wine, and olive oil had begun centuries earlier. Toward the end of the third millennium B.C., Indo-European-speaking peoples seem to have infiltrated Anatolia from the northwest, causing considerable political unrest. Despite these upheavals, the volume of trade between Anatolia and Mesopotamia reached new heights, as the two areas were becoming part of an ever-more closely meshed economic system. By 3900 years ago, for example, there was a sizable Assyrian merchant colony outside the city of Kanesh, one of several important trading centers *(karums)* that were staging posts for long-distance commerce in minerals and other commodities (Lloyd, 1967). The karums served as marketplaces and caravan termini, natural entrepots where prices for goods were carefully regulated. Local rulers levied taxes on the caravans, which brought important Assyrian ideas to Anatolia and reinforced the economic and political power of the elite at both ends of the trade routes.

Kanesh
3900 B.P.

BALANCE OF POWER: THE HITTITES

All these developments were symptomatic of ever-closer economic ties between different regions of the Near East. These ties were a symbol of an economic interdependency that persisted regardless of political change or war. The desert caravans of black asses and the ships that plied Mediterranean waters were symptomatic of this interdependency, of a more durable world system that transcended the boundaries of local societies and even entire civilizations. At the center of this world system lay the strategic Levant, a coastline with few natural harbors but with important trade routes to Mesopotamia, Anatolia, and the Nile.

During the second millennium B.C. the eastern Mediterranean coastlands were divided up among a network of small and prosperous states. They lived in the shadow of the great kingdoms that lay inland: Egypt to the south, Mitanni to the east of the Euphrates, and Hatti (the kingdom of the Hittites in Anatolia). Each controlled a large area of territory surrounded by a hinterland that lay more or less under their influence (Figure 20.3). The three states competed directly in the Levant, and they had complex dealings on all frontiers. Mitanni, for example, tried to prevent the city-state of Assur in northern Mesopotamia from going its own way, and the famous Amarna tablets, an archive of Egyptian diplomatic correspondence, tell of shifting allegiances among the city-states of the Levant. By this time, the Levant was a land of many cities, a regular military and diplomatic battlefield for its powerful neighbors.

The Hittites were the newest, and perhaps the most able, diplomatic players. They appear to have been a group of talented Indo-European people from the vast steppes north of Anatolia who infiltrated the plateau and seized power from the leaders of Kanesh and other cities, probably just before 3650 years ago (Lehmann, 1977; MacQueen, 1987). A foreign minority, the Hittites rose to political power by

Hittites
3650 to 3280 B.P.

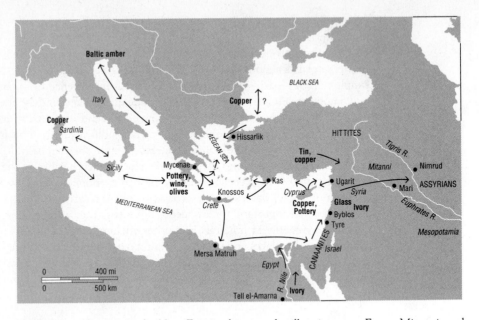

FIGURE 20.3   The balance of power in the Near East in the second millennium B.C.: Egypt, Mitanni, and the Hittite Empire.

judiciously melding conquest and astute political maneuvering, quickly becoming acculturated into their new milieu, while preserving their traditional values and outlook on life. They were not intellectuals, but religion was important to them. The king was not deified until after his death, if then. His duties were well defined: to ensure the state's welfare, wage war, and act as high priest under clearly defined circumstances. A hierarchy of officials supported the king, ruling an empire based on a rigid feudal system of land ownership and governance.

Hittite kings exercised enormous political influence in the Near East from their capital at Boghazkoy, with its 4 miles (6.4 km) of city walls. In the fifteenth century B.C., Syria had been a province of the Egyptian empire. The Hittites pressed hard on the Egyptians on both diplomatic and military fronts, until the Great King of Hatti, Suppiluliumas I (1375–1335 B.C.), could claim Lebanon as his frontier. The conflict culminated in the indecisive Battle of Kadesh between the forces of pharaoh Rameses II and the Hittite ruler Muwatallis in 1286. Egypt was exhausted by this effort, and diplomatic archives in Akkadian cuneiform contain records of the peace treaty of about 1269 between the Hittite and Egyptian kings, which confined Egyptian interests to southern Palestine. The same treaty is also recorded on the walls of the temple of Karnak at Thebes. The grandiloquent public architecture of the period commonly depicted Egyptians and Hittites locked in battle with state-of-the-art weaponry. This included light, two-wheeled chariots manned by archers and new siege machinery for use against the many walled cities in the disputed areas.

All of this diplomatic and military activity on the part of the great kingdoms was aimed at control of the lucrative gold, copper, and pottery trade of the eastern

Battle of Kadesh
1286 B.C.

Mediterranean, a trade in the hands of Levant and Mycenaean traders vividly illustrated by investigations of Bronze Age shipwrecks off the southern Turkish coast.

Kas

The advantage of shipwrecks from the archaeological point of view is that they provide sealed capsules of maritime trade frozen at a moment in time. The famous Kas ship, excavated by George Bass from the waters off southern Turkey, was shipwrecked in the fourteenth century B.C. The ship carried 200 copper ingots, each weighing about 60 pounds (27 kg), a load of 6 tons, enough to equip a small army with weapons and armor (Figure 20.4). A ton of resin traveled in two-handled jars made by people living in the Levant; it was used, so Egyptian records tell us, as incense for Egyptian rituals. There were dozens of blue glass disks, ingots being sent to Egypt from Tyre. The cargo also included hardwood, Baltic amber, tortoise shells, elephant tusks and hippopotamus teeth, ostrich eggs, jars of olives, and even large jars holding stacked Canaanite and Mycenaean pottery. Judging from a gold scarab found on board, at least one of the crew members was Egyptian. The Kas ship's cargo contains items from Africa, Egypt, the Levant, the Greek mainland and the Aegean, Cyprus, and even copper from Sardinia. It is a dramatic reflection of the truly international nature of eastern Mediterranean trade in the second millennium B.C., when the Hittites were at the height of their power. It is hardly surprising that the great powers of the day competed savagely

FIGURE 20.4 Excavations on the Bronze Age wreck at Kas, southern Turkey.

for control of the Levant, for it lay at the very center of an interlocking maze of trade routes that spanned the entire civilized world.

This maritime trade was still expanding in Hittite times. It played a major role in the diffusion of iron tools and weapons over the eastern Mediterranean. Iron is thought to have been first smelted in the middle of the first millennium B.C., perhaps in the highlands immediately south of the Black Sea. The new metal had many advantages, for its tough, sharp edges were invaluable for military tasks and for farming and carpentry. Iron was plentiful, unlike the tin used to alloy bronze. Iron tools soon became commonplace over a wide area of Europe and the Near East, although it was some time before domestic artifacts such as axes and hoes were invariably made with the new technology (Wertime and Muhly, 1980).

3200 B.P.   By 3200 years ago, Hatti was in trouble. The Hittites had prospered by virtue of their well-organized, professional army, long a stabilizing influence in the eastern Mediterranean. They were expert diplomats, who controlled what is now northern Syria through their rule over two great cities—Carchemish on the Euphrates and Alalakh of Mukish in the west. There were also important treaty relationships with other powerful neighbors, including Ugarit (Ras Shamra) on the northern Levant

Ugarit   coast. Ugarit was a cosmopolitan city ruled by a monarch who was almost like a merchant-prince. He controlled vast supplies of gold and a fleet of more than 150 ships, some of considerable size. These ventured as far afield as Cyprus and the Nile, the former being an important center of exchange with the Aegean. Ugarit was vital to the Hittites, for they depended on its ships and never became a maritime power.

3200 B.P.   Both the lack of maritime power and a rigid feudal system contributed to Hatti's undoing. About 3200 years ago, repeated migrations of foreigners flowed into Anatolia from the northwest, whence the Hittites had come only four centuries earlier. These population movements came to a head when the Phrygian peoples from Thrace ravaged the plateau as far south as the Taurus Mountains. Central Hittite government collapsed, partly because of attacks from outside but also because powerful vassals threw off their allegiance to the king. The rulers appealed to Ugarit and other maritime neighbors for assistance, but it was not forthcoming. Anatolia dissolved into the homeland of dozens of small city-states, each striving to maintain its independence. Only a few Hittite communities survived in small states in northern Syria that lasted until they were engulfed in the vast Persian Empire of the first millennium B.C.

THE SEA PEOPLES AND THE
RISE OF ISRAEL

The situation in the Levant was explosive, for the withdrawal of the great powers left a political vacuum that could not be filled by local rulers, who depended heavily on mercenary armies. With the collapse of the Mycenaean trade at about the same time, there was a general weakening of authority. The imperial powers and petty kingships that made up the world system of 3200 years ago were governed by highly centralized palace bureaucracies. The systems they controlled were very specialized, allowing for significant economies of operation and dense population concentrations. This very specialization made the entire system vulnerable to the effects of local upheavals, for a collapse in one area, say, the Hittite Empire, reverberated through the entire system. The exact causes of the almost dominolike collapse of Hittite and Mycenaean civilization, and the weakening of the Egyptian, are still a mystery. The abrupt collapse of the trade weakened urban elites and the foundations of their power (Coote and Whitelam, 1987).

The same interdependencies also affected the nomads and peasants who lived in the hinterlands of Levantine cities, both on the coast and on the mainland. The cuneiform tablets from the city of Mari, at the head of a powerful state on the Euphrates centuries earlier, provide compelling evidence of the intricate relationships between the cities and those who herded their flocks on the outskirts. These groups were also dependent on the international trade, but as the trade declined, they became increasingly politically independent during the period of destruction, a "Dark Age" that lasted more than 300 years. This was a time of piracy and widespread suffering, much of it at the hands of warlike bands, known to archaeologists as "The Sea Peoples."

In the Levant, many rural groups moved to the highlands inland during these centuries, relying more heavily on pastoralism and agriculture as their dependence on trading centers diminished. Village communities, nomadic herders, and even bandits lived in close proximity outside the reach of state power. It was in this milieu that a loose federation of highland villages, small towns, pastoral nomad groups, and former bandits formed a loose federation to preserve and defend their sovereignty in the face of outside states. This federation became the state of Israel, which acquired its own monarchy after 1000 B.C. and protected itself with a network of walled cities. By this time, eastern Mediterranean trade was recovering and the hillside federation expanded into lowland territory, circumscribed by the sea and the desert and by the still powerful Egyptian and Mesopotamian civilizations on either side.

Israel
1000 B.C.

THE PHOENICIANS

The general economic recovery of the first millennium B.C. was in large part attributable to the Phoenicians. They had first come into prominence in the Levant by acting as middlemen in a growing trade in raw materials and manufactured goods (Harden, 1962; N. K. Sanders, 1978). Their ships were soon carrying Lebanese cedarwood to Cyprus and the Nile. North of Israel, powerful Phoenician cities like Tyre, Sidon, and Byblos now expanded this trade. Their ships took over the copper and iron ore trade of the Mediterranean. Their trading networks later extended as far as the copper and tin mines of Spain, and Phoenician merchants made enormous profits from purple dye extracted from seashells and much used for expensive fabrics. By 800 B.C., Phoenician merchants were everywhere in the Mediterranean. A century later, the great Phoenician cities were forced to acknowledge Assyrian rule and to pay tribute to foreign masters. Magnificent Phoenician ivories come from the royal palaces at Nimrud on the Tigris, perhaps tribute or plunder from military campaigns. As for Israel, it, too, was absorbed into the Assyrian Empire in the eighth century B.C., as

800 B.C.

the Levant came under the sway of alien empires for many centuries, right into modern times.

THE AEGEAN AND GREECE

12,000 B.P. Even as early as 12,000 years ago, seagoing ships were plying the waters of the Aegean, trading obsidian from the islands to mainland Greece. Seagoing trade got under way

6000 B.P. in earnest after 6000 years ago, as long-distance exchange networks expanded rapidly. In a real sense, the history of Aegean and Greek early civilizations is the story of the growth of international trade in eastern Mediterranean waters.

Olives, Vines, and Seagoing Trade

Parts of mainland Greece and the Aegean were settled by farming peoples as early

8500 B.P. as 8500 years ago, but more intensive settlement of western Greece, the islands, and Crete did not occur until much later.

Sesklo   The Sesklo village in Thessaly was occupied approximately 7000 years ago and

7000 B.P. is typical of northern Greek sites of the time (Warren, 1975). The people lived in stone and mud houses connected by courtyards and passages. Their mixed farming economy depended heavily on cereal cultivation. Somewhat similar villages are found on Crete, where farming settlement dates back to at least 7500 years ago.

5500 B.P. There were radical changes in the settlement pattern after 5500 years ago, when villages were established in the Cyclades, throughout Crete, and on the Ionian islands of the west. In contrast, northern Greece seems to have lagged behind. The reason may have been agriculture, for southern Greece and the islands are ideal environments for the cultivation of olives and vines, with cereal crops interspersed between them (C. Renfrew, 1972). There was a veritable explosion in village crafts as well, in the manufacture of fine painted pottery, marble vessels, and magnificent stone axes (Figure 20.5). Stone vases and fine seals were made by Cretan workers; the seals were used to mark ownership of prized possessions or pots full of oil or other commodities. By 5500 years ago, the peoples of the Aegean and Greece were smelting copper and making bronze artifacts as well as ornaments in gold and silver. These included exquisite gold and silver drinking cups and the elaborate ornaments found at Troy II, which included more than 8700 gold beads, wire ornaments, chain links, and objects of fine gold sheet. The achievements of the Aegean metallurgists in part resulted from the rapid expansion of trading throughout the Aegean, far into Anatolia, and to Cyprus, with its rich copper outcrops (see Renfrew and Wagstaff, 1982).

The Aegean is well endowed with comfortable ports and alternative trading routes that provided easy communication from island to island for most of the year. Even relatively primitive vessels could coast from one end of the Aegean to the other in easy stages. Sailing vessels are depicted on Cretan seals dating to approximately 4000 years ago. The Aegean trade flourished on olive oil and wine, metal tools and ores, marble vessels and figurines, and pottery. The success of the trade led to a

4500 B.P. constant infusion of new products and ideas to Greece and the Aegean. By 4500 years

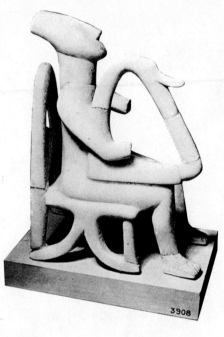

FIGURE 20.5   Harpist in marble, executed by a crafts-
worker on the Island of Keros in the
Aegean.

ago, numerous small towns housed farmers, traders, and skilled craftsworkers on the
mainland and the islands.

The beginnings of town life created considerable cultural diversity in the Aegean,
a diversity fostered by constant trading connections and increased complexity in
social and political organization. Nowhere is this better documented than on Crete,
where a brilliant civilization flourished in towns and palaces throughout the island.
In contrast, mainland Greece lagged somewhat behind, its many small towns having
only occasional contact with the Aegean islands and Crete.

THE MINOANS

The development of the Minoan civilization of Crete was almost certainly the result
of many local factors, among them the intensive cultivation of the olive and the vine.
Its development is best documented at the famous Palace of Knossos near Heraklion
in northern Crete (Figure 20.6) (Hood, 1973; Warren, 1975).

Knossos

**8100 to 3400
B.P.**

The first prehistoric inhabitants of Knossos settled there approximately 8100
years ago. No fewer than 23 feet (7 m) of early farming occupation underlie the
Minoan civilization. The first Knossos settlement was founded at approximately the
same time that Çatal Hüyük was first occupied in Anatolia. The Knossos farmers lived

FIGURE 20.6   General view of the Palace of Minos at Knossos.

5730 B.P.

in sun-dried mud and brick huts of a rectangular ground plan that provided for storage bins and sleeping platforms. By 5730 years ago, signs of long-distance trading increase in the form of exotic imports such as stone bowls. The first palace at Knossos was built approximately 3930 years ago; it is a large building with many rooms grouped around a rectangular central court.

Minoan civilization

c. 4000 to 3400 B.P.

At least nine periods of Minoan civilization have been distinguished by pottery styles found in the later levels of the Knossos site. Even during the earlier periods of the civilization, the Minoans were trading regularly with Egypt, for their pottery and metal objects have been found in burials there. About 3700 years ago, the earlier palaces were destroyed by an earthquake.

3700 B.P.

The high point of Minoan civilization followed that destruction, occurring between 3700 and 3450 years ago, when the Palace of Knossos reached its greatest size. This remarkable structure was made mainly of mud-brick and timber beams with occasional limestone blocks and wood columns. Some buildings had two stories; the plaster walls and floors were decorated initially with geometric designs and, after 3700 years ago, with vivid scenes or individual pictures of varying size. Sometimes the decorations were executed in relief; in other cases, colors were applied to the damp plaster (Figure 20.7).

Artistic themes included formal landscapes, dolphins and other sea creatures, and scenes of Minoan life. The most remarkable art depicted dances and religious ceremonies, including acrobats leaping vigorously along the backs of bulls (Figure

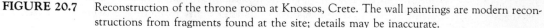

FIGURE 20.7   Reconstruction of the throne room at Knossos, Crete. The wall paintings are modern reconstructions from fragments found at the site; details may be inaccurate.

20.8). Writer Mary Renault (1963) has vividly reconstructed Cretan life at Knossos in novels that bring Minoan culture to life.

At the height of its prosperity, Crete was self-supporting in food and basic raw materials, exporting foodstuffs, cloth, and painted pottery all over the eastern Mediterranean. The Cretans were renowned mariners. Their large ships transported gold, silver, obsidian, ivory, and ornaments from central Europe, the Aegean, and the Near East, and ostrich eggs probably were traded from North Africa.

We know very little of Minoan religious beliefs, except for some chilling finds made by Peter Warren (1984) in a house on the north side of Knossos. This fine building had collapsed in the great earthquake of 3450 years ago. The first-floor ceiling fell into the basement, taking a magnificent set of ritual vessels with it. The basement fill also contained the scattered bones of two children in perfect health. A microscopic examination of the limb bones showed that knives had been used to remove flesh from the bone. Warren believes that this may be evidence not only of human sacrifice but, perhaps, of ritual cannibalism as well, possibly related to a fertility rite associated with the Cretan Zeus and the Earth Mother.

A major event during the later stages of the Minoan civilization was the massive

FIGURE 20.8   A Minoan bull and dancers, as painted on the walls of the Palace of Knossos. The bull, a domesticated form, has a piebald coat. This very fragmentary scene has been reconstructed from rather inadequate original pieces and is somewhat controversial. (After Evans, 1921.)

volcanic explosion on the island of Thera, a Minoan outpost 70 miles (113 km) from Crete, probably during the late seventeenth century B.C. (Manning, 1988). The eruption probably caused destruction on the north coast of the Minoan kingdom, but Knossos continued to flourish long afterward. This event is equated by some people with the eternal legend of Atlantis, the mysterious continent said to have sunk to the ocean bottom after a holocaust thousands of years ago (Luce, 1973). The Thera eruption may have accelerated the decline of Minoan civilization, which was already showing signs of weakness. Fifty years later many Minoan sites were destroyed and abandoned. Warrior farmers, perhaps from mainland Greece, established sway over the empire and decorated the walls of Knossos with military scenes. Seventy-five years later the palace finally was destroyed by fire, thought to have been the work of Mycenaeans who razed it. By this time the center of the Aegean world had shifted to the Greek mainland, where Mycenae reached the height of its power.

?3400 B.P.

3375 to 3350 B.P.

The dramatic flowering of Minoan civilization stemmed from the intensified trading contacts and the impact of olive and vine cultivation on hundreds of Greek and Aegean villages. As agricultural economies became more diversified and goods and commodities could be exchanged both locally and over longer distances, a far-reaching economic interdependence resulted. Eventually this led to redistribution systems that were organized and controlled by the inhabitants of Minoan palaces and elsewhere in the Aegean where there were major centers of olive production.

The redistribution networks carried metal objects and other luxury products the length and breadth of the Aegean. Interest in long-distance trading brought about some cultural homogeneity from trade, gift exchange, and perhaps piracy. The skills of craftsworkers were highly valued in village and palace alike. Specialized artisans practiced their crafts in the major palaces; they lived well, in stone buildings with well-designed drainage systems, and had wooden furniture.

Colin Renfrew (1973) describes both Minoan society and that of its successors, the Mycenaeans of the Greek mainland, as civilizations. He points to their sophisticated art and metalwork, to the complex palaces organized around specialized craftsworkers, and to their developed redistribution networks for foods. The Minoans and Mycenaeans did not build vast temples like those at Tikal in Guatemala (Chapter 22) or those in Egypt. They also did not live in cities. Palaces and elaborate tombs were the major monuments. Renfrew looks for the origins of Minoan and Mycenaean civilization within Greece and the Aegean and considers them to be the result of local social change and material progress, not external population movements. His theory sharply differs from earlier hypotheses that claimed migration of new peoples into Greece from the north or diffusion of new culture traits from Anatolia or the eastern Mediterranean were responsible (Childe, 1956).

THE MYCENAEANS

Mycenaeans
**3600 to 3200
B.P.**

The Mycenaean civilization, centered on the fertile plain of Argos on the Greek mainland, began to flourish about 3600 years ago (Taylour, 1990). The chieftains who ruled over the walled fortress of Mycenae (Figure 20.9) were buried in spectacular

FIGURE 20.9 The Lion Gate at Mycenae.

shaft graves that contained weapons adorned with copper and gold as well as fine gold face masks modeled in the likeness of their owners (Figure 20.10). Their wealth and economic power came from far-flung trading contacts and from their warrior skills (Figure 20.11). The kings were skilled charioteers and horsemen, whose material

 FIGURE 20.10   Gold mask of a bearded man, from Shaft Grave V at Mycenae, 3600 B.P.

**FIGURE
20.11**

Impression of a warrior fighting an enemy with a dagger, from an engraved gold ring, shaft graves, Mycenae, Greece.

culture and lifeway are immortalized in the Homeric epics. These epics, however, were written many centuries after the Mycenaeans themselves had become folk memories (Fagles, 1990).

Mycenaean commerce took over where Minoan left off. Much of the rulers' prestige was based on their contacts in the metal trade. Minerals were in constant demand in the central and eastern Mediterranean, especially tin for alloying copper to make bronze. Both copper and tin were abundant in central Cyprus and Anatolia, and the Mycenaeans developed the necessary contacts to obtain regular supplies.

The Mycenaeans also prized Baltic amber, a yellow-brown fossil resin that when rubbed seems to be "electric." Occasional pieces of this precious substance reached Mycenae, and amber is found in the royal graves there (Piggott, 1965). Just how extensive the Mycenaeans' European trading activities were has been much debated. They may well have been minimal (for a discussion, see Harding, 1984).

So complex did their trading transactions become that the Mycenaeans found it necessary to establish a writing system. They refined one that had been developed by the Minoans. The Mycenaeans used a form of script written in the Greek language, known now as Linear B (Chadwick, 1958; Diringer, 1962). Eighty-nine characters make up Linear B, 48 of which can be traced back to Minoan writing, Linear A. Linear A probably originated in the simple pictographic script of the earliest Minoans (Figure 20.12). The terms *Linear A* and *Linear B* were coined by Sir Arthur Evans when he first studied Minoan writing. Linear B was in more widespread use than A, partly because the Mycenaeans exerted greater political and economic power than their Cretan neighbors.

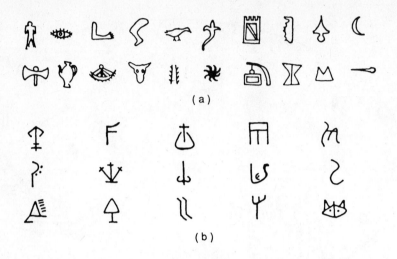

(a)

(b)

FIGURE
20.12

Early forms of writing: (a) Cretan pictographic script; (b) Linear A signs.

3150 B.P.

Mycenae continued to dominate eastern Mediterranean trade until about 3150 years ago, when its power was destroyed by warrior peoples from the north. In the same century, other northern barbarians overthrew the Hittite kingdom in Anatolia. These incursions into the Mediterranean world were caused by unsettled political conditions in Europe, at least partly the result of population pressures and tribal warfare (Chapter 21).

GREECE AFTER MYCENAE

3200 B.P.

700 to 600 B.C.

After Mycenae fell 3200 years ago, small-town merchants on the Greek mainland continued to trade, monopolizing commerce in the Aegean and Black seas. By the seventh and eighth centuries B.C., small colonies of Greek settlers lived on the northern and western shores of the Black Sea and along the north coast of Anatolia and developed trade in gold, copper, iron, salt, and other commodities (Bonzek, 1985). Other Greeks voyaged westward and settled in southern France; they soon had a brisk trade in wine and other commodities with central Europe (Morris, 1989).

The Greek City-States

In Greece many fertile agricultural areas are separated by ranges of mountains. Traders and seafarers of the Aegean islands and the Greek mainland therefore formed a network of small city-states that competed with one another for trade and political power. Athens was one of the larger and more prosperous states. The island of Sifnos in the Aegean was another, famous for its gold and silver. Paros marble was known all over the eastern Mediterranean, and Milos provided obsidian for many centuries.

Greek states unified only in times of grave political stress, as when the Persian

King Xerxes sought to add Greece to his possessions. Xerxes's defeats at Marathon (490 B.C.) and ten years later in a naval battle at Salamis ensured the security of Greece and made classical Greek civilization possible. Athens was foremost among the Greek states (Morris, 1989), becoming head of a league of maritime cities, which

was soon turned into an empire. This was the Athens that attracted wealthy immigrants; built the Parthenon; and boasted of Aeschylus, Sophocles, and other mighty playwrights. Classical Greek civilization flourished for 50 glorious years.

However, throughout the brilliant decades of Athenian supremacy, bickering with Sparta in Peloponnesus never abated. A deep animosity between the two cities had its roots in radically different social systems. Sparta's government was based on military discipline and a rigid class structure. Athenians enjoyed a more mobile society and democratic government.

The long rivalry culminated in the disastrous Peloponnesian War, from 431 to 404 B.C., which left Sparta a dominant political force on the mainland. The contemporary historian Thucydides documented the war, which was followed by disarray (Livingston, 1943). Greece soon fell under the sway of Philip of Macedonia, whose

rule between 359 and 336 B.C. began to develop political unity. His son Alexander the Great then embarked on a campaign of imperial conquest that took him from Macedonia into Persia and then to Mesopotamia. Alexander was welcomed as a hero and a god in Egypt, where he paused long enough to sacrifice to local deities and have himself proclaimed pharaoh. His continued quests took him as far east as the Indus

Valley and back to Babylon, where he died of fever in 323 B.C. By the time of his death, Alexander had united an enormous area of the ancient world under at least nominal Greek rule. His extraordinary empire fell apart within a generation, but his conquests paved the way for the uniform government of Imperial Rome.

THE ETRUSCANS AND ROMANS

During the first millennium B.C., the Mediterranean world was linked from one end to the other by highly intricate mercantile ties. Phoenicians and Greeks controlled much of this trade in metals and other essentials as well as exotic luxuries. The trade extended into temperate Europe and throughout the Italian peninsula, helping set the stage for large-scale Etruscan and Roman urban civilization in later centuries.

The Etruscans

Approximately 3000 years ago, some Urnfield peoples (named after their habit of burying cremated ashes in clay urns) from central Europe (Chapter 21) had settled south of the Alps in the Po Valley (Wells, 1981). They developed a skilled bronze-working tradition, in which products were traded far into central Europe and

throughout Italy. This people evolved into the Villanovan culture, which appeared in the ninth century B.C. and was soon in touch with Greek colonies in southern Italy

and perhaps with the Phoenicians (Piggott, 1965). Ironworking was introduced to the Villanovans in approximately the ninth century B.C. Iron tools and extensive trading contacts won the Villanovans political control over much of northern and western Italy. They established colonies on the islands of Elba and Corsica. Several centuries of trade and other contacts culminated in a literate Etruscan civilization.

Etruscans
650 to 450 B.C.

Like classical Greece, Etruscan civilization was more a unity of cultural tradition and trade than a political reality (Pallotino, 1977). The Etruscans traded widely in the central Mediterranean and with warrior peoples in central Europe. Etruscan culture was derived from the Villanovan, but it owed much to eastern immigrants and trading contacts that brought Oriental influence to Italian towns.

Etruscan territory was settled by city-states with much independence, each with substantial public buildings and fortifications. Their decentralized political organization made them vulnerable to foreign raiders. Warrior bands from central Europe overran some Etruscan cities in the centuries after 450 B.C., at which time Etruscan prosperity began to crumble.

450 B.C.

By the time of Etruscan decline, however, the Mediterranean was a civilized lake. Phoenician colonists had founded Carthage and other cities in North Africa and Spain and controlled the western Mediterranean. The rulers of Greece and Egypt and later Philip of Macedonia controlled the east, and the Etruscans were in control of most of Italy and many central European trade routes.

The Romans

Romans
509 B.C.

The Etruscans had been the first people to fortify the seven famed hills of Rome. In 509 B.C., a foreign dynasty of rulers was evicted by these native Romans, who began to develop their own distinctive city-state. The next few centuries saw the emergence of Rome from a cluster of simple villages by the Tiber River to the leadership of the Mediterranean and far beyond. The Romans inherited the mantle of classical Greece and added their own distinctive culture to this foundation. They then carried Greco-Roman civilization to many parts of the world that were still inhabited by preliterate peasant societies. Roman legions campaigned not only in Egypt and Mesopotamia and as far as India but also in central and western Europe and in Britain. If it were not for the Romans, the administrative and linguistic face of Europe would be very different today (Grant, 1960; Vickers, 1977).

295 B.C.

By 295 B.C., the power of Rome dominated the whole of Italy. At this time Rome was a form of democracy, governed by a delicate balance of aristocratic and popular authority. This type of governance was appropriate for a large city-state but was hopelessly inadequate for the complexities of a huge empire. Eventually, civil strife led to autocratic rule of the empire under the emperors, the first of whom was Julius Caesar, familiar to every student of Roman history for his epic conquest of Gaul (France). (His great-nephew Augustus was the first ruler actually to claim the title of emperor.)

200 to 133 B.C.

After two vicious wars with their rich rival, Carthage, the Romans achieved mastery over the western Mediterranean by 200 B.C., and by 133 B.C. much of Asia was under uneasy Roman domination. Unfortunately, the Romans lacked the mechanisms to administer their empire successfully until the Emperor Augustus reorganized the civil service and established the Pax Romana over his vast domains. There ensued a period of great material prosperity and political stability, at the price of political freedom of speech.

The stresses that led to the collapse of the Roman Empire first began to appear on the European frontiers in the second and third centuries A.D. Roman power began to decline as ambition and sophistication grew among the Iron Age tribes living on the edges of Roman territory. The "barbarians" on the fringes of the empire were mainly peasant farmers who had obtained iron by trading and intermarriage with La Tène peoples (Chapter 21). Many served as mercenaries in the Roman armies, acquiring wealth and sophistication and, perhaps most important of all, an insight into Roman military tactics.

A.D. 395

A.D. 410

Shortage of farming land and increasing disrespect for Rome caused many Germanic tribes to raid Rome's European provinces. The raids were so successful that the imperial armies were constantly campaigning in the north. In A.D. 395, after Emperor Theodosius died, the Roman Empire was split into eastern and western divisions. Large barbarian invasions from northern Europe ensued. Fifteen years later, a horde of Germanic tribesmen from central Europe sacked Rome itself; then the European provinces were completely overrun by warrior peoples. Other Germanic hordes disturbed North Africa and crossed much of Asia Minor but left little lasting mark on history there.

What was the legacy of Rome? Its material legacy can be seen in the road system, which still provides a basis for many of Europe's and the Near East's communications, and in the towns, like London, which are still flourishing modern cities. In cultural terms, its principal legacy was the legal system, which lies at the core of most Western law codes. Roman literature and art dominated European culture for centuries after the Renaissance. Their spoken and written language, Latin, survived for centuries as the language of the educated person and as the principal means of business communication between nations. Latin lies at the base of many modern European languages and was only recently abandoned as the liturgical language of the Roman Catholic Church. The Romans and their culture lie at the foundations of our Western civilization.

GUIDE TO FURTHER READING

Coote, Robert B., and Whitelam, Keith W. 1987. *The Emergence of Early Israel.* Sheffield, Eng.: Almond Press.
   A closely argued account of the rise of Israel, based on prehistoric archaeology and ecology. Provocative and convincing.

Hood, Sinclair. 1973. *The Minoans.* London: Thames and Hudson.
   A superb summary of the origins, history, and decline of the Minoan civilization for the informed layperson. Excellent illustrations.

Luce, J. V. 1973. *Atlantis.* New York: McGraw-Hill.
   A fascinating account of the Atlantis legend and a possible explanation for it in the eruption and explosion at Santorini (Thera) in the Aegean.

MacQueen, J. G. 1987. *The Hittites.* London: Thames and Hudson.
  An admirable summary of Hittite civilization. Lavishly illustrated.

Renfrew, Colin. 1972. *The Emergence of Civilization.* London: Methuen.
  A study containing a mass of information about Aegean civilization and trade that adopts a systems approach. Technical, but invaluable to the general reader.

Taylour, Lord William. 1990. *The Mycenaeans,* rev. ed. London: Thames and Hudson.
  Mycenaean civilization described by a leading authority; a companion volume to Hood on the Minoans. Lavishly illustrated.

Warren, Peter. 1975. *The Aegean Civilizations.* Oxford, Eng.: Elsevier Phaidon.
  A synthesis of Bronze Age Greece and its antecedents for the beginner. Excellent illustrations and thoughtful text.

CHAPTER 21   TEMPERATE EUROPE BEFORE THE ROMANS

no

Preview

- In contrast to earlier hypotheses, archaeologists now believe that copper working was developed independently in southeast Europe about 6800 years ago. The Varna Cemetery in Bulgaria shows just how elaborate the gold and copper metallurgy of the area became. The industry flourished because of a demand for the fine metal ornaments. Copper working also developed early in southern Spain and northern Italy.

- Copper working was a logical outgrowth of earlier stone and ceramic technologies. Its more widespread use coincides with the spread of Beaker and Battle Ax artifacts throughout much of Europe.

- Bronze working began at an unknown date but was widespread in what is now Czechoslovakia by 4500 years ago, as part of the Unetice culture. The trading networks of earlier times expanded to meet increased indigenous demand for metal artifacts during a period of rapid technological change after 3700 years ago. Some rich chieftaincies developed in the temperate zones.

- After 1200 B.C., new "Urnfield" burial customs and more advanced bronze-working techniques spread over much of central and western Europe. These were associated with an intensification of trading activity and greater social ranking: an elite warrior class.

• After 1000 B.C., ironworking techniques spread into temperate Europe and diffused through the Hallstatt and La Tène cultural traditions during the first millennium B.C.

The fundamental question about the emergence of complex societies in temperate Europe is simple: Did they emerge as a result of indigenous cultural evolution or because of diffusion of people and ideas from the Near East?

V. Gordon Childe (1956), Stuart Piggott (1965), and others have argued that the constant demands by Near Eastern societies for copper, tin, and other metals led to cultural development in the backwater that was temperate Europe. However, this traditional viewpoint has been challenged by the calibrated radiocarbon chronologies that place the appearance of copper working in the Balkans earlier than in Greece or the Aegean. Many people now believe that Europeans were just as innovative as their eastern neighbors (Champion et al., 1984; Melisauskas, 1978).

EARLY COPPER WORKING

Colin Renfrew (1978) and Ruth Tringham (1971) have argued that the farmers of southeast Europe developed copper smelting independently, partly because they already used improved pottery-firing techniques that were very suitable for copper smelting (Figure 21.1). Cited as proof of the early development are the finds at the Varna Cemetery near the Black Sea in Bulgaria.

The Varna Cemetery

Varna
6600 to 6200
B.P.

At the Varna Cemetery, more than 130 richly decorated graves have yielded dozens of fine copper and gold tools and ornaments. Colin Renfrew (1978) has described the Varna finds as "the earliest major assemblage of gold artifacts to be unearthed anywhere in the world," for they date to approximately 6600 to 6200 years ago. Both the copper and the gold are of Balkan origin; indeed both metals were being worked here earlier than they were in the Near East. (Such a statement reflects findings thus far; it does not preclude future discoveries of earlier metals in the Near East.) The Balkan copper industry was quite sophisticated and was organized to serve trading networks over a wide area. At Rudna Glava in Yugoslavia, fissures mark the places where early miners followed ore veins deep into the ground. One mine in Bulgaria has ancient shafts more than 32 feet (10 m) deep. These copper mines are the earliest so far discovered in the world and show that metallurgy developed rapidly into a considerable industry in the Balkans during the fifth millennium B.C. (Jovanovic, 1980).

The Varna burials provide striking evidence for differential wealth; some of the graves are richly decorated with gold ornaments whereas others contain few artifacts. Unfortunately, the settlement associated with the Varna Cemetery has yet to be found, but Renfrew (1978) has suggested that the users of the burial ground were part of a chiefdom in which the leaders used gold and copper ornaments to fulfill the social

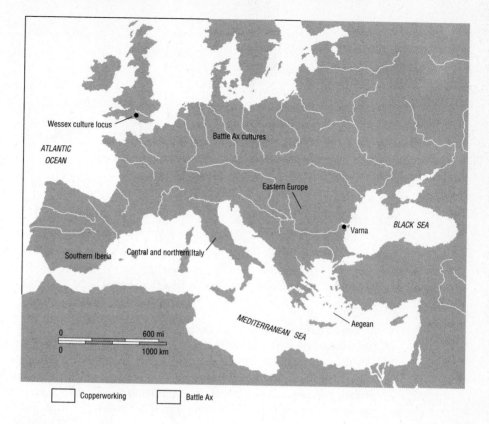

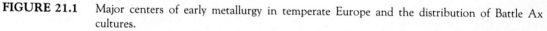

FIGURE 21.1   Major centers of early metallurgy in temperate Europe and the distribution of Battle Ax cultures.

need for conspicuous display. As he points out, the problem with explaining the rise of metallurgy is not a technical but a social one—defining the social conditions under which metal objects first came into widespread use. The earliest copper artifacts had few practical advantages over stone axes. Both copper and gold were used mainly for ornamental purposes (Figure 21.2). Perhaps it was no coincidence that the first metallurgists in temperate Europe developed a wide range of ornaments, luxury items traded through exchange networks that accelerated the spread of copper working to other parts of temperate Europe.

BATTLE AXES AND BEAKERS

The technology of copper working is really an outgrowth of that used for pottery manufacture and probably arose after many experiments with fire, clay, and stone. The beginnings of copper metallurgy in temperate Europe were probably almost imperceptible since a handful of simple, hammered copper artifacts date to as early as 5500 years ago. At least two possible areas of indigenous copper working have been

5500 B.P.

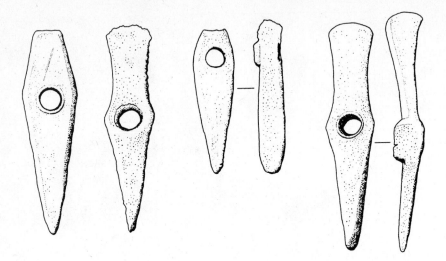

FIGURE 21.2   Copper ax heads from Czechoslovakia (one-third actual size).

identified in southern Europe, both near copper outcrops. One is in southern Spain (Iberia) and the other in northern Italy. In both regions, the copper workers started smelting approximately 4000 years ago. Britain is also rich in copper ores, and the metal was exploited early there, too. Wherever it developed, coppersmithing was probably a seasonal or at best a part-time occupation, and it was not until much later that tougher bronze artifacts came into daily use in the field and the chase.

The archaeological record of the period between 5500 and 4000 years ago is incredibly complicated, but we can discern two broad groupings of societies, the so-called Battle Ax and Beaker peoples, who ultimately mingled.

In east Europe, settled farming societies had lived on the edge of the huge Russian steppe for hundreds of years. Like the peoples of Anatolia and Greece, they had sporadic contacts with the nomads who roamed the plains to the east; about these we know little. In the southern Russian region, a widespread population of copper-using agriculturalists lived in rectangular, thatched huts, cultivated many crops, and also tamed domestic animals, possibly including the horse. This loosely defined **Kurgan culture** was remarkable for its burial customs, depositing each corpse under **5000 B.P.** a small mound (Piggott, 1965). The Kurgans used wheeled vehicles and made the copper or stone battle ax a very important part of their armory. The wheeled cart and the battle ax had spread widely over central and parts of northern Europe by 5000 years ago. The globular pots associated with these characteristic artifacts, many of them bearing characteristic cord-impressed decorations, have been found at hundreds of sites. The same artifacts have often been found in megalithic tombs. These new cultural traits were absorbed into the millennia-old European cultural tradition, and many experts feel that the Indo-European language spread into Europe at about this time. (Indo-European speech is thought to have originated in the region between the Carpathian and Caucasus mountains. The entire Indo-European controversy is complex and outside the scope of this book, but interested readers should consult Mallory, 1988; C. Renfrew, 1987.)

It was at about this time that new house forms appeared in temperate zones. Smaller timber dwellings, just large enough to house a single family, replaced the Danubian longhouse. Warriors were buried with their battle axes under small mounds, a reflection of new cultural traditions that were to persist in Europe for thousands of years. The warrior leaders who descended from Bronze Age chieftains were the German tribesmen that the Romans encountered on the frontiers of their European empire.

Beakers
4700 to 4000
B.P.

Between 4700 and 4000 years ago, a series of highly characteristic artifacts came into fashion over a large region of Europe: coastal Spain, southern France, Sardinia, northern Italy, east and central Europe, the Low Countries, and Britain (Figure 21.3) (Harrison, 1980). These include finely made bell-shaped beakers found in hundreds of graves and burial mounds. Archaeologists such as V. Gordon Childe thought in terms of tribes of "Beaker Folk," who spread the length and breadth of Europe, bringing a new culture and copper working with them. It seems more likely that these vessels spread widely not as a result of itinerant merchants or great population movements but simply because beakers, as well as other trinkets such as metal brooches, became prized status symbols throughout Europe. Perhaps they became valued heirlooms, priceless grave furniture, and artifacts exchanged as bride wealth

FIGURE 21.3   Beaker vessels and other artifacts, including arrowheads, from various localities in south central Britain.

or displayed at tribal gatherings. Beakers were only one of several innovations that were changing the face of European society. Another was the plow, which came into widespread use about 4200 years ago, opening the way for the cultivation of heavier soils and much larger acreages.

THE BRONZE AGE

In the Aegean, there was steady development from this early threshold of metalworking toward complex state organizations, but Europe remained settled by small village societies. The temperate zones were densely occupied and exploited, and vast acreages of forest had been cleared and brought under cultivation by 4000 years ago. The villagers managed woodland carefully, engaged in hunting to supplement their diet, and mined both hard ax stone and soft copper ore. They also panned for gold. Communal burials and individual interments were part of tribal tradition. If ambitious community works were needed, the basic metal technologies were known, and both boats and wheeled transport were available, as well as the humanpower and resources. European village society was stable and self-sufficient, with thousands of communities connected by ties of kin and family and by long-established paths that led from valley to valley along well-drained ridges. Above all, European society enjoyed assured and reliable food supplies that helped bind the communities together.

The European Bronze Age began not as a result of dramatic events and military conquest nor because of some startling invention (Coles, 1982; Coles and Harding, 1979). It was merely a gradual and inevitable quickening of responses to a number of new opportunities. Many of these changes were in material culture and settlement patterns. A series of landscape surveys in southern Britain, for example, has revealed vast networks of fields and land boundaries joining river valleys, ridges, and watersheds into a managed landscape, in which different communities owned closely defined agricultural land. One Dorsetshire, England, Bronze Age agricultural system encompassed 494 acres (200 ha), with settlements of four to five huts linked to enclosures with sunken herd paths. There were fields, hoe plots, stock corrals, and homesteads, all joined in single managed agricultural units. By 900 B.C., Bronze Age food production was sophisticated. It relied heavily on plow agriculture and field fallowing as well as manuring, and it was based on the rotation of many different cereal and root crops.

From about 4000 years ago, metallurgy was a growth industry throughout temperate Europe. A series of local bronze industries developed in different parts of Europe, bringing with them a whole range of related activities: trading of ores and finished artifacts from major mining centers and the barter of both prosaic and prestigious artifacts and ornaments over considerable distances. For the first time, a major European industry was practiced in areas where supplies of raw materials were scarce. For instance, Bronze Age communities in Scandinavia, which had no metals, went to considerable trouble to acquire metal ore and finished tools both from tribes in Britain and from central European sources. European smiths produced some of the finest bronze artifacts ever made in the ancient world: axes and adzes, battle axes, daggers, swords, spearheads, shields, and an enormous range of brooches, pins, and other ornaments. They also made delicate, prestigious gold ornaments that were highly prized and buried with important chieftains.

For all these metallurgical innovations, the basic tenor of agricultural life remained unchanged, except for gradual evolution in the structure of European society—the emergence of social ranking. Just what form this ranking took is a matter of lively controversy (Coles, 1982) since it is reflected only in a differentiation of grave goods between a few individuals and the rest of society. In Denmark, for example, excavations on the island of Fyn have revealed rich Bronze Age burials and a nearby settlement with a wealth of gold and bronze. This is clear evidence that there was a powerful community there, having extensive trading connections with metal-rich regions to the south. The evidence from Bronze Age graves across Europe shows that the rich and the poor were buried side by side, the former with substantial quantities of valuable metal artifacts that were thus lost to the people burying them. This can only mean that some members of society, perhaps important traders, more probably influential kin leaders, were aggrandized at the expense of others and became a new elite in European society (Coles and Harding, 1979).

Although the first occurrence of bronze may one day be shown to date to some 6000 years ago in southeast Europe, the earliest widespread use of tin-copper alloys was approximately 4500 years ago in what is now Czechoslovakia (Coles and Harding, 1979). The new bronze implements with tougher working edges (Figure 21.4) were initially in short supply, but their use spread gradually as new trade routes were opened across central and west Europe. The earliest bronze working was centered in

**Unetice culture
4500 B.P.**

Unetice, an industry manufacturing axes, knife blades, halberds, and many types of ornaments (Piggott, 1965). The bronze workers themselves obviously belonged to cultural traditions long established in the area, for their burial customs are identical to those of earlier centuries. Some believe that the art of alloying tin with copper, as well as casting techniques, came to Europe from Syria. Most people now argue, however, that bronze working developed independently in Europe in that the calibrated C14 dates from the Unetice industry are earlier than those for the Near Eastern prototypes from which the other school of thought assumes Unetice to have evolved.

Bronze working soon appeared in southern Germany and Switzerland as well, where deposits of copper and tin were to be found. Other places with copper outcrops were soon using the new methods, including Brittany, the British Isles, and northern Italy, all more remote from the initial centers of bronze working. The period between

**3700 to 3300
B.P.**

approximately 3700 and 3300 years ago was one of rapid technological progress and considerable social change, generated in large part by the reinforcing effects on the local centers of bronze working of persistent demand for critical raw materials and finished tools.

By this time, European trading networks carried far more than bronze artifacts and metal ores. The amber trade went from the shores of the Baltic to the Mediterranean, following well-established routes (Figure 21.5) (P. Phillips, 1980). Seashells, perhaps faience (glass) beads, and other exotic luxuries were dispersed northward into the temperate zones in exchange for raw materials. Some centers of bronze production became major places for redistributing other goods as well. The salt miners of Austria also were very active in the long-distance trade.

3300 B.P.

By 3300 years ago, even societies remote from metal outcrops were engaged in

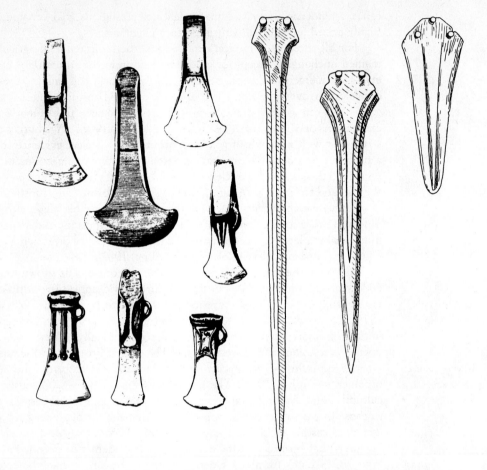

FIGURE 21.4   Copper and bronze implements from Britain: Simple flat axes and flanged and socketed axes (*left*, one-third actual size); a dagger and sword blades (*right*, one-fourth actual size).

metallurgy; the archaeological record tells little of increased specialization, although many richly adorned burials testify that the trade was concentrated among wealthy chieftains. The surplus food and energy were not devoted to generating additional surpluses and extra production but, in some societies, were channeled into erecting majestic religious monuments, of which Stonehenge in southern Britain is probably the most celebrated (Figure 21.6).

Stonehenge

Shrouded in fantasy and speculation, associated by many people with the ancient Druids' cult, Stonehenge is in fact a fantastically old religious temple (Chippindale, 1983). It began as a simple circle of ritual pits approximately 4700 years ago and went through vigorous reconstructions, reaching the zenith of its expansion in the late second millennium B.C. That Stonehenge was associated with some form of astronomical activity seems unquestionable, although the details are much debated.

The inhabitants of southern Britain also erected enormous earthwork enclosures and huge circles of timber uprights known as *henges* (see Chapter 11 and C.

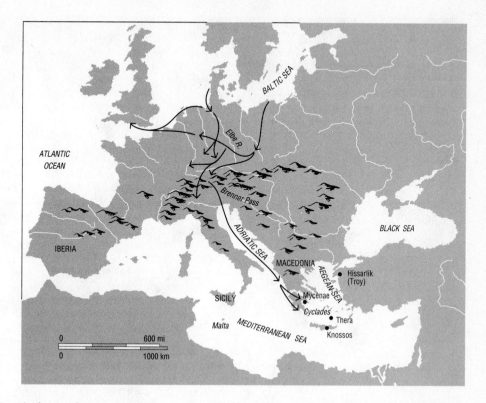

FIGURE 21.5 Amber trade routes in Europe and to Mycenae. The northern coastlines were the primary sources of Baltic amber. Amber was being passed southward to the Mediterranean by the time the Mycenaeans came to power.

Renfrew, 1983). Doubtless special priests were needed to maintain these spectacular monuments and to perform the rituals in their precincts. Religious activity was supported by the food surplus, not the increased productivity that generated spectacular social evolution in the Near East. Thus, during the third and part of the second millennia B.C., little social evolution went on in Europe; political power and wealth belonged to the chieftains and warriors rather than to divine kings and a hierarchic society.

BRONZE AGE WARRIORS

European societies became more socially ranked as time went on. As trade intensified, local monopolies over salt and other supplies became concentrated in the hands of comparatively few individuals. Population growth and perhaps some climatic deterioration put new pressure on agricultural land (P. Phillips, 1980; Piggott, 1965). All of this may have led to considerable political instability in Europe and to alliances of small tribes under the rule of powerful and ambitious chieftains, themselves once

FIGURE 21.6   Stonehenge as seen from the air. This photograph was taken before modern tourism caused development at the site.

minor village leaders. Some warrior groups even began to strike at the edge of the Mediterranean world, destroying Mycenae and the Hittite Empire.

As time went on, many more copper and bronze artifacts became available for domestic consumption. Some new tool forms were introduced by central European smiths, including socketed axes, varied woodworking tools, and the *ard* (a scraping plow drawn by oxen). The ard was a particularly important innovation, for it allowed deeper plowing, more advanced agricultural methods, and higher productivity. The new farming techniques were vital to feed the many new mouths, and prime farming land was harder to find than ever before.

Between 3200 and 2800 years ago, the population movements associated with central European peoples introduced a more consolidated system of agriculture to much of Europe, which allowed exploitation of much heavier soils as well as stock breeding (J. G. D. Clark, 1952; Dennell, 1983). For the first time, stock were fully integrated into the food-producing economy, and cattle were used for meat, milk, and draft work, though sheep were bred as much for wool as for their flesh. Improved technology for new implements of tillage was fully exploited to achieve a truly effective economic symbiosis between flora and fauna, carefully balancing forest clearance with cultivation and pasturage.

Urnfield culture
1250 B.C.

One powerful group of warrior tribes in west Hungary is known to archaeologists as the Urnfield people because of their burial customs: Their dead were cremated and their ashes deposited in urns; huge cemeteries of urn burials are associated with fortified villages, sometimes built near lakes. Urnfield people began to make full use of horse-drawn vehicles and new weaponry. Skilled bronze smiths produced sheet-metal helmets and shields. Warriors used the slashing sword, a devastating weapon far more effective than the cutting swords of earlier times.

The emergence of warrior elites was accompanied by a quickening of trade, reflected in a remarkable standardization of weapons and burial customs throughout much of central and western Europe. Within a couple of centuries, characteristic slashing swords and other central European tools had been deposited in cemeteries in Italy, the Balkans, and the Aegean. Exploitation of copper mines such as those in Austria's Tyrol was intensified. There, bands of miners used bronze-tipped picks to dig deep into the ground for copper ore. Their efforts increased the supplies of copper and tin available to central Europe (J. G. D. Clark, 1952; Coles and Harding, 1979).

The Scythians and Other Steppe Peoples

The vast rolling grasslands and steppes from China to the Ukraine were not settled by farming peoples until they had a culture enabling them to survive in an environment with extreme contrasts of climate and relatively infertile soils. The carrying capacity of the land is such that only a vast territory can support herds of domestic stock. The prehistory of this huge area is obscure until the first millennium B.C., when

Scythians
c. 500 B.C.

the Scythians (from Scythia, an area in southeast Europe) and other steppe peoples first appeared in the historical record. No one should doubt, however, the importance of nomads in the prehistory of Europe in earlier millennia (E. D. Phillips, 1972). The Kurgan people and other possible Indo-European speakers were familiar with the vast open spaces of the steppes (Figure 21.7).

As early as 6000 years ago, people living at the Dereivka site on the Ukraine's Dnieper River were riding horses with rope bits. Their successors roamed the steppes for centuries before the Scythians came out of history's shadows, living in stout felt tents and subsisting mostly on horse's milk and cheese as well as on food from hunting and fishing. The nomadic life, though, leaves few traces in the archaeological record, except when permafrost has preserved burials in a refrigerated state.

400 B.C.

We are fortunate in having extensive data about the vigorous society of nomad peoples from the spectacular frozen tombs of Siberia. Russian archaeologist Sergei Rudenko (1970) has excavated several nomad burial mounds erected in 400 B.C. at Pazyryk in northeast Siberia. The chiefs of Pazyryk were elaborately tattooed, wore

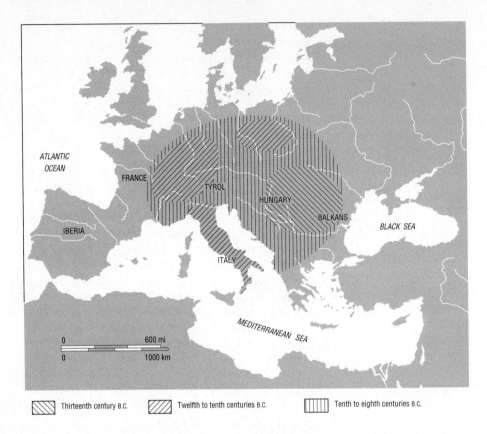

| Thirteenth century B.C. | Twelfth to tenth centuries B.C. | Tenth to eighth centuries B.C. |

FIGURE 21.7   Approximate distribution of Urnfield cultures in Europe.

woollen and leather clothes, and employed skillful artists to adorn their horse trappings and harnesses with exuberant, elaborate, stylized animal art. A powerful chief was accompanied to the next world by his wife and servants, horses and chariots, and many of his smaller possessions. The Pazyryk burials contain fragments of woven rugs, the earliest examples of such art in the world.

The steppe peoples lived to the north of the well-traveled trade routes of Greek merchants, but their territory was constantly being explored and sometimes colonized by farmers whose lands were becoming overpopulated or overgrazed. Enormous areas of steppe were needed to support even a small band of horse riders, for just a slight increase in population could drastically affect the food supplies of the original inhabitants. The result was constant displacement of populations as the nomads sought to expand their shrinking territory to accommodate their own population pressures. The nomads menaced the northern frontiers of the Mediterranean world throughout classical and more recent times.

The Eurasian nomad population flourished during the closing millennia of prehistory. The Pazyryk finds let us glimpse a prehistoric way of life that in some areas survived unchanged into historic times.

THE EMERGENCE OF IRONWORKING

Ironworking
c. 1000 B.C.

Late Bronze Age Europeans were effective farmers as well as traders and metallurgists capable of exploiting Europe's forested environment far more efficiently than their predecessors could. They lived amid a complicated network of trade that carried not only metals but also salt, grain, gold, pottery, and many other commodities. Their economic organization probably included community smiths, specialists supported by the village, but still no centralized state system of the Near Eastern type.

These exchange networks facilitated the spread of ironworking techniques across Europe with considerable rapidity after 1000 B.C. In widespread use for both weapons and utilitarian objects by 700 B.C., ironworking is much more difficult than bronze working, for the technology is harder to acquire and takes much longer; however, once it is learned, the advantages of the new metal are obvious. Because the ore is found in many more places, the metal is much cheaper and can be used for weapons and utilitarian artifacts as well. These would, of course, include axes, hoes, and plowshares, all of which contributed much to agricultural efficiency, higher crop yields, and greater food surpluses. The population increases and intensified trading activities of the centuries immediately preceding the Roman Empire are partly attributed to the success of iron technology in changing European agriculture and craftsmanship (Collis, 1984).

As iron technology spread into the country north of the Alps, new societies arose whose leaders exploited the metal's artistic and economic potentials. The tribal chieftaincy was the structure of government; the most coherent broader political unit was a loose confederacy of tribes formed in time of war or temporarily under the aegis of a charismatic chieftain. Despite the onslaught of Roman colonization and exploitation, culture beyond the frontiers retained its essentially European cast, an indigenous slant to cultural traditions that began when farming did (Wells, 1981).

Hascherkeller
3000 to 2800 B.P.

For all the technological changes, farming life continued much as before. Peter Wells (1984) has excavated an Iron Age farming community near Hascherkeller in lower Bavaria, Germany, where he found three enclosed farmsteads. The farmstead complexes included dwellings, barns, sheds, and workshops, with between 15 and 30 people living in each settlement. Occupied between 3000 and 2800 years ago, they were self-sufficient communities without iron tools that traded foodstuffs for such items as imported bronze scraps, beads, and graphite, the latter used for pottery decoration. Hascherkeller was apparently without iron, which was still a new metal. But it was occupied at a time when the first towns were emerging in central Europe,

Heuneburg
800 to 400 B.C.

communities like the Heuneburg, a significant cluster of timber houses occupied between 800 and 400 B.C. by about 200 people. The Heuneburg was a market town, one of many such local centers that were the forerunners of much later medieval communities of the same type.

The Hallstatt Culture

Hallstatt
730 B.C.

One strong culture was the Hallstatt, named after a site near Salzburg, Austria (Rowlett, 1967; Wells, 1981). Hallstatt culture began in the seventh and sixth centuries B.C. and owed much to Urnfield practices; the skillful bronze working of earlier times was still practiced, although some immigrants from the east may have achieved political dominance over earlier inhabitants. Bronze, however, was still the dominant metal for horse trappings, weapons, and ornaments. Chiefs were buried in large mounds within wooden chambers, some in wagons (Figure 21.8).

The Hallstatt people and their culture spread through former Urnfield territories as far north as Belgium and the Netherlands and into France and parts of Spain (Figure 21.9). Many Hallstatt sites are particularly notable for their fortifications. The Hallstatt people traded with the Mediterraneans along well-traveled routes up the Rhone River and through the Alps into central Europe. A significant import was the serving vessel for wine; containers of Mediterranean wine were carried far into central Europe as Hallstatt chieftains discovered wine drinking.

FIGURE 21.8   Bronze ritual cart from a Hallstatt grave in Austria, approximately 1 foot (0.3 m) long.

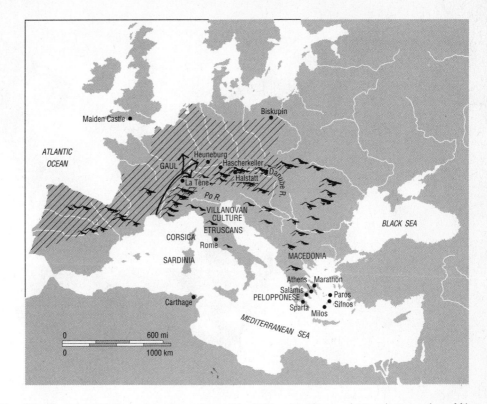

FIGURE 21.9   Distribution of Hallstatt Iron Age cultures (shaded area) in Europe during the seventh to fifth centuries B.C. The trade routes in southern France are also shown.

The La Tène People

La Tène
450 B.C.

By the last quarter of the fifth century B.C., a new and highly distinctive technology, La Tène, had developed in the Rhine and Danube valleys (Jacobsthal, 1944; Megaw, 1970). An aristocratic clique of chieftains in the Danube Valley enjoyed implements and weapons elaborately worked in bronze and gold. Much of their sophisticated art had roots in classical Greek and Mediterranean traditions, for La Tène craftsworkers were quick to adopt new motifs and ideas from the centers of higher civilization to the south (Figure 21.10). The La Tène people spoke Celtic, a language that spread widely through Europe from perhaps as early as the ninth century B.C. Greek and Roman writers referred to these people as Celts, a term that has survived in their linguistic label.

350 B.C.

La Tène technology was a specific adaptation of ironworking to woodland Europe. The culture extended north into the Low Countries and Britain in the fourth century B.C. La Tène art is deservedly famous, and the hill forts and defensive settlements of this Iron Age culture are widespread in west Europe. The superior military tactics of the La Tène people introduced the Romans to the short sword, for

**FIGURE
21.10**   Iron Age helmet from the bed of the River Thames in London, 8.07 inches (205 cm) at
the base.

Celts sacked Rome in about 390 B.C. The last three centuries before Christ saw
considerable change in Europe, with the appearance of coinage, the development of
small autonomous states, and the foundation of large settlements known to archaeologists and historians as *oppida,* the Latin word for "towns." Many were fortified and
somewhat similar to later towns in medieval Europe. La Tène peoples survived long
after France and southern Britain had been conquered by Rome in 55 B.C. (Cunliffe,
1974). Much territory in the temperate zones came under Roman domination, an
uneasy frontier province that eventually crumbled before the inexorable pressure of
the warlike tribes on its boundaries. The illiterate peoples who eventually sacked
Rome and ravaged its provinces were the descendants of prehistoric Europeans whose
cultural traditions had been evolving ever since the first farming cultures developed
north of the Mediterranean Basin.

*Roman conquest
55 B.C.*

GUIDE TO FURTHER READING

Champion, Timothy G., 1984. *Prehistoric Europe.* New York: Academic Press.
    *A textbook on European prehistory from the earliest times to the expansion of the
    Roman Empire. Major emphasis on subsistence, trade, and social organization.*

Coles, J. M., and Harding, A. F. 1979. *The Bronze Age in Europe.* London: Methuen.
An authoritative account of the complexities of the European Bronze Age that covers the topic far more fully than we can in this book.

Collis, John. 1984. *The European Iron Age.* London: Batsford.
A useful introduction to European ironmaking cultures.

Cunliffe, Barry. 1974. *Iron Age Communities in Britain.* London: Routledge & Kegan Paul.
The literature on the European Iron Age is scattered and published in many different languages. Cunliffe's account of Iron Age hill forts and other settlements in Britain will give you a general impression of the archaeology of the period.

Phillips, Patricia. 1980. *The Prehistory of Europe.* Bloomington: Indiana University Press.
A detailed synthesis of west European prehistory from the earliest times. Particularly good on the later periods.

Piggott, Stuart. 1965. *Ancient Europe.* Chicago: Aldine.
Somewhat outdated, an account of prehistoric Europe that is closer to Childe than to current evolutionary thinking but is still authoritative, with excellent illustrations.

PART VI

STATE-ORGANIZED SOCIETIES IN THE AMERICAS

(3550 YEARS AGO TO A.D. 1530)

PART VI CONTAINS DESCRIPTIONS OF THE GREAT AND COMPLEX STATES OF THE NEW WORLD. THE THEORETICAL LITERATURE SURROUNDING THE EMERGENCE OF STATES IN MESOAMERICA AND PERU IS ENORMOUS, AND INTERESTED READERS ARE REFERRED TO CHAPTER 15 FOR SOME OF THE PRINCIPAL ARGUMENTS SURROUNDING THE SUBJECT.

What, then, must have been the emotions of the Spaniards, when, after working their toilsome way into the open air, the cloudy tabernacle parted before their eyes, and they beheld these fair scenes in all their pristine magnificence and beauty. It was like the spectacle which greeted the eyes of Moses from the summit of Pisgah, and, in the warm glow of their feelings, they cried out, "It is the promised land!"

W. H. Prescott,
The Conquest of
Mexico, 1843

Chronological Table L

Calibrated Dates a.d./b.c./b.p.	C14 Years A.D./B.C.	MESOAMERICA		
			Lowlands	Highlands
1310–1515	1500		Spanish Conquest	
				AZTECS
		Postclassic		
870–1230	1000			TOLTECS
	500	Classic	MAYA CIVILIZATION	
				TEOTIHUACÁN
		Late Preclassic		MONTE ALBÁN
450–5 b.c.	A.D. 1		Regional Olmec styles	
820–480	500 B.C.	Middle Preclassic	OLMEC CULTURE	
3530–2905 b.p.	3000 B.P.			
4345–3660	3500	Early Preclassic		
			Well-established village agriculture	
4830–4303	4000			
5503–4925	4500		Chapter 14 ↑	

CHAPTER 22   MESOAMERICAN CIVILIZATIONS

Preview

- The Preclassic period of Mesoamerican prehistory lasted from approximately 4000 years ago to A.D. 250, a period of major cultural change in both lowlands and highlands. Sedentary villages traded with each other in raw materials and exotic objects. These exchange networks became increasingly complex and eventually came under the monopolistic control of larger villages. Increasing social complexity went hand in hand with the appearance of the first public buildings and evidence of social stratification.

- These developments are well chronicled in the Valley of Oaxaca and in the Olmec culture of the lowlands, which flourished from approximately 3500 to 2500 years ago. Olmec art styles and religious beliefs were among those that spread widely over lowlands and highlands during the late Preclassic period.

- The complex societies that developed in the Mesoamerican lowlands and highlands depended on diverse agricultural techniques. In the lowlands, Maya farmers not only used slash-and-burn methods but also raised swamp gardens. Some of the largest areas of the latter are close to major Maya centers, where highly organized food production was necessary. In the highlands, agricultural environments were very diverse. Many early communities relied on simple "pot irrigation." Later farmers used dry farming, slash-and-burn methods, and cultivated slopes, occasionally using terracing. Valley of Mexico societies used raised fields known as *chinampas*, reclaimed swamps, to feed large urban and rural populations.

- The Preclassic cultural developments culminated in the highlands in a number of great cities, among them Monte Albán and Teotihuacán. The latter housed more than 120,000 people and covered more than 8 square miles (20.7 sq. km) at the height of its prosperity. Teotihuacán collapsed approximately A.D. 700, probably as a result of warfare with other rival states in the highlands.

- Maya civilization arose in the lowlands after 3000 years ago. Religious ideologies, ritual organization, and extensive trading networks were key factors in the development of Maya society. The late Preclassic city of El Mirador endured more than 900 years. It covered about 10 square miles (25.9 sq. km), most of its temples and pyramids being built between 150 B.C. and A.D. 50. The city was controlled by a highly organized elite.

- Classic Maya civilization flourished from A.D. 250 to 900 and was remarkable for its sophisticated trade networks, great ceremonial centers, and elaborate ceremonies, known to us through sculptures, murals, and hieroglyphs. Maya rulers sought to appease their many gods with the aid of an elaborate sacred calendar based on astronomical events.

- Maya glyphs have recently been deciphered. They show that Maya civilization was far from uniform. Emblem glyphs identify individual rulers and ruling dynasties. Each center developed its own cultural traditions. The Maya were unified more by religious beliefs than by political or economic interests. Their political mechanisms included warfare, diplomacy, and arranged marriages to create alliances between neighboring centers.

- Maya political history is known through deciphered glyphs. Until about A.D. 600, the largest states were in northeast Petén, with a multicenter polity headed by the "Sky" rulers of Tikal. Maya civilization reached its height in the southern lowlands after the seventh century. By A.D. 800, Maya populations were declining rapidly.

- Maya civilization collapsed suddenly in the Yucatán after A.D. 900; the reasons for the collapse are still uncertain, but pressure on the labor force and food shortages doubtless were among them.

- Teotihuacán's collapse in the highlands resulted in a political vacuum for some centuries, which eventually was filled by the Toltecs and then the Aztecs, whose bloodthirsty civilization was dominant in the Valley of Mexico at the time of the Spanish conquest in A.D. 1519.

- Aztec civilization was unable to resist the Spanish and collapsed suddenly, partly as a result of serious internal stresses and rebellion by subject tribes.

Chronological
Table L

Few topics are surrounded by more fantasy, myth, and archaeological lunacy than the origins of pre-Columbian civilization in the Americas. Ever since Columbus first set foot in the Bahamas, scholars and others have speculated about the origins of the American Indians. The discovery of the Aztec and Inca civilizations fueled speculation and mythmaking to new and even more frenzied heights. The Ten Lost Tribes of Israel, the Canaanites, and all manner of other strange candidates have been invoked as the first civilized peoples to settle in the Americas. The survivors of the lost continents of Atlantis and Mu have been prime candidates for generations (Wauchope, 1962). Nineteenth-century readers were entranced by stories of a great mound builder civilization that flourished in the Midwest, only to perish under attack from savage hordes (Silverberg, 1968). Today, we are treated to sagas about ancient astronauts who colonized the Americas from space and then departed, leaving the roots of civilization behind them (von Däniken, 1970; Feder, 1990).

In the latest attack of incredible speculation, a respected Harvard zoologist tells us that America was settled by colonists from Europe and North Africa in the first millennium B.C., long before the Vikings or Columbus (Fell, 1976, 1980). His evidence consists of a comparison of alleged ancient American inscriptions and "timeworn" ruins in the lands from which the "Colonists" came. According to Barry Fell's theories, the settled civilizations of America, which were founded by Old World colonists, were subjected to upheaval and disaster in approximately A.D. 1000, just as the Vikings arrived. Hundreds of people have written to him, he claims, some of them American Indians trying to relate his fables to their own cultural traditions of people who arrived across the water centuries before. In other words, the inspiration for pre-Columbian civilization came from the Old World, perhaps only 3000 years ago.

What are we to make of these centuries of fantasy? Why is American archaeology so surrounded by crazy myths with no basis in scientific reality? One obvious explanation is people's appetite for a good adventure story, for epic heroes and transoceanic voyages. Another is that stories such as Barry Fell's or Erich von Däniken's are based on a haphazard collection of facts strung together into a convincing pattern without the rigor of systematic scientific analysis: This approach makes an adventure story easy to compile and to enjoy. Third, unlike Europeans, most Americans, because they are immigrants, feel no cultural identity with the Indians or their history. They feel more comfortable believing stories of age-old colonization by familiar peoples from the world of Egypt and the Near East. For many people, history is a faith, too, something to cling to and to believe against all scientific odds. Most of the strange works that purport to describe early civilization in the Americas play on such faith. They invite the reader to join with the group that knows the "truth" and either attack scientists as frauds or simply ignore their work. It is significant, for example, that Fell (1980) cites no works of archaeological scholarship in his *Saga America* except some descriptions of American Indian rock art. One can conclude only that scientific archaeological research is irrelevant to his tale or that he is unfamiliar with it or that it challenges the "faith."

The account of early American civilization that follows is based on scientific archaeological excavations and surveys by which evidence has been accumulating for the indigenous origins of New World civilization for more than a century. The cumulative scientific evidence is overwhelming and impressive in its consistency. No one can dismantle a sincerely held faith, and so I shall make no attempt to destroy the illusions of those who believe that America was settled by Atlanteans, ancient Egyptians, or anyone else: To do so is a waste of time. The irony is that the unfolding story of New World civilization revealed by science is far more fascinating and intellectually stimulating than any outer-space adventure story, however well conceived or marketed. (For more serious accounts of transoceanic voyaging, see Carter, 1981; Davies, 1979.)

AGRICULTURAL TECHNIQUES

Slash and burn

Early Mesoamerican farming communities lived in dispersed villages and used only slash-and-burn agriculture, which as we have seen cannot support high population densities (R. E. W. Adams, 1977a). In fact, there are many highly diverse agricultural environments in both highlands and lowlands, which were exploited in many different ways, probably long before more complex societies appeared.

Raised fields

Some fascinating experiments have involved scanning the Maya lowlands with side-scanning radar. They revealed that areas of wet-season swamp near known Maya sites often have many irregular grids of gray lines in ladder, lattice, and curvilinear patterns. These are thought to represent long-forgotten raised field systems built in swamps (Adams, Brown, and Culbert, 1981). The Maya and, perhaps to a lesser extent, their predecessors, drained and canalized swamps for agricultural and communication purposes, so the swamps became assets rather than liabilities, artificial environments where substantial food surpluses of maize and beans could be grown and then transported readily by canoe. The preparation and maintenance of raised fields were well within the capabilities of individual households and small hamlets (Culbert, 1981b). Most lowland agricultural techniques did not require large numbers of people until there was *intensification* of agricultural production as population densities rose in late Preclassic times. It is significant that some of the largest areas of raised fields are close to major Classic Maya centers like Tikal.

The Mesomerican highlands are highly diverse agricultural environments, as we have seen in the Tehuacán Valley (Chapter 14). The earliest farming villages in Oaxaca are concentrated in the valley floors, where water is within easy reach of the surface. Modern farmers choose similar villages for simple "pot" irrigation, where they plant their maize and other crops near small shallow wells. They simply dip pots into the wells and water surrounding plants from the shallow water table. Flannery (1968b) has argued that the Oaxacans used the same technique in prehistoric times, for it does not require large numbers of people. In time, as population densities rose, the Oaxacans were able to build on their simple and highly effective farming techniques, expanding onto slopes and into more arid lands with great success. Eventually, the economic power generated by these rising populations gave highland areas like this a decided edge in cultural evolution.

Pot irrigation

Chinampas

Similar diversity of agricultural techniques is found in the Valley of Mexico, where slash-and-burn methods, dry farming, and irrigation agriculture all were in use. The farmers used both floodwaters and canals to bring water to dry gardens. The most famous of all raised field techniques, however, is the *chinampa*, or floating garden technique, a highly intensive and productive agricultural system based on the reclaiming of swamps. The farmers piled up natural vegetation and lake mud to form huge grids of naturally irrigated gardens. The chinampas were used very systematically to grow a variety of crops, so timed that different crops came into harvest throughout the year (Sanders et al., 1970). This system is amazingly productive and is estimated to have supported approximately 100,000 people from 25,000 acres (10,117 ha) in 1519, the time of Spanish contact. Each chinampa produced large food surpluses that could be used to feed thousands of nonagricultural workers and specialists. William Sanders has argued that these 25,000 acres (10,117 ha) of chinampas actually could have supported approximately 180,000 people. That this highly effective agricultural system was the basis of early civilization and urban life in the Valley of Mexico is beyond question.

Market economy

The agricultural system of the Valley of Mexico may seem complicated, but it supported and was part of a far more elaborate system of food marketing, which provided not only tribute for taxes but also opportunities for the trading of special foodstuffs from one area of the highlands to another. The highland peoples relied on elaborate markets that were strictly regulated by the state and conducted on a barter system. The Valley of Mexico was an economic unit before Teotihuacán made it a political one as well. It was the great agricultural productivity of the valley and the sophisticated market economy of the emerging city that made the prodigious social and religious as well as material developments of later centuries possible. This economic system fostered the development of specialist crafts that were sold in the city markets and exported over wide areas.

PRECLASSIC PEOPLES IN MESOAMERICA

Preclassic
**c. 4000 b.p. to
a.d. 250**

By 4000 years ago, sedentary farming villages were common in most of Mesoamerica (R. E. W. Adams, 1977a; Sanders and Price, 1968; Weaver, 1981). In their agriculture, people relied on many plant species, and slash-and-burn farming methods were in wide use in the lowlands. With such methods people could clear small gardens in the forest by cutting tree trunks and brush and carefully burning branches to fertilize the soil with a layer of wood ash. Using pointed digging sticks, they planted maize and other crops. A few seasons later they abandoned the land, planting less important crops on older plots or leaving them to the forest. The search for new lands was constant, even when slash-and-burn was combined with irrigation or riverside agriculture.

Early Preclassic

Cuello
**c. 3000 b.p. to
a.d. 300**

Many centuries elapsed between the beginnings of village life and that of Mesoamerican civilization. The first signs of political and social complexity appear in many regions of Mesoamerica between about 4000 and 2900 years ago, during the early part of an era named the *Preclassic* or *Formative* by archaeologists, a period that lasted as late as A.D. 250. In many regions, small but often powerful chiefdoms headed by a chief and an elite appeared. The elite dominated economic, political, and religious life and ruled over large nonelite populations. A similar pattern of emerging social and political complexity has been documented in Mesopotamia, Egypt, China, and other areas where early state-organized societies evolved. In Mesoamerica, as elsewhere, the new chiefdoms can be identified by differences in house designs, by the appearance of small shrines, by social rankings detectable through grave goods, and from prestigious as opposed to more utilitarian artifacts. This process is well documented at Cuello in lowland northern Belize, which is radiocarbon dated to between c. 3000 years ago and A.D. 300 (Figure 22.1) (N. Hammond, 1980, 1982). The inhabitants of this site were maize farmers, who also relied heavily on wild plant foods for their diet.

There was no one region where this emerging sociopolitical complexity occurred first. Rather, it was a development that took place more or less simultaneously in many regions of Mesoamerica, not in isolation but with each region interacting with others (Sharer and Grove, 1989). The most famous of these societies is that of the Olmec.

Middle Preclassic: The Olmec and Theories of a Mother Culture

The Olmec people lived on the Mexican south Gulf Coast from about 3500 to 2500 years ago (Figure 22.1) (Bernal, 1969; Coe and Diehl, 1980). Their homeland is low-lying, tropical, and humid with fertile soils. The swamps, lakes, and rivers are rich in fish, birds, and other animals. It was in this region that the Olmec created a highly distinctive art style. Olmec art was executed in sculpture and in relief. The artists concentrated on natural and supernatural beings, the dominant motif being the "were-jaguar," or humanlike jaguar. Many jaguars were given infantile faces; droop-

Olmec
3500 to 2500
B.P.

FIGURE 22.1   Mesoamerican archaeological sites mentioned in this chapter. Approximate distributions of various traditions are shown.

ing lips; and large, swollen eyes, a style also applied to human figures, some of whom resemble snarling demons. Olmec contributions to Mesoamerican art and religion were enormously significant. For years, scholars have believed that elements of their art style and imagery were diffused southward to Guatemala and San Salvador and northward into the Valley of Mexico. In short, the Olmec was the "mother culture" of Mesoamerican civilization (Sharer, 1989). Increasingly, this theory is being questioned (Sharer and Grove, 1989).

San Lorenzo
3250 B.P.

The origins of the Olmec are a complete mystery, but the culture probably has strong local roots. The earliest traces of Olmec occupation are best documented at San Lorenzo, where Olmec people lived on a platform in the midst of frequently inundated woodland plains. They erected ridges and mounds around their platform, upon which they built pyramids and possibly ball courts and placed elaborate monumental carvings overlooking the site. The earliest occupation of San Lorenzo shows few Olmec features, but by 3250 years ago the inhabitants were beginning to build some raised fields, a task that required organized labor forces. By that time, too, distinctive Olmec sculpture began to appear. A century later, magnificent monumental carvings adorned San Lorenzo (Figure 22.2), distinctive and often mutilated by the Olmec themselves, perhaps when rulers died (Coe and Diehl, 1980).

One archaeologist has estimated the population of San Lorenzo at 2500 (Coe and Diehl, 1980). The inhabitants enjoyed extensive trade, especially in obsidian and other semiprecious materials obtained from many parts of Mesoamerica. San Lorenzo fell into decline after 2900 years ago and was surpassed by La Venta, the most famous Olmec site, nearer the Gulf of Mexico.

La Venta

La Venta
800 to 400 B.C.

The La Venta ceremonial center was built on a small island in the middle of a swamp (Drucker, 1959). A rectangular earth mound, 393 feet long by 229 feet wide and 105 feet high (120 m by 70 m by 32 m), dominates the island. Long, low mounds surround a rectangular plaza in front of the large mound, faced by walls and terraced mounds at the other end of the plaza (Figure 22.3). Vast monumental stone sculptures litter the site, including some Olmec heads bearing expressions of contempt and savagery. Caches of jade objects, figurines, and a dull green rock (serpentine) are common, too (Figure 22.4). Every stone for sculptures and temples had to be brought from at least 60 miles (96 km) away, a vast undertaking, for some sculptured blocks weigh more than 40 tons. The people traded ceremonial jade and serpentine from as far away as Costa Rica. La Venta flourished for approximately 400 years from 800 B.C. After approximately 400 B.C., the site probably was destroyed; we deduce this occurrence from signs that many of its finest monuments were intentionally defaced.

San Lorenzo and La Venta, with their relatively small populations, are manifestations of a much more complex social and political order, not in the fashion of a state-organized society, as earlier scholars suggested, but a series of chiefdoms with powerful leaders who maintained contacts with other such societies in the lowlands and perhaps further afield (Diehl, 1989). This is very different from characterizing the Olmec as the mother culture of all Mesoamerican civilization or as a great imperial empire, whose tentacles reached as far as the Mexican highlands. Arthur Demarest

FIGURE 22.2 Giant stone head from San Lorenzo made from basalt, approximately 8 feet (2.4 m) high. These heads may be portraits of rulers. David Grove (1973) has identified what he thinks are name glyphs on the "helmets."

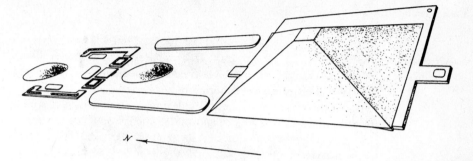

FIGURE 22.3   La Venta, site 4: layout of the major structures.

FIGURE 22.4   An Olmec altar or throne sculpture from La Venta. The sculpture is approximately 6 feet (2 m) high. At least one of these thrones shows the ruler in front connected to his parents on the side by umbilical cords.

(1989) points out that Olmec society changed over the centuries. At first, during the early Preclassic, it was a set of chiefdoms along the Gulf Coast of Veracruz and Tabasco, which may have exercised some influence over adjacent areas of Chiapas and Central Mexico. Later, during the middle Preclassic, Olmec society flourished during a period when art motifs, religious symbols, and ritual beliefs were shared between developing chiefdoms in many regions through the regular contacts between elites and day-to-day trade from region to region. It was what Demarest calls a "lattice of Middle Formative interaction" over many centuries that produced the complex and sophisticated traditions of Mesoamerican civilization that were to follow.

Late Preclassic

Late Preclassic
300 B.C. to A.D. 250

The trajectory of rapid cultural change continued in many regions during the late Preclassic (300 B.C. to A.D. 250). This was the period when a common religious system and ideology began to unify large areas of Mesoamerica. The leaders of the new orders validated their rule with elaborate public ceremonies in spectacular ceremonial centers, commemorating potent and widely recognized deities. Distinctive art and architecture went with the new religion, the practice of which required precise measurements of calendar years and of longer cycles of time. Writing and mathematical calculations were developed to affirm religious practices, a unifying political force in the sense that they welded scattered village communities into larger political units. By the time the classic Mesoamerican civilizations arose, dynasties of elites had been ruling parts of Mesoamerica along well-established lines for nearly 1000 years (Sabloff, 1989).

THE RISE OF COMPLEX SOCIETY
IN OAXACA

The Preclassic cultures of the Valley of Oaxaca have been studied intensively by Kent Flannery and his students, using highly sophisticated systems approaches to document changing settlement patterns and economic and demographic trends (Flannery, 1976; Flannery and Marcus, 1983). Something like 90 percent of the Preclassic Oaxaca villages were little more than hamlets of 50 to 60 people and the remainder were much larger settlements of 1000 to 1200, with populations of priests and craftspeople.

The evolution of larger settlements in Oaxaca and elsewhere was closely connected with the development of long-distance trade in obsidian and other luxuries such as seashells and stingray spines from the Gulf of Mexico. The simple barter networks for obsidian of earlier times evolved into sophisticated regional trading organizations in which village leaders controlled monopolies over sources of obsidian and its distribution. Magnetite mirrors, seashells, feathers, and ceramics were all traded on the highlands, and from the highlands to the lowlands as well. Olmec pottery and other ritual objects began to appear in highland settlements between 3150 and 2650 years ago, many of them bearing the distinctive were-jaguar motif of the lowlands, which had an important place in Olmec cosmology.

San José Mogote
3400 to 3150 B.P.

Public buildings began to appear in villages such as San José Mogote between 3400 and 3150 years ago. Many of them were oriented 8° west of north; they were built on adobe and earth platforms. Conch shell trumpets and turtle shell drums from the Gulf of Mexico are associated with these buildings, as are clay figurines of dancers wearing costumes and masks (Figure 22.5). There were marine fish spines, too, probably used in personal bloodletting ceremonies that were still practiced even in Aztec times. The Spanish described how Aztec nobles would gash themselves with knives or with the spines of fish or stingray in acts of mutilation before the gods, penances required of the devout (Saunders, 1989). It has been suggested that the

FIGURE 22.5   Four clay figurines shaped and posed deliberately to form a scene, buried beneath
an early Preclassic house at San José Mogote, Oaxaca.

diffusion of common art styles throughout Mesoamerica resulted both from an
increased need for religious rituals to bring the various elements of society together
and because the Oaxacan elite, aspiring to the status of their chiefly neighbors, took
to the new beliefs in slavish conformity (Flannery, 1976; Flannery and Marcus, 1983).
This diffusion took place after long-distance trading had been in existence for centuries and probably signaled an increase in larger villages such as San José Mogote.

Monte Albán

By 400 B.C., there were at least seven small states in the Valley of Oaxaca, of
which the one centered at Monte Albán soon became dominant. Although massive population growth and increased economic power were among the interacting
factors that aided in the rise of Monte Albán, its special terrain may have been of
vital importance in its ascendancy (Blanton, 1978, 1983). Richard Blanton has sur-
veyed more than 2000 terraces on the slopes of Monte Albán, terraces used for
agriculture and housing areas. Monte Albán commanded the best terrain in the

valley, sloping land that was organized for agriculture and dense settlement by a population of several thousand people, far larger than that of most major settlements in Mesoamerica at the time. Even as early as 400 B.C., some of the terraces were in use by a highly organized population whose leaders resided in a ceremonial and civic center built on the summit of the Monte Albán ridge. Although the large-scale buildings of later times have contoured the summit beyond recognition, it is clear that the first leaders to live there undertook major public works, many of them wood and thatch buildings that had incised sculptures of what may be dead and tortured enemies set into the walls.

Monte Albán went on to develop into a vast ceremonial center with splendid public architecture; its settlement area included public buildings, terraces, and housing zones that extended over approximately 15 square miles (40 sq. km) (Figure 22.6). The more than 2000 terraces all held one or two houses, and small ravines were dammed to pond valuable water supplies. Blanton suggests that between 30,000 and 50,000 people lived at Monte Albán between A.D. 200 and 700. Many very large villages and smaller hamlets lay within easy distance of the city. The enormous platforms on the ridge of Monte Albán supported complex layouts of temples and pyramid-temples, palaces, patios, and tombs. A hereditary elite seems to have ruled Monte Albán, the leaders of a state that had emerged in the Valley of Oaxaca by A.D. 200. Their religious power was based on ancestor worship, a pantheon of at least 39 gods, grouped around major themes of ritual life. The rain god and lightning were associated with the jaguar motif; another group of deities was linked with the maize god, Pitao Cozabi. Nearly all these gods were still worshiped at the time of Spanish contact, although Monte Albán itself was abandoned after A.D. 700, at approximately the same time as another great ceremonial center, Teotihuacán, in the Valley of Mexico, began to decline.

FIGURE 22.6   Monte Albán, Valley of Oaxaca—Zapotec ruins, 1951.

TEOTIHUACÁN

We have already referred to the Valley of Mexico as an economic unit, a network of markets that probably flourished long before large states came into being in the highlands. Perhaps the sequence of events that led to the founding of such polities, especially Teotihuacán, began with the buildup of agricultural populations in diverse environments such as the Valley of Oaxaca in the first and second millennia B.C. This population growth led to the development of more intensive agricultural methods, including both irrigation and chinampa systems. At the same time, different areas were linked by increasingly sophisticated trading networks and by an emerging market economy, perhaps with some specialized merchants.

Religious activity was stimulated by the introduction of beliefs and sacred objects from the lowlands. Trade in exotic luxuries increased as ceremonial centers and stratified societies were founded. By 200 B.C., the effects of increased religious activity, intensified trading, and the production of huge food surpluses from the diverse environment had led to the founding of at least two major cities in the Valley of Mexico. One of these, Teotihuacán, reached an enormous size and enjoyed vast political, economic, and religious power in the centuries that followed. In the Valley of Oaxaca, Monte Albán achieved a similar dominance. The two great states probably enjoyed an uneasy alliance.

Teotihuacán lies northeast of Mexico City and is now one of the great archaeological tourist attractions of the world. It was one of the dominant political and cultural centers of all Mesoamerica in approximately A.D. 500, the culmination of centuries of vigorous cultural development in the Valley of Mexico (Millon, Drewitt, and Cowgill, 1974).

Teotihuacán
200 B.C. to A.D. 700

The first buildings appeared at Teotihuacán in approximately 200 B.C., making up a handful of villages, at least one of which may have specialized in obsidian manufacture. By 100 B.C., Teotihuacán had begun to expand rapidly, and the scattered villages became a settlement covering more than 3.5 square miles (9.06 sq. km). Much of this early settlement is covered by the vast structures of later times. It is estimated that 600 people inhabited this early town. There were several public buildings.

René Millon, who carried out a systematic survey of Teotihuacán, found that by A.D. 150 the city extended over 5 square miles (12.9 sq. km) and housed more than 20,000 people. Obsidian trade and manufacture were expanding fast (Parsons and Price, 1971). There were two major religious complexes for which, among other structures, the Pyramids of the Sun and Moon were first built at this time.

City layout

Between A.D. 150 and 750, Teotihuacán exploded in size. Anyone traversing the Valley of Mexico had to pass through the city with its diverse population of priests, merchants, craftspeople, and other specialists. The rulers of the city erected hundreds of standardized apartment complexes and continued a master plan that laid out the city on a north-south axis, centered on the Avenue of the Dead (Figure 22.7), with another great avenue oriented east-west. The 8 square miles (20.7 sq. km) of Teotihuacán consisted of avenues and plazas, markets, temples, palaces, apartment buildings, and complex drainage and agricultural works. The entire city was dominated by the Pyramid of the Sun (an Aztec name), a vast structure of earth, adobe, and piled rubble. The pyramid, faced with stone, is 210 feet (64 m) high and 650 feet

(198 m) square. A wooden temple probably sat on the summit of the terraced pyramid. The long Avenue of the Dead passes the west face of the pyramid, leading to the Pyramid of the Moon, the second largest structure at the site (Figure 22.7). The avenue is lined with civic, palace, and religious buildings, and the side streets lead to residential areas. A large palace and temple complex dedicated to the Plumed Serpent (Quetzalcóatl), with platform and stairways around the central court, lies south of the middle of Teotihuacán, across from a central marketplace. Mass graves lie close by, probably those of sacrificial victims.

The Avenue of the Dead and the pyramids lie amid a sprawling mass of small houses. Priests and craftsworkers lived in dwellings around small courtyards; the less privileged lived in large compounds of rooms connected by narrow alleyways and patios. By any standard, Teotihuacán was a city, and it once housed up to 120,000 people. Although some farmers probably lived within the city, we know that rural villages flourished nearby. These were compact, expertly planned, and administered by city rulers.

FIGURE 22.7   Aerial view of the ceremonial precincts at Teotihuacán, with the Pyramid of the Moon in the foreground. At left in the background (to the left of the Avenue of the Dead) is the Pyramid of the Sun. (From *Urbanization at Teotihuacán, Mexico,* I, Part 1, 1973. © 1973 by René Millon.)

The comprehensive settlement pattern data from the Millon survey enable us to say something about the structure of Teotihuacán society. The food surpluses to support the city were produced by farmers who lived both in the city and in satellite villages nearby. Tribute from neighboring states also helped feed the city, and control of large areas of the plateau ensured that adequate food supplies came to Teotihua-

Agriculture

cán's huge market. Most of the people lived in the city. It is not known how important chinampa agriculture was for Teotihuacán, but irrigation farming was a key element in subsistence. Craftspeople accounted for perhaps 25 percent of the urban population; they lived in compounds of apartments near the more than 500 workshops that produced everything from obsidian tools to clay vessels. Merchants probably were an important class in the city, as were civil servants, who carried out the routine administration of Teotihuacán. There were even foreign quarters, one of which housed Oaxacans. The elite included priests, warriors, and secular leaders, who controlled the vast city and its many dealings through a strictly class society. Religious beliefs continued the rituals of earlier times, but it appears that cannibalism and human sacrifice became increasingly important in later centuries as the leaders of the city became more and more militaristic, a trend that was to continue into Aztec times.

Teotihuacán ruled the Valley of Mexico and parts of Puebla, but its influence through alliance, tribute, and warfare, as well as trading, extended over a far larger area of Mesoamerica. As in later times, the rulers of Teotihuacán probably controlled some highly strategic and economically important zones, but there were large areas where their influence was minimal. In the final analysis, Teotihuacán probably was a huge city-state bound to other city-states by uneasy alliances and tribute exchanges.

By A.D. 600, Teotihuacán probably was governed by a secular ruler who was looked upon as a divine king of some kind. A class of nobles controlled the kinship groups that organized the bulk of the city's huge population. In approximately A.D. 650, Teotihuacán was deliberately burned down. Only 50 years later its population was scattered in a few villages. Much of the former urban population settled in neighboring regions, which thereby reaped the benefit of Teotihuacán's misfortunes. No one knows exactly why this great city collapsed so suddenly. Its rapid development may have resulted in serious internal weaknesses that made Teotihuacán vulnerable to easy overthrow. A drought may also have weakened the city and provided an opportunity for jealous rivals to attempt an attack.

The very success of Teotihuacán may have accelerated its downfall. The new orders of society and politics spawned by the city may have been copied by other leaders, perhaps more aggressive and less tradition-bound than those of the mother city. Teotihuacán was not the only sophisticated city-state in the highlands between A.D. 500 and 700. William Sanders (1965) has argued that Teotihuacán was overthrown by a coalition of city-states that included, Xochicalco in the southwest and Cholula to the southeast. All these expanded after the downfall of Teotihuacán, and all had been powerful regional states at the time of the former's collapse.

Whatever the cause of Teotihuacán's collapse, its heyday marks the moment when one can begin to think of the Mesomerican world in more than purely local, and even regional, terms. Teotihuacán's political and social influence was enormous, and its traders ventured to many parts of the highlands and lowlands. For example, the ways in which Maya kings went to war were profoundly affected by the military practices and war-making rituals of Teotihuacán. The greatest legacy of Teotihuacán was not merely its cosmology, ideology, and trade networks but a new interconnectedness between the many societies of prehistoric Mesoamerica. In the centuries that followed the fall of Teotihuacán, this interconnectedness was an important factor in the development of more imperial civilizations in the Valley of Mexico. Before examining these civilizations, however, we must go back in time and describe the Maya civilization, whose roots and inspiration came from Preclassic societies elsewhere in Mesoamerica.

MAYA CIVILIZATION

The Maya civilization is probably the best known of all early American civilizations, one that has excited the imagination of scholars for more than a century. It took shape in lowland rain-forest areas that provided a highly varied environment in which people grew maize and other crops and harvested trees such as the ramon.

Maya Origins

Although the ultimate roots of Maya culture go back far into the Preclassic period, considerable debate surrounds the origins of Maya civilization, partly because until recently virtually nothing was known about Maya subsistence patterns (R. E. W. Adams, 1977a; N. Hammond, 1982). Perhaps the initial Maya settlement was dispersed, with villages scattered through the rain forest, in situations that seemed to militate against political or economic unity. The people flourished in a fundamentally empty landscape, where there was plenty of room for slash-and-burn agriculture and little incentive for cooperation. Their predecessors were hunter-gathers, small groups occupying tiny campsites who made no pottery. One such Archaic camp is known from the Colha site in Belize, in a level overlain by farming occupation that dates to later than 1000 B.C. (Schele and Freidel, 1990). This farming settlement is well documented at the Cuello site, where it dates to the early first millennium B.C. or perhaps a little earlier (Andrews and Hammond, 1990). It is not known whether the Colha and Cuello sites date the changeover from hunting and gathering to farming in this part of the lowlands, but a date of around 1000 B.C. would not be unexpected.

Colha
1000 B.C.
Cuello

Middle Preclassic
1000 to 400 B.C.

The earliest certain Maya communities come from the middle Preclassic (1000 to 400 B.C.). Some experts believe that large numbers of farmers moved into the lowlands during this period, bringing with them settled village life, the use of fine clay vessels, and domesticated plants. Migrations from the highlands into the lowlands were commonplace in later times, so it is entirely possible that such migrations took place during the middle Preclassic. What is known is that the lowland Maya experienced a very rapid in-migration of farmers and then a fast population buildup over a wide area during this period. The Maya were well established at Komchen in the Yucatán by 800 B.C., and they were constructing massive pyramids at several sites in the central Petén by 600 B.C. No one has yet accounted for this rapid buildup, but there are reasons to suspect that it was connected with a growing demand for such lowland products as animal pelts and brightly colored bird feathers by elites elsewhere. A growing volume of long-distance exchange contributed, then, to an efflorescence of indigenous lowland civilization within a few centuries.

Nakbe
600 to 400 B.C.

Between 600 and 400 B.C., the middle Preclassic inhabitants of Nakbe were constructing elaborate complexes of finely finished stone buildings that stood on huge platforms. Within a few centuries, they began erecting carved stelae that are thought to depict the center's rulers. Certainly by late Preclassic times the lords of Nakbe were commissioning beautiful masonry and plaster masks of the gods and ancestors on their pyramids. These façades seem to relate directly to the emerging

Divine kingship

notion of divine kingship, Ch'ul Ahau, in Maya civilization, a form of kingship that developed rapidly out of some earlier form of central authority between 600 and 100 B.C. (Freidel and Schele, 1988a, b). Another site of the same general antiquity that has yielded images of kings with deity masks wearing the Jester God crown of kingship is Uaxactun.

El Mirador
150 B.C. to
A.D. 50

By far the largest Preclassic Maya center is El Mirador, which was built between about 150 B.C. and A.D. 50. El Mirador covered about 6 square miles (16 sq. km), lying on low, undulating land; parts of the area flooded during the rainy season. The scale of El Mirador is vast, but it bears all the complicated iconography associated with Maya kingship. Archaeologists from Brigham Young University have uncovered more than 200 buildings; among them are great complexes of pyramids, plazas, causeways, and buildings (Matheny, 1986; Sabloff, 1990).

The Danta pyramid at the east end of the site dominates El Mirador. It rises from a natural hill more than 210 feet (70 m) high. The western face of the hill is sculpted into large platforms that are surmounted by buildings and temples. A little over a mile (2 km) west rises the Tigre complex, a pyramid 182 feet (55 m) high surrounded by a plaza, a small temple, and several smaller buildings (Figure 22.8). The Tigre complex covers about 58,000 square meters—an area a little larger than the base of Teotihuacán's Pyramid of the Sun. Three buildings, with the largest in the center, are on a truncated landing on the pyramid. This "triad" theme is also found at later sites such as Tikal.

El Mirador is unique because it was not altered in any significant way after the Preclassic. As excavations proceed, it should be possible to compare Preclassic with Classic occupation and to study the evolution of Maya architecture, city planning, and social and political organization. El Mirador is yielding some of the earliest examples of Maya writing. They appear on an inscribed potsherd, and some symbols are inscribed on the Tigre sculpture. El Mirador itself was an elaborate city and was probably controlled by a highly organized elite. They used artisans, priests, architects, and engineers, as well as traders and thousands of unskilled villagers. This stupendous city flourished successfully for centuries before it suddenly collapsed in the early Christian era. The dynamics of this collapse are little understood but are mirrored at other Preclassic Maya communities, where the institution of kingship arose and was then apparently abandoned. The volatility of many centers may be connected to endemic warfare, but despite this constant change, many centers, among them Tikal and Uaxactun, developed continuously into Classic times.

Cerros
50 B.C.

In 50 B.C. the small late Preclassic town of Cerros near the eastern coast of the Yucatán housed fisherfolk and traders. Within two generations, this tiny community transformed itself into a large center. The village disappeared under plazas and

FIGURE 22.8   Archaeologists at work on the east stucco mask on the Tigre Temple, El Mirador. The building and mask date to the late Preclassic. *Inset:* El Mirador, Petén: reconstruction of the Tigre complex of buildings and platforms. The entire complex dates to the late Preclassic period, c. 100 B.C. to A.D. 50.

temples, deliberately abandoned in favor of houses erected around the new sacred center. The unknown leaders of Cerros built their new temple according to pyramid designs that had developed among earlier peoples like the Olmec, designs that invoked a symbolic landscape in which religious activity took place (Schele and Freidel, 1990). Everyone in the community shared in the communal labor of building the sacred mountain, a gateway to the Otherworld that was so important in Maya religion. It was a symbolic act that acknowledged the arrival of kingship in the community. The first temple at Cerros was followed by later shrines, the settings for the ritual bloodlettings and sacrifices that served to legitimize the roles of the emerging nobility and of the leader. Kingship flourished at Cerros for a short time, then collapsed, for reasons that are still a mystery. Perhaps there were problems in transferring power from one generation to the next, or the experiment simply failed, as it did in other Maya communities of the day. In any event, the great temples went into disuse, but people still lived around the ruined structures, living off fishing and trade (Schele and Freidel, 1990).

Kingship: Sacred Space and Time

The leaders of Cerros and other Preclassic Maya communities are anonymous. They left no record of their names or personal histories. Their only heritage to their successors was a distinctive architectural heritage that stressed social ranking and the use of the large-scale architecture as a means of perpetuating royal dynasties. The rituals performed by these shaman-lords were performed on pyramids and in plazas of the great Maya centers, which were symbolic replicas of the sacred landscape created by the gods at the beginning. The architecture of the great ritual structures replicated forests, mountains, and caves as stelae, pyramids, and temple openings. These were powerful rituals, so powerful that the places where they were conducted became more and more sacred as successive rulers built new temples on the same spots. Generations of rulers replicated the iconography and sculpture of earlier buildings, elaborating on them to produce the sacred settings within which the strategies of political competition between neighbors were carried out.

Maya civilization was also embedded in a matrix of unfolding, cyclical time. Maya priests used the movements of planets and stars to mark the passage of time. They tried to understand the cycles of the cosmos, deciding which days were propitious for ritual, trade, royal marriages, war, and so on. Religious events were regulated according to a sacred year (*tzolkin*) with 13 months of 20 days each. The 260 days of the sacred year were unrelated to any astronomical phenomenon, being closely tied to ritual and divination. The length of this year was arbitrary and probably established by long tradition. Tzolkins were, however, closely intermeshed with a secular year (*haab*) of 365 days, an astronomical calendar based on the solar cycle. The *haab* was used to regulate state affairs, but the connections between sacred and secular years were of great importance in Maya life. Every 52 years a complete cycle of all the variations of the day and month names of the two calendars occurred, an occasion for intense religious activity.

The calendar was vital to Maya life, for the complex geography of sacred time was just as important as that of space for determining political strategies and social moves. Each day had a character, a distinctive identity in the tzolkin and haab, and a position in all the permutations of cyclical time. The records kept by Maya scribes in hieroglyphic codices (books) were incredibly intricate records of divine actions on each day of the cyclical calendar (Figure 22.9). Each Maya king developed a relationship to this constantly moving time scale. Some events, like planting and harvest, were regular events on the calendar. Others, like dates of accession, important victories, and royal deaths and births, left their marks on the calendar, sometimes as days that assumed great significance to the history of an individual dynasty. Maya rulers linked their actions to those of the gods and the ancestors, sometimes legitimizing their descent by claiming that it reenacted mythical events. In a real sense, Maya history was linked to the present and the Otherworld, to the legendary Olmec civilization of the past. Society was embedded in a matrix of sacred space and time (Schele and Freidel, 1990).

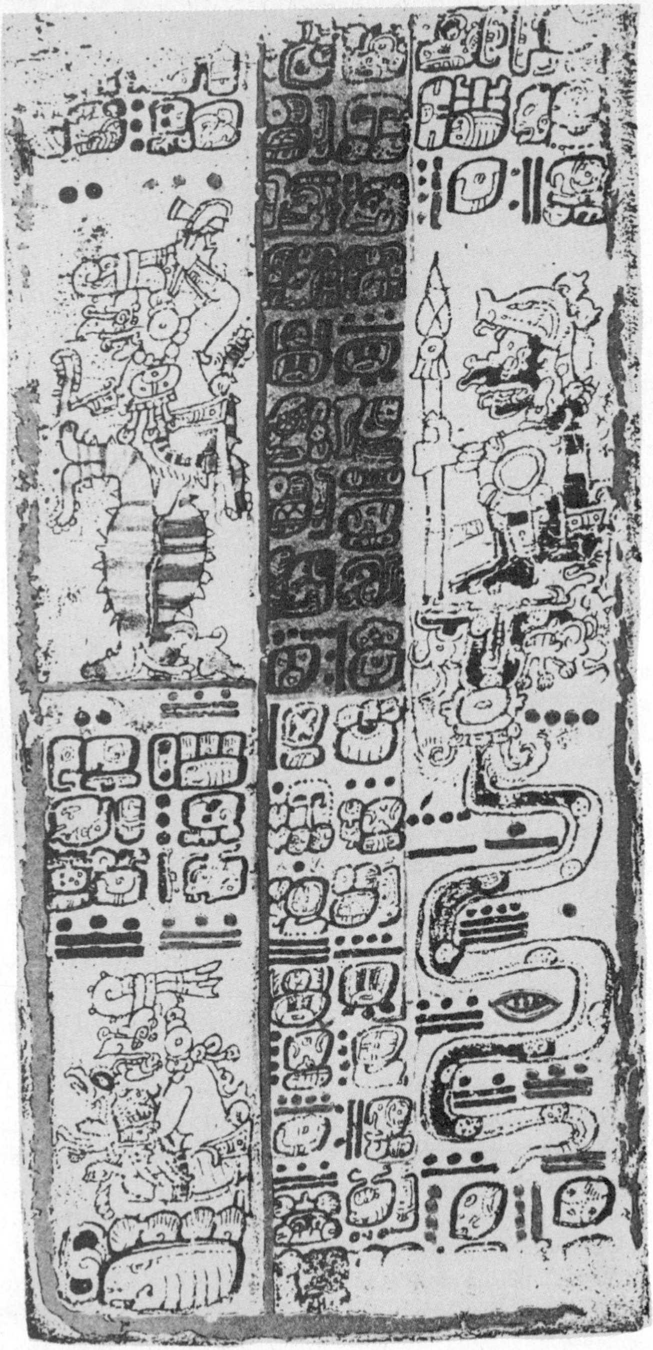

FIGURE 22.9 Only three certain, and perhaps one doubtful, Maya codices (books of picture writing) are known to have survived destruction by the Spanish. Here is a page from the so-called Dresden Codex, which records astronomical calculations, ritual detail, and tables of eclipses.

The Maya developed a hieroglyphic script used for calculating calendars and regulating religious observances (Coe, 1984; C. Jones, 1984). The script was also much used for recording genealogies, king lists, conquests, and dynastic histories. The symbols are fantastically grotesque, consisting mostly of humans, monsters, or god's heads (Figure 22.9). Partly because of the Spanish Bishop Diego de Landa, who recorded Maya dialects surviving in the mid-sixteenth century, scholars have been able to decipher part of the script that was written on temple walls or stelae and modeled in stucco.

These hieroglyphic records were of cardinal importance in Maya life, for the institution of kingship was based on the principle that the royal crown passed from father to son, or brother to brother to son, in a line that led back to a founding ancestor. From there, families and clans were carefully ranked by their distance from the central royal descent line. This system of family ranking and allegiance was the basis of political power, a system that worked well but that depended on careful documentation of genealogies. Social status was highly prized in Maya society, as we can see at the great center of Copán, a major frontier capital of the Maya world at the edge of the Central American chiefdoms. Its pyramids, temples, and stelae are a remarkable record of Maya kings exercising political and social power. Although cosmology was a feature of Copán's building designs, the main function of the civic structures there, as elsewhere, was to commemorate major events in the lives of kings and the political histories of kingdoms. Each building was dedicated by the king who built it in the context of a specific event, everything from a royal accession to an important victory or a new alliance. Among its many buildings, Copán features a ball court, a stadium used for an elaborate ceremonial contest in which sacrificial victims and kings descended through a symbolic "abyss" into the Otherworld. The players wore protective padding and used a rubber ball, which perhaps they aimed at markers—sometimes stone rings or macaw heads high on the side walls. We do not know the rules of the ball game, but the games were associated with human sacrifice and much pomp and circumstance.

By combining archaeological excavation at Copán with historical art interpretation and text translations, scholars have been able to trace a lineage of nobles who specialized in hieroglyphic writing, a skill that gave them special prestige (Fash, 1989). Members of another noble rank, the sahalob ("vassals"), served as expert administrators and received many privileges for their skill. Status was inherited and was one way in which the legitimacy of society as a whole was maintained.

Copán is just one of many sites where archaeologists have documented the complicated political and social history of Maya civilization. The public monuments erected by the Classic Maya emphasize not only the king's role as shaman, as the intermediary with the Otherworld, but also his position as family patriarch. Genealogical texts on stelae legitimize his descent, his close relationship to his often long-deceased parents. Maya kings used both the awesome regalia of their office and elaborate rituals to stress their close identity with mythical ancestral gods. This was a way in which they asserted their kin relationship and political authority over subordinate leaders and every member of society.

The king believed himself to have a divine covenant with the gods and ancestors, a covenant that was reinforced again and again in elaborate private and public rituals.

The king was often depicted as the World Tree, the conduit by which humans communicated with the Otherworld. Trees were the living environment of Maya life and a metaphor for human power. So the kings of the Maya were a forest of symbolic human World Trees within a natural, forested landscape. The Maya calendar ensured a constant round of ceremonies and rituals at the great ceremonial centers erected by the labors of hundreds of people, farmers who also fed kings, priests, and artisans. Yet the Maya world view created serious and binding obligations among the king and his nobility and all the people, reflected in the king's responsibilities in gathering and redistributing commodities of all kinds and in implementing agricultural schemes that turned swamps into organized, productive landscapes. The lives of Maya rulers and all their subjects were interconnected in vital, dynamic ways. The king was state shaman, the individual who enriched everyone's life in spiritual and ceremonial ways. His success at organizing trade and agriculture gave all levels of society access to goods and commodities. The great ceremonial centers built by Maya leaders created a setting in which elaborate rituals and ceremonies took on intense significance. The "histories written and pictured by the kings on the tree stones standing before human-made mountains gave form to time and space in both the material and spiritual worlds" (Schele and Freidel, 1990; readers interested in exploring Maya history and iconography are referred to this remarkable work, from which this brief account has been drawn).

Political Organization

Maya civilization was far from uniform, as recent advances in glyph decipherment have shown. It appears to have been a mosaic of political units, large and small, and it is difficult to be specific about the political relationships between Maya settlements, divided as the people were into a myriad of small and multicenter polities. One possible approach is through the identification of "emblem glyphs," titles that were carried by kings and their highest nobility in the major kingdoms. The emblem glyph of Palenque is *Ch'ul Bac Ahaw* ("Holy Bone Lord"), and that of Tikal is *Ch'ul Bal(am) Ahaw* ("Holy Jaguar Lord"). The emblem glyphs can operate as statements of political affiliation with particular kingdoms, for subordinate centers would sometimes use their overlord's glyph. They would identify political control over a territory by stating that events occurred *u cab* ("in the land of"). There appears to have been some form of hierarchical political organization within Maya domains, even if most of the details elude us (Culbert, 1988b).

There were many elements common to all Maya polities, among them the calendar and hieroglyphic script, essential to the regulation of religious life and the worship of the gods. Architectural and artistic styles in ceramics and small artifacts varied from center to center as each developed its own characteristics and cultural traditions (Coe, 1984). The Maya were unified more by religion than by political or economic interests, in much the same way, perhaps, as the spread of Islam unified diverse cultures.

The political mechanisms used by the Maya included warfare, which had strong ritual overtones and was probably very destructive in its consequences. It is questionable how important it was in territorial expansion and may have been aimed more at economic hegemony. Much art and many inscriptions concentrate on the ceremonial and ideological aspects of war—the capture and sacrifice of prisoners as a way of validating political authority (Schele and Miller, 1986). Whether this was the primary purpose of going to war is uncertain. However, judging from emblem glyphs, most wars were between immediate neighbors, with the capture and sacrifice of a ruler sometimes leading to dominance of one center by another for generations, at others apparently having little effect. Intermarriage between ruling families of neighboring sites was also a significant political device among the Maya. The marriage of women into other dynasties even allowed some sites to acquire lasting political control over others. The inscriptions tell us that visits by rulers or their representatives to other centers were important occurrences, usually commemorating significant political events such as an accession or occasions when a ruler designated his heir (Culbert, 1988b; Schele and Freidel, 1990; Schele and Miller, 1986).

CLASSIC AND LATE CLASSIC POLITICAL HISTORY

Cerros and El Mirador were important centers during the late Preclassic, but even as they prospered, important new centers were emerging a short distance away. Tikal and Uaxactun were growing in importance during the late Preclassic and stepped into the political vacuum left by the decline of El Mirador. The two centers were less than 12 miles (20 km) apart, too close for bitter
Tikal Uaxactun   rivals to coexist. Tikal had expanded greatly during the first century B.C., as large public buildings rose on the foundations of earlier, more humble structures. Clearly, the intent was to rival, and outdo, El Mirador's splendor. During this century, an elite emerged at Tikal, people represented by the burial of a noblewoman under a shrine and tomb paintings of richly decorated nobles. One burial contained a headless and thighless corpse tied up in a bundle, with a green fucsite portrait head that was once the chest pectoral of the deceased. The human face on the pectoral wears the Jester God headdress that kings wore for centuries afterward. Uaxactun just to the north underwent a similar transition during the same century. Here, Preclassic temples bear stucco masks and façades that depict the Maya world and the king who built the structures. At both Tikal and Uaxactun, Maya kings memorialized themselves on their temples, but the two centers were political and economic equals during this century.

Tikal's inscriptions are the chronicle of a remarkable dynasty that ruled its kingdom from the early Classic until the ninth century A.D. The earliest recorded monarch is Yax-Moch-Xoc, who is thought to have reigned between A.D. 219 and
A.D. 219   238. He was not the earliest king but was the one who served as founding ancestor for the great royal clan of Tikal that ruled in coming centuries. Uaxactun also fostered a powerful royal dynasty, whose monuments, like those of the Tikal kings, soon depict rulers with sacrificial victims cowering at their feet, noble victims taken in hand-to-hand combat for later sacrifice in public rituals. These portraits signal a crucial

development in Maya history—the increasing role of warfare and campaigns of deliberate conquest.

A.D. 320

Between A.D. 320 and 376, Great-Jaguar-Paw, the ninth successor of Yax-Moch-Xoc, came to the throne of Tikal. Great-Jaguar-Paw was not only long lived but also a formidable warrior. It was he who defeated the armies of Uaxactun on January 16,

A.D. 378

A.D. 378, in a conquest war under the generalship of one Smoking Frog that subjugated Tikal's long-term rival. His army ignored long-established rules of combat and sacked Uaxactun, setting up Smoking Frog as the founder of a new dynasty. The war was associated with new rituals first developed at Teotihuacán on the highlands, and it linked the god Tlaloc and the planet Venus. This was a period of regular trading contacts between Teotihuacán and many Maya centers, as evidenced by many finds of the distinctive green obsidian mined by the great city. The same contacts may have brought new philosophies of war and conquest and the rituals associated with them. These rituals were to become part of the Mesoamerican religious tradition for many centuries.

Tikal's royal dynasty prospered in coming centuries. They eventually headed a multicenter polity, extending their influence by conquest and long-distance trade and by judicious political marriages that gave neighboring rulers maternal kin ties to the center. At the height of its powers, Tikal's territory covered 965 square miles (2500 sq. km), with an estimated population of more than 360,000 people. After a period

A.D. 593

of apparent political trouble between A.D. 534 and 593, Tikal continued to prosper into the late Classic (Figure 22.10).

The city of Palenque also played a major role in Maya history and is remarkable not only for its fine buildings but also for its rulers' obsession with their ancestry. Two Palenque rulers, Pacal ("shield") and his oldest son, Chan-Bahlum ("Snake-Jaguar"), who ruled in the seventh century A.D., stand out for their vision and wisdom. Palenque's dynastic history began on March 11, A.D. 431, when Bahlum-Kuk

Palenque
A.D. 431 to 799

("Jaguar-Quetzel") became ruler, and lasted until sometime after A.D. 799. The experts have used the rich inscriptions left by Pacal and others to reconstruct a dynasty of no fewer than 12 kings, with, however, what Schele and Freidel (1990) call some "minor sidesteps." These sidesteps accounted for the obsession with history that was so remarkable in Pacal and Chan-Bahlum's day. Succession was through the male line, yet Pacal inherited the throne from his mother, Lady Zac-Kuk, who served for a time as ruler. (Figure 22.11). She must have been a remarkable woman, although we know nothing of her. Pacal claimed the throne as her son, and in so doing had to change the genealogical rules so that he could override the age-old rule of descent through the father and claim succession. In short, he and his son orchestrated orthodox belief with clever fictions. First, they declared Lady Zac-Kuk to be equivalent to the first mother of gods and kings at the beginning of the present creation. This mother deity was the mother of the three major gods of Maya religion. Next, Pacal and Chan-Bahlum claimed that Pacal was born on the very day of the calendar that coincided with that of the goddess's birth. Thus, both Pacal and the goddess were of the same divine substance. Pacal inherited the throne from his mother because this was what had happened at the beginning of creation—authority had been transmitted through both males and females. It may have helped that Pacal ascended to the throne at the age of 12, while his mother was still alive, and that she

FIGURE
22.10   Temple I at Tikal, Guatemala, which dates to about A.D. 700.

lived for another 25 years. The real power may have been in her hands for all those years, for it is only after her death in 640 that Pacal commissioned major inscriptions that justified his own rule. Toward the end of his long reign, which lasted 67 years, Pacal built the Temple of the Inscriptions, a masterpiece of Maya architecture under which his tomb lies. His artists carved the images of his direct ancestors around his coffin deep under the temple, on which his strategy of dynastic legitimization was recorded (Schele and Freidel, 1990). Chan-Bahlum continued his father's preoccupation with dynastic succession. Both rulers made Palenque a major power during their lifetimes, between A.D. 603 and 702, but the dynasty survived for only another century or so after Chan-Bahlum's death.

The late Classic period of Maya civilization, after A.D. 600, has been described as a period of warring states. It was a period of profound change in the lowlands, which started when Lord Water of Caracol attacked his mighty neighbor, Tikal, in

Kuk

Zac- Lady

Kina Ah-Nab-Pacal

Pacal just before
he receives the
crown from his
mother

Lady Zac-
Kuk, Pacal's
mother

Double-headed
Jaguar Throne

**FIGURE
22.11**

Pacal the Great, ruler of Palenque from A.D. 603 to 683, reigned for 67 years. This oval tablet commemorates his receipt of the crown from his mother, Lady Zac-Kuk. By using the name of a Maya goddess to refer to his mother, Pacal declared her to be the equivalent of a mother of the gods, making him divine offspring. (After Schele and Freidel, 1990.)

**Caracol
A.D. 556**

A.D. 556. Five years later, another war ended the domination of Tikal, which became a shadow of its former self. In the years that followed, successive lords of Caracol surrounded both Tikal and a neighboring state to the east, named Naranjo, with a circle of allies that were enemies of both states. Repeated attacks reduced Naranjo to a political shadow. With no standing armies, Maya kings could not garrison defeated towns. Not that this was necessary, for if the nobility were removed, there was no one to attract wealth and precious commodities or political influence. There was no way to recruit populations to support the center.

Caracol and its close ally to the north, Calakmul, never succeeded in forging an empire out of the ruins of their conquests and their many alliances. Tikal at the height of its power named its ruler Chac-Te ("Great Tree"), and his subordinate king was named Y'Ahaw ("His King"). The title Chac-Te reappears many times, but there is no evidence that the Maya developed any effective imperial form of government. In the three centuries that followed, the balance of power shifted many times, to Dos Pilos and back to Tikal, in the hands of the famous and vigorous ruler Ah-Cacaw (Figure 22.12). The diplomatic and military landscape was constantly changing. During the very late Classic, after A.D. 771, a new political pattern emerged, indicative of changed conditions and stressful times. Carved inscriptions began to appear in the houses of local nobles at Copán and other sites, as if the rulers were now granting the privilege of using inscriptions to important individuals, perhaps as a way of gaining their continued support in times of trouble. This proliferation of inscriptions in the Petén and elsewhere may also reflect minor nobles taking advantage of con-

A.D. 771

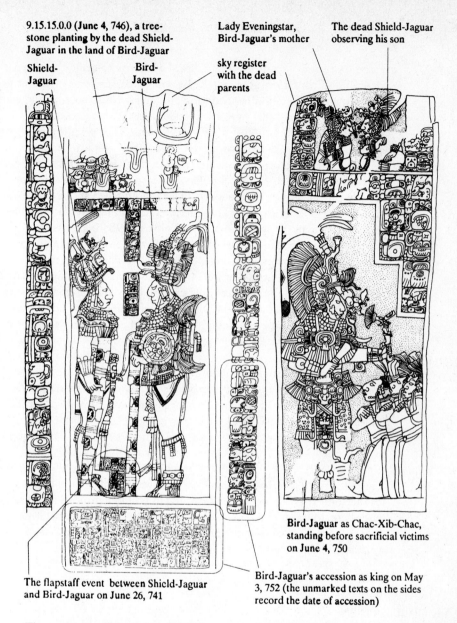

9.15.15.0.0 (June 4, 746), a tree-stone planting by the dead Shield-Jaguar in the land of Bird-Jaguar

Shield-Jaguar

Bird-Jaguar

Lady Eveningstar, Bird-Jaguar's mother

sky register with the dead parents

The dead Shield-Jaguar observing his son

The flapstaff event between Shield-Jaguar and Bird-Jaguar on June 26, 741

Bird-Jaguar as Chac-Xib-Chac, standing before sacrificial victims on June 4, 750

Bird-Jaguar's accession as king on May 3, 752 (the unmarked texts on the sides record the date of accession)

FIGURE 22.12 The aged ruler of Yaxchilan, Shield-Jaguar, conducts a flapstaff ritual with his son Bird-Jaguar on June 26, 741 *(left).* The flapstaff was a long wooden staff with a cloth tied down its middle. The nature of the ritual is unknown. *Right,* on June 4, 750, Bird-Jaguar wears the mask of the god Chac-Xib-Chac as he presents three unarmed victims for sacrifice. The stela on which these inscriptions were made was erected by Bird-Jaguar as part of a successful campaign to legitimize his claims to the throne of Yaxchilan. (After Schele and Freidel, 1990.)

fused times and a disintegrating political authority to claim their own brief independence. The confusion accelerated. By A.D. 800, Maya populations were declining sharply, and both monument carving and major construction soon came to an end.

Most Maya polities were small-scale, independent units that rarely interfered with their neighbors. The lowlands were never unified politically during the classic period. What the elite did share was a set of highly complex traditions and a network of contacts between rulers that transcended the local interests of individual polities and considerable local cultural diversity. Maya civilization was a local phenomenon. Only when a few aggressive, successful leaders emerged at places like Tikal did larger, multicenter polities emerge. These tended to disintegrate within a few generations.

As Norman Yoffee (quoted by Culbert, 1988b) points out, there are some parallels between the Classic Maya and early Mesopotamian civilizations. The Sumerians were governed by independent rulers with strong ritual powers, presiding over independent polities that were in a constant state of change and interaction. The city-state remained the practical political unit long after Sargon created a theoretically unified Mesopotamia about 4400 years ago (Chapter 16). Just as in the Maya lowlands, larger political units forged by leaders of exceptional ability soon fragmented back into their city-state parts. Maya civilization was a local phenomenon in the sense that its constituent states were relatively small, short-lived, and stable kingdoms. Regional ties were crucial, probably far more so than in Mesopotamia. These ties were forged through common religious beliefs, alliances, and marriage ties. For example, the mother of a ruler of Copán named Yax-Pac was a royal princess of Palenque, 1000 miles (3000 km) away. Despite these ties, however, the realities of social and economic instability militated against the long-term stability of any of the multicenter states that rose and fell with such bewildering rapidity during the late Classic.

The central institution of Maya civilization was the kingship, for it was the concept that unified society as a whole. Maya kings lived and carried out their deeds in the context of a history they recorded in building projects at Tikal, Palenque, and elsewhere. Maya elites lived out their lives in the context of the kings that ruled them, and in turn, thousands of commoners lived their lives with respect to the nobility (Figure 22.13).

THE COLLAPSE OF CLASSIC MAYA CIVILIZATION

A.D. 900

Collapse hypotheses

The Maya civilization flourished until about A.D. 900, when it suddenly and inexplicably collapsed. Maya civilization reached its peak after A.D. 600. Then, at the end of the eighth century, the great ceremonial centers of the Petén and the southern lowlands were abandoned, the long court calendar was discontinued, and the structure of religious life and the state decayed. No one has been able to explain this sudden and dramatic collapse of Maya civilization, which is the subject of a prolonged debate in American archaeology (Culbert, 1973; 1988a).

The Classic Maya collapse has fostered varied traditional explanations, most of them unilinear and monocausal. They have included catastrophes, such as earthquakes, hurricanes, and disease. Ecological theories mention exhausted soils, water loss, and erosion. Internal social revolt might have led the peasants to rebel against

**FIGURE
22.13**

A portion of the famous Bonampak murals at Chiapas, Mexico. This segment is in Room 4, showing Maya ruler, warriors, and war captives.

cruel rule by their elitist overlords. Each of these hypotheses has been rejected because either the evidence is insufficient or the explanation is oversimplified. Another popular hypothesis is that there was a disruptive invasion of Maya territory by peoples from the highlands. Certainly evidence reports Toltec intrusions into the lowlands, although it is hard to say how broad the effects of the invasions were or what damage they did to the fabric of Maya society.

The late Classic was a period of great activity and rapid population growth at almost all major sites in the Maya lowlands. The collapse began at some sites early in the ninth century. Major centers were abandoned, monumental inscriptions and major public building ceased, and populations declined rapidly. The effects were most strongly felt in the south. Within a century, huge sections of the southern lowlands were abandoned, never to be reoccupied (Culbert, 1988a). At Tikal, perhaps the greatest Maya center, the elite vanished and the population declined to a third of its earlier level. The commoner survivors clustered in the remains of great masonry structures and tried to retain a semblance of earlier life. Within a century, even they were gone. All this is not to say that Maya civilization vanished completely, for new centers may have emerged in neighboring areas, taking in some of the displaced population. Maya civilization continued to flourish in the northern Yucatán (Sabloff and Freidel, 1984).

Multiple factors

Everyone studying the Maya collapse agrees that a multiplicity of factors led to catastrophe in the southern lowlands (Culbert, 1973). The theories of the 1970s argued that the collapse of Teotihuacán gave the Maya a chance to enlarge their managerial functions in Mesoamerican trade. The elite became increasingly involved in warfare and competition between regions. The late Classic saw a frenzy of public building and increased pressure on commoners, the source of both food and labor for prestige projects. Agricultural productivity fell, disease may have reached epidemic proportions, and population densities plummeted, making recovery impossible.

These theories have been subjected to exhaustive analysis in recent years by researches that involve both simulation studies and examination of trading patterns and demographic and ecological stresses that could have affected population densities (for a detailed discussion, see Culbert, 1988a). Patrick Culbert has examined population densities and the potential for agricultural production in the southern lowlands. He shows that population densities rose as high as 77 persons per square mile (200 per km) during the late Classic over an area so large that it was impossible for people to adapt to bad times by moving to new land or emigrating. He believes that the magnitude of the population loss during the two centuries after A.D. 800 was such that social malfunction alone cannot account for it. Failure of the agricultural base must have been an important component in the collapse equation.

Agricultural collapse

Maya agriculture became increasingly intense as populations rose, with both terrace and raised-field systems covering large areas in many parts of the lowlands. At some of the larger sites like Tikal, the people may have been transporting great quantities of foodstuffs from distances of between 31 and 62 miles (50 and 100 km) away. In the short term, the intensification strategies worked, but they carried the seeds of collapse. The risks of climatic change, plant disease, erosion, and long-term declines in soil fertility were always present in such enterprises. To continue functioning efficiently, the newly intensified systems would have to be managed constantly. Just the repair of field systems after floods and rains would have required watchful effort on a large scale. There are no signs that the Maya made any social changes that enabled them to achieve such a level of management, especially when so many people were engaged in public construction projects and, apparently, in military activity (perhaps the Maya were under pressure from the north).

There are so few data that we can reconstruct almost any scenario of agricultural collapse. Culbert (1988a) believes that long-term environmental degradation was an important element in the scenario, where short-term gains in productivity were followed by catastrophic declines. For example, as populations rose, fallow cycles may have been shortened, leading to increased competition between crop plants and weeds; this is a problem that can be solved only by constant weeding, a very labor-intensive activity. Shortened fallow cycles also lead to lower levels of plant nutrients and declining crop yields. We do not know if the Maya counteracted these trends by systematic mulching or by planting soil-restoring crops. The problem of erosion may have been even more acute. There are signs that the people lost much soil to runoff in the lowlands, for they did not build the terraces needed in time to retain the soil. Some of this erosion may have resulted from extensive deforestation.

The Maya collapse may have had many interlocking causes, but Culbert (1988a) makes a convincing case for a major demographic and subsistence disaster. He draws an interesting parallel with Mesopotamia, where at Ur an abundance of water from an expanded canal system led to overirrigation, shortened fallow cycles, and high levels of salt in the soil (R. M. Adams, 1981). To quote Robert Adams, "long-term agricultural decline was in some ways a direct consequence of its earlier apparent success." The expanding Maya population was dependent on an agricultural system that made no allowance for long-term problems. Eventually the system could produce no further riches, could not expand, and could only decline—with catastrophic results.

THE TOLTECS

Although by A.D. 900 the Classic period had ended, Maya religious and social orders continued in northern Yucatán (Figure 22.14). The continuity of the ancient Mesoamerican tradition survived unscathed. Basic economic patterns and technological traditions were retained, although religious and ideological patterns and priorities

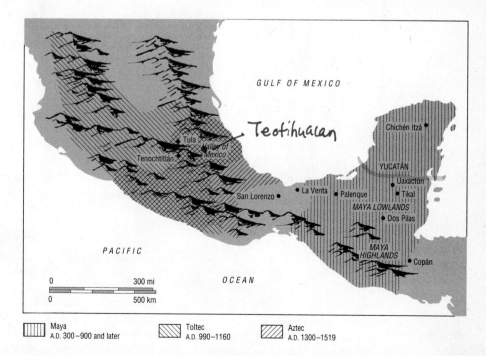

FIGURE 22.14   Distribution of Classic Maya, Toltec, and Aztec civilizations.

were disarranged. New ceremonial centers were built, but war and violence became primary as militaristic rulers achieved dominance in Mesoamerica (Davies, 1973, 1977, 1980). (See McVicker, 1985, for a discussion of Maya roles in the highlands.)

We have mentioned the unsettled Postclassic political conditions caused by population movements and tribal warfare. Many groups of invaders vied for political power in central Mexico until the Toltecs achieved dominance in the tenth century. The oral legends of the Aztec rulers, who followed the Toltecs, describe how the Toltecs came into Mesoamerica from the northwest frontiers beyond the civilized world. They settled at Tula, 37 miles (57 km) north of the Valley of Mexico, where they built a ceremonial center dedicated to their serpent god, Quetzalcóatl (Figure 22.15) (Davies, 1977; Diehl, 1984; Hanson, 1989). Tula is notable for its animal sculpture and pottery styles, but it did not have a long life, for in approximately A.D. 1160 some newcomers with a less developed religious organization arrived from the north and destroyed the temples.

Chichén Itzá in northern Yucatán was an important Maya ceremonial center in

Postclassic
A.D. 900 to 1521

Toltecs

Tula
A.D. 900

A.D. 1160

Chichén Itzá

FIGURE 22.15   Tula. The summit of its pyramid bears statues of richly adorned warriors with elaborate breastplates. These once supported the roof of the temple of the feathered serpent god, Quetzalcóatl.

Postclassic times (Figure 22.16). In the ninth century A.D., Chichén Itzá came under Toltec influence (Coggins, 1985; Roys, 1972; Weaver, 1981). The extent of this influence is much debated, but it probably represented a new political order, a complex mixing of Mexican and Maya factions among the elite. They developed new artistic and political styles that separated political functions from the personality of an individual ruler. The Chichén Toltecs developed a flexibility and a resilience that enabled them to be far more adaptive to changing political conditions than their southern neighbors had been. The leaders of Chichén Itzá developed a truly regional state. They controlled the two great resources of the northern Yucatán: a talented, well-organized population and massive salt fields along the coast. The site was aban-

Mayapán

doned in the thirteenth century, but the city of Mayapán, a walled settlement clustered around a ceremonial center, rose to prominence elsewhere in northern Yucatán. At least 12,000 people lived in this Maya city, which was ruled by the Cocom family. Maya civilization enjoyed a resurgence in this area, although Mayapán declined during the civil wars of the fifteenth century. A century later, the Spanish found Yucatán ruled by numerous petty chiefs.

The militaristic Toltecs were the leading military and political force in Mesoamerica for such a short time that their influence evaporated rapidly when Tula was destroyed. Another period of political chaos in the Valley of Mexico ensued, as more barbarians from the north (Chichimecs) maneuvered for political power (Davies, 1980).

FIGURE 22.16   Chichén Itzá, Temple of the Warriors.

THE AZTECS AND THE
SPANISH CONQUEST

When the first Spanish conquistadores arrived in highland Mexico in 1519, they were astounded by the rich civilization they found. The capital city of Tenochtitlán was the headquarters of a series of militaristic Aztec kings, who ruled over a wide area by religious decree, constant human sacrifice, and bloodthirsty campaigning. Within a few years of Spanish contact, Aztec civilization literally ceased to exist. Tenochtitlán was reduced to rubble after a siege that lasted 91 days.

The Aztecs were one of several nomadic, semicivilized Chichimeca groups who settled in the Valley of Mexico after the fall of Tula (Davies, 1973). They arrived during the early twelfth century, a politically weak but aggressive group who barely retained their own identity. After years of military harassment, the Aztecs fled into the swamps of Lake Texcoco in about 1325. There they founded a small hamlet named Tenochtitlán (now Mexico City). Less than two centuries later, this village had become the largest city in pre-Columbian America (Conrad and Demarest, 1984).

At first the Aztecs lived peaceably with their neighbors, and Tenochtitlán flourished as an important market center. By judicious diplomacy, discreet military alliance, and well-timed royal marriages, the Aztecs quietly advanced their cause until they were a force to be reckoned with in local politics. Then, in the early fifteenth century, they changed their foreign policy abruptly and embarked on a ruthless campaign of long-term military and economic conquest. Soon they controlled a loosely connected network of minor states and cities that extended across Mesoamerica. The real leader behind this change was a counselor and general named Tlacaelel, who was adviser to a series of aggressive Aztec rulers. It was he who encouraged the use of terror and human sacrifice as a means of controlling conquered territory. The rich tribute from conquered states and cities made Tenochtitlán the center of the Mesoamerican world, the hub of a political and economic confederacy that extended from near the Pacific Ocean to the Gulf of Mexico and from northern Mexico as far south as Guatemala.

Tenochtitlán, a city of more than 200,000 people, was a spectacular sight in the sixteenth century, with markets where more than 60,000 people are said to have assembled every day (Diaz, 1963; J. B. Morris, 1962). The market sold every form of foodstuff and provided every luxury and service. The principal streets of Tenochtitlán were of beaten earth, and there were at least 40 pyramids adorned with fine, decorated stonework (Moctezuma, 1988). Tenochtitlán certainly was larger, and probably cleaner, than many European cities of the time (Figure 22.17).

Large residential areas surrounded the central precincts, and houses with chinampa gardens lay on the outskirts of the city. Six major canals ran through Tenochtitlán, and there were three causeways that connected the city with the mainland. At least 200,000 canoes provided convenient transport for the people of the city, which was divided into 60 or 70 well-organized wards. Tenochtitlán was a magnificent city set in a green swath of country near a clear lake, with a superb backdrop of snow-capped volcanoes (Fagan, 1984b).

Aztec society was moving closer and closer to a rigid, highly stratified class system

**FIGURE
22.17**   A general view of the excavations and restoration at the Aztec Temple of Huitzilopochtli and
Tlaloc, the Templo Major, Tenochtitlán.

at the time of Spanish contact. No commoner was allowed to enter a waiting room
in the palace used by nobles. The king was revered as a semigod and had virtually
despotic powers. He was elected from a limited class group of *pipiltin,* or nobles. There
were full-time professional merchants called *pochteca,* and also a class of warriors
whose ranks were determined by the number of people they had killed in battle.
Groups of lineages called *calpulli* (big house) were the most significant factor in most
people's religious, social, and political life. Many of them coincided with wards in the
city. The great mass of the people were free people, or *macehualtin,* and serfs, landless
peasants, and slaves made up the bottom strata of society.

Much of Aztec society's efforts went toward placating the formidable war and
rain gods, Huitzilopochtli and Tlaloc, whose benevolence was assured by constant
human sacrifices. These sacrifices reached their peak at the end of each 52-year cycle,
like those of the Maya, when the continuity of the world would be secured by
bloodthirsty rites.

By the time of the Spanish conquest in 1519, Aztec society seems to have been
functioning in a state of frenetic and bloody terrorism that flourished at the behest
of arrogant, imperial rulers. The Aztecs had learned the fine art of terror as a political
instrument and regularly staged elaborate public displays in Tenochtitlán to which

subject leaders were invited. The Spaniards estimated that at least 20,000 people were sacrificed to the gods throughout the Aztec empire each year. This figure may be an exaggeration, but there is no doubt that a considerable number of prisoners of war and slaves perished by having their hearts ripped out in the presence of the gods. There was also a steady flow of sacrificial victims from the Aztecs' constant military campaigns. Indeed, the finest death for an Aztec warrior was to perish under the sacrificial knife after honorable capture in battle. Such a fate was known as the "flowery death."

The Aztecs have acquired a formidable reputation from historians—and, it must be confessed, from some archaeologists—because of their penchant for human sacrifice and cannibalism. That they were addicted to human sacrifice is certain, the cannibalism less so. Some believe that the Aztec nobles ate human flesh to compensate for a lack of meat in their diet, but the beans they ate as a staple were more than sufficient as a source of protein. It seems more likely that the Aztec nobles and priests engaged in occasional ritual cannibalism as part of their intensely symbolic religious beliefs (for a discussion, see Fagan, 1984b).

By the time the Spaniards landed on the Mexican lowlands, Aztec civilization was in danger of being torn apart. The society was becoming top-heavy with nobles because they were allowed to marry commoners and their children automatically became aristocrats. The demands for tribute both from subject states and from the free people of the city became ever larger and more exacting. There may well have been intense philosophical disagreements between the militant priests and warriors, who increasingly encouraged conquest and human sacrifice, and those more sophisticated and educated Aztecs who believed in a gentler, less aggressive world. It is fascinating to speculate what would have happened had Cortés not landed in Mexico. Given the past history of Mexico, it seems likely that Aztec civilization would have collapsed suddenly, to be replaced in due time by another society much like it. In truth, Aztec civilization had reached a point of complexity that was beyond the capacity of its rulers to control and administer, a complexity that Old World civilizations had brought under control, and we can be certain that the Aztecs' successors would have eventually done so as well.

The Aztecs were one of the most important groups in Mesoamerica when the Spaniards first explored the New World. From coastal villagers in the lowlands they heard stories of the fabled rich kingdoms in the high interior. Soon the conquistadores pressed inland. Hernán Cortés was the first Spaniard to come into contact with the Aztecs, now ruled by Moctezuma II, a despotic ruler who assassinated most of his predecessor's counselors and had himself deified. Moctezuma's reign was disturbed by constant omens of impending doom and predictions that the god Quetzalcóatl would return to reclaim his homeland (Dibble and Anderson, 1978). The king was deeply alarmed by the reports of Spanish ships on the coast. There were, then, considerable internal psychological stresses on Moctezuma and his followers before the Spaniards arrived.

It took Cortés two tough years to reduce the Aztecs to slaves and their marvelous capital to rubble. A handful of explorers on imported horses, armed with a few muskets, were able to overthrow one of the most powerful tribute states in the history of America. Without question, Cortés's task was made easier by both rebellious subjects of the Aztecs and the extraordinary stresses the Aztecs had placed on themselves.

By 1680, the Indian population of the Aztec heartland was reduced from approximately 1.2 million to some 70,000—a decimation resulting from war, slavery, disease, overwork and exploitation, famine, and malnutrition. Mesoamerica as a whole lost between 85 and 95 percent of its indigenous population during that 160-year period. Only a few fragments of the fabulous Mesoamerican cultural tradition survived into modern times, and the Indian population faced a new and uncertain chapter in their long history (Gibson, 1964).

GUIDE TO FURTHER READING

Davies, Nigel. 1973. *The Aztecs.* Norman: University of Oklahoma Press.
> *A skillfully assembled narrative of the rise of the Aztecs, largely compiled from oral histories and codices as well as archaeological evidence. Complicated but authoritative.*

Fagan, Brian M. 1984. *The Aztecs.* New York: Freeman.
> *A straightforward description of the Aztecs written for the general public. Strong description and narrative; little theoretical argument.*

Hammond, Norman. 1982. *Ancient Maya Civilization.* New Brunswick, NJ: Rutgers University Press.
> *Authoritative synthesis of the Maya civilization by an expert on the lowlands and on Maya ecology. A good starting point, with an excellent theoretical underpinning.*

Sabloff, Jeremy A. 1989. *The Cities of Ancient Mexico.* New York: Thames and Hudson.
> *A straightforward account of major Mesoamerican centers and cities for a general audience.*

Schele, Linda, and Freidel, David. 1990. *A Forest of Kings.* New York: Morrow.
> *A superb popular account of Maya history as known from glyphs. Entertaining, provocative, and challenging.*

Schele, Linda, and Miller, E. 1986. *The Blood of Kings.* Austin: University of Texas Press.
> *A brilliant, definitive account of Maya civilization and political history based on inscriptions and glyphs. An exemplary piece of long-term research.*

Weaver, Muriel Porter. 1981. *The Aztecs, Maya, and Their Predecessors,* 2d ed. New York: Academic Press.
> *A culture history that has been a standard reference for a decade; the second edition is even more thorough than the first. Strongly recommended for detailed reading. Comprehensive illustrations of sites and artifacts.*

Chronological Table M

Calibrated Dates a.d./b.c./b.p.	C.14 Years A.D./B.C.		PERU	
			Highlands	*Lowlands (Coast)*
	1532	Colonial Period	Spanish conquest	
a.d. 1310–1515	1500	Late Horizon	INCA	INCA
		Late Intermediate Period		
870–1230	1000	Middle Horizon	WARI TIWANAKU	CHIMU
265–640	500	Early Intermediate Period		NASCA MOCHE
450–5 b.c.	A.D. 1			
820–480	500 B.C.	Early Horizon	CHAVÍN	
3530–2905 b.p.	3000 B.P.			
		Initial Period	Large settled communities on the coast (well-established agriculture)	
4345–3660	3500			
4830–4305	4000			
5503–4925	4500		Chapter 14	

CHAPTER 23   ANDEAN STATES

Preview

- The earliest complex societies of coastal Peru may have developed as a result of intensive exploitation of maritime resources, especially small fish easily netted from canoes. In time, abundant food surpluses, growing population densities, and larger settlements may have preadapted coastal people for adopting intensive irrigation agriculture. These societies were organized in increasingly complex ways.

- During the so-called Initial Period of Peruvian prehistory, large monumental structures appeared, many of them U-shaped, just before and during the transition toward greater dependence on maize agriculture. This was also a period of continuous interaction and extensive trade between coast and highlands.

- This florescence of social complexity, new art traditions, and monumental architecture coincided with the emergence of several small polities in river valleys on the coast. The culmination of this trend is seen in various local traditions, among them the famous Chavín style. This central Peruvian style, once thought to have been the source of Peruvian civilization, is now known to be a late manifestation of cultural trends that began as early as 3800 years ago.

- After the Early Period ended in about 200 B.C., a series of coastal kingdoms developed, the political and economic influence of which spread beyond their immediate valley homelands. These states included the Moche, Nasca, and Recuay, which were remarkable for their fine pottery styles and expert alloy and gold metallurgy. They flourished in the first millennium A.D.

- The Middle Horizon lasted from A.D. 600 to 1000 and saw the rise of numerous small states that traded with one another and depended heavily on irrigation agriculture. In the highland empires of Tiwanaku and Wari, an acceleration of the process of broader unification took place.

- Approximately A.D. 1000, Chimu, with its great capital at Chan Chan on the northern coast, dominated a wide area of the coast. Its compounds reflect a stratified state, with many expert craftspeople and a complex material culture.

- During the Late Horizon of Peruvian prehistory, there was unification of highlands and lowlands under the Inca Empire, which may have emerged as early as A.D. 1200 and lasted until the Spanish conquest in A.D. 1534. The Inca rulers were masters of bureaucracy and military organization and governed a highly structured state—one, however, that was so weakened by civil war and disease that it fell easily to the conquistador Francisco Pizarro and his small army of adventurers.

Chronological
Table M

Andean civilization, is unique among the early civilizations for its mastery of remarkable environmental extremes. In its late fifteenth-century heyday, the vast Inca empire, known as Tawantinsuyu ("The Land of the Four Quarters"), extended from high-altitude mountain valleys in the Andes through dry highland plains to foothills to tropical rain forests and to coastal deserts, some of the driest landscape on earth. Each environment of the highlands and lowlands posed different environmental challenges, that is, confronted the Andeans with radically different climatic conditions and entire disparate food resources. Thus, Andean civilization pursued many different evolutionary pathways, which came together in a remarkable mosaic of states and empires, in large part as a result of widely held spiritual beliefs and by constant interchange between the coast and the highlands and between neighboring valleys and large population centers. Tawantinsuyu itself was a unique political synthesis sewn together by the Inca lords of the Andes in the centuries just before European contact. It was the culmination of centuries of increasing social complexity throughout the Andean area. How did such complex states arise in this landscape of extraordinary contrasts? Recent archaeological researches have generated some sophisticated hypotheses to account for them (Keatinge, 1988).

THE MARITIME FOUNDATIONS OF
ANDEAN CIVILIZATION

The rugged central Andean mountains are second only to the Himalayas in height, but only 10 percent of their rainfall descends the Pacific watershed. The foothill slopes and plains at the western foot of the mountains are mantled by one of the world's driest deserts, which extends virtually from the equator to 30° south, much of it along the Peruvian coast. Yet ironically, the richest fishery in the Americas hugs the Pacific shore, yielding millions of small schooling fish such as anchovies. These easily netted shoals support millions of people today, and they supported dense prehistoric populations. In contrast, the cultivation of this dry landscape requires controlling the runoff from the Andes with large irrigation systems that use long canals built by the coordinated labors of hundreds of people. Only 10 percent of this desert can be farmed, so its inhabitants rely heavily on the incredible bounty of the Pacific. Surprisingly, perhaps, this apparently inhospitable desert was a major center of complex early states, which traded with neighbors in the highlands and built large ceremonial centers.

The mechanisms by which complex states arose on the Peruvian coast are still little understood, partly because research has tended to concentrate on larger, more spectacular sites (Haas et al., 1987; Moseley, 1975b, 1986; D. J. Wilson, 1983). Such researches tell us little about the relative size of different communities or about population densities, which are critical measures of an evolving state society. It is only recently that larger-scale river valley surveys have collected such data, researches like Gordon Willey's (1963) classic work on the Virú and Donald Proulx's (1973, 1985) fieldwork in the Nepeña Valley. These investigations have shown that there were major changes in site clustering through time, especially after the introduction of maize agriculture and irrigation to the coast after 4500 years ago.

Maritime
foundations
theory

In the 1970s, archaeologist Michael Moseley (1975b) proposed what he called the "maritime foundations of Andean civilization" hypothesis. He argued that the unique maritime resources of the Pacific coast provided sufficient calories to support rapidly growing, sedentary populations, which clustered in large communities. In addition, the same food source produced sufficient surplus to free up time and people to erect large public monuments and temples, work organized by the leaders of newly complex coastal societies. This scenario runs contrary to conventional archaeological thinking, which regards agriculture as the economic basis for state-organized societies. In the Andes, argued Moseley, it was fishing. For thousands of years coastal populations rose, and their rise preadapted them to later circumstances, under which they would adopt large-scale irrigation and maize agriculture.

Moseley (1975b) implied that mollusks and large fish were vital resources on the coast, but marine biologists drew his attention to the incredible potential of anchoveta and other small schooling fish. Anchoveta can be easily netted throughout the year from small canoes. The fish offer predictable food supplies that can be dried or ground into fine meal. Such harvests would provide an abundance of protein. Judging from modern yields, if prehistoric coastal populations had lived at 60 percent of the carrying capacity of the fisheries and eaten nothing but small fish, the coast could have supported more than 6.5 million people. That is not to say that it did, but the figures make the point that the exploitation of small fish would have provided a more than adequate economic base for the emergence of complex societies on the coast. It is interesting that small mesh nets and floats have come from earlier coastal sites such as Paloma (Chapter 14).

Critiques of
maritime
foundations

Several critiques of the maritime foundations hypothesis have appeared, all of them based on the assumption that large coastal settlements could not have been supported by maritime resources alone (see, for example, D. J. Wilson, 1981, 1983). Most of these critiques have tended to ignore the potential of anchovetas. Another argument revolves around the famous El Niño phenomenon, the periodic changes in Pacific currents that reduce the fisheries to a shadow of their normal selves for several years at a time. In fact, as Moseley (1986) points out, El Niño brings unfamiliar fish species to the coast as well as violent rainfall that has the potential to disrupt irrigation systems with catastrophic results, some of which are now being identified in the archaeological record. Overall, the maritime foundations hypothesis has stood the test of time well, provided it is seen as a component in a much broader evolutionary process, which also took place inland, in the highlands, and in areas where the width of the coastal shelf precluded extensive anchoveta fishing.

Richard Burger (1985) argues that changing dietary patterns in the highlands, where agriculture became increasingly important, would have created a demand among farmers for lowland products—salt, fish, and seaweed. Seaweed is rich in marine iodine and could have been an important medicine in the highlands, used to combat endemic goiter and other conditions. By the same token, carbohydrate foods like oca, ullucu, and white potatoes that could not be grown on the coast have been found in preceramic sites in the Ancón-Chillón area of the Pacific lowlands. Thus, the formation of states in both lowlands and highlands may have been fostered by continuous, often highly localized interchange between coast and interior.

Michael Moseley believes that this reliance on maritime resources led to a preadaptation in the form of large, densely concentrated populations, whose leaders were able to organize the labor forces needed not only for building large ceremonial centers but also for transforming river valleys with sizable irrigation schemes. Under this scenario, irrigation farming was in the hands of a well-defined group of authority figures, who took advantage of existing simple technology and local populations to create new economies. This transformation, based as it was on trade, maize agriculture, and a maritime diet, acted as a "kick" for radical changes in Andean society (for discussion, see Moseley, 1986). But the transformation was based on ancient fishing traditions, which can be documented thousands of years earlier at Paloma and other early coastal villages.

Moseley's key point is that Andean civilization evolved in many ways, in a wide variety of ecological zones, from highland, tropical rain-forest, and lowland strategies that were all of great antiquity, some dating to the earliest millennia of human settlement. Thus, the maritime foundations hypothesis may help explain the development of states on the Peruvian coast, but it cannot account for parallel developments elswhere in South America.

COASTAL FOUNDATIONS:
THE INITIAL PERIOD

Sometime between 4500 and 3800 years ago, maize agriculture came to the Peruvian coast, and many villages moved inland. By this time the coastal fishing villages were much larger communities with highly organized social structures, as reflected in the first signs of communal structures, such as an 80-foot-high (24-m) temple mount at Salinas de Chao. The people may have cooperated in fishing and food gathering, but the cooperative effort in erecting large earthen platforms for temples or other public buildings satisfied entirely different needs and requires explanation.

This Initial Period of Andean civilization was an important millennium, for new concerns both with the cosmos and with religion permeated the Andes. The new beliefs manifested themselves in a wave of monumental construction in both lowlands and highlands. By 2400 years ago, the inhabitants of the Casma Valley on the coast were building the huge stone-faced 130-foot-high (40-m) platform of Sechin Alto. This mound, nearly 1000 feet (300 m) long and over 800 feet (250 m) wide, formed the base of a huge U-shaped ceremonial center with sunken courts, plazas, and flanking mounds. A vast sprawl of houses and platforms lies around this largest of all early ceremonial structures on the coast. Only small parts of the site have been excavated, including a small building, erected about 3300 years ago, surrounded by a mosaic of carved monoliths depicting a procession of armed men and dismembered human remains.

The shrines at Sechin Alto employ one of the persistent themes of ceremonial architecture in the Andes and on the coast, that of artificially raising or lowering sacred spaces relative to one another in what Michael Moseley (1985) calls "complementary opposition arranged linearly along a horizontal axis." On the coast, early ceremonial sites feature rectangular platform mounds fronting on a circular, sunken court that is usually housed in a rectangular forecourt (for discussion, see Donnan, 1985). This form of architecture appeared at least 4000 years ago. It had people enter the forecourt of the sacred complex at ground level, descend into the sunken court, and then climb the temple platform.

After 4000 years ago, coastal ceremonial buildings were greatly elaborated, with new architectural devices being adopted, among them a distinctive U-shaped platform, often associated with elaborate adobe friezes. This arrangement is found in the great Río Rímac complex of Huaca Florida, built about 3700 years ago.

El Paraíso, close to the mouth of the Chillón River near Lima, is the oldest of these U-shaped ceremonial complexes, and the closest one to the Pacific (Figure 23.1) (Bankes, 1977; Engel, 1957; Quilter, 1985). This vast site consists of at least six huge square buildings constructed of roughly shaped stone blocks cemented with unfired clay. The people painted the polished clay-faced outer walls in brilliant hues. Each complex consisted of a square building surrounded by tiers of platforms reached by stone and clay staircases. The largest is more than 830 feet (250 m) long and 166 feet (50 m) wide, standing more than 30 feet (10 m) above the plain. The rooms apparently were covered with matting roofs supported by willow posts. Perhaps as many as 100,000 tons of rock excavated from the nearby hills were needed to build the El Paraíso buildings. There are few signs of occupation around them, though, as if they were shrines and public precincts rather than residential quarters. The two largest mounds of collapsed masonry lie parallel to one another, defining a vast, elongated patio covering more than 6 acres (2.5 ha). This U-shaped layout is thought to be the precursor of this intrusive architectural style on the coast after 4000 years ago.

What is most surprising is that these huge structures were erected by people from

FIGURE 23.1   El Paraíso.

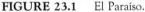

dozens of scattered villages. For reasons not yet understood, they united in a building project that channeled most of their surplus energies into a vast monumental center, a place where few people lived but where everyone apparently congregated for major public ceremonies. The people themselves lived a life of seeming simplicity. They owned only simple stone and wooden artifacts and wore cotton clothing decorated with basic geometric patterns and stylized animal-like motifs. They buried their dead in several layers of garments, nets, or looped sacks. Why should such a village society build such enormous structures, and who were the leaders who organized these massive public works?

El Paraíso is thought to have been built by people who subsisted off a fish-meal diet from the incredibly rich fisheries close offshore and who traded extensively with communities inland. Its U-shaped layout coincides with the florescence of similarly shaped ceremonial centers in the interior, at a time when coastal people began to consume much larger amounts of root crops, to make pottery, and to shift their settlements inland to river valleys. Some scholars believe that this move coincided with the introduction of large-scale canal irrigation (for discussion, see Moseley, 1985). Perhaps the spread of U-shaped ceremonial centers reflects a radical restructuring of society that coincided with major economic change. Moseley argues that the introduction of irrigation technology required a major reorganization of labor, which coincided with the appearance of new artistic traditions and architectural devices.

What does this mean in ritual terms? In many parts of the Americas the ritual manipulation of smoke and water served as a way of bridging stratified layers of air, earth, and bodies of water in the cosmos (Lathrap, 1985). Thus, it is argued, the early ceremonial centers of the coast and highlands (Figure 23.2) reflect an ancient tradition of using these substances to maintain communication with the cosmos. Burnt offerings are found at some Andean sites, among them Kotosh. Water flowed through masonry channels and cut stone ways at many highland sites and also at the famous ritual center at Chavín de Huántar. There, galleries and ritual waterways flowed through the ceremonial platform and beneath a circular, sunken court, connections

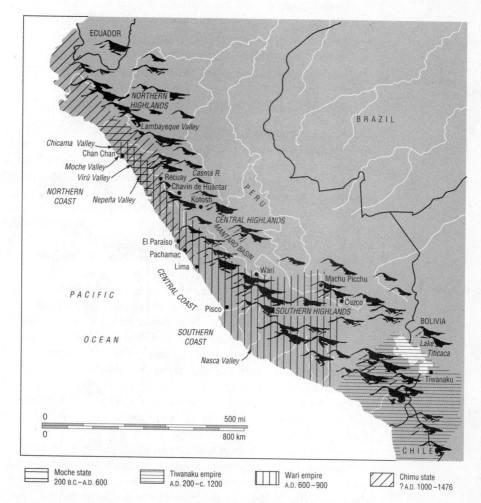

FIGURE 23.2   Peruvian archaeological sites mentioned in this chapter. Approximate distributions of various traditions are also shown.

that allowed the water to resonate under the ground so that the temple "roared." The vast, open courts of coastal U-shaped ceremonial complexes may have housed sacred orchards and gardens irrigated with specially manipulated water supplies. These ritual waterways were to reach their greatest elaboration with the Chimu state of the coast and the great imperial Inca capital at Cuzco thousands of years later (for discussion, see Donnan, 1985).

In social and political terms, the Initial Period remains somewhat of a mystery. There are few signs in burial rituals of any social ranking or of personal wealth. It is as if decision making and leadership were either not inherited or rotated from one person to the next on a regular basis. The many ceremonial centers suggest that different kin groups commemorated their identities by erecting their own shrines, perhaps on a competitive basis. There were probably some larger polities extending over several river valleys, one centered on the Casma Valley, three others along nearby parts of the coast (Pozorski and Pozorski, 1987); but who held sway over each of these political units is unknown.

THE EARLY HORIZON, CHAVÍN, AND THE INITIAL PERIOD

In 1943, archaeologist Julio Tello identified a distinctive art style in stone, ceramics, and precious metals over a wide area of highland Peru, a style he named *Chavín* after a famous prehistoric ceremonial center at Chavín de Húantar in central Peru. Tello's research led to a long-held belief among Peruvianists that the widespread Chavín art style was a "mother culture" for all later Andean civilizations, somewhat equivalent to the Olmec phenomenon in Mesoamerican prehistory (Pozorski and Pozorski, 1987). This became a distinctive "Early Horizon" in Peruvian prehistory, dating to about 900 B.C., a period when there was a great expansion of indigenous religious belief by conquest, trade, and colonization—the time when civilization began.

Chavín de
Húantar
900 B.C.

There is no doubt that Chavín de Húantar is testimony to an elaborate, well-developed iconography. The temple area is terraced with an impressive truncated pyramid on the uppermost level. The 32-foot-high (10-m) pyramid appears solid but is in fact hollow, a honeycomb of stone passages and rooms. The galleries are ventilated by special rectangular tubes. The temple housed a remarkable carving of a jaguarlike human with hair in the form of serpents (Figure 23.3) (Burger, 1984; Rowe, 1962). Chavín art, like this carving, is dominated by animal and human forms: Jaguar motifs predominate; humans, gods, and animals have jaguarlike fangs or limbs; snakes flow from the bodies of many figures. The art has a grace that is grotesque and slightly sinister. Many figures were carved in stone, others in clay or bone (Benson, 1971).

With its tangled animal and human motifs, Chavín art has all the flamboyance and exotic touches of the tropical forest. The animals depicted—cayman, jaguar, and snake—are all forest animals. The art may have originated in the tropical forests to the east of the Andes, but the Early Horizon Chavín temple has a U shape with a sunken central plaza, an architectural design documented centuries earlier at other coastal and highland sites (Burger, 1981, 1985; Pozorski and Pozorski, 1987).

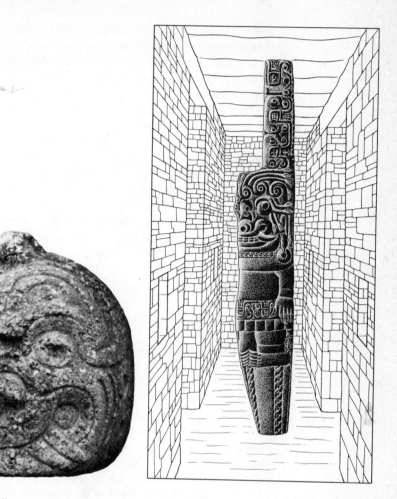

FIGURE 23.3   (*Left*) a Chavín wall insert, approximately 7.8 inches (20 cm) high, showing feline features, from Chavín de Huántar and (*right*) a Chavín carving on a pillar in the temple interior at Chavín de Huántar. Stone insets such as these are common on the walls of the Chavín ceremonial buildings.

Chavín de Huántar is far more than just a temple. Richard Burger (1981) has excavated areas outside the well-known ceremonial precincts and established that the site was occupied between about 850 and 200 B.C. At first the population was small, perhaps few more than 100 people. It seems to have expanded considerably by the fourth century B.C., at which point as many as 2000 to 3000 people may have been living near the temple precincts. Chavín de Huántar was certainly a large center, probably an influential place within its local area, and one of the largest settlements in Peru at the time of its occupation. It failed to expand into a fully developed urban center, however, and the nascent civilization that worshiped there collapsed, leaving nothing more than a small town and a persistent art style and iconography.

The Chavín style may have influenced artistic traditions over a wide area of Peru, and it may also be that the religious beliefs behind the motifs were more important than the art itself. Settlements like Chavín de Huántar were important ceremonial centers that unified surrounding farming villages with a common religious belief, but Chavín de Huántar was not unique. There were many other, often much earlier centers with the same general architectural and iconographic style.

For example, from about 4000 to 2200 years ago, the small ceremonial center at Huaricoto in the highlands, only 34 miles (55 km) from Chavín de Huántar, was the home of a religious ideology (Burger and Salazar-Burger, 1985). This "Kotosh Religious Tradition" is known to us by sacrificial hearths in which ceremonial offerings were burnt. These included animal bones and grain. The ritual hearth was sunk into the floor with a ventilator leading to the outside. Once the sacrifice was complete, the hearth was filled in. At first the rituals were performed in the open, but by the late Initial Period the hearths were surrounded by larger superstructures. The rituals may have been performed sporadically at certain times of the year, with the audience watching in the open. The Kotosh religious tradition appears to have flourished over an area of at least 155 miles (250 km) north to south in the highlands in the region where the Chavín cult, with its wild and extravagant animal motifs, was to gain strength.

The so-called Early Horizon associated with Chavín has often been assumed to have been a period of unification and coalescence of early Peruvian culture under the rubric of a single theology. In fact, state formation occurred far earlier, during the Initial Period among the north and central ports of the coast, where a set of interacting polities arose after 3800 years ago. Political units centered on the Moche, Casma, Chillón, and other river valleys where irrigation agriculture developed. Centuries before, when pottery was unknown on the coast but cotton was already widely cultivated, communication networks had arisen that linked not only neighboring coastal river valleys but lowlands and highlands as well. These trade routes, which straddled all manner of environmental zones, helped spread technology, ideology, pottery making, and architectural styles over large areas, giving a superficial sense of unity that was reflected in the widespread use of common art motifs.

Initial Period sites are known from many coastal river valleys (see Haas et al., 1987, for details). For example, Huaca Florida is an imposing mound of boulders and adobe lying approximately 8 miles (12.8 km) inland of El Paraíso (Patterson, 1985). Built somewhat later, about 3700 years ago, and on an even larger scale, the great platform is more than 840 feet (252 m) long, 180 feet (54 m) wide, and towers 100 feet (30 m) above the valley. A rectangular court lies close to the north side of the platform, but here the landscape is revealing, for Huaca Florida lies in the midst of an artificial environment created by irrigation. The focus of human settlement had moved inland, and the subsistence base changed from fishing to large-scale irrigation agriculture.

This was by no means the earliest irrigation in Peru, for even the first farmers probably made some limited use of canals to water their riverside gardens. However, the new works were on a far larger scale, spurred by the availability of an army of workers fed by abundant Pacific fish; by the presence of gentle, cultivable slopes inland; and by the expertise of the local people in farming cotton, gourds, and many lesser crops such as squashes and beans. Huaca Florida's leaders organized the reclamation of the desert by building canals along the steeper areas of the coastal valleys, in places where the gradients made the diversion of river water an easy task. This earliest of irrigation works may seem straightforward, but considerable organization was required to coordinate and develop it, and many people were needed to supervise the digging, to mediate land ownership disputes, and to maintain canals.

At first, each family may have worked together to irrigate its own sloping gardens, but gradually each community grew so much that essential irrigation works could be handled only by cooperative effort. Organized irrigation perhaps began as many minor cooperative works between individual families and neighboring villages. These simple projects eventually evolved into elaborate public works that embraced entire inland valleys, controlled by a corporate authority who held a monopoly over both the water and the land it irrigated. The process of organization, which may have taken centuries, was the result of many complex interacting factors, among them population growth and the emergence of increasing numbers of nonfarming society members such as priests and artisans, whose food needs had to be met by other people. By the time El Paraíso and Huaca Florida were built, it is possible that public works such as irrigation canals and temples were constructed through a form of taxation by labor. Perhaps the rulers devised a forerunner of the *mita* tax employed 2000 years later by the Inca, by which people worked a certain number of days per year for the state, as either construction laborer or farmers. When one worked for the state, pay was given in food and shelter, sometimes in the form of a share of the yield from the land allocated to the state (Donnan, 1985).

As for Chavín itself, it is a late manifestation of a primeval Andean architectural style, a coalescence of traits and ideas from both the coast and the forest that formed a flamboyant cultural manifestation over a local area of the highlands. The Early Horizon itself, rather than being a catalytic time of unification, may well have been a long period of disruption of age-old communication networks and well-established small polities on the coast. For instance, the Casma polity was invaded by foreigners from the highlands, who forged the coastal valley and neighboring highlands into a single political unit for the first time in prehistory. This development was the precursor of far larger states. Perhaps it is better to refer to the Early Horizon as the Early Period, a prolonged time of cultural change and political adjustment.

Textiles and Coastal Prehistory

Initial and Early Period sites are remarkable for their fine textiles. Few prehistoric societies rivaled the textile artistry of the coastal Peruvians. They lived in an environment in which both animal and plant (especially cotton) fibers were plentiful, and they were able to create fine and complex fabrics adorned with colorful, intricate patterns (Figure 23.4). The textiles have survived remarkably well in the dry coastal environment, in huge cemeteries where the dead were wrapped in fabric burial shrouds. The most spectacular textile finds come from huge cemeteries of mummified Indians on the sandy, desolate Paracas Peninsula south of the modern town of Pisco. The (Early Horizon) Paracas bodies lie in bottle-shaped chambers or stone-lined subterranean vaults with wooden roofs approximately 16 ft (4.87 m) high and 13 ft

FIGURE 23.4   A border motif from a Paracas mantle showing an anthropomorphic figure wearing a tunic and skirt similar to those found on Paracas mummy bundles.

(3.90 m) across cut through sand into soft rock. The sepulchers were divided into small chambers, where dozens of mummy bundles were placed. The Indians did not practice mummification in the formal ancient Egyptian sense. They simply took advantage of the exceptionally dry climate. Each corpse was disemboweled and then allowed to dry out in the hot sand in a fetal position with the knees at the chin. Eventually, the bodies were wrapped in brightly colored cotton, wool, or both. Sometimes the dead wore decorated mantles, shirts, turbans, or loincloths tailored to the size of the mummy bundle rather than the living person. Occasionally, the mourners attached small ornaments to the mummies or buried tools, food, or even pet monkeys or parrots with the deceased (Figure 23.5).

It is from these mummies that we learn the most minute details of Peruvian textiles, for the wrapping cloths are often almost perfectly preserved. The earliest textiles preserved on the coast date to approximately 6500 years ago, soon after cotton was first cultivated. The weavers were expert dyers and used more than 190 hues from plant dyes. The earliest dye in common use was blue, followed by red and then a multitude of bright colors. Decorative motifs included simple checkerboards; filled squares; and stylized depictions of birds, felines, and other animals. The oldest textiles had rather coarse and uneven yarns produced by twisting untreated yarn.

FIGURE 23.5   Archaeologist excavating an effigy pot of a kneeling warrior at a burial site at the Pyramid of the Sun and the Moon, Chan Chan, Peru.

After 4000 years ago, however, the weavers began to use delicate wood and thorn spindles mounted in a special pottery, gourd, or wooden cup that minimized vibration. Thus they could produce much finer cloth. Most of the textiles found in coastal tombs were made on backstrap looms just like those still in use in Peru today (Figure 23.6). Two sticks carry the lengthwise threads, the upper one suspended from a post and the lower tied to a belt around the weaver's back. As the work proceeds, the fabric is unrolled from the upper bar and the finished cloth is rolled onto the lower stick. The yarn is wound with a figure-eight motion between the two stakes and is laced fast to the loom sticks so that the edges of the fabric are uniformly finished off. The disadvantage of this type of loom is that the width of the cloth is limited by the span of the weaver's arms. The Indians sometimes combined several backstrap looms to create wider cloths.

From the Initial Period onward, the Andean region witnessed an extraordinary array of state-organized societies that displayed a remarkable diversity of culture, art, organization, and religious belief. At the same time, there were broad similarities in cosmology and culture that distinguish these societies from states elsewhere in the prehistoric world. As Michael Moseley and many others have pointed out, we are

FIGURE 23.6   Backstrap loom in use.

only now beginning to understand just how diverse and complicated the evolution of state-organized societies was in this region (see Haas et al., 1987).

THE EARLY INTERMEDIATE PERIOD

By 200 B.C., irrigation agriculture had developed on a very large scale on the coast, so much so that some settlements, such as Cerro Arena in the Moche Valley, covered more than a square mile. Excavations during the 1970s revealed more than 2000 separate structures, some with as many as 20 rooms (Bankes, 1977). A small group of 25 finely finished houses may have formed the administrative and residential quarters of Cerro Arena. There were considerable variations between these quarters and the humbler dwellings that surrounded them, as if Cerro Arena society was more complex than that of earlier settlements. This and other large settlements were supported by irrigation systems that required organized labor to construct and maintain them as well as strict water controls. Most of the cultivated land lay along the terraced edges of the valleys, where the soils were better drained and easily planted with simple wooden digging sticks, just as they are to this day. Even today the local people divert the seasonal river water into side canals by building dams of stakes and boulders into the streams. There is no reason to suppose that the same simple but effective technique was not used in antiquity. The ancient irrigation canals wound along the sides of the valleys, a series of narrow channels approximately 4 ft (1.2 m) wide, set in loops and S-shaped curves, watering plots approximately 70 ft (21.3 m) square. The surplus flowed off into the Pacific.

Moche

Moche
200 B.C. to A.D. 600

By 200 B.C., the Moche state had begun in northern coastal Peru, flourishing for 800 years. Its origins lay in the Chicama and Moche valleys, with great ceremonial centers and huge irrigation works (Donnan and McClelland, 1979). Information about the Moche peoples of 2000 years ago comes not only from irrigation systems and spectacular monuments but also from hundreds of finely modeled clay pots and human burials preserved in the dry desert sand of their cemeteries. Unfortunately, these burials are a prime target of commercial grave robbers. Many Moche cemeteries look like battlefields after heavy bombardment, for their pots fetch astronomical prices on the international art market.

The spectacular discovery of an undisturbed Moche tomb near the village of Sipan about 420 miles (680 km) northwest of Lima has revolutionized our knowledge of Moche's elite. Peruvian archaeologist Walter Alva (1988) uncovered an unlooted burial chamber containing a plank coffin that held the extended skeleton of a man in his thirties lying on his back with his arms along his sides. He wore gold nose and ear ornaments, gold and turquoise bead bracelets, and copper sandals. A ceremonial rattle, crescent-shaped knives, scepters, spears, and exotic seashells surrounded the body. Three young women, each about 18 years old, lay at the head and foot of the coffin, and two males in their mid-thirties on either side. A dog, two sacrificial llamas, and hundreds of clay vessels lay in the grave. Comparing the objects found in the tomb with people depicted in Moche art, Christopher Donnan (1989) has identified the man as a warrior-priest. Such individuals are shown on Moche pots presiding over sacrifices of prisoners of war, and they played a very important role in Moche society. In the earliest level (1990) of the same platform, Alva has also unearthed the richly decorated burial of an early warrior-priest, an older man with a gold funerary mask, a magnificent necklace of golden spiders atop their webs, and a gilded copper crab effigy of a deity more than 2 feet (6 m) tall that was once mounted on a fabric banner (Donnan, 1990).

What little we know about Moche society comes from undisturbed burials, and from museum studies of looted pots. They show that Moche society consisted of farmers and fisherfolk as well as skilled artisans and priests, who are depicted on pots with felinelike fangs set in their mouths and wearing puma-skin headdresses. A few expert craft potters created superb modeled vessels with striking portraits of arrogant, handsome men who can only have been the leaders of Moche society (Figure 23.7). The potters modeled warriors, too, complete with shields and war clubs, well-padded helmets, and colorful cotton uniforms. Moche burials show that some members of society were much richer than others, lying in graves filled with as many as 50 vessels or with weapons or staffs of rank. We do not know exactly how Moche society was

FIGURE 23.7   Moche portrait vessel approximately 11.4 in. (29 cm) high.

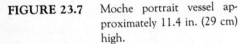

organized, but we can assume that the ruler wielded authority over a hierarchical state of warriors, priest-doctors, artisans, and the mass of the agricultural population. For instance, there was at least one Moche-style settlement in each subject valley.

Fortunately, the Moche artists and artisans gave us some more intimate glances at their society than do many civilizations (Figure 23.8). Their paintings show the ruler with a fine feather headdress seated on a pyramid, while a line of naked prisoners parades before him. A decapitated sacrifice at the base of one painting reminds us that human sacrifice may have been the fate of some prisoners of war. We see Moche soldiers in battle, charging their opponents with raised clubs. The defenders raise their feather-decked shields in defiance as the battle is fought to the death. The potters modeled maize-beer-befuddled drunks being supported by their solicitous friends, women giving birth with the midwife in attendance, and wives carrying babies on their backs in shawls and in wooden cradles suspended by nets. The women carried out all domestic activities, and the men served as warriors, farmers, and fishermen. We see them on a seal hunt, clubbing young seals on the rocky coast as their prey scurries in every direction. A clay llama strains reluctantly under its load, and a mouse eats a maize cob.

The pots also depict vividly what the Moche people wore. The men worked in short loincloths or cotton breeches and short sleeveless shirts underneath tunics that ended above the knee, fastened around the waist with colorful woven belts. More important people wore large mantles and headdresses made from puma heads or feathers from highland jungles. Nearly everyone donned some form of headgear: Brightly decorated cotton turbans wound around small caps and held in place with

FIGURE 23.8   Moche vessel depicting an owl-woman healer.

fabric chin straps were in common use. A small cloth protected the back of the neck from the burning sun. Moche women dressed in loose tunics that reached the knee and went bareheaded or draped a piece of cloth around their heads. Many men painted their lower legs and feet in bright colors and tattooed or daubed their faces with lines and other motifs. They often wore disk or crescent nose ornaments and cylindrical bar earrings, sometimes modeled in gold. Their necks bore large collars of stone beads or precious metal, and bracelets covered their arms and legs. Many people wore fiber sandals to protect their feet from the hot sand.

By this time the coastal people were expert metalworkers (Benson, 1979). They had discovered the properties of gold ore and extracted it by panning in streambeds rather than by mining. Soon they had developed ways of hammering it into fine sheets and had learned how to emboss it to make raised designs (Figure 23.9). They also had worked out the technique of annealing, making it possible to soften the metal and then hammer it into more elaborate forms, and they joined sheets with fine solder. The smiths used gold as a setting for turquoise and shell ornaments, crafted crowns, circlets, necklaces, pins, and tweezers. Gold was in such short supply

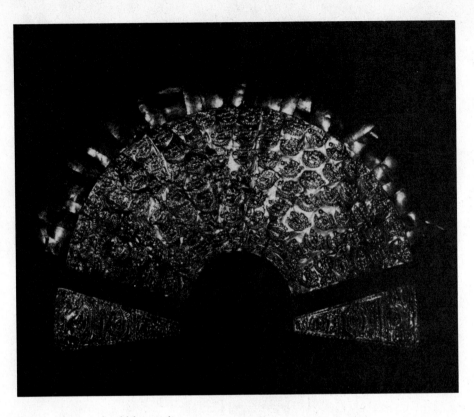

FIGURE 23.9   Moche hammered gold breastplate.

in prehistoric times that the metalworkers became expert at depletion gilding, an annealing technique that oxidizes the metal in an alloy of copper and gold to give the finished product a goldlike appearance even when the gold content is as low as 12 percent by weight. Many of the large gold objects such as animals and plate decorations seized from the Inca by Pizarro's soldiers were in fact made of an elaborate alloy of some gold, silver, and copper.

The greatest efforts of the Moche people were devoted not to irrigation systems or elaborate burials but to the erection of vast monumental platforms and temples on the southern edge of the cultivated land in the Moche Valley, approximately 4 miles (6.4 km) southeast of the modern city of Trujillo. They used tax labor to build a huge adobe temple platform rising 76 feet (23 m) above the plain at the foot of a conical hill named Cerro Blanco. The Spaniards called this complex *Huaca de la Luna*, the Temple of the Moon. *Huaca del Sol* (Temple of the Sun) stands close to the west, a confused mass of mud brick that once consisted of a ramp that gave access to five temple platforms, the highest, to the south, towering 135 feet (41 m) above the ground. The sides of the pyramid were steeply terraced and have been badly damaged by erosion and looters. Both platforms once supported courts, corridors, and room complexes, perhaps roofed with matting. Huaca del Sol may have been a palace, for there are deep rubbish heaps on the summit of the platform. In contrast, Huaca de la Luna is spotlessly clean, its temple buildings painted with brightly colored murals.

The Moche was a multivalley state that may have consisted of a series of satellite centers that ruled over individual valleys but owed allegiance to the great centers of the Moche Valley. At one time the Moche Valley presided over the coast as far south as the Nepeña Valley. Where possible, the Moche extended their ambitious irrigation systems to link several neighboring river valleys and then constructed lesser copies of their capital as a basis for secure administration of their new domains. Their traders were in contact with the north and with the Nasca people on the south coast as well (Proulx, 1983a). In approximately A.D. 600, the Moche people moved their center of administrative activity north to the Pampa Grande in the Lambayeque Valley. By this time the southern centers were abandoned, as the political and economic influence of the southern highlands and coast began to rise. The agricultural system of the southern valleys may have collapsed, perhaps as a result of major droughts, so the people moved north to an area where there was more water. They may also have been under pressure from people inland.

THE MIDDLE HORIZON:
THE FIRST EMPIRES

A series of brilliant states had flourished on the coast and in the highlands during the Early Intermediate Period—Moche on the north coast, Nasca in the south, and Recuay in the northern highlands, to mention only a few. The same period also saw the beginnings of monumental building at a highland site that would influence much of the Peruvian world—Tiwanaku (Proulx, 1983).

Middle Horizon
A.D. 600 to
1000

Between A.D. 600 and 1000 (the so-called Middle Horizon), the wealthiest highland districts lay at the southern end of the central Andes, in the high flat country surrounding Lake Titicaca. This was fine llama country. The local people maintained enormous herds of these beasts of burden and were also expert irrigation farmers. The *altiplano* supported the densest population in the highlands, and almost inevitably, the Titicaca region became an economic and demographic pole to the prosperous northern coast. By A.D. 200 Tiwanaku, on the eastern side of the lake, was becoming

Tiwanaku
?A.D. 200 to c.
1200

a major population center as well as an important economic and religious focus for the region (Kolata, 1982, 1986). The arid lands on which the site lies were irrigated and supported a population of perhaps 20,000 around the monumental structures near the center of the site. By A.D. 600 Tiwanaku was acquiring much of its prosperity from trade around the lake's southern shores. Copper working was especially important and probably developed independently of the well-established copper technology on the northern coast.

Tiwanaku was not only an economic force; it was a very important religious one as well. The great enclosure of Kalasasaya is dominated by a large earth platform faced with stones. Nearby, a rectangular enclosure is bounded with a row of upright stones and there is a doorway carved with an anthropomorphic god, believed to be the creator deity, Viracocha (Figure 23.10). Smaller buildings, enclosures, and huge

FIGURE 23.10   Gateway of the Sun at Tiwanaku, made from one block of lava. The central figure is known as the Gateway god; notice its jaguar mouth and serpent-ray headdress. The running figures flanking the god often are called messengers.

states are also near the ceremonial structures. One recently excavated temple contained the skeleton of a young warrior, perhaps a captive, sacrificed in A.D. 600.

It is the Tiwanaku art style that is most striking. Like Chavín, this tradition probably represents a powerful iconography. Tiwanaku's art motifs include jaguars and eagles as well as anthropomorphic gods being attended to by lesser deities or messengers. They occur over much of southern Peru as well as in Bolivia, the southern Andes, and perhaps as far afield as northwest Argentina. So powerful was the iconography and, presumably, the political and economic forces behind Tiwanaku that there was a serious political vacuum in the south after A.D. 1200, when Tiwanaku inexplicably collapsed into obscurity.

The influence of Tiwanaku can be seen at Wari in the Mantaro Valley, an important lowland ceremonial center that stands on a hill (Isbell and Schreiber, 1978; Rowe, Collier, and Willey, 1950). It is associated with huge stone walls and many dwellings that cover several square miles. The Wari art styles show some Tiwanaku influence, especially in anthropomorphic, feline, eagle, and serpent beings depicted on ceramic vessels. Like their southern neighbors, the Wari people seem to have revered a Viracocha-like being. By A.D. 800, their domains extended from Moche country in the Lambayeque Valley on the northern coast to south of Nasca territory and into the highlands south of Cuzco. They were expert traders, who probably expanded their domain through conquest, commercial enterprise, and perhaps religious conversion. Storehouses and roads probably were maintained by the state. As with the Inca of later centuries, the state controlled food supplies and labor (Schreiber, 1987).

Wari
?A.D. 600 to 900

Wari itself was abandoned in the ninth century A.D., but its art styles persisted on the coast for at least two more centuries. Both Wari and Tiwanaku were a turning point in Peruvian prehistory, a stage when small regional states became integrated into much larger political units. This unification may have been achieved by conquest and other coercive means, but the iconography shared by many coastal and highland Peruvians at the time must have been a powerful catalyst for closer political unity. There was constant and often intensive interaction between two poles of Andean civilization in the highlands and lowlands, each with quite different food resources and products. This interaction, long a feature of Andean life, was to intensify in the centuries that lay ahead.

These two great polities collapsed toward the end of the first millennium, leaving a vast political vacuum of small, competing tribes that was filled by the Inca after a period of conflict and warfare.

THE LATE INTERMEDIATE PERIOD: LATE COASTAL STATES

Chimu

The highland states traded regularly with several emerging polities on the coast, each of them founded on extensive irrigation systems. Of these, the most famous is the Chimu kingdom, centered on the Moche Valley of the northern coast, the same area inhabited 400 years earlier by the Moche people. The Moche Valley had long been densely cultivated, but the Chimu people now embarked on much more ambitious irrigation schemes; they built large storage reservoirs and terraced hundreds of miles of hillside to control the flow of water down steep slopes. One channel extended nearly 20 miles (32 km) from the Chicama Valley to the capital, Chan Chan, designed to supplement the relatively limited water supplies that came from the nearby Moche Valley (Figure 23.11). Even in periods of extreme drought these canals carried water from the deep-cut riverbed to terraces long distances away. Thus, the Chimu created thousands of acres of new fields and used water from great distances to harvest two or three crops a year from plots where only one crop had been possible before, and

Chimu
?A.D. 1000 to 1476

**FIGURE
23.11**   Chan Chan. Oblique air photograph of a walled enclosure or compound.

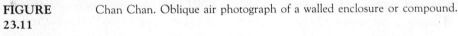

that at the time of the annual flood. So effective were these irrigation techniques that the Chimu controlled more than 12 river valleys with at least 125,000 cultivable acres, all of it farmed with hoes or digging sticks. Today, the local Indians water their maize crops approximately every ten days, and this probably was the practice in Chimu times as well (Bankes, 1977).

According to seventeenth-century Spanish chroniclers, the Chimu always maintained that their domains were originally ruled over by petty chiefs, but when the Inca conquered them between 1462 and 1470 they were led by a ruler named Michancamán, who governed through a network of hereditary local nobility. His courtiers held specific ranks, such as "Blower of the Shell Trumpet"; "Master of the Litter and Thrones"; and "Preparer of the Way," the official who scattered powdered shell dust wherever the ruler was about to walk. An archaeologist working at Chan Chan in 1969–1970 found a layer of powdered shell dust on a bench in a forecourt, perhaps evidence that the Preparer of the Way had been at work. The various provinces of the kingdom were ruled by loyal local leaders. They enjoyed not only tribute privileges but also rights to crops and land and to agricultural labor by commoners. Perhaps the most privileged members of society were the *Oquetlupec*, herb curers paid by the state to look after the sick. This was a hierarchical, highly organized society with strict social classes of nobles and commoners. Perhaps to enforce the social hierarchy, the legal system was very strict (Rowe, 1946).

The focus of the Chimu state was Chan Chan, a huge complex of walled compounds lying near the Pacific at the mouth of the Moche Valley. Chan Chan covers nearly 4 square miles (10.3 sq. km), the central part consisting of nine large enclosures laid out in a sort of broken rectangle. Each enclosure probably functioned as the palace for the current ruler of Chan Chan, who probably built himself a new headquarters near those of his predecessors (Lanning, 1967; Moseley, 1975a; Moseley and Day, 1982). The adobe walls of these compounds once stood as high as 33 feet (9.9 m) and covered areas as large as 670 by 2000 feet (201 by 600 m). The walls were not constructed to defend the rulers but to provide privacy and some shelter from the ocean winds. Each enclosure had its own water supply, a burial platform, and lavishly decorated residential rooms roofed with cane frames covered with earth and grass. The same enclosure that served as a palace during life became the ruler's burial place in death. The common people lived in tracts of small adobe and reed-mat houses on the western side of the city. Similar dwellings can be seen on the coast to this day.

Oral traditions tell us that the Chimu rulers practiced the institution of split inheritance, whereby each ruler inherited no material possessions to finance his reign. Split inheritance was to play a major role in Inca civilization (described on p. 623). Chimu rulers had access to and control of a huge labor pool. They employed laborers to expand and maintain irrigation works, and they served as military levies to acquire new lands and expand the tax base (Pozorski, 1987). Rulers soon learned the value of efficient communications, of officially maintained roadways that enabled them to move their armies from one place to the next with rapid dispatch. They constructed roads that connected each valley in their domain with the capital. The rural routes were little more than tracks between low adobe walls or widely spaced posts, mostly following centuries-old paths through the fields. In the densely populated valleys, Chimu roads were between 15 and 25 feet (4.5 and 7.5 m) across. In some places the roadway widened dramatically to 80 feet (24 m) or more. These were the roads that carried gold ornaments and fine hammered vessels to Chan Chan and textiles and fine, black-painted vessels throughout the empire. The traveler occasionally would encounter heavily laden llamas carrying goods to market, but most loads were carried on people's backs, for the Chimu never developed the wheeled cart. All revenues and tribute passed along the official roadways, as did newly conquered peoples being resettled in some area far from their original homeland. This draconian resettlement tactic was so successful that the Inca adopted it. The ruler then would install his own appointee in the new lands, in a compound palace that was a smaller version of Chan Chan itself.

The Chimu Empire extended far south, at least to Casma and perhaps reaching to the vicinity of modern Lima, for the main focus of civilization lay on the northern Peruvian littoral, where the soils were fertile and large-scale irrigation was a practical reality. Chimu armies fought with powerful neighbors to the south, among them the chief of Pachácamac, who controlled some narrow valleys south of Lima. Pachácamac had long been a venerated shrine and already boasted a terraced temple covering two-thirds of an acre (0.3 ha). Pachácamac has been a grave robbers' paradise for centuries. Later, the Inca built a vast Temple of the Sun at Pachácamac, an irregular trapezoid in a commanding position on a rocky hill.

For all its wide-ranging military activities and material wealth, the Chimu Empire was very vulnerable to attack from outside. The massive irrigation works of the northern river valleys were easily disrupted by an aggressive conqueror, for no leader, however powerful, could hope to fortify the entire frontier of the empire. We know little of the defenses, except for Paramonga in the Fortaleza Valley, a massive terraced structure built of rectangular adobes that overlooks the probable southern limits of Chimu territory. The Chimu were vulnerable to prolonged drought, too, for the storage capacity of their great irrigation works was only sufficient to carry them over one or two lean seasons. Perhaps, too, the irrigated desert soils became too saline for agriculture, so that crop yields fell drastically at a time when population densities were rising sharply. Since the Chimu depended on a highly specialized agricultural system, once that system was disrupted—whether by natural or artificial causes—military conquest and control of the irrigation network was easy, especially for aggressive and skillful conquerors such as the Inca, who conquered the Chimu in the 1460s.

THE LATE HORIZON: THE INCA STATE

Late Horizon
A.D. 1476 to
1534

The Late Horizon of Peruvian archaeology was also the shortest, dating from A.D. 1476 to 1534. It is the period of the Inca Empire, when those mighty Andean rulers held sway over an enormous area of highland and lowland country (Bankes, 1977; Rowe, 1946).

The Inca were born into an intensely competitive world, their homeland lying to the northwest of the Titicaca basin in the area around Cuzco (for an extended description, see Conrad and Demarest, 1984). They were a small-scale farming society living in small villages, organized in kin groups known as *ayllu,* groups claiming a common ancestry and also owning land in common. The Inca were a self-sufficient people, and their ayllu leaders contributed labor to one another as a means of organizing and distributing labor on a reciprocal basis. The ayllu was legitimized in its land ownership and protected by the ancestors. It was small wonder that the Inca always took good care of their ancestral mummies. The bodies of the dead, their tombs, and their fetishes, as well as numerous other sacred places and phenomena, were known as *huaca.*

Inca
A.D. 1200 to
1534

The later Inca rulers clothed their origins in a glorious panoply of heroic deeds. It is likely, however, that the Inca were a fractious, constantly quarreling petty chiefdom. The chronicles of early conquest reflect the constant bickering of village headmen, and the earliest Inca rulers were probably petty war leaders (*sinchi*), elected officials whose success was measured by their victories and booty. To stay in office, they had to be politically and militarily adept so that they could both defeat and appease their many potential rivals. The official Inca histories spoke of at least eight Inca rulers between 1200 and 1438, but these genealogies are hardly reliable (Rowe, 1946). They probably depict little more than legendary figures. During the fourteenth century, a number of small tribal groups in the southern highlands began to develop a more powerful military confederacy, but the Inca flourished in this competitive atmosphere because their leaders were expert politicians as well as warriors. A leader named Viracocha Inca rose to power at the beginning of the fifteenth century. Unlike his raiding predecessors, however, he turned to permanent conquest and soon presided over a small kingdom centered in Cuzco. Viracocha Inca became the living god, the first in a series of constant religious changes that kept the new kingdom under tight control. At about the same time a new religious cult emerged, that of Inti, a celestial divine ancestor who was part of the sky god. (We say *part* because Inti was more of a cluster of solar aspects than the sun god.)

Around 1438, a brilliant warrior named Cusi Inca Yupanqui was crowned Inca after a memorable victory over the neighboring Chanca tribe. He immediately took the name Pachakuti ("He Who Remakes the World") and set about transforming the Inca state. In particular, he and his henchmen developed a form of royal ancestor cult. This in itself was not especially significant since Pachakuti simply reworked an age-old Andean tradition, but the law of split inheritance that went along with it had a lasting and profound significance. A dead ruler was mummified. His palace, servants, and possessions were still considered his property and were maintained by all his male descendants *except* his successor, normally one of his sons. The deceased was not considered dead, however. His mummy attended great ceremonies and would even visit the houses of the living. Those entrusted to look after the king ate and talked with him, just as if his life were still going on. This element of continuity was extremely important because it made the royal mummies some of the holiest artifacts in the empire. Dead rulers were living sons of Inti, visible links with the gods, the very embodiment of the Inca state and of the fertility of nature. Meanwhile the ascending ruler was rich in prestige but poor in possessions. The new king had to acquire wealth so he could both live in royal splendor and provide for his mummy in the future—and the only wealth in the highland kingdom was taxable labor.

Therefore, every adult in Inca country had to render a certain amount of labor to the state each year after providing for the basic subsistence needs of his own ayllu. This *mita* system repaired bridges and roads, cultivated state-owned lands, manned the armies, and carried out public works. It was a reciprocal system. The state, or those benefiting from the work, had to feed and entertain those doing it. The split inheritance of the Inca rulers meant that all taxes levied by their predecessors went to them and not to the newcomer. He had to develop a new tax base and could do so in only two ways: by levying more labor from existing taxpayers or by conquering new lands. Since the Inca rulers needed land to provide food for those who worked for them and the earlier kings owned most of the land near Cuzco, the only way a new ruler could obtain his own royal estates was by expansion into new territory. This expansion could not take the form of temporary raids. The conquest had to be permanent, the conquered territory had to be controlled and taxed, and the ruler's subjects had to be convinced of the value of a policy of long-term conquest.

The Inca rulers turned into brilliant propagandists, reminding everyone that they were gods and that the welfare of all depended on the prosperity of all rulers, past and present, and on constant military conquest. There were initial economic advantages, too, in the form of better protection against famine. Also, the rulers were careful to reward prowess in battle. Nobles were promoted to new posts and awarded insignia that brought their life-style ever closer to that of the king, and even a brave commoner could become a member of the secondary nobility. A highly complicated set of benefits, economic incentives, rewards, and justifications fueled and nourished the Inca conquests. Their successful ideology provided them with a crucial advantage over their neighbors, and within a decade of Pachakuti's accession they were masters of the southern highlands. Their army had become an invincible juggernaut, and in less than a century the tiny kingdom taken over by Pachakuti had become a vast empire. Topa Yupanqui (1471–1493) extended the Inca Empire into Ecuador, northern Argentina, parts of Bolivia, and Chile. His armies also conquered the Chimu state, whose water supplies Topa already controlled. The best Chimu craftsworkers were carried off to work for the court of the Incas. Another king, Huanya Capac, ruled for 34 years after Topa Inca and pushed the empire deeper into Ecuador.

The Inca rulers developed an efficient administrative system to run their empire, one based firmly on the precedents of earlier societies. *Tawantinsuyu,* "The Land of the Four Quarters," was divided into four large provinces known as *suyu* (quarters), each subdivided into smaller provinces, some of them coinciding with older, conquered kingdoms. The conquered peoples in the Inca Empire were usually ruled by a leading member of a local family, known as a *curaca.* These hereditary chiefs were a form of secondary non-Inca nobility who governed a taxpaying population of 100 people or more, but all the really important government posts were held by Inca nobles. The Inca rulers realized, however, that the essence of efficient government in such varied topography was efficient communications, so the road builders commandeered a vast network of age-old Indian highways from the states they conquered. They linked them in a coordinated system with regular rest houses so that they could move armies, trade goods, and messengers from one end of the kingdom to the other in short order (Hyslop, 1984).

The Incas' passion for organization impinged on everyone's life. Their society was organized into 12 age divisions for the purposes of census and tax assessment, divisions based on both physical changes like puberty and major social events like marriage. The most important stage was adulthood, which lasted as long as one could do a day's work. All the census and other data of the empire were recorded not on tablets but on knotted strings. The *quipu* were a complex and sophisticated record-keeping system that seems to have been so efficient that it more than made up for the lack of writing (Ascher and Ascher, 1981). They also were a powerful instrument for enforcing social conformity, codifying laws, and providing data for the inspectors, who regularly visited each household to check that everyone was engaged in productive work and living in sanitary conditions. No one could travel without official permission. Everything about the Inca lifeway stressed conformity and the need to respect and obey the central government.

At the time of the Spanish conquest, the Inca controlled the lives of as many as 6 million people, most of them living in small villages dispersed around religious and political centers. It was here that Inca artisans labored, producing major works of art in gold and silver. Brightly painted Inca pottery is found throughout the empire; it is decorated with black, white, and red geometric designs. Despite the widespread distribution of Inca pots and artifacts, however, regional pottery styles flourished because the village potters, many of whom were conquered subjects, continued the cultural traditions of earlier centuries.

Cuzco
Machu Picchu

Inca political and religious power was centered on major urban complexes like Cuzco in the Andes, where the ceremonial center was built of carefully fitted stones (Figure 23.12) (Protzen, 1986). Such locations as Machu Picchu, high in the Andes (Figure 23.13), are famous for their fine masonry structures (Gasparini and Margolies, 1980). The Inca ruler held court in Cuzco, surrounded by plotting factions and ever-changing political tides. One villain was the very institution of split inheritance that fueled Inca military conquest. Every ruler faced increasingly complex governance problems as a result. The need for more and more conquests caused great military, economic, and administrative stress. The logistics of long-distance military campaigns

**FIGURE
23.12**   Inca masonry from the fortress of Sacsahuaman, near Cuzco.

were horrendous, and the soldiers had to be fed from state-owned land, not royal estates. Moreover, although their tactics were well adapted to open country, where their armies were invincible, the rulers eventually had to start fighting in forest country, where they fared badly. Meanwhile the empire had grown so large that communication became a lengthier and lengthier process, compounded by the great diversity of people living within the Inca domain. Also, the increasing number of high-ranking nobles devoted to the interests of dead rulers led to chronic factionalism in Cuzco. Under its glittering façade, *Tawantinsuyu* was becoming a rotten apple. In the end, the Inca Empire was overthrown not by Peruvians but by a tiny band of foreigners with firearms who could exploit the inherent vulnerability of such a hierarchical, conforming society.

THE SPANISH CONQUEST: 1532–1534

This vulnerability came home to roost in 1532, when a small party of rapacious Spanish conquistadores landed in northern Peru. When Francisco Pizarro arrived,

**FIGURE
23.13**   Machu Picchu. Forgotten for 400 years after the Spanish conquest, it was rediscovered by
the American explorer Hiram Bingham in 1911.

the Inca state was in some political chaos, its people already decimated by smallpox
and other diseases introduced by the first conquistadores. Inca Huayna Capac had
died in an epidemic in A.D. 1525. The empire was plunged into a civil war between
his son Huascar and another son, Atahuallpa, half brother to Huascar. Atahuallpa
eventually prevailed, but as he moved south from Ecuador to consolidate his territory, he learned that Pizarro had landed in Peru.

The Spaniards had vowed to make Peru part of Spain and were bent on plunder
and conquest. Pizarro arrived in the guise of a diplomat, captured Atahuallpa by
treachery, ransomed him for a huge quantity of gold, and then brutally murdered
him. A year later the Spaniards captured the Inca capital with a tiny army. They took
over the state bureaucracy and appointed Manco Inca as puppet ruler. Three years

A.D. 1533
A.D. 1536   later, Manco Inca turned on his masters in a bloody revolt. Its suppression finally
destroyed the greatest of the Peruvian empires.

The Spanish conquest of Mexico and Peru saw the first major confrontation
between the forces of an expanding Europe emerging from centuries of feudalism and
complex non-Western societies that were still living with the full legacy of prehistoric
times.

THE END OF PREHISTORY

The four and a half centuries since the Spanish conquests of Mexico and Peru have seen European settlement in all corners of the globe, the emergence of the industrial state, and the acting out of the last, tragic chapter of human prehistory: the clash between the Western and non-Western worlds (Fagan, 1984b; Wolf, 1984). The basic scenario was relived again and again. A small party of European explorers arrived, as did Captain James Cook in Tahiti or the French voyager Marion du Fresne in Tasmania. The first encounter was a fleeting kaleidoscope of curiosity, sometimes horrified fascination, and often romantic excitement. Sometimes even experts like Cook had trouble understanding peoples like the Tasmanians or Australian Aborigines. "They wander about in small parties from place to place in search of food," he wrote. "They are all together an ignorant, wretched race of mortals, though at the same time the natives of a country capable of producing every necessity of life." Right from the beginning there was incomprehension.

Even in paradisal areas like the South Seas, initial romance soon turned to bitter disillusionment on both sides. Sometimes the people thought their strange visitors were gods, as the Aztec did Hernán Cortés. An elderly Maori chief in New Zealand told a nineteenth-century official that the priests had told them the whites were goblins with eyes in the back of their heads, an apparent reference to their oarsmen facing the stern in their boats. Soon, the strangers proved to be aggressive, warlike, and acquisitive, all too human in their ambitions and goals. Their exotic diseases decimated tens of thousands of people, in Mexico alone millions of Indians within a few generations (Wolf, 1984).

At first the contacts were brief ones, with Europeans coming to trade furs, refit their ships, or search for gold. Then the missionaries arrived, seeking to convert the heathen and save their souls. They were followed by colonists, often impoverished, land-hungry farmers who saw a better life in the fertile soils of Tasmania, New Zealand, British Columbia, and the African interior. It was then that the process of catastrophic culture change began, and indigenous hunters, foragers, fisherfolk, and farmers started competing for land with the newcomers. Inevitably, the strangers with their iron tools and firearms won, and the indigenous population retreated into marginal areas and enclaves, where they preserved a shadow of their former culture and lifeway, if they were able to survive at all.

Today, the clash of cultures is still in inexorable progress, deep in the Amazon rain forest and in highland New Guinea, where rain forests are felled and age-old lifeways destroyed forever. The world lives with a tragic legacy of misunderstanding as we face what will probably be the question of questions for the twenty-first century: How do we bridge the great gulf of incomprehension that exists between the Western and non-Western worlds, between the rich and the poor? How can we begin to understand human biological and cultural diversity in all its bewildering complexity? Our journey through over 2 million years of human prehistory has shown you just how similar humans are in their general behavior and responses to a multitude of environmental challenges. We are all part of the same human family, and archaeology is just about the only way we have to understand many of the forces that shaped today's world. We hope *People of the Earth* has given you some understanding of the compelling biological and cultural forces that have shaped our past and will help shape our future.

GUIDE TO FURTHER READING

Bankes, George. 1977. *Peru Before Pizarro.* Oxford, Eng.: Phaidon.
   A useful introduction to Peruvian archaeology that examines different aspects of prehistoric life. Good for the beginner.

Conrad, Geoffrey W., and Demarest, Arthur A. 1984. *Religion and Empire: The Dynamics of Aztec and Inca Expansionism.* Cambridge, Eng.: Cambridge University Press.
   A clear and succinct analysis of two imperial, preindustrial civilizations. A sophisticated, well-argued book. Strongly recommended.

Haas, Jonathan, Pozorski, S., and Pozorski, T., eds. 1987. *The Origins and Development of the Andean State.* Cambridge, Eng.: Cambridge University Press.
   A useful series of essays on the complex processes of state formation in the Andean region. Not for beginners.

Keatinge, Richard, ed. 1988. *Peruvian Prehistory.* Cambridge, Eng.: Cambridge University Press.
   Essays reviewing the current state of Peruvian archaeology.

Moseley, Michael E. 1975. *The Maritime Foundations of Andean Civilization.* Menlo Park, CA: Cummings.
   A short essay that argues that the foundations of Peruvian civilization lay on the coast in subsistence patterns that relied heavily on maritime resources. Controversial but convincing for the most part.

Rowe, John H. 1946. *Inca Culture at the Time of the Spanish Conquest.* Vol. 2, *Handbook of South American Indians.* Washington, DC: Smithsonian Institution.
   The classic account of Inca culture reconstructed from historical documents and limited archaeological investigations.

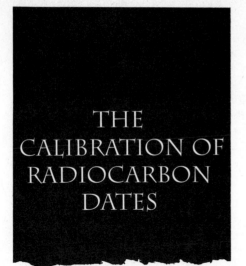

THE CALIBRATION OF RADIOCARBON DATES

IMPORTANT NOTE

It has been apparent for some time that the ages provided by most radiocarbon samples suffer from considerable inaccuracies because of variations in cosmic ray bombardment of the earth. As is explained in Chapter 1, dates from sites to about 7250 years old (about 5300 B.C.) can be calibrated by using tree rings to provide absolutely accurate ages.

These calibrations place me in somewhat of a chronological dilemma. Calibrated radiocarbon dates are used regularly only in a few parts of the world, noticeably in Europe, whereas many American archaeologists ignore them. Should we use calibrated dates in *People of the Earth?*

I have set up the text in such a way that you can use calibrated dates if you wish. Each chronological table for which calibrated dates are relevant has one column giving radiocarbon ages, and another giving the calibrated dates. You can read from whichever column you wish.

The dates in the margins are uncalibrated except in the European chapters, where such dates are commonly used. You can convert them to C14 ages by referring to the requisite chronological table. The following conventions are used:

Radiocarbon ages and dates established by historical chronologies, tree-ring dating, and other methods are expressed as follows: A.D. 1225 or 3250 B.C., with the A.D./B.C. convention in small capital letters.

Calibrated dates are expressed in tables as follows: a.d. 1225 or 3250 b.c., with lowercase letters. (See also Pearson, 1987.)

The most recent calibration tables are the result of extensive collaboration among radiocarbon laboratories around the world. The figures in the table that follows are based on the tables in *Radiocarbon*, vol. 6 (1986), and on Jeffrey Klein, J. C. Lerman, P. E. Damon, and E. K. Ralph, "Calibration of Radiocarbon Dates: Tables Based on the Consensus Data of the Workshop on Calibrating the Radiocarbon Time Scale," *Radiocarbon* 24, no. 2 (1982):103–149.

Calibrating radiocarbon dates is not easy and is a matter for specialist expertise. The following are approximate calibrations for 500-year intervals from A.D. 1500 to 7250 years ago.

Calibration Table

Calibrated Date[a] or a.d./b.c./b.p.		Radiocarbon Age A.D./B.C./B.P.
a.d.	1500	1501 ± 6 A.D.
	1000	932 ± 10
	500	385 ± 13
	10	38 ± 10 B.C.
b.c.	500	472 ± 13
b.p.	3000	2898 ± 10 B.P.
	3500	3280 ± 16
	4000	3698 ± 13
	4500	5505 to 4925
	5000	5950 to 5640
	5500	6545 to 5960
	6000	7235 to 6575
	6500	7705 to 7205
	7000	8285 to 7445
	7300	8585 to 8595
Before 7500		Outside calibration range

[a]Calibrated dates are based on an assumed standard deviation of 100 years. The date range varies with the standard deviation (see tables).

BIBLIOGRAPHY OF WORLD PREHISTORY

The literature of world prehistory proliferates more and more every year, to the point that it is now beyond the ability of any one scholar to keep abreast of it. This bibliography is not intended as a comprehensive reference guide to world prehistory. Rather it is a compilation of both the majority of sources used to write this book and a cross section of the most important monographs and papers relating to all parts of the world. Readers interested in probing more deeply into the literature should pursue the references given in the publications listed here or consult a specialist.

Adams, R. E. W., ed. 1977a. *The Origins of the Classic Maya.* Albuquerque: University of New Mexico Press.

———. 1977b. *Prehistoric Mesoamerica.* Boston: Little, Brown.

Adams, R. E. W., Brown, W. E., and Culbert, T. Patrick. 1981. "Radar Mapping, Archeology, and Ancient Maya Land Use." *Science* 213 (4515):1457–1462.

Adams, Robert M. 1966. *The Evolution of Urban Society.* Chicago: Aldine.

———. 1981. *Heartland of Cities.* Chicago: University of Chicago Press.

Adams, Robert M., and Nissen, Hans J. 1972. *The Uruk Landscape.* Chicago: University of Chicago Press.

Adovasio, James M., et al. 1981. *Meadowcroft Rockshelter and the Archaeology of the Cross Creek Drainage.* Pittsburgh: University of Pittsburgh Press.

———. 1984. "Meadowcroft Rockshelter and the Pleistocene/Holocene Transition in South-West Pennsylvania." In Hugh Genoways and Mary Dawson, eds., *Contributions in Quaternary Vertebrate Paleontology,* pp. 1–56. New York: Carnegie Museum of Natural History.

———. 1986. "Who Are Those Guys? An Examination of the Pre-Clovis Flintworking Complex from Meadowcroft Rockshelter and the Cross Creek Drainage." *American Antiquity* 62: 117–124.

Adovasio, J. M. and Carlisle, R., eds. 1988. *Americans before Columbus: Ice Age Origins.* Pittsburgh: University of Pittsburgh Ethnology Monographs 12.

Adovasio, J. M., Donahue, J., and Stuckenrath, R. 1990. "The Meadowcroft Rockshelter Radiocarbon Chronology, 1975–1990." *American Antiquity* 55 (2): 348–354.

Agrawal, D. P. 1982. "The Indian Bronze Age Cultures and Their Metal Technology." *Advances in World Archaeology* 1:213–264.

Aigner, Jean S. 1970. "The Unifacial, Core, and Blade Site on Anagula Island, Aleutians." *Arctic Anthropology* 7 (2):59–88.

Aikens, C. Melvin. 1970. *Hogup Cave.* Salt Lake City: University of Utah Press.

Aikens, C. Melvin, and Higuchi, Takayasu. 1981. *Prehistory of Japan.* New York: Academic Press.

Aitken, M. J. 1985. *Thermoluminescence Dating.* Orlando, FL: Academic Press.

———. 1990. *Science-Based Dating in Archaeology.* Reading, MA: Addison Wesley.

Akazawa, Takeru. 1982. "Cultural Change in Prehistoric Japan." *Advances in World Archaeology* 1:151–212.

Aldred, Cyril. 1968. *Akhenaten.* London: Thames and Hudson.

———. 1986. *The Egyptians,* 2d ed. New York: Thames and Hudson.

Allan, William. 1965. *The African Husbandman.* Edinburgh: Oliver and Boyd.

Allchin, Bridget. 1966. *The Stone Tipped Arrow.* New York: Barnes and Noble.

Allchin, Bridget, and Allchin, Raymond. 1983. *The Rise of Civilization in India and Pakistan.* Cambridge, Eng.: Cambridge University Press.

Allen, J. 1969. "The Hunting Neolithic: Adaptations to the Food Quest in Prehistoric Papua, New Guinea." In J. V. S. Megaw, ed., *Hunters, Gatherers, and First Farmers Beyond Europe* pp. 167–188. Atlantic Highlands, NJ: Humanities.

———. 1989. "When Did Humans First Colonize Australia?" *Search* 20 (5):149–154.

Allen, J., Golson, J., and Jones, Rhys, eds. 1977. *Sunda and Sahel: Prehistoric Studies in Southeast Asia, Melanesia, and Australia.* New York: Academic Press.

Allen, J., Gosden, C., and White, J. P. 1989. "Pleistocene New Ireland." *Antiquity* 63 (240):548–561

Allen, J., and White, J. P. 1989. "The Lapita Homeland: Some New Data and an Interpretation." *Journal of the Polynesian Society* 93:129–146.

Alpers, Edward A. 1975. *Ivory and Slaves in East Central Africa.* Berkeley and Los Angeles: University of California Press.

Alva, Walter. 1988. "Discovering the New World's Richest Unlooted Tomb." *National Geographic Magazine* 174 (4):510–548.

———. 1990. "New Royal Tomb Unearthed." *National Geographic Magazine* 177 (6):2–16.

Ambrose, Stanley H. 1984. "The Introduction of Pastoral Adaptations to the Highlands of East Africa." In J. Desmond Clark and Steven A. Brandt, eds., *From Hunters to Farmers,* pp. 212–239. Berkeley and Los Angeles: University of California Press.

Ammerman, A., and Cavalli-Sforza, L. 1973. "Measuring the Rate of Early Farming in Europe." In Colin Renfrew, ed., *The Explanation of Culture Change,* pp. 343–357. London: Duckworth.

Anderson, Arthur O., and Dibble, Charles, eds. 1978. *The Florentine Codex.* Salt Lake City: University of Utah Press.

Anderson, Atholl. 1987. "Recent Developments in Japanese Prehistory: A Review." *American Antiquity* 61 (232):270–281.

Anderson, D. G., and Hanson, Glen T. 1988. "Early Archaic Settlement in the Southeastern United States: A Case Study from the Savannah River Valley." *American Antiquity* 53 (2):262–286.

Anderson, Douglas. 1970. "Akmak." *Acta Arctica* 15:1–25.

———. 1979. "Archaeology and the Evidence for the Prehistoric Development of Eskimo Culture." *Arctic Anthropologist* 16 (1):16–26.

Anderson, J. E. 1969. *The Human Skeleton: A Manual for Archaeologists.* Ottawa: National Museum of Canada.

Andrews, E. W., and Hammond, Norman. 1990. "Redefinition of the Swasey Phase at Cuello, Belize." *American Antiquity* 55 (3):570–584.

Ascher, Marcia, and Ascher, Robert. 1981. *The Code of the Quipu.* Ann Arbor: University of Michigan Press.

Bahn, P., and Vertut, Jan. 1988. *Images of the Ice Age.* New York: Viking Press.

Bailey, G. N. 1978. "Shell Middens as Indicators of Postglacial Economies: A Territorial Perspective." In Paul Mellars, ed., *The Early Post Glacial Settlement of Northern Europe,* pp. 235–261. London: Duckworth.

Baillie, M. G. L. 1982. *Tree Ring Dating and Archaeology.* New York: Columbia University Press.

Bankes, George. 1977. *Peru Before Pizarro.* Oxford, Eng.: Phaidon.

Bannister, Bryant, and Robinson, William J. 1975. "Tree-Ring Dating in Archaeology." *World Archaeology* 7 (2):210–225.

Barker, Graham. 1985. *Prehistoric Farming in Europe.* Cambridge, Eng.: Cambridge University Press.

Barker, Phillip. 1983. *Techniques of Archaeological Excavation,* 2d ed. London: Batsford.

Barnard, Noel. 1961. *Bronze Casting and Bronze Alloys in Ancient China.* Canberra: Australian National University.

Barry, John C., et al. 1985. "Neogene Mammalian Faunal Change in Southern Asia: Correlations with Climatic, Tectonic, and Eustatic Events." *Geology* 13:637–640.

Bar-Yosef, O. 1975. "Archaeological Occurrences in the Middle Pleistocene of Israel." In Karl Butzer and Glynn Ll. Isaac, eds., *After the Australopithecines,* pp. 571–604. Chicago: Aldine.

———. 1986. "The Walls of Jericho." *Current Anthropology* 27 (2):157–162.

———. 1987. "Late Pleistocene Adaptations in the Levant." In Olga Soffer, ed., *The Pleistocene Old World: Regional Perspectives,* pp. 219–236. New York: Plenum.

Bar-Yosef, O., and Belfer-Cohen, A. 1989. "The Origins of Sedentism and Farming Communities in the Levant." *Journal of World Prehistory* 3 (4):447–498.

Bayard, Donn T. 1970. "Excavations at Non Nok Tha, Northeast Thailand, 1968: An Interim Report." *Asian Perspectives* 13:109–144.

———. 1972. "Early Thai Bronze: Analysis and New Dates." *Science* 176:1411–1421.

———. 1977. "Phu Wiang Pottery and the Prehistory of Northeastern Thailand."

In G. Bartstra et al., eds., *Modern Quaternary Research in Southeast Asia,* pp. 57–102. Rotterdam: Balkema.

———, ed. 1984. *The Origins of Agriculture, Metallurgy, and the State in Mainland Southeast Asia.* Dunedin, New Zealand: University of Otago Press.

———. 1986. "Agriculture, Metallurgy, and State Formation in Southeast Asia." *Current Anthropology* 25 (1):103–105.

Beadle, George. 1981. "The Ancestor of Corn." *Scientific American* 242 (1):96–103.

Beaumont, Peter. 1980. "On the Age of Border Cave Hominids 1–5." *Palaeontologica Africana* 23:21–33.

Bellwood, Peter. 1970. "Fortifications and Economy in Prehistoric New Zealand." *Proceedings of the Prehistoric Society* 37 (1):56–95.

———. 1979. *Man's Conquest of the Pacific.* Oxford, Eng.: Oxford University Press.

———. 1985. *The Prehistory of the Indo-Malaysian Archipelago.* North Ryde, NSW: Academic Press.

———. 1987a. *The Polynesians.* London: Thames and Hudson.

———. 1987b. "The Prehistory of Island Southeast Asia: A Multidisciplinary Review of Recent Research." *Advances in World Archaeology* 1 (2):171–224.

Bellwood, Peter, and Koon, J. 1989. "Lapita Colonists Leave Boats Unburned." *Antiquity* 63 (240):613–622.

Bender, Barbara. 1985. "Emergent Tribal Formations in the American Midcontinent." *American Antiquity* 50 (1):52–62.

Benfer, Robert. 1982. "The Lomas Site of Paloma (5000 to 7500 B.P.), Chilca Valley, Peru." In Ramerio Matos, ed., *Andean Archaeology,* pp. 27–54. New York: Academic Press.

Benson, Elizabeth, ed. 1971. *Dumbarton Oaks Conference on Chavín.* Washington, DC: Dumbarton Oaks.

———. 1979. *Pre-Columbian Metallurgy of South America.* Washington, DC: Dumbarton Oaks.

Bernal, Ignacio. 1969. *The Olmec World.* Berkeley and Los Angeles: University of California Press.

Bettinger, R. L. 1987. "Archaeological Approaches to Hunter-Gatherers," *Annual Review of Anthropology* 16:121–142.

Binford, Lewis R. 1964. "A Consideration of Archaeological Research Design." *American Antiquity* 29:425–441.

———. 1968. "Post-Pleistocene Adaptations." In L. R. Binford and S. Binford, eds., *New Perspectives in Archaeology,* pp. 313–341. Chicago: Aldine.

———. 1978. *Nunamiut Ethnoarchaeology.* New York: Academic Press.

———. 1979. "Organization and Formation Processes: Looking at Curated Technologies." *Journal of Anthropological Research* 35 (3):225–273.

———. 1980. "Willow Smoke and Dog's Tails: Hunter-Gatherer Settlement Systems and Archaeological Formation Processes." *American Antiquity* 45 (1):4–20.

———. 1981. *Bones.* New York: Academic Press.

———. 1983. *In Pursuit of the Past.* New York: Thames and Hudson.

———. 1984. *Faunal Remains from Klasies River Mouth.* New York: Academic Press.

Binford, Lewis R., and Binford, Sally. 1966. "A Preliminary Analysis of Functional

Variability in the Mousterian of Levallois Facies." *American Anthropologist* 68 (2):238–295.

Binford, Lewis R., and Chuan Kun Ho. 1986. "Taphonomy at a Distance." *Current Anthropology* 26 (4):413–442.

Binford, Lewis R., and Stone, Nancy. 1986. "Zhoukoudien: A Closer Look." *Current Anthropology* 27 (5):453–475.

Birdsell, J. 1977. "The Recalibration of a Paradigm for the First Peopling of Greater Australia." In J. Allen, J. Golson, and R. Jones, eds., *Sunda and Sahul*, pp. 113–167. Orlando, FL: Academic Press.

Blanc, Alberto C. 1961. "Some Evidence for the Ideologies of Early Man." In S. L. Washburn, ed., *The Social Life of Early Man*, pp. 119–136. New York: Viking Fund.

Blanton, Richard E. 1978. *Monte Albán: Settlement Patterns at the Ancient Zapotec Capital.* New York: Academic Press.

———. 1983. "Advances in the Study of Cultural Evolution in Prehispanic Highland Mesoamerica." *Advances in World Archaeology* 2:245–288.

Blegen, Carl. 1971. *Troy.* London: Thames and Hudson.

Bogucki, Peter, and Grygiel, Ryszard. 1983. "Early Farmers of the North European Plain." *Scientific American* 248 (4):105–115.

Bonsell, Clive. ed. 1989. *The Mesolithic in Europe.* Edinburgh: Edinburgh University Press.

Bonzek, Jan, ed. 1985. *The Aegean, Anatolia, and Europe in the 2nd Millenium B.C.* New York: Academic Press.

———. 1988. *Forest Farmers and Stockherders.* Cambridge, Eng.: Cambridge University Press.

Bordes, François. 1968. *The Old Stone Age.* New York: McGraw-Hill.

Boserup, Ester. 1965. *The Conditions of Agricultural Growth: The Economics of Agrarian Change Under Population Pressure.* Chicago: Aldine.

Boule, Marcellin, and Vallois, H. 1957. *Fossil Men.* London: Thames and Hudson.

Bovill, E. W. 1968. *The Golden Trade of the Moors.* London: Heinemann.

Bowdler, J. M., Jones, R., and Thorne, A. G. 1970. "Pleistocene Human Remains from Australia: A Living Site and Human Cremation from Lake Mungo, Western New South Wales." *World Archaeology* 2:39–60.

Bower, John R. F. 1984. "Settlement Behavior of Pastoral Cultures in East Africa." In J. Desmond Clark and Steven A. Brandt, eds., *From Hunters to Farmers*, pp. 252–259. Berkeley and Los Angeles: University of California Press.

Braidwood, L. S., ed. 1982. *Prehistoric Village Archaeology in South-eastern Turkey.* Oxford, Eng.: British Archaeological Reports, International Series, no. 138.

Braidwood, R. J., and Braidwood, L. S., eds. 1983. *Prehistoric Archaeology Along the Zagros Flanks.* Chicago: Oriental Institute.

Braidwood, R. J., and Cambel, H. 1980. *Prehistoric Research in Southeastern Anatolia.* Istanbul: Edebiyat Facultesi Basimevi.

Brain, C. K. 1981. *The Hunters or the Hunted: An Introduction to African Cave Taphonomy.* Chicago: University of Chicago Press.

Brauer, Günter. 1984. "A Craniological Approach to the Origin of Anatomically

Modern *Homo sapiens* in Africa and Implications for the Appearance of Modern Europeans." In Fred Smith and Frank Spencer, eds., *The Origins of Modern Humans*, pp. 327–410. New York: Liss.

Breuil, Henri. 1908. *La Caverne d'Altamira*. Paris: Payot.

————. 1952. *Four Hundred Centuries of Cave Art*. Montignac, France: Centre d'Etudes et de Documentation.

Briggs, L. Cabot. 1951. "The Ancient Khmer Empire." *Transactions of the American Philosophical Society*, no. 41.

Brodie, Fawn. 1957. *The Devil Drives*. London: Eyre and Spottiswoode.

Brose, David C. 1979. "A Speculative Model of the Role of Exchange in the Prehistory of the Eastern Woodlands." In David C. Brose and N'omi Greber, eds., *Hopewellian Archaeology*, pp. 3–8. Kent, OH: Kent State University Press.

Brose, David C., and Greber, N'omi. 1979. *Hopewellian Archaeology*. Kent, OH: Kent State University Press.

Brothwell, Don R. 1985. *Digging Up Bones*. London: British Museum.

Browman, David L. 1978. "Toward the Development of the Tiahuanaco (Tiwanaku) State." In David L. Browman, ed., *Advances in Andean Archaeology*, pp. 327–349. The Hague: Mouton.

Brown J., and Phillips, J., eds. 1983. *Late Archaic Hunter-Gatherers in the Midwest*. New York: Academic Press.

Brumfiel, Elizabeth. 1983. "Aztec State Making: Ecology, Structure, and the Origin of the State." *American Anthropologist* 85 (2):261–284.

Bryan, Alan Lyle, ed. 1978. *Early Man in America from a Circum-Pacific Perspective*. Edmonton: University of Alberta.

————. 1986. *New Evidence for the Pleistocene Peopling of the Americas*. Orono, ME: Center for the Study of Early Man.

Bryant, Vaughn. 1974. "Prehistoric Diet in South Texas: The Coprolite Evidence." *American Antiquity* 39:100–109.

Bunn, Henry, and Kroll, J. 1986. "Systematic Butchery by Plio/Pleistocene Hominids at Olduvai Gorge, Tanzania." *Current Anthropology* 27 (5):431–451.

Bunn, Henry, et al. 1980. "FxJj50: An Early Pleistocene Site in Northern Kenya." *World Archaeology* 12 (2):109–136.

Burger, Richard L. 1981. "The Radiocarbon Evidence for the Temporal Priority of Chavín de Huántar." *American Antiquity* 46:592–602.

————. 1984. *The Prehistoric Occupation of Chavín de Huántar*. Berkeley and Los Angeles: University of California Press.

————. 1985. "Prehistoric Stylistic Change and Cultural Development at Huaricoto, Peru." *National Geographic Research* 1 (4):505–534.

Burger, Richard L., and Salazar-Burger, Lucy. 1985. "The Early Ceremonial Center of Huaricoto." In Christopher Donnan, ed., *Early Ceremonial Architecture in the Andes*, pp. 111–138. Washington, DC: Dumbarton Oaks.

Butzer, Karl. 1971. *Environment and Archaeology*. Chicago: Aldine.

————. 1974. *Environment and Archaeology*, 3d ed. Chicago: Aldine.

————. 1976. *Early Hydraulic Civilization in Egypt*. Chicago: University of Chicago Press.

————. 1981. "Civilizations: Organisms or Systems?" *American Scientist* 68:517–524.

————. 1982. *Archaeology as Human Ecology: Method and Theory for a Contextual Approach.* Cambridge, Eng.: Cambridge University Press.

Butzer, Karl, and Isaac, Glynn Ll., eds. 1975. *After the Australopithecines.* Chicago: Aldine.

Byrd, B. F. 1989. "The Natufian: Settlement Variability and Economic Adaptation in the Levant at the End of the Pleistocene." *Journal of World Prehistory* 3 (2): 159–198.

Caldwell, Joseph R. 1958. *Trend and Tradition in the Prehistory of the Eastern United States.* Washington, DC: American Anthropological Association Memoir 88.

Campbell, Bernard. 1985. *Humankind Emerging,* 3d ed. Boston: Little, Brown.

Canby, Thomas. 1979. "The Search for the First Americans." *National Geographic Magazine,* September, 1979, pp. 330–363.

Caneva, I., Frangipane, M., and Palmiere, A. 1987. "Predynastic Egypt: New Data from Maadi." *African Archaeological Review* 5:105–114.

Cann, R. L., et al. 1987. "Mitochrondrial DNA and Human Evolution." *Nature* 325:31–36.

Carneiro, Robert L. 1970. "A Theory of the Origin of the State." *Science* 169:733–738.

Carter, George F. 1981. *Earlier Than You Think.* College Station: Texas A & M University Press.

Carter, Howard. 1923. *The Tomb of Tut-ankh-Amun.* London: Macmillan.

Caton-Thompson, G., and Gardner, E. W. 1934. *The Desert Fayum,* 2 vols. London: Royal Anthropological Institute.

Ceram, C. W. 1953. *Gods, Graves and Scholars.* New York: Knopf.

Chadwick, John. 1958. *The Decipherment of Linear B.* Cambridge, Eng.: Cambridge University Press.

Chagnon, Napoleon, and Irons, J., eds. 1979. *Evolutionary Biology and Social Behavior.* North Scituate, MA: Duxbury.

Champion, Timothy G., et al. 1984. *Prehistoric Europe.* New York: Academic Press.

Chang Kwang-Chih. 1980. *Shang Civilization.* New Haven, CT: Yale University Press.

————. 1981. "In Search of China's Beginnings: New Light on an Old Civilization." *American Scientist* 60:148–160.

————. 1986. *The Archaeology of Ancient China,* 4th ed. New Haven, CT: Yale University Press.

Chapman, Jefferson, et al. 1982. "Man-Land Interaction: 10,000 Years of American Indian Impact on Native Ecosystems in the Lower Little Tennessee Valley, Eastern Tennessee." *Southeastern Archeology* 1:115–121.

Childe, V. G. 1936. *Man Makes Himself.* London: Watts.

————. 1942. *What Happened in History.* London: Routledge & Kegan Paul.

————. 1952. *New Light on the Most Ancient East.* London: Routledge & Kegan Paul.

————. 1956. *Piecing Together the Past.* London: Routledge & Kegan Paul.

————. 1958. "Retrospect." *Antiquity* 32:69–74.

Chippindale, Christopher. 1983. *Stonehenge Complete.* London: Thames and Hudson.

Chung Tang and Pei Gai. 1986. "Upper Palaeolithic Cultural Traditions in North China." *Advances in World Archaeology* 5:339–364.

Cinq-Mars, Jacques. 1979. "Bluefish Cave I: A Late Pleistocene Eastern Beringian Cave Deposit in the Northern Yukon." *Canadian Journal of Anthropology* 3:1–32.

Clark, Geoffrey, and Yi Seonbok. 1983. "Niche-Width Variation in Cantabrian Archaeofaunas." In Juliet Clutton-Brock and Caroline Grigson, eds., *Hunters and Their Prey.* Vol. 1, *Animals and Archaeology,* pp. 183–208. Oxford, Eng.: British Archaeological Reports, International Series No. 163.

Clark, J. Desmond. 1959. *The Prehistory of Southern Africa.* Baltimore: Pelican.

———. 1967. "The Problem of Neolithic Culture in Sub-Saharan Africa." In W. W. Bishop and J. Desmond Clark, eds., *Background to Evolution in Africa,* pp. 601–628. Chicago: University of Chicago Press.

———. 1970. *The Prehistory of Africa.* London: Thames and Hudson.

———. 1971. "A Re-examination of the Evidence for Agricultural Origins in the Nile Valley." *Proceedings of the Prehistoric Society* 37 (2):34–79.

———. 1983. "The Significance of Culture Change in the Early Later Pleistocene in Northern and Southern Africa." In Erik Trinkhaus, ed., *The Mousterian Legacy,* pp. 1–12. Oxford, Eng.: British Archaeological Reports, International Series, No. 151.

———. 1984. "Prehistoric Cultural Continuity and Economic Change in the Central Sudan in the Early Holocene." In J. Desmond Clark and Steven A. Brandt, eds., *From Hunters to Farmers,* pp. 113–126. Berkeley and Los Angeles: University of California Press.

Clark, J. D., and Brandt, Steven A., eds. 1984. *From Hunters to Farmers.* Berkeley: University of California Press.

Clark, J. Desmond, and Harris, J. W. K. 1985. "Fire and Its Roles in Early Hominid Lifeways." *African Archaeological Review* 3:3–28.

Clark, J. G. D. 1952. *Prehistoric Europe: The Economic Basis.* Palo Alto, CA: Stanford University Press.

———. 1954. *Star Carr.* Cambridge, Eng.: Cambridge University Press.

———. 1958. "Blade and Trapeze Industries of the European Stone Age." *Proceedings of the Prehistoric Society* 24:24–42.

———. 1965. *Archaeology and Society.* New York: Barnes and Noble.

———. 1975. *The Earlier Stone Age Settlement of Scandinavia.* Cambridge, Eng.: Cambridge University Press.

———. 1979. *Mesolithic Prelude.* Edinburgh: Edinburgh University Press.

Clutton-Brock, Juliet. 1981. *Domesticated Animals from Early Times.* Austin: University of Texas Press.

Coe, M. D. 1968. *America's First Civilization: Discovering the Olmec.* New York: American Heritage.

———. 1984. *The Maya,* 3d ed. London: Thames and Hudson.

Coe, Michael D., and Diehl, Richard. 1980. *In the Land of the Olmec,* 2 vols. Austin: University of Texas Press.

Coe, William, and Haviland, William A. 1982. *Introduction to the Archaeology of Tikal, Guatemala.* Philadelphia: University Museum, University of Pennsylvania. (The first of a projected 39 reports on Tikal.)

Coggins, Clemency. 1985. *The Sacred Cenote of Sacrifice.* Austin: University of Texas Press.

Cohen, Mark, 1977. *The Food Crisis in Prehistory.* New Haven, CT: Yale University Press.

———. 1988. *Health and the Rise of Civilization.* New Haven, CT: Yale University Press.

Cohen, Mark, and Armelagos, G., eds. 1984. *Paleopathology at the Origins of Agriculture.* Orlando, FL: Academic Press.

Coles, J. M. 1973. *Archaeology by Experiment.* London: Heinemann.

———. 1982. "The Bronze Age in North West Europe: Problems and Advances." *Advances in World Archaeology* 1:266–321.

Coles, J. M., and Harding, A. F. 1979. *The Bronze Age in Europe.* London: Methuen.

Collis, John. 1984. *The European Iron Age.* London: Batsford.

Colwell, R. N., ed. 1983. *Manual of Remote Sensing,* 2d ed. Falls Church, VA: American Society of Photogrammetry.

Connah, Graham. 1987. *African Civilizations.* Cambridge, Eng.: Cambridge University Press.

Conrad, Geoffrey W., and Demarest, Arthur A. 1984. *Religion and Empire: The Dynamics of Aztec and Inca Expansionism.* Cambridge, Eng.: Cambridge University Press.

Cooper, J. S. 1983. *Reconstructing History from Ancient Inscriptions: The Lagash-Umma Border Dispute.* Malibu, CA: Undena Publications.

Cordell, Linda. 1984a. *The Archaeology of the Southwest.* New York: Academic Press.

———. 1984b. "Southwestern Archaeology." *Annual Review of Anthropology* 13:130–132.

Cosgrove, R., Allen, J., and Marshall, B. 1990. "Pleistocene Occupation of Tasmania." *Antiquity* 64 (242):59–78.

Courand, Claude. 1985. *L'Art Azilien.* Paris: Gallia Prehistoire.

Covey, Curt. 1984. "The Earth's Orbit and the Ice Ages." *Scientific American* 280 (2):58–77.

Cranstone, B. A. L. 1972. "The Tifalmin: A Neolithic People in New Guinea." *World Archaeology* 3 (2):132–142.

Crawford, O. G. S. 1953. *Archaeology in the Field.* New York: Praeger.

Creamer, Winifred, and Haas, Jonathan. 1985. "Tribes versus Chiefdoms in Lower Central America." *American Antiquity* 50 (4):738–754.

Croes, Dale, and Hackenberger, S. 1988. "Hoko River Archaeological Complex: Modelling Prehistoric Northwest Coast Economic Evolution." *Research in Economic Anthropology* Supplement 3: 19–85.

Culbert, T. Patrick, ed. 1973. *The Classic Maya Collapse.* Albuquerque: University of New Mexico Press.

———. 1988a. "The Collapse of Classic Maya Civilization." In Norman Yoffee and George Cowgill, eds., *The Collapse of Ancient States and Civilizations.* Tucson: University of Arizona Press.

———. 1988b. "Political History and the Decipherment of Maya Glyphs." *Antiquity* 62 (234): 135–152.

Cunliffe, Barry. 1974. *Iron Age Communities in Britain.* London: Routledge & Kegan Paul.

D'Acevedo, Warren. 1986. *The Great Basin.* Vol. 5, *Handbook of North American Indians.* Washington, DC: Smithsonian Institution.

Dalrymple, C. Brent, and Lamphere, Mason. 1970. *Potassium Argon Dating: Principles, Techniques and Applications in Geochronology.* San Francisco: Freeman.

Daniel, Glyn E. 1973. *Megaliths in History.* London: Thames and Hudson.

———. 1981. *A Short History of Archaeology.* London: Thames and Hudson.

Dart, Raymond A. 1925. "*Australopithecus africanus:* The Man-Ape of Southern Africa." *Nature* 115:195.

———. 1957. *The Osteodontokeratic Culture of Australopithecus prometheus.* Pretoria: Transvaal Museum.

Davidson, Janet. 1985. "New Zealand Prehistory." *Advances in World Archaeology* 4:239–292.

Davies, Nigel. 1973. *The Aztecs.* Norman: University of Oklahoma Press.

———. 1977. *The Toltecs.* Norman: University of Oklahoma Press.

———. 1979. *Voyages to the New World: Fact or Fantasy.* London: Macmillan.

———. 1980. *The Toltec Heritage.* Norman: University of Oklahoma Press.

Davis, Richard S. 1987. "Regional Perspectives on the Soviet Central Asian Paleolithic." In Olga Soffer, ed., *The Pleistocene Old World: Regional Perspectives,* pp. 121–134. New York: Plenum.

Deacon, Hilary. 1979. "Excavations at Boomplas Cave: A Sequence Through the Upper Pleistocene and Holocene in South Africa." *World Archaeology* 10:241–257.

Deetz, James. 1967. *Invitation to Archaeology.* Garden City, NY: Natural History Press.

Delcourt, P. A., and Delcourt, H. R. 1981. "Vegetation Maps for Eastern North America." *Geobotany* 2:123–165.

Delson, Eric. 1986. "Human Phylogeny Revised Again." *Nature* 322:496–497.

Demarest, Arthur. 1989. "The Olmec and the Rise of Civilization in Eastern Mesoamerica." In Robert Sharer and David Grove, eds., *Regional Perspectives on the Olmec,* pp. 303–344. Cambridge, Eng.: Cambridge University Press.

Dennell, Robin C. 1983. *European Economic Prehistory: A New Approach.* New York: Academic Press.

Diaz, Bernal. 1963. *The True History of the Conquest of New Spain.* Translated by J. M. Cohen. Baltimore: Pelican.

Dibble, Charles E., and Anderson, Arthur J. O. 1978. *Florentine Codex,* Vol. 14. Salt Lake City: University of Utah Press.

Dibble, Harold. 1987. "Reduction Sequences in the Manufacture of Mousterian Implements of France." In Olga Soffer, ed., *The Pleistocene Old World: Regional Perspectives,* pp. 33–46. New York: Plenum.

Diehl, Richard. 1989. "Olmec Archaeology: What We Know and What We Wish We Knew." In Robert Sharer and David Grove, eds., *Regional Perspectives on the Olmec,* pp. 17–32. Cambridge, Eng.: Cambridge University Press.

———. 1984. *Tula.* London: Thames and Hudson.

Dillehay, Tom. 1984. "A Late Ice Age Settlement in Southern Chile," *Scientific American* 254 (4):100–109.

———. 1990. *Monte Verde: A Late Pleistocene Settlement in Chile.* Washington, DC: Smithsonian Institution.

Dincauze, Dena. 1983. "An Archaeo-Logical Evaluation of the Case for Pre-Clovis Occupations." *Advances in World Archaeology* 3:275–324.

————. 1989. "Meadowcroft Questions and Answers." *Quarterly Journal of Archaeology* 10 (1):144–146.

Di Peso, C. C., et al. 1974. *Casas Grandes: A Fallen Trading Center of the Gran Chichimeca.* Flagstaff, AZ: AmerInd Foundation.

Diringer, David. 1962. *Writing.* New York: Praeger.

Dolukhanov, Paul H. 1982. "Upper Pleistocene and Holocene Cultures of the Russian Plain and Caucasus." *Advances in World Archaeology* 1:323–358.

————. 1986. "The Late Mesolithic and the Transition to Food Production in Eastern Europe." In Marek Zvelebil, ed., *Hunters in Transition,* pp. 109–120. Cambridge, Eng.: Cambridge University Press.

Donnan, Christopher B., ed. 1985. *Early Ceremonial Architecture in the Andes.* Washington, DC: Dumbarton Oaks.

————. 1989. "Unraveling the Mystery of the Warrior Priest." *National Geographic Magazine* 174 (4):550–555.

————. 1990. "Master Works Reveal a Pre-Inca World." *National Geographic Magazine* 177 (6):34–49.

Donnan, Christopher B., and McClelland, Donna. 1979. *The Burial Theme in Moche Iconography.* Washington, DC: Dumbarton Oaks.

Dorn, R. I., Nobbs, M., Cahill, T. A. 1988. "Cation-ratio Dating of Rock Engravings." *Antiquity* 62 (237):681–689.

Dortch, Charles, and Merrilees, Duncan. 1973. "Human Occupation of Devil's Lair, Western Australia, During the Pleistocene." *Archaeology and Physical Anthropology in Oceania* 8:89–115.

Dragoo, Don W. 1976. "Some Aspects of Eastern North American Prehistory: A Review 1975." *American Antiquity* 41 (1):3–27.

Drucker, Phillip. 1959. *La Venta, Tabasco: A Study of Olmec Ceramics and Art.* Washington, DC: Smithsonian Institution.

Dumond, Don. 1987a. *The Eskimos and Aleuts.* London: Thames and Hudson.

————. 1987b. "A Reexamination of Eskimo-Aleut Prehistory." *American Anthropologist* 89 (1):32–56.

Dunnell, Robert C. 1971. *Systematics in Prehistory.* New York: Free Press.

————. 1980. "Evolutionary Theory and Archaeology." *Advances in Archaeological Method and Theory* 3:35–99.

Earle, Timothy. 1978. *Economic and Social Organization of a Complex Chiefdom: The Halelea District, Kaua'i, Hawaii.* Ann Arbor: Museum of Anthropology, University of Michigan.

Ebert, J. I. 1984. "Remote Sensing Applications in Archaeology." *Advances in Archaeological Method and Theory* 7:293–362.

Edwards, I. E. S. 1973. *The Pyramids.* New York: Viking Press.

Eisenberg, J. F. 1981. *The Mammalian Radiation.* London: Athlone.

Eliade, Mircea. 1954. *The Myth of the Eternal Return.* New York: Pantheon.

————. 1959. *The Sacred and the Profane.* New York: Harcourt, Brace.

El Mahdy, Christine. 1989. *Mummies, Myth, and Magic in Ancient Egypt.* New York: Thames and Hudson.

Elphick, Richard. 1977. *Kraal and Castle.* New Haven, CT: Yale University Press.

Emory, Kenneth P. 1972. "Easter Island's Position in the Prehistory of Polynesia." *Journal of the Polynesian Society* 81:57–69.

Engel, Frederic. 1957. "Early Sites on the Peruvian Coast." *Southwestern Journal of Anthropology* 13:54–68.

Evans, Sir Arthur J. 1921. *The Palace of Minos at Knossos*, 4 vols. Oxford, Eng.: Clarendon.

Fagan, Brian M. 1979. *Return to Babylon*. Boston: Little, Brown.

——. 1984a. *The Aztecs*. New York: Freeman.

——. 1984b. *Clash of Cultures*. New York: Freeman.

——. 1985. *The Adventure of Archaeology*. Washington, DC: National Geographic Society.

——. 1987. *The Great Journey*. London: Thames and Hudson.

——. 1990. *The Journey from Eden*. New York: Thames and Hudson.

——. 1991a. *Ancient North America*. New York: Thames and Hudson.

——. 1991b. *Archaeology: A Brief Introduction*, 4th ed. New York: HarperCollins.

——. 1991c. *In the Beginning*, 7th ed. New York: HarperCollins.

Fagan, Brian M., and van Noten, F. 1971. *The Hunter-Gatherers of Gwisho*. Tervuren. Belgium: Musée Royal de l'Afrique Centrale.

Fagles, Robert. 1990. *The Iliad*. New York: Viking.

Fairbanks, Richard G. 1989. "A 17,000-year Glacio-Eustatic Sea Level Record: Influence of Glacial Melting Rates on the Younger Dryas Event and Deep Sea Circulation." *Nature* 342:637–642.

Fairservis, Walter A. 1976. *The Roots of Ancient India*, 2d ed. New York: Macmillan.

——. 1983. "The Script of the Indus Valley Civilization." *Scientific American* 243 (3):58–77.

Falk, Dean. 1984. "The Petrified Brain." *Natural History* 93 (9):36–39.

Farnsworth, Paul, et al. 1985. "A Re-evaluation of the Isotopic and Archaeological Reconstruction of Diet in the Tehuacán Valley." *American Antiquity* 50 (1):102–116.

Fash, William. 1989. "The Sculpture Façade of Structure 9N-82: Content, Form, and Meaning." In David Webster, ed., *The House of the Bacabs*, pp. 212–237. Washington, DC: Dumbarton Oaks.

Fedden, Robin. 1977. *Egypt*. London: Murray.

Feder, Kenneth L. 1990. *Frauds, Myths, and Mysteries*. Mountain View, CA: Mayfield.

Fedigan, L. M. 1986. "The Changing Role of Women in Models of Human Evolution." *Annual Review of Anthropology* 15:25–66.

Fell, Barry. 1976. *America B.C.* New York: Times Books.

——. 1980. *Saga America*. New York: Times Books.

Finley, M. I. 1963. *The Ancient Greeks*. London: Chatto & Windus.

Finney, Ben R. 1967. "New Perspectives on Pacific Voyaging." In Genevieve Highland et al., eds., *Polynesian Culture History*, pp. 141–166. Honolulu: Bishop Museum.

Fish, P. R., and Fish, S. R. 1977. *Verde Valley Archaeology: Review and Perspective*. Flagstaff: Museum of Northern Arizona.

Fitzgerald, Patrick. 1978. *Ancient China*. Oxford, Eng.: Elsevier Phaidon.

Fladmark, Knud. 1978. *A Palaeoecological Model for Northwest Coast Prehistory*. Ottawa: National Museums of Canada.

Flannery, Kent V. 1965. "The Ecology of Early Food Production in Mesopotamia." *Science* 147:1247–1256.

———. 1968a. "Archaeological Systems Theory and Early Mesoamerica." In Betty Meggers, ed., *Anthropological Archaeology in the Americas*, pp. 67–87. Washington, DC: Anthropological Society of Washington.

———. 1968b. "The Olmec and the Valley of Oaxaca: A Model for Interregional Interaction in Formative Times." In Elizabeth Benson, ed., *Dumbarton Oaks Conference on the Olmec*, pp. 79–110. Washington, DC: Dumbarton Oaks.

———. 1969. "Origins and Ecological Effects of Early Domestication in Animals." In Peter J. Ucko and G. W. Dimbleby, eds., *The Domestication and Exploitation of Plants and Animals*, pp. 207–218. London: Duckworth.

———. 1972. "The Cultural Evolution of Civilizations." *Annual Review of Ecology and Systematics.* 4:399–426.

———. 1973. "The Origins of Agriculture." *Annual Review of Anthropology* 2:271–310.

———, ed. 1976. *The Early Mesoamerican Village*. New York: Academic Press.

———, ed. 1982. *Maya Subsistence*. New York: Academic Press.

———. 1983. "Settlement, Subsistence, and Social Organization of the Proto-Otomangueans." In Kent V. Flannery and Joyce Marcus, eds., *The Cloud People*, pp. 32–36. New York: Academic Press.

Flannery, Kent V., and Marcus, Joyce, eds. 1983. *The Cloud People*. New York: Academic Press.

Flannery, Kent V., et al. 1981. "The Preceramic and Formative of the Valley of Oaxaca." In Jeremy A. Sabloff, ed., *Archeology*. Vol. 1, *Supplement to the Handbook of American Indians*, pp. 48–93. Austin: University of Texas Press.

Flannery, Kent V., et al. 1986. *Guilá Naquitz*. Orlando, FL: Academic Press.

Fleischer, Robert L. 1975. "Advances in Fission Track Dating." *World Archaeology* 7 (2):136–150.

Flenniken, Jeffrey. 1988. "Morphological Projectile Point Typology: Replication Experimentation and Technological Analysis." *American Antiquity* 62:111–121.

Flint, R. F. 1971. *Glacial and Quaternary Geology*. New York: Wiley.

Folan, William J., et al. 1983. *Coba: A Classic Maya Metropolis*. New York: Academic Press.

Foley, Robert. 1981. *Off-site Archaeology and Human Adaptation in Eastern Africa*. Oxford, Eng.: British Archaeological Reports, International Series, No. 97.

———. 1984a. "Early Man and the Red Queen." In Robert Foley, ed., *Hominid Evolution and Community Ecology*, pp. 85–110. London: Academic Press.

———, ed. 1984b. *Hominid Evolution and Community Ecology: Prehistoric Human Adaptation in Biological Perspective*. London: Academic Press.

———. 1984c. "Putting People into Perspective." In Robert Foley, ed., *Hominid Evolution and Community Ecology*, pp. 1–24. London: Academic Press.

———. 1987. "Hominid Species and Stone-Tool Assemblages: How Are They Related?" *Antiquity* 61:380–392.

Ford, Richard I., ed. 1985. *Prehistoric Food Production in North America*. Ann Arbor: University of Michigan Museum of Anthropology.

Forest, J. D. 1986. "Tell el-Oueili: Preliminary Report on the 4th Season." *Iraq* 44 (1–2):55–60.

Fowler, Melvin L. 1958. *Modoc Rockshelter*. Springfield: Illinois State Museum.

———. 1969. "The Cahokia Site." In Melvin L. Fowler, ed., *Investigations in Cahokia Archaeology*, pp. 1–14. Urbana: Illinois Archaeological Survey.

———. 1978. "Cahokia and the American Bottom: Settlement Archaeology." In Bruce D. Smith, ed., *Mississippian Settlement Patterns*, pp. 455–478. New York: Academic Press.

Freeman, Leslie, and Echegaray, Jesús. 1981. "El Juyo: A 14,000-Year-Old Sanctuary from Northern Spain." *History of Religions* 21:1–19.

Freidel, David, and Schele, Linda. 1988a. "Kingship in the Late Preclassic Lowlands." *American Anthropologist* 90 (3):547–567.

———. 1988b. "Symbol and Power: A History of the Lowland Maya Cosmogram." In Elizabeth Benson and Gillett Griffin, *Maya Iconography*. Princeton, NJ: Princeton University Press.

Frison, George C. 1978. *Prehistoric Hunters of the High Plains*. New York: Academic Press.

Galinat, Walter C. 1985. "Domestication and Diffusion of Maize." In Richard I. Ford, ed., *Prehistoric Food Production in North America*, pp. 245–278. Ann Arbor: University of Michigan Museum of Anthropology.

Galloway, P., ed. 1989. *The Southeastern Ceremonial Complex*. Lincoln: University of Nebraska Press.

Gamble, Clive. 1986a. "The Mesolithic Sandwich." In Marek Zvelebil, ed., *Hunters in Transition*. pp. 33–42. Cambridge, Eng.: Cambridge University Press.

———. 1986b. *The Palaeolithic Settlement of Europe*. Cambridge, Eng.: Cambridge University Press.

Gardner, R. Allen, and Gardner, Beatrice A. 1969. "Teaching Sign Language to a Chimpanzee." *Science* 163:664–672.

Garlake, Peter. 1973. *Great Zimbabwe*. New York: McGraw-Hill.

Garrod, D. A. E. 1951. "A Transitional Industry from the Base of the Upper Palaeolithic in Palestine and Syria," *Journal of the Royal Anthropological Institute* 81:121–129.

Garrod, D. A. E., and Bate, Dorothea. 1937. *The Stone Age of Mount Carmel*. Cambridge, Eng.: Cambridge University Press.

Gasparini, Graziano, and Margolies, Luise. 1980. *Inca Architecture*. Bloomington: Indiana University Press.

Gingerich, Phillip D. 1985. "Nonlinear Molecular Clocks and Ape-Human Divergence Times." In Philip V. Tobias, ed., *Hominid Evolution: Past, Present, and Future*, pp. 441–466. New York: Liss.

Giteau, M. 1966. *Khmer Sculpture and the Angkor Civilization*. London: Thames and Hudson.

Golson, Jack. 1977. "No Room at the Top: Agricultural Intensification in the New Guinea Highlands." In J. Allen, J. Golson, and Rhys Jones, eds., *Sunda and Sahel*. pp. 602–638. New York: Academic Press.

———. 1986. *The Chimpanzees of Gombe.* Cambridge, MA: Harvard University Press.

Gorman, Chester A. 1969. "Hoabhinian: A Pebble-Tool Complex with Early Plant Associations in Southeast Asia." *Science* 163:671–673.

———. 1971. "Hoabhinian and After: Subsistence Patterns in Southeast Asia During the Late Pleistocene and Early Recent Periods." *World Archaeology* 2 (3):300–320.

Gosden, C., Allen, J., et al. 1989. "Lapita Sites of the Bismarck Archipelago," *Antiquity* 63 (240):561–586.

Goudie, Andrew. 1983. *Environmental Change,* 2d ed. Oxford, Eng.: Clarendon Press.

Gould, Richard A. 1977. *Puntutjarpa Rockshelter and Australian Desert Culture.* New York: American Museum of Natural History.

———, ed. 1978. *Explorations in Ethnoarchaeology.* Albuquerque: University of New Mexico Press.

———. 1980. *Living Archaeology.* Cambridge, Eng.: Cambridge University Press.

Gould, S. J. 1977. *Ever Since Darwin: Reflections in Natural History.* Baltimore: Penguin.

Gowlett, John. 1978. "Culture and Conceptualization: The Oldowan-Acheulian Gradient." In G. N. Bailey and P. Callow, eds., *Stone Age Prehistory,* pp. 243–260. Cambridge, Eng.: Cambridge University Press.

———. 1984. "Mental Abilities of Early Man." In Robert Foley, ed., *Hominid Evolution and Community Ecology,* pp. 167–192. London: Academic Press.

———. 1986. "Culture and Conceptualization." In G. N. Bailey and P. Callow, eds., *Stone Age Prehistory,* pp. 243–260. Cambridge, Eng.: Cambridge University Press.

———. 1987. "The Archaeology of Radiocarbon Accelerator Dating." *Journal of World Prehistory* 1 (2):127–170.

Grant, Michael. 1960. *The Romans.* London: Weidenfeld and Nicholson.

Grasiosi, Paolo. 1960. *Palaeolithic Art.* New York: Abrams.

Grayson, Donald K. 1983. *The Search for Human Antiquity.* New York: Academic Press.

Green, R. C. 1969. "Lapita." In Jesse D. Jennings, ed., *The Prehistory of Polynesia,* pp. 27–60. Cambridge, MA: Harvard University Press.

Greenberg, Joseph. 1987. *Language in the Americas.* Palo Alto, CA: Stanford University Press.

Griffin, J. B. 1967. "Eastern North American Prehistory: A Summary." *Science* 156:175–191.

Grootes, P. M. 1978. "Carbon-14 Time Scale Extended: Comparison of Chronologies." *Science* 200 (4337):11–15.

Groube, L. M. 1970. "The Origins and Development of Earthwork Fortifications in the Pacific." In R. C. Green and M. Kelly, eds., *Studies in Oceanic Culture History,* pp. 133–164. Hawaii: Bishop Museum.

Groube, L., et al. 1986. "40,000-Year-Old Human Occupation Site at Huon Peninsula, Papua, New Guinea." *Nature* 324:453–455.

Grove, David. 1973. "Olmec Altars and Myths." *Archaeology* 26:128–135.

Groves, Colin P. 1989. "A Regional Approach to the Problem of Modern Humans in Australasia." In Paul Mellars and Christopher Stringer, eds., *The Human Revolution,* pp. 274–285. Edinburgh: Edinburgh University Press.

Grygiel, Ryszard, and Bogucki, P. 1986. "Early Neolithic Sites at Brzesc Kujawski, Poland." *Journal of Field Archaeology* 13 (2):121–138.

Guidon, Niede, and Delibrias, G. 1986. "Carbon 14 Dates Point to Man in the Americas 32,000 Years Ago." *Nature* 321:769–771.

Haas, Jonathan, et al., eds. 1987. *The Origins and Development of the Andean State.* Cambridge, Eng.: Cambridge University Press.

Haland, Randi, and Shinnie, Peter. 1985. *African Iron Working—Ancient and Traditional.* Bergen: Norwegian University Press.

Hall, Kenneth R. 1985. *Maritime Trade and State Development in Early Southeast Asia.* Honolulu: University of Hawaii Press.

Hallam, Sylvia. 1975. *Fire and Hearth.* Canberra: Australian Institute of Aboriginal Studies.

Hamden, G. 1961. "The Evolution of Irrigation Agriculture in Egypt." *Arid Zone Research* 17:119–142.

Hammond, F. 1981. "The Colonization of Europe: The Analysis of Settlement Process." In Ian Hodder et al., eds., *Pattern of the Past,* pp. 211–248. Cambridge, Eng.: Cambridge University Press.

Hammond, N. 1980. "Early Maya Ceremonial at Cuello, Belize." *Antiquity* 54:176–190.

———. 1982. *Ancient Maya Civilization.* New Brunswick, NJ: Rutgers University Press.

———. 1986. "New Light on the Most Ancient Maya." *Man* 21:299–413.

Hanson, D., ed. 1989. *Tula of the Toltecs.* Iowa City: University of Iowa Press.

Hapgood, Phillip J. 1989. "The Origin of Anatomically Modern Humans in Australasia." In Paul Mellars and Christopher Stringer, eds., *The Human Revolution,* pp. 245–273. Edinburgh: Edinburgh University Press.

Haq, J., et al. 1977. "Corrected Age of the Pliocene Boundary." *Nature* 269:483–488.

Harding, A. F. 1983. "The Bronze Age in Central and Eastern Europe: Advances and Prospects." *Advances in World Prehistory* 2:1–50.

———. 1984. *The Mycenaeans and Europe.* New York: Academic Press.

Harlan, J. R. 1967. "A Wild Wheat Harvest in Turkey," *Archaeology* 19 (3):197–201.

Harlan, J. R. et al. eds. 1976. *Origins of African Plant Domestication.* The Hague: Mouton.

Harris, David R. 1978. "Alternative Pathways Toward Agriculture." In Charles A. Reed, ed., *The Origins of Agriculture.* The Hague: Mouton.

———, ed. 1980. *Human Ecology in Savanna Environments.* New York: Academic Press.

Harris, D., and Hillman, G. 1989. *Foraging and Farming.* London: Unwin Hyman.

Harris, Marvin. 1968. *The Rise of Anthropological Theory.* New York: Crowell.

Harrison, Richard J. 1980. *The Beaker Folk.* London: Thames and Hudson.

Hasegawa, T. et al. 1983. "New Evidence of Scavenging Behavior in Wild Chimpanzees." *Current Anthropology* 24:231–232.

Hassan, Fekri. 1981. *Demographic Archaeology.* Orlando, FL: Academic Press.

———. 1986. "Desert Environment and Origins of Agriculture in Egypt." *Norwegian Archaeological Review* 19 (2):63–76.

———. 1987. "High Precision Radiocarbon Chronology of Ancient Egypt, and

Comparisons with Nubia, Palestine, and Mesopotamia." *Antiquity* 61 (231):119–135.

———. 1988. "The Pre-Dynastic of Egypt." *Journal of World Prehistory* 2 (2):135–186.

Hatch, Elvin. 1973. *Theories of Man and Culture.* New York: Columbia University Press.

Haury, Emil. 1936. *The Mogollon Culture of Southwestern New Mexico.* Globe, AZ: Gila Pueblo.

———. 1976. *Hohokam, Desert Farmers and Craftsmen: Excavations at Snaketown.* Tucson: University of Arizona Press.

Hayden, Brian. 1981. "Research and Development in the Stone Age: Technological Transitions Among Hunter-Gatherers." *Current Anthropology* 22 (5):519–548.

Haynes, C. Vance. 1982. "Were Clovis Progenitors in Beringia?" In David M. Hopkins et al., eds., *Paleoecology of Beringia,* pp. 383–398. New York: Academic Press.

Hays, T. R. 1984. "A Reappraisal of the Egyptian Predynastic." In J. Desmond Clark and Steven A. Brandt, eds., *From Hunters to Farmers,* pp. 65–73. Berkeley and Los Angeles: University of California Press.

Heizer, R. F., and Berger, Rainer. 1970. "Radiocarbon Age of the Gypsum Cave." *Contributions of the University of California Archaeological Research Facility* 7:1–12.

Henry, Donald O. 1989. *From Foraging to Agriculture.* Philadelphia: University of Pennsylvania Press.

Higgs, Eric S., and Jarman, P. 1969. "Origins of Agriculture." *Antiquity* 43:31–41.

Higham, Charles F. W. 1972. "Initial Model Formation in Terra Incognita." In David L. Clarke, ed., *Models in Prehistory,* pp. 453–476. London: Methuen.

———. 1984a. "The Ban Chiang Culture in Wider Perspective." *Proceedings of the British Academy* 110:1–30.

———. 1989. *The Archaeology of Mainland Southeast Asia.* Cambridge, Eng.: Cambridge University Press.

Hill, Andrew. 1984. "Hyaenas and Hominids." In Robert Foley, ed., *Hominid Evolution and Community Ecology,* pp. 111–128. London: Academic Press.

Hillman, G. C. and Davis, M. S. 1990. "Measured Domestication Rates in Wild Wheats and Barley Under Primitive Cultivation, and Their Archaeological Implications." *Journal of World Prehistory* 4 (2):157–222.

Ho Ping-Ti. 1969. "Loess and the Origins of Chinese Agriculture." *American Historical Review* 75:1–36.

Hodder, Ian, ed. 1982. *Symbolic and Structural Archaeology.* Cambridge, Eng.: Cambridge University Press.

Hoffecker, J. F. 1988. "Early Upper Palaeolithic Sites of the European USSR." In J. F. Hoffecker and C. A. Wolf, eds., *The Early Upper Palaeolithic,* pp. 237–272. Oxford: British Archaeological Reports, International Series, No. 437.

Hoffman, Michael A. 1979. *Egypt Before the Pharaohs.* New York: Knopf.

Hoffman, Michael A., et al. 1982. *The Predynastic of Hierakonpolis.* Cairo: Egyptian Studies Association.

Hole, Frank, Flannery, Kent V., and Neely, J. A. 1969. *The Prehistory and Human Ecology of the Deh Luran Plain.* Ann Arbor: University of Michigan Museum of Anthropology.

Holmes, Charles. 1987. "Prehistoric Maritime Adaptations in Southeast Alaska and

Adjacent Canada." Paper presented at symposium, Prehistoric Maritime Adaptations Around the North Pacific Rim, October 15–17, 1986. Hokkaido: Sapporo Abashiri.

Hood, Sinclair. 1973. *The Minoans.* London: Thames and Hudson.

Hooton, E. A. 1948. *Up from the Ape.* New York: Macmillan.

Hopkins, David M., et al., eds. 1982. *Paleoecology of Beringia.* New York: Academic Press.

Howell, F. Clark. 1966. "Observations on the Earlier Phases of the European Lower Palaeolithic." *American Anthropologist* 68 (2):111–140.

———. 1974. *Early Man.* Chicago: Time-Life.

Howell, F. Clark, and Clark, J. Desmond. 1963. "Acheulian Hunter-Gatherers of Sub-Saharan Africa." *Viking Fund Publications in Anthropology* 36:458–533.

Howell, John M. 1987. "Early Farming in Northwestern Europe." *Scientific American* 237 (11): 118–126.

Hunwick, John D. 1971. "Songhay, Bornu and Hausaland in the Sixteenth Century." In Jacob F. Ajayi and Michael Crowder, eds., *History of West Africa,* Vol. 1, pp. 120–157. London: Longmans.

Huxley, Thomas H. 1863. *Man's Place in Nature.* London: Macmillan.

Huyen Pham Minh. 1984. "Various Phases of the Development of Primitive Metallurgy in Viet Nam." In Donn T. Bayard, ed., *The Origins of Agriculture, Metallurgy, and the State in Mainland Southeast Asia,* pp. 173–182. Dunedin, New Zealand: University of Otago Press.

Hyslop, John. 1984. *The Inca Road System.* New York: Academic Press.

Hyslop, John, et al. 1987. *Huaca Prieta.* New York: American Museum of Natural History.

Ikawa-Smith, Fumio. 1978. "Lithic Assemblages from the Early and Middle Upper Pleistocene Formations in Japan." In Alan Lyle Bryan, ed., *Early Man in America from a Circum-Pacific Perspective.* Edmonton: University of Alberta.

———. 1980. "Current Issues in Japanese Archaeology." *American Scientist* 68 (2):134–145.

Institute of Vertebrate Paleontology and Paleoanthropology, Chinese Academy of Sciences. 1981. *Atlas of Primitive Man in China.* New York: Van Nostrand Reinhold.

Irwin, G., Brickler, S., and Quirke, P. 1990. "Pacific Voyaging by Canoe and Computer." *Antiquity* 64 (242):34–50.

Irwin, H. T., and Wormington, H. M. 1970. "Paleo-Indian Tool Types in the Great Plains." *American Antiquity* 325:24–34.

Irwin-Williams, C. 1973. "The Oshara Tradition: Origins of Anasazi Culture." *University of New Mexico Contributions in Anthropology,* No. 4.

———. 1978. "Summary of Archaeological Evidence from the Valsequillo Region, Puebla, Mexico." In David L. Browman, ed., *Cultural Continuity in Mesoamerica,* pp. 7–22. The Hague: Mouton.

Isaac, Glynn 1981a. "Emergence of Human Behavior Patterns." *Philosophical Transactions of the Royal Society of London* 292:177–188.

———. 1984. "The Archaeology of Human Origins: Studies of the Lower Palaeolithic in East Africa, 1971–1981." *Advances in World Archaeology* 3:1–89.

Isaac, Glynn Ll., and Harris, J. W. K. 1978. "Archaeology." In M. D. Leakey and Richard E. Leakey, eds., *The Fossil Hominids and an Introduction to Their Context, 1968–1974.* Vol. 1, *Koobi Fora Research Project,* pp. 47–76. Oxford, Eng.: Clarendon.

Isbell, William, and Schreiber, Katharina J. 1978. "Was Huari a State?" *American Antiquity* 43:372–389.

Jacobsen, Thomas W. 1981. "Franchthi Cave and the Beginning of Village Settled Life in Greece." *Hesperia* 50:303–319.

———. 1987ff. *Excavations at Franchthi Cave, Greece.* Many volumes. Bloomington: Indiana University Press.

Jacobson, Jerome. 1979. "Recent Developments in South Asian Prehistory and Protohistory." *Annual Review of Anthropology* 8:467–502.

Jacobsthal, P. 1944. *Early Celtic Art.* Oxford, Eng.: Oxford University Press.

Jarrige, J., and Meadow, R. 1979. "The Antecedents of Civilization in the Indus Valley." *Scientific American* 240 (1):122–133.

Jeffries, R. W. 1987. *The Archaeology of Carrier Mills.* Carbondale: Southern Illinois University Press.

Jelinik, Arthur. 1981. "The Middle Paleolithic of the Levant." In J. Cauvin and P. Sanlaville, eds., *Prehistoire de Levant,* pp. 299–302. Paris: CRNS Publications.

Jennings, Jesse D. 1957. *Danger Cave.* Salt Lake City: University of Utah Press.

———, ed. 1979. *The Prehistory of Polynesia.* Cambridge, MA: Harvard University Press.

———, ed. 1983. *Ancient Native Americans,* 2d ed., 2 vols. New York: Freeman.

Jochim, Michael. 1976. *Hunter-Gatherer Subsistence and Settlement.* New York: Academic Press.

———. 1981. *Strategies for Survival: Cultural Behavior in Ecological Context.* New York: Academic Press.

———. 1983. "Paleolithic Cave Art in Ecological Perspective." In G. N. Bailey, ed., *Hunter-Gatherer Economy in Prehistory,* pp. 212–219. Cambridge, Eng.: Cambridge University Press.

Johanson, Donald C., and Edey, Maitland A. 1981. *Lucy: The Beginnings of Humankind.* New York: Simon & Schuster.

Johanson, Donald C., and White, Tim. 1979. "A Systematic Assessment of Early African Hominids." *Science* 202:321–330.

Johanson, Donald C., et al. 1987. "New Partial Skeleton of *Homo habilis* from Olduvai Gorge, Tanzania." *Nature* 327:205–211.

Johnson, Paul. 1978. *The Civilization of Ancient Egypt.* London: Weidenfeld and Nicholson.

Jones, Christopher. 1984. *Deciphering Maya Hieroglyphs.* Philadelphia: University Museum, University of Pennsylvania.

Jones, Rhys. 1989. "East of Wallace's Line: Issues and Problems in the Colonization of the Australian Continent." In Paul Mellars and Christopher Stringer, eds., *The Human Revolution,* pp. 743–782. Edinburgh: Edinburgh University Press.

Joukowsky, Martha. 1981. *A Complete Manual of Field Archaeology.* Englewood Cliffs, NJ: Prentice Hall.

Jovanovic, Borislav. 1980. "The Origins of Copper Mining in Europe." *Scientific American* 242 (5):152–168.

Judd, Neil M. 1954. *The Material Culture of Pueblo Bonito.* Washington, DC: Smithsonian Institution.

———. 1964. *The Agriculture of Pueblo Bonito.* Washington, DC: Smithsonian Institution.

Kalb, J. F., et al. 1984. "Early Hominid Habitation of Ethiopia." *American Scientist* 72:168–178.

Kano, Chiaki. 1979. *The Origins of the Chavín Culture.* Washington, DC: Dumbarton Oaks.

Keatinge, Richard, ed. 1988. *Peruvian Prehistory.* Cambridge, Eng.: Cambridge University Press.

Keeley, Lawrence H. and Cahen, Daniel. 1989. "Early Neolithic Forts and Villages in NE Belgium: A Preliminary Report," *Journal of Field Archaeology* 16 (2):157–176.

Keeley, Lawrence H. and Toth, Nicholas. 1981. "Microwear Polishes on Early Stone Tools from Koobi Fora, Kenya." *Nature* 293:464–465.

Keightley, David N. 1978. *Sources of Shang History: The Oracle Bone Inscriptions of Bronze Age China.* Berkeley and Los Angeles: University of California Press.

———, ed. 1983. *The Origins of Chinese Civilization.* Berkeley and Los Angeles: University of California Press.

Kelly, R. C., and Todd, L. C. 1988. "Coming into the Country: Early Paleoindian Hunting and Mobility." *American Antiquity* 53 (2):231–244.

Kemp, Barry. 1989. *Ancient Egypt: The Anatomy of a Civilization.* London: Routledge.

Kennedy, David. 1987. *Rise and Fall of the Great Powers.* New York: Vintage Books.

Kenyon, Kathleen. 1981. *Excavations of Jericho,* Vol. 3. Jerusalem: British School of Archaeology.

Kidder, A. V. 1927. *An Introduction to the Study of Southwestern Archaeology, with a Preliminary Account of the Excavations at Pecos.* New Haven, CT: Yale University Press.

Kiernan, F. A., and Fairbank, J. K. 1974. *Chinese Ways of Warfare.* Cambridge, MA: Harvard University Press.

Kinnes, Ian. 1982. "Les Fouaillages and Megalithic Origins." *Antiquity* 56:24–30.

Kirch, Patrick V. 1982. "Advances in Polynesian Prehistory: Three Decades in Review." *Advances in World Archaeology* 2:52–102.

———. 1984. *The Evolution of the Polynesian Chiefdoms.* Cambridge, Eng.: Cambridge University Press.

———. 1985. *Feathered Gods and Fishhooks.* Honolulu: University of Hawaii Press.

———, ed. 1986. *Island Societies.* Cambridge, Eng.: Cambridge University Press.

———. 1988. "The Talepakemalai Lapita Site and Oceanic Prehistory." *National Geographic Research* 4 (3):328–342.

Kirk, Ruth. 1975. *Hunters of the Whale.* New York: Morrow.

Kirkbride, Diana. 1975. "Umm Dabaghiyah 1974: A Fourth Preliminary Report." *Iraq* 37:3–10.

Kirkby, Anne V. T. 1973. *The Use of Land and Water Resources in the Past and Present Valley of Oaxaca.* Ann Arbor: University of Michigan Museum of Anthropology.

Klein, Jeffrey, et al. 1982. "Calibration of Radiocarbon Dates." *Radiocarbon* 24 (2):103–150.

Klein, Richard G. 1969. *Man and Culture in the Late Pleistocene.* San Francisco: Chandler.

———. 1979. "Stone Age Exploitation of Animals in Southern Africa." *American Scientist* 67:23–32.

———. 1984. "The Prehistory of Stone Age Herders in South Africa." In J. Desmond Clark and Steven A. Brandt, eds., *From Hunters to Farmers,* pp. 281–289. Berkeley and Los Angeles: University of California Press.

———. 1989. *The Human Career.* Chicago: University of Chicago Press.

Knudsen, Ruthann. 1986. "Contemporary Cultural Resource Management." In David Meltzer, Don D. Fowler, and Jeremy Sabloff, eds., *American Archaeology Past and Future,* pp. 395–413. Washington, DC: Smithsonian Institution.

Kohl, P. 1975. "Carved Chlorite Vessels: A Trade in Finished Commodities in the Mid-Third Millennium." *Expedition* (Fall): 18–31.

———. 1978. "The Balance of Trade in Southwestern Asia in the Mid-Third Millennium B.C." *Current Anthropology* 19:463–492.

Kolata, Alan L. 1982. "Tiwanaku: Portrait of an Andean Civilization." *Field Museum of Natural History Bulletin* 53 (8):13–28.

———. 1986. "The Agricultural Foundations of the Tiwanaku State: A View from the Heartland." *American Antiquity* 51 (4):748–762.

Kornietz, Ninelj L., and Soffer, Olga. 1984. "Mammoth Bone Dwellings on the North Russian Plain." *Scientific American* 251 (5):164–175.

Kramer, Samuel. 1963. *The Sumerians.* Chicago: University of Chicago Press.

Kristiansen, K. 1981. "A Social History of Danish Archaeology." In Glyn E. Daniel, ed., *Towards a History of Archaeology,* pp. 20–44. London: Thames and Hudson.

Kurtén, Björn. 1968. *Pleistocene Mammals in Europe.* Chicago: Aldine.

Kurtén, Björn, and Anderson, E. 1980. *Pleistocene Mammals of North America.* New York: Columbia University Press.

Laitman, Jeffrey T. 1984. "The Anatomy of Human Speech." *Natural History* 93 (9):20–27.

Lamberg-Karlovsky, C. C. 1973. "Urban Interactions on the Iranian Plateau: Excavations at Tepe Yahya, 1967–1973." *Proceedings of the British Academy* 59:5–43.

———. 1978. "The Proto-Elamites and the Iranian Plateau." *Antiquity* 52:114–120.

Lancaster, Jane, and Whitten, Phillip. 1980. "Family Matters." *The Sciences* 1:10–15.

Lanning, Eric P. 1967. *Peru Before the Incas.* Englewood Cliffs, NJ: Prentice Hall.

Larichev, Vitaliy, et al. 1987. "Lower and Middle Paleolithic of Northern Asia: Achievements, Problems, and Perspectives." *Journal of World Prehistory* 1 (4):415–464.

———. 1988. "The Upper Paleolithic of Northern Asia." *Journal of World Prehistory* 2 (4):359–396.

Lathrap, Donald W. 1985. "Jaws: The Control of Power in the Early Nuclear American Ceremonial Center." In Christopher Donnan, ed., *Early Ceremonial Architecture in the Andes,* pp. 241–268. Washington, DC: Dumbarton Oaks.

Laughlin, William S. 1980. *Aleuts, Survivors of the Bering Land Bridge.* New York: Holt, Rinehart & Winston.

Laughlin, William S., Marsh, G. H., and Harper, A. B., eds. 1979. *The First Americans: Origins, Affinities and Adaptations.* New York: Fisher.

Laville, Henri, Rigaud, Jean-Philippe, and Sackett, James. 1980. *Rock Shelters of the Perigord.* New York: Academic Press.

Leakey, L. S. B. 1951. *Olduvai Gorge, 1931–1951.* Cambridge, Eng.: Cambridge University Press.

Leakey, M. D. 1971. *Olduvai Gorge,* Vol. 3. Cambridge, Eng.: Cambridge University Press.

———. 1978. "Pliocene Footprints at Laetoli, Tanzania." *Antiquity* 52:133.

Leakey, M. D., and Harris, J. D. 1990. *Laetoli: A Pliocene Site in Northern Tanzania.* Oxford, Eng.: Oxford University Press.

Leakey, Richard, and Lewin, Roger. 1977. *Origins.* New York: Dutton.

Lee, Richard B. 1979. *The !Kung San.* Cambridge, Eng.: Cambridge University Press.

Lee, Richard B., and DeVore, Irven, eds. 1976. *Kalahari Hunter-Gatherers.* Cambridge, Eng.: Cambridge University Press.

Legge, A. J., and Rowley-Conwy, Peter. 1987. "Gazelle Hunting in Stone Age Syria." *Scientific American* 238 (8):88–95.

Lehmann, Johannes. 1977. *The Hittites: People of the Thousand Gods.* London: Collins.

Leroi-Gourhan, Andre. 1965. *Treasures of Palaeolithic Art.* New York: Abrams.

———. 1984. *The Dawn of European Art: An Introduction to Palaeolithic Cave Painting.* Cambridge, Eng.: Cambridge University Press.

Leveque, François, and Vandermeersch, Bernard. 1982. "Les découvertes de restes humains dans un horizon Castelperronien de Saint-Césaire (Charente-Maritime)." *Bulletin de la Société Préhistorique Française* 77:35.

Levetzion, Nehemiah. 1973. *Ancient Ghana and Mali.* London: Methuen.

Lewin, Roger, 1987. *Bones of Contention.* New York: Simon & Schuster.

———. 1988a. *Human Evolution,* 2d ed. Oxford, Eng.: Blackwell.

———. 1988b. "A Revolution of Ideas in Agricultural Origins." *Science* 240:984–986.

Lewis, David. 1972. *We the Navigators.* Honolulu: University of Hawaii Press.

Lewis-Williams, David. 1981. *Believing and Seeing: Symbolic Meanings in Southern San Rock Art.* New York: Academic Press.

Lhote, Henri. 1959. *The Search for the Tassili Frescoes.* London: Hutchinson University Library.

Lipe, William D. 1978. "The Southwest." In Jesse D. Jennings, ed., *Ancient Native Americans,* pp. 403–454. San Francisco: Freeman.

Livingstone, Sir R., trans. 1943. *Thucydides' History of the Peloponnesian War.* Cambridge, Eng.: Oxford University Press.

Lloyd, Seton. 1963. *Mounds of the Near East.* Chicago: Aldine.

———. 1967. *Early Highland Peoples of Anatolia.* New York: McGraw-Hill.

———. 1980. *Foundations in the Dust.* London: Thames and Hudson.

———. 1983. *The Archaeology of Mesopotamia,* 2d ed. London: Thames and Hudson.

Lourandos, Henry. 1987. "Pleistocene Australia: Peopling a Continent." In Olga Soffer, ed., *The Pleistocene Old World: Regional Perspectives,* pp. 147–166. New York: Plenum.

Luce, J. V. 1973. *Atlantis.* New York: McGraw-Hill.

Lumley, Henry de. 1969. "A Paleolithic Camp near Nice." *Scientific American* 87:23–32.

Lynch, Thomas F. 1980. *Guitarrero Cave.* New York: Academic Press.

———. 1989. "Glacial-Age Man in South America? A Critical Review." *American Antiquity* 55 (1):12–36.

McBurney, C. B. M. 1976. *Early Man in the Soviet Union.* London: British Academy.

McGhee, Robert. 1984. "Contact Between Native North Americans and the Medieval Norse: A Review of Evidence." *American Antiquity* 49 (2):4–26.

McGimsey, Charles R. 1973. *Public Archaeology.* New York: Academic Press.

McIntosh, Susan Keech, and McIntosh, Roderick J. 1981. "West African Prehistory." *American Scientist* 69:602–613.

McIntosh, S. K., and McIntosh, R. J. 1988. "From Stone to Metal: New Perspectives on the Later Prehistory of West Africa." *Journal of World Prehistory* 2 (1):89–131.

MacNeish, Richard, ed. 1970. *The Prehistory of the Tehuacán Valley.* Austin: University of Texas Press.

———. 1971. "Early Man in the Andes." *Scientific American,* no. 4, pp. 36–46.

———. 1978. *The Science of Archaeology.* North Scituate, MA: Duxbury.

———. 1979. "Earliest Man in the New World and Its Implications for Soviet-American Archaeology." *Arctic Anthropology* 16 (1):2–15.

———. 1983. "Mesoamerica." In Richard Shutler, Jr., ed., *Early Man in the New World,* pp. 125–136. Beverly Hills, CA: Sage.

———. 1986. "The Preceramic of Middle America." *Advances in World Archaeology* 5:93–130.

MacNeish, Richard, and Nelken-Terner, Antoinette. 1983. "The Pre-Ceramic of Mesoamerica." *Journal of Field Archaeology* 10 (1):71–84.

MacNeish, Richard, et al. 1980. *The Prehistory of the Ayacucho Basin, Peru.* Ann Arbor: University of Michigan Press.

———. 1980, 1981. *The Prehistory of the Ayacucho Basin, Peru.* University of Michigan: Ann Arbor. Vol. 2: *Excavations and Chronology* (1981); Vol. 3: *Nonceramic Artifacts* (1980).

MacQueen, J. G. 1987. *The Hittites.* London: Thames and Hudson.

McVicker, Donald. 1985. "The 'Mayanized' Mexican." *American Antiquity* 50 (1):82–101.

Malinowski, Bronislaw. 1922. *Argonauts of the Western Pacific.* London: Routledge & Kegan Paul.

Mallory, J. P. 1988. *In Search of the Indo-Europeans.* New York: Thames and Hudson.

Manning, Stuart. 1988. "The Bronze Age Eruption of Thera." *Journal of Mediterranean Archaeology* 1 (1):17–82.

Marks, Anthony E. 1983. "The Middle to Upper Palaeolithic Transition in the Levant." *Advances in World Prehistory* 2:51–98.

Marquardt, William H. 1978. "Advances in Archaeological Seriation." *Advances in Archaeological Method and Theory* 1:1–26.

Marshack, Alexander. 1972. *The Roots of Civilization.* New York: McGraw-Hill.

———. 1975. "Exploring the Mind of Ice Age Man." *National Geographic* 154:62–89.

Martin, Paul, and Klein, Richard, eds. 1984. *A Pleistocene Revolution.* Tucson: University of Arizona Press.

Martin, Paul, and Wright, H. E. 1967. *Pleistocene Extinctions: The Search for a Cause.* New Haven, CT: Yale University Press.

Mason, Ronald J. 1981. *Great Lakes Archaeology.* New York: Academic Press.

Matheny, Ray. 1986. "Early States of the Maya Lowlands during the Late Preclassic Period." In Elizabeth P. Benson, ed., *City-States of the Maya: Art and Architecture,* pp. 1–44. Denver: Rocky Mountain Institute of Pre-Columbian Studies.

Maxwell, Moreau S. 1985. *Prehistory of the Eastern Arctic.* New York: Academic Press.

Mayr, Ernst. 1982. *The Growth of Biological Thought.* Cambridge, MA: Harvard University Press.

Megaw, J. V. S. 1970. *Art of the European Iron Age.* Bath, Eng.: Baker.

Meggers, Betty. 1973. *Prehistoric America.* Chicago: Aldine.

Melisauskas, Saraunas. 1978. *European Prehistory.* New York: Academic Press.

Mellaart, James. 1967. *Çatal Hüyük.* New York: McGraw-Hill.

———. 1975. *The Neolithic of the Near East.* London: Thames and Hudson.

Mellars, Paul. 1973. "The Character of the Middle-Upper Palaeolithic Transition in Stone-tool Assemblages." In Colin Renfrew, ed., *The Explanation of Culture Change: Models in Prehistory,* pp. 255–276. London: Duckworth.

———. 1985. "The Ecological Basis of Social Complexity in the Upper Palaeolithic of Southwestern France." In T. Douglas Price and James Brown, eds., *Prehistoric Hunter-Gatherers: The Emergence of Cultural Complexity,* pp. 271–297. Orlando, FL: Academic Press.

———. 1989. "Technological Changes at the Middle-Upper Palaeolithic Transition: Economic, Social, and Cognitive Perspectives." In Paul Mellars and Christopher Stringer, eds., *The Human Revolution,* pp. 338–365. Edinburgh: Edinburgh University Press.

Meltzer, David. 1988. "Late Pleistocene Adaptations in Eastern North America." *Journal of World Prehistory* 2 (1):1–52.

———. 1989. "Why Don't We Know when the First People Came to North America?" *American Antiquity* 54 (3):471–490.

Mendelssohn, Kurt. 1974. *The Riddle of the Pyramids.* New York: Praeger.

Menzel, Dorothy, et al. 1964. "The Paracas Pottery of Ica." *University of California Bulletins in American Archaeology and Ethnology,* Vol. 50.

Michels, Joseph W. 1973. *Dating Methods in Archaeology.* New York: Seminar.

Milanich, Jerald, et al., eds. 1984. *McKeithen Weeden Island: The Culture of Northern Florida, A.D. 200–900.* Orlando, FL: Academic Press.

Milisaukas, S., and Kruk, J. 1989. "Neolithic Economy in Central Europe." *Journal of World Prehistory* 2 (3):403–446.

Miller, Daniel. 1985. "Ideology and the Harappan Civilization." *Journal of Anthropological Archaeology* 4:1–38.

Millon, R., Drewitt, R. Bruce, and Cowgill, George. 1974. *Urbanization at Teotihuacán, Mexico.* Austin: University of Texas Press.

Minnis, Paul. 1985. "Domesticating People and Plants in the Greater Southwest." In Richard I. Ford, ed., *Prehistoric Food Production in North America,* pp. 309–339. Ann Arbor: University of Michigan Museum of Anthropology.

Mithen, Stephen. 1989. "Evolutionary Theory and Postprocessual Archaeology." *Antiquity* 63 (240):483–495.

Mochanov, Yuri A. 1978. "Stratigraphy and Chronology of the Paleolithic of Northeast Asia." In Alan L. Bryan, ed., *Early Man in America from a Circum-Pacific Perspective,* pp. 67–68. Edmonton: University of Alberta.

Moctezuma, Eduardo Matos. 1988. *The Great Temple of the Aztecs.* New York: Thames and Hudson.

Moore, Andrew, T. 1979. "A Pre-Neolithic Farming Village on the Euphrates." *Scientific American* 241 (2):62–70.

———. 1985. "The Development of Neolithic Societies in the Near East." *Advances in World Archaeology* 4:1–70.

———. 1989. "The Transition from Foraging to Farming in South West Asia." In D. Harris and G. Hillman, eds., *Foraging and Farming,* pp. 620–631. London: Unwin Hyman.

Moorey, P. R. S. 1982. "The Archaeological Evidence for Metallurgy and Related Technologies in Mesopotamia, c. 5500–1200 B.C." *Iraq* 44:13–38.

Moratto, Michael. 1985. *California Archaeology.* New York: Academic Press.

Morenz, Siegfried. 1973. *Egyptian Religion.* London: Macmillan.

Morgan, Lewis. 1877. *Ancient Society.* New York: Holt, Rinehart, and Winston.

Morison, Samuel Eliot. 1971. *The Northern Voyages.* Vol. 1, *The European Discovery of America.* New York: Oxford University Press.

Morlan, Richard E. 1983. "Pre-Clovis Occupation North of the Ice Sheets." In Richard Shutler, Jr., ed., *Early Man in the New World,* pp. 47–66. Beverly Hills, CA: Sage.

Morlan, Richard E., and Cinq-Mars, Jacques. 1982. "Ancient Beringians: Human Occupation in the Late Pleistocene of Alaska and the Yukon Territory." In David M. Hopkins et al., eds., *Paleoecology of Beringia,* pp. 353–382. New York: Academic Press.

Morris, Ian. 1989. "Tomb Cult and the 'Greek renaissance': The Past in the Present in the 8th Century B.C." *Antiquity* 62 (237):750–761.

Morris, J. Bayard, ed. 1962. *Five Letters of Cortes to the Emperor, 1519–26.* New York: W.W. Norton.

Morse, Dan, and Morse, P. A. 1983. *Archaeology of the Central Mississippi Valley.* New York: Academic Press.

Moseley, Michael. 1975a. "Chan Chan: Andean Alternative to the Preindustrial City." *Science* 187:219–225.

———. 1975b. *The Maritime Foundations of Andean Civilization.* Menlo Park, CA: Cummings.

———. 1978. "The Evolution of Andean Civilization." In Jesse D. Jennings, ed., *Ancient Native Americans,* pp. 491–541. San Francisco: W. H. Freeman.

———. 1985. "The Exploration and Explanation of Early Monumental Architecture in the Andes." In Christopher Donnan, ed., *Early Ceremonial Architecture in the Andes,* pp. 28–58. Washington, DC: Dumbarton Oaks.

———. 1986. "Maritime Foundations in Retrospect: A Fishy Hypothesis." Paper to the Society for American Archaeology, New Orleans.

———. 1991. *Peru.* London: Thames and Hudson.

Moseley, Michael, and Day, Kent C., eds. 1982. *Chan Chan: Andean Desert City.* Albuquerque: University of New Mexico Press.

Movius, Hallam L. 1944. "Early Man and Pleistocene Stratigraphy in South and East Asia." *Papers of the Peabody Museum* 19:3.

———. 1973. "Quelques commentaires supplémentaires sur les sagaies d'Isturitz: données de l'Abri Pataud." *Bulletin de la Société Prehistorique Française* 70:85–89.

———. 1977. *Excavation of the Abri Pataud, Les Eyziés (Dordogne).* Cambridge, MA: Peabody Museum.

Mueller, James A., ed. 1975. *Sampling in Archaeology.* Tucson: University of Arizona Press.

Mughal, R. M. 1974. "New Evidence of the Early Harappan Culture from Jalipur, Pakistan." *Archaeology* 27 (2):106–113.

Muller, Jon D. 1983. "The Southeast." In Jesse D. Jennings, ed., *Ancient Native Americans,* 2d ed, pp. 222–326. San Francisco: Freeman.

———. 1986. *Archaeology of the Lower Ohio River Valley.* New York: Academic Press.

———. 1989. "The Southern Cult." In Patricia Galloway, ed., *The Southeastern Ceremonial Complex: Artifacts and Analysis,* pp. 11–26. Lincoln: University of Nebraska Press.

Muller-Beck, Hansjurgen. 1961. "Prehistoric Lake Dwellings." *Scientific American* 211 (4):36–44.

———. 1982. "Late Pleistocene Man in Northern Eurasia and the Mammoth-Steppe Biome." In David M. Hopkins et al., eds., *Paleoecology of Beringia,* pp. 329–352. New York: Academic Press.

Murdock, George Peter. 1968. "The Current Status of the World's Hunting and Gathering Peoples." In Richard B. Lee and Irven DeVore, eds., *Man the Hunter,* pp. 13–20. Chicago: Aldine.

Nassaney, Michael S. 1987. "On the Causes and Consequences of Subsistence Interactions in the Mississippi Alluvial Valley." In William Keegan, ed., *Emergent Horticultural Economies of the Eastern Woodlands,* pp. 129–151. Carbondale: Center for Archaeological Investigations, Southern Illinois University.

Nelson, Sarah. 1982. "Recent Progress in Korean Archaeology." *Advances in World Archaeology* 1:103–150.

———. 1990. "The Neolithic of China and Korea." *Antiquity* 64 (243):234–248.

Nilsson, Tage. 1983. *The Pleistocene.* Stuttgart: Enke Verlag.

Nissen, Hans J. 1988. *The Early History of the Near East 9000–2000 B.C.* Chicago: University of Chicago Press.

Oakley, K. P. 1964. *Frameworks for Dating Fossil Man.* Chicago: Aldine.

Oates, David, and Oates, Joan. 1976. *The Rise of Civilization.* Oxford, Eng.: Elsevier Phaidon.

Oates, Joan. 1973. "The Background and Development of Early Farming Communities in Mesopotamia and the Zagros." *Proceedings of the Prehistoric Society* 39:147–181.

Oliver, Douglas. 1977. *Ancient Tahitian Society.* Honolulu: University of Hawaii Press.

Oliver, Roland, and Fagan, Brian M. 1975. *Africa in the Iron Age.* Cambridge, Eng.: Cambridge University Press.

Oliver, Roland, and Fage, John D. 1963. *A Short History of Africa.* Baltimore: Pelican.

Olivier, Robert C. D. 1982. "Ecology and Behavior of Living Elephants: Bases for

Assumptions Concerning the Extinct Woolly Mammoth." In David M. Hopkins et al., eds., *Paleoecology of Beringia,* pp. 291–306. New York: Academic Press.

Olsen, S. J. 1987. "The Practice of Archaeology in China Today." *Antiquity* 61 (232):282–290.

Otto, Martha Potter. 1979. "Hopewell Antecedents in the Adena Heartland." In David C. Brose and N'omi Greber, eds., *Hopewellian Archaeology,* pp. 9–14. Kent, OH: Kent State University Press.

Ovey, C. D., ed. 1964. *The Swanscombe Skull: A Survey of Research on a Pleistocene Site.* London: Royal Anthropological Institute.

Pallotino, Massimo. 1977. *The Etruscans.* Translated by David Ridgeway. Harmondsworth, Eng.: Lane.

Parkington, John. 1987. "Prehistory and Paleoenvironments at the Pleistocene-Holocene Boundary in the Western Cape." In Olga Soffer, ed., *The Pleistocene Old World: Regional Perspectives,* pp. 349–364. New York: Plenum.

Parsons, Lee, and Price, Barbara. 1971. "Mesoamerican Trade and Its Role in the Emergence of Civilization." *Contributions of the University of California Archaeological Research Facility* 11:169–195.

Patterson, Thomas C. 1985. "The Huaca La Florida, Rímac Valley, Peru." In Christopher Donnan, ed., *Early Ceremonial Architecture in the Andes,* pp. 59–70. Washington, DC: Dumbarton Oaks.

Pearsell, Deborah. 1987. *Paleoethnobotany.* Orlando, FL: Academic Press.

Pearson, G. W. 1987. "How to Cope with Calibration." *Antiquity* 61:98–103.

Pearson, Richard. 1981. "Social Complexity in Chinese Coastal Neolithic Sites." *Science* 213:1078–1088.

Pearson, Richard J., et al., eds. 1986. *Window on the Japanese Past: Studies in Archaeology and Prehistory.* Ann Arbor: Center for Japanese Studies, University of Michigan.

Pelto, Peter J. 1966. *The Nature of Anthropology.* Columbus, OH: Merrill.

Penck, Albrecht, and Brückner, Edward. 1909. *Die Alpen im Eiszeitalter.* Leipzig: Tauchnitz.

Penniman, T. K. 1965. *A Hundred Years of Anthropology.* New York: Humanities.

Peringuey, Louis. 1911. *The Stone Age in South Africa.* Capetown: South African Museum.

Perkins, Dexter. 1964. "The Prehistoric Fauna from Shanidar, Iraq." *Science* 144:1565–1566.

Peyrony, Denis. 1934. "La Ferrassie." *Prehistoire* 3:1–54.

Pfeiffer, John E. 1982. *The Creative Explosion.* New York: Harper & Row.

———. 1985. *The Emergence of Man,* 4th ed. New York: Harper & Row.

Phillips, E. D. 1972. "The Scythian Domination in Western Asia." *World Archaeology* 4:129–138.

Phillips, J., and Brown, J. A. eds. 1983. *Archaic Hunter-Gatherers in the Midwest.* Orlando, FL: Academic Press.

Phillips, Patricia. 1980. *The Prehistory of Europe.* Bloomington: Indiana University Press.

Phillipson, David. 1977. *The Later Prehistory of Eastern and South Africa.* London: Heinemann.

————. 1984. *African Archaeology.* Cambridge, Eng.: Cambridge University Press.

Pickersgill, Barbara. 1972. "Cultivated Plants as Evidence for Cultural Contacts." *American Antiquity* 37 (1):97–103.

Piggott, Stuart. 1965. *Ancient Europe.* Chicago: Aldine.

Pilbeam, David. 1985. "Patterns of Human Evolution." In Eric Delson, ed., *Ancestors,* pp. 51–59. New York: Liss.

————. 1986. "Distinguished Lecture: Hominoid Evolution and Hominoid Origins." *American Anthropologist* 88 (2):295–312.

Piperno, D. R. 1988. *Phytolith Analysis: An Archaeological and Geological Perspective.* Orlando, FL: Academic Press.

Plog, Fred T., and Upham, Steadman. 1983. "Analysis of Prehistoric Political Organization." In Elizabeth Tooker, ed., *The Development of Political Organization in Native North America,* pp. 199–213. Washington, DC: American Ethnological Society.

Plomley, N. J. B. 1969. *An Annotated Bibliography of the Tasmanian Aborigines.* London: Royal Anthropological Institute.

Pope, Geoffrey G. 1984. "The Antiquity and Paleoenvironment of the Asian Hominidae." In R. O. I. Whyte, ed., *The Evolution of the East Asian Environment,* pp. 922–947. Hong Kong: Center of Asian Studies, University of Hong Kong.

————. 1989. "Bamboo and Human Evolution." *Natural History* 10 (89):49–56.

Pope, Geoffrey G., et al. 1986. "Earliest Radiometrically Dated Artifacts from Southeast Asia." *Current Anthropology* 27 (3):275–279.

Pope, Michael. 1973. *Decipherment.* London: Thames and Hudson.

Possehl, Gregory L., ed. 1979. *Ancient Cities of the Indus.* Durham: University of North Carolina Press.

————. 1980. *Indus Civilization in Saurashta.* Delhi: B. R. Publishing.

————, ed. 1982, *The Harappan Civilisation.* London: Aris and Phillips.

————. 1986. *Kulli.* Durham: University of North Carolina Press.

Possehl, Gregory L., and Raval, M. H. 1989. *Harappan Civilization and Rojdi.* New Delhi, India: Oxford and IBH Publishing.

Postgate, Nicholas. 1977. *The First Empires.* Oxford, Eng.: Elsevier Phaidon.

Potts, Richard. 1984a. "Home Bases and Early Hominids." *American Scientist* 72:338–347.

————. 1984b. "Hominid Hunters? Problems of Identifying the Earliest Hunter-Gatherers." In Robert Foley, ed., *Hominid Evolution and Community Ecology,* pp. 129–166. London: Academic Press.

Powers, William R., and Hamilton, Thomas D. 1978. "Dry Creek: A Late Pleistocene Human Occupation in Central Alaska." In Alan L. Bryan, ed., *Early Man in America from a Circum-Pacific Perspective,* pp. 72–78. Edmonton: University of Alberta.

Pozorski, Thomas. 1987. "Changing Priorities Within the Chimu State: The Role of Irrigation Agriculture." In Jonathan Haas et al., eds., *The Origins and Development of the Andean State,* pp. 111–120. Cambridge, Eng.: Cambridge University Press.

Pozorski, Thomas, and Pozorski, Sheila. 1987. "Chavín, the Early Horizon, and the Initial Period." In Jonathan Haas et al., eds., *The Origins and Development of the Andean State,* pp. 36–46. Cambridge, Eng.: Cambridge University Press.

Premack, Ann James, and Premack, David. 1972. "Teaching Language to an Ape." *Scientific American* 241 (1):92–99.

Price, T. Douglas. 1983. "The European Mesolithic." *American Antiquity* 48:761–778.

———. 1985. "Foragers of Southern Scandinavia." In T. Douglas Price and James Brown, eds., *Prehistoric Hunter-Gatherers: The Emergence of Cultural Complexity*, pp. 212–236. New York: Academic Press.

———. 1987. "The Mesolithic of Western Europe." *Journal of World Prehistory* 1 (3):225–305.

Price, T. Douglas, and Brown, James, eds. 1985. *Prehistoric Hunter-Gatherers.* New York: Academic Press.

Price, T. Douglas, et al. 1982. "Thermal Alteration in Mesolithic Assemblages." *Proceedings of the Prehistoric Society* 48:467–485.

Prickett, Nigel, ed. 1983. *The First 1000 Years: Regional Perspectives in New Zealand Archaeology.* Palmerston North: New Zealand Archaeological Association.

Protzen, Jean-Pierre. 1986. "Inca Stonemasonry." *Scientific American* 254 (2):94–105.

Proulx, Donald. 1973. *Archaeological Investigations in the Nepeña Valley, Peru.* Amherst: University of Massachusetts Press.

———. 1983a. "The Nasca Style." In Lois Katz, ed., *Art of the Andes: Pre-Columbian Sculptured and Painted Ceramics from the Arthur M. Sackler Collection,* pp. 87–104. Washington, DC: Arthur M. Sackler Foundation.

———. 1983b. "Tiahuanaco and Huari." In Lois Katz, ed., *Art of the Andes: Pre-Columbian Sculptured and Painted Ceramics from the Arthur M. Sackler Collection,* pp. 107–114. Washington, DC: Arthur M. Sackler Foundation.

———. 1985. "An Analysis of the Early Cultural Sequence in the Nepeña Valley, Peru." *Research Report of Department of Anthropology, University of Massachusetts, Amherst,* no. 25.

Quilter, Jeffrey. 1985. "Architecture and Chronology at El Paraíso, Peru." *Journal of Field Archaeology* 12 (3):274–298.

Raab, Mark L., and Goodyear, Albert C. 1984. "Middle Range Theory in Archaeology: A Critical Review of Origins and Applications." *American Antiquity* 49:255–268.

Raikes, Robert. 1967. *Water, Weather, and Prehistory.* London: Baker.

Rak, Yoel. 1983. *The Australopithecine Face.* New York: Academic Press.

Ramenovsky, Ann. 1987. *Vectors of Death.* Albuquerque: University of New Mexico Press.

Ranov, V. A., and Davis, R. S. 1979. "Toward a New Outline of the Soviet Central Asian Paleolithic." *Current Anthropology* 20 (2):249–270.

Raymond, J. Scott. 1981. "The Maritime Foundations of Andean Civilization: A Reconsideration of the Evidence." *American Antiquity* 46:806–820.

Redman, Charles L. 1978. *The Rise of Civilization: From Early Farmers to Urban Society in the Ancient Near East.* San Francisco: Freeman.

———. 1987. "Surface Collection, Sampling, and Research Design: A Retrospective." *American Antiquity* 52 (2):249–265.

Reeves, Nicholas. 1990. *The Complete Tutankhamun.* New York: Thames and Hudson.

Renault, Mary. 1963. *The King Must Die.* New York: Random House.

Renfrew, Colin. 1970. "The Tree-Ring Calibration of Radiocarbon: An Archaeological Evaluation." *Proceedings of the Prehistoric Society* 36:280–311.

———. 1972. *The Emergence of Civilization.* London: Methuen.

———. 1973. *Before Civilization.* New York: Knopf.

———. 1978. "Varna and the Social Context of Early Metallurgy." *Antiquity* 52: 199–203.

———. 1983. "The Social Archaeology of Megaliths." *Scientific American* 249:152–163.

———, ed. 1984. *The Megalithic Monuments of Western Europe.* London: Thames and Hudson.

———. 1987. *The Archaeology of Language.* London: Cape.

Renfrew, Colin, and Bahn, Paul. 1991. *Archaeology: A Handbook of Ideas and Methods.* New York: Thames and Hudson.

Renfrew, Colin, and Dixon, J. E. 1976. "Obsidian in Western Asia: A Review." In Ian Longworth and K. E. Wilson, eds., *Problems in Economic and Social Archaeology,* pp. 137–150. London: Duckworth.

Renfrew, Colin, Dixon, J. E., and Cann, J. R. 1966. "Obsidian and Early Cultural Contact in the Near East." *Proceedings of the Prehistoric Society* 32:1–29.

Renfrew, Colin, and Shennan, S. J. eds. 1982. *Ranking, Resource and Exchange: Aspects of the Archaeology of Early European Society.* Cambridge, Eng.: Cambridge University Press.

Renfrew, Colin, and Wagstaff, J. M., eds. 1982. *An Island Polity: The Archaeology of Exploitation in Melos.* Cambridge, Eng.: Cambridge University Press.

Renfrew, Jane. 1973. *Palaeoethnobotany: The Prehistoric Food Plants of the Near East.* London: Methuen.

Reynolds, Robert. 1986. "Computer Simulation." In Kent Flannery, ed., *Guilá Naquitz,* pp. 263–289. Orlando, FL: Academic Press.

Reynolds, T. E. G., and Barnes, G. L. 1984. "The Japanese Palaeolithic: A Review." *Proceedings of the Prehistoric Society* 50:49–62.

Rindos, David. 1984. *The Origins of Agriculture: An Evolutionary Perspective.* New York: Academic Press.

Rizkana, I., and Seeher, J. 1984. "New Light on the Relation of Maadi to the Upper Egyptian Cultural Sequence." *Mitteilungen des Deutchen Archaologischen Instituts Abteilung Kairo* 40:237–252.

Roberts, Neil. 1984. "Pleistocene Environments in Time and Space." In Robert Foley, ed., *Hominid Evolution and Community Ecology,* pp. 25–54. London: Academic Press.

Roberts, R. G., et al. 1990. "Thermoluminescence Dating of a 50,000-year-old Human Occupation Site in Northern Australia." *Nature* 345:153–156.

Roe, Derek, 1981. *The Lower and Middle Palaeolithic Periods in Britain.* London: Routledge & Kegan Paul.

Rognon, Pierre. 1981. "Interprétation paleoclimatique des changements d'environments en Afrique du Nord et au Moyen Orient durant les 20 derniers millénaires." *Palaeoecology of Africa* 13:21–44.

Romer, John. 1981. *The Valley of Kings.* New York: Morrow.

Ronen, Avraham, ed. 1982. *The Transition from Lower to Middle Paleolithic and the Origins of Modern Man.* Oxford, Eng.: British Archaeological Reports, International Series, No. 151.

Roosevelt, Anna. 1980. *Parmana: Prehistoric Maize and Manioc Subsistence Along the Amazon and Orinoco.* Orlando, FL: Academic Press.

Rose, M. D. 1984. "Food Acquisition and the Evolution of Primate Behavior: The Case of Bipedalism." In D. J. Chivers et al., eds., *Food Acquisition and Processing in Primates,* pp. 509–524. New York: Plenum.

Roth, H. Ling. 1887. "On the Origins of Agriculture." *Journal of the Royal Anthropological Institute* 16:102–136.

Rowe, John H. 1946. *Inca Culture at the Time of the Spanish Conquest.* Vol. 2, *Handbook of South American Indians.* Washington, DC: Smithsonian Institution.

———. 1948. "The Kingdom of Chimor." *Acta Americana* 6:26–59.

———. 1962. *Chavín Art: An Inquiry into Its Form and Meaning.* New York: Museum of Primitive Art.

Rowe, John H., Collier, John, and Willey, Gordon R. 1950. "Reconnaissance Notes on the Site of Huari, near Ayacuchu, Peru." *American Antiquity* 16:120–137.

Rowlett, Ralph. 1967. "The Iron Age North of the Alps." *Science* 161:123–134.

Rowley-Conwy, Peter. 1986. "Between Cave Painters and Crop Planters: Aspects of the Temperate European Mesolithic." In Marek Zvelebil, ed., *Hunters in Transition,* pp. 17–32. Cambridge, Eng.: Cambridge University Press.

Roys, R. 1972. *The Indian Background of Colonial Yucatán.* Norman: University of Oklahoma Press.

Rudenko, Sergei. 1970. *The Frozen Tombs of Siberia: The Pazyryk Burials of Iron Age Horsemen.* Translated by M. W. Thompson. Berkeley and Los Angeles: University of California Press.

Ruffle, John. 1977. *Heritage of the Pharaohs.* Oxford, Eng.: Phaidon.

Rukang Wu and Shenglong Liu. 1983. "Peking Man." *Scientific American* 248 (6):80–95.

Sabloff, Jeremy A. 1989. *The Cities of Ancient Mexico.* New York: Thames and Hudson.

———. 1990. *The New Archaeology and the Ancient Maya.* New York: Scientific American Library.

Sabloff, Jeremy A., and Freidel, David A. 1984. *Cozumel: Late Maya Settlement Patterns.* New York: Academic Press.

Sabloff, Jeremy A., and Lamberg-Karlovsky, C. C., eds. 1975. *Ancient Civilization and Trade.* Albuquerque: University of New Mexico Press.

Sahlins, Marshall, and Service, Elman, eds. 1960. *Evolution and Culture.* Ann Arbor: University of Michigan Press.

Sanders, N. K. 1977. *The Sea People.* London: Thames and Hudson.

Sanders, William T. 1965. *The Cultural Ecology of the Tehuacán Valley.* University Park: Pennsylvania State University Press.

Sanders, William T., Parsons, Jeffrey R., and Santley, Robert S. 1979. *The Basin of Mexico: Ecological Processes in the Evolution of a Civilization.* New York: Academic Press.

Sanders, William T., and Price, Barbara J. 1968. *Mesoamerica: The Evolution of a Civilization.* New York: Random House.

Sanders, William T., and Webster, David. 1978. "Unilinealism, Multilinealism, and the Evolution of Complex Societies." In Charles L. Redman et al., eds., *Social Archaeology,* pp. 249–302. New York: Academic Press.

Sanders, William T., et al. 1970. *The Natural Environment: Contemporary Occupation and Sixteenth Century Population of the Valley: Teotihuacán Valley Project Final Report.* University Park: Pennsylvania State University Press.

Sarich, Vincent. 1971. "A Molecular Approach to the Problem of Human Origins." In Phyllis Dolhinow and Vincent Sarich, eds., *Background for Man,* pp. 60–81. Boston: Little, Brown.

———. 1983. "Retrospective on Hominoid Macromolecular Systematics." In R. L. Ciochon and R. S. Corrucini, eds., *New Interpretations of Ape and Human Ancestry,* pp. 137–150. New York: Plenum.

Sauer, Carl O. 1952. *Agricultural Origins and Dispersals.* New York: American Geographical Society.

Saunders, Nicholas. 1989. *People of the Jaguar.* London: Souvenir Press.

Schapera, Isaac. 1930. *The Khoisan Peoples of South Africa.* New York: Humanities.

Schele, Linda, and Freidel, D. 1990. *A Forest of Kings.* New York: Morrow.

Schele, Linda, and Miller, E. 1986. *The Blood of Kings.* Austin: University of Texas Press.

Schiffer, M. B. 1983. "Towards the Identification of Site Formation Processes." *American Antiquity* 48:675–706.

———. 1987. *Site Formation Processes of the Archaeological Record.* Orlando, FL: Academic Press.

Schiffer, M. B., and House, John. 1977. *The Cache River Archaeological Project.* Fayetteville: Arkansas Archaeological Survey.

Schledermann, Peter. 1990. *Crossroads to Greenland.* Calgary, Alta.: Arctic Institute of North America.

Schmandt-Besserat, D. 1978. "The Earliest Precursor of Writing." *Scientific American* 238 (6):50–59.

Schreiber, Katharina J. 1987. "Conquest and Consolidation: A Comparison of the Wari and Inka Occupation of a Highland Peruvian Valley." *American Antiquity* 52 (2):266–284.

Scudder, Thayer. 1962. *The Ecology of the Gwembe Tonga.* Manchester, Eng.: Manchester University Press.

———. 1971. *Gathering Among African Woodland Savannah Cultivators.* Lusaka: University of Zambia.

Serge, Aldo, and Asconzi, Antonio. 1984. "Italy's Earliest Middle Pleistocene Hominid Site." *Current Anthropology* 25 (2):230–235.

Service, Elman. 1962. *Primitive Social Organization.* New York: Random House.

———. 1975. *The Origins of the State and Civilization.* New York: W. W. Norton.

Shackleton, N. J., and Opdyke, N. D. 1973. "Oxygen Isotope and Paleomagnetic Stratigraphy of Equatorial Pacific Ocean Core V28–238." *Quarternary Research* 3:38–55.

Sharer, Robert. 1989. "Olmec Studies: A Status Report." In Robert Sharer and

David Grove, eds., *Regional Perspectives on the Olmec*, pp. 3–7. Cambridge, Eng.: Cambridge University Press.

Sharer, Robert, and Grove, David. eds. 1989. *Regional Perspectives on the Olmec*. Cambridge, Eng.: Cambridge University Press.

Sharer, Robert J., and Ashmore, Wendy. 1987. *Archaeology: Discovering Our Past*. Palo Alto, CA: Mayfield.

Sharman, G. R., et al. 1980. *Beginning of Agriculture*. Allahabad, India: University of Allahabad.

Sharp, Andrew. 1957. *Ancient Voyagers in the Pacific*. Baltimore: Pelican.

Shawcross, Kathleen. 1967. "Fern Root and Eighteenth-Century Maori Food Production in Agricultural Areas." *Journal of the Polynesian Society* 76:330–352.

Shennan, S. J. 1982. "Ideology, Change, and the European Early Bronze Age." In Ian Hodder, ed., *Symbolic and Structural Archaeology*, pp. 235–247. Cambridge, Eng.: Cambridge University Press.

Sherratt, Andrew G. 1981. "Plough and Pasture." In Ian Hodder et al., eds., *Patterns of the Past*, pp. 344–361. Cambridge, Eng.: Cambridge University Press.

Shinnie, Peter. 1967. *Meroe*. London: Thames and Hudson.

Shipman, Pat. 1984. "Scavenger Hunt." *Natural History* 93 (4):20–28.

Shipman, Pat, and Rose, J. 1983. "Evidence of Butchery and Hominid Activities at Torralba and Ambrona." *Journal of Archaeological Studies* 10 (5):475–482.

Silverberg, Robert. 1968. *The Mound Builders of Ancient America*. New York: New York Graphic Society.

Simons, Elwyn. 1984. "Dawn Ape of the Fayum." *Natural History* 93 (5):18–20.

Singer, Ronald, and Wymer, John. 1982. *The Middle Stone Age at Klasies River Mouth in South Africa*. Chicago: University of Chicago Press.

Singer, Ronald, et al. 1973. "Clacton-on-Sea, Essex: Report on Excavations 1969–1970." *Proceedings of the Prehistoric Society* 39:6–74.

Smith, Andrew B. 1984. "Origins of the Neolithic in the Sahara." In J. Desmond Clark and Steven A. Brandt, eds., *From Hunters to Farmers*, pp. 84–92. Berkeley and Los Angeles: University of California Press.

Smith, Bruce D. ed. 1978a. *Mississippian Settlement Patterns*. New York: Academic Press.

———. 1978b. "Variations in Mississippian Settlement Patterns." In Bruce D. Smith, ed., *Mississippian Settlement Patterns*, pp. 479–503. New York: Academic Press.

———. 1986. "The Archaeology of the Southeastern United States: From Dalton to De Soto, 10,500–500 B.P." *Advances in World Archaeology* 5:1–92.

———. 1989. "The Independent Domestication of Indigenous Seed-Bearing Plants in Eastern North America." In William F. Keagan, ed., *Emergent Horticultural Economies of the Eastern Woodlands*, pp. 3–48. Carbondale: Center for Archaeological Investigations.

Smith, M. T. 1987. *Archaeology of Aboriginal Culture Change in the Interior Southeast*. Gainesville, FL: University of Florida Presses.

Smith, P. E. L. 1978. "An Interim Report on Ganj Dareh Tepe, Iran." *American Journal of Archaeology* 82:538–540.

Snow, Dean. 1980. *Archaeology of New England.* New York: Academic Press.

Soffer, Olga. 1977. "Upper Palaeolithic Connubia, Refugia, and the Archaeological Record from Eastern Europe." In Olga Soffer, ed., *The Pleistocene Old World,* pp. 333–348. New York: Plenum Press.

———. 1985. *The Upper Palaeolithic of the Central Russian Plains.* New York: Academic Press.

Soffer, Olga, and Gamble, Clive, eds. 1990. *The World in 18,000 B.P.* Edinburgh: Edinburgh University Press.

Solheim, William. 1971. "An Earlier Agricultural Revolution." *Scientific American* 133 (11):34–51.

Sollas, W. J. 1910. *Ancient Hunters.* London: Macmillan.

Spencer, Herbert. 1855. *Social Statistics.* London: Macmillan.

Speth, John. 1983. *Bone Kills and Bone Counts: Decision Making by Ancient Hunters.* Chicago: University of Chicago Press.

Spooner, Brian, ed. 1972. *Population Growth: An Anthropological Perspective.* Cambridge, MA: MIT Press.

Spriggs, Matthew. 1989. "Dating the Island Southeast Asian Neolithic." *Antiquity* 63 (240):587–613.

Stahl, Ann Bower. 1984. "Hominid Dietary Selection Before Fire." *Current Anthropology* 25 (2):151–168.

Stark, Barbara. 1986. "Origins of Food Production in the New World." In David Meltzer et al., eds., *American Archaeology Past and Future,* pp. 277–322. Washington, DC: Smithsonian Institution.

Starling, N. J. 1985. "Colonization and Success: The Earlier Neolithic of Central Europe." *Proceedings of the Prehistoric Society* 51:41–57.

Steinkeller, P. 1989. *Sales Documents of the Ur III Period.* Stuttgart, Germany: Steiner Verlag.

Steponaitis, V. 1986. "Prehistoric Archaeology in the Southeastern United States 1970–1985." *Annual Review of Anthropology* 15:363–404.

Steward, Julian. 1970. *A Theory of Culture Change.* Urbana: University of Illinois Press.

Steward, Julian, et al. 1955. *Irrigation Civilizations: A Comparative Study.* Washington, DC: Pan American Union.

Stoltman, James B. 1978. "Temporal Models in Prehistory: An Example from Eastern North America." *Current Anthropology* 19:703–746.

Stoltman, J. B., and Barreis, D. A. 1983. "The Evolution of Human Ecosystems in the Eastern and Central United States." In H. E. Wright, ed., *The Holocene.* Vol. 2, *Late Quaternary Environments of the United States,* pp. 252–268. Minneapolis: University of Minnesota Press.

Street, F. Alayne. 1980. "Ice Age Environments." In Andrew G. Sherratt, ed., *The Cambridge Encyclopaedia of Archaeology,* pp. 52–56. New York: Cambridge University Press and Crown Publishers.

Stringer, C. B. 1984. "Human Evolution and Biological Adaptation in the Pleistocene." In Robert Foley, ed., *Human Evolution and Community Ecology,* pp. 55–84. London: Academic Press.

Stringer, C. B., and Andrews, P. 1988. "Genetic and Fossil Evidence for the Origin of Modern Humans." *Science* 239:1263–1268.

Stringer, C. B., et al. 1979. "The Significance of the Fossil Hominid from Petralona, Greece." *Journal of Archaeological Science* 6:235–253.

———. 1984. "The Origin of Anatomically Modern Humans in Western Europe." In Fred Smith and Frank Spencer, eds., *The Origins of Modern Humans*, pp. 51–136. New York: Liss.

Struever, Stuart, ed. 1971. *Prehistoric Agriculture.* Garden City, NY: Natural History Press.

Struever, Stuart, and Holton, Felicia Antonelli. 1979. *Koster: Americans in Search of Their Past.* New York: Anchor Press/Doubleday.

Suess, Hans. 1965. "Secular Variations of the Cosmic-Ray-Produced Carbon 14 in the Atmosphere." *Journal of Geophysical Research* 70:23–31.

Tainter, Joseph. 1988. *The Collapse of Civilizations.* Cambridge, Eng.: Cambridge University Press.

Taylor, R. E., and Meighan, C. W., eds. 1978. *Chronologies in New World Archaeology.* New York: Academic Press.

Taylour, Lord William. 1990. *The Mycenaeans,* 2d ed. London: Thames and Hudson.

Telegin, D. J. 1987. "Neolithic Cultures of the Ukraine and Adjacent Areas and Their Chronology." *Journal of World Prehistory* 1 (3):307–331.

Terrace, H., Petitto, L., Sanders, R., and Bever, T. 1979. "Can an Ape Create a Sentence?" *Science* 206:891–902.

Terrell, John. 1989. "Commentary: What Lapita Is and What Lapita Isn't." *Antiquity* 63 (240):623–626.

Thomas, David. 1989. *Archaeology,* 2nd ed. New York: Holt, Rinehart & Winston.

Thomas, David, and Bettinger, Robert. 1983. *The Archaeology of the Monitor Valley.* New York: American Museum of Natural History.

Thomas, Julian. 1987. "Relations of Production and Social Change in the Neolithic of Northwestern Europe." *Man* 22 (3):405–430.

Torrance, Robin. 1986. *Production and Exchange.* Cambridge, Eng.: Cambridge University Press.

Tosi, Maurizo, ed. 1983. *Prehistoric Sistan I.* Rome: ISMEO.

Toth, Nicholas. 1985. "The Oldowan Reconsidered: A Close Look at Early Stone Artifacts." *Journal of Archaeological Science* 12:101–120.

Toth, Nicholas, and Schick, K. D. 1986. "The First Million Years: The Archeology of Protohuman Culture." *Advances in Archeological Method and Theory* 9:1–96.

Toynbee, Arnold. 1962. *The Study of History.* Oxford: Oxford University Press.

Trigger, Bruce G. 1980. *Gordon Childe: Revolutions in Archaeology.* London: Thames and Hudson.

———. 1981. "Anglo-American Archaeology." *World Archaeology* 13:138–145.

———. 1989. *A History of Archaeological Thought.* Cambridge, Eng.: Cambridge University Press.

Trigger, Bruce G., et al. 1983. *Ancient Egypt: A Social History.* Cambridge, Eng.: Cambridge University Press.

Tringham, Ruth. 1971. *Hunters, Fishers, and Farmers of Eastern Europe: 6000–3000 B.C.* London: Hutchinson University Library.

———. 1983. "V. Gordon Childe 25 Years After." *Journal of Field Archaeology* 10 (1):85–100.

Tringham, Ruth, et al. 1980. "The Early Agricultural Site of Selevac, Yugoslavia." *Archaeology* 33 (2):24–32.

Trinkaus, Erik. 1982. "Evolutionary Continuity Among Archaic *Homo sapiens.*" In Avraham Ronen, ed., *The Transition from Lower to Middle Paleolithic and the Origins of Modern Man,* pp. 301–320. Oxford, Eng.: British Archaeological Reports, International Series, No. 151.

———, ed. 1983a. *The Mousterian Legacy.* Oxford, Eng.: British Archaeological Reports, International Series, No. 151.

———. 1983b. *The Shanidar Neanderthals.* New York: Academic Press.

Trinkaus, Erik, and Howells, W. W. 1979. "The Neanderthals." *Scientific American* 241:118–133.

Turner, Christy. 1984. "Advances in the Dental Search for Native American Origins." *Acta Anthropogenetica* 8:23–78.

Tuttle, Russell, ed. 1972. *The Functional and Evolutionary Biology of Primates.* Chicago: Aldine-Atherton.

Tylor, Edward. 1871. *Anthropology.* London: Macmillan.

Ucko, Peter J., and Dimbleby, G. W., eds. 1969. *The Domestication and Exploitation of Plants and Animals.* London: Duckworth.

Upham, Steadman, et al. 1987. "Evidence Concerning the Origin of Maize de Ocho." *American Anthropologist* 89 (3):410–419.

Vavilov, N. I. 1951. "Phytogeographic Basis of Plant Breeding." *Chronica Botanica* 13:14–54.

Vickers, Michael. 1977. *The Roman World.* Oxford, Eng.: Elsevier Phaidon.

Villa, Paola. 1983. *Terra Amata and the Middle Pleistocene Archaeological Record of Southern France.* Berkeley and Los Angeles: University of California Press.

Vinnecombe, Patricia. 1976. *People of the Eland.* Pietermaritzburg: Natal University Press.

von Däniken, Erich. 1970. *Chariots of the Gods.* New York: Bantam.

Walker, Alan. 1981. "Dietary Hypotheses and Human Evolution." *Philosophical Transactions of the Royal Society of London* 292:56–64.

Walker, Alan, et al. 1986. "*Australopithecus* Finds from West of Lake Turkana." *Nature* 322:517.

Wallerstein, Immanuel. 1974. *The Modern World System.* New York: Academic Press.

Ward, S. C., and Kimbel, W. H. 1983. "Subnasal Alveolar Morphology and the Systematic Position of *Sivapithecus.*" *American Journal of Physical Anthropology* 61:157–171.

Warren, Peter. 1975. *The Aegean Civilizations.* Oxford, Eng.: Elsevier Phaidon.

———. 1984. "Knossos: New Excavations and Discoveries." *Archaeology* 37 (4):48–57.

Watson, Patty Jo, LeBlanc, Steven, and Redman, Charles L. 1984. *Archeological Explanation: The Scientific Method in Archeology.* New York: Columbia University Press.

Wauchope, Robert. 1962. *Lost Tribes and Sunken Continents.* Chicago: University of Chicago Press.

Weaver, Muriel Porter. 1981. *The Aztecs, Maya, and Their Predecessors,* 2d ed. New York: Academic Press.

Webb, Clarence H. 1968. "The Extent and Content of Poverty Point Culture." *American Antiquity* 33:297–331.

Webb, W. S. 1974. *Indian Knoll*, new ed. Knoxville: University of Tennessee Press.

Weidenreich, Franz. 1946. *Apes, Giants, and Men.* Chicago: University of Chicago Press.

Weiss, Harvey, ed. 1986. *The Origins of Cities in Dry-Farming Syria and Mesopotamia in the Third Millennium B.C.* Guildford, CT: Four Quarters Publishers.

Weiss, Mark L., and Mann, Alan E. 1988. *Human Biology and Behavior*, 5th ed. Boston: Scott, Foresman/Little, Brown.

Wells, Peter. 1981. *Culture Contact and Culture Change.* Cambridge, Eng.: Cambridge University Press.

———. 1984. "Early Iron Age Community in Central Europe." *Scientific American* 249 (6):68–93.

Wendorf, Fred, ed. 1968. *The Prehistory of Nubia.* Dallas, TX: Southern Methodist University Press.

Wendorf, Fred, and Schild, Romuald. 1980. *Prehistory of the Eastern Sahara.* New York: Academic Press.

———. 1981. "The Earliest Food Producers." *Archaeology* 34 (5):30–36.

Wendorf, Fred, et al., eds. 1984. *Cattle Keepers of the Eastern Sahara: The Neolithic of Bir Kiseiba.* Dallas, TX: Southern Methodist University Press.

Wenke, R. J., Long, J. E., and Buck, Paul E. 1988. "Epipaleolithic and Neolithic Settlement in the Fayyum Oasis of Egypt." *Journal of Field Archaeology* 15 (1):29–51.

Wertime, Theodore A., and Muhly, James D., eds. 1980. *The Coming of the Age of Iron.* New Haven, CT: Yale University Press.

Wheat, Joe Ben. 1972. *The Olsen-Chubbock Site.* Washington, DC: Society for American Archaeology.

Wheatley, Paul. 1971. *The Pivot of the Four Quarters.* Chicago: Aldine.

———. 1975. "Satyarta in Suvarnadvipa: From Reciprocity to Redistribution in Ancient Southeast Asia." In Jeremy A. Sabloff and C. C. Lamberg-Karlovsky, eds., *Ancient Civilization and Trade*, pp. 227–284. Albuquerque: University of New Mexico Press.

———. 1979. "Urban Genesis in Mainland Southeast Asia." In R. B. Smith and W. Watson, eds., *Early Southeast Asia.* pp. 288–303. Oxford, Eng.: Oxford University Press.

———. 1980. *Kings of the Mountain.* Kuala Lumpur: University of Malaysia Press.

Wheeler, Sir Mortimer. 1954. *Archaeology from the Earth.* Oxford, Eng.: Clarendon Press.

———. 1962. *The Indus Civilization*, 2d ed. Cambridge, Eng.: Cambridge University Press.

———. 1968. *Early India and Pakistan.* New York: Praeger.

White, Joyce C. 1982. *Ban Chiang: The Discovery of a Lost Bronze Age Civilization.* Philadelphia: University of Pennsylvania Press.

White, J. P., Allen, J., and Specht, J. 1988. "The Lapita Homeland Project." *Australian Natural History* 22 (9):410–416.

White, J. Peter, and O'Connell, James. 1982. *A Prehistory of Australia, New Guinea, and Sahul.* Sydney: Academic Press.

White, Leslie. 1949. *The Science of Culture.* New York: Grove.

White, Randall. 1982. "Rethinking the Middle/Upper Paleolithic Transition." *Current Anthropology* 23 (2):169–191.

———. 1986. *Dark Caves and Bright Visions.* New York: American Museum of Natural History.

Whitelaw, K. W., and Coote, R. B. 1987. *The Emergence of Israel in Historical Perspective.* Sheffield, Eng.: Almond Press.

Whittle, Alasdair. 1985. *Neolithic Europe: A Survey.* Cambridge, Eng.: Cambridge University Press.

Wickler, Stephen, and Spriggs, Matthew. 1988. "Pleistocene Occupation of the Solomons." *Antiquity* 62 (237):703–707.

Wilcox, David R. 1980. "The Current Status of the Hohokam Concept." In D. E. Doyel and Fred T. Plog, eds., *Current Issues in Hohokam Prehistory: Proceedings of a Symposium,* pp. 236–243. Tempe: Arizona State Museum.

———. 1985. "The Tepiman Connection: A Model of Mesoamerican-Southwestern Interaction." In Randall H. McGuire and Francis Joan Mathier, eds., *Ripples in the Chichimec Sea,* pp. 86–94. Carbondale: Southern Illinois University Press.

Wilk, R. R., and Ashmore, Wendy, eds. 1987. *House and Household in the Mesoamerican Past.* Albuquerque: University of New Mexico Press.

Willey, Gordon R. 1953. *Prehistoric Settlement in the Virú Valley, Peru.* Washington, DC: Smithsonian Institution.

———. 1963. *The Archaeology of the Virú Valley, Peru.* Cambridge, Eng.: Peabody Museum.

———. 1966. *North and Middle America.* Vol. 1, *An Introduction to American Archaeology.* Englewood Cliffs, NJ: Prentice Hall.

———. 1971. *South America.* Vol. 2, *An Introduction to American Archaeology.* Englewood Cliffs, NJ: Prentice Hall.

Willey, Gordon R., and Sabloff, Jeremy A. 1980. *A History of American Archaeology,* 2d ed. San Francisco: Freeman.

Wills, S. H. 1989. *Early Prehistoric Agriculture in the American Southwest.* Santa Fe, NM: School of American Research.

Wilson, David J. 1981. "Of Maize and Men: A Critique of the Maritime Hypothesis of State Origins on the Coast of Peru." *American Anthropologist* 83: 931–940.

———. 1983. "The Origins and Development of Complex Prehispanic Society in the Lower Santa Valley, Peru: Implications for Theories of State Origins." *Journal of Anthropological Archaeology* 2:209–276.

Wilson, Edward O. 1980. *Sociobiology: The Abridged Edition.* Cambridge, MA: Harvard University Press.

Wilson, J. A. 1951. *The Burden of Egypt.* Chicago: University of Chicago Press.

Windels, Ferdinand. 1965. *The Lascaux Cave Paintings.* London: Faber & Faber.

Winters, Howard. 1967. *The Riverton Culture.* Springfield: Illinois State Museum.

Wittfogel, Karl W. 1957. *Oriental Despotism: A Comparative Study of Total Power.* New Haven, CT: Yale University Press.

Wobst, H. M. 1978. "The Archaeo-ethnology of Hunter-gatherers or the Tyranny of the Ethnographic Record in Archaeology." *American Antiquity* 43:303–309.

Wolf, Eric. 1984. *Europe and the People Without History.* Berkeley: University of California Press.

Wolpert, Stanley A. 1977. *A New History of India.* London: Oxford University Press.

Wolpoff, Milford H., et al. 1984. "Modern *Homo sapiens* Origins: A General Theory of Hominid Evolution Involving the Fossil Evidence from East Asia." In Fred Smith and Frank Spencer, eds., *The Origins of Modern Humans,* pp. 411–484. New York: Liss.

Woolley, Sir Leonard. 1934. *The Royal Cemetery.* Vol. 2, *Ur Excavations.* London: British Museum.

Worsaae, J. J. A. 1849. *The Primeval Antiquities of Denmark.* London: Murray.

Wright, Gary. 1971. "Origins of Food Production in Southwestern Asia: A Survey of Ideas." *Current Anthropology* 12:447–478.

Wright, Henry T. 1977. "Recent Researches on the Origin of the State." *Annual Review of Anthropology* 6:379–397.

Wright, Henry T., and Johnson, G. 1975. "Population, Exchange, and Early State Formation in Southwestern Iran." *American Anthropologist* 77:267–289.

Wright H. T., and Pollock, Susan. 1986. "Regional Socio-Economic Organization in Southern Mesopotamia: The Middle and Late 5th Millennium." *Prehistoire de la Mesopotamie,* pp. 317–329.

Wright, R. V. S. 1971. *Archaeology of the Gallus Site, Koonalda Cave.* Canberra: Australian Institute of Aboriginal Studies.

———. 1977. *Stone Tools as Cultural Markers.* Canberra: Australian Institute of Aboriginal Studies.

Wylie, Alison. 1985. "The Reaction Against Analogy." *Advances in Archaeological Method and Theory* 8:63–111.

Wynn, T., and McGrew, W. C. 1989. "An Ape's View of the Oldowan." *Man* 24 (3):383–398.

Yellen, John E. 1977. *Archaeological Approaches to the Present.* New York: Academic Press.

Yen, Douglas E. 1977. "Hoabhinian Horticulture: The Evidence and Questions from Northwest Thailand." In J. Allen, J. Golson, and Rhys Jones, eds., *Sunda and Sahel,* pp. 567–600. New York: Academic Press.

Yerkes, Richard. 1988. "The Woodland and Mississippian Traditions in the Prehistory of Midwestern North America." *Journal of World Prehistory* 2 (3):307–358.

Yesner, David K. 1987. "Life in the Garden of Eden: Causes and Consequences of the Adoption of Marine Diets by Human Societies." In Marvin Harris and Eric B. Ross, eds., *Food and Evolution,* pp. 111–131. Philadelphia: Temple University Press.

Zohary, D., and Hopf, Marie. 1988. *Domestication of Plants in the Old World.* Oxford, Eng.: Oxford University Press.

Zubrow, Ezra. 1971. "Carrying Capacity and Dynamic Equilibrium in the Prehistoric Southwest." *American Antiquity* 36:127–138.

Zvelebil, Marek, ed. 1986. *Hunters in Transition.* Cambridge, Eng.: Cambridge University Press.

Zvelebil, Marek, and Rowley-Conwy, Peter, eds. 1984. "Transition to Farming in Northern Europe: A Hunter-Gatherer Perspective." *Norwegian Archaeological Records* 17:104–128.

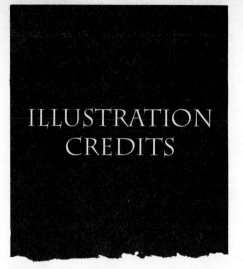

ILLUSTRATION CREDITS

Frontispiece: Granger

CHAPTER 1

Page 7: © British Museum. *Page 8:* (upper right) © Tortoli, Photo Researchers; (upper left) © Georgia, Photo Researchers; (lower left) Reprinted courtesy of The Colonial Williamsburg Foundation; (lower right) © Rakoczy, Photo Researchers. *Page 9:* (upper left) Reprinted courtesy of The University of California/W. Swalling photographer; (upper right) Reprinted courtesy of The University Museum, University of Pennsylvania/Nick Hartman photographer; (lower left) © Wolfgang Kaehler; (lower right) Photo by D. C. Ochsner, © UCLA Institute of Archaeology and JoAnne Van Tilburg, Director Moai Documentation Project, Easter Island 1984. *Page 18:* Barkley, Union County Advocate/Kentucky Heritage Council. *Figure 1.3:* From *Invitation to Archaeology* by James Deetz. Copyright © 1967 by James Deetz. Reprinted by permission of Doubleday, a division of Bantam, Doubleday, Dell Publishing Group, Inc. *Figure 1.4:* (left) Vida Freeman/Earthwatch; (right) Courtesy of the Society of Antiquaries of London. Figure 1.5: From *Invitation to Archaeology* by James Deetz. Copyright © 1967 by James Deetz. Reprinted by permission of Doubleday, a division of Bantam, Doubleday, Dell Publishing Group, Inc.

CHAPTER 2

Figure 2.1: From Karl W. Butzer, *Archaeology as Human Ecology* (New York: Cambridge University Press), 1982, p. 16. Reprinted by permission. *Figure 2.2:* From Karl W. Butzer, *Archaeology as Human Ecology* (New York: Cambridge University Press), 1982, p. 31. Reprinted by permission. *Figure 2.3:* Reproduced with permission from Colin Renfrew and Paul Bahn, *Archaeology: Theories, Methods, and Practice,* Thames and Hudson, London and New York 1991. *Figure 2.4:* Museum of Anthropology, University of Michigan. *Figure 2.5:* Shostak, Anthro-Photo.

CHAPTER 3

Figure 3.1: From Alison Jolly. 1985. *The Evolution of Primate Behavior.* New York: Macmillan. Used by permission of the author. *Figure 3.2:* Redrawn with permission of Macmillan Publishing Co., Inc. from *The Ascent of Man* by David Pilbeam. Copyright © 1972 by David Pilbeam. *Figure 3.3c:* Redrawn with permission of Bantam Books, Inc. from *Monkeys and Apes* by Prudence Napier, copyright © 1972. All rights reserved. *Figure 3.5:* Photograph by courtesy of the Transvaal Museum, South Africa. *Figure 3.6:* Courtesy of Alan R. Hughes, University of the Witwatersrand. *Figure 3.7:* Institute of Human Origins. *Figure 3.8:* Photograph by John Reader, courtesy of Mary Leakey. *Figure 3.9:* © Copyright held by The National Museums of Kenya, P.O. Box 40658, Nairobi, Kenya. Reprinted by permission. *Figure 3.10:* Institute of Human Origins. *Figure 3.12:* Robert Foley/Antiquity Publications Ltd. *Figure 3.13:* Henry T. Bunn. *Figure 3.14:* Photographed by Hugo van Lawick © National Geographic Society. *Figure 3.15:* From *Life Nature Library/Early Man.* Redrawn from Lowell Hess © 1980 Time-Life Books Inc. *Figure 3.16:* (top) From *Life Nature Library/Early Man.* Redrawn from Lowell Hess © 1980 Time-Life Books Inc.; *(bottom)* Adapted by permission from *Olduvai Gorge: Excavations in Beds I and II* by M. D. Leakey, © 1971, Cambridge University Press. *Figure 3.17:* From John Gowlett in Robert Foley, ed., *Hominid Evolution and Community Ecology* (New York: Academic Press), 1984, p. 176, Fig. 7.1.

CHAPTER 4

Page 122: From N. J. Shackleton and N. D. Opdyke, "Oxygen Isotope and Paleomagnetic Stratigraphy of Equatorial Pacific Ocean Core V28-238," in *Quaternary Research* 3:38–55. Reprinted by permission. *Figure 4.1:* After Flint. 1971. *Glacial and Quaternary Geology.* New York: Wiley. Adapted by permission of John Wiley & Sons. *Figure 4.2:* © Copyright held by The National Museums of Kenya, P.O. Box 40658, Nairobi, Kenya. Reprinted with permission. *Figure 4.3:* Cambridge Museum of Archaeology and Anthropology. *Figure 4.4a:* AP/Wide World. *Figure 4.4b:* From H. L. Movius, Jr., "The Lower Paleolithic Structures of Southern and Eastern Asia," *Transactions of the American Philosophical Society,* Vol. 38, Pt. 4 (1948). Reprinted by permission of the Society and the author. *Figure 4.5:* © Brake, Photo Researchers. *Figure 4.6:* (top) From Grahame Clark, *Aspects of Prehistory.* Copyright © 1970 by the Regents of the University of California. Reprinted by permission of the University of California Press; *(bottom)* Redrawn by permission for Ronald Singer et al., "Excavation of the Clactonian Industry," *Proceedings of the Prehistoric Society,* by permission of the Society. *Figure 4.7:* (top) From John Gowlett in Robert Foley, ed., *Hominid Evolution and Community Ecology* (New York: Academic Press), 1984, Figs. 7.3, 7.5, and 7.6. *Figure 4.8:* (top) Acheulian hand ax from Figure 26 *The Swanscombe Skull: A Survey of Research on Pleistocene Site* (Occasional Paper No. 20, Royal Anthropological Institute of Great Britain and Ireland), by permission of the Society; *(bottom left)* From *The Distribution of Prehistoric Culture in Angola* by J. D. Clark, Companhia de Diamantes de Angola, Africa, 1966; *(bottom right)* Adapted from *Prehistory of Africa* by J. D. Clark, Thames and Hudson, Ltd., London. *Figure 4.9:* From John Gowlett in Robert Foley, ed., *Hominid Evolution and Community Ecology* (New York: Academic Press), 1984, p. 176, Fig. 7.1. *Figure 4.11:* Robert Foley/Antiquity Publications Ltd. *Figure 4.12:* Robert Foley/Antiquity Publications Ltd. *Figure 4.13:* Robert Foley/Antiquity Publications Ltd. *Figure 4.14:* Courtesy of F. Clark Howell. *Figure 4.15:* Karl Butzer, *Environment and Archaeology,* Cambridge University Press, 1982. Reprinted with permission of Cambridge University Press. *Figure 4.16:* By permission of Henry de Lumley, Laboratoire de Paléontologie Humaine et de Préhistoire, Marseilles. *Figure 4.17:* Drawings by Janis Cirulis from *Mankind in the Making* by William Howells. Copyright © 1959, 1967 by William Howells. Reprinted by permission of Doubleday, a division of Bantam, Doubleday, Dell Publishing Group, Inc. *Figure 4.18:* Drawings by Janis Cirulis from *Mankind in the Making* by William Howells. Copyright © 1959, 1967 by William

Howells. Reprinted by permission of Doubleday, a division of Bantam, Doubleday, Dell Publishing Group, Inc. *Figure 4.19:* From Jacques Bordaz, *Tools of the Old and New Stone Age,* copyright 1970 by Jacques Bordaz. Copyright © 1958 by the American Museum of Natural History. Reprinted by permission of the author. *Figure 4.20: (bottom left)* Adapted from *Prehistory of Africa* by J. D. Clark, Thames and Hudson Ltd., London; *(bottom right)* Redrawn from J. M. Coles and E. S. Higgs, *The Archaeology of Early Man* by permission of Faber and Faber Ltd. *Figure 4.21:* From A. C. Blanc, "Torre in Pietra Saccopastore, Monte Circeo: On the Position of the Mousterian in the Pleistocene Sequence of the Rome Area," in *Hundert Jahre Neanderthaler* (Cologne: Bohlau Verlag, 1958).

CHAPTER 5

Figure 5.2: From Karl W. Butzer, *Environment and Archaeology,* 2nd edition (Hawthorn, N.Y.: Aldine Publishing Company), 1971. Reprinted by permission of the author. *Figure 5.3:* From Karl W. Butzer, *Environment and Archaeology,* 2nd edition (Hawthorn, N.Y.: Aldine Publishing Company), 1971. Reprinted by permission of the author. *Figure 5.4:* Courtesy of Milford Wolpoff. *Figure 5.5: (left a and left b)* Adapted from *The Old Stone Age* by F. Bordes. Copyright © 1968 by McGraw-Hill, Inc. Used with permission of McGraw-Hill Book Company and Weidenfeld & Nicholson Ltd.; *(right a)* From Jacques Bordaz, *Tools of the Old and New Stone Age,* Copyright 1970 by Jacques Bordaz. Reprinted by permission; *(right b)* Adapted by permission from *Le Paléolithique supérieur en Périgord* by Denise de Sonneville-Bordes, Directeur de recherches au Centre national de la Recherche scientifique, Institut du Quaternaire, Université de Bordeaux. *Page 181* (Table 5.1): Adapted by permission from the following sources: H. Breuil; *Le Paléolithique supérieur en Périgord* by Denise de Sonneville-Bordes, Directeur de recherches au Centre national de la Recherche scientifique, Institut du Quaternaire, Université de Bordeaux; Lowell Hess, *Early Man,* Life Nature Library, © 1965 Time Inc. by permission of the publisher, Time-Life Books Inc.; *The Old Stone Age* by F. Bordes. Copyright © 1968 by McGraw-Hill Book Company and Weidenfeld & Nicolson Ltd. *Figure 5.6:* Collection Musée de l'Homme. *Figure 5.7:* Collection Musée de l'Homme. *Figure 5.8:* Coxe, American Museum of Natural History. *Figure 5.9:* Collection Musée de l'Homme. *Figure 5.10:* © Alexander Marshack, 1972. *Figure 5.11:* From O. Soffer, *The Upper Paleolithic of the Central Russian Plain,* Academic Press, 1985, Fig. 2.67. Reprinted with permission of Academic Press and the author. *Figure 5.12: (top)* From Richard G. Klein, *Man and Culture in the Late Pleistocene,* © 1969 by Chandler Publishing Company. By permission of Dun-Donnelley Publishing Corporation; *(bottom)* From *The Archeology of the USSR* by A. L. Mongait, Mir Publishers, Moscow. *Figure 5.13:* Reprinted by permission of Faber and Faber Ltd. From J. M. Coles and E. S. Higgs, *The Archaeology of Early Man.* *Figure 5.14:* From C. B. M. McBurney, *Early Man in the Soviet Union,* Fig. 6, p. 44. Published by Oxford University Press for The British Academy; from the Proceedings of the British Academy, Volume LXI, 1975.

CHAPTER 6

Figure 6.1: Adapted from Fekri Hassan. 1981. *Demographic Archaeology.* Orlando. Academic Press. Adapted by permission. *Figure 6.2:* From Jaques Bordaz, *Tools of the Old and New Stone Age.* Copyright 1970 by Jaques Bordaz. Reprinted by permission. *Figure 6.3:* Stark Museum of Art, Orange, Texas. *Figure 6.4:* Courtesy of the Smithsonian Institution. Photo No. T13301. *Figure 6.5:* South African Archeological Bulletin and Professor V. Riet Lowe. *Figure 6.7:* WSU Hoko River Archaeological Project. *Figure 6.9:* From O. Bar-Yosef and A. Belfar-Cohen. 1989. The Origins of Sedentism and Farming Communities in the Levant. *Journal of World Prehistory* 3(4): 460. Used by permission of Plenum Publishing Corporation. *Figure 6.10:* From Donald O. Henry. 1989. From *Foraging to Agriculture: The Levant at the End of the Ice Age.* Philadelphia:

University of Pennsylvania Press. Used by permission. *Figure 6.11: Left:* Redrawn from D.A.E. Garrod and D.M.A. Bate, *The Stone Age of M. Carmel* by permission of Oxford University Press. *Right:* From James Mellaart, *The Earliest Civilizations of the Near East.* Reprinted by permission of Thames and Hudson Ltd., London.

CHAPTER 7

Figure 7.2: Redrawn with permission of the Glencoe Press from *Foundations of Archeology* by Jason W. Smith. Copyright © 1976 by Jason W. Smith. *Figure 7.3:* From Brian M. Fagan, *The Great Journey* (London: Thames and Hudson), 1987, p. 93. Julie M. Longhill, artist. *Figure 7.4:* Redrawn from Gordon R. Willey, *An Introduction to American Archaeology, Vol. I: North and Middle America,* © 1966. Reprinted by permission of the author and Prentice Hall, Inc., Englewood Cliffs, N.J. *Figure 7.5:* Tom D. Dillehay. *Figure 7.6:* Teiwec, Arizona State Museum. *Figure 7.7:* Courtesy of University of Colorado Museum, Joe Ben Wheat photo. *Figure 7.8:* Redrawn by permission of McGraw-Hill Book Company from *PreHistory of North America* by Jesse D. Jennings. Copyright © 1968 by McGraw-Hill, Inc. *Figure 7.9:* Drawing by Thomas R. Whyte. Courtesy of The Frank H. McClung Museum, The University of Tennessee, Knoxville. *Figure 7.10:* From Brian M. Fagan, *The Great Journey* (London: Thames and Hudson), 1987, p. 162. *Figure 7.11:* Field Museum of Natural History (Neg. #953.5.73.6), Chicago. *Figure 7.12:* U.S. Information Agency No. 11-SC-33831 in National Archives Building. *Figure 7.13:* University of Alaska Museum.

CHAPTER 8

Figure 8.2: South African Archaeological Bulletin and Murray Schoonraal. *Figure 8.3:* Paul den Hoed and Thomas A. Dowson, Rozk Art Research Unit, University of Witwatersrand. *Figure 8.4:* Marshall/!Kung San Foundation. *Figure 8.5:* F. Peron. *Figure 8.6:* Reproduced with permission of the publishers from Bellwood, P., *Prehistory of the Indo-Malaysian Archipelago,* Academic Press, Sydney, Australia, 1985. *Figure 8.8:* Reprinted by permission from *Nature,* Vol. 324, pp. 453–455. Copyright © 1986 Macmillan Magazines Limited. *Figure 8.9:* Stephen Wickler. *Figure 8.11:* Australian Information Service. *Figure 8.13:* Rudy Frank, Courtesy R. F. Cosgrove. *Figure 8.14:* Redrawn by permission from Richard A. Gould, "The Archaeologist as Ethnographer," *World Archeology* 3,2 (1971), 143–177, Fig. 18.

CHAPTER 9

Figure 9.1: Adapted by permission from *The Material Culture of the People of the Gwembe Valley* by Dr. Barrie Reynolds, published by Manchester University Press for the Livingstone Museum, Zambia. *Figure 9.2:* From Roger Lewin, *Human Evolution,* Blackwell Scientific Publications Ltd., 1984. Reprinted by permission. *Figure 9.3:* S. von Herbenstain. *Figure 9.4:* Used by permission of Dr. Gordon Hillman. *Figure 9.5:* Used by permission of Dr. Gordon Hillman. *Figure 9.6, Top:* Wyatt Davis, Courtesy Museum of New Mexico (Neg. 44191); *Bottom left:* Tyler Dingee, Courtesy of Museum of New Mexico (Neg. 73453); *Bottom right:* Tyler Dingee, Courtesy of Museum of New Mexico (Neg. 73449). *Figure 9.7:* Reproduced courtesy of the Trustees of the British Museum.

CHAPTER 10

Figure 10.2: Courtesy of Tell Abu Hureyra excavation. *Figure 10.4:* British School of Archaeology in Jerusalem. *Figure 10.5:* Peter Dorrell & Stuart Laidlaw, Institute of Archaeology, University of London. *Figure 10.6:* Redrawn from James Mellaart, *Çatal Hüyük* by permission of Thames and Hudson, Ltd., London. *Figure 10.7:* Redrawn from James Mellaart, *Çatal Hüyük* by permission of Thames and Hudson, Ltd., London.

CHAPTER 11

Figure 11.1: From *Proceedings of the Prehistoric Society* by permission of the Society. *Figure 11.3:* From *Prehistory* by Derek Roe, with permission of the Biologisch-Archaeologisch Instituut der Rijksuniveristeit Gronongen, the Netherlands. *Figure 11.4:* From Grahame Clark, *World Prehistory,* 3rd. ed., p. 140: © 1977 Cambridge University Press. *Figure 11.6:* From *Prehistory* by Derek Roe, with permission of Presses Universitaires de France. *Figure 11.7:* Neg. #39604, Courtesy Department of Library Services, American Museum of Natural History. *Figure 11.8:* Redrawn from *Ancient Europe* by Stuart Piggott, with permission of Edinburgh University Press. Copyright © Stuart Piggott, 1965.

CHAPTER 12

Figure 12.1: Grossgold, Photo Researchers.

CHAPTER 13

Figure 13.3, Figure 13.4, and Figure 13.6: Reprinted by permission from *The Archaeology of Ancient China,* 3rd ed. by Kwang-chih Chang (New Haven: Yale University Press, 1977). *Figure 13.7:* Scala/Art Resource, N.Y. *Figure 13.9:* Courtesy of Professor R. C. Green. *Figure 13.10:* Field Museum of Natural History (Neg. #100629), Chicago. *Figure 13.11:* Courtesy of The British Library.

CHAPTER 14

Figure 14.1: Reprinted by permission from *Prehistoric Food Production in North America,* ed. by Richard Ford, University of Michigan Museum of Anthropology. *Figure 14.3:* Photo by Thomas F. Lynch. *Figure 14.4:* From Gordon R. Willey, *An Introduction to American Archaeology Vol. II: South America,* © 1971. Reprinted by permission of Prentice Hall Inc., Englewood Cliffs, N.J. *Figure 14.5:* Drawing by Junius Bird. Courtesy of The American Museum of Natural History. *Figure 14.7:* Photograph taken by Jonathan E. Reyamn. *Figure 14.8:* Courtesy of the Louisiana Office of State Parks. *Figure 14.9:* Redrawn by permission of McGraw-Hill Book Company from *Prehistory of North America* by Jesse D. Jennings. Copyright © 1968 by McGraw-Hill, Inc. Used with permission of McGraw-Hill Company. After W. S. Webb, University of Kentucky Reports in Anthropology and Archaeology, no. 2. *Figure 14.10 a and c:* Courtesy of the Werner Forman Archive Limited. *Figure 14.10 b:* Field Museum of Natural History (Neg. #90925), Chicago. *Figure 14.11:* Artist's reconstruction by William Iseminger.

Photograph courtesy of Cahokia Mounds State Historic Site. *Figure 14.12:* Courtesy of Cahokia Mounds State Historic Site.

CHAPTER 15

Figure 15.1: Adapted from *Physical Anthropology and Archaeology* by Clifford J. Jolly and Fred Plog. Copyright © 1976 by Alfred A. Knopf, Inc. Reprinted by permission of Alfred A. Knopf, Inc. *Figure 15.2:* From *The Rise of Civilization: From Early Farmers to Urban Society in the Ancient Near East* by Charles Redman. W.H. Freeman and Company. Copyright © 1978. Reprinted by permission.

CHAPTER 16

Figure 16.2: Courtesy of the Oriental Institute, University of Chicago. *Figure 16.3 and Figure 16.4, bottom:* Fotoarchiv Hirmer Verlag Munchen. *Figure 16.4, Top:* From *Early Mesopotamia and Iran* by Max E. Mallowan. Thames and Hudson, Ltd., London. *Figure 16.5:* From Samuel Noah Kramer, "The Sumerians," *Scientific American,* October 1957. Reprinted with permission of W.H. Freeman and Company. Copyright © 1957 by Scientific American, Inc. All rights reserved. *Figure 16.6:* Courtesy of The University Museum, University of Pennsylvania.

CHAPTER 17

Figure 17.3: © George Holton, Photo Researchers. *Figure 17.4:* Michael Holoford, London. *Figure 17.5:* All rights reserved, The Metropolitan Museum of Art. *Figure 17.7:* Courtesy of the Rhodesian National Tourist Board.

CHAPTER 18

Figure 18.2: Roger-Viollet Documentation Generale Photographique, Paris. *Figure 18.5:* Courtesy of the University Museum, The University of Pennsylvania. *Figure 18.6:* Magnum Photos, Inc./Mark Riboud.

CHAPTER 19

Figure 19.2: Peabody Museum, Harvard University, © President & Fellows of Harvard College. Photo by Hillel Burger #N28172 © 1978. *Figure 19.4:* Courtesy of Smithsonian Institution. *Figure 19.5:* The China Friendship Society: from Grahame Clark, *World Prehistory,* 3rd edition, p. 306, © 1977 Cambridge University Press.

CHAPTER 20

Figure 20.2. left: From *Ancient Europe* by Stuart Piggott, with permission of Edinburgh University Press. Copyright © Stuart Piggott, 1965. *Figure 20.2. right:* Reproduced by Courtesy of the Trustees of the British Museum. *Figure 20.4:* Donald A. Frey, Institute of Nautical Archaeology. *Figure 20.5:* Ekdotike Anthenon S. A. Athens. *Figure 20.6:* Fotoarchiv Hirmer Verlag Munchen. *Figure 20.11:* From *Ancient Europe* by Stuart Piggott, with permission of Edinburgh University Press. Copyright © Stuart Piggott, 1965. *Figure 20.12:* Adapted from *Writing* by David Diringer, with permission of Thames and Hudson Ltd., London © David Diringer, 1962.

CHAPTER 21

Figure 21.1 and Figure 21.2: From *Ancient Europe* by Stuart Piggott, with permission of Edinburgh University Press. Copyright © Stuart Piggott, 1965. *Figure 21.3:* Courtesy of the Ashmolean Museum. *Figure 21.4:* From R.F. Tylecote in *The Prehistory of Metallurgy in the British Isles,* 1986. Reprinted by permission of R.F. Tylecote. *Figure 21.6:* Aerofilms Library, London. *Figure 21.7:* From *Ancient Europe* by Stuart Piggott, with permission of Edinburgh University Press. Copyright © Stuart Piggott, 1965. *Figure 21.10:* Reproduced courtesy of the Trustees of The British Museum.

CHAPTER 22

Figure 22.2: Courtesy of Franklin Graham. *Figure 22.3 and Figure 22.4:* From Gordon Willey, *An Introduction to American Archeology, Vol. I: North and Middle America.* © 1966. Reprinted by permission of the author and Prentice Hall, Inc., Englewood Cliffs, N.J. *Figure 22.5:* From Robert D. Drennan, "Contextual Analysis of Ritual Paraphernalia from Formative Oaxaca," in Kent V. Flannery (ed.), *The Early Mesoamerican Village* (Orlando, Fla.: Academic Press, 1976). Reprinted by permission of the author and the publisher. *Figure 22.6:* Arizona State Museum, The University of Arizona, E.B. Sayles, photographer. *Figure 22.7:* From *Urbanization at Teotihuacán, Mexico,* I, Pt. 1, 1973. © 1973 by Rene Millon. *Figure 22.8, photo:* Copyright © Project El Mirador. *Figure 22.8, drawing:* Copyright © Richard Hansen. *Figure 22.9:* Courtesy of Smithsonian Institution, National Anthropological Archives. *Figure 22.10:* Photo Researchers/Carl Frank. *Figure 22.11:* From Linda Schele and David Freidel, *A Forest of Kings.* New York: William Morrow, Fig. 6.7. Copyright © 1990 by Linda Schele and David Freidel. Used by permission of William Morrow and Company, Inc./Publishers, New York. *Figure 22.12:* From Linda Schele and David Freidel, *A Forest of Kings.* New York: William Morrow, Fig. 7.8. Copyright © 1990 by Linda Schele and David Freidel. Used by permission of William Morrow and Company, Inc./Publishers, New York. *Figure 22.13:* Peabody Museum, Harvard University © President and Fellows of Harvard College. Neg. #21622 F.P. Orchard © 1953. *Figure 22.14:* Courtesy of Smithsonian Institution. *Figure 22.15:* Lesley Newhart. *Figure 22.16:* Courtesy of Franklin C. Graham. *Figure 22.17:* Lesley Newhart.

CHAPTER 23

Figure 23.1: Photo by Jeffery Quilter. *Figure 23.3, left:* Courtesy Gordon Willey. *Figure 23.3, right:* Courtesy of Franklin Graham. *Figure 23.4:* Anne Paul/Earthwatch. *Figure 23.5:* M. Moseley/Anthrophoto. *Figure 23.6:* McIntyre, Woodfin Camp. *Figure 23.7:* Peabody Museum, Harvard University © President and Fellows of Harvard College. David de Harpoort © 1958. *Figure 23.8:* Peabody Museum, Harvard University © President and Fellows of Harvard College. Hillel Burger © 1982. *Figure 23.9:* Lee Boltin. *Figure 23.10:* Bettman Archive, Inc. *Figure 23.11:* M. Moseley/Anthrophoto. *Figure 23.12:* Courtesy of Franklin C. Graham. *Figure 23.13:* George Holton/Photo Researchers, Inc.

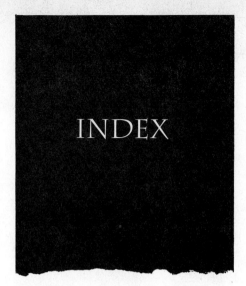

INDEX

Note: An italicized page number indicates a page on which an illustration appears.